Ball

RED BOOK

Greenhouse Growing   *14th Edition*

Vic Ball, Editor
Geo. J. Ball, Inc.

Reston Publishing Company, Inc.
A Prentice-Hall Company
Reston, Virginia

Library of Congress Cataloging in Publication Data

Main entry under title:

The Ball red book.

Includes bibliographical references.
1. Floriculture.   2. Plants, Ornamental.
3. Ornamental plant industry.   I. Ball, Vic.
II. Bachman, Todd.
SB405.B254 1985   635.9   84–11559
ISBN 0–8359–0382–6

Production supervision/interior design: Tally Morgan

Printed in the United States of America

PRINCIPAL CONTRIBUTORS

Todd Bachman	Bulb Crops
Vic Ball	Bedding Plants, Chrysanthemums, Geraniums—Hybrid (Seed)
Frank Batson	Azaleas
Michael Behnke	Gerberas
Charles Conover	Foliage Crops
Robert Danielson	Roses, Cut
Paul Ecke, Jr.	Poinsettias
Ralph Freeman	Carbon Dioxide
Ed Harthun	Miscellaneous Crops
Robert Hartman	Tissue Culture
Roy Larson	Irrigation
Ian Mackay	Roses, Garden & Pot
Robert Miller	Lilies
Robert Oglevee	Geraniums, Cutting
Marlin Rogers	Air Pollution
Ed Rose	Carnations
James Shanks	Hydrangeas

We also acknowledge help on many chapters in this book by the following Ball staff people: Ronald Adams, Teresa Aimone, William Hamilton, Janet Langefeld, Carl Loeb, Werner Rader, Jim Schield, Mark Snyder, Scott Trees, and Jan Umstead. Also, Ken Horst of Cornell.

CONTENTS

*SECTION III   OTHER BASICS FOR PROFITABLE
CROPS, 119*

DEDICATION

This fourteenth edition of the BALL RED BOOK is dedicated to my father, George J. Ball, founder of the BALL RED BOOK tradition—and of the organization which it represents.

George J. Ball, founder of the Ball Company and of the Ball Red Book—*with a house of his fine asters, early 1930s.*

INTRODUCTION— WHAT YOU'LL FIND HERE

First a bit of celebration!

Believe it or not, this is the 50th anniversary edition of the BALL RED BOOK! The first edition was written (by hand) by my father, George J. Ball, in 1933. He was then an emerging new seedsman. Price of the book—20¢; a modest 64 pages. Close to 100,000 copies of the many following editions have been sold worldwide since then.

But back to the BALL RED BOOK, 14th edition—and the future!

As this edition goes to press, U.S. and Canadian growers are knee deep in the painful realities of free trade. Imports! Cut pompons and carnations are badly hurt, roses feeling the pinch. Pot plants seriously threatened. Bedding plants so far so good—but no guarantee here either. A key goal of our new edition is to include a thorough briefing on state-of-the-art mechanization and computerization. Labor saving! Basic to cost efficiency—which is our *real defense* against imports.

The good news about all this: Production of most ornamental crops worldwide is moving rapidly toward mechanization—so far, in fact, that growing most crops need no longer be a labor-intensive job. Those who will survive economically in the years ahead (we feel) really must accept and move into this mechanized /computerized world. Many of our major crops will no longer be grown where labor is cheapest—the job will go to the most mechanized, most efficient country. Example: The Boekestijn range in Holland: Here over 2 million 4- and 5-inch pot mums are grown in a 7-acre, totally mechanized range—incredibly, by only 12 people. And, the Middelburg family (again, Holland) grows, harvests, and packs 6 acres of year-round pompons—with only 4 people: Senior and his three hard-working sons.

The BALL RED BOOK has always aimed to be a basic text on the commercial culture of the crops of the day. The book is both for the many newcomers to our industry and for experienced growers trying a new crop or a new, better way to do the job. Or perhaps an old hand having a problem—and looking for answers. And certainly much used by student groups. It will be that again, completely updated. You will find the practical basics needed to grow most any commercial crop of the '80s—bedding, pot, foliage, or cut flower.

Ours is and always has been the business-oriented approach to growing. Not how to grow the biggest, showiest, longest stem flower, but how to plan and grow the crop for maximum profit in the marketplace of today.

All the major crop chapters have been rewritten and updated. You'll find a new chapter by Paul Ecke, Jr., on poinsettias; Bob Miller on lilies; the Oglevees on geraniums; on bedding plants, mums, and dozens of lesser crops by the Ball staff. And Charles Conover on foliage. Bob Danielson, a very practical man, on roses. Jim Shanks on hydrangeas. And Ed Harthun of Ball on updating the 65 minor (but often important) miscellaneous crops.

Warm thanks to these many specialists who have contributed generously to this 50th anniversary edition of the BALL RED BOOK. And to brother Carl Ball, whose encouragement and interest in our various publications is much appreciated. And to the dedicated Ball staff people, many of whom have helped editorially—and others who have done the job of producing this book: Robert Petrucci, Gene McCormick, Janet Langefeld, Steve Wedemeyer. And to Rosalie Katz for typing it all plus resolving hundreds of questions. And to Lulu Warkentin for seeking out 99% of the glitches (you never get them all!). And lastly, to Catherine Rossbach, Carl Lindholm, and Tally Morgan of Reston Publishing Company—our new partners in the project—for their good support.

I hope you'll find it a useful book.

Vic Ball
West Chicago, Illinois

P.S. There are numerous references throughout this book to *Grower Talks*. This is a grower publication available by writing *Grower Talks*, P.O. Box 501, West Chicago, Illinois 60185. Back copies subject to availability.

SECTION I

The Physical Plant—A Labor/Fuel/Cost-Efficient Physical Plant for the '80s

Chapter 1

GROWING STRUCTURES

First, some general considerations.

START FRESH!

So often we see growers struggling to adapt old ranges to modern mechanization, heating, etc. In many cases, it just won't work. We do see quite a few growers who simply move a few miles out of the city, find some fresh open land, spend some money leveling it—and then they are ready to really start building a modern greenhouse range. Examples: Alexander Masson, Kansas City, or really any one of the Van Wingerden ranges anywhere. Mechanization demands, first of all, flat well-drained land to build on; second, wide hard-surfaced aisles. And of course any new project of this kind should have ample land available for expansion.

There is something psychological about doing all this—it says that you and your staff are committed to the future. Bankers like that. Note the section "To Remodel or Rebuild" later in this chapter.

One possible exception to all this: We do often see growers with a smaller old greenhouse range which the city has grown around. And such growers do convert such places into retail outlets. The public likes to buy from the grower—

and when they see a glass roof they think everything was grown there by the proprietor. Besides, the public just loves to wander around a glass greenhouse. Often such growers build attractive "store front" structures upfront. And of course always good signs and parking. It may be tough—but we've seen a lot of growers buy expensive next-door lots for just parking (Kramers, Neenah, Wisconsin).

And one more thought on all this: If you're going to pull up stakes from the old family range and build a modern producing unit, are you sure you're in the right part of the country? We see a light scattering of northern growers moving into the Southeast and Texas. This does mean moving from the population center (the market), but there are major advantages in winter light and fuel costs. Many larger growers operate both northern ranges and new operations in the South. Or the Far West!

Speaking of all this, there is a point that has puzzled us for a long time: Why are bedding plants grown in the North and shipped to the South? There would be a lot of reasons for doing it just the other way around. Again, winter/spring light is better in the South, fuel cost is lower, and labor might tend even to be less expensive. A few growers are moving this way—a classic example is Dick Hazeleger and son, Dirk, a Michigan bedding grower who moved to Atlanta and built 16 acres of modern bedding production.

WHICH STRUCTURE, WHICH ROOF?

A rather tough complicated question—and often a very difficult choice for the grower. Here, briefly, are the chief contenders as of the mid-1980s. And some pros and cons, rough costs, for each.

Glass

Good glass has been the basic house on which our industry has been built. It is still widely used. Where management has long-range intentions, and is reasonably well capitalized, glass is still good business. No roof permits a higher percent of precious winter light to reach the crop than glass. If equipped with good single, or better yet, double, thermal sheets, glass will be a reasonably fuel-efficient roof. So often, even here in our own operation, we have figured costs of various other materials, and whenever you apply a 10- or 20-year look at the cost per year, glass wins. One compelling argument for glass: Virtually all the 25,000 acres of greenhouses in Holland today are glass. And much of Germany and England. Modern glass with aluminum bars, bar caps that protect the putty, and galvanized metal structures offer a very low maintenance cost.

Good American glass—as of the 1980s. This is IBG's standard glass house (Glas-Acre III). Note wide bar spacing and narrow bars—a very light house!

One of the decisions facing the North American grower is—which manufacturer? There are excellent greenhouse builders in the U.S., in Canada, and certainly in Europe, especially Holland. We will not attempt to list suppliers.

Here's a very low-priced structure—great for bedding plants only, in the Midwest. Structure material costs about 35¢ a square foot! Note the carefully ventilated heater. The grower: Pat Bellrose, Fahr Greenhouse, Glencoe, Missouri.

For one thing, the trade press carries the ads from all of them constantly. One point: In comparing bids, do compare carefully the liveload (weight of the roof itself) plus the windload for which the roof is designed. If in doubt, have these figures checked from the specifications by a structural engineer.

Dutch houses, in general, are mass produced for volume—typically Dutch. The result is that they tend to be somewhat lower in cost but sometimes less flexibility is available to the grower. Then, too, as of the mid-1980s, the major currency differences tend to favor Canadian or Dutch suppliers over the U.S. builder. On the other hand, the U.S. supplier tends to get the job done a little quicker and has replacement components more readily available.

Costs vary widely! Good ridge-and-furrow glass, one-acre blocks, the shell only, labor and material, will vary from $3.25 up to $4–$4.25 per square foot. This does not include site preparation, fan/pad cooling, heat, temperature control, benches, cement floors, heat sheets, water—plus a headhouse. All this tends to double or triple the total cost against the cost of the original shell. But this is a permanent, very low maintenance, fuel-efficient (with thermal sheets), and often labor-efficient range. Winter light availability will be the best available. And it will stay that way for a long time.

Inflated double poly for comparison, shell only (roof and sides), labor and material, for a one-acre block, ridge-and-furrow, will be a bit under $2 a square foot. Again, no cooling, no heat, no benches, etc. Add 50¢ for pad/fan cooling, add $1, at least, for thermal sheets, mechanized. And for poly add about 25¢ a square foot each time you re-cover the roof (12¢ for poly, 13¢ for labor, our estimate).

Major rose-growing areas across the northern U.S. typically are of glass. Roses demand maximum winter light. Also, the better holiday pot-plant growers tend to go to glass these days. Several major midwestern growers recently have switched from inflated double poly to glass. The problems: Lack of midwinter light and disease problems brought on by the high humidity under polyethylene.

Inflated Double Poly

This is very widely used in the U.S. and Canada today. Our personal guess is that inflated double poly is the most widely used roof in North America today. And there's lots of it being built each year. Virtually all of the large Van Wingerden ranges across the U.S. are inflated poly.

The great case for the inflated poly roof The great case for the inflated poly roof is most of all low initial cost. Perhaps 60% as much as good glass.

Inflated double poly—and note the use of a two-bay greenhouse roof to cover the headhouse (on the right). Jack Mast range, Grand Rapids area, Michigan.

Good example of a modern, gutter-connected, inflated double poly range. Moderate cost, high fuel efficiency; main limitation is winter light on light-sensitive crops in northern areas. This is the Sentry World (Insurance Company) range— used to produce 18000 square feet of 3½" annuals for their golf course. Location: Wausau, Wisconsin.

Also in its favor, especially when combined with a single thermal sheet, is that it is a very fuel-efficient roof. We hear on the order of 40% to 45% less fuel than glass without a thermal sheet.

Probably the most severe limitation of an inflated polyethylene roof is the relatively lower light penetration compared to good glass. In general, roses in the northern U.S. are not successful under double poly, and most holiday pot plants, including Valentine's and Easter mums, are marginal. A lot of them are grown under double poly and sometimes are very good quality. But the best growers seem to move to glass as soon as they can. The two reasons always given are the quality difference and disease problems because of the humidity under poly.

There are specific situations where double poly is in heavier use:

- The major bedding-plant grower who typically includes a crop of poinsettias, often shuts down in January and early February. This grower avoids the penalty of poor winter light, retains the advantage of fuel economy and low initial cost.

• Either a year-round pot-plant/bedding grower or a retail grower starting in business with limited capital will often go the double-poly way, simply because of lower initial cost. In a word, you can recover your invested capital out of earnings faster with double poly than you can with glass.

All of this looks a little different as you go farther south. A good example: Norm White, Chesapeake, Virginia, who is certainly at least one of the top-quality pot-plant growers in the U.S. All under inflated double poly. Note, though, that his location in Chesapeake, Virginia means a good bit higher winter light than areas such as Chicago and Cleveland.

Another example of the top-quality northern grower under double poly: Greilings at Denmark (Green Bay), Wisconsin. About a 10-acre range, again bedding plants in the spring followed with foliage baskets and poinsettias in the fall. This is one of the very low winter light areas in the U.S. Quality of what we see here is first class.

Then there is Seattle. Some of the quality growers in this area will tell you that you just can't do quality crops under double poly in Seattle. And yet there are growers who are making a commercial success in that area under poly.

Growers so often express concern about heavy snow or wind destroying a poly greenhouse. And it does happen. However, growers using a top-quality fastener to secure the poly—and who know how to put it on right—seem to rate poly even a better bet under heavy snow than glass.

One negative for double-poly bedding plants: On the warm days of late April and early May, it just gets too warm under poly for quality bedding plants. And there isn't much the grower can do about it—still faced with the threat of occasional frost. Quality deteriorates very rapidly under such conditions, except of course for the few pioneers who are equipped to "roll their crops outdoors" during April/May.

HID Lights Plus Inflated Poly

Here's an interesting option especially for high-light crops in low winter light northern areas. The plan: Install HID lights under an inflated double-poly roof. The lights will give off ample light for the critical Christmas, Valentine's, and Easter rose crops. Bill Vermeer, Toronto grower, uses double poly with HID lights on his roses, and along with the improved lighting on the crop, the HID lights also give off a lot of heat. "With temperatures down to 45°, the HID lights radiate enough heat so that virtually no added heat is needed—assuming a tight poly house." HID lights under a Quonset roof would require quite a high gutter to permit placing the bulbs high enough for efficient light distribution. Power cost is another critical point. Many growers will negotiate special rates for off-hours of light. After 10 or 11 p.m.

We're hearing recently of a new HID light (called "Poot Light") that delivers light on a more horizontal plane than the traditional bulb. Result: You need not position the bulbs so high up in the air. Source: PL Light Systems, St. Catharines, Ontario and Ball-Superior, Ltd. in Mississauga, Ontario.

Wash the Roof

A little trick on poly: Monsanto's 603 is generally accepted as a two-year roof in northern areas. We learned from Monsanto recently that if it were hosed off under high pressure and with an appropriate solvent or hot soapy water after two years, that the light reduction from dust can be effectively removed. And, the grower can get a third year from the roof. Not often done—but perhaps should be.

Rigid Double Plastics (Structured Sheets)

They've been around for a decade or more. As of the mid-1980s there are dozens of substantial ranges covered with them, including several substantial northern rose growers. Who, by the way, are reporting excellent quality and production—just as good as glass. Certainly the past year or two they have attracted substantially more attention than ever before. There have been dozens of new installations going in in the past year or two. They are definitely on the way up.

The case for structured sheets:

Fuel economy   Generally we hear about 40% to 50% less fuel than a single sheet of glass without thermal sheets. That's a lot of saving—and a key case for structured sheets.

Good light transmission   The U factor of these materials is about 0.65. Inflated double poly 0.7 to 0.75, glass 1.13. Of course, the lower the factor, the less the fuel loss. So let's say perhaps 10% more fuel efficiency than double poly and 40% to 45% less than glass.

Ten-year reasonable life expectancy   With almost zero maintenance. Growers seem to expect a maximum of 5% loss of light after ten years on the roof. And again, northern rose crops, quality and production—every bit as good as glass.

Retrofit   It is relatively easy to refit the roof bars to accommodate structured sheets.

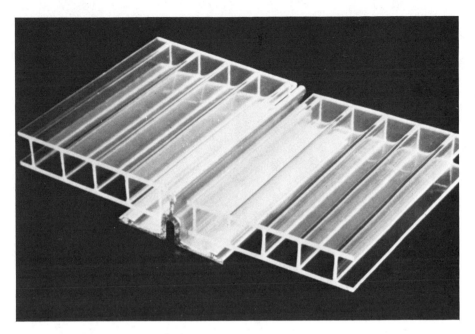

*An example of a structured sheet. It's two layers of rigid plastic perhaps ¼"
apart. Structured sheets show a lot of promise as North American greenhouse
roof coverings.*

Now the down side:

- Probably most of all, lack of in-depth experience with them.
- Gradual loss of light—5% in ten years with acrylic is not bad,—poly-
carbonates are not that good.
- Fire—the acrylics are as fire-vulnerable as fiberglass.
- Yellowing—the polycarbonates yellow over a period of time.
- Snow—the top layer of a structured sheet will be cool; snow melts
slowly. But it doesn't seem to have been a problem with growers so
far.

Principal Contenders

The three contenders:

- Acrylic—as can be seen by the accompanying table, offers the best
light transmission over a period of years.

11

Structured sheets are widely used for ends and sidewalls of double poly ranges. Good light penetration, very fuel efficient, and they resist breakage from vandalism.

- Polycarbonates—lowest cost.
- The new combos—an interesting combination of the above two—apparently capturing most of the good qualities of its two parents, without the problems.

A few suppliers of these materials, by the way: Poly Growers, Inc. (717) 546-3216. Stuppy Greenhouse Supply (816) 842-3071; Nexus Greenhouses (303) 457-9199; and Double A Truss (209) 239-1271.

Table 1-1 STRUCTURED SHEETS*

	Acrylics (Exolite, Acrycel Techlite, Exo-glaze)[1]	Polycarbonates (Polygal, Qualex, Cyroflex)	Combo (Polygal S.G.[2] Profile sheet)
How many years without serious loss of light transmission?	Good—typically only 5% light loss in ten years.	Not as good, can lose up to 15% light transmission in ten years. Very much faster light loss in Florida—Southern California.	Good. 5% loss in ten years.[3]
Does it yellow as it ages?	It does not yellow.	It does yellow.	Good—no yellowing.[3]
High impact strength—not subject to hail or vandalism damage.	Can be broken with a hammer or severe hail.	Very high impact strength. You can walk on this roof.	Good—high impact strength.
Does it burn?	It will burn—about like fiberglass.	Highly flame resistant.	Good—highly flame resistant.
Can it be bent around a hoop house roof?	Does not bend. Some new acrylics do bend a bit.	Yes! It can be bent around a hoop roof.	Good—it can be bent.
Cost, very rough—depending on quantity, etc.	Around $2 a square foot of panel.[4]	From $1.25 to $1.50 per square foot of panel.	From $1.40 to $1.60 per square foot.

[1]Rough Bros. are marketing both acrylic and polycarbonate under the Techlite name. (513) 242-0310.
[2]Poligal USA, Inc. (608) 884-6394.
[3]Apparently the thin layer of acrylic on top of the polycarbonate sheet screens out the damaging ultraviolet—and now the polycarbonate lasts longer. Same thing for the yellowing problem.
[4]We're hearing of a new 8-mm-thick acrylic (vs. the normal 16 mm) which we hear will be priced competitive with polycarbonates. Phone Ball Seed's Jim Schield (312) 231-3500 for details.
*Thanks to David Bilhorn for help on this table.

13

An interesting sawtooth application—aluminum frame and fiberglass roof. Open sides here allow ample ventilation. Photo taken at Pan American Plant Company, Parrish, Florida. Bob Danielson, left, and Steven Peters of PAP in the photo. And note photo on the right, an inflated tube to close the "tooth" of the saw.

Fiberglass

There was a major surge of new fiberglass structures built in the 1970s. Clearly that has slowed down—but there are still substantial new ranges being built. Somehow you see most of it in California and the Southeast and Southwest.

Light transmission initially is quite good—but over a period of eight or ten years, most present materials deteriorate rather badly. We are hearing of a new fiberglass that carries a 20-year guarantee. So perhaps progress is being made on this point. Another plus: There are no bar cracks allowing cold air to enter the greenhouse. On the other hand, the wavy configuration of a fiberglass roof means more exposed area, so that's a negative in terms of fuel.

Fiberglass will burn, and there have been disastrous flash fires of major ranges. Growers learn to build fiberglass in smaller blocks to isolate the fire. Also, a metal or cement wall from the ground up 30" or 35" will prevent grass fires from igniting the house.

To build an acre of fiberglass, ridge-and-furrow, again the shell only, costs around $3.25 a square foot. The roof material cost is about comparable, but labor is substantially less for fiberglass. It is, of course, not as permanent as glass.

About Sedo

There is much engineering detail on all these roof materials in *Grower Talks*, September 1981. Sedo is a different approach to the greenhouse roof problem. This time it's two sheets of glass glazed or welded together—with a

9 mm ($\frac{3}{8}$") space between the sheets for insulation. The weld is so tight and permanent that there is almost no problem of air or moisture penetration or of algae forming. CO_2 is introduced into the space between the sheets to prevent condensation. The upper sheet is an extremely strong tempered glass. Very heavy hail may break the top sheet occasionally but it has never gone through both layers. Fuel economy reported is about 40% saving vs. single glass. Light transmission: The Germans say about 90% as much light as with single glass. It is of course permanent and totally fire resistant. There is a snow problem—obviously snow will melt slower on a Sedo roof (cooler top surface). However, the experience in Germany has been encouraging here. The panels are very heavy. A 14 square foot panel weighs about 66 lbs. One result is that the trusses that support it must be roughly twice as strong as with single glass.

As of this writing, there are almost no serious installations of Sedo in the U.S.

Double Glaze on the Bar (Winandy)

Another alternative—now *two* layers of glass glazed to a conventional roof bar in the usual way. The E. G. Hill Company, Richmond, Indiana, has substantial area in this type of roof and reports major fuel economy and "good roses." The manufacturer reports about 50% to 60% fuel saving vs. single glass. Again, it is heavier than single glass and that does put more pressure on the structure. As to longevity, again it's permanent, and that's great. Experience as of this writing is relatively limited. Source: Winandy Greenhouse Company Inc., 2211 Peacock Road, Richmond, Indiana 47374. (317) 935-2111.

Listen to IBG's Roger Hertel, general manager of greenhouse production, on what growers are building in the mid-1980s. "In broad sweep, inflated poly is probably number one, then glass and fiberglass are about a tie for number two. Areas like Michigan, heavy in bedding plants, use a lot of poly. California is building a lot of both glass and fiberglass for cut flowers. We are selling a lot of rigid double plastics for northern rose growers although the West Coast growers are building more glass."

SEPARATE HOUSES WASTE FUEL!

Not generally realized: A series of separate Quonset plastic houses will burn from 30% to 40% more fuel vs. the same area covered by gutter-connected houses. Same general comparison between separate glass houses and a ridge-and-furrow or connected glass range. The reason is obvious. The total exposed wall surface is much higher on an acre of separate houses vs. an acre of gutter-connected houses. On separate houses, each house has a lot of exposed side-wall. On a gutter-connected range, there is only one exposed sidewall.

We heard recently of a Jersey grower who was talked into tearing down a 20,000 square foot range of separate hoop houses (report from Bill Roberts at Rutgers, New Jersey). He replaced them with gutter-connected inflated poly plus thermal sheets. Result: His annual fuel cost dropped from $1.63 per square foot to 83¢. An important plus in the connected houses is that you have far better control over working crews. And of course as you get into mechanization, gutter-connected houses are a must.

There is another related point here. There are many different designs of even gutter-connected houses. Some have a relatively flat roof, others have a higher arched roof—from gutter to ridge and back to gutter. The higher arched roof again will have more exposed vertical surface than the flat roof. Again, fuel savings. Of course, a flatter roof could be a problem in the matter of snow removal.

TO REMODEL OR REBUILD?*

Another tough and very important question facing many growers today. A brand new range can save a lot on labor, on fuel costs—and many times, will produce better quality. Yet it costs a lot of money to rebuild and in balance, it may not be good business for you today. Often there are tax and interest rate considerations. Also available capital.

Here again, were several knowledgeable, experienced growers who have been through this quite in depth:

Tom Doak—Yoder's   Tom brings much experience to this question from his long involvement in Yoder operations. A few comments:

> If you do go to the expense of rebuilding, be certain that when you are through you will have important savings in both energy costs and labor costs to show for your investment. Example: double poly, we find, does save an honest 25–30% against a single glass roof. Also heat sheets (gutter-to-gutter applied at night) yield between 25–40% savings in our experience. We just did three acres of heat sheets at Leamington, Ontario, cost about $1.00 per sq. ft. of ground covered. We figure it will pay off in about one and one-half years in fuel savings. You do have to watch snow load here, though. When snow accumulates to dangerous weight loads, you want the outside of the roof warm—to melt that snow off. That means no heat sheet. Automated heat sheets also mean automated shade for mums, etc.
>
> We figure fuel cost alone, about $1.00 per sq. ft. per year for 60° house in the North today. So if you can save one-third of your fuel bill, you are saving $15,000 a year. How many years will it take to pay for your new heat sheets or Lapseal?

*Based on presentation at The Ohio Short Course, reported in *Grower Talks*, 1980–81.

Certainly crop turnover has to be watched, too. It is simply that more dollars per bench per year increases your ability to carry overhead costs such as fuel and labor.

Moving benches, however you do it, eliminate most of that walk space. You not only cut the fuel bill 15–20% but really you can build 20% less greenhouse area and turn out the same amount of crops.

We think a lot about material handling devices. Unfortunately, most old greenhouses were built in an era of cheap labor and often don't lend themselves well to this.

Decisions on rebuilding or remodeling also have to be looked at from a tax point of view. Talk to your tax accountant. Remember that repairs and modifications generally do not qualify for investment tax credit savings.

Another point: it takes a lot of money to rebuild—and even for extensive modifications. In some cases it may be a question of whether capital is available for this purpose. Greenhouses are not the best collateral—to many bankers.

Tom talked about industrial revenue bonds—which, in effect, make capital available for improvements or rebuilding at "tax-free bond" rates. Generally 7.5% to 9% interest and, in some cases, you can get 100% financing. Usual range seven to ten years. They are done in cooperation with the local municipality. One requirement is they must create new jobs or save existing ones. But the low interest rate is very helpful.

Finally, the question of rebuilding or remodeling boils down to which route will enable you to recover your investment sooner. But to make an intelligent decision you really have to put down all the factors involved. Tom displayed a table which we thought was an excellent approach to the problem (see p. 18).

Robbie Roberson—Oakdell   Robbie is Service Director of Weyerhaeuser's large range in Apopka, Florida. They are major wholesale producers, especially of foliage and flowering pot plants. Robbie also had some constructive points—on the question of rebuilding or remodeling.

Important to think first of your personal and corporate long-term objectives. Are you in business for the long haul—or do circumstances force you to short-term thinking?

Think also of industry trends—the long range outlook, especially for the crops in which you specialize.

Certainly a consideration is simply availability of capital. At 13-15%, the businessman of today has to think twice before assuming major debts for either remodeling or rebuilding. You have to ask yourself—are there alternatives? Can we remodel and achieve much of our goals—without the expense of a major new physical plant? Don't forget, rebuilding itself is a big headache.

Important question—do I really want this business to expand importantly over the years ahead?

Flower growing is by nature a labor-intensive industry. And labor is getting scarcer and more costly every day. Therefore, we base our plans here on maximum mechanization—even though it costs a lot of money. We want to make people more productive.

CASH FLOW ANALYSIS
(only on money saved)

Effect on:	Yr.1	Yr.2	Yr.3	Yr.4	Yr.5	Yr.6	Yr.7	Yr.8	Yr.9	Yr.10
Net Investment										
Wages & Fringes										
Utilities										
Production Supplies										
Freight										
Maintenance										
Interest										
Miscellaneous										
Total										
After Tax Effect										
(at your tax rate) of:										
Investment Tax Credit										
Depreciation										
Total Cash In (Out)										
Cumulative										

1. Net Investment—Let's say we are considering a new block of greenhouses that will cost $100,000. Under Year 1, show $100,000 cash outflow.

2. Wages and Fringes—If labor efficiencies in the new range will save $10,000 per year, show $10,000 saved for each year from Year 1 through Year 10.

3. Utilities—Let's say thermal sheets or a double poly roof will save $12,000 per year on fuel, show $12,000 for each year—for Year 1 through Year 10.

And so on through the other items. Don't forget added interest cost for money borrowed—a minus cash flow.

Watch tax implications: Fuel saving is only saving net after taxes. Fuel is a deductible expense of operations. Same for labor saved. Interest expense also tax deductible.

Depreciation—Not a direct cash outflow—but, there is a tax saving each year as you depreciate the new greenhouses—a cash inflow.

Investment Tax Credit—Certainly this is a cash saving—a cash flow plus.

At the bottom, add up your cash gains and losses. How many years of more efficient operation will it take to recover your $100,000 investment? What net reduction in operating expenses after that?

Done carefully, this table will give you a realistic basis for a go or no go decision. Certainly such a matrix accurately prepared will be a major help in borrowing money from your banker. Bankers understand this kind of talk!

Certainly it is important to plan carefully before either rebuilding or committing to a major new facility. Plan in complete detail certainly including cash flow for the immediate future; you have got to do this before you go to the banker, and then you have to keep them informed as you go along.

A good starting point for a decision on remodeling or rebuilding is to get the hard information on your operating costs today. Example, what are the real costs in labor to pot a mum—and then to move it to the flowering bench? And how much cost to space it? How much labor cost per bed for spraying, watering, feeding? A good way to do this is to account for every minute of all your employees for a sample week—perhaps three or four times a year. You will learn a lot!

Another good approach to this planning is to visit other growers. Often you will gain good practical ideas.

Robbie talked a good bit on portable beds (*Grower Talks,* January 1980, page 5). These are the 20-25 ft. "tables" which can be moved into the potting room for potting, then back out to the greenhouse where they become the growing bench. Sounds like a lot of work—and only for the very large grower—but, says Robbie, "Not so. We find major economies in moving as much as possible of our greenhouse operations into the headhouse. We get much better control of labor, realize important savings in unit cost of typical greenhouse operations. I believe this would apply even to a smaller range."

Potting machines—"We can't afford to do without one. Again it just makes our people more productive. We work hard, by the way, on mechanizing all movement of soil—keep it easy." Continues Robbie:

Central irrigation control, again, can be a labor saver. You can water a range without walking all over the place.

Some Dutch growers do excellent pot plants right on the ground—and often use overhead monorail systems to move things around. Monorails are also used over the tops of many benches over there. Also pallets can be great labor savers. We use carts—and often with trailers. Up to six carts drawn by one tractor. Always rubber-tired. Be certain everything possible is put on wheels. Sprayers, hoses, even trash cans. Put telephones all over the place so they are convenient. Again, always wide, good cement walks.

Finally, our goal is to be more capital intensive and less labor intensive.

G.V.B.

Chapter 2

A FUEL-EFFICIENT HEATING SYSTEM*

UNIT HEATERS VS. CENTRAL BOILERS

This is the first basic decision—and again pros and cons each way. Not generally realized: the fact that central boilers in general are about 10% more fuel efficient than unit heaters. We hear often 75% for a boiler, 65% for unit heaters. Plus the fact that central boilers typically are quickly convertible from oil to gas or propane. These are two very big advantages!

On the downside, unit heaters take less initial investment. And there's less to go wrong (heating mains, return systems, condensate pumps, etc.). And, of course, if one unit heater fails, the others pick up the slack. Plus—if you add a house, you add a couple more heaters and away you go. But a 10% penalty in fuel cost over ten years is a lot of money. Another plus for unit heaters: You simply don't need a boiler room. Which together with the difference in cost between unit heaters and boilers adds up to a substantial economy in favor of unit heaters.

Appropriate to all of this is a story in the *North Carolina Flower Growers Bulletin*, December 1982, by Dr. D. H. Willits. What he is saying in effect is with the typical on-off controls, some heat is wasted because the whole unit

*Parts of this chapter are based on stories by the author that appeared in *Grower Talks* 1982–1983.

 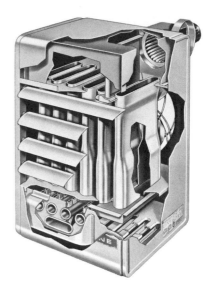

Here is the new Modine "high-efficiency" gas-fired unit heater. Modine reports that it achieves 83% average thermal efficiency vs. older units at about 76%. It recirculates exhaust gases. Also, the fan only operates when there is heat to distribute. Progress! At right is a cutaway view of the heater.

The Incendo boiler. Very low operational labor cost, burns certain low-cost fuels mechanically, and initial cost substantially lower. Promising!

shuts down (fan and all) while there is still a lot of heat energy in the unit heater. Conversely, there can be fan operation when the heat exchanger is not ready for the fan. He proposes a thermal switch (Grainger model #2E245) which will turn the fan off at 110° and open it at 90°F. He projects saving of the installation cost in less than one year. For a copy of the Bulletin, write Roy Larson, Department of Horticultural Science, North Carolina State University, Raleigh, NC 27607.

Another basic penalty of unit heaters: They are almost always installed overhead. And as will be developed later in this chapter, systems that introduce the heat up in the attic of the house are very wasteful compared to heat distributed down at the soil surface. We have seen heat from unit heaters ducted down to the ground—under the benches—but it's awkward and ra.ely done.

Recent improvements in unit heaters are improving their efficiency importantly. Modine now offers a "high efficiency heater" that passes hot gases through a second heat exchange area. And other improvements—for which Modine claims a 20% plus improvement in efficiency. Contact Modine Manufacturing Co. for details (1500 Dekoven Ave., Racine, WI 53401.)

Another improvement is a new system of installing a horizontal steam heat exchange unit overhead, directing the warm air down below the bench

This unit will raise 4,000 gallons of water per hour by 20°. Unit costs roughly $10,000. Bob Bernacchi (left), the grower, reports "very noticeable difference in take-off of such crops as lilies with warm water."

(through poly tubes). Then under the bench to distribute the heat (poly tubes). Important benefits from all of this. All of which is covered in detail in *Grower Talks,* April 1984.

MODERN HOT WATER CIRCULATING SYSTEMS

Most of the major new ranges we've seen in recent years are heated with quite sophisticated hot water systems. These systems are costly—but efficient. Basic to the system is the capability of varying the temperature of hot water in the circulating pipes in the greenhouses according to the need. Now add computer control to this and it anticipates coming sudden heat load—so the boiler can start working ahead of time to handle it. In the same way, it will pull back the boiler in case of an anticipated drop in the load. Like the sun coming out on a cloudy day.

The systems—and the computer involvement in them—are complex, but offer major economies in fuel.

A good example: the Greiling range at Denmark, Wisconsin. For anyone interested, this system was engineered by The Van Wingerden Plastic Greenhouse Company, (704) 891-7389. The boiler for this system was supplied by Kewanee Boiler Corp. (314) 532-7755. The Greilings add that there have been improvements in the boilers since they installed theirs. They might use a different approach if they did the job again.

Interesting point: Growers just aren't using steam for sterilizing soil as much since most crops are grown in artificial mixes. Which takes away one of the important cases for a steam system. Plus the greater efficiency of modern hot water circulating heat.

STEAM HEAT

For whatever reason, a great many of the major greenhouse ranges across North America today were established two generations ago—and at that time, steam was used in most cases. So there are lots of steam heating systems in use today. Steam works. And it does supply steam for sterilizing soil—and any other process work requiring heat, like heating water for crops.

However, from all we can gather at this time, new ranges being built today generally use hot water. First, you dispose of the need for a whole condensate return system, pumps, traps, etc. Second, to our knowledge, hot water, if anything, tends to be a bit more efficient. Also, a hot water system provides a more even heat. Also, modern computerized environmental control systems work well with hot water systems. The computer can control the temperature of the water in response to the heat demand in the greenhouses. Also, the computer can turn off the water circulating system when it's not needed.

On the other side of the coin, a steam system can respond quickly to a sudden heat load—faster than hot water. However, doing a lot of this sort of thing puts a severe strain on the boiler. Sudden expansion of metal is not good. Also, the steam pipes are full of cold water—and as steam hits this water more problems develop.

Of course, there will be situations in any individual case that may work in favor of either steam or hot water. Better talk to a heating engineer—and the suppliers of equipment involved.

INFRARED HEAT

Seems to attract strong proponents and many test installations here and there—but the mainstream of heating still seems to be going toward hot water or steam systems. Infrared is extremely efficient in terms of percent of heat recovered from the fuel—but there seem to be limitations.

We hear of maintenance problems. Burners fail. Exhaust stacks corrode. And the system is more costly than unit heaters or steam boilers. Plus the need to adjust cultural practices. Like timing lilies. Infrared heats only the object it reaches—it may heat the upper leaves, but not lower foliage and the soil (especially if there is a heavy canopy of leaves, and plants are closely spaced). Many growers do succeed well with a variety of crops under infrared. Perhaps part of the problem is getting used to working with this system of heating.

All this will bring letters from infrared partisans. And of course, all heating systems have problems. If infrared is tempting, try a house. Certainly progress is being made in making infrared do the job for the grower.

HEAT THE PLANT, NOT THE AIR*

From talking with growers who have used soil heating both in the U.S. and in Holland we get the feeling that soil heating might be a real sleeper. It's not new—but a scattering of solid grower experiences are turning up some almost unbelievable fuel economy. And accelerated plant to sell crop times. And better quality. Most crops like warm feet. Gerberas, for example, produce a lot better with warm feet. Bedding and pot crops mature faster.

*Much of this section is based on a story in *Grower Talks,* April 1983, by the author.

The Rutgers University floor heating plan (Bill Rogers). Plants grow so much faster with warm feet and fuel bills are so much lower with the heat down at the plants—not up near the roof.

For some reason, growers generally don't seem to have realized its potential. Two approaches we see: burying hot water pipe in soil—or in a layer of concrete 3–4" deep. Plan #2: Biotherm. First we'll talk buried pipe.

The mechanics are simple. You level the floor, lay out ¾" plastic pipe spaced 12" apart. On top of this goes 3" of porous concrete. You pipe warm water through the plastic pipes at 90° to 100°F—and that's it. Pot plants or bedding plants can be grown right on the floor—or cut flowers the same way—with simple sideboards.

Bill Roberts, Rutgers Ag Engineer, is closely identified with all this, and reports that polyethylene is the best tube. By the way, Bill reports roughly 150 acres of floor heating installed across the U.S. today—much of it as a result of Bill's talks, publications, etc.

Poinsettias—with ⅙ as much oil per plant! Here's one of several striking examples we've come across of this soil heat idea at work. The growers: the Swanekamps, Kube-Pak Garden Plants. The Swanekamps operate about 500,000 square feet of bedding plants/pot plants in Allentown, N.J. The case in point: a 60,000 square foot block of poinsettias grown on the normal fall schedule. 35,000 6" plants.

In 1978, the Swanekamps had no thermal sheets, no floor heat, and they used 28,000 gallons of oil (0.8 gallons per plant). By 1982, they'd installed

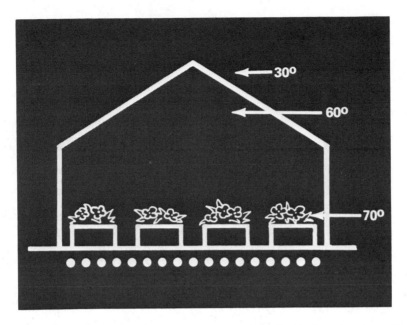

Another way to save big on fuel: With the heat installed below the plants (buried pipe here), the plant temperature will be warm (70°), the attic temperature cooler—maybe 60° to 65°. The same house with overhead unit heaters and polyethylene tube distribution might well have 75° to 80° (attic temperature). And always remember, if you cut the difference between inside and outside roof temperature in half, you cut the fuel bill in half.

floor heat and a single-sheet, aluminized blanket and cut fuel use to 5,000 gallons (0.14 gallons per plant—about 17% as much as four years earlier).

Typically, it was not a precise scientific experiment—the thermal sheets did help—but certainly not that much. Poinsettia temperatures, by the way, were 68° until October 1 (quite warm to get them going), 65° through October, then gradually to 55° through December. The poinsettia crop was reported as first class.

Another example—again at Swanekamps. This time bedding plants. First, Bill Swanekamp reports "With floor heat we can transplant the crop three to four weeks later than without it. Therefore, our January fuel cost took a huge dive after we installed floor heat. We simply weren't using space, except for seed germination during January. In fact, we burned 70,000 gallons of oil in January 1978, and we are using 8,000 gallons for the same month today!"

About costs: We took the figures from Bill Roberts and Swanekamps—on tubes, pouring the concrete, etc. The total conversion from bare ground to soil heat/concrete floor. Labor and material comes out to about 70 cents per square foot. Roughly $30,000 per acre.

A great way to get heat down below the crop: First, install an overhead heat exchange unit (left photo); duct the heat down below the bench, then distribute it to the end of the bench in a second poly tube (above right photo).

Biotherm—a different approach Again, plastic tubes piping warm water to the crop. Yes, heating the plant and not the whole house. Biotherm delivers heat more precisely where it's needed. Therefore, it's more economical in terms of fuel used. But initial installation cost is higher than for other heating systems. Most installations are used for some forms of propagating—seed, cuttings, etc. Source: Biotherm Engineering, 421 Second Street, Petaluma, CA 94952 (704) 763-4444. Competitive producers of similar equipment: G.H. Energy Systems Ltd., 926 E. Smith Rd., Bellingham, WA 98226, (604) 383-5424; and Bio-Energy Systems Co., 221 Canal St., Ellenville, NY 12428, (914) 647-6700.

We've seen dozens of 4' × 10' or 4' × 20' benches equipped with Biotherm—for seed germination of bedding plants. The system adapts itself well to this. And, by the way, provides heat at a fraction of the energy cost of electric cables.

We have one grower report (Keith Talbot of Wolfe's, Waco, TX) on a Biotherm installation. Keith reported about 7,000 square feet of bench area heated, including tubes, controls, etc. Complete labor and material about $10,000. A larger installation would cost less per square foot.

By far the largest installation of Biotherm we know of is at Frank Cobb's, Sandyland, Las Cruces, NM range. The range covers about 500,000 square

Biotherm—an interesting way to put heat just under the crop—where it's needed. Great for germinating seed, rooting cuttings, etc.

feet. About 80,000 square feet of greenhouse are equipped with Biotherm here—all of it for propagating mums. 6" pots are filled (by potting machine at the greenhouse bench), are moved by pot-moving belt to the growing bench equipped with Biotherm tubes. The pots are then watered, and unrooted cuttings are stuck directly into the pot. The tubes are spaced 2" apart down the bench. It's, of course, a closed circulating system. Temperatures seem to be quite uniform from end to end of a 150' bench.

Result of all this: In 10 to 11 days, an unrooted cutting becomes a well established mum plant—roots all over the top half of the pot. It's an impressive example of what warm soil can do for a crop. Frank is quite pleased with the whole installation—and it is a sort of classic use of the Biotherm tube. One obvious plus for Biotherm: You don't heat the walks—just the growing area. Temperature at the plant level will be perhaps 65°; up in the attic it will be 50° or less.

Why the huge savings with soil heat? Back to Bill Swanekamp—and eliminating ⅚ of the oil cost for a poinsettia.

A little of it Bill Roberts feels is a result of sun heating of the soil. Especially during August and September there's a lot of bright sunshine—and Bill reports that there will be very little fuel needed to heat water for the tubes until 10 p.m. or 11 p.m.—following a bright day.

Another part of the saving is the obvious reduction in crop time—fewer weeks plant-to-sell. Which translates into fewer gallons of oil per poinsettia.

29

But the really big economy is another story. To get the idea, you have to go back to the basics of how many BTUs or horsepower it takes to heat a given amount of greenhouse. In other words, what is the theoretical base for heat load for which heating systems are designed? In a word, the heat load is calculated on:

- Total square feet exposed to outdoor temperature.

- Multiplied by the difference between inside and outside temperatures.

Obviously, with a given amount of exposed roof and sidewall surface, if you can reduce the spread between inside and outside temperature by half, you will cut the fuel cost by half. And something like that seems to be what happens in a soil-heated greenhouse. Down at the ground among the plants, the temperature will be 60° to 65°—as needed for the crop. But up in the attic, the temperature can be 10° or 20° less. Which, interestingly enough, is the opposite of the way most greenhouses are heated. Typically, unit heaters or steam pipes are located overhead with the result that the attic will be the warmest place in the greenhouse, not the coolest.

So you begin to realize that, in fact, soil heating may often result in as much as 20° or 30° less difference between inside the greenhouse and outside temperatures. And that, we suspect, is where the huge savings are coming from.

One negative: Everything here grows on the ground. And, of course, it's hard to disbud a pot mum—in fact, you would certainly set it up on a stand to do the job. But, on the other hand, many pot crops can be, and are, grown very well on the ground. Certainly bedding plants. By the way, what a great way to keep the soil warm for growing plugs.

We know of almost no cut flower applications of soil heating today—but there should be an obvious advantage for roses, mums, etc. in northern areas.

Again: We suspect the soil heat idea has major savings potential for many growers! And will grow better crops in less time.

BASIS FOR CALCULATING BTU REQUIREMENTS*

Not that every grower should be a heating engineer—but it will help growers appreciate the factors that influence heat loss in a greenhouse if they understand how the BTU capacity of a heating system is calculated.

In principle, it's rather simple. The heat loss (in British thermal units per hour) will equal the area (roof, sides, and ends of the greenhouse) times the

*Thanks to Werner Rader, of Geo. J. Ball, for technical details here.

Important point on fuel! An acre of separate *hoop houses (above) will almost double the fuel cost vs. the same acre gutter-connected (below). It's simply that you eliminate all those sidewalls—which means about half as much exposed surface.*

difference between inside and outside temperature, divided by the *R* factor (rate of heat loss through the roof).

Let's assume that the total square foot area of the roof, sides, and ends of a greenhouse equal 10,000 square feet. Let's assume also that we want the capability of maintaining 60°F with 0°F outside—a 60° difference. 10,000 square feet times 60 (degrees difference) divided by 1.13 (U factor of glass) will result in a BTU demand of 530,973 BTU capacity. Which can be satisfied by one 600,000 BTU heater or six heaters each with a 100,000 BTU capacity.

There are other considerations! Condition of the roof—important glass slippage, or even the glass lap cracks can affect this. High winds will obviously increase the demand for heat. A glass roof with lap cracks will freeze over on a very cold night, greatly reducing the heat demand. And of course, different roof materials each have their own U factor or heat loss factor.

Another factor: Where heat distribution system (pipes or poly tubes) are positioned below the bench and below the crop or better yet in the soil, the temperature up just under the roof tends to be a good bit lower—which will influence heat load importantly.

Lastly, we again urge talking with heating engineers or suppliers of this equipment.

OTHER HELPFUL DATA

First, here are the U factors for various greenhouse roofing materials. The lower the factor, the more fuel efficient the roof:

Material	U factors
glass, single layer	1.13
glass, double layer	.65
polyethylene, single film	1.15
polyethylene, double-film inflated	.70
fiberglass	1.0
acrylic, double sheet	.56
polycarbonate, double sheet	.62
concrete block 8″	.51
asbestos board ¼″	1.10
polyurethane foam applied at site, 1″ thick	.14
black sateen	.65
polyester fabric, spun bound, reemy 2016	1.20

Which Month Uses the Fuel?

HEATING REQUIREMENTS BY MONTH AT STATE COLLEGE, PA, EXPRESSED IN DEGREE DAYS AND PERCENTAGE OF TOTAL

	Average degree days per heating season	Percent of total heating season
July	0	0
August	12	0
September	83	1
October	439	7
November	766	13
December	1,130	19
January	1,401	24
February	933	16
March	608	10
April	379	7
May	139	2
June	44	1
Total	5,934	

Credit: Penn State Dept. of Hort.

How Much Saved When You Lower Temperatures?

PERCENT REDUCTION IN FUEL USE WHEN GREENHOUSE TEMPERATURES ARE LOWERED

Average outside temperature	A B	Inside greenhouse temperature reduction from A to B					
		65° to 60°F %	65° to 55°F %	60° to 55°F %	60° to 50°F %	55° to 50°F %	55° to 45°F %
(°F)	(°C)						
20	6.7	11	22	12	24	14	28
24	4.4	12	24	14	28	16	32
28	2.2	13	26	16	32	19	38
32	0	15	30	18	36	22	44
36	2.2	17	34	21	42	26	52
40	4.4	20	40	25	50	33	66
44	6.7	24	48				
48	8.9	29	58				

Equivalents 45°F—7.2°C; 50°F—10°C; 55°F—12.8°C; 60°F—15.6°C; and 65°F—18.3°C
Credit: Penn State Dept. of Hort.

Typical Boiler Efficiency

From Roses, Inc. Bulletin #83, February 1982, here's an interesting table on "typical" efficiencies of boilers commonly used for greenhouses.

Boiler type	CO_2(%)	Exhaust gas temp. (°F)	Typical combustion efficiency (%)
Economic packaged (3-pass)	13	450	85
3-pass economic	11½	500	82
2-pass Scotch Marine	11	550	79
Cast iron sectional	10	600	77
Vertical, firetube type	10	700	75
Lancashire (and similar)	9	650	74
Vertical, cross tube type	8	1000	58

Dutch Re-Burner

A system you see a good bit in Holland. Here the flue gases coming from the boiler and normally headed for the chimney are instead diverted to a special chamber. This chamber includes provision for converting some of the heat from this flue gas into warm water—which is piped into the greenhouse. Also, the carbon dioxide content is removed and again piped into the crop area. Result: Fuel efficiency up in the 95%+ range. And temperature on this final "stack" down in the 160° to 170°F range. In fact, you can hold your hand over the top of the chimney!

G.V.B.

Chapter 3

OTHER MAJOR FUEL SAVERS

WHICH FUEL?

A very critical decision! In some situations growers can realize major savings by switching fuels. But to appraise *your* potential for such savings you must first reduce the available alternatives to a common language. You've got to compare apples with apples!

The most practical language: rate each fuel according to cost per BTU. That's a British Thermal Unit—a basic way to measure heat. Don't worry about the details. Just know, for example, that if your grade of oil at your cost delivers 100,000 BTUs for 90¢—and gas BTU cost is 60¢—well, let's switch to gas! This comparison is so easy to do—the accompanying charts are self-explanatory. Remember, you're not buying coal or oil or gas—you're buying heat. And buy it as cheap as you can.

Coal—Pro and Con

Under certain conditions, coal can cut a grower's fuel bill in half, or even to one quarter.

The first "condition" concerns the fuels available to you—and their cost. Example: If you're paying 70¢ a gallon for propane—and if you can buy very

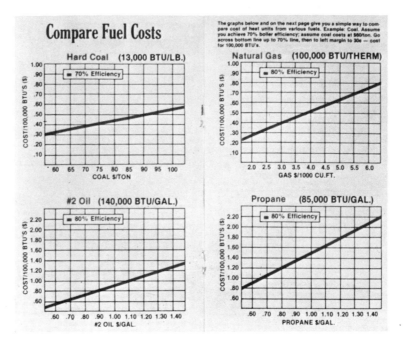

Compare Fuel Costs

The graphs below and on the next page give you a simple way to compare cost of heat units from various fuels. Example: Coal. Assume you achieve 70% boiler efficiency; assume coal costs at $60/ton. Go across bottom line up to 70% line, then to left margin to 30¢ — cost for 100,000 BTU's.

Hard Coal (13,000 BTU/LB.)

COST/100,000 BTU'S ($)

70% Efficiency

COAL $/TON

Natural Gas (100,000 BTU/THERM)

COST/100,000 BTU'S ($)

80% Efficiency

GAS $/1000 CU.FT.

#2 Oil (140,000 BTU/GAL.)

COST/100,000 BTU'S ($)

80% Efficiency

#2 OIL $/GAL.

Propane (85,000 BTU/GAL.)

COST/100,000 BTU'S ($)

80% Efficiency

PROPANE $/GAL.

A very important chart for all growers! Think cost per 100,000 BTUs—not cost per gallon. Example: One grower found that going from 50¢/therm gas to $50/ ton coal cut his fuel cost from 60¢ per 100,000 BTUs to 25¢. And that was $1 million a year difference! All of which comes to light from these charts. Think BTU cost!

cheap coal, then you have a real bargain available to you. But, if you're paying 35¢ for gas, and if coal FOB your greenhouse is on the expensive side, then coal may be no bargain at all. And here's a classic case where reducing the fuels available to you to a common BTU cost is a must. You simply have to compare apples with apples.

The second limitation of coal is EPA. Regulations and their interpretations seem to vary even from city to city. If you can make your peace with EPA on a reasonable basis, then barrier #2 is out of the way. Often it's a politicking job. Many growers seem to win, by the way!

Third limitation: Storing coal is a lot different from turning on the gas main. You're going to have piles of coal on your premises. Some growers (Jack Van de Wetering of Long Island) build silos to keep the coal out of sight—plus it avoids freezing problems. Also, better availability for mechanical conveyors. But silos cost money, too.

The fourth limitation is that even though the new modern coal stokers are relatively labor free, there is still some maintenance, etc. However, all the newer coal burners we see reduce ash handling to minutes a day—and it's mostly mechanized. You just don't see many clinkers at all. Flue blowing is

36

mechanized, or in some boilers, completely eliminated. And coal feeding is again mechanized and a once-a-day, 10-minute chore. But, again, it isn't 100% clean and labor-free like gas.

We came across one Philadelphia area grower who was deluged with soot and fly ash from a so-called "modern" boiler. Obviously a malfunction, maintenance problem of some sort. This just shouldn't happen with modern stokers. Even with "cheap" coal.

For one example of where coal really did the trick, see *Grower Talks* September 1981, page 16. John Van Bourgondein paid off the costly equipment in one year and is immensely pleased with the whole operation.

The last limitation of coal is simply expensive equipment—compared to oil and gas burners. Example: One coal burner supplier reported rough cost for a 145-horsepower Scotch Marine boiler with burners (or stokers) of roughly $30,000 for the gas/oil burner vs. $90,000 for coal. At the 580-horsepower level, it was about $80,000 for a gas/oil burner vs. $150,000 for coal.

So it takes more capital for coal-burning equipment than for gas or oil. Which is okay if you can pay it back in two to three years—and if you have the money.

There are two principal suppliers of these "modern" coal burners that we are hearing about today. First, Russ Weiss, Durable Greenhouses, P.O. Box 641, Center Moriches, NY 11934. The Van Bourgondein installation—

The new look in greenhouse coal piles—a metal silo. Note the loading crane. The grower: Ivy Acres, Calverton, Long Island.

and many others in the northeastern U.S. have been engineered, and in some cases, installed by Russ Weiss. Russ, by the way, was working on a new smaller coal stoker for perhaps ¼-acre bedding plant growers—again, fully mechanized. We hear soon to be available.

Another brand new, and again, very interesting piece of coal-burning equipment is from Kewanee Boiler, 101 Franklin St., Kewanee, IL 61443, (309) 853-3541. They call it their Incendo coal boiler. It's a new patented package boiler/burner combination. It has been used quite extensively for several years in England. Kewanee recently acquired the patents and U.S. rights. They have sent 20 of these boilers to the U.S. Army for use in Germany; first U.S. installations are just being negotiated. Kewanee claims that, using even relatively inexpensive soft coal, it will be 5% to 10% more efficient than "conventional" stokers and boilers. They quote 80% to 84% efficiency under clean, good operation for Incendo vs. 70% to 75% for conventional boilers and stokers. Another important claim is that the Incendo stoker/boiler combination is ¼ to ⅓ less expensive than most conventional U.S. stoker/boilers. Third, it is quite mechanized. No soot blowing, almost no clinkers, ash removal easily done once a day, semi-mechanized. And very important: The burner does seem to adapt itself to less expensive soft coals. Again, these are manufacturer's claims— but certainly Kewanee is a reputable manufacturer.

A classic example of everything being "right" for coal: the grower Hans Pein, Urbana, IL. Hans operates 120,000 square feet of bedding/pot plants. It's all inflated double poly.

Based on these figures, Hans hopes to pay off his investment in a new Incendo boiler in well under three years. His figures are shown in Table 3-1.

Table 3-1 ESTIMATED FUEL SAVINGS FROM HANS PEIN'S INSTALLATION OF A KEWANEE INCENDO COAL BOILER

	Fuel used	Cost per 100,000 BTUs	Annual fuel cost
Today	LP gas, 68¢ gallon	84¢	$120,000 ($1 per square foot per year)
With Kewanee Incendo	Illinois coal, $36 FOB the greenhouse	20¢	Under $30,000 per year (estimate)

Coal, Gas, and Oil

These are the three most commonly used alternatives today. The other choice mainly for larger growers would be #6, or the heavier oil which must be preheated. But it does generally yield a lower BTU cost. And again, the choice between these three and coal is mainly an economic one.

Occasionally we see growers using cheap, locally available sawdust or wood shavings. Some growers do very well with it—in spite of some work involved in handling and feeding the burner. Occasionally growers have installed expensive equipment and suddenly found their source of cheap wood shavings vanished.

THERMAL SHEETS—BIG FUEL SAVERS

Thermal sheets are fast becoming standard practice in greenhouses the world over. In effect, the grower extends a sheet of insulation out from gutter to gutter at sunset, leaves it in place until sunrise. Sometimes the sheet is extended lengthways of the house up close to the roof. More and more, the "extending" of these sheets is being mechanized. Often they also serve to provide daylength control: short days for mums, kalanchoes, etc. Many growers also use them in summer to achieve partial light reduction in hot, bright weather.

And now, more recently, a whole new batch of double and triple thermal sheets are coming onto the market. And they, again, show great promise. The now standard Dutch double sheet—extended lengthways of the house mechanically and up under the roof—cuts the fuel bill roughly in half. Cost is minimal (we hear $1.25 to $1.50 per square foot of ground). Almost zero interference with precious winter light. That's the kind of thing that makes us feel that the fuel problem, in many cases, is no longer a pressure point.

Thermal sheets just can't be used in houses with purlin posts and other interferences. They're fine in a Quonset house, free-standing, or, better yet, gutter-connected.

Thermal Sheets—Pro and Con

Question: What's happening in the real world with thermal sheets? Are growers really moving on them? What are the pluses and negatives?
We talked all this in detail with three "expert witnesses":

- Nick Van Wingerden, grower—with 16 acres of inflated double poly, northern Illinois, all with thermal sheets.

- Wadsworth Equipment Company's Bob Klaeser.

- Ball Seed's Jim Schield.

Nick Van Wingerden Nick, the practical grower, says "My gut feeling is we are saving 25% to 30% on fuel, though accurate figures are hard to come by. I know that without heat sheets, we had real trouble holding temperatures on sub-zero nights. With them, we can easily hold temperatures in any weather.

Here's a double-layer overhead thermal sheet installed at Neal Mast's, Grand Rapids, Michigan. Note the two rolls of material across the house. Each one extends lengthways from truss to truss. The lower sheet is perforated polyethylene; the top is white polyester fiber. Result: about a 50% fuel saving vs. single glass.

I predict we will get our investment back on the thermal sheets in three years. Maybe a bit longer if fuel cost drops."

Another strong plus Nick brings up is light reduction in summer. His basic thermal sheet is the white polyester fiber—which serves both to insulate in winter and reduce the summer light by about 45%. "It's a big help on warm days in May and throughout the summer. Also, it was simple to clip black sateen cloth to the heat sheet on several mum sections for daylength control. Worked OK."

On drip: "Sheets of polyethylene can be used for thermal sheets—but water collects in 'bellies' and makes big problems. It almost tore down a greenhouse for us one time. The polyester fiber that we use now absorbs moisture and, while there is some drip, it usually doesn't accumulate and make problems.

"I wouldn't consider building without thermal sheets."

Wadsworth—Bob Klaeser Bob's comment on payoff: "I'd say three to five years, depending on how cold the climate, how tight the installation. Certainly slower payoff in the South."

On light reduction in the summer: "It is important. Fuel saving is the primary concern, but light reduction is big. The sheets also help make air conditioning more effective. As far as switching from sheets in the spring to black cloth—it's a real job. Generally not practical."

We asked Bob about rough cost figures—he reported a little under $1 a square foot (by the acre) for material for mechanical single-layer thermal sheet. With labor, well over $1 a square foot.

Question: How about black poly instead of white fiber? "It can be used, but it's a sort of expedient. Costs a lot less, but doesn't last as long—not more than three years. Then there are those pools of water that make such big, big problems."

Another interesting comment from Bob: "Wadsworth sales of thermal sheets are a very important part of our operation these days. Lots of activity—mainly in northern states."

Ball Seed's Jim Schield Jim was a bit less bullish on thermal sheets. From his daily contact with growers he got a feeling that the saving, even in a northern range, would be more like 15% or 20%—and the payoff five years plus. All this based on inflated double poly. Jim also reported, in his opinion, that 90% plus of all greenhouses being built this year will be double poly.

The standard, single thermal sheet mechanically applied—in this case in a double poly range. The sheet of poly extends from your right to your left—in the photo, it's about half extended. Cost about $1.25 a square foot installed. The grower: Nick Van Wingerden, Granville, Illinois.

On thermal sheets, Jim much favors the white polyester fabric. "Drip from overhead is spread out—it seems to penetrate the cloth and then most of it evaporates. Black poly is just as good an insulator—but the drip forms into pools of water that make big problems."

Jim confirmed the importance of light reduction using the white polyester fabric materials. On converting from the white cloth to black poly for mums, "Switching to poly is a big, costly job. It means handling hundreds of clips. Besides, so many of the small- to middle-sized growers grow half a house or a bench of mums and don't want to shade the whole house.

"Starting with single-layer glass, heat sheets will save a full $\frac{1}{3}$. But the grower using inflated double poly has already reduced his fuel cost by perhaps 30%. Somehow I don't think you get another 30% cut by adding thermal sheets to the double poly."

Some sources for the white polyester cloth heat sheet so widely used: Thermoshade II from Simtrac—(312) 679-7970. Nick Van Wingerden uses Floratex 60 from Europe. Wadsworth offers 6-ounce white polyester cloth— (303) 424-4461. Ball Seed offers Sto-Cote Heatshield, a plastic sheet—(312) 231-3500.

A point on all thermal sheets: In case of a heavy snow at night, growers are learning that it's better to leave the thermal sheet retracted—to help melt the snow away. If you don't, you're very apt to find snow frozen to the roof for the next day or two. You do lose some fuel, but winter light is so critical! Also, in case of heavy snow, deflate the roof. Now heat will get to the outer layer, and melt the snow. There is a tendency for snow to form into pockets. Beware!

Double Thermal Sheets

The more recent development—a *two-layer* thermal sheet that typically reduces fuel cost from 50% to 60%.

One of the most important and promising installations we've seen are the Dutch thermal sheets. We saw an installation by the Verzuu Company— Utrecht, Holland—at the Neal Mast range, Grand Rapids, MI. Here the two sheets are extended lengthways of the house from truss to truss 1' to 3' below the roof. On Neal's range, the lower sheet is polyethylene with tiny perforations to allow moisture to pass. The upper sheet is again the fabric insulation material, which permits moisture to pass and can provide partial light reduction in summer.

A most important point that we observed: the very minimal amount of loss of precious winter light with this installation. Particularly this Verzuu equipment has an ingenious device to force the cloth up into small-diameter rolls during the day. Result: The houses we saw in mid-December at Mast's seemed to be getting virtually all of the available outdoor light.

Structured sheets—a cymbidium orchid house.

Managing double sheets   Neal Mast and son, Jim, make several points about managing such a double-sheet system. First, at sunrise, the top sheet is retracted. The lower sheet (perforated poly) is left in place until perhaps 9 a.m. or 10 a.m. Two reasons. First, if both sheets are withdrawn at sunrise, there is a heavy load on the boiler to heat the upper air and glass surfaces. And sudden, heavy loads on boilers are not good. Also there is a tendency for the cold air in the attic to rush down onto the crop, condense moisture, and make problems. Doing it in two steps, the cold air from above gradually filters down through the porous plastic onto the crop—so there is no sudden change of temperature at the crop level. Also, Neal points out: The upper white fiber sheet reduces light by about 45%. If this is withdrawn at sunrise, you lose little growing light—since the lower polyethylene level permits 90% + of the light to pass to the crop.

Neal makes a third point about these two layers: Sometimes on cloudy days there is a major demand for heat to maintain temperature. It is possible to extend only the poly sheet on such a day. Now you have the efficiency of a thermal sheet working for you—but only a 10% loss of light.

Neal's other son, Arie, at Sun Hill Greenhouses, a mile or two south, had a similar insulation—but now with two layers of black poly. Actually it is roughly ⅛" strips of black poly woven into a fabric. Again, double layer and fully mechanized. Reason for the black poly: to provide short days for mums, which are an important crop here. And, the woven strips allow moisture to pass through.

Movement of the two layers of two sheets of cloth on both ranges can be timeclock controlled.

Other comments from Neal Mast "I'm already noticing a big difference in fuel consumption with the double insulation. On a recent trip to Holland I saw thermal sheets on most ranges—and quite a lot of double-thermal sheets showing up today."

On installation: "I understand there is a Canadian branch of Verzuu that will install single-layer insulation for 30¢ a square foot, two layers probably twice that." Telephone (416) 939-7833.

"The sections of cloth are extended and withdrawn with cables—which are powered by six shafts which run from gutter-to-ridge and back to gutter across the 42' house. In other words, these shafts move the sheets back and forth throughout a 175' house.

The whole 60,000 square foot range is equipped with slider benches— one walk per house now."

Double Sheets—Together

We saw recently in Holland an installation of two thermal sheets that were fastened together at the outer edges, but allowed to separate throughout the width of the sheet. They were handled as one sheet—an important economy in mechanical equipment vs. two separate sheets handled separately. The grower reported within 5% as much fuel economy as he would expect from two separate sheets handled separately. See accompanying photo.

A new approach to a double thermal sheet. Here the two sheets are joined together at the edges and will lay roughly together or an inch or two apart across the house from gutter to gutter. Preliminary reports from Holland (above) indicate about 45% saving vs. 50% for two sheets separated a foot apart. The left sheet is synthetic, the right sheet (#2) is a black plastic.

EFFICIENT GREENHOUSE CLIMATE CONTROLS

Environmental Control—Computerized

In the past several years, a variety of excellent equipment has come on to the market to manage greenhouse environment in general. Including temperature, humidity, light intensity, application of black cloth shade, light reduction as needed, ventilation fans and irrigation pads for cooling, etc. Manufacturers of this equipment are claiming, and often delivering, 15% to 25% fuel economy vs. the old thermostats. Bob Oglevee, one of the principal suppliers, commented at GrowerExpo '84, "We are seeing equipment now that can maintain temperatures within $\frac{1}{10}$ of a degree vs. the 2 to 3 degree spread of the past. And that means a lot of fuel saving."

There is a detailed report on a good example of this type of equipment—and just what it can do—in *Grower Talks,* January 1984, page 26. The other payoff you realize, talking to growers who have this equipment, is that it unburdens the grower just a whole lot! The endless minute adjustments in heat, ventilation, fans, pads, cooling, black cloth application, etc., that are part of the grower's day—can now largely be computerized. It just makes life a whole lot easier. Said Mr. Koole, rose grower from Vancouver, "Definitely easier on me. I set the limits. After that the computer makes it happen. 24 hours a day."

For details on equipment available—and what it can do—see the chapter on computers elsewhere in this book.

SLIDING BENCHES—AISLE ELIMINATORS

Here's the plan where benches may be rolled sideways. A typical house with four benches and normally four walks will now have only one walk (plus a gutter walk). And that one walk can be positioned anywhere the grower wishes, by rolling the benches sideways. Normally the rolling is accomplished by turning a crank that's at the head of the bench. It's not hard to do. As of early 1984, many conversions to "rolling benches" were being done across the U.S. and Canada. One supplier reported about double the demand for these benches in 1984 vs. 1983.

The obvious advantage is that you now use perhaps 86% or 88% of the available space for crops vs. 62% to 66% with the old-style walks. Stated a different way, that means perhaps 30% less fuel cost and 30% less of all overhead cost (depreciation, salary, taxes, insurance, etc.)—per plant. And that is a major cost reduction. And actually the grower still has access to his crop.

Inevitably we find ourselves comparing slider benches with the tray mechanization concept. Both plans offer a much higher percentage of space utilization. In fact, the trays do even better than sliders. Both provide access to the crop—trays can be spread a foot or so apart anywhere for this purpose. Of course, the major feature of the tray approach is very fast and very low cost movement of the crop from headhouse to bench and back to headhouse. Again, these tray conversions are certainly more costly. It's a whole different way of managing a greenhouse!

One American manufacturer of rolling benches, Rough Brothers, Inc., P.O. Box 16010, Cincinnati, Ohio 45216, (513) 242-0310, offers a commercial version of the slider bench. Rough is, as of this date, busy installing such equipment in greenhouses across the country. Figure about $2 per square foot of bench cost.

G.V.B.

Chapter 4

COOLING SYSTEMS AND FAN JETS

FAN/PAD COOLING

Nearly all serious production of year-round pot plants and major cut crops such as roses, etc., are equipped with fan/pad cooling. Only exception would be cool summer areas such as Washington State and Vancouver. A pot mum crop without cooling even in the Midwest or the East is a good bet for major losses from heat stalling in summer. And further south or in the Southwest, cooling is an absolute must. Surprisingly, there are major greenhouse areas even in Florida with fan/pad cooling. In spite of the relatively high humidity, there is enough cooling to make it economical.

The rapid rise of the cost of electricity has caused growers in some areas to reconsider rows of giant fans and pad cooling systems. A big example: Aldershot Greenhouses near Toronto, with many acres of year-round pot mums, are taking a serious try at relying on 50" roof ventilators to do the cooling job. Their climate (almost between two of the Great Lakes) takes a lot of the hot weather pressure away.

But still, nearly all serious production of pot plants and cut flowers in North America is fan/pad cooled.

47

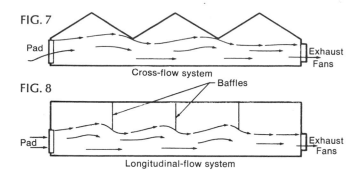

FIG. 7

Pad

Cross-flow system

Exhaust
Fans

FIG. 8

Baffles

Pad

Exhaust
Fans

Longitudinal-flow system

A good schematic drawing of cooling. The top range: ridge and furrow. Note how the gutter keeps the cool air down near the crop. The lower sketch is a separate house, the cool air now drawn lengthways from pad (left) to fans. In this case, baffles are needed to keep the cool air down at the crop level. Drawing credit: Acme Engineering Company, Muskogee, Oklahoma.

How It Works

Evaporative cooling of greenhouses is accomplished by drawing air through a wet pad and evaporating water, cooling the air by absorbing 8,100 BTUs of heat energy for each gallon evaporated.

A wet wall, consisting of pads, water distribution system, water pump and sump, is erected continuously along one side or end wall of the greenhouse. The pads must be kept wet to facilitate the evaporation process. On the opposite wall, exhaust fans properly sized for the greenhouse size and location are installed and placed to provide smooth airflow across the greenhouse. Pads should be sized to provide the most economical and efficient system possible. Cellulose pads 4″ and 6″ thick operate best at an air speed of 250 feet per minute through the pad and 2″ aspen pads work best at 150 feet per minute.

How Cool?

The amount of cooling achievable by evaporative cooling varies with the differential between the wet bulb and dry bulb temperatures. This differential varies not only with location and season, but also during each day. Although the dry bulb could vary as much as 25°F in one day, the wet bulb varies approximately ⅓ as much. Therefore, cooling could be accomplished even in normally high humidity areas in the middle of the day when it is really needed.

A well-designed evaporative cooling system should be able to reduce the dry bulb temperature inside the wet wall to approximately 85% of the difference between the outside dry bulb and wet bulb temperature. A temperature rise of about 5°F to 7°F from the pad to the exhaust fans should be expected.

48

Please do not "cheat" on the size of the intake air openings—the larger the better. A smaller size than called for creates static resistance, which greatly reduces the efficiency of the fans and causes increased electricity usage. We prefer continuous vents whenever possible.

How Many Fans—How Big a Pad?

The calculations are simple—the problem is that the need varies by localities. Some areas have consistently high 90% humidity summer days (Dallas, Texas for example). Others like Chicago will be typically low 90s many days. Generally, fan and pad systems work best in dry climates. Systems must be "oversize" in high humidity areas like Houston, Texas and Florida.

To give a rough idea of equipment needed for cooling an acre of conventional gutter-connected greenhouses, here's the way it's figured: Length of the houses × width × the distance from the ground to the gutter height tells the CFM required for air movement. To figure pad area required, divide that total CFM by 250 and that total by the number of linear feet of wall the pad vent will cover—this last number will tell you how tall the system will have to be. In humid climates, we recommend oversizing fan and pads 20%. For growers interested in calculating pad and fan requirements we suggest writing to Acme Engineering Co., P.O. Box 978, Muskogee, OK 74401, for a copy of a manual entitled *Controlled Environment Equipment for Greenhouses,* their form number C29L-582.

Good example of a "wet pad" installed across the end of a pot plant range. Air is drawn from the outside, through the wet pad, and then to the crop. The evaporation occurring as air rushes through the pad does the cooling.

Cautions on pad installations: Pads cause resistance to airflow, so be sure that all air passes through the pads, and that all other openings are closed. Even an open fan-jet shutter will greatly reduce pad efficiency.

Sample Calculations

Example: Fourteen bays each 21' wide by 144' long greenhouses have a total area of 42,336 square feet. With an 8' gutter height, this section of greenhouse requires moving 338,688 cubic feet of air per minute—for proper fan/pad cooling. Divided by the factor "250," this means the range will require a minimum of 1,355 square feet of pad area. Assuming the pads are mounted to the gables, we have 294' available to mount the system (14 bays × 21'). The square feet required divided by the available linear feet of mounting space means the pads will have to be at least 4.61' tall to do the job. Always figure pads up to the next even foot, not down. In this example, then, 5' tall pads should be used.

When the house temperature becomes too high and cooling is needed, the equipment controller or cooling thermostat simultaneously opens the motorized shutter and energizes exhaust fans. When the desired temperature has been reached, the equipment controller or thermostat closes the inlet shutter and turns off the exhaust fan, thereby shutting off the supply of outside air.

When the relative humidity in the house exceeds the desired level it can be reduced by bringing in cooler outside air that has a lower water vapor content. The humid house air is expelled by the exhaust fan while the drier incoming air is heated and mixed with the house air.

Which Pad?

In recent years, new types of pads have come on the market that offer important advantages. Here they are—pro and con—vs. the traditional aspen pad.

There are four main types of cooling pads on the market today. Aspen, paper/honeycomb, concrete, and lastly, aluminum pads. Each has its own pluses and minuses to consider when choosing a pad system.

Aspen pads The least expensive from an initial investment standpoint, aspen pads are about the oldest form of cooling pads. Because of limited surface area for evaporation to occur they may be less effective than the other types of pad. Main drawback, though, is the high degree of maintenance required, usually yearly replacement. Still it is the least expensive alternative.

Paper pads   A patented design of paper coated with a special glue formed into a honeycomb shape. One manufacturer in Florida provides all the paper/honeycomb pads in this country regardless of the manufacturer of the pipe distribution and retur system. The paper pad has a much greater surface area than aspen per square foot of pad, thus providing more cooling per square foot of pad. Pd life varies from two to seven years depending on how many months a year they are used and the pH of the water. High alkaline water seems to deteriorate or dissolve the glue that holds the pads together. Water should be pH adjusted to provide the longest life. Algae buildup on the pads can be controlled chemically with algaecides. These "paper pads" are very widely used—and in fact aspen pads are almost off the market at present. Additional manufacturers of paper pads are expected as the patents for paper pad systems expire.

Concrete pads   Made of wood fiber sprayed with concrete, concrete pads are a good alternative to paper pads in high alkaline water areas. Guaranteed for 10 years by the manufacturer. These pads have significant mass to help absorb incoming heat. Because of some inconsistency in the air porosity inherent to the design, 20% to 30% greater pad area is required when compared with paper pads. To keep resistance to airflow at a minimum, the pads should be oversized when compared with paper by this amount. Cost is about $2 to $3 per square foot of pad area more than the paper system.

Aluminum pads   Now on the market. Aluminum pads are made of a number of layers of expanded aluminum metal with a special surface texture to help hold moisture. They are too new for much testing to have been done at this printing. Because the pads are made completely of aluminum they should last a long time. Cost is approximately $1 per square foot more than paper pads. Worth looking into. Just remember that some of the engineering and testing under various climates is yet to be done.

As of mid-1984, 90% plus of pads in North America are paper. The aluminum pad is promising, but as yet unproven.

Fan Maintenance

For fans to work at peak efficiency with the minimum amount of electrical usage, certain maintenance steps and general guidelines should be followed. All the belts should be kept very tight to eliminate slippage, which reduces not only the air output of the fans but can also increase electrical use on the motor. Be sure that all air leaks in the greenhouse are kept plugged in order to get top efficiency from your pads. The pads create an air resistance, and air leaks in the greenhouse can increase temperatures in the greenhouse 4° to 10°

because the air intake is going through the air leaks and not the pads themselves. Be sure that the pad area is kept completely wet without any dry spots. Algae can be controlled by the use of chemical algaecides or even common bleach. During the winter months, check for air intrusion through the fan shutters or inlet shutters to reduce heat loss. These simple steps will keep your greenhouse cooler in the summer and warmer in the winter.

FAN-JET SYSTEMS

An ingenious and widely used system of fans/inlet louvers/polyethylene tubes— used both to distribute heat and to ventilate greenhouses.

A typical fan jet installation (this time at the DuPage Horticultural School green- houses, West Chicago, Illinois). The unit heater (above right) blows hot air to the left. It is drawn into the poly tube by a fan in the end of the tube. Then it's blown on down the house, distributed by the holes. The heat is also pushed from the heater by the fan (on the right of the unit heater), again toward the poly tube. The louver (open in this photo) is closed in cold weather but can be opened to draw in a bit of fresh air on early spring days. Note the exhaust tube, above right.

Stage I—Ventilation

The fan-jet systems provide for necessary ventilation, especially on warm spring days—without a rush of cold air hitting the crop. This is done by drawing air in through the louver by means of a fan—then forcing it through a large 18–24″ diameter polyethylene tube which runs overhead the length of the greenhouse. A series of small holes down the length of the tube permits small amounts of outside air to enter the greenhouse atmosphere—without damage to crops.

The same fan and polyethylene tube system is used to distribute heat from overhead unit heaters. Now the heat is simply drawn from the outlet of the unit heater into the fan jet and again it's distributed down the length of the house through the perforated polyethylene tube. The system does provide a quite uniform temperature from one end of the greenhouse to the other during heating operations.

We thought the following paragraphs from *The Greenhouse Climate Control Handbook,* 1980, published by Acme Engineering and Mfg. Corp., Muskogee, OK were helpful in understanding this equipment.

Fan-Jet Minimum Ventilation Systems

During cool nights of spring, summer and fall and on most sunshiny winter days, minimum ventilation is needed to control the house temperature. This type of ventilation, using cool or cold outside air, is quite different from summer ventilation and evaporative cooling. The flow must be turbulent with small to moderate quantities of air required, while in the summer the flow should be smooth and use large quantities of air.

The minimum ventilation system is an important part of the climate control system and requires several distinct characteristics. First, it must have ample air flow capacity to maintain a proper heat balance by removing the excess solar heat on mild sunlit days.

Second, the minimum ventilating system must be able to introduce the very cold winter air into the greenhouse without producing cold drafts on the plants. This requires a very thorough mixing of the cold outside air with the warm inside air before the plant level is reached. Since powered ventilating has the energy available to produce the turbulence necessary for thorough mixing, it supplies properly tempered fresh air.

Third, it is important that all parts of the greenhouse be at the same temperature. To achieve this, the ventilating system must distribute the air very uniformly throughout the house and maintain positive air movement and continuous circulation. A powered ventilating system has a real advantage over gravity systems that rely on thermal air currents, since it has the energy required to provide uniform air distribution and mixing. Continuous circulation also produces a gentle air movement that maintains a better leaf surface micro climate and prevents pockets of disease-producing high humidity.

For average conditions an airflow of 1½ to 2 cfm per square foot of floor space will hold the house temperature within 15°F of outside temperature.

The use of exhaust fans for mechanical ventilation of greenhouses combined with perforated transparent plastic tubes makes an ideal method of introducing cold air into a greenhouse in the winter without cold drafts. The development of these principles has produced the Acme Fan-Jet Climate Control System. This is a multi-purpose system that can alternately heat, dehumidify, ventilate or recirculate the air in a greenhouse for proper climate control in the fall, winter and spring seasons. This system is not designed to provide temperature control in warm seasons. Moreover, the exhaust fans of this system can also serve as the fans for the summer fan and pad cooling system.

The Fan-Jet system consists of a specially constructed pressurizing fan attached to a custom-designed perforated plastic tube located in the upper section of the house that extends along the length of the greenhouse with its far end closed.

The pressurizing fan runs continuously, inflating the tube and blowing air through the holes in the form of jets into the greenhouse space. This uniformly distributes the air for the full length of the tube creating turbulence, thorough mixing and active air motion throughout the entire greenhouse. It maintains a more uniform temperature and humidity, and prevents cold spots.

The fan is mounted inside the greenhouse at a specified distance from the gable end wall in front of a special-sized motorized shutter that functions as the fresh air inlet. Several sizes of Fan-Jets with matching air inlet shutters and perforated tubes are offered for different requirements and often two or more units are needed for a greenhouse depending on its size.

Supplying Heat

Quoting from the Acme bulletin—on the role of this Fan-Jet system and distributing heat:

Since the Fan-Jet ventilating system provides excellent distribution and circulation of air it can also serve as a highly efficient heat distribution system. When equipped with an accessory "heat kit" package it becomes part of a heating system without affecting its other functions of minimum ventilation and recirculation. The heat kit comprises a baffle arrangement that permits the use of conventional horizontal-discharge-type unit heaters in combination with Fan-Jet units to make an efficient and economical heating system.

Since the Fan-Jet Climate Control System works directly with the air it reacts quickly to changes in requirements. By using high velocities and the rapid mixing turbulence of the jets, it achieves the maximum capability of the equipment in a matter of seconds and provides the quick response necessary for maintaining a uniform climate.

The Fan-Jet system is designed to both heat and ventilate in fall, winter, and spring. However, when high summer temperatures arrive, larger fans and usually a fan/pad cooling system are needed.

Rough cost for the Fan-Jet system—for the fan, the shutter, the poly tube, tube hangers, tube support systems and heat accessories, not including the heater—on a 150-foot gutter-connected greenhouse is about $525 FOB factory.

G.V.B.

Chapter 5

HEADHOUSES

An adequate headhouse (workroom) is absolutely basic to any efficient growing operation. Also, it's essential for much of modern mechanization. Potting machines for pot plant growers, flat fillers and seeders for bedding growers. They all need a good, dry, well-lighted area—with reasonable temperature control, certainly with cement floors. Most pot plant specialists are designing loading ramps so that trucks can be backed up to the headhouse doors—with the truck bed the same level as the headhouse floor.

One of the basics of tray mechanization (see Chapter 7) is that potting can be done in the headhouse, the crop moved to the growing area, then back to the headhouse for packing. All of which demands adequate work area.

Probably most headhouses we see are metal roof or sometimes fiberglass roof structures. But several quality growers with good physical plants we know of do this job under an inflated double-poly roof. Examples are Van de Weterings on Long Island.

Depending on the operation, the headhouse is normally the storage place for major supplies. Soil mix, packing boxes for bedding growers, trays, and packs. For pot growers, flower pots and shipping boxes. For cut flower growers, space for grading, bunching. And for refrigeration. Plus space for tray storage.

All this brings to mind the massive work area at Hazelegers, Alpharetta Greenhouse, Alpharetta, Georgia. For roughly 500,000 square feet of greenhouse area, this work area covers 45,000 square feet. By the way, very adequate office space is contiguous to this work area. The work area breaks down to 9,000 square feet for soil mixing/storage, 6,000 square feet for planting area, 30,000 square feet for warehouse and shipping area.

And don't forget parking space! Often for large trucks, too.

Here are some examples of good operations, amount of headhouse provided.

Grower	Greenhouse area (sq. ft.)	Headhouse area (sq. ft.)	Work area is what % of total range?	Crop	Remarks
G & E Greenhouse Batavia, IL	136,000	12,560	9.2	Pot plants	Not including cooler
G & E Greenhouses Elburn, IL	69,000	5,805	8.4	Pot plants	
Alpharetta Greenhouses Alpharetta, GA	500,000	45,000	9	Bedding plants Pot plants	
Masson's Linwood, KS	240,000	40,000	16.5	Bedding plants Pot plants	[1]
Frank Cleason South Elgin, IL	137,000	11,760	8.5	Pot plants	
Mid-America Growers Granville, IL	688,000	56,000	8.1	Bedding plants Pot plants	[2]
Nick Van Wingerden Ivy Acres Calverton, LI, NY	860,000	73,000	8.5	Bedding plants Pot plants	[3]

[1]Alexander Masson:
"Our ratio is 1:6. Keep in mind, however, we garage most delivery trucks inside. And secondly, we produce and market a diversified line of product and this activity needs more space than, say, the producer of just potted mums."

[2]Nick Van Wingerden: "We are planning to expand our support buildings by 10,000 square feet as we have a third of our peat moss outside and we are just too tight now. Our support buildings, by the way, include soil mixing, peat storage, transplanting, sowing area, offices, cafeteria, bathrooms, shipping pick up area, storage, cooler, shop, chemical room."

[3]Ivy Acres: Their new range consists of a 10-acre block (430,000 square feet) plus an additional 10 acres created by their unique roll-out system (see mechanization section). Interestingly, if you add the two 10 acre areas together, you, again, come up with a headhouse area about 9% of the total area of greenhouse.

An adequate headhouse, cement floor, light, heat are essential to a good operation—and particularly vital when mechanized equipment is used. Here's a good example—done with inflated poly, by the way. Fuel efficient! The grower, Ivy Acres, Calverton, Long Island.

Interesting conclusion: The remarkable consistency of work area to total glass area—very close to 9%. Except Alexander Masson who keeps trucks inside—and who does substantial assembly and packing of other related products in his work area.

The percent of headhouse area needed seems to stay fairly constant regardless of the size of the operation.

Hearty thanks to these growers for providing this enlightening picture.

G.V.B.

SECTION II

Labor-Saving Mechanization

Chapter 6

SOME BACKGROUND ON MECHANIZATION

As this fourteenth edition goes to press, U.S. and Canada growers are clearly facing an imperative to mechanize—if they mean to be competitive in the ever-more free trade world we seem to face. Certainly this must include pot plants and bedding growers. And, cut flower crops, too.

At this stage (early 1984) the comments of a leader in this tough transition are to us relevant. The grower: Alexander Masson, large wholesale pot producer, Kansas City: "Our basic decision made three years ago to move toward tray mechanization now seems to have been not only sound—but the most important basic change in the history of our company. The tray concept is sound—and we're immensely pleased that our new facility out at Linwood is being developed around them."

And, certainly Masson and many other farsighted growers are relying heavily on potting machines, various forms of automatic irrigation, and much other available technology.

Interesting leaders in bedding plant mechanization to us are the Van de Weterings of Ivy Acres, Calverton, Long Island. They are far into plugs, flat fillers of course, and are just developing tray mechanization to move their crop to the growing area and back to the shipping area. And, to eliminate aisles. And now they are reaching aggressively for better ways to mechanically sort out orders for annuals.

One of the secrets of the great Dutch success in mechanizing is specializing. Not necessarily only one crop—but typically where you see advanced tray mechanization and other major efforts to mechanize, you see perhaps a maximum of several crops a year grown on that range. You just can't do this sort of mechanizing where you have a bench each of five different crops in a house. And that's the way so many U.S. growers do things. And it's hard to change. We make the point here though because if the U.S. grower is going to be competitive he's going to have to move as rapidly as possible toward fewer crops, and specializing, studying, and doing the best job possible on the ones that he does grow. Pick the things that you seem to make money on and with which you do well and which you find a market for and push them. And cut out a few of your "other" crops each year. You'll be a lot more efficient.

Fact: Dutch specialization has its roots in their very efficient auctions.

One of the conflicts here is the classic retail grower. From 10,000 to 40,000 square feet of greenhouse sold through a retail garden center in the spring. One of his strengths in drawing people to his place is having a wide variety of things to offer in the spring. Typically half a dozen of the colorful "other" pot plants. Like New Guinea impatiens, Rieger begonias, Browallia, pot dahlias, hibiscus, etc. One way to offer this wide variety of material and not complicate your growing is to buy at least some of these things from specialists. Or at least buy them in the 2¼" stage so you need only finish the crop.

But for the larger wholesale pot plant specialist, the decision about specializing is coming into sharp focus. Even very large pot plant growers typically will produce a dozen or two different crops a year—which certainly doesn't lend itself to mechanization. Their response when you talk about this with them is always the same—"We just have to have this variety to market our product."

And yet competition is coming from specialists. Again, isn't the answer to gradually move toward few crops? We wonder at times whether our giant supermarket chains aren't going to sponsor more specialization in a certain way. Perhaps one grower can be the specialist producer of Rieger begonias for a chain like Kroger with 800 florist shop stores. Somebody else can be their violet supplier, someone else does perhaps the rotation of primula in winter and maybe a hibiscus crop in the spring.

The other basic question involved here is simply the problem of financing—money to pay for it. Mechanization is costly—even though it may well pay the grower back quickly in savings.

Somewhat, this goes back to profitability of an operation. If a grower is earning only 5% on the capital invested in his range, it's not easy to borrow from a bank. A grower earning twice or more that much will find it a lot easier to borrow—and easier to repay the loan.

But the flip side of all this is that the very mechanization the grower wants may very well permit him to boost his return on his investment substantially.

Somehow the Dutch (champion mechanizers) do seem to borrow heavily to finance their modern mechanized ranges. Maybe too much. We hear (early 1980s) of a rash of bankruptcies among Dutch growers. Yet most of them survive—and run very efficient operations.

TAX SAVING

There is important help from taxes, depreciation, etc. Examples:

Depreciation   On equipment such as potting machines, tray mechanization, and automated thermal sheets, normal write-off is on a five-year basis. That means that in five years, probably half the cost of the equipment has been paid for out of depreciation.

Investment tax credit   Now on a new greenhouse range and most capital expenditures, the government allows you to deduct 8% of the cost of the equipment—from your next tax statement. A $100,000 greenhouse means that you pay $8,000 less taxes the next year. This credit was recently nearly dropped by the government—but the Society of American Florists successfully lead efforts that saved the credit.

Energy credit   No longer available.

LEASING

Another answer to the "money for mechanizing" problem: equipment leasing. This is a realistic alternative source of financing. Such financing is available today—to pay for a new range plus equipment for it. You pay current interest cost and treat the investment as an expense item. After a period of time, often five years, the grower may, and typically does, buy the whole thing—for a nominal amount.

One more general point on mechanization—which seems to us an excellent starting place in your planning: For one week, several times a year, carefully record all hand labor expenditures that you make. One grower just

65

took a minute with each employee at the end of each day and sorted out the crops and activities he spent his time on. It can be done with cards filled out by the employee. However you do it, even at a little expense, it provides a basis for decisions on where to spend money on mechanization. After all, no mechanized equipment is good business unless you can save enough labor cost to recover your investment in a couple of years. So the question is: What is my investment in each of these jobs?

Not opinions—but facts.

The wheelbarrow and the hose must go!

G.V.B.

Chapter 7

TRAY MECHANIZATION —HOW AND WHY*

Tray mechanization (some growers say "container" mechanizing) is an extremely promising approach to the problem of minimizing labor cost especially on pot plants, foliage, and certainly bedding plants. The strength and the genius of tray mechanization is that it provides an extremely low-cost way to move plants from headhouse to greenhouse and back to headhouse. It was originated in Holland (Boekestijn's in the Westland area) in the mid-1970s, and is used today in dozens of ranges in Holland and is starting to appear across the U.S. and Canada.

The system is built around a tray. This is an aluminum sort of "box" varying from perhaps 4' by 12' to 5' by 20'. Normally 4"–5" deep. They are nearly always made of aluminum, and are quite lightweight. A man can easily pick up an empty tray!

The tray serves as the bench. Plants are grown in the trays. And again, the point of this system is that trays full of plants can be moved very rapidly and at minimal cost from headhouse to growing area and back to the headhouse. How? The answer comes in two parts:

*Parts of this chapter are based on several stories in *Grower Talks,* 1983–84, by the author.

A typical tray (above left)—in this case, 5' by 13'. Note the two pipe "rails" on which the tray is rolled from the house to the center walk. Note, also, the water hose available to each tray. Photo (right): Trays roll from the right to the center walk; a temporary pipe rail carries them across the walk to the roller conveyor, then to the headhouse—self-propelled! Both photos at Burnaby Lakes Greenhouse, Vancouver, British Columbia.

Moving trays up and down the length of the greenhouse This is always done by rolling the tray on two lengths of normally about 1½" to 2" pipe. Thanks to ingenious rollers built onto the bottom of the trays, these trays can be pushed very easily—even though they are full of plants. We've seen one person push 1500 6" mums down the length of a greenhouse—with ease.

The trays are positioned crosswise in a row down the length of the house. Narrow houses may accommodate one row of trays (crossways), wider houses may accommodate two or even three rows of trays—between gutters. (See photos).

Again, these trays, full of plants or empty, can be moved up and down the length of the house with great ease.

Moving the trays down the center walk The next step is moving trays from the end of the bench (adjacent to the center walk). How are the trays picked up at this point and moved to the headhouse? Here we've seen half a dozen different systems. Simple, lower cost installations simply roll the tray onto a four-wheeled cart—and the grower can pull it by hand up to the headhouse. Or anywhere.

From here there are a variety of more sophisticated systems. One of the best and most common is a sort of self-propelled track. The trays are just rolled up to the center walk and onto the track and the track itself propels the tray right on into the headhouse. All by itself! (See photo.) Other growers use, again, the two rows of 1½" pipe and hand propel the trays from greenhouse to headhouse. See photos of a variety of these systems along with the story.

There are installations in Holland where this movement of trays from headhouse or work area to the growing bench is not only self-powered, but computer-controlled. It can be done—and is, in several installations in Holland.

The result of all this: Again, pot plant crops (or bedding plants) can be moved very rapidly, easily, and inexpensively from the headhouse or work area to the growing bench. And, conversely, back from growing bench to headhouse. And, that does some great things for crop labor cost! Don't forget, moving things is the number one cost of growing most pot plants and bedding plants. And foliage. And mum propagation. And plug production.

Here are some of the things that tray mechanization ranges do with this easy, low-cost mobility:

Potting   Take for example a crop of pot mums. The soil, the cuttings, the pots, are all stored and available in the headhouse. In the headhouse—and close to the potting machine. Now, when mums are to be potted, the pots are filled on the potting machine, cuttings stuck into the pots, and they are rolled onto the tray. There is mechanization available to move the pots from

Part of the 7-acre tray installation at Boekestijn's, de Lier, Holland. Note that trays here are moved down the center in a sort of train. The three trays on the left are moving toward the headhouse.

the potting machine to the tray—mechanically! In fact, new Javo* equipment even permits variable spacing of these pots. Anywhere from pot-tight to whatever you wish. Once the tray is full of pots, it is rolled off to the growing area.

Disbudding Since one man can move 1250 to 1500 pots from greenhouse to work area in perhaps ten minutes, it becomes economical to move the crop to the headhouse for such operations as disbudding mums. And, in fact, growers do just that. And, here is one of the great benefits of the tray system. It's simply that crews do accomplish a great deal more work in a day when the job is brought to them in a convenient dry, well-heated headhouse. The crews spend less time wandering about from job to job, less time getting to their coffee break and restroom facilities. Growers with such systems (including Pan-American Plant Company's mum rooting operation in Florida, which is all tray mechanized) report major gains in productivity of their crews— when the job is done in the headhouse.

Spacing Let's say that the crop of pot mums is originally sent out to the greenhouse pot-tight. Weeks later it's ready to space. You roll the crop back to the headhouse, put empty trays alongside of full ones, and respace the crop—and roll it back. Again, this respacing can be done completely with a minimum of handwork.

Lilies Let's say we have a crop of lilies, and typically some plants are coming faster than others. You roll the whole crop into the headhouse, move the slower plants from the original tray out to separate trays—which can be put into a warmer house. And of course reconsolidate the more advanced plants. No lugging!!

Refrigerating crops Example: A crop of pot tulips. The tulips are potted in the headhouse using the potting machine. They are then watered, and rolled into the refrigerator. Again, these trays can be raised to the upper shelves of the refrigerator either mechanically or by handcrank devices. After the necessary number of weeks, the trays are moved down to the ground level, and off to the greenhouse for forcing. Such crops of pot bulbs in fact today are never touched as individual pots from potting until sleeving.

Packing/shipping One of the major payoffs of tray mechanization is in shipping such crops as poinsettias, pot mums, etc. A house or an acre or ten acres of poinsettias can be easily rolled into the headhouse when they are ready for shipping. There the crew again has sleeving facilities handy to the tray. Also, packing boxes. And, a few feet away are the loading dock and the truck. Clearly there is major economy of labor in getting that poinsettia from the growing bench through sleeving and boxing and into the truck—with trays.

*Javo USA, Inc., 1109–1111 Cobb Parkway, Marietta, Georgia 30062 (404) 428-4491.

A point: Some crops will not mature all at one time. Example: Cyclamen. Some "cherry picking" is often necessary. In such cases, a gantry overhead tray can be rolled up and down the bench, plants selected for today's shipping, then the tray rolled up to the center walk and off to the headhouse.

It's possible to pick up a single tray down in the middle of the house and bring it up to the center walk. It seems that almost anything can be done—but the more you do, the more it costs!

The Payoff

To summarize: The principal advantages of tray mechanization are:

- Greatly reduced cost of moving crops from headhouse to growing area and back to the shipping room. And, this is important since moving things is almost always the number one labor cost of growing the crop.

- Major decrease in cost of hand operations done in a headhouse vs. doing the job in the greenhouse. Greenhouses are hot in summer, cold

Trays at Masson's, Linwood, Kansas. The Massons have made a major investment in tray mechanization at their new Linwood range. Shown above, on the right, Alexander Masson; on the left, Larry Thomas of Masson's. Alexander considers tray mechanization the "most important decision we've made in our business career."

71

in winter, sometimes wet under foot, drafty. Not at all ideal conditions for doing hand jobs. On the other hand, facilities in the headhouse certainly should be ideal for such operations.

- Reduction in aisle space. Since nearly all the crop labor is done in the headhouse, there is no longer a need for all that expensive aisle space. Typically tray growers have one aisle per house. This means an increase in usable space in a greenhouse from around 65% to 85 or 90%. And that translates into 25 to 35% less for all overhead cost per plant. Certainly including fuel, manager's salary, taxes, insurance, etc. Conversely it means that you can get 25% more plants from the same acre of greenhouse.

- Not a major point, but the pipes on which the trays are rolled also serve as heating pipes—typically in such ranges with a hot water system.

Cost

Cost for all this equipment varies so widely that it is hardly useful to try to spell it out. But just to get a rough idea, one of the more sophisticated new systems built recently, for a 100,000-square-foot pot plant range, cost on the order of $250,000–$300,000 for all the trays, tracks, and self-powered center walk track needed for the job. And, again for the record, good floating aisle metal benches for the same 100,000 square feet would probably cost approximately $200,000.

And of course there is a whole array of depreciation, investment tax credit, etc., which is a major offset to such capital investments.

Smaller Growers

How about a one-acre tray range? Can a smaller range, let's say an acre of pot plants, use the tray system efficiently? Answer: We've seen ranges of such size in Holland—often with less sophisticated equipment, but certainly growing in trays, doing a good job, and reaping the important benefits of labor saving.

One point that should be made: Crops with fast turnover adapt themselves obviously very well to the tray system. A crop that will be three months or even less on the bench makes sense with trays. A crop that will take six months to mature tends not to involve enough moving cost to warrant the cost of trays. Rooting mum cuttings by specialist propagators is a natural for the tray system and in fact both Yoder and Pan-American Plant Company in the U.S. are fully tray-mechanized.

Trays are for the smaller grower, too. This is the Strybis range in Holland—
50,000 square feet of mainly 4" pot mum production. It's all rolling trays, almost
no walk space. Here's one tray, on the cart used to move trays from greenhouse
to headhouse. Note the little guide wheel in front of the cart.

Other Points

Boekestijn   This remarkable range in de Lier, Holland, includes a seven-acre block devoted to year-round 4" and 5" pot mums, two plus million a year. Up to the mid-1970s, it was normal benches and hand moving of crop. At that point, it was converted to tray mechanization. To our knowledge, one of the first (if not the first). The labor crew needed to produce and pack and box this production was reduced from 50 to 12 when the job was converted from conventional system to trays! And that's a remarkable record for cutting labor cost. For details on this interesting range, see *Grower Talks*, December, 1983.

It's not just trays—there are many critically important tricks of management here. For example, none of the pot mums are disbudded—they're all daisies and really look not bad as you see them going out. Unrooted cuttings are directly stuck and covered with sheets of polyethylene until rooted rather than bothering with mist. Irrigation as we recall is a mat system perhaps involving flooding of the aluminum trays. Not sure on this point.

A typical house of established 4" pot mums at Boekestijn's. Note the absence of aisles—access is from the gutter walk—and by moving the trays apart lengthways it is possible to access any plant in the house by hand. Impressive!

Interesting: One man is the "grower" on this entire seven-acre range. One person is the "internal transport" person—he moves all the plants from work area to greenhouse and back to work area. This plus ten women who do the potting (in fact, just drop unrooted cuttings into the pots as they go by), plus the sleeving and boxing of plants. All of which is done in the headhouse.

You just don't see very many people around that seven acres of greenhouse! And you sure don't see any walks—except the one very wide center cement walk.

Irrigation of pot plants Chapin-type tubes are used very widely. In many cases, growers have headers and tubes installed permanently into the trays. Then as the tray is rolled into position in the greenhouse bench, it is quick coupled to a water line—to provide both water and feed.

Bedding plant application Van de Weterings at Calverton, Long Island, are one of the first, to our knowledge, to use the tray system to move flats of annuals from headhouse to growing area and back. They initiated new equipment in spring 1984 which they report enables one man to move 3,000 flats of annuals from the growing bench to the shipping room in one hour!!! We figure that is somewhere on the order of 3¢ or 4¢ per flat to move the flat from greenhouse to headhouse. And that is major progress.

Also, another striking advantage and innovation here: The Van de Weterings have developed a system of rolling whole houses of flat annuals outdoors in early spring. As soon as the crop is established, it can be rolled out of the greenhouse on tracks to the area adjacent to the end of the greenhouses. Again, just minutes per house to do the job. The crop can be left out during the cool early spring days. If frost threatens, it can be rolled in very easily. Five minutes per greenhouse.

Two great advantages of this "roll-out" system: First, a second crop can be grown on the ground in the same house—thus, the grower gets two simultaneous crops from the house. Second point, the crop that is finished outdoors develops a superb quality—just like the old German cold-frame system. Cool nights, lots of rain, and lots of light.

Foliage crops   We know several major foliage growers who are completely tray-mechanized. The largest one clearly is Oakdale in Apopka, Florida—here at last reading were about nine acres of trays devoted almost entirely to production of potted foliage plants.

Access to crop   Under the tray system, it is possible for the grower to access any plant in the house. You can push two trays apart anywhere you wish and walk in between the trays and get at any part of the operation.

Suppliers of tray equipment: Hawe-Dexco USA, Inc., 611 Industrial Ave., Boynton Beach, Florida 33435 (305) 734-1661; Intransit, de Hondert, Magen 6, P.O. Box 87, 2678 ZG de Lier, Holland; and, Wevab B.V., Kerklaan 19, 2678 ST de Lier, Holland.

G.V.B.

Chapter 8

BELT
MECHANIZATION

A different approach to the problem of moving crops. It's built around a self-propelled moving belt, normally provided in 10′ sections. Normally you'll see a 6″ wide plastic endless belt built in 10′ sections. Joined together, these sections can move pot plants or flats or almost anything almost any distance across a greenhouse. They can go uphill, downhill, through tunnels, around corners, etc. Which can be a great help in many cases—and which we believe we'll see a lot more of, especially on smaller ranges and perhaps some retail growing ranges. They can be used to unload a truckload of peat, to move plants to and from the shipping room—to move anything really. And, hand moving costs $$!

The most striking example of belt mechanization we know of today is the Aldershot range, Burlington, (Toronto) Ontario, Arie VanderLugt and his two sons, Peter and Gerald. Here on about 250,000 square feet, the VanderLugts produce about 900,000 6″ mums a year—with a total workforce of well under 30. Which is a sharp reduction from most similar operations. Nearly all moving of pot mums from start to finish is on belts. See *Grower Talks,* September, 1983, for details.

Here, the pots are filled in the work area (using a potting machine). They're moved by belt to a potting area where rooted cuttings are planted into the pots. From there by belt to the starting houses—for several weeks of high

A major and very interesting belt application. Aldershot Greenhouses, near Toronto (the Van der Lugt family), produces one million pot mums per year. And, nearly all the moving of the crop is done on belts. Result: major labor saving. The man above is picking up plants from the starting area (70°, long days); the belt will move them to the finishing bench. Photo courtesy of Aldershot Greenhouses.

temperature, high humidity, and long days. Then again by moving belt to the flowering bench.

An important part of this scheme is a folding 100' section of belt that can be collapsed into perhaps a 6' or 8' unit on wheels and moved from house to house. When needed, it's wheeled half way down a 100' walk then spread out both ways—to provide moving belt from end to end of the 100' walk. (See photo elsewhere in this chapter.)

At order-filling time, plants here are sleeved on the bench, moved to the center walk (on belts in special trays), then on small trucks on to the headhouse.

The overall efficiency of the operation is a major step forward and is clearly making waves in the pot plant industry. Full details, by the way, in *Grower Talks,* September, 1983. The VanderLugt range, by the way, is entirely equipped with slider benches (floating aisles)—so they have gained the advantage of higher space utilization.

An interesting bedding plant application of belts is Jeffery's, St. Catharines, Ontario. They are basically bedding plants, 120,000 flats a year, wholesale.

Also, several greenhouses of poinsettias. They have several hundred feet of belt equipment, again in 20' sections, which they move freely about their operation and use heavily in both bedding plants and poinsettias.

They report a cost of about $100 Canadian for a 20' section (10" wide) and $70 for a 20' section (6" wide) including electric power. To extend this further, you buy additional sections without power—they hook onto the original axle-driven powered section. Jeffery uses the belts in 100' sections, one powered unit and four "free-loaders" costing about $7,000.

TRAYS OR BELTS—WHICH IS BEST?

The big question now: Which is the more efficient way for the specialist pot or bedding grower—trays or belts? The Vander Ende family (Burnaby Lakes in Vancouver) have just completed (1984) a new 100,000 square foot range fully

Belts are much used in Holland! Here is foliage production at Boekestijn's, de Lier. The plants moving off to the right have just turned a corner (behind the plants)—and will go off to the shipping room via belts. Speaking of belts, don't miss the Jeffery's belt application under Bedding Plant Mechanization, elsewhere in this book.

equipped with trays—taking full advantage of all that trays have to offer. (See Chapter 7, on trays.) As of this writing, it hasn't really been in operation long enough for a fair appraisal. The Massons at Kansas City also have a major tray installation. There is about a nine-acre tray installation at the Oakdale range in Apopka, Florida—nearly all foliage plants, which has been in operation for several years. Gene Greiling has just completed about three acres of trays for his specialized plug production in Apopka.

It would probably be premature to attempt a judgement on which is the "best" system. Certainly belts have an important place in production of pot plants and bedding plants and foliage. Often we see belts used in combination with trays. For a preliminary guess, it would seem that the tray system does the job with substantially fewer people—but at substantially higher initial investment. Also, trays do provide a bit more space utilization than even sliders.

Three suppliers are: Bouldin & Lawson Inc., Rt. 10, Box 208, McMinnville, TN 37110 (615) 668-4090. Chris Industries Corp., 4001 7th Terrace South, St. Petersburg, FL 33711 (813) 327-3908. And, Javo USA Inc., 1109 Cobb Parkway, Marietta, GA 30062 (404) 428-4491.

G.V.B.

Chapter 9

PLUGS—BIG SPACE- AND LABOR-SAVERS

Plugs are the big news in bedding plants for the 1980s. Growers large and small are in most cases at least starting to move that way. Larger specialists are often doing 70-80% of their bedding flats from plugs (early 1980s).

How does it work? In effect, the petunia or impatiens is "direct seeded" to a tiny 1/2"–5/8" diameter "pot." Then weeks later this little plug is transplanted to the bedding plant pack, etc. Then it's grown on to a salable-size bedding plant. Sounds like much work and more cost—but in fact, it's less of both.

The starting phase is done on 11" × 21" plastic sheets, which have been pressed to form several hundred tiny cups (see photo). Typically one cup (holding one plant) will form a root ball 5/8" in diameter × 1" high. There's always drainage provision in the bottom of each cup.

The cup is first filled with a carefully prepared germinating mix. It's watered, the seed (or seeds) is sown, and we're off.

Weeks later this plug annual is ready to be "shifted"—many to regular bedding plant packs or cell packs, maybe 8 or 12 packs per flat. Some go to 3", 4" pots. Some to hanging baskets.

A sheet of well-done plugs. In the photo: Mike Pointer, Skagit Gardens, Mount Vernon, Washington.

ADAPTABILITY TO MECHANIZATION

The heart of the case for plug-grown annuals (or other crops) is first greatly reduced crop time. Also, it's the high level of mechanization possible under this system. Examples:

Filling the cups   With a little adaptation, the typical bedding plant flat-filler will fill trays for starting plug annuals. Very important that each cell or cup be really filled—no airspace in the lower half of the cell. We saw equipment at Grow Show '82 (see *Grower Talks*, September 1982, page 35) which mechanically filled the cells, then gave them a hard shaking for a few seconds. Then brushed them lightly over the top with a sort of broom. Result, full mechanization and well-filled cells.

Seed sowing   There's a whole array of mechanical seed sowers to do this job. Full specifications, performance, etc., are covered later in this chapter. The point for the moment though, is that sowing a seed, with several exceptions, is a fully mechanized operation. Several seeds such as very small begonias and marigolds with "tails" are just now starting to be handled by mechanical seeders.

Covering the seed   If necessary, a fine coating can be applied over the cup to cover the seed mechanically.

82

Irrigation/feeding of the sheets of plugs Fully mechanized—with automatically timed misting equipment—and fertilizer injectors.

Removing the plugs Again, mechanical equipment is now available (see *Grower Talks*, September 1982 for Boulding & Lawson equipment) to remove the plugs, spread them out on a belt—to be moved to the transplanting crew.

Transplanting The technology for mechanically planting these plugs into packs or pots is available. But growers are finding that by organizing the work properly, they can reduce transplanting cost to 10¢-15¢ per flat (72 plants).

THE CASE FOR PLUG ANNUALS

Why is the plug idea moving so rapidly into the bedding plant industry? Several answers:

Labor saving For the reasons outlined above, the seed sowing and transplanting into packs of annuals is already semi-mechanized—and will soon be more so. And that's an important economy to the grower!

Less bench time Individual crops vary widely—but in general good plugs planted to a typical bedding plant pack will be salable in at least 1/3 fewer days than in the case where bare root seedlings are dug and transplanted. See photo for comparison of plug and bare root impatiens.

When you save 1/3 of the time from plant to sell, you're reducing all overhead costs (very important) by 1/3. The same greenhouse structure, the same grower and manager, the same fuel cost now will produce 1/3 more flats of annuals per season.

Put a different way, a bedding plant specialist can turn out 1/3 more flats of annuals or pot annuals or hanging baskets per season than he could with transplanted bare root seedlings. And that, again, is a big difference.

New rotation opportunities The shorter crop time plug annual opens some interesting rotation possibilities. Example: One midwestern grower had a 1/2 acre glass area used for Easter pot mums. The mums were out early, mid-April. There just wasn't time for a followup crop of bedding plants. But with plugs, especially on a reasonably early Easter, he could turn out good quality flat annuals by early to mid-May by following the Easter mums with plug-planted pack annuals.

John Hughes, Ontario extension man, reported one grower shipping out Mother's Day pot mums April 30 (they do normally go out a week ahead of

Well-developed impatiens plugs were transplanted to the cell pack on the right October 15. At the same time, bare-root seedlings were transplanted to the left pack—and took 3 more weeks to mature. Which makes a point that plugs save several weeks' growing time. Result: 25% to 30% more flats per bench per year.

the holiday). Followed at once by plug-started annuals, which were salable three weeks later. Still right for the peak bedding plant season. Another of John's clients shipped out benches of pansy plants April 30, again followed by plug-started petunias. There were salable by late May.

Labor saving is important and obvious to the grower. However, to us the shorter crop time and the capability of fitting in tighter rotations in the all-important spring weeks is the real heart of the case for plug annuals. That's the reason we believe so many growers are moving that way quite rapidly.

Plugs Plant Faster

One of the key advantages of plug annuals is faster transplanting. The point was brought to sharp focus by a report from John Hughes, Toronto area extension man, at a recent BPI conference.

In effect, John working with local growers set up a comparison between: Seedlings hand dug, hand sorted, and planted. One planter, one flat. Now plugs. Holes predibbled in each pack to accommodate the six plugs. And the whole operation set up on an assembly line basis. The flats were moved slowly past the transplanters. Each person responsible for planting one of the 12 packs.

Obviously, the second grower's transplanters had only to pick up the plug and drop it in a hole. No digging of seedlings, no sorting of small and large seedlings, no firming in of the seedling.

The result was an incredible 11¢ per flat transplant labor cost vs. 50¢ a flat for the hand dug, one-person, one-flat system.

DISADVANTAGES OF PLUGS

There are several:

- Clearly it takes a lot more 70° bench space to germinate seed in plugs vs. the old open flat of seedlings. And that means more cost. However, in a week, or ten days at most, plug sheets can normally be moved to a cooler house.

- Germinating seed and growing the plugs in the tiny cells is tough—very demanding. Many growers lose half or more of their plugs, especially the first year or two.

- Machines for the mechanical seeding are expensive.

It's important that the plugs have bottom heat—to maintain 70° to 75° soil temperature for most annuals. Also, that they be exposed to the air on the underside—to prevent masses of root-through. The above bench developed at Meiring's, Carleton, Michigan. It does the job well.

SUGGESTIONS FOR GROWING PLUGS

We've made the point several times—growing plugs in those tiny cells is a very tough challenge. In fact, it's so tough that a great many smaller growers are simply buying plugs rather than having to organize themselves for the strict discipline of successful plug growing. Much good detail on all of this is in *Grower Talks,* October 1982. But many growers *are* growing their own. And many are successful—certainly not all.

So here are pointers on how to do it:

1. *Use a good mix and fill the cells carefully.* The mix should be sterile, certainly porous, and fine enough so that the plugs will actually fill. Chunks of peat or sticks that will cause air spaces in the plugs are bad news. The plug must be full of mix—all the way from top to bottom. Be sure the salt level in the mix is moderate or low.

2. *Soil temperature.* For most annuals—70° or even 75° is a must. That's soil temperature. Irrigating the plugs with 45° or 50° water will mean a soil temperature near that level—far too cool for good germinations. Many growers we see are using heated water for their plugs. See *Grower Talks,* April 1984, for Bernacchi's equipment.

3. *Mist.* Irrigating with a mechanical mist system is, again, really a must to succeed with plug growing. Typically we hear 12 seconds of mist every 12 minutes on cloudy days and 12 seconds every 6 minutes on sunny days, which is adjusted as these seedlings develop. By the way, a plastic skirt a foot or two above the bench sideboard protects the surface of the plug sheet from drafts—very helpful.

4. *After germination.* As soon as the seeds sprout, it's important to move the plug sheets to a cooler, drier climate—55° or even less for petunias and 60° for begonias, impatiens, salvia, etc. Ventilation is critical here—not drafts, but certainly fresh air circulation.

5. *Feeding.* Most growers use a germinating mix which has enough nutrients and minor elements to carry the plant through the first week or so. But certainly at about that time some feeding should be included in the mist. We hear most often 50 to 75 parts per million of nitrogen and potash. And, again, minor elements: pH is often a serious problem with plug growing where hard waters are encountered. Bicarbonates in the water will drive the pH up to 7.5–8.0 in no time. Result: iron and other essential elements are not available to the plant. And it dies. It's very important to check pH regularly—especially when you're first starting with plugs.

6. *Length of time in plugs*. How long can plants be left in the plug? A very important point. We've seen impatiens held in plugs until buds were actually starting to be visible. A well-developed, mature plug plant will take off and grow very rapidly after transplanting. However, there is a limit. If the plant stays in the plug too long it will become checked and hardened—and will take even longer to get growing again. We've seen geraniums left in plugs for several months—and really get out and go after planting. It's really a matter of judgement.

Plug Sizes

There are several sizes of plugs currently available to growers. All are formed into sheets to fit in 11″ × 21″ flats. Here they are:

Plugs per 11″ × 21″	Flat size of plug
648	$^{6}/_{16}$″ × $^{6}/_{16}$″
400	$^{9}/_{16}$″ × 1″
273	$^{10}/_{16}$″ × 1″

Here are the principal sizes of plug or waffle sheets used. All fit into a 21″ long flat. The 648 grows twice as many plants or more—but is twice the challenge to the grower because of the small soil volume.

Which is the correct one to use?

First suggestion: If you're starting out growing plugs for the first time, we strongly urge use of the 273—the larger plug. It's just a lot easier to succeed with perhaps twice the volume of soil.

After you've had some experience and if you are pressed for space, try going down to a 400 or even a 648 plug per flat size. It does save a lot of space, especially on a large operation. Some growers do a very good job with a 648 plug. But it is certainly more foolproof and easier to use a larger size.

Just for the record, here's an interesting figure on space required by plugs:

Grown in	Square inches per plant
⅝" plug	0.9"
4" pot	25.0"

In a way, that's really the case for plugs. You get 28 times more plants per square foot!

For 10,000 Flats
72 plants/flat

Type:	Square Ft.	% finished ar
Mass	1,330	6 ½
648	2240	11
400	3,640	18
273	5,330	26

An interesting table—again by Meiring's, Carleton, Michigan. 10,000 21" flats will need 16,000 to 18,000 square feet. To fill them with 273 (large) plugs, it will take 5,330 square feet—or about 26% of the area of the finished flats.

THE CASE FOR BUYING PLUGS

Almost predictably, the intensive level of care required to grow plugs successfully has resulted in a great many of especially the smaller growers buying them from specialists. And probably if such a smaller grower had really good cost records, he would find himself ahead of the game for buying them. Many larger growers do grow their own—although we keep coming across growers such as Norm White, Chesapeake, Virginia (4–5 acres and a major bedding grower) who buys rather than grows his own. And Norm is a top-notch grower.

Probably the classic case for buying plugs would be the smaller wholesale, even retail grower, who does a lot of hanging baskets and 4" annuals. A 5¢ or 6¢ plug can be turned into a 70¢, 4" impatiens in just a couple of weeks. Such growers understandably tend to buy the plugs.

The other point here is, again, the question of the specialist. A man who does only bedding plants (on a large scale) is a lot more apt to succeed, both in quality and in cost, growing his own plugs. The fellow who grows a wide variety of crops—either wholesale, or especially the retail grower—has really a strong case for buying, rather than growing his own. A place with several dozen different crops in ½ an acre in busy spring months is a poor bet for "grow your own" plugs.

Seed Sowers Available

Table 9-1 (p. 90) lists the four principal seeders available in the mid-1980s—and brief comments on each.

Suggestion: If you're interested in this equipment, write to all four and get their updated specifications, prices, etc. Addresses are on the table.

TABLE OF SEEDER SPECIFICATIONS

In developing Table 9-1 on seeders (1984), some very interesting trends come to light—from the seeder manufacturers.

Plug trend up All four manufacturers reported strong demand for seeders. As of January 1, 1984, three out of four manufacturers were sold out until mid-February.

Smaller growers are buying seeders Especially from Bob Dekker of Old Mill a report that "we have sold a lot of seeders to smaller growers—even sometimes retail growers down to a quarter of an acre."

Lots of seeding direct to the pack Again Bob Decker, "We're getting a lot of orders from smaller growers who plan to direct seed into the cell pack." Farmer Grant, Ann Arbor, Michigan, has a single head model 615. Flats move directly from the flat filler to the seeder on a power belt—then to the greenhouse growing area—again, via power belt. Soil-heated ground for germination used here.

Table 9-1 PLUG SEEDERS

	Speed per hour One seed per plug	Handles begonia seed raw?	Handles marigolds?
Blackmore Blackmore Transplanter Co. 725 N. Huron Street Ypsilanti, MI 48197 (313) 483-8661 Mr. Skip Blackmore	Reliably 50,000 seeds/hr. with 200 plug flats, a bit less with a 400 & 648 flat.	Yes. Widely used. 95%–98% will be all doubles, some 3–4. 1% skips. Non-Stops sown one per plug. See introduction—begonias.	Skip Blackmore, "Present equipment delivers a seed to 90% of plugs, 10% skips. Probably better next year. Germination outlook for detailed marigolds for spring 1984—about normal.
Hamilton (Pneumatic machine) BFG Supply Company 14500 Kinsman Road Burton, OH 44021 (216) 834-1883 Mr. Dick Bonner	Dick Bonner reports 50,000 petunia seeds/hr. using 273 tray. Maximum speed 80,000 seeds/hr. with "optimum configuration."	Yes. Maximum "10% double or multiple, a few skips, all the rest singles."	Will handle detailed marigolds. Skips near zero, doubles-triples 10%, the balance singles. "There is widespread use of Hamilton with detailed marigolds."
Old Mill (Electronic) Old Mill Company Savage Industrial Center Savage, MD 20763 (301) 725-8181 Mr. Bob Decker	One head delivers 11,000–15,000 seeds/hr., three heads about 40,000 seeds/hr. (this from model 615—using petunia seed). With optimum seed & conditions, maximum up to 20,000 seeds/hr. (615).	Yes: 75% single, 20–30% double, 2% skips.	Detailed seed goes just like petunias. With tails marigolds move slowly.
Vandana (Manual) Vandana Growing Systems, Inc. 2950 N. Weil Street Milwaukee, WI 53212 (414) 263-3131 Mr. Dana Cable	Speed depends on operator's skill. A complete tray is sown at one time. Capacity: 30,000–60,000/hr. depending on seed variety.	Ball Seed's Jim Schield: "We have a few success stories with growers doing clump sowing 2–4 seeds/plug. Low cost per seed helps here."	Not yet—plate coming for detailed seed soon.

Note: All specifications are from the manufacturer.

90

	Handles all other seeds except:	Self-cleaning discharge?	Does it feed & expel flats mechanically?
Blackmore	Tomatoes OK if defuzzed. Without defuzz, 10% double, 2% skips. Zinnias—no.	Blackmore now applies normal pressure to move seed through tube & to the flat. Plus a second "strong blast." Result: 1–2% maximum stick. High-pressure blowout in conjunction with rubber tips eliminates plugged holes.	Feed yes; expel, yes.
Hamilton	Tomatoes: OK in defuzzed seed. Without defuzzing, not satisfactory. Zinnias—no.	A needle pokes through each nozzle after each delivery. For two or more seeds per plug, Hamilton cleans between each delivery. Also, on conveyor model machine, there is a dial type selector. Growers can select from one to nine seeds per plug by just dialing.	Yes.
Old Mill	Tomatoes defuzzed go normally just like petunias. Without defuzzing, no.	"Not a problem with Old Mill equipment."	Yes, both ways.
Vandana	Can do raw tomatoes, defuzzed tomatoes faster. No marigolds or zinnias.	Seed is held in each hole of the template by vacuum. The template is inverted, vacuum is released, and seed drops into individual tubes. The operator may (some do) reverse air pressure between drops to clean the template. Visual inspection is a great advantage.	No.

91

Table 9-1 (continued)

	Can it handle all sizes & spacing of plug sheets?	Automatic transplanter available?	If unattended machine runs out of seeds or flats what happens?
Blackmore	Blackmore handles 400-648— and the new 200. No others.	Yes. Skip reports a few more growers each year using the automatic punch-out system."	Nothing.
Hamilton	Virtually any configuration. By the way, with Hamilton equipment, the grower can dial in a change from 1 to 2 seeds quickly.	"On the shelf for the moment."	Nothing.
Old Mill	Yes, handles a wide variety of configurations.	"Prototype being tested." See introductory notes on this.	The machine stops immediately if seed or flats not available.
Vandana	273 & 406 plugs per sheet are normal equipment. Also, on special order other configurations are available.	No transplanter. Vandana offers a semi-automatic plug dislodger available for all models of commercial plug trays.	Nothing.

	Is seed covering available? Does it stick labels?	What provision to prevent seed bounce?	Does it dibble holes for seed?
Blackmore	Seed covering—no Labels—no	Not a problem—rather a low-pressure delivery plus specialist tube which decelerates speed of the seed at delivery point.	No
Hamilton	Seed covering—yes Labels—no	Conical seed discharge cup slows seed, eliminates bounce.	Yes
Old Mill	Covering—yes Labels—yes	"It's only a 1"–2½" drop from seed delivery point to plug. Not a problem."	No
Vandana	Covering—yes Labels—no	"Not a problem."	No

Table 9-1 *(continued)*

	Delivery on equipment ordered Jan. 1, 1984	Provision for static electricity	Models, features, prices
Blackmore	6 weeks	Grounded & constructed of metal to bleed static. No plastic tubes.	$5800—3rd generation basic model, 60,000 seeds/hr. vs. 20,000 old model. Strong air pressure blast to clean nozzle. Flat counter on machine. Feed two flats at once. $6400—will seed 200—400—400—648. Base model does any one of the three.
Hamilton	6 weeks		$5665—flats handfeed, expelled automatically. $7900—conveyor model, automatic feed & ejection. Includes dibbling, sowing & applies covering after sowing. See column 5 regarding multiple seeder. $600—side loader option—flats can be loaded from the side.
Old Mill	6 weeks		$9800 (model 615)—single head for small growers. Automatic flat-feed, handles wide range of waffle sheets, & seed from begonias to watermelons & marigolds with tails. Change from variety A to B in 1 min. Handles up to a 400 flat (600 flat special order). $30,000 (model 620)—with one head, automatic flat feeder, covers seed, accumulates flats, all capabilities of 615. $33,000 (model 620-2) two heads. $36,000 (model 620-3) three heads. Sows about 2½ times as much as 620. $6000—option to handle a 600 plug sheet. $4500—option for automatic tag inserter. $4750—option for automatic watering of flats after seeding.
Vandana	At once		$2395 (model 273)—handles 273 plugs per tray only $2910 (model 400)—handles 400 plugs per tray $2595 (model 288)—handles 288 plugs per tray $3110 (model 406)—handles 406 plugs per tray Above models complete with table-cart, four templates. $87.50—option for variable vibrator on template heads on all models. Additional templates available.

Begonia pellet trend Especially smaller growers seem to be using more pelleted begonias. Comments: "It's easier to see the seed—same for petunias." This is in spite of the fact that germination is generally not as good in pellets. From Ball Seed's Anna Ball: "Our experience recently is that germination is not a problem with pelleted begonias if the pellets are kept evenly moist. Don't wet them and then let them dry. Also, don't store pellets more than 90 days. Pellet use seems to be going up some."

Tag inserters Automatic insertion of Tag Along®—interest up. Even at $4500 it mechanizes a laborious task.

Think seed cost—especially for begonias Skip Blackmore: "If a seeder drops two begonia seeds in a plug, it will produce a fine looking cell pack or 4-inch begonia plant. At maybe a quarter cent, the seed cost is not a problem. With hybrid tomatoes, it's a different story—seed costs more, and two tomato plants in a plug don't look great. Again, seed cost on Non-Stops is quite a bit higher than for a fibrous begonia. More case for one seed per plug or hand transplanting."

The following varieties available in defuzzed tomatoes spring 1984: *Champion, Better Boy, Big Boy, Superfantastic, LaRoma, and Early Girl.*

Detailed marigolds Word from several seed sources: Spring 1984 should bring detailed seeds of both African and French, which will germinate normally. Lots of progress here recently. The Africans have been okay, the French not always strong germination—but now okay. Skip Blackmore: "The economics of marigolds don't press that hard on plugs. They are very fast to remove from the seed flat and transplant. No sorting really necessary. Also, they are a very fast crop—often only four weeks from transplant to sell. Less case here for plugs than most annuals. Also, very little transplanting shock."

Speedy transplanters From Skip Blackmore: "Allen Smith (Detroit area) reports 600 flats (72 plants) transplanted per hour using predibbled flats, plugs plus the assembly approach. Crew of six plus several suppliers. Ed Pinter about the same. Jim Jeffery (St. Catharines, Ontario) about the same experience."

Automated transplanters Interest cooling! With plugs and assembly lines, cost to transplant a flat (72 plants) is down to 10¢ or so. Just not enough potential to save labor to warrant costly automated planter.

General Comments on the Seeders

Blackmore First on the market (early 1970s), certainly reliable, fast, and good equipment. Handles a wide range of seeds. Blackmore also offers a transplanting system. Price range $6000 to $7000.

Here's the Blackmore Seeder—the first of this type of mechanical seeders—and Mr. Blackmore, Sr., the inventor and producer. It took 10 years to be appreciated—but seeders and plugs are fast becoming standards for the North American bedding crop!

Hamilton   Pneumatic, again, well-built good equipment, fast, and again handles a wide range of seed. Price range $6000 to $8000.

Old Mill   Electronic, more sophisticated equipment, moderately fast, can handle almost any kind of seed. Shuts itself off when it runs out of seed. Includes automated label sticking, watering, and covering flats. Starts at about $10,000 and up.

Vandana   Widely used, semi-manual machine. Low cost ($2500 to $3000). Good equipment to start out on.

As we go to press we have word of a new seeder: Seed-Rite from Seed-Rite Seeder Company, Rt. 1, Box 198, Prairie du Sac, WI 53578. It's a manually operated seeder, about $550. Telephone (608) 643-4008 for details.

G.V.B

Chapter 10

AUTOMATIC IRRIGATION*

Watering of floricultural crops is a cultural practice filled with contrasts and contradictions. It is perhaps the most important task to be accomplished if high quality crops are to be produced, yet it is an assignment often given to the youngest or least experienced employee who is receiving the least amount of pay. Water in most areas is one of the cheapest raw materials used in the commercial production of floricultural crops, yet it is the commodity most often withheld and limited. Greenhouse operators might tell employees who are watering plants to quickly finish so they can do something important, such as spray fungicides on those plants infected with disease organisms, whose spores were dispersed with hasty and careless watering in the first place.

Most growers do recognize the extreme importance of water and of the people applying the water. They are aware that in most greenhouse ranges it does require more labor than any other task. They do realize that to many employees it is a boring, tedious job that does not require much thought or concentration. An employer might not be able to persuade employees that watering is exciting, but hopefully employees could be convinced that the job is essential.

*Contributed by Roy A. Larson, Department of Horticultural Science, North Carolina State University, Raleigh.

COSTS OF MANUAL WATERING

Manual watering is still perhaps the most frequently used method for irrigating floricultural crops, if one were to survey all commercial flower growers, but automatic watering systems have become increasingly popular. Greenhouse operators are now aware that manual watering is not as cheap as they thought, even if the one doing the watering might be getting the lowest wages on the greenhouse staff.

Paul Nelson, in his text *Greenhouse Operation and Management* (Reston Publishing Company, 1981), did some calculations to show the cost of manual watering. He used a crop which was growing on a bench 400 square feet in size, and which required watering twice a week, or 104 times a year. He calculated a water-flow rate of 8 gallons per minute through a ¾" hose, so 25 minutes were required at each watering to apply 200 gallons to the bench. A total of 43.3 hours was required to water that crop 104 times in one year. An hourly pay scale of $3.50 would still result in a labor cost of $151.55. Some crops can require daily watering, increasing the costs even more.

There are other costs of manual watering that might be regarded as hidden costs. It is difficult to put a price tag on plants lost, or at least with the quality impaired, because watering was not done on time or was done improperly and carelessly. Many pathogens causing plant diseases are spread by splashing water, increasing costs for fungicides, labor, and increased shrinkage.

WHAT ARE THE ADVANTAGES OF MANUAL WATERING?

The list of advantages of manual watering gets constantly shorter as automatic watering systems are improved in efficiency and flexibility, and labor costs continue to rise. Some growers might state that when crops are manually watered, the person with the hose can make instant decisions as to which plants need water and which ones do not. That justification is true, if the employee is experienced and alert. The person with the hose is also often the one who spots the insect infestation or disease infection and calls them to the attention of the supervisor. That justification is also true, again if the employee is experienced and alert.

Initial costs of manual watering are low, in contrast to many automatic systems, as only a spigot, a garden hose, and in some instances a water breaker, are needed. Potted plants can be moved about, without the need for removing or adding tubes, and plants in different sized pots can be grown on the same benches.

The list of advantages of automatic watering gets longer while the list in favor of manual watering gets shorter. The initial cost, both for equipment and installation, will be higher for the automatic watering systems, but these costs are much more acceptable if the grower knows that future labor costs will be less. An analysis of cost can give a greenhouse operator some very definite ideas about expenses and savings. Current prices are readily available from the watering system manufacturers.

Watering Can Be Done Carefully

It is difficult to place a price tag on money that can be saved, or earned, because crop losses are decreased with careful watering. The mechanism of watering with most automatic systems avoids splashing water. In contrast to the "fire hose" method of watering so frequently encountered with manual watering, water comes out with very little force from some automatic watering dispensers. There is no splashing and no dispersal of spores. Compaction of the medium in the pot or the bench is minimized. So many times one can visit greenhouse ranges where a slow-release fertilizer or an insecticide such as Temik® (Aldicarb) has been placed on the "soil" surface, and immediately washed out with an unnecessary force of water from a hose. Automatic watering systems usually avoid this, though it wouldn't have to occur with manual watering, either.

Pot Plants Are More Likely to Be Properly Spaced

Growers often believed that a strong disadvantage of automatic watering of pot plants with tubes was that the system lacked flexibility. Labor costs would be too high if pots, with tubes, had to be moved as the plants increased in size, and space would be wasted if plants were immediately given their final spacing, as soon as the plant material was potted. This debate still goes on, as labor and fuel costs both increase. Shrinkage, or loss of plants, does decrease, however, when plants are given the final spacing when first placed in the greenhouse. Growers could have very strong intentions to never let plants get crowded, but other tasks with apparently higher priorities delay the moves, and quality is impaired. Labor still accounts for more of the total production costs than does fuel, so frequent moving and spacing of plants usually is not economical.

There are automatic watering systems, such as mat or capillary watering, with flexibility, if growers are concerned about "wasted" space.

Plants Can Be Watered Efficiently

The task of watering greenhouse crops manually is truly looked upon as a task by many greenhouse employees. They regard the job as tedious, often boring, not very challenging, and time-consuming. Automatic watering is free of such criticism, as often the employee simply has to turn on one valve, the crops get watered while the employee might be doing something else, and after an appropriate period of time the valve gets turned off again. Such a system is actually semi-automatic, as someone had to turn the valve on, time the watering duration, and then turn off the valve.

Watering systems can be truly automatic. A timeclock can activate a solenoid valve, water can be applied for a determined period of time, and then automatically be shut off. A sensing device, monitoring sunlight or temperature, can be used instead of a timeclock, coordinating water requirements with other environmental factors. With either system a grower conceivably could be absent, such as on weekends, and the crops would still be watered, "untouched by human hands." Most growers do not have such strong faith in solenoid valves or timeclocks, so they would want personnel there to make certain the system is working. The mechanism is there, however, for very efficient, labor-saving watering.

THE "MECHANICS" OF AUTOMATIC WATERING

The duration of watering has been mentioned, and the original decision about duration has to be made by the grower. Growers can readily calculate how much time is required for 10% of the water to be leached through the soil, and on-off riders on the timeclock can be adjusted to provide that duration. One of the earliest methods used for automatic watering of pot plants was based on weight of the water. The grower would calculate how many ounces of water were needed for proper watering, and this quantity would be pre-set on a Moist scale. The water would be automatically shut off when that quantity of water had been added to the representative plant on the scale.

Mat or capillary watering of potted plants can be readily controlled, as the major requirement of the mechanism is simply to keep the mat wet, so capillarity will not be lost. This can be achieved by using a timeclock to turn on the solenoid valve to apply the water. We applied water for 5 minutes at 10 a.m. and for 5 minutes at 2 p.m. every day, regardless of weather, and kept the mats wet and grew very acceptable potted plants. Other researchers have been successful with very brief periods of watering (6 seconds), applied frequently (every 6 minutes) from 8 a.m. to 7 p.m. One supplier of mats recommends a constant application of water to their mat to ensure capillarity. Growers can make mat watering semi-automatic by simply using a hose to wet the mat periodically but some advantages of the system are lost with this approach.

Automatic watering of cut flower crops has a longer history than for potted plants, and some growers have developed sophisticated systems for automatic watering of roses, carnations, chrysanthemums, and other cut flower crops. A former carnation grower in western North Carolina used tensiometers throughout his range as indicators when water should be applied, and plants were then irrigated with a perimeter watering system. Cut flower growers with ground beds do have to know all about the medium in which they are growing their crops, and know how much water they must add to get some leaching, because they cannot always tell when leaching is occurring.

A guideline of 2 quarts per square foot has been suggested for cut flower crops, but that guideline was for soil and did not consider the depth of the medium in the bench or bed. A more detailed guideline is to apply $1/15$ of a gallon of water per square foot for each inch of depth (P. V. Nelson, *Greenhouse Operation and Management*). If the bench has 8" sidewalls and has 7" of medium in it, then $7/15$ gallons of water or approximately 2 quarts would be applied per square foot. Adjustments in quantity of water would be made if the depth of medium was more or less than 7". Growers who know their water flow rate (gallons per minute) can then calculate how long they must irrigate to apply the proper amount of water, and this amount can be controlled with a timeclock. The guideline above is for a medium containing some soil in it. Many media popular now do not contain soil as an ingredient and are better drained than most media containing soil. More frequent applications, of shorter durations, might be advised for soilless mixes. The duration must still be long enough for some leaching to occur, however, to avoid a buildup of soluble salts.

ONE HAS A CHOICE OF AUTOMATIC WATERING SYSTEMS

Over the years several systems have been developed, and there have been refinements within those systems. Space does not permit a thorough evaluation of all the systems and refinements, but major ones will be discussed. Advantages and disadvantages will be considered. Precise costs of equipment will not be reported, as such costs are too subject to change.

Systems for Pot Plants

Tube watering   This system is the most widely used in the United States and has affected other cultural practices besides watering. Fertilizer injection to pot plant crops is possible with tube watering. Systemic fungicides and insecticides have been applied through tubes when the physical characteristics of the pesticides made such a practice possible. Growth regulators, such as

Insertion of tube with anchor, for tube watering of geraniums. Photo courtesy of Chapin Watermatics, Inc., Watertown, New York.

Cycocel® to poinsettias, have been applied to crops with the tube watering system. Tube watering has had an impact on the spacing of pot plants, as mentioned earlier.

Tube watering, as the name implies, is the placement of the end of a thin plastic tube on the surface of the potting medium in each pot (see photo). Some form of anchor at the end of the tube is always needed, to keep the tube in place. Each tube is inserted to a header, which is connected to ¾″ polyethylene or PVC pipe, and is connected to the water line. The header might be very short, with 20 tubes coming from it (photo), or run the length or width of the bench. Holes can be plugged, if all tubes are not needed.

Advantages of tube watering are its efficiency, foliage remains dry, soil is not compacted, and each pot remains isolated from others, reducing opportunities for the spread of root-rot, causing disease organisms. Disadvantages occasionally mentioned are initial cost, labor required to install tubes, and lack of flexibility to have different pot sizes on the same bench. Growers must inspect the system regularly to make certain tubes are inserted to each pot and that tubes remain open and free of soil particles and other debris.

Overhead irrigation   Water can be automatically applied to the canopy of plants with spray nozzles or sprinklers. This method is used more frequently on bedding plants than it is on flowering pot plants. Different types of nozzles can be used. Coverage can be controlled by the height of the risers. This system is readily mechanized and easy to install. A major disadvantage is that foliage does get wet, increasing the likelihood of disease problems, particularly foliar diseases. Many growers are reluctant to apply water to open flowers, and that

Short header, with 20 tubes, connected to ¾" pipe for automatic watering of potted plants. Photo courtesy of Chapin Watermatics, Inc., Watertown, New York.

cannot be avoided with overhead irrigation. Frequent examination of nozzles and plants is essential to make certain all nozzles are working and plants are being watered.

Capillary watering (mats) This is not a new concept of watering as it has been tried for many years. Previously, plants were placed on sand; water was applied to the sand and moved upward into the potting medium by capillarity. The new aspect of this system is the reservoir for holding water. Sand has been replaced by mats (see photo, p. 104) often made of synthetic fibrous material. The mats might resemble cheap carpeting, and several layers of newspapers have even been used successfully. Black polyethylene film is placed on a flat bench, the mat is placed on top of the polyethylene, and some method to apply water is installed. Tubes or special type hoses can be used to supply the water, but the grower must be certain there are enough tubes to apply water uniformly on the mat. The system can be completely automatic, or semi-automatic if greenhouse personnel turn the water on and off. Some greenhouse operators keep water dripping constantly on the mats while others apply larger volumes, when needed, to keep mats wet.

We have used mats for several years, and many of the negative things we thought would happen never occurred. We did not get into difficulty with high soluble salts, even though very little leaching of nutrients might be expected when movement of water is upward. The potting medium remained moist constantly, diluting the soluble salts effect. We did not encounter root-rot problems, which one might expect when the medium is moist continuously and, it seems, when spread of an organism such as Pythium, a water mold, would be likely. The potting media we used were pasteurized and we tried to

103

Illustration of mat watering of chrysanthemums. Black tubing provides water to the mat. Photo courtesy of Chapin Watermatics, Inc., Watertown, New York.

follow good greenhouse sanitation practices, and we avoided diseases. We have grown many crops on mats, and we have had success with all of them. Occasionally plants on mats have been taller than plants watered with tubes or with the hose but the differences usually have been approximately only 1" to 2". We have had plants in 4" and 6" pots on the same mat at the same time, with no watering problems. Incorporation of slow-release fertilizer in the potting medium, or as a top-dressing after potting, resulted in plants which were free from nutrient deficiencies. The severity of the algae problem is less with the slow-release fertilizers than when soluble fertilizers are applied to the mats.

Advantages of mat watering are flexibility, as pots of different sizes can be placed on the same mat; ease of installation; moving plants to increase spacing as the plants enlarge can be done easily and quickly, compared to tube watering. Plugging of tubes or nozzles is eliminated. Disadvantages or precautions with mat watering are that benches must be quite level for the system to work properly; algae does become unsightly and a nuisance, particularly on white mats where algae can be so noticeable; some mats do have a relatively short span of usefulness before they must be discarded; pots must have adequate drain holes in the bottom of the pot so capillarity can start and continue; capillarity must be maintained, or excessive soluble salts could be damaging.

Several procedures have been used to control algae, including the use of black polyethylene film placed on the mat with holes for contact of the pot with the wet mat. Some algaecides have been phytotoxic.

Insect infestations, such as fungus gnats, can be severe, as apparently the wet mats serve as breeding sites. Other insect troubles do not seem to increase.

A unique way of automatically watering pot plants is to place plants on troughs made of extruded aluminum. Bubble plastic film is placed on the trough, and a thin mat strip is placed on the plastic. Water is applied to the troughs and moves down the trough, as one end is slightly lower than the other end. Capillarity again is involved in the movement of water from the mat strips into the pot and to the surface of the potting medium.

Advantages of the system are similar to those described above under capillary watering. Water can be collected at the low end of the trough and recirculated, reducing runoff from the greenhouse premises. The system does take longer to install than the more conventional use of wider mats, and cost of extruded aluminum troughs must be considered when the system used for automatic watering of pot plants is selected.

Nutrient film technique   This system was developed in England and is used there and in some other countries in Europe. Water and nutrients move on polyethylene sheeted troughs and are absorbed by the plant. Surprisingly good root systems have been produced with NFT. Advantages and disadvantages are similar as for mat watering, except algae might be even more of a problem on the film plastic.

Systems for Cut Flowers

Cut flower crops have been watered automatically for many years in some greenhouse ranges, and systems used today are similar to systems used years ago. Subirrigation and gravel culture are not the popular topics now, but they were among the earliest systems used. Growers seemed to walk a "tightrope" with regard to nutrition and disease control and found that other automatic or semi-automatic watering systems were less likely to have some of the troubles.

Perimeter watering systems   Perimeter watering of cut flower crops has been used by growers for many years, but some recent improvements have made the system even more acceptable. Plumbing is so much easier now with the improved plastic or PVC pipe and fittings. White PVC pipe does not expand and move out of the bed or bench as would occur with black plastic pipe. Nozzles with different distribution patterns (45°, 90°, or 180°) can be easily installed.

The system can be operated semi-automatically or automatically, with timeclocks turning the water on and off. There are some precautions that must be observed if watering is to be done successfully. Long benches require that water mains come to the middle of the benches so the distance water must travel down the perimeter pipes will not be excessive. There must be sufficient water pressure so plants in the center of the bench will get watered. Some growers remove the bottom foliage on chrysanthemums, as they believe the larger leaves block the dispersal of water. This perhaps is true on wide benches and with low water pressure, but we do not remove leaves on chrysanthemums growing on benches 42" wide. Removing bottom foliage is labor- and time-consuming, and those larger leaves are very beneficial to the plants, particularly in the early stages of growth. A grower must be able to disconnect the system from the water main and raise the pipe during soil pasteurization or the fittings will be damaged by the high temperatures. It is also a good practice for the pipe and fittings to be surface-sterilized with a disinfectant, prior to re-installation on the soil surface.

Perimeter watering is often used on carnations and roses. Some rose growers have quit putting corn cobs, straw, and similar mulches on the soil surface, as perimeter watering has made the important task of watering so much simpler than watering with the hose. An interesting statistic is that one carnation flower reportedly can use one gallon of water by the time it is harvested, indicating the volume of water utilized by a carnation crop.

Advantages of perimeter watering are the savings in labor and time achieved with this system of watering, and it is relatively easy to install and to maintain. Water quantity and pressure must be adequate to provide uniform irrigation. A newly planted crop of snapdragon seedlings might be blown over with excessive force, while a mature mum or carnation crop might have dry plants in the center with inadequate pressure.

Polyethylene tubing   There are different types within this system (see photo). One of the earliest types consisted of flat black plastic tubing, placed lengthwise on the bench, with at least two tubes per bench. Water would move down the tubing, which would swell, and water would then be dispersed through holes spaced regularly in the tubing. A newer system consists of a perforated plastic pipe within a flat polyethylene tube, and the water slowly seeps through the stitching in the tube. Such tubes should not be further apart than 8", as the lateral movement of water will only be about 4" from each side of the tube.

Tubes are attached to ¾" plastic pipe at one end of the bench, and that pipe is connected to the water main. Tubes are plugged at the other end of the bench. The length of the tubes on the bench should not exceed 60', and water pressure should be within the range of 4 to 9 lbs. per square inch (psi).

There is no splashing of water with this latest system, installation is quite easy, and the tubing lasts longer than material used in earlier systems. As with perimeter watering systems, the tubing must be removed between crops and should be surface-sterilized if the soil is pasteurized.

A similar system can be installed across the bench rather than down the length of the bench. A polyethylene pipe is installed on one side of the bench, and a thin polyethylene tube is connected to the pipe, at 8" intervals. Water is slowly applied to the crop.

Polyethylene tubes used for watering cut flower crops. Photo courtesy of Chapin Watermatics, Inc., Watertown, New York.

Installation perhaps takes longer for this system than when fewer tubes are run the length of the bench but the advantages and disadvantages are similar.

The nutrient film technique (NFT) system has also been used on cut flower crops in Europe. It perhaps is more popular among tomato and cucumber growers, but it is a system to watch with interest.

Tremendous advances have been made in automatic watering of floricultural crops. It is difficult to predict what innovations in watering practices will be in the future, but only the most foresighted of growers of 25 years ago might have guessed at some of the systems available now. There is no reason to believe that ingenuity among manufacturers and growers will cease suddenly and no further advances will be made.

Chapter 11

FIVE OTHER PRACTICAL LABOR SAVERS

POTTING MACHINES—FLAT FILLERS*

Over the years there have been many potting machines developed for the greenhouse and nursery market. Worldwide, the Javo potting machine is the leader in the market. We also see Bouldin and Lawson. Besides potting machines, many growers have adapted their flat fillers to fill pots. Examples of flat fillers that can be adapted to fill pots are the Ball flat filler, the Bouldin and Lawson combo flat and pot filler, and Gleason flat and pot-filling equipment.

Source/locations on the various machinery:

1. Javo USA, Inc., 1109 Cobb Parkway, Marietta, GA 30062. Phone number (404) 428–4491. $10,000 and up.

2. Bouldin and Lawson, Inc., Rt. 10, Box 208, McMinnville, TN 37110. Phone number (615) 668–4090. $10,000 and up.

*Contributed by Ronald Adams, Ball Seed Co.

3. The Ball flat fillers made by Strong Manufacturing Co., Pine Bluff, AK. Phone number (501) 535–4753. $6,500 and up.

4. Gleason Equipment Co., Clackamas, OR. Phone number (503) 658–5504. $5,000 and up.

Potting Machines, Pro and Con

Potting machines and flat fillers are definite labor savers, but before making a buying decision there are certain requirements that should be analyzed.

1. Is labor relatively available on short notice?

2. Would having a machine allow you not to hire inexperienced temporary help?

3. Would the investment be recovered in a maximum of 2–3 years in cost of labor saved?

Potting machines are a vital part of modern pot plant production. Many growers of one acre or less are finding them economical—especially where they specialize in only several major crops. The above photo is Javo equipment.

POTTING MACHINE PAYBACK POTENTIAL THROUGH LABOR SAVINGS

Labor Task: Fill 10,000 6" pots with growing medium and place in the greenhouse.
Methods

Manual System
3 laborers fill pots (200 pots per hour)
1 laborer supplies pots and medium
3 laborers bring pots to bench (final location)

Potting Machine with Automatic Dispenser
1 standard machine fills 1,500 pots per hour
1 laborer works machine
1 laborer supplies machine with medium and pots
1 laborer removes pots
3 laborers bring pots to final location

Analysis

---

7 laborers @ $3.50 per hour
Total labor costs: 7 men × $3.50 per hour × 50 hours = $1,225 for 10,000 pots. (200 pots per hour possible, 10,000 ÷ 200 = 50 hours to complete task.)

6 laborers @ $3.50 per hour for about 7 hours (10,000 pots ÷ 1,500 pots)
Total labor costs: 6 men × $3.50 per hour × 7 hours = $147 for 10,000 pots.
Labor savings alone for filling 10,000 6" pots = $1,225 − $147 = $1,078.
Potting machine cost with automatic pot dispenser about $11,200 (approximate). Therefore, if customer produces about 104,000 pots per year, payback would be in about one year *on labor savings alone:* that is, every time 10,000 pots are filled customer saves $1,078. Customer must do this filling 10.4 times (11,200 ÷ 1,078) for 10.4 × 10,000 pots = 104,000.*

*These are only rough approximations. We urge growers to do this sort of calculation—based on your own figures.

Labor Task: Fill 10,000 standard flats with growing medium and place in greenhouse.
Methods

Manual System	Potting Machine with Flat Filler Attachment
2 laborers fill flats (200 flats per hour)	
1 laborer supplies flats and medium	1 machine fills 600 flats per hour
3 laborers bring flats to final location	1 laborer works machine
	1 laborer supplies machine with medium and flats
	3 laborers remove flats and bring to final location

Analysis

---

6 laborers @ $3.50 per hour	5 laborers @ $3.50 per hour
Total labor costs: 6 men × $3.50 per hour × 50 hours = $1,050.	Total labor costs: 5 men × $3.50 per hour × 17 hours = $298.
	Total labor savings = ($1,050 − $298 = $752) per 10,000 flats. Flat filler attachment costs $3,850. Therefore, if customer produces 51,000 flats (3,850 ÷ 752 × 10,000 flats) per year, payback would be in about one year on *labor savings alone.**

*These figures are approximate. Actual labor figures and procedures will vary. Machine costs do not include borrowing costs *or* depreciation. Also, these figures are *conservative* on the manual system aspect; therefore, payback may be less than one year. *Important:* This machine may qualify for an 8% investment tax credit, which means that the purchaser may directly decrease his taxes by 8% of the purchase price.

FERTILIZER INJECTORS—LABOR SAVER!

Fertilizing of virtually all commercial flower crops today is done along with irrigation. The fertilizer is injected into the irrigation water just ahead of application to the crop. And it's done automatically. Modern injectors permit varying the concentration of the fertilizer being injected. Also, these injectors will handle other chemicals in some cases.

Full details on these automated fertilizer injectors will be found in Section III, "Other Basics for Profitable Crops."

We're talking shortening daylength to control flowering of mums, kalanchoe, etc. Also summertime partial light reduction on crops that can't stand full sun. Both operations are very much a part of many growing ranges. Both are energy-related. And both certainly offer mechanization possibilities. So let's pull it all together in this chapter.

Short-Day Control First

The classic old way to create short days—just pull a big piece of black sateen over the bench—supported by a metal and wire framework. Applied at 5 p.m. removed at 7 a.m. And, of course, done manually. In some cases done with sheets of black poly—but it won't stand much of this kind of wear.

Years ago growers found that they could stretch a sheet of black poly from gutter to gutter—supported by wires drawn across the house. You just fasten the sheet to one gutter and draw it across the house—often securing it to a wire at the other gutter with clothespins. Still a manual operation—but a great deal less man hours than pulling shade over individual benches. The obvious disadvantage: you've got to shade the whole house as one. No more individual bench shading.

The next step—and actually a byproduct of energy conservation—was to mechanize that sheet of material that was drawn across the house. Gutter to gutter. Ideas to mechanize this were spawned as result of the roughly ⅓ fuel saving effected by stretching such a sheet from sunset to sunrise during winter weather. And the same sheet, if it's opaque, will do the short-day job in spring and summer. And now fully mechanized. Just set it up on a timeclock. And the whole installation for both energy saving and short-day control was not that terribly expensive. $1.25–$1.50 per sq. ft. for starters.

And that's the way a great many of the larger pot and cut mum ranges are being black cloth shaded today. With competitive pressures of the 1980s, pulling cloth by hand is going out fast.

Double heat sheets The most recent innovation here are systems that spread two layers of some sort of fabric or plastic sheeting across the house, either gutter to gutter or more often, recently, up a foot or two below the glass roof and extended lengthways of the house. From truss to truss. One of the sheets can very easily be an opaque plastic. We see a black polyethylene material made of ⅛" wide strips of black poly woven into a sort of fabric. It seems to work well. Water won't form pockets! The first system we saw was produced by Verzuu of Utrecht, Holland—first installation at Neal Mast's, Grand Rapids, MI. Shortly after that we saw a different double heat-sheet system produced by George Dean of Wadsworth Controls in Denver. First installation at Burnaby Lakes Greenhouse in Vancouver. Different in detail—but they both do the same thing.

Light Reduction

Many crops just can't stand the full 10,000–12,000 foot-candles of mid-summer sunlight—especially under a glass roof. Which aggravates the problem. Also, by the way, in many cases people have the same problem standing this intensive heat and sunlight. Result of all this: almost a majority of crops are put under some sort of light reduction in hot summer weather.

Here again the old plan was just to make up whitewash and buckets and using a tin can the grower just threw it up over the roof. It did the job—but, of course, with a lot of hand labor. And, maybe worst of all, it was so hard to get it off in the fall. Result of this was that so often you see that shade still there in November when the crop desperately wants every bit of light it can get. By the way, such shade can be—and really should be—removed in late September. Simply make up solution of Lightening Crystals available from Florist's Products, Inc. (312) 885–2242, spray it on the roof, and hose it off with water. It should leave the glass clear.

Mechanized light reduction Again, the job now can be mechanized. And it's easily done with the same mechanical equipment that applies both black cloth for daylength control—and the white polyester fabric for energy conservation. It is, again, just spreading a basic sheet of fabric across from one gutter to the other—across the house. And, of course, mechanically. Fortunately the white polyester fabric that is so widely used for energy conservation also provides about a 45% reduction in summer sunlight. So it's widely used, especially for foliage crops—and also for other crops that just don't want that intensive light and heat. We see many acres of greenhouses these days over which this white polyester fabric does provide light and heat reduction.

Double thermal sheets Again, the double thermal sheets discussed under energy on page 42 will provide this partial light reduction in summer. The Dutch system installed at Neal Mast's, Grand Rapids, MI provides the 45% light reduction when the white polyester sheet is used as the top layer of the two. This can be extended anytime during the day when summer light becomes too intensive. Again, fully mechanized. By the way, we have seen growers who put this light reduction on a foot candle meter. Now whenever the light intensity under the roof exceeds a set point, the light reduction automatically extends over the crop. We've seen this on one large Bay area range. Also in Germany.

And, of course, the same can be said for the Wadsworth double-energy curtain system.

G.V.B.

AUTOMATED CUT FLOWER HARVESTING

There is a whole array of equipment available both in the U.S. and in Holland that will do a variety of things related to harvesting of cut flowers. All of the following examples are offered by Olimex in Holland. U.S. address: Olimex USA, P.O. Box 729, Watsonville, CA 95077. Telephone (408) 722–0831.

- *Rose graders:* Equipment that will electronically sort roses according to stem length.

- *Carnation counters:* Equipment that will count carnation stems into bunches of 25 or whatever.

- *Mum stem strippers:* Will quickly and easily remove leaves from the lower several inches of the stem.

- *Stem cutters:* After bunching, this cutter will quickly and mechanically cut the entire bunch off at a designated length from the flower head.

- *Bunch tiers:* Equipment that will quickly tie a bunch of pompons or 25 carnations or roses or whatever.

Speaking of all this, we should mention some remarkable success stories by commercial growers in cutting unit labor cost through incentives. We think of Ted Palpant at Ashne Farms, near Santa Maria, CA. Such operations as grading, stripping, and tying roses, same for carnations, same for other cut flowers—Ashne has reduced unit labor cost to half and even one-third in some cases—by carefully administered and developed incentive compensation. The workers earn more, go home when they're finished, have more time with their families—and the owner's unit costs are way down. Much more detail in *Grower Talks,* March 1983, page 16.

Another little interesting combination of labor-saving equipment and ingenuity: The Dutch pompon harvester. We visited recently a grower named Middelburg in the Westland area of Holland. He and his three sons grow and harvest a remarkable six acres of pompons—with no outside help. Four people— six acres of year-round pompons!

The point of our story: the harvesting system. They have built a 3' by 5' tray which is suspended by two overhead rails. On this tray from left to right you will see a stem cutter, a leaf stripper, a bunch tier, and suspended from in front of the shelf is a pack of sleeves. The grower quickly pulls up five stems of pompons, puts the ends into the stem cutter, then the stem stripper, then the tier. Now the bunch is put stems down into the pack of sleeves and quickly picked up with one sleeve around the bunch of pompons. To finish it off, there is a proper corrugated box on the shelf into which the bunch is placed—and it's all ready to go to the auction next morning. No, they're not put in water overnight.

G.V.B.

OTHER WAYS TO MOVE THINGS

There are so many of them and they are widely used today by all sorts of growers. A couple of highlights:

Racks on wheels   These are wire racks typically 24 or 30" wide and maybe 3 to 5' long—and mounted on wheels which can be pivoted. They are used to move pot crops, bedding plants, almost anything. Only requirement is cement walks. One major supplier: Cannon Equipment Company, 324 W. Washington, Cannon Falls, MN 55009 (507) 263–4231. Often these carts are moved about with a forklift. And often we see them loaded up onto trucks with a forklift, then wheeled down to the end of the truck.

Roller tracks   These are aluminum tracks in typically 10' sections with rollers. You just lay them down the length of the bench or down a walk hooked end to end, and you can push all sorts of stuff back and forth on the roller track. Most often used for filling a bench with pot plants. You just put the pots in flats on the track and push them down the bench.

Overhead monorails   Hundreds of greenhouses use them to move things back and forth. Often adaptations of the manure rack used by farmers.

G.V.B.

Simple conveyor tracks can do wonders to save labor of moving things around greenhouses.

Many growers find that overhead monorail carts are helpful in moving material from bench to shipping room.

SECTION III

Other Basics for Profitable Crops

Chapter 12

PLAN AHEAD!

Like any well-run business, a greenhouse operation very much needs a carefully developed, written plan kept at least one year ahead. It makes such a lot of good sense to put down the full details of what you're going to do in the 12 months ahead—and what you'll end up with in the way of profits. All done *before* the year—rather than afterwards. Once the crops are grown and sold there is, of course, nothing you can do about problems and losers.

The plan should include:

WHAT WILL BE GROWN AND WHEN?

For each crop, the number of potted plants or flats of bedding plants or bunches of cut flowers. When the crop moves onto the bench, then it is harvested. By varieties. And, of course, always specifying spacing. Terribly important in the case of pot crops like poinsettias.

ACCOUNT FOR ALL YOUR BENCH SPACE YEAR-ROUND

A good plan should obviously provide for a crop to occupy all benches throughout the 12 months. Empty bench space is a luxury few growers can afford these days. Exception: a few bedding growers we know who simply prefer to go full steam in the spring—then just close up for the rest of the year. And done right, they make a good living at it.

HOW WILL THE CROP BE MARKETED?

Obviously important: a written plan for how everything on the year's production plan will be sold. And as far as possible, some sort of commitment as definite as possible with the buyers. We do see more and more of major pot plant and bedding plant crops these days for which a market is committed in writing by major chains—before the crop is even planted. Yes, it's subject to minor adjustment toward the end, but it is a definite marketing agreement for the crop.

DO FORECAST PROFITS—AT LEAST ON MAJOR CROPS

It's not that complicated or difficult to set up at least a rough cost and dollar sales on at least your major crop. Like poinsettias, pot mums. Or if you're a bedding grower, flats of bedding plants. Doing this sort of thing ahead of time often provides some unpleasant facts about lack of profitability of the crop. But the big thing is, the grower still has a chance to adjust the crop—*before it's grown*. In some cases the crop time from start to finish can be reduced—by bringing in 2¼" or "pod pack" geraniums, poinsettias, New Guinea impatiens, etc. In other cases, spacing can be adjusted downward. We've seen growers do acres of poinsettias in as little as 9" by 10" spacing. And make a very good profit at it. No, it's not a deluxe crop—but it can be produced at a price the mass outlets like—and still at a quality that will provide people with welcome color in their homes. That's not saying that there isn't a place for 14 × 14 6" poinsettias—but it's got to bring something like $4.50 or more—to pay for all that space it used. And we see many crops done just this way too.

Profit for the Year

Few growers today can forecast their profit for the year ahead—with any degree of accuracy. But it's coming—and it's certainly good business to do it.

January and June—the two bad months Typically thousands of poinsettias roll out in mid- to late December. And suddenly there are those houses and houses of empty benches. What a classic case for planning ahead! *There*

122

are crops that can be brought in to use this costly space—and, in fact, turn a profit on it. But it sure won't happen unless it is planned well in advance. Typically we see 2¼" material such as primula veris, kalanchoes pot-tight on such places in late November. It occupies very small space—and is ready to space out as the poinsettias start to go. Also another good prospect: St. Valentine's pot mums, either 6" or 4". And, of course, budded azaleas are prime candidates for such space.

The June space problem The same problem happens on many places in June. House after house of bedding plants roll out in April and May, and after Memorial Day there's again all that empty space. We've seen acres of such space filled with hanging baskets, mainly foliage. And 4" or 6" potted foliage plants. Some growers we've seen succeed very well with summer 4" annuals. The Long Island growers seem able to sell a lot of 6" summer annuals. Sold through June, July, and even August. The major supermarket, garden center, discount chains can and do move large quantities of such summer annuals. One upstate New York grower filled several such houses with summer tomatoes. He had potted plants ready to roll in late May and was on the market midsummer—well ahead of the outdoor garden crops.

The point of all this: There are lots of ways to solve the problem—but they all require good, prior planning. Which usually means ordering plant material—or starting it from seeds yourself—so that the plants will be ready to roll in as soon as the bench space is empty.

By the way, we hear occasionally of growers who simply close down houses in January or February. In some circumstances this might be the best answer. However, we have to wonder. First there is a potential for making a profit on crops that can be produced at that time. Second, the simple problem that most of the expense of running those greenhouses through January and February goes on whether you have a crop there or not. Most of the staff, including yourself, will be there. The houses must be kept above freezing. All the depreciation, insurance, taxes, etc. go right on, crop or no crop. And most of all, so many of the important Easter, Mother's Day pot crops are started back in December and January. Like pot mums. And lilies. Some growers just shrink down a bit!

The Computer's Role in All This

Probably the biggest change in this edition of our *Red Book* is the arrival of computers on the scene of greenhouse management. So many of the points that we've discussed above—space planning, cost forecasting, etc.—can be and are being done accurately and effectively with computers. And it's being done with a lot less manual record keeping. Yes, it's new. Only a handful of growers are actually using this technology today. But it appears to us that it is a very valuable tool to make the grower more efficient on space and cost planning. Plus a lot of other help in managing his operation. Like anticipating major labor and space requirements. You'll find a full chapter describing such equipment and its application to greenhouse management elsewhere in this book.

G.V.B.

Chapter 13

SOIL MIXES*

Using the correct soil mix is just as important as choosing the right variety or proper control of temperature. The soil mix serves several important functions:

Provides for air and water exchange   If a mix is too tight with too little porosity, then it will hold too much water in its pore spaces, not allowing sufficient air for developing a healthy, well-branched root system. This will slow down growth, oftentimes missing scheduled flower dates. On the other hand, if the mix is too open, it will require too much water too often, increasing production labor cost, not to mention the quantity of water and nutrients needed to produce the crop.

Serves as a reservoir for nutrients   While it serves as a reservoir for nutrient exchange, it also is critical for buffering the pH and fertilizer salts. Soil pH is extremely critical for optimum nutrient uptake. With such a soil mixture as one part soil, one part peat, and one part perlite, the optimum soil pH should be approximately 6.2; whereas with an organic mixture of bark, peat, perlite, and vermiculite, the optimum pH is 5.2 to 5.5, a whole unit lower. Also, the ability of the soil to hold and release nutrients will help maximize the efficiency of the fertilizer, whether it's a slow release or water soluble.

*Contributed by Ron Adams, Ball Seed Co.

Should adequately support the plant Keep in mind, though, a plant in a bedding plant container requires a different support than does a tall pot plant such as a 4" geranium. If a plant is not properly supported, then extra care will have to be taken to stake or tie up the plant. This means extra labor, increasing your cost of production. An inadequately supported plant with poor soil structure or too lightweight soil can also reduce the shelf life. For instance, many times when plants are being shipped, they are jostled during shipping. In a lightweight mix, the plants will not be adequately supported and will be floppy and loose when they reach their destination—not being of excellent quality.

Should be reproducible You should be able to consistently reproduce that mix time after time, season after season. Just imagine growing on a year-round pot mum schedule and changing your mix every week. This would definitely increase your frustrations in handling that crop, trying to adapt to each drainage or fertilizer requirement.

Should be readily available Historically, this item has not been a traditional function of the soil mix, but today as we're dealing with larger production areas, any soil mix or the materials for the soil mix should be readily available when you need it, be it a commercial mix from a factory or be it local components. For instance, if you are making your own mix and peat moss is a standard ingredient, we have seen seasonal outages of peat moss due to poor harvest conditions at the peat bogs.

Another aspect of it is where you store your mix. Is it properly stored where the mix is available? For instance, if you store it outside and you encounter an extremely wet and rainy period, can you get out and bring your mix into the greenhouse? Another example is in the middle of winter—is your soil mix pile frozen to the point that it is unavailable? These are things that you want to consider whether it's your own mix or whether it's a commercial mix—the availability of the material when you need it.

Commercially prepared soil mixes are currently receiving much attention. These mixes contain ingredients from straight peat moss to blends using bark, perlite, vermiculite, and peat. It is important to understand that you can grow in almost any medium. But if you compare the media functions to your own conditions there will be one best medium that fits your needs.

The Case for Specialized Mixes

There are several factors that have created this shift away from growers making their own soil mix, and let's take a look at some of these.

Consistency A large firm making soil mixes on a year-round basis can specialize and consistently make the same mix to the same standards. Therefore, you have peace of mind when you place an order that the mix is the same as in the previous batch that you have been using.

Scarcity of materials As communities have developed around greenhouses and major metropolitan areas, good top soil has either become unavailable or very expensive to prepare and store on site. Weed killer contamination is a very real problem in field soils today. Other ingredients can also become scarce, such as Canadian peat moss during a year of poor harvest or a local supplier of bark not having his normal quantity of supplies because the housing industry has not created the demand for lumber, slowing down the production of bark.

Large specialist firms making mixes are able to overcome these commodity shortages and are able to maintain larger supplies because of economy of sale. Therefore, they can ensure a consistent supply to the marketplace.

Cost More growers have recognized that considerable man hours have gone into soil preparation, competing with the time that could be spent in production. It not only takes time to put the mixes together, but it also requires management time and organizing planning and resource commitment, such as inventory dollars for raw materials. As with any production materials, you want to tie up as few dollars as necessary in materials or labor. Buying mixes has freed up this time and resource dollars so you only have to inventory finished, ready-to-use mix and you can schedule it to arrive when you need it.

Convenience Using a commercially prepared mix allows you to concentrate your efforts on other areas of the growing operation. Let's face it, there are several things to consider in making your own mix, such as particle size, pH adjustments, soluble salt levels, sterility. It is much more convenient to depend on an outside supplier who specializes in mixes and manufacturing than to dilute your own time in resources.

Cost Estimates

Next, just to give you an idea of what it costs to make mixes, Paul Nelson at North Carolina State University sat down and figured it out using a fixed-cost determination method of preparing mixes depending on management size and how much it would cost where he figured in all of the components as well as the physical equipment required. This just goes to show, if you take the same factors into consideration that most commercial manufacturers use, that the mix cost range per cubic yard that he showed was anywhere from $48 to $131, depending on the size of your operation. Commercial mixes are available in the marketplace from approximately $30 a yard, depending on where you are located, up to $70 a cubic yard depending on the type and quality of the mix.

Chapter 14

STERILIZING SOIL

HEAT STERILIZING

Soil sterilizing (more correctly, "pasteurizing") is done both with steam and with various chemicals. Since the great majority of sterilizing by commercial flower growers is done with steam, we will cover that first.

What does steaming accomplish? Properly done, it should kill weeds practically 100%, kill all soil-borne insects (on raised benches), and in general all of the bacteria and fungi and virus organisms that are harmful to commercial crops. In addition, it makes heavy soils more granular, greatly improving drainage and aeration. This granulation often brings the greatest growth improvement of all!

Sources of Steam

There is so much equipment available today that will provide steam for greenhouse sterilizing that lack of steam-generating equipment is no longer the problem that it was. Suggestions:

Use existing boilers Many places have steam boilers already installed and in use for heating. A boiler capable of heating a range of glass is always

129

The time-honored system of sterilizing benches of soil in the greenhouse. You rototill, turn in the edges from the sideboards, cover it with a steaming cover, and then pipe in the steam. Note the header at the center of the bench. Important: Use a thermometer to ensure that desired soil temperature is reached even at the bottom of the bench. Photo at Ball greenhouses, West Chicago, Illinois.

adequate for sterilizing. Low-pressure boilers are entirely adequate—just be sure the mains are amply large all the way to the bench being steamed.

Some ranges have hot water boilers. In nearly all cases, such boilers can be easily converted into steam generators. Best procedure is to contact the manufacturer of the boiler, to be sure. Among boilers that *cannot* be converted: Lord & Burnham Heavy-Duty hot water boilers W36, W30, W24, and W18, also Kroeschell hot water boilers of the old type. Reason: these boilers are so designed that there is not enough room in the top of the boiler to collect and separate the steam from hot water without running the water level dangerously low.

Conversion of most hot water boilers to steam consists of valving off the flow and return lines, installing a water bottle with tri-cocks and gauge glass, and a safety valve set to blow steam at 15 lbs. Also, automatic water feed, and low-water alarm are usually installed. For full details see your local boiler dealer.

In most cases such equipment will be bought for the dual purpose of heating the greenhouses and sterilizing soils. Probably the minimum size we are talking about here would be a 25 hp boiler which would be capable of steaming a 500 sq. ft. bench in two or three hours.

An increasing number of package steamers are going into greenhouses both for steaming and for general heating (even up to 300–400 hp). All costs considered, they tend to be cheaper. A big advantage, especially in the larger sizes, is that the package-steamer deal includes both boiler and burner— designed by the factory to work properly *together*. The buyer doesn't have to work the "bugs" out of the job after it's installed. By the way, there's much less installation involved, too.

The package steamers are generally rated at their full capacity—no overload factor as is usually figured in a regular boiler. Bricked-in permanent boilers have been considered a little more rugged, simple, easier to keep clean. Generally they are "fire tube" while the package steamers could be "fire tube" or "water tube." The latter work on much less volume of water. However, growers who have the package steamers are generally quite satisfied with them. Most 50–150 hp boilers used today are packaged—some go up to 500 hp.

Among the more generally used makes are:

- Cleaver-Brooks. Source: Fred W. Kramer & Associates, 5314 W. Harrison, Chicago, Illinois.

- York. Source: York-Shipley Inc., York, Pennsylvania.

- Kewanee Boiler Inc., Kewanee, Illinois.

- Superior Boiler Co., Hutchinson, Kansas.

To get a rough idea of cost on package steamers, here are f.o.b. factory prices on one of the popular makes (low pressure). This price includes boiler and oil burner all put together ready to hook up and turn on, but remember this is only a rough figure. Prices can vary $2,000 to $3,000 because of the many combinations of pressures, fuels, and electrical characteristics. Therefore, in quoting prices, manufacturers will want to know what particular unit is involved and the auxiliary equipment required.

All these are packaged units, all horizontal fire tube except as noted.

- 30 hp costs $10,200, vertical tubeless boiler, burns #2 oil or gas in areas where available.

- 50 hp costs $14,000, burns #2 oil or gas in areas where available.

- 100 hp costs $19,750, burns #2 oil or gas in areas where available.

- 250 hp costs $39,800, burns #2 oil or gas in areas where available.

- 500 hp costs $55,500, burns #2 oil or gas in areas where available.

For the record, the traditional old greenhouse boiler was a bricked-in permanent type boiler. It involved lining the fire chamber with fireproof brick, also installing stokers or burners.

High Pressure—or Low?

A few years ago, it was generally believed that 75 or 100 lbs. of steam pressure was needed to do a real job of steaming. Gradually, experience has shown that a large enough boiler with adequate main sizes can do the job just as well for practical purposes with 10 or 12 lbs. pressure—or even with 5.

Steaming Outdoor Areas

Outdoor beds for asters, mums, young carnation stock, etc. can be sterilized by various means. Actually, sterilizing of such beds is becoming general practice. Methods:

Conventional Thomas-method covers Plastic covers are laid over the area to be steamed.

Steam rake In effect, a large (12'-wide) rake is pulled through the soil. "Teeth" are 10–15" long. The rake is so designed that a jet of steam escapes from the tip of each of the "teeth." A large sheet of canvas is attached to the rake, trailing 20'–30' feet behind the rake as it is dragged through the soil. Since the rake moves very slowly, this "skirt" acts as a cover, holds the steam down in the soil (for about an hour). Thus, a given point, as the rake and trailing skirt pass by, is heated to 180° or better for almost an hour. The steam can be introduced as much as 12"–14" below the surface in soft and sandy soils, thus catching nematodes from below (so they can't dig deeper to escape the heat).

A 12'-wide rake teamed up with an adequate boiler can do an acre in about 4 to 5 days. Cost for the rake (as made by a local machinist for a Florida grower) around $1,500—including a winch to pull it, not including boiler cost.

Similar devices are used in injecting chemicals for sterilizing soils. Out West they are known as "chisels." The teeth are, in effect, a chisel with the sharp blade on the front edge.

Chemical sterilization Outdoor growers, in the West and Northwest and in Florida, are showing increasing interest in various chemicals for sterilizing soils. They are generally less expensive and less trouble to apply. Up to now, the big problem has been that they tended to fall short of desired results in controlling disease organisms. Also, great care must be used to ensure that all the gas is aired out of a soil before planting. However, newer materials are coming onto the market which are making a better showing than the older materials. The Florida mum growers are following these materials quite closely. Several recent cases have shown much of the same remarkable "boost" in growth following chemical sterilizing that has been experienced with steam—no explanation, but impressive results.

Three rather serious crop losses have come to our attention in the past year or two where crops were planted on land sterilized with chemicals—evidently, before the material had been entirely leached or aerated out of the soil. There was one major crop loss of this type on mums. Various smaller losses have occurred to greenhouse crops. Carnations are reported to be very susceptible to injury from traces of some of these materials. This "after-sterilizing-injury" problem is one that must certainly be watched closely where chemicals are used on growing soils.

Steaming Bulk Soils

Many pot plant and bedding growers of today are using commercial mixes—and have no need to sterilize. A lot of others though are mixing their own media—or in many cases, using some of commercial mixes along with some local soil. Such growers often do sterilize.

The two most practical answers to how to do it seem to be:

Commercially produced soil steaming wagon   Source: Lindig Mfg. Co., St. Paul, MN. These are simply 8' or 10' long carts, usually rubber tired, which provide a large box capable of holding 4 to 5 cubic yards of soil. Across the bottom is a precise pattern of equally spaced pipes with holes for uniform steam distribution. They work fine. And especially they are great because after sterilizing, the wagon can be wheeled around and used for a potting bench. See photo.

Concrete mixers   We see many growers today often using salvaged concrete mixers both to mix soil and to do the steaming job. Sometimes they are mounted on wheels, sometimes on a permanent base. They are quite easy to load (using conveyor belts) and equally easy to unload—just tip the mixer back and out comes the soil. Again, see photo (p. 134).

G.V.B.

CHEMICALS FOR STERILIZING*

A number of chemicals have been formulated as liquids to be applied in the soil for killing nematodes, certain insects, weeds, and more recently, fungi. Most of these chemicals become gases and diffuse in the soil to bring about the kill. The soil temperature must be 50°F or above at the 6" level to permit good gas dispersion. Soil must be tilled to reduce or bury crop debris and be in good planting condition when treated.

*Contributed by Dr. Kenneth Horst, Cornell University.

A widely used wagon that both sterilizes soil and serves as a potting bench. One source: Lindig, Minneapolis, Minnesota.

One of the problems arising from the sterilization or near sterilization of soil with materials such as chloropicrin, methyl bromide, or steam is that such treatment removes most organisms—beneficial as well as disease-producing—from the soil. Under such conditions, the first organisms to be introduced have very little competition and can develop very rapidly. If a disease-producing organism is introduced first, serious problems may result. For this reason, when using soil treated this way, it is imperative to use clean planting containers, tools, and other equipment, and especially clean or pathogen-free planting stock. Because of the difficulty of doing this under most nursery conditions, other approaches to the problem need to be found.

Of course, nearly all steaming of soils in the U.S. is done to the 180°F, 30-minute standard. However, where less than a complete kill of soil life is wanted, one approach is to *pasteurize* the soil at temperatures of 160°F for 30 minutes—the so-called aerated-steam method. Another approach is through the use of fungicides applied either as drenches or as additives to the soil. These may either prevent the re-entry of disease-producing organisms or prevent their development in the soil, should they become introduced.

(a)

(b)

(c)

Tractor-mounted rig for injecting gaseous chemicals into field soil for pasteurization. (a) Chisels extend into the soil. Behind each is a tube that delivers the
gas into the soil. A rake follows to seal the holes made by the chisels. (b) A roll
of polyethylene film is located behind the rake. At the beginning of the row the
end of the polyethylene is anchored by burying it in the soil. As the tractor
moves across the field, the film unrolls. (c) One side of the film is buried by a
disc while the other side is glued to the previous sheet of plastic. Up to five
acres of field can be treated by three people in one day with a single tractor.
(Photo courtesy of W. A. Skroch, Department of Horticultural Science, North
Carolina State University, Raleigh, North Carolina 27607)

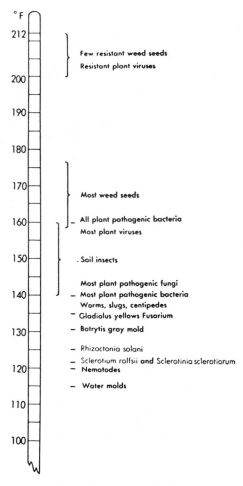

Temperature necessary to kill pathogens and other organisms harmful to plants. Most of the temperatures indicated here are for 30-minute exposures under moist conditions. (From Baker, K. F., ed., "The U. C. System for Producing Healthy Container-Grown Plants," California Agriculture Experiment Station and Extension Service Manual 23, *1957)*

Chemicals—Pro and Con

While steam sterilization is the most popular, the most reliable, and generally the most economical method of soil sterilization, many occasions arise where steam is not available and chemicals would be less expensive than setting up a steam system. Certainly, over the last several years, progress has been made in the field of chemicals.

Dr. Donald E. Munnecke, plant pathologist, U.C.L.A., says, "An ideal chemical for treating soil is one that kills a variety of fungi, bacteria, insects and weeds; is inexpensive and harmless to the operator and equipment; is quick-acting and effective deep in the soil as well as on the surface; is harmless to nearby plants, and is not toxic to subsequent plantings in the soil."

As yet, the above-described chemical has not been developed. Therefore, there are three general types of material available: those that will control diseases, those that will control insects and nematodes, and herbicides that will control weeds. Of the classes of organisms to be controlled, the diseases are the most difficult. If a chemical will control the soil-borne fungi, chances are it will control the other organisms as well.

One major drawback of chemicals for treatment of greenhouse soils is the time required for complete aeration of the chemicals after treatment. Planting too soon will result in loss of roots—or even the crop. Waiting two weeks for soil aeration is an expensive process. This period for aeration is much less critical in terms of outdoor areas that are cropped only once a year. Also, great care must be used in working with chemicals under glass to ensure that gas escaping from a bed doesn't get to other plants in the house.

There are several materials available now that can be used safely in the greenhouse with no damage to the crops. These will be discussed separately.

Which Chemical?

There are dozens of materials sold for this purpose. We don't claim to have carefully analyzed the performance of them. Tables 14-1 and 14-2 (see pp. 138–142) reflect mostly the experience of commercial growers and pathologists around the country as we have observed them. They have been prepared by the Department of Plant Pathology at Cornell University.

Before discussing individual materials, it should be pointed out that the results of chemical treatment may vary widely according to soil texture, moisture, and temperature. Dosage should vary accordingly. Heavy, dry, cold soils generally require more chemical to get the same results.

Terraclor® (PCNB)   This material, though commonly grouped with the fungicides, is not really a fungicide, but a fungistat. This means that it does not kill most of the organisms against which it is effective, but prevents their development. However, it is extremely good for controlling certain soil-borne disease-producing organisms such as rhizoctonia and various species of sclerotinia. In addition to this, it has the advantage that it has a relatively long residual action and is practically insoluble in water. Thus, once it has been added to the soil, it will remain effective for periods as long as six months to a year.

Terraclor is best applied to the soil prior to planting. One to two pounds of the 75% wettable powder per 1000 sq. ft. should be worked into the top 2

137

Table 14-1 SOIL FUMIGANTS

Accepted common name	Some trade names	Application rate	Effective against	Min. soil temp.	Cost (approx.) $/100 sq. ft. ($/unit)	Comments
chloropicrin*	Larvacide Picfume Acquivite Tri-Clor	3 cc on 12″ centers or per cu. ft. of soil (480 lbs./acre)	Weeds, most fungi, nematodes, soil insects. Controls verticillium.	60°F	$2.55 $2.25/ lb.	Soil must be covered with gas-proof cover for at least 24 hrs. It is most effective at soil temperatures from 60°F to 90°F. Soil must be well aerated for 10–21 days before planting. Fumes are toxic to living plants.
98%* methyl bromide 2% chloropicrin. Under pressure in 1 lb. cans and 30 lb. cylinders	Dowfume MC-2 Pestmaster Soil Fumigant-1	4 lbs. per 100 sq. ft. or 100 cu. ft. of soil applied under tarp.	Weeds and insects at lower rates; bacteria and most fungi at higher rates. Inadequate verticillium control.	50°F	$10.00 $2.50/ lb.	It can be used in houses where plants are growing, although slight leaf injury has been observed on carnations, mums, geraniums, and lilies. In clear, warm weather, air sandy, arid, and other light soils, for 3–4 days; heavier soils, for 7–12 days. Fumes slightly toxic to plants. Do not use for treating soils to be planted to carnations, salvia, and snapdragons.

138

*Indicates that the usage of the material is restricted and can be used by permit only in certain states.

Accepted common name	Some trade names	Application rate	Effective against	Min. soil temp.	Cost (approx.) $/100 sq. ft. ($/unit)	Comments
67%* methyl bromide 33% chloropicrin	Dowfume MC-33	½ lb. per 100 sq. ft. or 250 lbs. per acre.	Weeds, insects, bacteria, fungi, including verticillium.	50°F	$1.17 $2.33/ lb.	Same as above.
Technical grade dichloropropene—dichloropropane mixtures	Vernafene D-D Vidden D Telone (100% dichloropropene, $2.40/gal.)	20–40 gals. per acre.	Nematodes and insects.	50°F	50¢ $5.56/ gal.	Apply with hand injector or tractor-mounted equipment. Wait 14–28 days before planting. Fumes toxic to living plants.
liquid carbamate SMDC	Vapam VPM Sistan Trimaton	Drench in 1 qt./100 sq. ft. Use at least 15 gals. water. Injected— 1 pt. per 100 sq. ft. (50 gals./acre).	Nematodes, most weeds, and insects	50°F	$5.30 $10.00/ gal.	Do not plant for 2 to 3 weeks after treatment, then make test plantings of seedlings or cuttings and wait a few days before planting entire crop. If soil is cold or excessively wet, wait 3 to 4 weeks. Fumes toxic to living plants.

Table 14-1 (continued)

Accepted common name	Some trade names	Application rate	Effective against	Min. soil temp.	Cost (approx.) $/100 sq. ft. ($/unit)	Comments
Mixture of 80% dichloro-propene-dichloro-propane, 20% methyl isothiocyanate	Vorlex Di-Trapex	25–40 gals. per acre.	Nematodes, weeds, and fungi.	50°F	$1.38 $20.00/ gal.	Apply with hand injector or tractor-mounted equipment. Wait 14–28 days before planting. Fumes toxic to living plants.
40% formaldehyde	Formalin	1 pt. in 6¼ gals. water applied at ½ gal. per sq. ft.	Fungi and bacteria.	60°F	$6.11 $6.11	Soil should be moist before treatment, tarp-covered for first 24 hrs. Aerate for 14 days. Treated soil may be used for potting if aired until all odor of formaldehyde has gone. Fumes toxic to living plants.

Table 14-2 SOIL DRENCHES

Accepted common name	Some trade names	Application rate	Effective against	Min. soil temp.	Cost (approx.) $/100 sq. ft. ($/unit)	Comments
PCNB	Brassiocol Terraclor	1½ lbs. (75%)/1,000 sq. ft. mixed with top 1–2″ of soil, or drenched on living plants at the rate of ½ to 1 lbs./100 gals. water. Drenched at 1 pt./sq. ft. or 100 gals. applied to 800–1,000 sq. ft. of bench	Rhizoctonia, sclerotinia.	—	$1.31 $3.50/ lb.	Specific for rhizoctonia, sclerotinia spp., and sclerotium spp. Not effective against water molds. Good residual action.
Thiram	Arasan (42S)	1 fl. oz. (42%)/6 gals. water. Higher dosages may cause injury. Use 1–2 pts./sq. ft.	Fungi.	—	84¢ $25.00/ gal.	Effective in preventing root-and-stem rot of poinsettias.
Nabam	Dithane D-14 Parzate liquid Ortho Nabam Thiodou liquid	1 fl. oz. (22%)/4 gals. water. Use 1–2 pts./ sq. ft.	Fungi.	—	10¢ $2.65/ gal.	Spot treatments to prevent disease spread. Little residual effect.
50% benomyl	Benlate (for turf— Tersan 1991, same % active and same price)	½–1½ lbs./100 gals. water; apply ½ pt./6″ pot.	Cylindrocladium, thielaviopsis, sclerotinia, fusarium, verticillium and rhizoctonia.	—	$5.65 $15.08/ lb.	Plant roots must be confined to the treated area's "container plantings." Results of field tests have been erratic but not inconsistent with the postulation that a large percentage of the root system is required to take up the fungicide.

141

Table 14-2 (continued)

Accepted common name	Some trade names	Application rate	Effective against	Min. soil temp.	Cost (approx.) $/100 sq. ft. ($/unit)	Comments
	Truban 30WP	4–6 ozs./100 gals. of water applied to 400 sq. ft. of bench area or ½ pt./6″ pot.	Pythium and phytophthora.	—	$1.55 $16.50/ lb.	Good residual qualities—treat at 4- to 12-week intervals, if necessary.
	Truban 25EC	3 oz./100 gals. 8 oz./200 gals.	Pythium and phytophthora.	—	3 oz. 63¢/8 oz. $3.35/ $27.00/qt.	
	Lesan-Terraclor®	8 ozs. 35% WP Lesan plus 4 ozs. 75% WP Terraclor per 100 gals. water applied to 400 sq. ft. or ½ pt./6″ pot.	Rhizoctonia and pythium.	—	$1.61 Lesan— $11.10/lb. Terraclor®— $3.50/lb.	Cover container with black cloth and apply immediately upon mixing, as Lesan deteriorates upon standing in solution and exposure to light.
	Lesan	8 ozs. 35% WP per 100 gals. water applied to 400 sq. ft. or ½ pt. per 6″ pot	Water molds (pythium, etc.)	—	$1.39 $11.10/ lb.	Cover container with black cloth and apply immediately upon mixing as Lesan deteriorates upon standing in solution and exposure to light.
	Banrot 40WP	4–8 ozs. per 100 gals. water applied to 400 sq. ft. or ½ pt. per 6″ pot	Water molds, rhizoctonia.	—	$2.88 $22.50/ lb.	
	Subdue 2E	¼–2 ozs. per 100 gals.	Water molds.	—	$2.47 $155.88/gal.	May be toxic at 2 oz. rate.

to 4" of soil. If a rhizoctonia problem should break out after the plants have been started, Terraclor can be drenched on at the rate of 1 to 1½ lbs. of 75% wettable powder per 100 gals. water and applied at the rate of 1 pt. per sq. ft. or 100 gals. applied to 400 sq. ft. of bed. Most plants are not injured at this concentration, but try it on a few plants first to make sure injury does not occur. Terraclor is not effective against pythium. Do not make repeated applications of Terraclor.

Lesan The water molds pythium and phytophthora are found occurring naturally in most soils, and in addition, they are rapid invaders of sterilized soil. Lesan is a fungicide which has been found to give excellent control against water mold root rots of many plants including gloxinias, African violets, chrysanthemums, poinsettias, azaleas, snapdragons, and geraniums. Recommendations regarding application rates vary between 100 and 200 parts per million. This is equivalent to 4 to 8 ozs. of the 35% wettable powder per 100 gals. of water to be applied at ½ pt. per 6" pot. For bench and field plants, apply 1½ lbs. 35% wettable powder per 100 gals. water to 400 sq. ft. of bed. A second applicaton may be made 2 to 4 weeks later if necessary, since Lesan does not have a long residual effect. The frequency of application depends partly on the crop and the disease severity, but with most susceptible crops, it is recommended that Lesan be put on every 7 to 10 days.

Cover pail with black cloth, as Lesan deteriorates upon standing in solution and exposure to light.

Lesan-Terraclor® mixtures A 35–65% mixture of Lesan-Terraclor® is available, which is effective against water molds and rhizoctonia. A first drench of 4 to 8 ozs. per 100 gals. of this material can be used, but repeat drenches should be of just Lesan alone, since Terraclor® does not break down in the soil and may build up to a toxic level.

Banrot Banrot is a broad spectrum fungicide made up of 15% wettable powder Ethazol plus 25% Thiophanate-m. Use as soil drench at 8 oz. per 100 gals. for control of root rots caused by pythium, rhizoctonia, sclerotinia, schlerotium, fusarium, and thielaviopsis. Use 100 gals. over 200 sq. ft. of bed, or 1600 6" pots. Drench every 4–6 weeks. Be sure to check label before using.

Benlate Benlate, a systemic fungicide, has given excellent control of a number of soil pathogens including rhizoctonia, sclerotinia, sclerotium, fusarium, thielaviopsis, verticillium, and cylindrocladium. The 50% wettable powder is available as Benlate for ornamentals and Tersan 1991® for turf. The rate of application is ½ to 1½ lbs. per 100 gals. of water applied at 1 pt. per sq. ft. Most plants are not injured at this concentration, but try it on a few plants first to make sure injury does not occur. Plant roots must be confined to the treated area as "container plantings." Results of field tests have been erratic, but not inconsistent with the postulation that a large percentage of the root system is required to take up the fungicide.

Chloropicrin and methyl bromide Combinations of chloropicrin and methyl bromide, either 55–45% or 66–34% mixtures, are more effective against fungi than the materials used alone. The combination must, of course, be covered with polyethylene sheeting. Some authorities state that, using chloropicrin sealed in with plastic, the control of verticillium approaches the results obtained with steam. However, chloropicrin applied under glass is apt to cause injury to other crops in the same house. Methyl bromide is less dangerous, but has been known (along with other chemicals containing bromine) to be toxic to some crops, especially carnations. Therefore, it is not wise to use methyl bromide on carnation soil. A good precaution, where chemicals are considered, is to try them on a small scale first to see how they affect specific plants grown under your conditions.

Truban (Ethazol) Specifically for water mold control, Truban is often combined with other materials in a soil drench program. Use 8 oz. per 100 gals. of water. Apply 100 gals. to 200 sq. ft. of bed, or 1 cup per 6" pot. Follow the application with an additional watering to improve the penetrability of the material into the soil. Drench every 6 to 8 weeks as necessary.

Cost

Ease and cost of doing the job vary greatly, depending upon which type of chemical is being used. For instance, applying such chemicals as methyl bromide is far from an agreeable task—and it is dangerous if not handled properly. Vapam is much easier to handle—but probably less effective. Approximate cost of using each of the various methods is indicated on the chart.

We may conclude from the above discussion that chemicals might be most profitably and effectively used under the following conditions:

1. Where overhead costs are low, so that time for aeration is not expensive. In general, this means outdoor areas that are cropped only once or twice a year.

2. Where weeds and perhaps soil-borne insects are the main reasons for sterilizing. Chemicals are generally not dependable for control of certain hard-to-kill disease organisms.

3. Chemicals are used more generally on less valuable crops—outdoor flower and vegetable crops—where the cost and potential return are lower than for more intensive forms of culture.

4. Chemicals tend to be used where steam boilers are not available. Boilers cost money! Rental of a portable boiler may be the best solution for some growers.

Safety Precautions

1. Always read the label before using pesticides. Note warnings and cautions each time before opening a container. *Read and follow directions for use.*

2. Keep pesticides away from children, pets, and irresponsible people. Store pesticides in a secure place away from food and feed.

3. Do not smoke while using pesticides, and avoid inhalation.

4. Do not spill pesticides on skin or clothing. If they are spilled, remove contaminated clothing and wash exposed skin areas thoroughly.

5. Dispose of empty containers so that they pose no hazard to humans, animals, or valuable plants.

6. If symptoms of illness occur during or shortly after using pesticides, call a physician or get the patient to a hospital immediately. Physicians now have available information for the quick and effective treatment of accidental overexposure to pesticides. If possible, take along a label from the pesticide container.

7. You may obtain prompt, up-to-date information on the symptoms and treatment of cases resulting from exposure to toxic agricultural chemicals by calling your "Poison Control Center."

Chapter 15

MODERN FERTILIZING METHODS*

FERTILIZER INJECTORS

Fertilizer injectors have become a standard piece of greenhouse equipment. They are necessary because greenhouses are using more open organic soil mixes. It has been found that the best sustained plant growth comes from constantly feeding with a water soluble fertilizer such as Peters or Millers through the water system. Fertilizer injectors allow the opportunity to make up ahead concentrated fertilizers that are proportioned by an injector directly into the water line at the desired parts per million required for feeding.

Because of the multitude of growing situations there are many different types of injectors available. Injectors can be portable or built into the main water line. The advantage of setting up portable injector units or using small injectors is for zone feeding, where it allows custom applications of fertilizer for different crops or different greenhouses. If one crop is grown primarily in the operation, then one formula fed through a centralized injector is highly desirable. Again, the operation will determine which is best.

*Contributed by Ron Adams, Ball Seed Co.

A Smith fertilizer injector—much used by commercial growers. Note the tank at the right, which is used to mix the concentrate.

How to Decide Which Unit to Buy

First, you have to know the minimum and maximum water flow rate for the area that's going to be fed. For example: A Smith R3 injector has a minimum flow requirement of 3 gallons per minute, and a maximum flow requirement of 12 gallons per minute. This means that to start feeding there have to be at least 3 gallons of water per minute flowing through the water line to drive the water motor pistons for accurate feeding. At a flow higher than 12 gallons per minute, water flow will be restricted coming through the injector, limiting how many hoses or drip irrigation stations can be used at one time.

Some of the smaller less expensive units have been developed for the animal health industry and have been used as feed medicators. They are the Merit Proportioner made by Merit Industries, P. O. Box 8075, Cranston, Rhode Island 02920. The Merit has a 1–128 proportioning ratio. Next, a Dosematic made in France, distributed by J-F Equipment Company, 10290 Monroe Drive, Suite 307, Dallas, Texas 75229. The Dosematic has an adjustable proportion setting from 1–100, 1–128, 1–200 and works in flow range of 8 to 420 gallons per hour, whereas the Merit is 2 to 400 gallons per hour. Both of these units are made of plastic bodies and can be used with ¾" water lines and can handle a small greenhouse up to 5,000–10,000 square feet. Again, these units are fine for small houses or temporary situations such as cold frames to handle surge business in the spring. These units retail for approximately $200.

For a more fixed permanent installation you might want to consider a Smith Proportioner, which can be built into the water line depending on your needs and have units that can handle from a ¾" water line up to a 6" water line. A Smith injector is a brass unit built to last a long time. The small units, the R3 or R4, can be cart-mounted and easily transported to the growing area. Smith injectors can also be optioned to handle standard fertilizers, acid injections for water pH control—such as sulfuric or phosphoric—or pesticides to be able to allow you to inject fungicides or insecticides on your crops. Standard proportions for Smiths are 1–100 or 1–200, but other proportions can be factory set. Cost of the Smith injector ranges from $800 to $2000 on standard units. Smith Measure Mix Company is located at 1299 Lawrence Drive, Newbury Park, California 91320. Another commercial unit is Gewa, made in Germany, distributed in the U.S., and works with water pressure in a tank to proportion. Cost for these units ranges from $400 to $1000 depending on unit size. Also, HPA, which uses a water meter to send electric signals to solenoid valves and works from a pressure-regulated injector pump. Cost for these units ranges from $1600 to $5000.

Table 15-1 (Ohio State) is for preparing concentrate for fertilizer injectors. Example: Using 30-10-10, to produce 100 ppm of nitrogen, make up a stock solution of 4.50 ozs. of 30-10-10 and set the injector to apply it at one part concentrate to 100 parts of water. This will provide 100 parts per million of nitrogen in the irrigation water.

Table 15-1 HANDY TABLES FOR INJECTION FEEDING

Use a dosage between 100 ppm and 200 ppm nitrogen. Let plant growth and soil tests determine which concentration and formula to use. ½ gallon per square foot is normal watering rate with constant feeding.

30% Nitrogen formulas (30-10-10, etc.)

Injector ratio	100 ppm nitrogen			150 ppm nitrogen			200 ppm nitrogen		
(1:300)	13.50	oz. (.8437	lb.)	20.25	oz. (1.2656	lb.)	27.00	oz. (1.6875	lb.)
(1:200)	9.00	oz. (.5625	lb.)	13.50	oz. (.8437	lb.)	18.00	oz. (1.125	lb.)
(1:150)	6.75	oz. (.4218	lb.)	10.125	oz. (.6328	lb.)	13.50	oz. (.8437	lb.)
(1:128)	5.76	oz. (.3599	lb.)	8.64	oz. (.5398	lb.)	11.52	oz. (.7198	lb.)
(1:100)	4.50	oz. (.2812	lb.)	6.75	oz. (.4218	lb.)	9.00	oz. (.5625	lb.)
(1:50)	2.25	oz. (.1406	lb.)	3.375	oz. (.2109	lb.)	4.50	oz. (.2812	lb.)
(1:30)	1.35	oz. (.08437	lb.)	2.025	oz. (.1265	lb.)	2.70	oz. (.1687	lb.)
(1:24)	1.08	oz. (.0675	lb.)	1.62	oz. (.10125	lb.)	2.16	oz. (.1350	lb.)
(1:15)	.675	oz. (.04218	lb.)	1.012	oz. (.06327	lb.)	1.35	oz. (.08437	lb.)

Table 15-1   (continued)

25% Nitrogen formulas (25-5-20, 25-10-10, 25-0-25 etc.)

Injector ratio	100 ppm nitrogen			150 ppm nitrogen			200 ppm nitrogen		
	per gallon of concentrate								
(1:300)	16.50	oz.	(1.0312 lb.)	24.75	oz.	(1.5468 lb.)	33.00	oz.	(2.0625 lb.)
(1:200)	11.00	oz.	(.6875 lb.)	16.50	oz.	(1.0312 lb.)	22.00	oz.	(1.375 lb.)
(1:150)	8.25	oz.	(.5156 lb.)	12.375	oz.	(.7734 lb.)	16.50	oz.	(1.0312 lb.)
(1:128)	7.04	oz.	(.4399 lb.)	10.56	oz.	(.6598 lb.)	14.08	oz.	(.8798 lb.)
(1:100)	5.50	oz.	(.3437 lb.)	8.25	oz.	(.5156 lb.)	11.00	oz.	(.6875 lb.)
(1:50)	2.75	oz.	(.1718 lb.)	4.125	oz.	(.2578 lb.)	5.50	oz.	(.3437 lb.)
(1:30)	1.65	oz.	(.1031 lb.)	2.475	oz.	(.1546 lb.)	3.30	oz.	(.2062 lb.)
(1:24)	1.32	oz.	(.0825 lb.)	1.98	oz.	(.12375 lb.)	2.64	oz.	(.1650 lb.)
(1:15)	.825	oz.	(.05155 lb.)	1.237	oz.	(.07734 lb.)	1.65	oz.	(.1031 lb.)

20% Nitrogen formulas (20-20-20, 20-5-30, 21-7-7, etc.)

Injector ratio	100 ppm nitrogen			150 ppm nitrogen			200 ppm nitrogen		
	per gallon of concentrate								
(1:300)	20.25	oz.	(1.2656 lb.)	30.375	oz.	(1.8984 lb.)	40.50	oz.	(2.5312 lb.)
(1:200)	13.50	oz.	(.8437 lb.)	20.25	oz.	(1.2656 lb.)	27.00	oz.	(1.6874 lb.)
(1:150)	10.125	oz.	(.6328 lb.)	15.187	oz.	(.9492 lb.)	20.25	oz.	(1.2656 lb.)
(1:128)	8.64	oz.	(.5398 lb.)	12.96	oz.	(.8097 lb.)	17.28	oz.	(1.0796 lb.)
(1:100)	6.75	oz.	(.4218 lb.)	10.125	oz.	(.6328 lb.)	13.50	oz.	(.8437 lb.)
(1:50)	3.375	oz.	(.2109 lb.)	5.0675	oz.	(.3164 lb.)	6.75	oz.	(.4218 lb.)
(1:30)	2.025	oz.	(.1265 lb.)	3.037	oz.	(.1898 lb.)	4.05	oz.	(.2531 lb.)
(1:24)	1.62	oz.	(.10125 lb.)	2.43	oz.	(.15188 lb.)	3.24	oz.	(.2025 lb.)
(1:15)	1.012	oz.	(.06327 lb.)	1.518	oz.	(.09492 lb.)	2.025	oz.	(.1265 lb.)

15% Nitrogen formulas (15-15-15, 15-30-15, 16-4-12, etc.)

Injector ratio	100 ppm nitrogen			150 ppm nitrogen			200 ppm nitrogen		
	per gallon of concentrate								
(1:300)	27.00	oz.	(1.6875 lb.)	40.50	oz.	(2.5312 lb.)	54.00	oz.	(3.3750 lb.)
(1:200)	18.00	oz.	(1.1250 lb.)	27.00	oz.	(1.6875 lb.)	36.00	oz.	(2.2500 lb.)
(1:150)	13.50	oz.	(.8437 lb.)	20.25	oz.	(1.2656 lb.)	27.00	oz.	(1.6875 lb.)
(1:128)	11.52	oz.	(.7200 lb.)	17.28	oz.	(1.0800 lb.)	23.04	oz.	(1.4400 lb.)
(1:100)	9.00	oz.	(.5625 lb.)	13.50	oz.	(.8437 lb.)	18.00	oz.	(1.1250 lb.)
(1:50)	4.50	oz.	(.2812 lb.)	6.75	oz.	(.4218 lb.)	9.00	oz.	(.5625 lb.)
(1:30)	2.70	oz.	(.1687 lb.)	4.05	oz.	(.2531 lb.)	5.40	oz.	(.3375 lb.)
(1:24)	2.15	oz.	(.1350 lb.)	3.21	oz.	(.20063 lb.)	4.32	oz.	(.2700 lb.)
(1:15)	1.35	oz.	(.08437 lb.)	2.025	oz.	(.1265 lb.)	2.70	oz.	(.1687 lb.)

It's clearly impossible to give any specific directions for applying fertilizers that will fit the needs of each of the dozens of greenhouse crops. However, we present the following, based on our experience with these materials, as at least reasonable rates of application where tests, growth, or your judgement have indicated the need.

Nitrogen

- *Ammonium sulfate,* sulfate of ammonia (21% nitrogen). 1 pound per 100 square feet, or in solution, 1 ounce to 2 gallons of water.

- *Sodium nitrate,* nitrate of soda (16% nitrogen). Use same as ammonium sulfate.

- *Dried blood* (about 10% nitrogen—not quite so quickly available as above). Usual application 2 to 3 pounds per 100 square feet.

- *Ammonium nitrate* (34% nitrogen). ½ pound per 100 square feet, or in solution, 1 ounce to 5 gallons of water.

- *Urea* (46% nitrogen). ½ pound per 100 square feet. In solution, 1 ounce to 7 gallons of water.

- *Calcium nitrate* (15% nitrogen). Use same as ammonium sulfate.

- *Ammonium phosphate* (di-ammonium phosphate contains 21% nitrogen, 53% phosphoric acid). Use ½ pound per 100 square feet, or 1 ounce to 5 gallons liquid.

Phosphorus

- *Superphosphate,* acid phosphate. Usually 20% phosphoric acid, sometimes 45%. The 20% material is usually used at 5 to 10 pounds per 100 square feet; 45% is used about half this strong.

- *Bone meal.* 20% phosphoric acid, but very slowly available. Superphosphate much better. Raw bone meal contains about 4% nitrogen, steamed bone meal half as much.

Potassium (Potash)

- *Potassium chloride* (muriate of potash). Contains about 50% potash and is used at about 1 pound per 100 square feet, or 1 ounce to 2 gallons of water.

- *Potassium sulfate* (sulfate of potash). Contains about 48% potash and is used at the same rate as the muriate.

- *MagAmp* (7-40-6). Use at 15 pounds per 100 square feet of bench space, or 10 pounds per cubic yard of potting soil.

- *Osmocote* (14-14-14). Use at 18 pounds per 600 square feet of bench area.

- *Osmocote* (18-9-9). Use at 14 pounds per 600 square feet of bench area.

For Lowering pH

- *Aluminum or iron sulfate*. Try 1 to 2 pounds per 100 square feet; more if needed. In solution, 1 ounce to 2 gallons of water.

- *Sulfur* (finely ground). 1 to 3 pounds per 100 square feet.

For Raising pH

- *Ground limestone* (calcium carbonate, lime, calcium hydroxide) or *dolomite* (calcium-magnesium carbonate). Application of 5 pounds per 100 square feet will raise pH from $1/2$ to 1 unit. The finer the grind of the limestone, the more quickly it will react.

SLOW-RELEASE FERTILIZERS

Using slow-release fertilizers to produce quality bedding and pot plants has become a routine practice in the greenhouse. In some cases slow-release fertilizers have reliably supplied all the nutrients necessary to produce an excellent crop. There are several advantages of using a slow-release fertilizer: (1) provides a constant source of fertilizer that can safely be incorporated into the soil mix prior to planting; (2) reduces the constant need to mix and proportion or apply dry soluble fertilizers; (3) maintains optimum fertility levels during winter months when waterings are not as frequent; (4) can be used with

152

capillary watering systems to minimize algae buildup on mats; and (5) increases the plant shelf-life by providing nutrients after plant leaves the greenhouse. This can be a real benefit in the case of hanging baskets, foliage, or house plants, such as African violets, by providing feed for a longer period of time.

Slow-release fertilizers have proven themselves over a number of years, but they have also shown us some disadvantages that we need to consider when using them: (1) cannot easily adjust the salt level or lower it for periods of slow growth; therefore, the plants can be affected by high soluble salts; (2) should be incorporated into the soil prior to planting for the most consistent release rate; (3) can feed at too high a nutrient level when the crop has finished, making it difficult to control growth at a retail sales area; (4) some slow-release material when top-dressed will float out of the pot under flooding conditions, reducing the effective rate; and (5) some slow-release fertilizers are temperature dependent or bacterial dependent; therefore, the release rate is affected by the temperature and bacterial activity.

Even though we can use either liquid feed or slow-release fertilizers to feed the plants, we have consistently seen the best growth when using a combination of slow-release fertilizer with a constant liquid feed of water-soluble fertilizer. By using the combination, the normal rate can be reduced sometimes as much as 50%, but for you to figure the best rate you should determine based on your own conditions which combination rate will work the best. For example, if the slow-release fertilizers recommend a 10 lb. per cubic yard rate, and you normally feed it 250 ppm nitrogen, then you would reduce the rate to 5 lbs. per cubic yard of slow-release and 125 ppm nitrogen respectively.

Coated Fertilizers

There are two basic types of complete slow-release fertilizers: coated and granulated. Coated fertilizers consist of water-soluble fertilizers coated with plastic or sulphur, which allows the fertilizers to become available over time. The most common coated fertilizer is called Osmocote, which uses a micro-porous plastic resin to lock up the fertilizer until osmotic pressure initiates the release, then the fertilizer diffuses through the coating until the fertilizer is depleted. Release times can be controlled by the coating thickness, and Osmocote formulas can feed crops anywhere from 3 to 4 months up to 12 months. The most common formula is 14-14-14, 3 to 4 months for pot and bedding crops. Osmocote can either be top-dressed or incorporated into the soil. It cannot be steam-sterilized once it is placed in the soil.

Another type of coated fertilizer is called sulphur-coated urea. It was first developed by the Tennessee Valley Authority Research Lab. It uses a waxed sulphur coat to cover the urea nitrogen, and through bacterial degradation the nitrogen becomes available over time. Other nutrients can be co-blended with this fertilizer, but they're usually not considered slow-release. Sulphur-coated fertilizers depend on bacterial breakdown of the coating for making the nutrients available. Because of this there is a high degree of variability. This particular fertilizer should definitely be tested under your conditions to determine its suitability.

Sources are Lakeshore Equipment Co., Elyria, Ohio; and O. M. Scott, Marysville, Ohio.

Granulated Fertilizers

Granulated slow-release fertilizer types are MagAmp and Choice 10-10-10.* MagAmp is a co-granulated blend of nitrogen, phosphorous, potassium, and magnesium giving a formula of 7-10-6 plus 12% magnesium. MagAmp, or ammonium phosphate, is what we consider a true control-release fertilizer, where only 1% of the fertilizer is available in a 24-hour period under saturated conditions. The MagAmp formula is high in phosphorous and could even be considered as a phosphorous source for soil mixes with the additional benefit of nitrogen, potassium, and magnesium. MagAmp is not temperature sensitive, and soils including MagAmp can be steam-sterilized prior to planting without any harmful effects. MagAmp release rates can be changed by varying the particle size. There are two grades commercially available: (1) the medium grade—the most desirable for greenhouse production—lasts 4 to 6 months in the soil, and (2) the coarse grade—typically suited for nursery stock and outdoor plantings—can last up to 24 months in the soil.

Choice 10-10-10, another non-coated fertilizer, is a homogeneous mixture containing all the necessary elements for good plant growth. Choice 10-10-10 blends various basic nutrients together to give time release. Once watered in, the Choice 10-10-10 dissolves into its basic form becoming available over time. To provide the long-term or slow-release portion of nitrogen, urea formaldehyde is used; whereas fritted phosphate, potash, and trace elements provide the slow dissolution rates for the other elements. Choice 10-10-10 can be applied as a top-dress or it can be incorporated into the soil. It should never be steam-sterilized or applied to wet foliage because it can cause damage.

*Source: Ball Seed Co.

RATE SHEETS

Osmocote

Osmocote 14-14-14 (3- to 4-month term).

Incorporating

Volume or area of mix. (Incorporating in soil mix for potting up or shifting.)	Low (sensitive plants)	Medium (nursery stock)	High (greenhouse crops)
Per cubic foot	2 oz.	3.5 oz.	7 oz.
Per cubic yard	3 lbs.	6 lbs.	12 lbs.
Per cubic meter	2 kg	3.5 kg	7 kg
Per 100 square feet (to 6" depth)	5 lbs.	10 lbs.	20 lbs.
Per square meter (to 15 cm depth)	0.25 kg	0.5 kg	1 kg

Top-dressing

Container size (top-dressing on established plants)	Approx. no. of containers per cubic yard	Low (sensitive plants)	Medium (nursery stock)	High (greenhouse crops)
5" standard round pot	800	2 g	4 g	8 g
6" standard round pot	450	3 g	6 g	12 g
1 gallon container	300	5 g	10 g	20 g
3 gallon container	80	20 g	40 g	80 g
5 gallon container	50	25 g	50 g	100 g

Choice Mix

Recommended rates of application for foliage and pot plants.

	When incorporating Choice 10-10-10 in soil mixes:		When using Choice 10-10-10 as a top dressing:	
Amount	Light, coarse-textured soil mixes, well-drained (ozs. = weight)	Heavier, medium-textured, moderately drained	Size	Maximum rate test trial before exceeding
1 cubic foot	6 oz.	4 oz.	4" standard pot	½ level tsp.
1 bushel	7.5 oz.	5 oz.	5" standard pot	¾ level tsp.
1 cubic yard	10 lbs.	7 lbs.	6" standard pot	1 level tsp.
			8" standard pot	1 level tsp.

Note: The above rates should be reduced by 50% when using a liquid-feed program at concentrations in excess of 150 ppm each of Nitrogen (N) and Potash (K_2O) in conjunction with Choice 10-10-10, 2 to 3 times a week.

MagAmp

#1 Combination program with liquid feed

MagAmp® plus liquid feed—Takes advantage of the best of both constant feed plus controlled release.

Crop	MagAmp rate per cu. yd.	MagAmp rate per bushel	Liquid feed notes
Bedding Plants	5 lbs. medium granule	3½ oz. medium granule	
Pot Plants	10 lbs. medium granule 5 lbs. medium granule	7 oz. medium granule 3½ ozs. medium granule	
Vegetable Bedding Plants	5 lbs. medium granule	3½ oz. medium granule	Combination feed system—when on a constant feed system feed every other watering.
Container Nursery Crops*	10 lbs. coarse granule	7 oz. coarse granule	
Cut Flowers	MagAmp per 100 sq. ft. (indoors or outdoors) 7½ lbs. medium granule		

*Azalea growers note: Many azalea growers have used MagAmp successfully at rates of 8–10 lbs. per cu. yd. However, because there are so many varieties, we recommend that trials be run first, before adopting a full program.

#2 Recommendation—used alone

MagAmp® used as the only source of N-K-P.

Crop	MagAmp rate per cu. yd.	MagAmp rate per bushel	Feed notes
Bedding Plants	10 lbs. medium granule	7 oz. medium granule	
Pot Plants	20 lbs. medium granule	14 oz. medium granule	
	10 lbs. medium granule	7 oz. medium granule	Adjust pH and add minor elements required for crop being grown. Incorporate MagAmp at the recommended rate throughout
Vegetable/ Bedding Plants	10 lbs. medium granule	7 oz. medium granule	the growing media. A 1-lb. coffee can holds approx. 1½ lbs. of MagAmp. A 6-oz. juice can holds approx. 6 oz. of MagAmp.
Container Nursery Crops*	20 lbs. coarse granule	14 oz. coarse granule	
Cut Flowers	MagAmp per 100 sq. ft. (indoors or outdoors) 15 lbs. medium granule		

*Azalea growers note: Many azalea growers have used MagAmp successfully at rates of 8–10 lbs. per cu. yd. However, because there are so many varieties, we recommend that trials be run first, before adopting a full program.

Chapter 16

GERMINATING SEED

Germinating seed is one of the more difficult parts of the growing job—so often seed is sown and germinated by the proprietor.

Here are some suggestions:

1. *Sow good seed.* Remember, seeds are living things! No one can guarantee a perfect stand. Reputable seedsmen, through dry storage, regular germination tests, generally supply good seed. There are low-priced flower seeds—but the occasional problems that result more than wipe out the savings.

2. *Soil medium—use the right kind.* A wide variety of soil (or no soil) mixes *will* germinate seed. To do the job it must be:
   a. Loose, porous, well-drained.
   b. Low in salts. High salts damage tender roots.
   c. Free of disease—you can't win if the soil is full of damp-off organisms. The mix must either be naturally sterile (Jiffy-Mix®, peat-vermiculite, or Ball Germinating Mix) or else be steamed 180°/30 minutes. Include flats, labels, etc.
   d. Be reasonably fine-textured. You don't sow petunia seeds in big lumps of soil.

CHECK LIST FOR GERMINATION TROUBLES

SUFFICIENT MOISTURE? ABSOLUTE NECESSITY — UNIFORM — NOT EXCESSIVE.

CORRECT TEMPERATURE? — USUALLY 65-70° — SOME PLANTS COOLER.

SEEDS COVERED TOO DEEP? AIR IS AS ESSENTIAL AS HEAT AND MOISTURE!!! FINE SEEDS REQUIRE LITTLE OR NO COVER — WILL "WASH" INTO SOIL.

ANTS-MICE — MORE OFTEN RESPONSIBLE THAN PEOPLE GENERALLY REALIZE — EVEN FLORISTS!

CLEAN, DISEASE-FREE STERILIZED MEDIUM?

YOUR SEEDSMAN IS ONLY HUMAN -- DOES HIS BEST. IF YOU THINK HE IS AT FAULT, WRITE AND GIVE HIM A CHANCE TO HELP!

ABOVE ALL, REMOVE SEEDLINGS TO COOL AIR AND PLENTY OF LIGHT AS SOON AS SPROUTED - - BEST DAMP-OFF PREVENTATIVE!

In fact, the majority of growers we see simply use Jiffy-Mix® or Ball Germinating Mix. It's sterile, has enough nutrients to make seedlings grow, texture is okay and it does drain. Some growers do add some sand to Jiffy-Mix®. Reason: separation of seedlings during transplanting goes faster (be sure to sterilize the sand).

Such mixes as Jiffy-Mix® have enough nitrate so that further fertilization is normally not needed. In mixes without fertilizer, use 1 ounce of 20-20-20 per three gallons of water.

3. *Keep soil warm.* Here must be the number one stumbling block—especially with the more "difficult" things like impatiens, geraniums. They really aren't difficult!!!

The majority of bedding annuals should have a *soil* temperature (day and night) of 75°F to achieve prompt germination. Not a house temperature, but actual temperature in the soil. This does apply to petunias, geraniums, impatiens, begonias, salvias, lobelias, marigolds and vincas. 70° honest soil temperature will sprout most of these annuals most of the time, but 75° does it more promptly, generally a better percentage. Why not!

You must have a suitable thermometer to know where you stand.

a. Moisture evaporation from the soil surface will cool the soil 5° to 10°. Ken Reeves, Toronto bedding-plant specialist, says, "Soil temperatures in my flats are frequently 10° or more below the house temperature. I check it!"

b. Water applied to seed flats (mist, etc.), often at 50° or 45°, will cool the soil down sharply. Tests at Michigan State show that 70°

160

soil took eight hours to get back up to 70° after an application of cold water.

The growers who consistently win with the tough ones (geraniums and impatiens) insist on "mid-70's in the soil."

A good way to really control soil temperature is by use of hot-bed cables. Depending on length, these cost around 50–70¢ per square foot. Now you set the thermostat (in the soil) where you want it. Growers often use steam pipe below the bench.

More recently we're seeing Biotherm and similar tiny hot water tubes running lengthwise down the bench 2" to 4" apart. They provide ample bottom heat—at a lot less energy cost and electricity. In fact, Swanekamp, major bedding grower in New Jersey, does much of his seed germination right on the ground—but with soil heat to maintain the necessary 70–75° soil temperature in the flats.

There is a group of bedding annuals that need a lower temperature for sprouting. Soil temperature of 65° is recommended for pansies, phlox, snapdragons.

4. *Keep soil surface always moist until sprouting.* Geo. J. Ball used to say that if a seed started to soak up moisture, then was allowed to dry, it would die. Once you start, the soil surface must be kept moist. Ways to do it:

   a. Mist—6 seconds per 10 minutes during sunny daylight only. Actually, the best growers seem to prefer misting by hand. They live with their flats that carefully. Says one good Virginia grower, "Automatic mist tends to get my seed flats too moist. I'd rather watch them myself."

   b. Another way: Wrap flats in poly, or cover the bed with a sheet of poly. If flats are well watered before sowing, there is normally ample moisture to sprout the seeds. Be sure to remove the poly as soon as the seedlings are through. Leonard Osborne, Piney Flats, Tennessee, says, "It gets too hot here under poly. I prefer to cover the seed flats with newspaper—and keep a close eye on them." Leonard always wins!

5. *Cover the seed?* The winners all leave the fine seed uncovered—petunias, begonias, etc. The tiny seeds soon wash down into the mix. Nearly all growers do cover the larger seeds, such as tomatoes, salvia, zinnia. Dr. Cathey, USDA, says that many seeds need three days of darkness to germinate. Examples: verbenas, larkspurs, dusty millers, pansies, phlox, portulacas.

Mist is a widely used tool in seed germination.

AFTER-SPROUTING CARE

Under the 75°/high-moisture regime, good seed should be well up in 5 days or less for most annuals. Very soon now these flats should be moved into a 50° house. Don't let them dry to wilting—but gradually withhold moisture. "Cool and dry" from here on produces well-rooted, sturdy seedlings—and a minimum of damp-off problems.

As seedlings mature, they're best with full sun, lots of fresh air.

GROWER COMMENTS

Jim Crouch, Jonesboro, Tennessee, "We had some damp-off after transplanting annuals—hit the flats with a drench of Dexon and Terraclor. It seemed to stop the problem."

Phil Couch, Rogersville, Tennessee, "It's important not to sow seed too thickly. You crowd the seedlings, encourage damp-off. I use 1/256 ounce of petunia seeds to a 24" flat. At 75° to 80° soil temperature, they jump through

162

in no time. Sowing in rows helps, too—if damp-off starts, it will just go down the row and stop."

From Val Maxwell of Green Thumb, large Apopka, Florida, producer, "All flats here are watered in with Dexon after transplanting. Everything."

BEGONIAS—AND OTHER TINY SEEDS

Special problem! How often have you seen a flat of fibrous begonias that sprout well—then most of them just fail to grow?

Usual cause: the seed (and seedlings) are both very small, very shallow-rooted. Especially under mist, all nutrients are promptly leached out of the surface of the mix—soon after sowing—so the tiny seedling simply starves! Answer: 1 ounce per 3 gallons of 20-20-20 applied as soon as seeds sprout.

G.V.B.

Chapter 17

HOW TISSUE CULTURE MAKES BETTER CROPS*

From the beginning of time, man has had a need to understand and control his destiny. In horticulture as man gained understanding of plant growth and development he modified his practice of foraging to extensive field culture, from managing his crops by hand to managing them with equipment, pesticides, and growth regulators. Gradually in an attempt to control the environment, he used saran-covered field structures, greenhouses, climate control systems, and finally growth chambers. In an attempt to control the root zone, man has gone from soil to semi-artificial mixes, to artificial mixes, and in nutrition, from manure as a fertilizer source to precise chemical formulations. In an effort to improve the yield from his efforts, man developed from saving the best seed to breeding programs which provided seed for the greatest yields. His greatest control over yield, however, was contained in vegetative propagation of selected high-yielding varieties where the genetic purity of a given line is guaranteed. With vegetative propagation came a myriad of systemic pathogens which altered the genetic potential of a given line and necessitated the development of certification programs to assure maintenance of clean stock. All of these advances have given him greater control over the results of his efforts.

*Contributed by Dr. Robert Hartman, president of Hartman (Tissue Culture) Nurseries, Palmdale, Florida.

In 1902, Haberlandt proposed that individual cells of plants under the influence of hormones had the capacity to develop into complete plants, and that this phenomenon could be demonstrated in cell cultures. Thus tissue culture, the ultimate in control over plant growth and response, had its birth. Haberlandt, however, was unable to demonstrate his concept, and it wasn't until 1939 that unlimited growth of plant cells could be demonstrated. Tissue culture developed since 1939 primarily as a tool for plant physiological investigations. In 1960, however, Morel published a paper that began tissue culture's impact on agriculture. Utilizing the concept that a plant systemically invaded by a pathogen was not uniformly infected and that if noninfected (clean) cells could be removed, made to live and develop into entire plants, then you would have a pathogen-free plant of the desired genotype. This he accomplished with an orchid, and in doing so he noted in his paper that his techniques not only allowed him to obtain a single disease-free plant, but many. Morel's concepts were immediately put into practice by the orchid industry. Its applicability to other crops also began to be explored. Thus, since the 1960s, the development of the application of tissue culture technology to man's effort ultimately controls every phase of plant development. Plant tissue culture, then, is the aseptic culture of cells, tissues, and organs in a controlled artificial medium and environment.

Today tissue culture has become the technique of preference for the propagation of a myriad of crops in the foliage, floriculture, ornamental, forestry, fruit, and vegetable industries. Tissue culture techniques are routinely used for the elimination of phytopathogens and for a host of genetic manipulations. In pharmacology, tissue culture is used in the production of secondary metabolites for medicinal purposes.

TISSUE CULTURE PROPAGATION PROCESS

For ease of understanding, the tissue culture propagation process can be defined in four stages.

Stage 1: initiation stage   Selected plants are taken from the greenhouse to a laboratory where parts are sterilized; from them a small, hopefully sterile piece of tissue is excised. This piece of tissue is placed into a defined medium. The various media used in tissue culture provide the life support and physiological manipulation systems for the cultured plant parts. The media constituents vary according to the plant species being cultured and the culture stage. However, the constituents generally consist of major/minor nutrients, water, an energy source (usually sucrose, table sugar), complex organic constituents such as vitamins and inositol, and hormones and hormone precursors. Plant hormones can be categorized into two groups: (a) *cytokinins,* first discovered in 1956, which are responsible for bud initiation and proliferation and (b)

Plants grow and multiply in vitro.

auxins, first discovered in 1934, which are responsible for, among other things, cell enlargement. It is the ratio of the hormones between these two groups and the specific hormones used within the groups that control the development of the excised plant part. The ingredients are used in a liquid state or suspended in a jelled condition. The mixed medium is then dispensed into containers ranging from test tubes and plastic boxes to Mason and baby food jars. The jelling agent is usually agar (a seaweed derivative). Once formulated, the media in its container is steam-sterilized in an autoclave. Media can also be filter sterilized. It is during this establishment state that the excised plant parts adjust to laboratory conditions.

Stage 2: multiplication stage   After the adjustment period, usually 4–8 weeks, the excised plant parts are placed in new media where they are induced to multiply. Multiplication can occur in a number of different ways, but commercially in 1983 it generally occurs in one of two ways: (a) adventitiously, where individual cells or cell groups from meristematic areas on a callous (undifferentiated cell mass) eventually develop into a normal plant, or (b) axillary branching, where the normally occuring vegetative axillary buds are encouraged to grow. The multiplication process usually takes from 4–8 weeks and is repeated many times depending on the level of plants desired.

Stage 3: rooting stage   Shoots, whether developed adventitiously or from axillary branches, are removed from stage 2 conditions and are placed in a medium that induces rooting. During this stage plantlets are often subjected to higher light intensities in preparation for stage 4.

Stage 4: establishment in the greenhouse stage Rooted plantlets are removed from the laboratory conditions and are placed in soil in the greenhouse.

Though these stages are convenient for describing the tissue culture process, in reality they are not as distinct as they sound. Often plants initiate roots simultaneously with shoots so that there is no need for stage 3. Similarly the rooting stage is often done in the greenhouse so that stages 3 and 4 occur simultaneously. In fact, plants are sold from the last three stages.

RECEIVING TISSUE CULTURE PLANTS

If plants are received as a stage 4 liner, then normal horticulture practices would be observed. However, if plantlets are received from stages 2 or 3, special care must be taken. The following is a typical set of instructions for handling stage 2 and 3 plantlets.

1. Remove plants from the containers or packages in which they were shipped as soon as possible after they are received.

2. Wash off any agar medium attached to the roots. If there is any variation in size of the plantlets, they should be graded into uniform lots prior to planting.

3. Plant in 1–2″ pots or cells containing sterile light potting mix. Commercial mixes such as Pro-Mix®, Metro Mix 300®, Vegetable Plug Mix®, Jiffy Mix®, etc. can be used successfully. It is a good practice to drench plants once with a soil fungicide (Banrot, Truban/Benlate, etc.) after they are planted. This may not be necessary if good sanitation is practiced. Keep plants moist and cool (70–80°F) while planting.

4. Place potted plants in reduced light (80–90% shade, 550 to 1000 foot candles) at high humidity (80–95% relative humidity) for 7–14 days. Temperatures are best kept between 80–85%F; however they should not go below 70°F or above 90°F. Bottom heat is especially helpful. High humidity can be created by infrequent misting or by a polyethylene tent. If a tent is used, be sure it doesn't get too hot. Many plants have been cooked in tents. A translucent plastic lid can be used effectively for plastic flats. Keep plants in reduced light (less than 2000 foot candles) with regular greenhouse conditions (i.e., fluctuating temperatures and humidities) for another 7–14 days. High temperatures

(above 90°F) should still be avoided. Plants should start getting fertilizer as soon as the roots are established. This usually occurs 5–7 days after planting, for rooted plants, and 10–14 days on root initiated plants.

5. After the 2–4 week establishment period (depending on a particular plant involved and the way in which it was received), plants are acclimated to the greenhouse and are ready to be handled as normal greenhouse plants. If plants are to be finished at high light intensities, above 3000 foot candles, then light intensity should be gradually increased to the final intensity so as not to burn plants.

Remember, the microplants you receive are accustomed to laboratory conditions which include 78°F, plus or minus 2°F, 200 to 1000 foot candles of narrow spectrum light, 98–100% relative humidity, roots if present not required, nonfunctional photosynthetic system, hormones in the media, and sterile conditions. From this condition you must make them adjust to greenhouse conditions which include 65–105°F, 1000–4000 foot candles of broad spectrum light, 40–100% relative humidity, functional necessary roots, functional necessary photosynthetic system, hormones produced by the plant internally, and nonsterile conditions. The above suggestions have worked successfully for many growers, allowing them to routinely accomplish the transition at greater than the 95% level.

TIME REQUIRED FOR THE TISSUE CULTURE PROCESS

It generally takes from 9–18 months (from the first piece of excised tissue) to get a new herbaceous plant variety on the market utilizing tissue culture techniques. Woodies often take longer, up to five years.

TISSUE CULTURE COST

The tissue culture process is cost effective if executed with precision. However, there have been many lab failures due to small mistakes in this cost-intensive process. Consider a few cost items. In 1983 dollars, for example, facilities normally cost between $100 to $150 per square foot to build and equip a working 2000 square foot lab. The average new variety or species takes from $1000 to $10,000 to develop into a working production system. It takes approximately $3000 to $8000 worth of equipment for a lab technician, and it typically takes 3–6 months to get a technician productive enough to reach the break-even point. Electricity costs alone for a 3200 square foot lab can exceed $1000 per week.

TISSUE CULTURE PLANTS FOR THE GROWER—PRO AND CON

Because of high laboratory overhead costs, a nursery will find that dealing with a tissue culture lab for plant material can be different from dealing with a conventional source. Labs are less able to adapt to the seasonal requirements of a customer. With the present state of the art, tissue culture is best suited to provide a steady stream of plant material. Most labs require a commitment of purchase from the customer (up to one year) as well as reasonable notice prior to quantity changes (usually three months or more) or cancellation (often six months). This requires long-range planning by the customers. Cost effectiveness is often a concern of growers. They often pay the same price for a smaller tissue culture plant than one conventionally propagated.

The advantages are that tissue culture plants, if properly handled by the labs, are genetically uniform and physiologically juvenile, which results in vigorous growth and often more branching providing finished plants with better habits. Plants tend to mature uniformly with very few culls and are most generally disease free. Shipping costs for laboratory plants are cheaper, as up

Tissue culture first became important in the orchid world. The ability to build up a new seedling rapidly changed the economics of the industry. Here's Hermann Pigors, Oakhill Gardens, Dundee, Illinois, in his orchid tissue culture "bottle room." With Hermann is tissue culture lab technician, Susan White.

to 2000 plants weighing less than five pounds can be shipped per cubic foot. Availability is not subject to season, peculiar weather conditions, or sudden disease or insect outbreaks. Since they are produced under laboratory conditions, few quarantine restrictions are placed on them. In fact, Australia, which allows only six conventionally propagated plants of a species into the country per year, will allow unlimited quantities of plants in tissue culture to be imported. Moreover, greenhouse production area formerly used for stock building and maintenance can now be turned into a finishing area. In many cases, tissue culture affords the only economic vegetative propagation means for many plants.

PROBLEMS

Contamination   The biggest problem facing most labs is contamination. For the tissue culture procedural magic to work, it must be done under sterile conditions. Almost any kind of micro-organism can contaminate a culture. Most contaminants are *not* pathogens, but they can rapidly grow on the medium and compete with the plant for nutrients. Furthermore, during their growth they excrete toxic waste products which will eventually kill the plant.

Most contaminants come from humans. The normal atmosphere we all breathe contains up to 1 million particles of 0.2 micron size or larger per cubic foot. The particles, many of which are bacterial or fungal spores, are charged and are attracted to other objects of opposite charge. Humans attract enormous numbers of particles to them which they carry into the lab. Besides wearing operating hoods to cover their hair, technicians are asked to scrub to their elbows with a disinfectant solution and are often required to wear a surgical mask. Furthermore, large air scrubbers operate 24 hours a day scrubbing particles out of the air. Some companies maintain two labs: in case they develop a problem in one lab, they can recover rapidly using stock from the other.

Mutation   Mutation can become a serious problem for labs. Under the high multiplying state, a mutated line, perhaps more suited for the tissue culture conditions, can inadvertently be selected. If a culture develops a detectable genetic change, the product coming out of the lab will be defective. To avoid this, many labs regularly restart their stock or maintain stock in culture in a nonmultiplying state. Storage techniques are being utilized and developed whereby plants can be stored for extended periods of time at refrigerator temperatures (34°F, plus or minus 2°F) or for years at liquid nitrogen temperatures.

Production control   As explained earlier, tissue culture is high-priced agriculture. Lab technicians must be highly skilled in their technique, and therefore, relative to other agriculture workers, are higher paid. This skill takes time to develop, which adds cost. Furthermore, the initial cost and operating costs per square foot are very high. To operate economically, labs must be run at least 8 hours per day (preferably 24 hours per day), 5 days per week, 52 weeks per year, utilizing to the fullest extent the trained, skilled employees in the expensive facility. Coupling that with the long crop buildup times has caused labs to be relatively unresponsive to seasonal demand. Today, because of limited supply, labs have been able to get away with this. As more labs become operational, competition will force labs to better address seasonal demands. This may require development of technology not now available.

SUMMARY

Tissue culture techniques offer man the most complete control over plant culture there is. With these techniques, one can control, maintain, and propagate plants with absolute precision. Formerly impossible, exotic, genetic, manipulative procedures are made routine and rare medicinals are available in quantities. Ultimately, techniques will be developed that will allow the above manipulations, where applicable, with all plants. It is just a matter of economics and time. Formerly prevalent devastating pathogens will become all but extinct with huge sustained influxes of pathogen-free material. Stock, once certified, will remain certified through stock maintenance procedures. Entirely new plants, which will significantly affect man's basic needs for food and fiber, will become a reality. Crops that are economically not feasible to clone will fall to suspension culture systems, which will give rise to direct embryogenesis from single somatic cells that can be mechanically sorted and sown, coated or uncoated, into stabilized greenhouse medium. These will ultimately be transplanted directly to the field.

The risks are great and much basic information is still lacking, but the potential this technology offers to the future of all agriculture, and therefore to mankind, is enormous.

Chapter 18

GROWING CONTAINERS—A SUMMARY*

An important and key decision for any grower today are the choices available for containers. It's important because

1. Choice of container is often an integral part of an overall marketing plan. Certain size containers appeal to one size market while others, particularly smaller containers, appeal to the mass market outlet.

2. Some containers cost more but may be well worth the difference to a crop and in a particular situation.

3. Your choice of containers has a definite effect on what material handling systems you can install to cut down on labor within your own business.

The purpose of this chapter is to offer a brief objective appraisal of the different growing containers on the market today and what's good—and perhaps what's not so good—about each. The chapter is divided into rooting containers, bedding plant containers, pots, hanging baskets, and nursery pots.

*Contributed by James Schield, Ball Seed Co.

Jiffy-7s and -9s®

Jiffy-7s® were first offered in this country in 1967 and have risen to prominence because of their versatility in rooting a large number of different types of crops. The grower gets a pellet about 1¾″ diameter by ¼″ thick. It's made of peat moss (and fertilizer) compressed to allow ⅟₇th of original volume and wrapped in a plastic mesh for a Jiffy-7® and just plain peat for the Jiffy-9®. After sitting out on a bench and watering, or under mist, they expand to a full pot of peat about 1¾″ diameter by 2″ high. Ready to plant seed, seedlings, or cuttings. There are several types available:

- #700, the original, pH 5.5 to 6.0 plus normal nutrients

- #703, pH 6.0 to 6.3, with reduced nutrients recommended for flower cuttings and has a pre-drilled hole

- Poly mats—these have a 703 Jiffy-7® attached to a perforated polyethylene sheet, prespaced on the poly mat to save you labor in setting out the Jiffys on a bench. Various spacings are available for various crops.

The Jiffy-7. It's a compressed pellet (right) which when moistened will expand and become a fine fiber-enclosed "flower pot—filled with peat" (left).

The Jiffy-Pot—also widely used in bedding plants. Especially by growers producing for the more affluent trade. Here's a strip of 12 2¼"s that fit into a plastic pack for growing and marketing (left).

Pro/Con Cost of Jiffy-7s® and Jiffy-9s®

Pro

1. Consistency. Jiffy-7s® are consistent in pH, nutrients, and water-holding capacity the first time and every time you open a new case, making it much easier to root whatever crop that you'd care to.

2. Convenience. Just take the pellets out of the box, water them, and you're ready to go. Nothing to add and you don't need a large storage area to keep a supply on hand.

3. Versatility. Almost all types of plants root and grow very well in a Jiffy-7 and -9®. I'd like to say that if it can be rooted at all it can be rooted in a Jiffy-7®.

Con

1. Tip Over. Used individually, Jiffy-7s and -9s® can be tipped over if hand watering is misapplied. One obvious answer to this problem is using the poly mat or the Jiffy tray application (#726 with 6 pellets or #720 with 10 pellets).

2. Handling of the Jiffy-9®. Because there is no protective netting on a Jiffy-9®, if it is handled excessively some crumbling of the peat moss in the root ball does occur. This problem usually only surfaces on plants that are being shipped.

Overall, the Jiffy-7® and Jiffy-9® have proven to be satisfactory rooting and germinating vehicles for the widest range of crops.

Artificial Rooting Blocks and Cubes

Under this heading comes an interesting array of products that are manufactured from plastic foam or wood fibers. They have been used successfully for a number of crops, depending upon the block, and have the advantage of being not only available but also completely sterile. Here's a brief rundown on two of these containers.

The Oasis block Oasis is an expanded plastic foam block best known today for poinsettia rooting. The pro side is that because they come in strips, Oasis blocks offer some convenience in handling and are a completely sterile rooting medium. In general, plants that prefer higher moisture levels such as certain foliage plants and poinsettias seem to do better in the Oasis block than crops that prefer to be on the dry side, such as geraniums. While geraniums may be rooted in Oasis blocks, extraordinary care must be taken in the watering and misting cycles to prevent stem rot.

On the con side, the water-holding capacity of the Oasis block is completely different from any of the soil media that you may be using to grow the plants once they've been rooted. Because of this fact, for the first week or two after transplanting Oasis block-rooted plants in the final container, extra care in watering must be taken to be sure that roots are getting out of the Oasis block and into the surrounding soil medium. Most problems with Oasis blocks occur because roots have not gone out of the Oasis block into the soil medium. Another potential hazard of Oasis blocks is that in the manufacturing process, the Oasis block contains a chemical which inhibits or prevents the rooting of plants. For this reason, the Oasis block must be *thoroughly* rinsed prior to sticking cuttings in order to prevent problems from occuring. Oasis blocks have gained a place as a viable rooting medium. More poinsettias currently are being rooted in Oasis blocks than by any other means.

BR8 block A treated cellulose fiber material that has met both success and encountered problems. Again, as in the case of Oasis blocks, watering the BR8 block properly seems to be the greatest problem. BR8 blocks are currently not as readily available as Jiffy-7s® or Oasis and are only being used on a limited basis.

Trends Difficult to fathom at this point; however, we see a lot of work done with peat moss being held together with soil binders. We also see a continuing trend toward direct sticking of cuttings to the final growing container, which has to a certain degree cut down on the potential market for Jiffy-7s® and artificial rooting blocks. Not all customers find this method to be either economical or desirable. It seems to depend upon the individual grower and his individual situation.

176

In bedding plant containers, one major trend that continues is the use of vacuum formed plastic cells and flats for bedding plant production. They have taken a large share of the market once held by molded fiber packs and compressed peat strips because of their economical price and relatively inexpensive freight costs. Although there is some variation from one area of the country to another, generally speaking the Handi-Flat, approximately 11" × 21", has become the standard size growing flat. Most popular cell sizes offer 72 plants/flat, 48s, 36s, and 18 plants/flat for instant color or seed geranium production. There are literally hundreds of variations in the number of packs per flat and the number of cells per flat available. Current trends see a move away from 96 plants per flat and in some instances away from even 72 plants per flat. This trend is utilized to reduce the total plant cost per pack. In many instances the larger plant (3"-4"-6") appeals to carriage trade garden center retail customers and late season retail customers.

Some of the advantages to the grower of these vacuum formed flats and packs include ease of handling, efficient use of storage space, and indeed, lower prices than might otherwise be available. Another major payoff in the standard flat is that there are a number of labor-saving mechanical devices, including the flat fillers and seeding machines which are built to accommodate the standard size flats.

The widely used cell pack—here with geraniums.

The very widely used Cell-Pak, the "AC 9/8." Eight packs of nine plants each. The most widely used container: the AC 6/12.

On the con side, plastic is simply not as forgiving of the grower who tends to overwater. This can be a special problem when the soil mix is a bit heavy. Since plastic has become the standard for the industry, some retail growers have found that they can differentiate their product by offering it in Jiffy-Strips or garden packs.

Cell packs versus more open packs The cell pack, which divides each plant from its neighbor to allow for easy transplanting by the consumer, continues to gain popularity. It's sort of a happy halfway ground between open plastic packs and individually potted plants. More cell packs are grown today than ten years ago (a reversal of the previous trend) because of the great customer acceptance of the individualized plant.

Fiber garden packs Garden packs, made of wood fibers bonded together with an asphalt product, have been around for a number of years and are still used successfully by a good number of growers. They are offered in a good variety of shapes and sizes and at one time formed the background of the bedding plant container business. Plastics have pretty much replaced the molded garden pack, but there are still some good reasons to use this product. First, molded fiber is a little easier to turn out a good plant because it is a porous product and has a lot of drain holes. Some retail customers like the earthy brown color as well. Some of the disadvantages of this product is that it does not permit easy separation of the plants for the home gardener, and from the grower's angle they are a little more expensive and have a much higher shipping cost than plastic containers. Trend on molded fiber is steadily down.

Jiffy-Strips and other peat pots   Jiffy-Strips are made of 70% European peat, 30% wood fiber, and soluble fertilizer. The strips offer both the advantages of the cell pack because of individualized plants and the advantages of the molded garden pack because they can breathe. Primary disadvantages include shipping expense and the fact that they are priced slightly higher than their plastic competitors.

Peat pots—Jiffy-Pots®   These were first offered in 1954 and subsequent imitators have proven to be very popular in the instant color market and with vegetable transplants. Retail customers like the convenience of being able to plant pot and all and growers appreciate the ease of growing with Jiffy-Pots®. Market has been fairly steady for the Jiffy-Pots®, primarily because of freight considerations.

FLOWER POTS

The last 20 years have seen a steady trend away from clay pots to the now standard injection-molded polypropylene plastic flower pot. Primarily because they're lighter weight for both shipping and handling and they're not nearly as breakable. From a grower's point of view a number of crops, including cyclamen, plainly do better in a clay container. Many retail customers also prefer to purchase plants in a clay pot as opposed to plastic.

Plastic pots are available in a very wide range of sizes, with the current trend being towards the "Azalea" sizes, which are slightly shorter than the standard pot. The prime consideration for the grower in choosing pots should be to only grow in pot sizes that his market is willing to accept and to try to reduce as much as possible the number of sizes he's producing in order to achieve economies of handling and in purchasing.

Trends in flower pots are hard to see, but as petroleum prices rise in the next few years, we can see growers looking for new flower pots made of less expensive material with the freight savings of plastics.

HANGING BASKETS

The largest increase in the whole world of containers up to last year has been in the hanging baskets. It's amazing the wide range of plant varieties that can be successfully grown and sold in hanging baskets from Cascade mums to petunias to broccoli and vinca. Most popular size today is the 10" diameter and the 8" diameter; 10" being most popular in garden center outlets and 8" for the mass merchants.

NURSERY POTS

Sold generally in quart sizes such as four-quart, six-quart and eight-quart, nursery pots are used for such items as garden roses, pot forcing roses, garden mums, and for stock plants in the bedding plant greenhouse industry. They are less rigid and less fancy than the injection molded pots and typically are made of molded fiber. Generally, they are reasonably priced and will, not being fancy, do the job that's asked of them.

LONG-RANGE TRENDS IN CONTAINERS

Where are we going in the next 5 or 10 years?

1. Clearly the trend, begun a number of years ago toward more individually grown plants, especially in bedding plants, continues. The most recent shift is away from 96 plants per flat and toward a fewer number of plants per flat.

2. Peat and fiber pots continue to be a factor in this area of growing containers. Sales on these two products have not grown as rapidly as plastic containers, not because they didn't provide a suitable container but rather because of price and freight considerations.

3. As the cost of plastic resins continues to rise, more work will be done to look at making packs, flats, and flower pots from renewable resources that have the shipping economies of plastic containers.

4. As more growers mechanize their operations, fewer container sizes will be available in the marketplace.

Chapter 19

THE IMPORTANCE OF CARBON DIOXIDE*

During the 1960s the subject of carbon dioxide (CO_2) was one of the "hottest" topics in the greenhouse industry. Everyone, it seemed, was asking "What is it?," "Is it really worth using?," "How much does it cost?," or "Will I obtain results?." All of these were valid questions. This presentation will attempt to answer each of these questions, and provide you with some realistic guidelines on how to use carbon dioxide as a production management tool for producing quality plants. Yet the question remains: "Does CO_2 benefit bedding plant growers?" In this chapter we'll attempt to answer that one also.

As the late 1960s and early 1970s passed, many growers of cut flowers invested in CO_2. The results were: quicker cropping, stronger stems, stockier stems, improved quality, and higher yields. Growers rapidly discovered that with CO_2 they needed to step up fertility programs, increase growing temperatures, and water more frequently. In the period 1968–73 there were crop changes from cuts to pots as well as more bedding plants grown. With all this activity, interest in CO_2 lessened. Then, in 1973–74, the "Energy Crisis" hit hard! Fuel prices quadrupled, resulting in only a small percentage of growers

*Contributed by Ralph Freeman, New York State Cooperative Extension.

continuing to invest in CO_2. These were primarily the rose growers. The attention previously focused on CO_2 was quickly drawn to conservation strategies.

WHAT IS CO₂?

Carbon dioxide (CO_2) is one of the basic compounds found in the atmosphere. The approximate concentration is about 300 ppm by volume. Generally, we refer to the concentration as being 300 ppm. CO_2 is one of the raw products required for photosynthesis.

The compound CO_2 is a colorless, noninflammable gas which is heavier than air. The gas solidifies under atmospheric pressure at $-78.5°C$ ($-109.3°F$). Solid CO_2 possesses the interesting property of passing directly into the gaseous state (sublimation) without going through the liquid state at atmospheric pressure.

PHOTOSYNTHESIS AND CO₂

Photosynthesis is a biochemical process using the sun's energy to chemically combine CO_2 and water (in the presence of the catalysts chlorophyll and solar radiation) to yield chemical energy in a usable form. The actual products of photosynthesis are carbohydrates (sugars and starches), complex chemical compounds, water and oxygen. A simplified explanation of the process of photosynthesis is seen in the following formula:

$$\boxed{\text{CarbonDioxide}} + \boxed{\text{Water}} \xrightarrow[\text{green plants}]{\text{Light Energy}} \boxed{\text{Carbohydrates}} + \boxed{\text{Oxygen}}$$

Carbon dioxide has been shown to be a limiting factor for proper growth and development of plants grown in greenhouses during the fall, winter, and spring. This occurs because greenhouse vents are normally closed to conserve heat for extended periods of time. Without adequate ventilation the CO_2 level drops below the normal 300 ppm atmospheric level. Plants have a tremendous need for CO_2. With vents closed the CO_2 is quickly used up, thus becoming a limiting factor for plant growth. Plant growth with inadequate CO_2 is put under stress, resulting in poorer growth than might be realized. Figure 19-1 shows approximate CO_2 levels measured in greenhouses and outdoors during the course of daylight hours.

182

Dramatic evidence of the effect of maintaining correct levels of CO_2. The two plants above were treated, the two lower plants not treated.

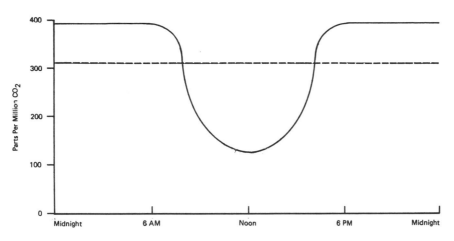

Figure 19–1. Carbon dioxide levels as measured in a greenhouse (solid line) and outdoors (dotted line) in a typical 24 hr. period.

Over the years research has shown that adding CO_2 during the daylight hours to the greenhouse atmosphere in concentrations of 3, 4, or 5 times greater than that found in the natural atmosphere will give increased yields, higher quality, and often shorter cropping times.

183

Adding CO_2 to the greenhouse environment is nothing new. This practice has gone on for many years. Europeans have been known to utilize manures, straw, and other organic mulches in the production of their crops. Since CO_2 was one of the by-products of decay, these practices aided those growers immensely.

Before the 1950s rose growers in the United States used tremendous quantities of manures, peatmoss, straw, and corncobs, either incorporated in growing mixes or used as mulches. Likewise, other cut flower growers, and especially cut chrysanthemum growers, followed suit. Veteran growers still recall the great quality, large stem and flower diameters, obtained in "the good old days." Much of this quality was perhaps due to the CO_2 given off by these mulches and soil incorporants.

Following World War II, as transportation costs and product costs increased, little by little less and less organic amendments were used. Thus, with less CO_2 in the greenhouses, the former quality was not maintained.

All during this time, other cultural techniques were being modified and recommended. Some of these included steam pasteurization, liquid fertilization, new and different pesticides, automatic and semi-automatic systems for irrigation, temperature control, ventilation, etc. These new practices took the brunt of the blame for any decrease in crop quality. Lest we forget, CO_2 was perhaps one of the limiting factors in plant growth after the mulching and organic amendment practices changed.

It wasn't until the late 1950s that CO_2 became an important topic in the greenhouse industry. Goldsberry and Holley at Colorado State University worked with roses and carnations, and reported very positive results when CO_2 was used in greenhouses.

Following their reports of CO_2 effects in greenhouses, the 1960s mushroomed with CO_2 research on all types of crops. Some of the reported results were:

- Carnations—faster crops, production up by one-third, stems stronger

- Chrysanthemums—longer and heavier stems; quicker crops

- Roses—significant production increases, improved grades, varietal differences, shorter cropping times

- Snapdragons—earlier flowering, better quality, heavier stems

- Geraniums—more cuttings from stock plants (30% more), cuttings rooted faster, plants from CO_2 cuttings were larger, more branching, faster cropping

- Bedding Plants—earlier flowering, larger leaves, taller, larger stem diameters, more fresh weight, seedling growth faster.

As one carefully analyzes each of the research reports, differences in the plant responses and in the opinions formed regarding the benefits of CO_2 become evident. Some of the negative findings may have been due, in retrospect, to variables other than CO_2.

WHEN TO USE CO₂

The results in Figure 19-1 demonstrate a very low level of CO_2 occurs in greenhouses for a significant portion of the daylight hours. Research has clearly shown that deficient levels of CO_2 occur in greenhouses generally between 9 a.m. through 3 p.m. during the fall, winter, and spring months. Therefore, if CO_2 is limiting at any time during the daylight hours, photosynthesis and, ultimately, plant growth will be limited. It is during these hours that CO_2 should be added to the greenhouse environment to help overcome this limiting factor.

Chrysanthemums, for example, have been found to respond more favorably in the young plant stage (up to the time of visible flower buds) than they will when mature. Other plants may respond similarly. In plants showing this response pattern a grower could stop using CO_2 in the finishing-off period.

WHICH CROPS RESPOND?

There are many crops that respond favorably to the addition of CO_2 to the greenhouse environment. Some of these that have been reported are:

Potted plants	Cut flowers
Azalea	Carnations
Begonias	Chrysanthemums
Begonia tuberous	Roses
Coleus	Snapdragons
Chrysanthemum	
Cucumber	
Cyclamen	
Geraniums	
Impatiens	
Lettuce	
Poinsettias	
Tomato	
Violets	

185

VARIETAL DIFFERENCES

There are distinct varietal differences in CO_2 response. For example, some chrysanthemum varieties may respond so favorably that as much as 50–60% increase in production may occur. In contrast, other chrysanthemum varieties grown under the same conditions may show no visible effect. This varietal difference is true with many different kinds of plants. So don't expect super-results and responses from all varieties of a given crop plant.

As you attempt to grow various kinds of plants and different varieties, record all your observations and measurements. Good management decisions can be made for future crops only if permanent records are available for analysis.

HOW MUCH TO ADD?

Research results have been inconsistent from university to university as to the exact amount of CO_2 to add to the greenhouse air for maximum growth and development of plants. There are many reasons for all this variability, but as one studies the various reports and takes into account growers' experiences we do find some common threads. Based on both research findings and commercial usage of CO_2, we can suggest that growers try to maintain levels between 600 and 1500 ppm.

Do not permit the CO_2 level to exceed 5000 ppm. First, it is wasteful (costly) and second, somewhere beyond that point headaches and listlessness may become troublesome.

SOURCES OF CO_2

There are many different sources of CO_2. Some are ventilation (exchanging greenhouse air with fresh outside air); decomposition of mulches; compressed CO_2 gas; dry ice; liquid CO_2 and combustion of various fuels (propane, natural gas, or kerosene). Many growers in Europe remove the CO_2 from flue gases after the boiler fuels have been burned. In order to do this, special stack scrubbers must be used that separate the CO_2 from the noxious gases. The CO_2 is then collected and injected into the greenhouses. Table 19-1 provides some basic information on each of the more commonly used fuels.

It is important that sufficient supplies of oxygen be provided to all burners of fossil fuels, so that noxious gases such as ethylene and sulfur dioxide do not cause deleterious effects to the plants.

Table 19-1 A LISTING OF SOME OF THE MORE COMMON SOURCES OF CO_2 AND GENERAL COMMENTS REGARDING EACH

Source of CO_2	Comments
Organic Matter	As organic matter breaks down, CO_2 is generated. In this aerobic process there is little control over the levels maintained in the greenhouse environment.
Solid CO_2	Dry ice is placed in special cylinders, and CO_2 is released as the dry ice sublimes. The amount of CO_2 going in the greenhouse is regulated with gas flow meters or pressure regulator valves.
Burning of Fossil Fuels[a]	Burning of kerosene, propane, or natural gas results in the generation of CO_2. The regulation of CO_2 concentrations is controlled by the rate of firing and/or the number of units being used.
Liquid CO_2	Stored in special vessels. The CO_2 is released at controlled rates via gas flow meters or pressure regulator valves.

[a]When purchasing fuel be sure the fuel supplier is aware that you'll be using fossil fuels for CO_2 generation. If by chance he has a lot with a sulfur content higher than normal, it would be undesirable for your purposes and he'll choose not to deliver it.

LIGHT, TEMPERATURE, FERTILITY

As carbon dioxide can become a limiting factor reducing growth of plants, likewise light, temperature, and fertility can become limiting factors in plant growth. If, for example, the ideal CO_2 levels for a particular crop were between 800 and 1000 ppm and either one or more of the light, temperature, or fertilizer levels were not up to par, growth would be restricted and the full potential of adding CO_2 would be lost. Therefore, each grower must discover the proper light levels, temperature, and fertilizer rates that would be optimal in his specific situation, as well as the levels and rates for the different seasons of the year. Now, this sounds difficult but experience has shown the following to be a starting guide:

Light Know your crop needs. Provide as much light as possible, yet not so much as to scorch leaves or blooms.

Temperature Higher levels may be needed. 62–65°F nights and up to 80°F days. Start ventilating at 80–82°F and turn CO_2 generators off automatically or manually when top vents are open 4".

Fertility Fertilizer programs will have to be stepped up. With increased growth more fertilizer and water will have to be applied. Keep fertility levels up at all times. Use soil tests and foliar analysis. Some growers have had to nearly double the amount formerly used when they start a CO_2 program.

Most important—for maximum growth, don't allow any growth factor to become a limiting factor.

CAUTION!!!!

Upper limits As growers may have a tendency to keep adding CO_2 to reach the "upper limits" a note of caution is in store here. The Mine Safety Appliance Company reported that a concentration of 8–10% CO_2 can be fatal. CO_2 concentrations of one percent (10,000 ppm) may cause headaches and listlessness. Concentrations too high make it impossible for the lungs to accomplish their function of eliminating CO_2 from the blood, and suffocation can result from prolonged breathing of such a high percentage of the gas. However, a small amount of CO_2 in the blood is necessary to stimulate the brain centers controlling respiration. Our basic guideline may be taken from the research. That is, most results indicate plants respond favorably to levels up to 2000 ppm. Let's not exceed this level.

Water When using CO_2 generated from open flame burners in greenhouses we must be cautious because tremendous quantities of water are generated as a by-product of combustion. Remember the formula:

$$\left.\begin{array}{l} \text{Natural gas} \\ \text{or LP gas} \\ \text{or kerosene} \end{array}\right\} + \text{oxygen} \rightarrow \text{carbon dioxide} + \text{water}$$

This clearly shows that the fuel used in the combustion process yields CO_2 + water. Where does this water go? It goes into the greenhouse atmosphere. The relative humidity increases. As we grow at high daytime temperatures, tremendous quantities of water are accumulated in the greenhouse air. This becomes troublesome when temperatures are lowered for nighttime growing. Then, on temperature fall, the moisture condenses out of the air as droplets on the plant tissues. If fungi spores are present, such as those of botrytis and powdery mildew, disease problems can develop quickly.

The purpose of mentioning this is to advise growers of this potential problem. The moisture in the air can be controlled by exchanging inside air with drier, outside air, or by leaving the vents cracked when the heat is turned on. The latter procedure warms the air allowing the air to pick up more moisture, and then causes it to be exchanged through the vents with the drier outside air. This successfully reduces the humidity of nighttime air in the greenhouse.

Safety controls   Each CO_2 generator should have approved safety controls. Some of these include a flame failure safety valve; solenoid valve which automatically switches the fuel on and off; gas filter; fine reading gauge showing true jet pressure; and a thermocouple which will shut off the gas flow if the pilot light is not functioning.

Use low sulfur fuels   When purchasing fuels for CO_2 generation, be sure your fuel supplier is aware that it will be used for CO_2. This will aid him in avoiding delivery of batches with abnormally high sulfur content.

Fuel leaks   Unburned fuels escaping into the greenhouse air can cause serious plant damage. Leakage from the piping system or from a burner operating incorrectly has resulted in flower and fruit abortion, abnormal growth, and numerous other problems.

AVOID AIR POLLUTION PROBLEMS

Self-induced air pollution problems are those caused by burners and furnaces in greenhouses that are not burning properly. Failures are usually due to inadequate amounts of oxygen supplied to the combustion process. Other causes may be dirty nozzles, off-center fires, delayed ignition, oil or gas leaks, pulsating fuel pressure, etc. Any of these factors, and more, can cause difficulties such as incomplete combustion resulting in noxious gases contaminating the greenhouse atmosphere. When these gases are present in excessive concentration for sufficient time, damage such as glazing of leaves; parallel veins; necrotic flecks, spots, and areas between veins; or twisted and distorted growth may occur.

The primary difficulty in greenhouses is a lack of oxygen, which will cause the fuel to burn improperly. This is a common problem because, in our "energy conscious" world, we're making greenhouses tighter and tighter. Those air leaks around the doors and other places are not there anymore, especially during the night when all cracks fill up with free moisture. When using CO_2 burners during the day, the same oxygen deficiency can occur, especially on those cloudy days when little or no venting occurs.

One method used to help avoid self-induced air pollution problems is to install a louver on the side of the greenhouse or inexpensive air duct such as a stovepipe from the outside to the burner. To help size the duct or louver, here's a rule of thumb: one square inch of cross-sectional area for each 2,000 BTU's. Therefore, a 100,000 BTU unit would require an air-intake duct of at least fifty square inches.

FACT: Every year at least 15–20% of the growers with heaters in greenhouses experience self-induced air pollution problems because they felt it would never happen to them. With CO_2 units the same can happen, particularly when houses are closed up in the daytime.

Provide plenty of air (oxygen) for combustion and you'll be safe.

DOES CO₂ BENEFIT BEDDING PLANT GROWERS?

Certainly! The literature reveals bedding plants such as geraniums, petunias, marigolds, tomatoes, lettuce, and numerous other crops benefit from the use of CO_2. If used, expectations should be faster seedling growth, faster crops, and improved quality.

The greatest responses and most benefit would take place in the young plant stages, not near maturity of the crop. One place where CO_2 could be particularly beneficial would be immediately following germination until bud set. Propagators could make real use of CO_2, especially during rooting of geranium cuttings as well as in growing seedlings and plugs to the point of transplanting.

Beware—if bedding plant growers use CO_2, expect all your scheduling to change. Plants do grow faster in CO_2-enriched environments. Watch your scheduling carefully.

COSTS

Even though growers today are "energy conscious," the costs of installing and operating CO_2 generators are not that expensive. Investments in CO_2 generators amount to approximately ten cents per square foot to install. Now, that's a one-time investment! Maintenance on the equipment is generally minimal.

The cost of generating CO_2 from either liquid carbon dioxide or fuels such as kerosene, propane, or natural gas amounts to approximately ten to fifteen cents per square foot per year. Keep in mind CO_2 will only be used during October through April with operational hours of 9 a.m. to 3–4 p.m. or a total of around 1,000 hours annually in the North.

When one considers the increase in production and improved quality as a result of using CO_2, there is no question about the economics. If used properly and the grower keeps all factors affecting growth of the plants managed well, the investments in equipment, maintenance, and costs of generating CO_2 are soon paid with a good return on the investment.

190

Over the years a number of different "CO_2 test kits" have been made available to the greenhouse industry. Their purpose was to provide an indispensable aid to help the grower measure the amount of CO_2 in the greenhouse at any time.

Grower reaction to many of these CO_2 test kits has varied. Some comments were positive, others negative. Costs of the kits and supplies were often another problem area. It seemed most of these kits soon found their way to dusty corners and were forgotten either due to their costs, time to take the test, inaccuracies, or whatever.

There are however, very accurate instruments available for measuring the concentration of CO_2 in air. Unfortunately, these are very expensive.

Well then, what is a grower to do? How can he know how much CO_2 is in the greenhouse air? First, he can calculate the volume of the greenhouse(s) in which CO_2 will be injected or generated. For example:

$$\text{Volume of Greenhouse} = (\text{width}) \times (\text{length}) \times (\text{avg. height of } 12')$$
$$\text{Volume} = (25') \times (100') \times (12')$$
$$\text{Volume} = 300,000 \text{ cu. ft.}$$

Second, calculate the hourly CO_2 requirements. To do this, keep in mind that plants on the average need at least 400 ppm (0.04%). Then,

$$\frac{(30,000 \text{ cu. ft.}) \times (400 \text{ ppm/hr.})}{1,000,000 \text{ ppm}} = 12 \text{ cu. ft. } CO_2/\text{hr.}$$

This is the CO_2 sensing equipment produced by Priva—which activates an additional flow of CO_2 into the atmosphere when levels fall below the set point.

Knowing that 12 cu.ft. of CO_2/hr. are required for 400 ppm, the grower can set the pressure regulator flow control valve on the liquid dry ice converter *or* set the gauge pressure (on gas-fired units) on the setting to deliver an adequate amount of CO_2 per hour. All reliable gas equipment should have charts to relate gauge pressure, propane or natural gas used/hr., and the number of pounds of CO_2 generated/hr. Although the exact concentration may not be known, good judgment, experience, and continued use should be combined to make necessary adjustments for the daily weather changes so excessive concentrations can be avoided.

EQUIPMENT SELECTION

There are numerous companies having equipment available for CO_2 injection. These include units which burn natural gas, propane, or kerosene. There is also equipment that stores pure CO_2 and is released through gas flow meters or pressure regulator valves and distributed into the greenhouse(s).

Selection of equipment should include a careful evaluation of the following factors:

- *Well constructed and engineered equipment* to avoid the disastrous results of plant damage from unburned gas and fume injury.

- *Dependable and reliable equipment* operating with minimal breakdowns.

- *Safety controls* to automatically stop the unit in the event the fuel supply is exhausted or the flame goes out.

- *Constant level control* to maintain oil or gas consumption and CO_2 output at a constant rate and assure steady CO_2 output at all times.

- *Economical to operate.*

SUMMARY

This chapter has attempted to review what CO_2 is and how to use it, and to describe some costs and benefits of its use.

Carbon dioxide, one of the essential ingredients in green plant growth, often becomes a limiting factor because the supply is rapidly used up in greenhouses. Natural replacement is difficult as greenhouses are becoming tighter and tighter in our energy-conscious age. Therefore, adding CO_2 at 2, 3, or 4 times natural concentrations will cause plants to grow faster, stems and flowers to increase in diameter, leaves to become larger, quality to improve, and cropping time to decrease. This will only occur, however, if all the other growth factors are in their proper supply and balance.

In summary:

- CO_2 is a gas present in the atmosphere but generally deficient in supply in greenhouses during the daylight hours of fall, winter, and spring. As a result, growth is impaired.

- Adding CO_2 during daylight hours, 9 a.m. to 4 p.m., at concentrations of 500 to 1500 ppm will help accelerate growth.

- CO_2 is generated from liquid carbon dioxide by sublimation or generated from burning fossil fuels such as natural gas, propane, or kerosene.

- Many of the commonly grown crops respond favorably to CO_2 enrichment of the greenhouse atmosphere. Expect varietal differences.

- Provide as much light to your crop(s) as possible without scorching the leaves and blooms.

- Growing temperatures need to be higher: 62–65°F nights and up to 80°F days. Start venting at 80–82°. When vents are 4" open, turn the CO_2 generators off.

- Fertility and irrigation programs may have to be stepped up. With more growth you can't afford to be lacking in plant nutrients or water. Use soil tests as a guide for determining nutrient levels in growing mixes.

- Don't exceed 5000 ppm CO_2 concentrations. Above this level, damage to humans can occur.

- Select and use quality equipment with the necessary safety controls.

- All fuels should be of extremely low sulfur content.

- The cost of generating CO_2 is approximately 10–15 cents per square foot per year.

- CO_2 is a good investment, especially when outdoor temperatures are low and little venting takes place.

- Open flame generators producing carbon dioxide in greenhouses should be supplied with sufficient oxygen for complete combustion of fuels to take place. Rule of thumb: 1 square inch of free air space per 2000 BTUs.

- Expect and reap the results!!!

Chapter 20

INSECT CONTROL— A TABULATION*

Table 20-1   SHELF LIFE OF SELECTED PESTICIDES*

Pesticide	Shelf life	Comments
Insecticides		
carbaryl, WP (Sevin)®	several years	WP formulations have been stored up to 5 years without loss of effectiveness—settling will occur in flowable formulations
diazinon (Spectracide)®	5 to 7 years	Diazinon formulations will last 5 to 7 years providing concentrate containers are tightly sealed (granular and dusts are kept dry)
disulfoton (DiSyston)®	2 years	Under normal conditions
azinphosmethyl, WP (Guthion)®	2 years	Under normal conditions
malathion, WP	indefinite	Very stable when stored under proper conditions (decomposes when exposed to high temperature)

*Prepared by Richard K. Lindquist and edited by Harry K. Tayama, Ohio State University.

Table 20-1   (continued)

Pesticide	Shelf life	Comments
oxydemeton-methyl (Meta-systox-R)®	2 years	Under normal conditions
methoxychlor, WP	indefinite	Stable under normal conditions
resmethrin (SBP-1382)®	6 mos–2 + years	Stable at 70°F for at least 2 years, at 80°F stable for 6 months
aldicarb (Temik® 10G)	indefinite if kept dry	Moisture causes active ingredient to be released from granules
acephate (Orthene 75SP)	2 + years	Under normal conditions
Bacillus thuringiensis Dipel	6 months– 3 + years	WP tormulations in closed containers, stored at 30% RH, should be stable for at least 3 years; use liquid formulations within 6 months
Fungicides		
benomyl, WP (Benlate)®	2 years	If kept tightly sealed, shelf life should be at least 2 years— keep dry (will decompose if exposed to moisture)
captan, WP	3 years	Under normal conditions
Herbicides		
ammonium sulfamate, soluble salt (Ammate)®	at least 2 years	Keep dry and under 100°F—no low temperature limit
DCPA, WP (Dacthal)®	at least 2 years	Under normal conditions
glyphosate, liquid (Roundup)®	at least 2 years	Quite stable when stored under 140°F (do not allow to freeze)
pronamide, WP (Kerb)®	at least 2 years	Under normal conditions
paraquat, liquid	indefinite	Extremely stable, but do not allow to freeze
simazine, G, WP (Princep)®	indefinite	Stored as long as 9 years under good conditions
oryzalin, WP (Surflan)®	3 years	If stored at high temperatures, it should be mixed well before using
trifluralin, G (Treflan)®	3 years	Lost 15 to 20 percent activity when stored at 100°F—will be stable 3 years when stored under dry conditions and temperatures no higher than 80°F

*Originally compiled by J. Carlson, Department of Entomology, University of Massachusetts; Revised by C. C. Powell and R. K. Lindquist, Ohio State University.

Table 20-2   INSECT AND MITE CONTROL CHART*

Insect or mite pests	Chemical control			Registered crops	Comments
	Common name	Brand name	Formulation		
Aphids	Acephate	Orthene	75SP	Anthurium, Cacti, Carnation, Chrysanthemum, foliage plants, Orchid, Poinsettia, Rose.	Foliar spray. Injures some chrysanthemum cultivars and foliage plants.
	Acephate	PT 1300	Aerosol	Airplane, Aloe, Begonia, Bird of Paradise, Bloodleaf, Boston Fern, Cacti, Calendulas, Carnation, Chicken Gizzard, Christmas Cactus, Chrysanthemum, Coleus, Columbine, Croton, Crown of Thorns, Cutleaf Philodendron, Devil's Ivy, Dieffenbachia, Dusty Miller, Euonymous, Gardenia, Geranium, German Ivy, Grapeleaf Ivy, Impatiens, Jade Plant, Moses in the Cradle, Nightblooming Cereus, Ornamental Peppers, Orchid, Pansy, Peperomia (solid and variegated), Philodendron, Poinsettia, Polka Dot Plant, Sanseveria, Santolina, Schefflera, Shrimp Plant, Snapdragon, Spider Plant, Sprengeri Asparagus, Velvetleaf, Wandering Jew, White-Edged Swedish Ivy, Zinnia.	
	Aldicarb	Temik	10G	Carnation, Chrysanthemum, Easter Lily, Gerbera, Rose, Snapdragon.	Granules on soil. Repeat at 3-5 week intervals.
	Diazinon Dichlorvos	Diazinon Vapona	Fog Several	Carnation, Chrysanthemum, Rose. All greenhouse ornamentals.	Fog, smoke, aerosol. Effective at cooler greenhouse temperatures.

197

Table 20-2 (continued)

Insect or mite pests	Chemical control			Registered crops	Comments
	Common name	Brand name	Formulation		
	d-Phenothrin	Sumithrin	2EC	Ageratum, Aphelandra, Aster, Azalea, Begonia, Calendula, Chrysanthemum, Coleus, Dracaena, Ficus, Fuchsia, Geranium, Ivy, Marigold, Peperomia, Petunia, Philodendron, Poinsettia, Pothos, Rose, Salvia, Schefflera.	Foliar spray. May not be effective against green peach aphid.
	Endosulfan	Thiodan	50WP, EC, Smoke	All greenhouse ornamentals.	Effective at warmer greenhouse temperatures.
	Fluvalinate	Mavrik	2F	All greenhouse ornamentals.	
	Insecticidal Soap	Safers	Conc.	All greenhouse ornamentals.	Wet foliage thoroughly by spraying or wiping.
	Kinoprene	Enstar	5E	All greenhouse ornamentals.	Foliar spray. Repeat application at 10-day intervals. Do not use on roses or poinsettias.
	Lindane	Lindane	Several	All greenhouse ornamentals.	Foliar spray, smoke, fog.
	Malathion	Malathion	Fog	Carnation, Chrysanthemum, Geranium, Snapdragon, Rose.	Fog only.
	Naled	Dibrom	Several	All greenhouse ornamentals.	Emulsion, smoke.
	Oxamyl	Oxamyl	10G	All Spice, Aluminum Plant, Ardisia, Artillery Plant, Asparagus Fern, Azalea, Bird's Nest Fern, Boston Fern, Caladium, Carnation, Chrysanthemum, Croton, Diffenbachia,	Granules may be broadcast on media surface or preincorporated.

Pest	Common name	Trade name	Formulation	Plants	Remarks
	Oxydemeton-methyl	Meta-Systox-R	2EC	Dracaena, Gardenia, Gladiolus, Gypsophila, Hoya, Iris, Ivy, Jade Plant, Leatherleaf Fern, Maranta, Palm (Neanthebella and Madagascar), Peperomia, Philodendron, Poinsettia, Rose, Sanseveria, Snapdragon.	Foliar spray or drench.
	Sulfotepp	Dithio, Dithione	Fog. Smoke	All greenhouse ornamentals.	May be formulated with tetradifon. With non-systemic insecticides, repeat application at 7-day intervals, as needed.
Cabbage Looper	Acephate	PT 1300	Aerosol	Same as for aphids.	
	Bacillus thuringiensis	Dipel	WP	All greenhouse ornamentals.	Foliar spray. Thorough coverage necessary.
	Fluvalinate	Mavrik	2F	All greenhouse ornamentals.	
	Lindane	Lindane	WP	All greenhouse ornamentals.	Foliar spray.
Fungus Gnats (adults)	Resmethrin	PT 1200	Aerosol	All greenhouse ornamentals.	Aerosol. Repeat applications at 4-5 day intervals (adults).
(larvae)	Oxamyl	Oxamyl	10G	Same as for aphids.	Apply as described for aphids. Repeat in 4-6 weeks.
Leafminers	Acephate	PT 1300	Aerosol	Same as for aphids.	Note: Leafminer adults and larvae may be tolerant or resistant to all pesticides listed here. Sanitation and crop rotation are very important in suppressing leafminers.

Table 20-2 (continued)

Insect or mite pests	Chemical control			Registered crops	Comments
	Common name	Brand name	Formulation		
	Aldicarb	Temik	10G	Chrysanthemum, Gerbera.	Granules on soil. Repeat at 3-5 week intervals.
	Diazinon		Fog	Aster, Carnation, Chrysanthemum, Snapdragon.	
	Dichlorvos	Vapona	Fog	All greenhouse ornamentals.	Effective at cooler greenhouse temperatures.
	Naled	Dibrom	Fog	All greenhouse ornamentals.	
	Nicotine	Several	Emulsion	All greenhouse ornamentals.	
	Oxamyl	Oxamyl	10G	Same as for aphids.	
	Parathion	Penncap M	F	Chrysanthemum.	Foliar spray. May be tank-mixed with Permethrin for better control.
	Permethrin	Pramex, Pounce	EC	Chrysanthemum.	Foliar spray. Repeat applications at 4-5 day intervals. Maximum label rate may be required.
Leafrollers	Acephate	Orthene	75SP	Rose.	Foliar spray. Very effective.
	Acephate	PT 1300	Aerosol	Same as for aphids.	
	Dichlorvos	Vapona	Fog	All greenhouse ornamentals.	Fog. Effective at cooler greenhouse temperatures.
	Lindane		WP	All greenhouse ornamentals.	Foliar spray.
	Naled	Dibrom	EC	All greenhouse ornamentals.	Vapor treatment.
Mealybugs	Acephate	Orthene	75SP	Anthurium, Cacti, foliage plants, Orchid, Poinsettia.	Foliar spray. Repeat at 2-3 week intervals. May injure some foliage plants.

Common Name	Trade Name	Formulation	Plants	Remarks
Acephate Aldicarb	PT 1300 Temik	Aerosol 10G	Same as for aphids. Poinsettia.	Granules on soil. Repeat at 3-5 week intervals.
Bendiocarb	Dycarb, Ficam, Turcam	76WP	African Violet, Ageratum, Aglaonema, Antirrhinum, Ascarina, Asparagus sprengeri, Asplenium, Azalea, Baby's-Breath, Begonia, Calathea, Calendula, Celosia, Chrysanthemum, Cineraria, Cissus, Coleus, Cyrtomium, Daffodil, Dahlia, Dianthus, Dieffenbachia, Dracaena, Dryopteris, Epipremnum, Fern spp., Ficus, Four-O-Clock, Fuchsia, Gardenia, Gazania, Geranium, Gladiolus, Guave, Hydrangea, Hypoestes, Impatiens, Iris, Ivy, Lily Of The Valley, Maranta, Marigold, Mondograss, Nasturtium, Nephrolepis, Nicotiana, Ochrosia, Pachysandra, Pansy, Petunia, Philodendron, Plumella, Poinsettia, Polypodium, Portulaca, Rose, Sagopalm, Salvia, Sansevieria, Schefflera, Shasta Daisy, Spathiphyllum, Vandaonomea, Verbena, Vinca, Wandering Jew, Zinnia.	Foliar spray. Avoid use of alkaline water for best results.
Dichlorvos	Vapona	Fog, Smoke, Aerosol	All greenhouse ornamentals.	Effective at cooler greenhouse temperature.
d-Phenothrin	Sumithrin	2EC	Same as for aphids.	Foliar spray. Repeat at 10-14 day intervals.
Insecticidal Soap	Safers	Conc.	All greenhouse ornamentals.	Repeat at 1-2 week intervals.

Table 20-2 *(continued)*

Insect or mite pests	Chemical control			Registered crops	Comments
	Common name	Brand name	Formulation		
	Naled Oxamyl	Dibrom Oxamyl	Vapor, Fog 10G	All greenhouse ornamentals. Same as for aphids.	Repeat at 3-5 week intervals.
	Sulfotepp	Dithio, Dithione	Smoke, Fog	All greenhouse ornamentals.	
	Kinoprene	Enstar	5E	All greenhouse ornamentals.	Foliar spray. Repeat applications at 1-2 week intervals. Do not use on roses or poinsettias.
Millipedes	Ethion	Ethion	EC	None.	Greenhouse bench spray.
	Malathion	Malathion	50WP	None.	Greenhouse bench spray.
Mites (Cyclamen Mite)	Endosulfan	Thiodan	WP, EC	All greenhouse ornamentals.	Foliar spray.
	Dicofol	Kelthane	WP, EC	All greenhouse ornamentals.	Foliar spray.
Two-Spotted Spider Mite	Acephate	PT 1300	Aerosol	Same as for aphids.	
	Aldicarb	Temik	10G	Carnation, Chrysanthemum, Cymbidium Orchid, Gerbera, Poinsettia, Rose, Snapdragon.	Granules on soil. Repeat at 3-5 week intervals. May not be effective on older woody plants.
	Cyhexatin	Plictran	50WP	Carnation, Chrysanthemum, Poinsettia.	Foliar spray.
	Dichlorvos	Vapona	Fog, Smoke	All greenhouse ornamentals.	Effective at cooler greenhouse temperature.

Pest	Common name	Trade name	Formulation	Plants	Remarks
	Dicofol	Kelthane	WP, EC, Fog	All greenhouse ornamentals. Carnation, Chrysanthemum, Rose.	Foliar spray.
	Dienochlor	Pentac	WP, F	All greenhouse ornamentals.	Foliar spray.
	Dienochlor	Pentac	Fog	Carnation, Chrysanthemum, Rose.	Foliar spray. Use maximum label rate.
	d-Phenothrin	Sumithrin	2EC	Same as for aphids.	Foliar spray.
	Fenbutatin-oxide	Vendex	WP, F	All greenhouse ornamentals.	Use higher rate for mite control.
	Fluvalinate	Mavrik	2F	All greenhouse ornamentals.	Repeat applications at 7-10 day intervals.
	Insecticidal Soap	Safers	Conc.	All greenhouse ornamentals.	
	Malathion		Fog	Carnation, Chrysanthemum, Geranium, Rose, Snapdragon.	
	Naled	Dibrom	EC	All greenhouse ornamentals.	Vapors.
	Oxamyl	Oxamyl	10G	Same as for aphids.	
	Propargite	Omite	WP	Carnation, Chrysanthemum, Rose.	Foliar spray. May injure some cultivars.
Plume Moth	Sulfotepp	Dithio, Dithione	Fog, Smoke	All greenhouse ornamentals.	
	Dichlorvos	Vapona	Fog	Carnation, Chrysanthemum, Rose.	
	Malathion		Fog	All greenhouse ornamentals.	
	Lindane		WP	All greenhouse ornamentals.	
	Naled	Dibrom		Carnation, Chrysanthemum, Poinsettia, Rose, Snapdragon.	
Scale Insects	Acephate	Orthene	75SP	Anthurium, Cacti, foliage plants, Orchid, Poinsettia.	Foliar spray. Repeat at 2-3 week intervals. May injure some foliage plants.
	Acephate	PT 1300	76WP	Same as for aphids.	
	Bendiocarb	Dycarb, Ficam, Turcam		Same as for mealybugs.	
	Kinoprene	Enstar	5E	All greenhouse ornamentals.	Foliar spray. Repeat applications at 2-week intervals.
	Malathion		Fog	All greenhouse ornamentals.	
	Oxamyl	Oxamyl	10G	Same as for aphids.	

Table 20-2 (continued)

Insect or mite pests	Chemical control			Registered crops	Comments
	Common name	Brand name	Formulation		
Slugs	Sulfotepp	Dithio	Fog, Smoke	All greenhouse ornamentals.	Bait, dust, emulsion.
	Metaldehyde	Snarol, Slugit, Bug-Geta	Several	All greenhouse ornamentals.	
	Methiocarb	Slug-Geta, Mesurol	Bait	All greenhouse ornamentals.	
Sowbugs	Malathion	Malathion	WP	None.	Spray or dust soil surface.
Springtails	Malathion	Malathion	WP	None.	Spray or dust soil surface.
Thrips	Acephate	Orthene	75SP	Anthurium, Cacti, Carnation, Chrysanthemum, foliage plants. Orchid, Poinsettia, Rose.	Foliar spray may injure some cultivars.
	Acephate	PT 1300	Aerosol	Same as for aphids.	
	Aldicarb	Temik	10G	Chrysanthemum.	Granules on soil surface. Not effective against flower thrips.
	Bendiocarb	Dycarb, Ficam, Turcam	76WP	Same as for mealybugs.	
	Diazinon		Fog	Aster, Carnation, Chrysanthemum, Snapdragon.	
	Dichlorvos	Vapona	Fog, Aerosol	All greenhouse ornamentals.	
	Fluvalinate	Mavrik	2F	All greenhouse ornamentals.	Foliar spray, dust, fog.
	Lindane	Lindane	Several	All greenhouse ornamentals.	
	Malathion	Malathion		Carnation, Chrysanthemum, Geranium, Rose, Snapdragon.	
	Naled	Dibrom	EC	All greenhouse ornamentals.	Vapors.
	Nicotine		Several	All greenhouse ornamentals.	Spray, dust, emulsion, smoke.

Pest	Insecticide	Trade name	Formulation	Plants	Remarks
	Oxydemeton-methyl	Meta-Systox-R	EC	All greenhouse ornamentals.	Foliar spray.
	Resmethrin Sulfotepp	PT 1200 Dithio, Dithione	Aerosol Fog, Smoke	Chrysanthemum. All.	Repeat applications of all materials (except granular formulations) at 4-5-day intervals to protect flowers.
Whiteflies	Acephate Aldicarb	PT 1300 Temik	Aerosol 10G	Same as for aphids. Chrysanthemum, Gerbera, Poinsettia.	Granules on soil. Repeat at 3-5-week intervals.
	Dichlorvos d-Phenothrin	Vapona Sumithrin	Several 2EC	All greenhouse ornamentals. Same as for aphids.	Fog, smoke, aerosol. Foliar spray. Apply in late afternoon or night. Repeat weekly.
	Endosulfan	Thiodan	Several	All greenhouse ornamentals.	Foliar spray, dust, smoke.
	Fluvalinate Insecticidal Soap Kinoprene	Mavrik Safers Enstar	2F Conc. 5E	All greenhouse ornamentals. Same as for aphids. All greenhouse ornamentals.	Foliar spray. Do not use on roses or poinsettias.
	Lindane	Lindane	Several	All greenhouse ornamentals.	Foliar spray, fog, smoke.
	Malathion	Malathion	Fog	Carnation, Chrysanthemum, Rose, Geranium, Snapdragon.	
	Naled	Dibrom	Vapor, Smoke	All greenhouse ornamentals.	
	Oxamyl Pyrethrins	Oxamyl Pyrenone	10G EC	Same as for aphids. African Violet, Aster, Azalea, Begonia, Camelia, Carnation, Chrysanthemum, Dahlia, Geranium, Gladiolus, Marigold, Rose, Rubber Plant, Wandering Jew.	

Table 20-2 (continued)

Insect or mite pests	Chemical control			Registered crops	Comments
	Common name	Brand name	Formulation		
	Resmethrin	SBP-1382	EC	Ageratum, Azalea, Aster, Begonia, Calendula, Chrysanthemum, Coleus, Geranium, Ivy, Petunia, Poinsettia, Rose, Salvia.	Foliar spray. Apply resmethrin during late afternoon or night. Repeat weekly.
		PT 1200	Aerosol Fog	All greenhouse ornamentals. Arum Lily, Azalea, Begonia, Bird of Paradise, Chinese Fan Palm, Coleus, Crane Lily, Dieffenbachia, English Ivy, Foundation Palm, Gardenia, Geranium, India Rubber Tree, Norfolk Island Pine, Poinsettia, Palms, Snapdragon, Wandering Jew, Zephyr Lily.	
	Pyrethrins Resmethrin	Py-Sy Greenhouse Concentrate, Rotospray Resmethrin	EC	All greenhouse ornamentals.	Can be used as high-volume or ULV spray.
	Sulfotepp	Dithio, Dithione	Fog, Smoke	All greenhouse ornamentals.	

*Before purchasing and using any pesticide, you must check all labels for registered use, rates, and application frequency. Generic names have been used for all pesticides. When possible, check the discussion of individual materials for examples of trade names. This list is presented for information only. No endorsement is intended for products mentioned, nor is criticism meant for products not mentioned.

206

Chapter 21

WHEN TO SOW—
A TABULATION*

A common question asked by growers is "When do they bloom?" In fact, a recent survey of bedding plant producers found that the dominant industry problem for bedding plant growers is the timing and scheduling of production to sales! No doubt this scheduling difficulty also applies to pot crops as well.

Many factors affect the flowering time of greenhouse crops. They include sowing date, weather variations, growing temperature, fertility, use of growth regulators, daylength, and general cultural practices. Weather variations are certainly beyond a grower's control. But the other factors can be controlled.

Sowing dates are the most critical factors that a grower can control. Once those dates are established, then other factors, such as temperature, fertility, and watering, can be modified as the weather dictates, to speed up or slow down a crop's flowering time.

The following schedules will provide a general guideline for establishing sowing dates. The schedules will need to be modified based on individual cultural practices, climate, and the time of year.

All of the following schedules came from carefully kept records. Keep in mind that the most accurate, complete scheduling information you will ever come across will be the information you find in your own records. Accurate records from your own greenhouse are invaluable tools in scheduling future production. If you do not have a record-keeping system, by all means, start one immediately.

*Contributed by Carol McShane, Bodger Seed Co.

Crop	Sow	To flower
AGERATUMS Use B-Nine to improve uniformity and to enhance dark green leaf color. For best performance, use F1 hybrids. Grow at 60°F.	Mar. 14 Feb. 21	Mid-May flats in the North Mid-April flats in the South
BEGONIAS, FIBROUS-ROOTED When grown during the summer, provide 60°F nights, humidity, and shade. Use small leaf varieties for flats or pots, and large leaf varieties for pots. Can be planted in sun or shade outdoors. Bronze leaf types are best for sun tolerance. 4½″ pots can be grown year-round. They are especially popular for holiday sales.	Jan. 24 Jan. 10 July 20 Dec. 26 Dec. 15 Nov. 20	Mid-May flats in the North Mid-April flats in the South 4½″ pots for Christmas 4½″ pots for Mother's Day Mid-May baskets Mid-April baskets
BEGONIAS, TUBEROUS-ROOTED During winter months, provide four hours of additional light at night from seed emergence until bud formation. Otherwise, plants may stop growing, and form tubers. For flats, use a 3″ cell, minimum. Use the F1 *Nonstop* series for dependable performance. Grow at 62°F.	Dec. 26 Dec. 12 Dec. 13 Nov. 15 Oct. 25	Mid-May flats in the North Mid-April flats in the South 4″ pots for Mother's Day Mid-May baskets Mid-April baskets
CALCEOLARIAS This is an easy to grow, cool crop for spring and holiday sales. Use the quick flowering *Anytime* series in 4½″ or 5″ pots. *Bright 'N' Early* is also a popular variety for 5 or 5½″ pots. Grow at 50°F and protect from the hot sun in the spring.	Sept. 1 Sept. 15	Early April sales Late April sales
CALENDULAS Grow under cool conditions and sell with pansies. For flats, use the dwarf *Fiesta Gitana* series.	Feb. 7 Jan. 12 Nov. 15 Aug. 2	Mid-April flats in the North Mid-March flats in the South Late Jan. 4″ pots in the Southwest Late Oct. 4″ pots in the Southwest
CELOSIAS Dwarf varieties can be sold in flower. Tall varieties should be sold green. B-Nine can be used to improve uniformity. There are two types of celosia, feathered and crested. For 4″ pots, use	Feb. 27 Mar. 20 Feb. 15 Feb. 25	Mid-May flats in the North Mid-May flats in the North Mid-April flats in the South Mid-April flats in the South (green plants)

Crop	Sow	To flower

Jewel Box Moisture (crested) or
Geisha Mixture (feathered). Grow
at 62°F.

CINERARIAS
An easy to grow pot crop. Grow
cool at 50°F. Use *Starlet & Ball
Florist Select* in 5 or 5½″ pots.

	Sept. 2	Late Feb. & early March
	Oct. 1	Late March & early April

COLEUS
Colorful in flats, pots, and baskets. Useful as part of an indoor
foliage plant program.

	Feb. 26	Mid-May flats in the North
	Jan. 24	Mid-April flats in the South
	July 1	4″ pots in October
	Feb. 1	Mid-May baskets
	Jan. 4	Mid-April baskets

CYCLAMENS
Use hybrids for faster flowering,
more uniform crops. Flowering
time varies with growing temperature, pot size, and by variety.

	Apr. 1	4″ pots in Dec. minia. varieties
	Feb. 1	5″ pots in Nov. hybrid varieties
	Jan. 2	5″ pots in Dec. hybrid varieties

DAHLIAS
Transplant into 2½″ cells or Jiffy-
Pots®. Shift into 4″ pots, covering
a portion of the stem if necessary. With adequate spacing,
pinching is not needed. Try *Dahl
Face Mix* for single flowers and
Rigoletto or *Figaro* for double
flowers. Can be sold in flower in
flats, using a 2¼″ cell, minimum. Grow at 62°F.

	Mar. 7	Mid-May flats in the North
	Feb. 15	Mid-April flats in the South
	Feb. 15	Mid-May 4″ pots in the North
	Feb. 3	Mid-April 4″ pots in the North
	Feb. 26	Mid-May flats in the North
	Feb. 10	Mid-April flats in the South

DUSTY MILLERS
Silver Dust is the most popular
variety.

	Jan. 3	Early May pots in the North

GAZANIAS
Hot weather tolerant, they are
good for flat & basket sales.
Flowers close up at night and on
cloudy days.

	Feb. 1	Mid-May flats in the North
	Jan. 2	Mid-April flats in the South
	Jan. 10	Mid-May baskets
	Dec. 15	Mid-April baskets

GERANIUMS
For all around good performance
(packs, pots, and outdoors), several good series are available.
The *Smash Hit* and *Ringo* series
are popular choices. For the earliest flowers, the *Hollywood* series. Other recommendations
include *Cameo, Red Elite,* and
Razzmatazz. Use *Cycocel* for
more compact plants. Silverthio-
sulfate is effective for controlling

	Jan. 3	Early May pots in the North
	Jan. 25	Mid-May pots in the North
	Jan. 10	Mid-April pots in the South
	Mar. 20	Mid-May flats in the North
	Feb. 15	(sell green)
		Mid-April flats in the South
		(sell green)

209

Crop	Sow	To flower
flower petal shatter.		
GERBERAS	Jan. 3	Early May sales
Happipot Mixture is the only	Dec. 14	Mid-April sales
dwarf variety from seed that is	June 1	October sales
suitable for 4″ pots. Flower stems		
range from 6″-12″ tall. The crop		
will come into flower over a		
three-week period.		
GLOXINIAS	June 1	Christmas sales
Grow at 65° minimum. Best in 5″	July 20	Valentine's Day sales
pots. Dwarf *Velvet Plush* can be	Apr. 20	Sweetest Day sales
grown in 4½″ pots.		
IMPATIENS	Mar. 2	Mid-May flats in the North
Use self-branching varieties for	Feb. 7	Mid-April flats in the South
compact flats and pots. Double-	Feb. 20	4″ pots in early May
flowered varieties are also avail-	Jan. 15	Mid-May baskets
able from seed and are best in 4″	Dec. 26	Mid-April baskets
pots. *Showstopper* and *Blitz* se-		
ries are best in baskets.		
LOBELIAS	Mar. 2	Mid-May flats in the North
Use 3 to 4 seedlings per cell	Feb. 12	Mid-May baskets
pack. Popular in cool climates,		
it's a favorite in the Pacific		
Northwest.		
MARIGOLDS, AMERICAN	Feb. 26	Mid-May flats in the North
This type is daylength respon-		(needs short-day treatment)
sive, blooming best under short	Mar. 25	Mid-May flats in the North
days. Sowings made before Feb.		(sell green)
15 bloom dwarf and early. Later	Feb. 1	Mid-April flats in the South
sowings need short-day treat-	Feb. 21	Mid-Apr flats in South (sell green)
ments to bloom. Use dwarf vari-	Feb. 10	4″ pots in early May
eties only. Sell tall varieties		
green.		
MARIGOLDS, FRENCH	Mar. 6	Mid-May flats in the North
Popular varieties include the *Boy*	Feb. 15	Mid-April flats in the South
series, the *Bonanza* series, and		
the *Janie* series. These strains are		
earlier to flower and more com-		
pact than older strains.		
MARIGOLDS, TRIPLOIDS	Mar. 15	Mid-May flats in the North
They are a cross between French	Feb. 22	Mid-April flats in the South
and American types. With the		
best heat tolerance of all mari-		
golds, they are the best choice		
for the South.		
PANSIES	Jan. 7	Mid-April flats in the North
Use F1 varieties instead of F2 or	Dec. 15	Mid-March flats in the South
open-pollinated types for their	July 20	Early October flats in the South
uniformity, earliness, and heat		

Crop	Sow	To flower
tolerance. Grow cool for quality plants.		
PEPPERS, ORNAMENTAL Popular 4″ pot plants with colorful fruits, they should be grown at 60-65°F. *Holiday Cheer* has round fruit and *Fireworks* has pointed fruit.	Dec. 20 Aug. 1 May 25	Early May 4″ pots December 4″ pots October 4″ pots
PERENNIALS For spring sales, they can be sown in late summer, transplanted and established in flats in the fall, and overwintered in cold frames in a cool greenhouse. Another alternative is to treat them like annuals, by sowing in the winter, transplanting into flats, growing warm in the greenhouse, and selling in the spring. A minimum 3″ cell pack is best, and color plant labels are helpful with perennials.	July-Aug. Jan.-Feb.	Spring sales in flats. Grow cool. Spring sales in flats. Grow warm.
PETUNIAS, DOUBLES Grow cool for well-branched plants. Use B-Nine to control height.	Jan. 30 Jan. 4	Mid-May flats in the North Mid-April flats in the South
PETUNIAS, SINGLES Grow cool for well-branched plants. Use the new *Floribunda* types for best pack and garden performance.	Feb. 15 Jan. 20 Jan. 18	Mid-May flats in the North Mid-April flats in the South Mid-May baskets
PHLOX, DWARF Sow direct into flats.	Mar. 6 Feb. 7	Mid-May flats in the North Mid-April flats in the South
PRIMULAS, MALACOIDES Fragrant plants for 4½″ pots, grow at 50°F for early spring sales. The best varieties are *Snow Cone* and *Pink Ice*.	Sept. 1	Valentine's Day
PRIMULAS, ACAULIS & VERIS Both types should be grown cool. They are popular for spring pot sales, in the Midwest and Northeast, and for winter bedding plant sales in the West.	Sept. 1 June 15– early fall	March 4″ pots Winter sales in the West
SALVIA Sell the dwarf varieties in flower and the tall varieties green. B-Nine helps control height.	Feb. 26 Mar. 22 Jan. 26 Feb. 16	Mid-May flats in the North Mid-May flats in North (sell grn.) Mid-April flats in the South Mid-April flats in South (sell grn.)

Crop	Sow	To flower
SHAMROCKS Direct sow several seeds into 3½" pots.	Jan. 1	St. Patrick's Day sales
SNAPDRAGONS, GREENHOUSE Dates are based on 50° growing temperature and raised benches.		
Single Stem—	Aug. 16 Oct. 6 Oct. 25 Nov. 14 Dec. 11 June 10	Dec. 16–Jan. 1 Mar. 16–Mar. 31 Apr. 5–Apr. 20 Apr. 25–May 5 May 10–May 15 Sept. 5–Sept. 10
Pinched—	July 20 Sept. 5 Nov. 15	Mid-December Early March Mid-March
SNAPDRAGONS, OUTDOORS Sell dwarf varieties in flower, and sell tall varieties green. After plants are established, grow cool.	Feb. 1 Mar. 24 Jan. 3 Feb. 22	Mid-May flats in the North Mid-May flats (sell green) Mid-April flats in the South Mid-April flats (sell green)
THUNBERGIAS This is a fast growing annual that's excellent in baskets. *Alata Mixture* or the *Susie* series.	Jan. 24 Jan. 2	Mid-May baskets Mid-April baskets
VERBENAS Germinate at alternating soil temperatures, 65°F nights and 75° days. Plants are sensitive to excess moisture.	Feb. 4 Jan. 24	Mid-May flats in the North Mid-April flats in the South
VINCAS Seeds need darkness to germinate and they are sensitive to overwatering. After transplanting, maintain 65°F growing temperature for at least three weeks. Use the *Little* series for flats and pots. Use *Polka Dot* and the *Carpet* series for baskets.	Jan. 20 Jan. 3 Jan. 3 Dec. 8	Mid-May flats in the North Mid-April flats in the South Mid-May baskets Mid-April baskets
ZINNIAS Sell dwarf varieties (*Pulcino, Peter Pan, Short Stuff, Dasher* series & *Thumbelina*) in flower in flats and pots. Tall varieties should be sold green.	Mar. 14 Apr. 3 Feb. 8 Mar. 1 Mar. 3	Mid-May flats in the North Mid-May flats (sell green) Mid-April flats in the South Mid-April flats (sell green) 4" pots for Mother's Day

Chapter 22
POLLUTION

AIR POLLUTION EFFECTS ON ORNAMENTAL CROPS*

As our world becomes more and more densely populated, our need for plants and flowers increases, but at the same time our ability to produce and distribute them in pristine condition becomes more challenging. More people and "people-related" activities give rise to air pollution problems that make it increasingly difficult to produce and maintain high-quality plants that are free from air pollution injury.

It is not surprising that among the various types of living organisms, plants are considered to be the most sensitive biological indicators of the presence of trace quantities of air pollutants. Let's stop a minute to consider how a plant is constructed and how it operates. To synthesize the carbohydrates needed for normal growth, a plant must "mine" vast quantities of air to collect carbon dioxide, a gaseous raw material needed to support photosynthesis. To grow a crop of corn yielding 100 bushels per acre requires ten tons of carbon dioxide gas. To secure this quantity, the corn plants growing on an acre of land must process 33,500 *tons* of air. A plant's anatomy is organized to "strain" such vast quantities of air to secure its basic building blocks for growth, but at the same time the plant vulnerably exposes itself to the damaging effect of trace quantities of other phytotoxic gases which might be present in the air it is processing.

*Contributed by Marlin N. Rogers, University of Missouri.

Although their relative importance may vary from place to place, damaging air pollutants may be nationally ranked in the following descending order of importance on the basis of their measured economic effects on all economic plants: sulfur oxides, ozone, fluorides, peroxyacyl nitrates, ethylene, chlorine, and nitrogen dioxide (Middleton, 1967). Estimates of the total monetary damage to agricultural crops amount to about $100 million annually in California and to more than $500 million in the U.S. as a whole.

General Symptoms of Air Pollutant Injury

The most common symptoms of air pollution injury to a plant are caused by loss of water (plasmolysis) from cells in the leaf, resulting in its death. This water loss appears to result from changes in the permeability of the membranes surrounding each cell that permit the water contained inside the cell to "leak out." Cells in different parts of the leaf appear to be affected differently by each specific toxicant. In some cases, only cells in the upper palisade layer may be affected; in others, only cells adjacent to the stomatal pores collapse, while in still other instances, groups of cells extending completely through the leaf may be killed. These differences help identify which specific pollutant material may be causing a particular phytotoxic effect (Brandt, 1962).

Physiological Effects of Air Pollutants on Plants

Not all air pollutant injuries to plants are expressed as distinct symptoms, particularly if plants are exposed to marginally low concentrations for extended time periods. In this case, conditions may simply cause slow, "unthrifty" plant growth with the plants never showing more distinctive symptoms. Such injury has been termed as "hidden," "chronic," or "invisible" in the past. Also, this type of injury is measurable only after the completion of detailed comparisons of growth between plants exposed to low levels of air pollutants and plants grown in air carefully filtered with adsorbents that remove toxic gases.

This stunting and poor growth of the affected plants is due to the damaging effects of the air pollutants upon sensitive cellular membranes and key enzyme systems that are mediating critical metabolic activities. For example, fluorides have been shown to inhibit the activity of peroxidase and cytochrome oxidase enzymes, and as a result to interfere with plant respiration, and carbohydrate synthesis and interconversion (McCune and Weinstein, 1971). Photosynthesis is also inhibited by most air pollutant chemicals, and different toxicants have been ranked in their ability to reduce the process as follows: $HF > O_3 > Cl_2 > SO_2 > NO_2 > NO$ (Bennett and Hill, 1973). Ozone damages plants by destroying the semi-permeability of the cellular membranes, thereby interfering with the plant's ability to regulate movement of water, mineral elements, and elaborated foods from one part of the plant to another (Rich, 1964). Peroxyacetyl nitrate (PAN) appears to be an important photosynthetic inhibitor also (Dugger and Ting, 1970). Ethylene accelerates senescence and aging and increases respiratory rates in many plants (Abeles, 1973).

Sulfur Dioxide

Sources The principal sources of sulfur dioxide in the air are electrical generating plants using low-quality, high-sulfur-content coal, the smelting or refining of sulfur-containing copper, lead, zinc, and nickel ores, and the production, refining, and use of high-sulfur petroleum and natural gas (Wood, 1968). Power generation by coal-burning plants is the most important single source of trouble. Since more and more of these large plants are being set up at mine-mouth locations, sulfur dioxide problems in the future will not necessarily be confined to metropolitan areas. Calvert (1967) has calculated, for example, that when three such plants are completed and in operation near mines in western Pennsylvania, about one-third of the southwestern part of the entire state will theoretically be subjected to ground-level concentrations of sulfur dioxide of 0.15 ppm (parts per million), which is approaching the threshold point for injury—particularly if ozone is also present at low concentrations (Menser and Heggestad, 1966). In many of our large cities SO_2 levels have actually *decreased* within recent years, as a result of "clean-up" actions taken by the utilities following the passage of restrictive legislation (Bates, 1972).

Necrotic symptoms On broad-leaved plants sulfur dioxide causes formation of necrotic (dead) spots in the parts of the leaf between the major veins (see photo). Both palisade and spongy parenchyma cells die, and the affected areas become papery in texture and usually ivory or light tan in color. The area immediately adjacent to the main veins usually remains green in color. Older florists, who, in their earlier days, burned poor-quality soft coal in boilers located in the end of their greenhouses, will remember this kind of injury which used to occur, at some time or other, nearly every winter. On grasses and other plants having parallel veins, injury is likewise pretty much confined to the interveinal areas, with the final bleached pattern giving a streaked effect (see drawing, p. 216). Chronic injury appears only as a generalized chlorosis (lightening of color between the veins) with the death of a few isolated cells being shown by white or brownish flecks.

As long as aerial concentrations of sulfur dioxide are low, the gas dissolves in the moisture present inside the leaf, forming sulfites, which are gradually changed into relatively harmless sulfates. However, if sulfites accumulate faster than this conversion can occur, cell permeability is affected and the cells begin to lose their water (Brandt, 1962).

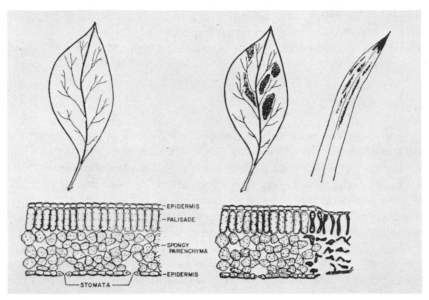

Normal dicotyledon leaf and cross section (left). Sulfur dioxide injury (right). Note blotchy interveinal areas of dicotyledon leaf and streaked areas on monocotyledon leaf (grass type).

Plants having succulent leaves of high physiological activity are most likely to be injured. The plants most susceptible to injury may be damaged after exposure to 0.48 ppm for four hours or 0.28 ppm for 24 hours (Thomas, 1961).

Table 22-1   BEDDING PLANTS SUSCEPTIBLE TO SULFUR DIOXIDE INJURY*

Susceptible		Intermediate	Resistant
Ageratum	Four O'Clock	Asparagus 'Sprengeri'	Cabbage
Begonia	Geranium	Cauliflower	Castor Bean
Broccoli	Hibiscus	Eggplant	Cellery
Brussels Sprout	Lettuce	Gladiolus	Chrysanthemum,
Canna	Mallow	Hollyhock	most cvs.
Centaurea	Marigold	Nasturtium	Cucumber
China Aster	Morning Glory	Parsley	Impatiens
Chrysanthemum,	Okra	Snapdragon	Muskmelon
some cvs.	Pepper	Sweet William	Pansy
Coleus	Poppy	Tomato	Periwinkle
Cosmos	Verbena		
Endive	Zinnia		

*The susceptibility ratings shown in this and subsequent tables have been compiled from numerous published sources. In cases of conflicting data, the author placed the plant in what he considered to be the most appropriate category.

Ozone

First discovered as a cause of trouble in 1956 in California, and now a major problem for the Connecticut Valley shade-grown tobacco producers, it has been claimed that, "in New Jersey, ozone is our most important single phytotoxic air pollutant, affecting, as it does, many plant species within our state" (Daines, *et al.*, 1960).

Sources   While there are naturally occurring sources of ozone in the atmosphere, the main source of this pollutant is photochemical reactions in polluted atmospheres. Oxides of nitrogen emitted into the air by any kind of combustion occurring at high temperatures (e.g., boilers, incinerators, automobile engines) react, in the presence of sunlight, with oxygen, to produce ozone, O_3, an extremely active chemical substance. If hydrocarbons are also present, ozone tends to accumulate to higher levels than it would otherwise.

Since motor vehicles are major sources of both hydrocarbons and nitrogen oxides, we would expect relatively high levels of ozone to build up daily in sunny climates in metropolitan areas with high traffic density—and such is the case (California Bureau of Air Sanitation, 1966). Although it is difficult to make precise measurements of ozone concentration with the currently available instrumentation, it has been found that naturally occurring levels range from zero up to about 0.50 ppm. Sensitive tobacco varieties may be injured by one-tenth this level for eight hours (Heggestad, 1969). Plant injury from ozone has been reported from most of the states along the eastern and western seacoasts, Utah, Wisconsin, and from most of the larger metropolitan areas of the country (Taylor, 1968).

Symptoms   The most common type of symptom resulting from exposure to ozone consists of tiny, discrete, usually light-colored spots, flecks, or stipples over part or most of the upper surfaces of the affected leaves of broadleaved plants, which are caused by the collapse of the upper palisade cells just under the upper epidermis of the leaf (see p. 218). (The ordinary florist's first impression might be that a sudden and massive invasion of red spiders had attacked his plants—but he would be unable to find any mites upon close examination of the leaves.) In plants without an upper palisade layer, the spots may go completely through the leaf and be visible on both surfaces. In grapes, the stippled spots are pigmented and dark brown in color rather than the lighter colors typical of most other plants. In some other plant species, a more general necrotic bleaching of the upper surface of the leaf appears (Heggestad, 1968). Leaf age may affect the severity of symptom expression in many plants, with the more mature leaves being more susceptible than very young leaf tissue.

Ozone injury to onions causes a tip burn of leaves, which may gradually increase in size and extent. In this plant, however, there are resistant cultivars in which the stomata close quickly after the pollutant contacts the guard cells. This prevents further entry of the ozone into the leaf and offers considerable

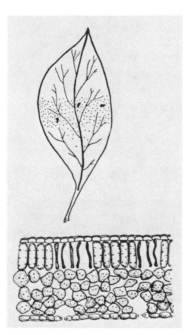

Ozone injury. Note flecking or stippled effect on leaf. On sectioning, only the palisade layer is affected.

protection. It has now been ascertained that this resistance mechanism is controlled by a single dominant gene pair, so with this crop, it has been relatively easy to develop ozone-resistant cultivars by plant breeding (Engle and Gableman, 1966).

Similarly, tobacco breeders have been able to produce ozone-resistant cultivars of cigar-wrapper tobacco which can continue to be grown profitably in the Connecticut Valley, where this crop has long been of great commercial importance, even in the presence of ozone concentrations that would be disastrous to most of the older cultivars. It appears, in fact, that the plant breeder may possess one of the important keys of the future to practical control of ozone injury to these and many of our other cultivated crops, including the different kinds of bedding plants susceptible to injury by this pollutant (Gableman, 1970).

Even though necrotic symptoms might not be apparent, long-continued exposure of plants to sublethal concentrations of ozone may result in reduced growth rates and the development of chlorotic symptoms indistinguishable from those typical of old age or iron, manganese, or nitrogen deficiency. Premature defoliation and abscission of blooms and young fruits of crops such as tomato, pepper, and citrus may also occur (Taylor, 1968).

Synergism between ozone and sulfur dioxide   Single air pollutant gases are rarely present around plants in a natural growing situation, as would be true in controlled experiments. Does the presence of mixtures of air pollutants cause different plant responses than the presence of individual toxicants?

At one time, researchers had evidence which they interpreted as showing an actual interference between materials. Sulfur dioxide was thought to interfere with the damaging effects of other air pollutants, such as the mixtures of oxidants present in Los Angeles air and the reaction products of ozone and gasoline.

More recent studies (Reinert, et al., 1975) have shown, however, that there are different kinds of interactions between different air pollutants. Abundant data regarding sulfur dioxide–ozone interactions now show us that with most plants, the damaging effects from such a mixture are either additive or greater than additive (synergistic), but that in a few cases, the damaging effects are less than additive (or competitive). Similar responses have been observed on plants exposed to combinations of SO_2 and NO_2, but much less information is available about this combination. Even less is known about the potential effects of other possible air pollutant combinations. Tobacco cultivars, which normally require exposures of about eight hours at 0.1 ppm of ozone alone to cause symptoms, were injured and showed typical ozone injury symptoms after two hours exposure to 0.03 ppm of ozone, if sulfur dioxide was also present simultaneously at about 0.25 ppm (Menser and Heggestad, 1966). Such findings only serve to point out some of the new subtle and potential dangers we face as we continue to add new gaseous components to our atmosphere.

Table 22-2   BEDDING PLANTS SUSCEPTIBLE TO OZONE INJURY

Susceptible		Intermediate	Resistant
Ageratums	Lettuce	Abutilons	China Asters
Asters	Mallow	Cabbage	Chrysanthemums,
Begonias	Marigolds	Coleus, some cvs.	most cvs.
Broccoli	Muskmelon	Cucumbers	Lobelias
Brussels Sprout	Onions	Eggplant	Peppers
Carnations	Pansies	Impatiens	Periwinkles
Celery	Petunias	Parsley	Snapdragons
Chrysanthemums,	Potatoes	Sensitive Plant	Stocks
some cvs.	Pumpkins	Squash	Sunflowers
Coleus, some	Salvias	Tomatoes, some cvs.	Sweet Pea
cvs.	Strawberries	Verbenas	Tolmiea
Dahlias	Sweet Basil		Zinnias
Dill	Sweet Potatoes		
Endive	Tobacco		
Fuchsias	Tomatoes		
Geraniums			
Gourds			

Fluorides

Although fewer kinds of plants may be susceptible to injury from fluoride air pollution than from other toxicants, plants that are sensitive are affected by exceedingly low concentrations of fluorides in the atmosphere. Gladiolus, for example, may be adversely affected by exposure to concentrations as low as 0.1 parts per billion (ppb) for 5 weeks. This is because such plants act as accumulators or biological concentrators of these substances, and are able to accumulate toxic levels in the apices and margins of leaves.

Sources   Plants receive fluorides from both their root environment and from their aerial environment. Soils or fertilizers (e.g. superphosphate) may be high in soluble fluorides, which can be absorbed by the plant's root system. Likewise, water sources high in fluorides can contribute to the problem. Finally, fluorides may also be absorbed by the foliage of plants directly from the air.

Atmospheric fluorides arise primarily from industrial sources; in the refining of aluminum ores, fluorides arise from the molten cryolite bath in which the alumina is reduced. Fluorides are also released in significant amounts by phosphate fertilizer plants, brick plants, steel manufacturing plants, refineries, pottery and ferro-enamel works, and in recent years, by rocket fuel combustion.

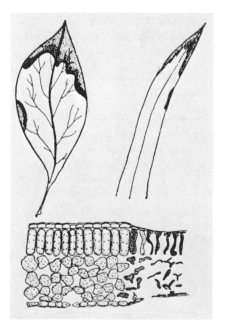

Fluoride injury. Note the tip and edge necrosis on both the dicotyledon leaf and the monocotyledon (grass-type) leaf with sharp line of demarcation. Section shows severe collapse and shrinking of internal structure.

Symptoms Inside the plant, fluorides move in the transpirational stream and concentrate in the marginal or apical portions of leaves. The fluoride in the leaf is immobile; it does not move to other parts of the plant. When toxic concentrations are reached in these localized areas, the affected cells collapse and die (see drawing). Then, the necrotic areas normally turn a reddish brown or tan color, which is fairly distinctive. The margin between the dead and uninjured tissue is often set off by a darker brown-red band of color.

In contrast to sulfur dioxide and ozone, open stomata do not appear to be essential for plant absorption of fluorides. This would suggest that absorption of fluorides occurs directly through the plant cuticle, although this has yet to be verified.

Table 22-3   BEDDING PLANTS SUSCEPTIBLE TO FLUORIDE INJURY

Susceptible	Intermediate	Resistant	
Cannas	Asters	Boston Ferns	Marigolds
Cyclamens	Azaleas	Broccoli	Morning Glory
Dracaenas	Baby's Breath	Brussels Sprout	Nasturtiums
Gladiolus	Begonias	Cabbage	Onions
Hemerocallis	Carnations	Caladiums	Periwinkles
Hyacinths	Coleus	Canterbury Bells	Petunias
Irises	Dahlias	Cauliflower	Phlox
Jerusalem Cherry	Geraniums	Celery	Portulacas
Lilies	Lettuce	China Asters	Potatoes
Poinsettias	Narcissus	Chrysanthemums	Roses
Spider Plants	Onions	Columbines	Salvias
Sweet Potatoes	Pelargonium	Cosmos	Snapdragons
Tulips	Peppers	Cucumbers	Stocks
	Strawberries	Dahlias	Sweet Pea
	Sunflowers	Eggplant	Tobacco
	Sweet William	English Daisies	Wandering Jew
	Tomatoes	Four O'Clocks	Zinnias
	Verbenas	Lobelias	
	Violets		

PAN—Peroxyacetyl Nitrate

During the mid-1940s, another type of plant injury began to be identified in Southern California as being associated with "smog" (Middleton, *et al.*, 1950). In this case, the injury consisted of silvering, glazing, bronzing, and sometimes death of the lower leaf surfaces of sensitive plants. More recently, this type of injury has been ascribed to "oxidants." Haagen-Smit *et al.* (1952) were later able to show that these symptoms could be produced artificially by exposing plants to the reaction products resulting from a mixture of ozone and vapors of certain unsaturated hydrocarbons, or by the photochemical reaction of nitrogen dioxide and hydrocarbons. Stephens, *et al.* (1961) later showed that these "silver-leaf" symptoms were due to peroxyacetyl nitrate (PAN) present in the air at very low concentrations. PAN concentrations of 20 to 30 ppb are common at Riverside, California, with peaks of 54 to 58 ppb having been reported there, and in Salt Lake City. Peaks as high as 210 ppb have been reported from Los Angeles, California (Taylor, 1969).

Sources This material is produced in the atmosphere as a secondary product from air pollutant substances already present, and results from a photochemical reaction between nitrogen dioxide and simple olefins. The concentration of this and other closely related compounds has a diurnal fluctuation, essentially disappearing during the hours of darkness, but building up to, and remaining at, maximum levels from shortly after sunrise until sunset (Jaffe, 1967). The most serious and widespread plant injury has been reported from around Los Angeles, California, even though occasional damage has been reported from at least 18 other states and several foreign countries (Middleton and Haagen-Smit, 1961; Taylor, 1969).

Symptoms Symptoms usually appear first on the lower surfaces of young, recently expanded leaves as a glazing or bronzing (see drawing, p. 224). At higher concentrations and longer exposures, more severe symptoms occur— complete collapse of transverse bands of tissue across individual leaves.

Leaf susceptibility is closely correlated with age and maturity of the cells. As a leaf expands, it matures first near the apex and finally near the base. For this reason, then, it is common to find bands of collapsed tissue near the tip of the upper leaves injured on the plant, in the middle of leaves further down, and near the base of the lower leaves affected, particularly if the plant has been subjected to a single exposure of the pollutant. This type of injury is typical in the case of petunia and tobacco. Repeated exposures, of course, would affect different areas of tissue each day, and would eventually result in overall injury to leaves extending over much of the stem of the plant (Taylor, 1969).

Since the injured tissue of the leaf usually stops expanding, a pinched or distorted leaf margin may result as the rest of the uninjured leaf tissue continues to expand. The glazing or silvering symptom has been found (Borbrov, 1965) due to drying and desiccation of cells just under the epidermis, and to the separation of the two cellular layers. Cellular death and injury began first in cells adjacent to the substomatal cavity.

Repeated exposure of plants to PAN and other forms of oxidant air pollution often results in accelerated senescence of leaf tissue, chlorosis, leaf abscission, etc. It has been suggested (Rich, 1964) that these effects may be caused by endogenous ethylene production within the plant, triggered by continuous or successive exposures to low concentrations of oxidants in the atmosphere.

Relation between light and PAN injury High light intensity greatly increases the severity of plant injury from PAN, and minimum exposures to light before, during, and after exposure of the plants to the toxicant are necessary for the development of visible symptoms (Dugger, et al., 1963; Taylor, et al., 1961; Taylor, 1969). Early in the morning, it was necessary for the plants to receive about three hours of light before they became susceptible to injury. If as little as a 15-minute period of darkness was given during the middle of the day preceding exposure of the plants to PAN, a full hour of sunlight was required to restore sensitivity. Likewise, almost three hours of light following exposure of plants was necessary to secure symptom development.

Dugger and Ting (1968) have shown a good correlation between a decreased sulfhydryl content in plants brought about by irradiation with far-red light and increased resistance to injury by PAN. Perhaps it may be possible in the future to protect some of our greenhouse plants by simply flicking on a source of far-red light during smog periods of high PAN concentrations.

Table 22-4   BEDDING PLANTS SUSCEPTIBLE TO PAN INJURY

Susceptible		Intermediate	Resistant	
African Violets	Peppers	Tobacco	Azaleas	Forget-me-not
Asters	Petunias		Begonias	Gaillardias
Carnations	Primroses		Broccoli	Ivies
Celery	Roses		Cabbage	Onions
Dahlias	Tomatoes		Calendulas	Pansies
Endive	Salvias		Cauliflower	Periwinkles
Fuchsias	Snapdragons		Chrysanthemums	Sweet Peas
Impatiens	Sunflowers		Coleus	Touch-me-not
Lettuce	Sweet Basil		Cucumbers	Violas
Muskmelons				

Ethylene

Forty or 50 years ago, ethylene injury was common to greenhouse plants due to leaks in gas mains carrying the manufactured or "illuminating gas" in use at that time, which normally contained 2% to 8% ethylene. However, with the gradual replacement of manufactured gas by natural gas, which has a much lower level of ethylene (usually none), many plants known to be especially sensitive to ethylene are not damaged by prolonged exposures to gas mixtures containing as much as one or two percent natural gas (Gustafson, 1944). Hasek, et al. (1969) have published an excellent and comprehensive review of the effects of ethylene on flower crops.

Although ethylene is well down the list as a major cause of economic losses to the growers of *all* kinds of plants, it is a much more serious problem for *greenhouse grown* plants. A detailed economic impact study carried out

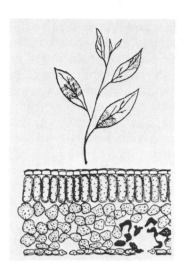

PAN injury. Note position effect with age of leaf. On sectioning, initial collapse is in the region of stomates.

in a densely populated, urbanized five-county area in Pennsylvania (in which there were located 177 commercial greenhouse production facilities) showed that almost half the plant losses in these greenhouses could be attributed to ethylene (Carroll and Jansma, 1972). The great susceptibility of many of our flower crops, and our tendency to concentrate their production in urbanized areas where ethylene is frequently present at injurious levels, causes it to be more damaging to floricultural crops in particular, than to other crops in general.

Sources The principal sources of ethylene gas now are (a) combustion products, particularly exhaust fumes from motor vehicles, and from dirty or improperly adjusted greenhouse heating devices; (b) effluents from industrial plants, such as polyethylene-manufacturing establishments (Hall *et al.*, 1957); and (c) the natural by-products of plant respiration, particularly those from diseased or damaged plant tissue. Ethylene from the latter source is particularly important as a cause of plant injury in flower storage rooms and refrigerators.

Symptoms Probably no other air pollutant causes as great a variety of symptom expression as does ethylene gas. In some cases, growth regulator types of injury occur, with the appearance of epinasty (bending down of petioles even though the plant is turgid) of foliage (Crocker and Zimmerman, 1932; Denny and Miller, 1935). In other cases, ethylene causes premature senescence, which shows up as yellowing and dropping of lower foliage, early ripening and dropping of florets in snapdragons, calceolarias, larkspur (Fischer, 1950) and roses (Shull, 1930), or "going to sleep" in carnation flowers (Crocker and Knight, 1908). Orchid flowers are very sensitive indicators of ethylene, with "dry sepal" injury showing up on cattleyas after exposure to concentrations as low as 0.1 ppm for eight hours (Davidson, 1949).

Plant stems and roots have been reported in other cases as losing their normal orientation to gravity. Cotton plants growing downwind from a polyethylene plant in Texas in fields where ethylene levels varied from 0.04 to 3.0 ppm lost apical dominance and became prostrate and vine-like in growth (Hall, et al., 1957). Plant roots have also lost their sense of direction and have actually grown up out of the ground instead of in the normal downward direction (Michner, 1938).

Ethylene, arising from incomplete fuel combustion in gas-fired unit heaters in tightly constructed plastic houses, has caused the production of thickened stems with short internodes and prolific development of side branches on carnations and chrysanthemums (Holley, 1960; Rogers, et al., 1969) (see photo). In addition, the latter workers were able to show that ethylene concentrations of one to two ppm in the air prevented or delayed flower bud initiation in short-day plants such as chrysanthemums and poinsettias, even though the plants were being subjected to flower-inducing day length treatments. Similar results have also been reported as being true for cocklebur, the classic "guinea-pig" plant for photoperiodic studies (Abeles, 1967). Thus, it would appear that this phenomenon could be true for short day plants in general.

Typical ethylene-injury symptoms on chrysanthemum. Left, control plant given 5 weeks of short-day treatment in an ethylene-free atmosphere. Right, plant of same age given same amount of short-day treatment in an atmosphere containing 1-2 ppm ethylene. Note the closely-spaced leaves, failure to initiate a flower bud, and loss of apical dominance as indicated by the breaking into growth of the axillary sideshoots. Similar symptoms developed on plants grown in tightly constructed plastic houses heated by gas-fired unit heaters lacking any special provision for air intake to supply the needs of the combustion.

One of the best ways for bedding plant producers to monitor their greenhouses for the possible presence of ethylene gas is to grow a few indicator plants along with their crops (see photo). Tomatoes, exposed to one ppm ethylene for three hours show epinasty, and African marigolds and sunflowers are even more sensitive, responding to 0.005 ppm ethylene. However, since tomato plants are usually easier to grow on a year round basis, they are probably the most logical and reliable indicator plant to use to warn flower growers of the presence of possibly harmful ethylene levels in the various growing areas.

Table 22-5   BEDDING PLANTS SUSCEPTIBLE TO ETHYLENE

Susceptible		Intermediate	Resistant
Calceolarias	Roses	Azaleas	Airplane Plants
Carnations	Snapdragons	Broccoli	Endive
Cucumbers	Stocks	Cabbage	Onions
Impatiens	Sunflowers	Cauliflower	Palms, Neanthe
Marigolds	Sweet Pea	Celosias	bella
Narcissus	Sweet Potatoes	Coleus	Podocarpus
Nasturtiums	Tomatoes	Fuchsias	Romaine lettuce
Orchids	Tulips	Gardenias	Sanseveria
Philodendrons		Lettuce	
		Pansies	
		Petunias	

Tomato test plants showing typical ethylene-injury symptoms. Left, untreated control plant; center, plant exposed to 1-2 ppm ethylene for 24 hours; right, plant exposed to 1-2 ppm ethylene for 1 week. A few tomato test plants in active growth should be maintained at all times by a grower who suspects that he might be experiencing ethylene problems. Then, if the plants begin to show these epinastic symptoms, he will be aware of his problem and may be able to correct it before it causes trouble to his other less-sensitive plants.

Effects of Environment on Toxicity by Air Pollutants

We have already seen that age and succulence of leaf tissue is often an important factor in determining relative susceptibility of different plant parts and that different pollutants act differently. Ozone, for example, affects the more mature tissue while PAN causes more damage on the younger leaves.

In addition to age of tissue, the environmental conditions under which the plants are grown are often of great importance in determining the extent and seriousness of damage. Here again we see variations from plant to plant and from pollutant to pollutant but, in general, it appears that those environmental conditions which favor the development of the most prolific and healthy plant growth result in the most severe air pollution injury. This is a particularly difficult problem because if we are to attempt to reduce damage from air pollutants by controlling the growing environment around the plants, it means that we might have to grow the plants under *less than ideal* conditions and be satisfied with a slow, poor quality plant growth in order to secure *any* growth. For the better bedding plant producers, this is not a very satisfactory alternative.

Moisture   Both soil moisture and the relative humidity of the air are known to affect stomatal opening, and if manipulated, can alter the degree of plant injury from air pollution exposures. Khatamian et al. (1973) were able to substantially reduce ozone injury to young tomato plants by subjecting them to mild moisture stress (but not sufficient to cause an actual reduction in total growth) prior to exposure to the pollutant. Similar results have been recorded for injury caused by SO_2. Withholding water from petunias prior to exposure to ozone and PAN also substantially reduced plant injury (Siedman et al., 1965). Moderate levels of salinity in the growing medium afforded considerable protection to alfalfa from high ambient levels of ozone (Hoffman et al., 1975), but building up soluble salt levels by bedding plant producers to protect their plants from air pollution injury is risky, and could easily result in greater losses of plant growth from salt injury than from the atmospheric problems.

Light   Since the major air pollutants (except for fluorides and nitrogen dioxide) enter leaves through open stomata, and since light is the major environmental factor controlling opening and closing of stomata, we would expect light to greatly affect plant sensitivity to air pollutants. Specific findings in this area have already been discussed in the section on PAN.

Experiments with *light intensity* have yielded conflicting results. In an experiment carried out using tobacco and beans, Dunning and Heck (1973) found that increasing light levels from 2,000 to 4,000 foot-candles resulted in greater ozone injury to bean, but had essentially no effect on tobacco. Dugger et al. (1963), to the contrary, found that bean plants grown under 900 ft-c of light were more susceptible to ozone injury than plants grown under 2,200 ft-c, and Noble (1965) and Menser and Street (1962) indicated that full sunlight reduced sensitivity in plants exposed to ambient levels of air pollutants. It would appear that the increasing susceptibility of plants as light levels increase from zero up to about 1,000 ft-c is related to the effects of light upon opening of the stomata, and that perhaps our observations of decreasing susceptibility of plants as light levels move even higher may be related to internal physiological changes leading to increased protoplasmic resistance.

Length of day (or *photoperiod*) has also been shown to affect plant susceptibility. Greater sensitivity to oxidant injury has been reported under 8-hour than under 16-hour photoperiods for annual bluegrass (Juhren, *et al.*, 1957), pinto beans (Heck and Dunning, 1967) and tobacco (Heck and Dunning, 1967; MacDowall, 1965).

Temperature   Temperature also has important effects on the response of plants to the photochemical pollutants such as ozone and PAN. Plants such as spinach, Romaine lettuce, and endive were as much as eight times more resistant to injury, if they were given a week of 55°F before exposure, instead of a more normal growing temperature of 75°F (Kendrick, *et al.*, 1956). In other cases, plant sensitivity has also been reported to decrease after a few days exposure to higher than normal temperatures of 85°F or higher. These changes in inherent plant sensitivity correlate well with changes in stomatal behavior, since pre-exposure of plants to either low or high temperatures for a few days prior to the air pollution exposure results in partial stomatal closure and reduced plant sensitivity (Feder, 1970). Bedding plant growers forced to grow their plants at lower temperatures because of the fuel shortage might reap an unexpected benefit—less air pollution injury.

Carbon Dioxide   Elevated levels of carbon dioxide in the air are known to cause partial stomatal closure, and it has been shown that exposure of tobacco plants to levels of 500 ppm CO_2 prior to exposure to damaging levels of ozone resulted in significantly less injury (Heck and Dunning, 1967). Since many commercial greenhouses are equipped for CO_2 enrichment of the air for improved plant growth, it might be possible to utilize control of this environmental variable for protection of susceptible plants from predicted air pollution episodes.

Plant Nutrition   Relationships between the level of plant nutrition for the different major mineral elements and the severity of air pollution damage from various substances are quite varied, but in most cases it seems that plants receiving optimum levels of nutrition, which cause lush, rapid growth, may be more susceptible to injury than plants whose growth has been partially inhibited by mineral element deficiencies or excesses. Fluoride susceptibility of tomato plants was least at deficient and at excessive levels of nitrogen and calcium (Brennan *et al.*, 1950), and ozone toxicity to tomato was minimal at low levels of phosphorus nutrition (Leone and Brennan, 1970).

228

In the case of sulfur dioxide injury, it has been shown that the severity of injury from exposures to this toxicant can be closely correlated with the level of sulfur nutrition provided by the growing medium. Sulfur dioxide fumigations caused more injury to tomato plants fertilized with high levels of sulfur than with low (Leone and Brennan, 1972); beans exhibited the same response (Adedipe et al., 1972). This is apparently due to the cumulative effects of sulfur uptake from both roots and leaves, which resulted in the accumulation of foliar sulfate levels in the toxic range. However, it was noted that beans which received high levels of sulfur nutrition from the roots were less susceptible to ozone injury than plants receiving lower levels of sulfur fertilization. It was hypothesized, in this situation, that the protective action of the high sulfur feeding may have resulted from increased numbers of sulfhydryl groups in the plant tissues, since it is known that such substances do offer some protection against oxidant injury (Fairchild et al., 1959).

Growing media   Today many florists are moving away from soil mixtures for growing their plants and are using lightweight artificial mixes more and more. These result in excellent plant growth with a minimum of problems, but the improved plant growth may become a partial liability in smoggy growing areas. Heck and Dunning (1967) found that bean plants grown in a mix consisting either of peat-perlite or vermiculite were more severely damaged by ozone than were plants of the same age grown in a soil mixture. This may be explained by the results obtained by Stolzy et al. (1961), who found that low oxygen diffusion rates in the growing medium made tomato plants more resistant to ozone injury, particularly when plant vigor was noticeably impaired.

Plant Protection Against Air Pollution

Research has suggested many measures that might be taken at specific times to protect individual kinds of plants from particular air pollutants. Due to the great diversity of toxicants and the great variability in the kinds of plants florists grow, however, there is not likely to be any one kind of treatment that will give perfect control of all problems for all kinds of plants except complete eradication of air pollutants from our plant growing atmospheres. This is unlikely to occur before we reach Utopia.

Legislative solutions   Air pollution problems are fundamentally "people" problems resulting from concentrated "people" activities—manufacturing, transportation, and all other endeavors presently considered necessary to provide us the "quality of life" we wish to attain. One possible long-range solution lies in the political arena, in the development and use of land use policy and air quality standards. Both processes must be made to work together. Good land use planning could prevent the location of agricultural enterprises in the vicinity of large specific sources of pollution, but this must be coupled with the enforcement of air quality standards in the areas designated for agricultural use at pollutant levels low enough to prevent serious plant injury. Admittedly this is a very difficult political combination to achieve, but slow progress is being made in many areas.

Breeding for plant resistance We already know that different plants vary widely in their inherent resistance to different air pollutants, and plant breeders have already made significant progress in developing resistant cultivars of several important crops. We have new cultivars of tobacco, onions, beans, and alfalfa (Rich, 1975); and sweet corn, tomatoes, petunias, red maples, and pines (National Research Council, 1977) resistant to different toxicants. Such programs are long-term in nature, however, and will require many years to be completed. Eighty-one petunia cultivars were screened (Cathey and Heggestad, 1973) and were divided into six classes ranging from very sensitive to very tolerant. Future cultivar development should take such information into account, along with all the other objectives considered in a plant improvement program.

Protectant sprays Immediate, short-term control measures are also important, especially until more permanent forms of control can be achieved. Allmendinger *et al.* (1950) showed that fluoride injury could be reduced in plants sprayed with alkaline substances such as lime. Ascorbic acid and other antioxidant sprays protect plants from oxidant air pollutants such as ozone and PAN (Freebairn and Taylor, 1960). Applications of several of the dithiocarbamate fungicides (zineb, maneb, or ferbam) have provided some protection from photochemical smog in California (Kendrick *et al.*, 1954). The above kinds of protection resulted from chemical reactions between the protectants on the surface of the leaf and the air pollutant, and broke down under long exposures and at high concentrations of the pollutants involved. Unsightly residues from the applied chemicals were also damaging on the plants used as ornamentals.

More recently, several of the newer *systemic* fungicides, such as benomyl, triarimol, carboxin, thiabendazole, and thiaphonate, have been shown to be even more effective than the dithiocarbamates (Ormrod, 1974; Rich, 1975). These materials have the advantage that they may be applied either as exterior sprays, or from the interior of the plant, in the form of soil additives or drenches, with essentially no surface residues. These substances show considerable promise and may be used for dual benefits—control of many common disease problems and simultaneous alleviation of air pollution injury on many kinds of ornamental plants. Concentrations and application rates normally used for fungicidal effectiveness would normally also be sufficient to provide pollution protection as well.

The chemical growth retardants chlormequat (Cycocel), SADH (B-Nine), and ancymidol (A-Rest) used on bedding plants to control plant height and improve "shelf-life" have also been shown to provide increased resistance to

230

air pollution stress (Cathey and Heggestad, 1972, 1973). These substances also increase plant tolerance to other kinds of stress—heat, cold, and drought. This results from the fact that such substances cause partial or complete closure of stomata for varying periods of time after application, which would decrease the entry of air pollutants into the leaves. They also cause many other metabolic changes in the plant, which could also be of importance. Given growth retardants affect only certain species of plants, and it has been shown that if the chemical is effective in shortening the plant, it will also provide air pollution protection. A high degree of protection results, however, *only* if the growth retardant chemical is used at about *twice* the concentration normally required for size control (e.g. SADH should be used as a 0.5% spray for air pollutant protection, rather than as 0.25%, which is the concentration used for height control in most plants).

A last-ditch control measure for air pollution injury for greenhouse plant growers is filtration of toxic gases from all air being brought into the growing structure. This has been done for a long time by research scientists studying air pollution problems in badly polluted areas. Darley and Middleton (1961) and Sherwood et al. (1970) described combination evaporative-cooler, activated-charcoal filtering units that can be fabricated for greenhouse use. Such a system costs money, of course, and adds to production costs, but in the most severe situations in highly urbanized areas, may be the last alternative available if a grower is to continue in business.

Air pollutants do not render it *impossible* for us to grow bedding plants in metropolitan areas, but they certainly make it more *challenging*. Only the most creative and inventive managers will have the ingenuity to stay ahead of these problems as we move toward the twenty-first century.

References

Complete reference citations to the papers cited in this chapter have not been included to save space. Anyone interested in specific citations may contact Dr. Marlin Rogers, Department of Horticulture, University of Missouri, Columbia, MO 65201.

BEWARE UNVENTED HEATERS!!

Every so often we come across a crop of bedding annuals or mums or something that is just plain unhappy. In obvious trouble. The grower doesn't really know why. But, there *is* a problem.

All too often, the culprit is an open-flame heater.

Each winter we come upon clear examples of gas damage from poorly vented unit heaters, or heaters with no provision for air inlet to the burner. In some cases, the damage is minor, just close to the heater. In others, it is devastating. One whole crop of bedding plants—40,000 square feet or so of poly greenhouses—perhaps a 60% loss. A pot-mum grower who lost 8,000 pots of mums—really a total loss. In another case, 35,000 square feet of cut mums—total loss.

Most of these problems occur in polyethylene greenhouses—probably because the poly houses are so airtight. But, one of the serious losses described above was in a glass greenhouse. So, it can happen under glass, too!

When you see these major losses, you wonder how many other crops are just not quite what they should be—again because of poorly vented heaters. And the grower never knows the difference.

So, we're taking a little space to describe the problem in some detail—and the remedy.

The Typical Problem

Most cases of injury from heaters look about like this. First, it is usually a polyethylene structure and usually almost airtight, which is easy to do with poly. The problem, of course, occurs only with open-flame unit heaters installed right in the greenhouse. Steam-unit heaters are never a problem, simply because there is no open flame.

The problem occurs where such open-flame gas or oil-fired heaters are either vented poorly or not at all. By venting, we mean that there is simply no provision for the "smoke" from the fire to get out of the greenhouse. What would happen if you tried to operate a regular coal boiler in your greenhouse without a chimney? There would be no place for the smoke and gases from the fire to escape—so they just all pour into the greenhouse. Some growers who had severe damage have reported the gases from the fire were so dense that they would make your eyes burn on cold nights. Obviously, there should be no noticeable smoke and gases from the fire in a greenhouse where the heaters are properly vented, even on a cold night.

The problem can also occur where there is no provision for an *air inlet* for the burner. When carbon-containing fuels are burned completely, the final end products are carbon dioxide and water vapor, but if incomplete combustion occurs because of oxygen deficiency, reduced substances such as ethylene, carbon monoxide and formaldehyde may be formed instead. Because large quantities of oxygen are needed for combustion during severely cold weather, and because the tight construction of plastic houses (particularly the popular, double-layer, air-inflated houses) prevents normal air infiltration or exchange with the outside atmosphere, inside oxygen levels can be reduced too low for complete fuel combustion, with the subsequent production of harmful air pollutants.

232

In regular glass greenhouse structures, there are usually two or more complete air changes per hour (depending upon outside conditions) by infiltration between the laps of the glass, which maintains an adequate supply of oxygen inside the structure for fuel combustion, except during extremely cold periods when the cracks might be filled with frozen condensate. For these reasons, it is *essential* that you provide a supply of fresh outside air to each burner unit, by installing a duct through the plastic wall, having a minimum cross-sectional area of 1 (one) square inch for each 2,000 BTU heat output rating of the heating device being used. For example, if you have a burner rated to put out 100,000 BTU of heat for your greenhouse, you need an air inlet pipe of a minimum of 8" in diameter.

What are some of the indications that you might be having self-induced air pollution problems? If you find that your heating units have gone out during the night during severely cold weather, you should consider the possibility of insufficient oxygen to support combustion of the fuel necessary to provide the large amounts of heat needed. If you detect unusual odors or smells emanating from your heater when you enter the house from the outside, you should also be suspicious. Both carbon monoxide and ethylene gases are basically odorless, but under combustion conditions where either or both of these might be produced, other substances such as aldehydes are also often produced which do smell, and might be detected by your nose. If you find that your heating unit is suddenly producing great quantities of soot, you should also have it checked, because this is another indication of poor combustion.

In addition to ethylene, burners can produce other harmful gases that can cause difficulty. We have often been consulted about cases in the early spring in which bedding plants or other young seedling plants were showing severe marginal leaf burns, stunting, and failure to grow—even in cases when tomato plants in the same greenhouse were *not* showing epinasty typical of ethylene injury. When we followed up on these cases, we generally found out that when outdoor temperatures moderated so that less heating and more ventilation was being used, the problem seemed to disappear and was no longer troublesome. Judd (1973) reported on such a case, in which sulfur dioxide was eventually determined to be the problem.

Symptoms

The several crops we have seen:

Bedding annuals   Serious injury from heaters will actually curl the leaves of such plants as tomatoes, petunias, salvias, and marigolds. Soon, the top growth is deformed, stunted, and obviously unhappy. Impatiens seem to be very susceptible. Tomatoes are especially unhappy in these fumes—again, leaves curl badly and the plants just stop growing. Actually, all plants seem to be more or less affected by it—perhaps tomatoes are particularly sensitive.

Mums Response of mums to fumes from heaters is very typical, really very easy to spot, once you get to know what to look for. As each stem comes up and starts to form its bud, the gas injury seems first to simply delay the development of the bud. The bud will grow to perhaps a $1/8''$ to $3/16''$ size, then it will stop developing. Soon vigorous side buds will start to grow out past the center bud. They will be typically halfhearted, semi-vegetative shoots. There is a bud in the tip of each of them, but something is holding the buds back from normal development. By the time all this has happened, the plant is weeks past its normal flowering date—and we still have only these halfhearted little $1/4''$ or less buds. It's a little like heat delay in midsummer. If the problem is caught in its early stages, and if the side buds are quickly removed, and the problem of the heater corrected, the buds might go on and develop. Once it gets out of hand, and once the side buds have passed the original center bud by an inch or two, probably the best thing is to discard the crop and start over.

Typically on the mum problem, by the time the crop should be in full flower and ready for market, we have only the aborted center bud and several $2''$ or $3''$ half-vegetative side shoots to show for our effort.

Remedy

When making a new installation, or trying to troubleshoot the problems of an old one, call upon the engineers and service personnel of the firm supplying the heaters for consultation and assistance. They are anxious to help you use their equipment so that it performs properly and successfully for you, so you will come back year after year with additional business.

It would be almost certain that any unit heaters installed by a reputable firm would have built into them an adequate-sized vent to allow for escape of smoke and gases from the fire. Be sure that the vent is carried out through the roof so that the gas can escape. To ensure a proper draft, the outside exhaust stack must be tall enough to be well above the roof peaks of nearby structures. It is also a good idea to have a proper cap on its top to prevent downdrafts, to prevent exhaust gases being carried back downward into your greenhouses by gusting winds. If exhaust fans for ventilation in the greenhouse go on while the burner is still operating or just after it has shut off, this may also pull exhaust gases back into the greenhouse. Many growers have interconnected controls to prevent such occurrences. Birds' nests built in your flues during the summer when the heating units were not in use have also been found, in a few cases, preventing escape of the exhaust gases.

Still one other point needs to be watched. Each unit heater needs to be disassembled regularly—at least once a year before the major heating season begins—so that the heat exchanger inside can be inspected for possible cracks or holes caused by rust. The flames and heated exhaust gases pass through the inside of the heat exchanger on their way up the exhaust stack, and if there are holes in it, or in your exhaust pipes, air pollutant gases may leak out into your greenhouse and cause problems. Since nearly all unit heaters are completely enclosed in an outer sheet metal cover, it means that you have to dismantle them to make your inspection possible, but it is an essential type of preventative maintenance that needs to be carried out each fall without fail. It is possible to purchase unit heaters in which the heat exchanger is constructed of stainless steel, but these are considerably more expensive than the stock models. However, if you lose a greenhouse full of saleable plants from self-induced air pollution, that might have been an inexpensive form of insurance.

Finally, be sure to have properly sized air intakes for each gas- or oil-fired heater unit. On the coldest nights, there is a great temptation to stuff an old sack in them to keep all that cold air from coming into the greenhouse unit, but that is the time when the air is needed most for combustion. If you try to save a few pennies during the night by doing this, you may have plant injuries worth dollars or hundreds of dollars the next morning!

G.V.B.

Chapter 23

NUTRIENT/pH ADJUSTMENTS FOR MODERN MIXES*

THE ROLE OF SOIL TESTING

Monitoring of plant nutrients has become an increasingly important aspect of the overall effort to enhance productivity and the quality of floral crops.

The uncontrollable, extremely high and low nutrient levels associated with the use of decaying organic matter or dry fertilizer applications have been dramatically reduced due to the adoption of constant liquid fertilization programs. Most floral crop growers have installed fertilizer injector systems which permit them to apply high analysis water soluble fertilizers through their irrigation lines with the aim of maintaining an optimal level of nutrients throughout the production period.

In spite of the fact that the producer has greatly improved control over fertilizer applications, a program for monitoring nutrient levels continues to be an important procedure to include in an overall production program. This is

*Contributed by John C. Peterson, Associate Professor, Department of Horticulture, Ohio State University. Editor's note: The light organic mixes so widely used today demand important different nutrient programs. We have called on John Peterson of Ohio State to spell out some of these points.

due to the fact that the nutrient content of fertilizer water and the level of nutrients within a growing medium is one of the new factors that influence plant growth which we as humans cannot readily detect. Whereas light, temperature, and moisture levels can be monitored in a relative manner using our human senses, the only manner in which we can detect fertilizer levels in water and growing media is by analytical testing. Therefore, periodic monitoring is critical.

The current system for providing nutrients to plants within irrigation water is based upon mechanical systems and human assistance, both of which can misfunction. Errors in mixing procedures and the malfunction of equipment can lead to situations where insufficient or excess fertilizer is applied.

In addition, the amount of fertilizer applied and retained within a growing medium can be influenced by the frequency and quantity of irrigation water applied. Since this can vary depending upon weather and worker activity, no accurate assumption can be made about the actual nutrient content within a growing medium.

A simple monitoring system can be employed whereby a conductivity (soluble salts) meter can be used to monitor the fertilizer in irrigation water and growing medium. The use of this type of program can permit a grower to easily monitor the general level of nutrient in water and growing media. Specifics about this type of monitoring program can usually be obtained from county extension agents or university floriculture specialists.

It is important to point out that the conductivity meter monitoring system provides a relative indication of how much fertilizer is contained within a solution or growing medium. It does not provide a perspective as to the specific plant nutrients that are contained in the solution or medium. For example, a desirable conductivity (soluble salts) level can be obtained by adding table salt to water or a growing medium, but this certainly would not allow for the growth of quality plants. For this reason a complete specific element analysis becomes important.

Many floral crop producers will regularly schedule sample collection and analysis into their production program. The findings of the analysis can be used to modify fertilization programs to avoid problems before they become serious. Relatively speaking, the use of a commercial or university growing medium analysis service is quite inexpensive, particularly if one considers the impact of losing just a few plants to fertilization problems.

Tissue Analysis

Yet another aspect of nutritional monitoring, which should be considered as part of an overall nutritional monitoring program, is foliar or tissue analysis. Tissue analysis allows a producer to gain one more additional perspective about the impact of a given fertilization program upon the nutritional status and in turn the quality of a crop.

Many factors can influence the uptake of nutrients into a plant other than the amount and type of fertilizers which are applied to a crop. Tissue analysis permits a grower to definitely determine if the nutrients which are being applied are actually being taken up into the plant in adequate quantities to optimize crop growth and quality. In light of the fact that many factors can influence nutrient uptake, a tissue analysis will enable a grower to identify fertilizer program modifications that must be made to compensate for other factors that may influence nutrients uptake. Tissue analysis is the definitive answer as to whether a fertilization program is working properly.

Growers are often faced with the question of when and how often should nutrient levels be monitored. There happens to be no clearcut answer to this question. Often the answer relates to the overall production precision within a production program. This includes employee efficiency, mechanical system accuracy, and any other factors which might alter the application, utilization, and leaching of nutrients within the growing medium. It all seems to boil down to the fact that the more frequent the monitoring the less likelihood that problems will occur and the greater the opportunity to produce a high-quality crop. Certainly, weekly or biweekly monitoring of fertilizer levels in irrigation water and growing media with a conductivity meter should not be a difficult or costly program to follow. A complete laboratory growing medium and tissue analysis should be easy to justify on a monthly or bimonthly basis, depending on total production time. Certainly, growing medium and tissue samples should be submitted when the first sign of a production problem appears.

It is interesting to note that very frequently the source of floral crop production problems relates to nutritional problems. Again, this probably results from our inability to readily detect fertility levels with our human senses. This fact alone should emphasize the need for a consistent nutrient monitoring program.

ADJUSTING pH/NUTRIENT LEVELS TO MODERN MIXES

Perspectives about nutrient levels and pH level for modern growing mixes clearly need to be modified. For many years floral crop producers have utilized information developed by agronomists who have worked with mineral field soils. Currently, very few growers, if any, are utilizing mineral soils for the production of their crops. In recent years the floriculture industry has witnessed a shift to "soilless" organic potting media.

Research indicates that the chemical and nutrient exchange properties of our modern organic potting media differ significantly when compared to mineral field soil. Findings indicate that the pH at which nutrient availability is optimized is approximately 5.5, a whole pH unit lower than the optimum pH for a mineral field soil. Furthermore, the levels of nutrients which must be applied to crops growing in organic mixes so as to optimize growth must also be modified. The 200 parts per million (ppm) fertilizer level of nitrogen (N) and potassium (K) for constant fertilization which was once thought to be optimal has been recognized to be generally too low for organic mixes. A fertilizer application level of 250 to 300 ppm N and K is now viewed to be the optimal concentration for most floral crops growing in organic potting mixes.

The move to modern organic mixes has also heightened our awareness of the need to provide certain major and trace nutrients. Sufficient residual trace and major nutrients were contained in field soil, and in the past growers did not need to be as concerned about them. Floral crop producers who use modern organic mixes must now heighten their concern about providing trace elements either as a preplant amendment (fritted trace elements) or in a soluble form as part of a soluble fertilization program.

As a result of the reduced amount of limestone which is being incorporated into organic mixes and the precipitation problems associated with formulating soluble fertilizers which contain both phosphorus and calcium or magnesium, low calcium and magnesium levels seem to be more prevalent. More attention must be given to supplying magnesium and calcium as preplant amendments in a manner that does not influence pH. Otherwise, a soluble form must be provided as part of a soluble fertilizer program.

Obviously, our growing medium composition has changed and so must our views about fertilization practices change.

SECTION IV

Computers!

Chapter 24

SUGGESTIONS ON GETTING STARTED

Already today (mid-1980s), at least some computers are a part of most substantial commercial growing operations. And their role in efficient production is expanding rapidly.

Typically in such a situation, many growers are anguishing over whether to move on computers. And since computers can do three basic jobs for the growers, the other question is—which one first? Let's take a try at that one.

Accounting   Printing invoices, statements, doing payroll (including checks), and creating monthly and annual operating statements and balance sheets. Computers can also do cash flow projection. Also, regular surveying and aging of accounts receivable and accounts payable. This application is clearly the most widely used by growers today.

Crop planning   Does such tasks as crop planning, space planning, keeping inventory of plants available for sale, providing cost data, and much more. They also provide much of the data helpful to the grower in planning his workload, his buying, etc.

Environmental control computers A newer, more specialized application widely used in Holland today, very little in the U.S. and Canada. The "EC" computers do the basic temperature control job. But, they also can and do much more—on hundreds of ranges. Key examples: controlling humidity, effecting major fuel savings (15–25% often) by more efficient operation of the heating system. And equally important, they can make life so much easier for the grower. See details later in this section.

WHICH ONE FIRST?

Our vote for number one: go first on accounting computers. To us they effect the most direct saving in labor. The fastest payback for equipment cost. But we do urge growers to install accounting equipment that can eventually "talk" to your crop planning computer. It's so sensible! You enter a sale for 500 pot mums, and this one data entry will create an invoice to the customer, update your sales totals, and at the same time, it updates your unit cost (cost per pot), your space control, and your inventory control. All that is done with just one entry—if your accounting and your crop planning computers are tied together. As of the mid-1980s, only Plant Master has both crop planning and accounting capabilities.

The choice between environmental and crop planning computers for number two in order probably depends on the grower's circumstances. A strong case for adopting crop planning as number two can be made—especially on ranges of fair size, in places with not too much diversity of crops.

Carl Loeb, Ball Technical Services, makes an interesting case for this approach.

> I would move crop planning to #2 for the reason that the average grower probably spends between 6 and 12% of his annual gross in energy. If he installs environmental control systems under ideal circumstances perhaps he saves 25% of that 6 to 12%. The potential savings, therefore, are between 1½ and 3% of the gross. Labor on the other hand ranges anywhere from 20–30%. Crop planning reduces labor. Therefore, the impact that crop planning can have on the grower's bottom line can be more substantial than the impact that environmental control systems can have. Additionally, the ability to get the maximum production out of one's greenhouses will contribute significantly to the bottom line in ways that are difficult to project because some growers may be more efficient than others. But in general, I think that the economic impact to the American grower of crop planning and good management information is of more economic importance than environmental control systems will be.

244

Large ranges in cold climates (heavy fuel expense) would probably realize more than average savings from environmental computers—and might well consider this approach as number two in their order of computerizing. We do hear of 15 to 25% fuel savings on such ranges after installation of good environmental control computers.

The following chapters provide more details on these three types of computers.

G.V.B.

Chapter 25

COMPUTERIZED ACCOUNTING

Let's consider mainly here a grower interested in installing computerized accounting today—but, also wanting in another year or two to go into crop planning, cost accounting, etc. A very typical situation. We do recommend that growers going into accounting only plan from the start to accommodate the addition of the crop planning function to their computer.

The key to this: To buy computer and accounting software which has the capacity to interact with crop planning software. It's possible to buy accounts receivable program from supplier A, a general ledger program (software) from supplier B, and crop costing software from supplier C. The problem: When you put it all together, the three programs would almost certainly not have the capability of sharing information from one to the other.

Let's put it a different way: The same grower installing accounting software today, but planning to go into crop accounting later, would certainly want to have the capability ultimately of making one entry—for example for a sale of 100 pot mums—and being sure that that entry would do all of the things needed throughout both of the accounting and crop costing systems. Specifically, entering the invoice for a sale of 100 pot mums to customer A must do the following things:

- Create the invoice to the customer

- Create shipping ticket

- Update accounts receivable

- Update the general ledger

- Update the financial statements

- Enter data for cost accounting

- Enter data for material handling

- Update greenhouse space available

Again, a grower going into an accounting computer only today, if he plans correctly, will be able to add software to his accounting computer system so that he can do all of the above things—from a single entry. Obviously important!

To do accounting, let's say on an acre of wholesale or a retail growing range, the grower will need:

- Computer

- Printer

- Hard disk drive—Floppy disks are slower, and most important in green-house applications, are subject to corruption from moisture and dust in the air.

- Appropriate software

Software needed for an accounting-only application would be as follows:

- Order entry/inventory control—This is the program used to enter all customer orders, sales tickets into your system. It is the basis for keeping inventory control records.

- Accounts receivable

- Accounts payable

- General ledger

- Payroll—ability to write checks and keep tax records

Each of these will come to the grower on a floppy disk—which the grower can immediately transfer to his hard disk.

Here's how we expect that the grower of the 1990s will be spending some part of his precious time—getting information from the computer and making management decisions with the computer—toward a more profitable operation. The grower here is Paul Dinkins, Eagle River, Alaska.

MULTI-USERS

The owners of a half-acre or perhaps an acre of wholesale pot plant range with a limited number of sales tickets can probably handle his entire workload of accounting and crop planning activities with one computer, one printer. However, the same acre of greenhouse with an active retail department with thousands of sales tickets, especially a lot of credit sales, would probably need several "terminals"—a terminal being a computer with a typewriter console.

A busy or larger retail operation might need half a dozen or even several dozen of these terminals depending on the volume, especially of invoices, to be written. An important point here: A single terminal might handle the job if you are willing to delay writing invoices in order to create payroll or to do financial statements, for example. But if a business is to be operated efficiently, there should be enough terminal capacity to keep both the flow of invoice writing and the other accounting activities up to date. It's the old story—how can you manage your business efficiently if you don't have up-to-date information?

Standard Plant Master equipment today is a multi-user system and can be run on up to six terminals.

George Lucht, who operates Malmborg's, Minneapolis, has moved into computers. Here is George getting some answers.

TRAINING

Another important point in selecting equipment is to select the supplier who offers good training for you or your staff person who will do the computer work. This should mean both initial training—upon receiving the equipment, also ongoing support. Answers to questions and problems, updating of software as better programs become available. And, software is constantly improving, of course.

SECURITY OF INFORMATION

A point in favor of computerizing: It permits real security. It's standard practice, and by the way highly recommended, that all computerized data be taken off the hard disk daily—and stored out of the building. This is no big job—perhaps 15 minutes for most operations. And what it means is in case of a fire no matter how severe, you will still have such vital records as your accounts receivable, accounts payable, etc. We've all heard the story that 80% of businesses who lose their accounts receivable in a fire never reopen their doors! With manual records, you just can't keep the copies elsewhere—it isn't practical.

HOW ABOUT NURSERY PRODUCTION?

Growers producing both flowers or bedding plants and hardwood nursery stock can certainly include their nursery production in all this computerized equipment. Of course nursery production only can also be handled with almost the same equipment.

PRESENT SUPPLIERS

There are two firms who presently supply crop costing software and computers: Ball Technical Services, 211 N. 1st Street, Mt. Vernon, Washington 98273 and Yoder Brothers, P.O. Box 230, Barberton, Ohio 44203. Since this equipment is changing rapidly, better consult these suppliers as to the capabilities of their equipment. And others as new suppliers enter the market. This section talks Ball Technical equipment—because as of this printing, it (and Yoder's in some cases) is the only supplier available.

G.V.B.

Chapter 26

CROP SPACE PLANNING, INVENTORY CONTROL, COSTING*

Here we're talking computerizing of production planning, inventory control, space control, and most important of all, unit cost. What does it cost me to grow and sell a 6" mum, for example?

All of these things can be and are being done today (mid-1980s) by real commercial growers. Across the U.S. and Canada. Very little of this in Europe so far, by the way. Strange.

We are quite aware of the many growers who have often bought very costly computers—and today they are gathering dust. But there is equipment now on the market which will really give the grower practical control of these important functions. And perhaps best of all, some suppliers of this equipment are providing thorough training and followup service—so important to success, especially with those unfamiliar with computers. As most of us are.

*Chapters 26 and 27 are based on material from 1983–84 *Grower Talks,* by the author.

The two suppliers of crop computers as of this date are Ball Technical Services, 211 N. 1st Street, Mt. Vernon, Washington 98273 and Yoder Brothers, P. O. Box 230, Barberton, Ohio 44203. Since we are more familiar with the Ball Technical Service equipment, we'll talk mainly about it. Both are reputable suppliers.

HOW BIG A GROWER?

Carl Loeb, Ball Technical Services, says that a range should be 25,000 to 50,000 square feet with $250,000 to $500,000 a year sales. We would add to this that the grower with fewer crops or, best of all, a one-crop specialty (like flat annuals) can get the most from this equipment with the least effort. Especially if he is wholesale, selling major quantities to a few customers. At the other extreme, the half-acre retail grower with small bits of dozens of crops on his range will have the hardest time using this sort of equipment on his crop planning. However, such a grower, with a large number of charge sales tickets would get a strong payback on an accounting computer. Back to the smaller retail grower with many crops, pressure seems to build from all sides on such growers to simplify their operations by growing a lot fewer items and more of them. And buying in semi-finished or finished the other items.

For the record, the Ball Technical package, and generally Yoder's equipment, is capable of handling the needs of a variety of growers. Certainly pot plant and foliage producers, bedding plant producers, nursery growers, and outdoor producers.

A COMPUTER CAN DO SO MANY THINGS!

We've seen so many growers recently who have bought computers. Some small Apples, some big $35,000 IBMs—and more. Up to $500,000! Typically, the grower had some one task in mind. Like inventory control. Many do parts of their accounting. But so often these computers are delivering only 10% or less of their potential. Few are doing effective crop/space planning, cost accounting, inventory control. The Ball Technical plan offers the capability of doing most or all of the crop planning—plus the accounting work—for a typical grower operation. Certainly including inventory control. Once you've fed all the details of your operation into the black box, it *can* give you back so very much. If you ask for it.

The paragraphs that follow will list and describe this flow of information. That's the job of a computer. To supply management information to the businessman.

So here we go:

We hate people who throw their favorite buzzwords up to us. But there are several that do help understand it all.

Database   All those details of what you grow—spacing, respacing, pot sizes, soil mixes, etc.

Disk (hard disk drive)   Think of it as a cross between a tape recorder and a phonograph record. But, instead of recording and playing music, it records and plays back all sorts of information you feed into it. Call it an electronic filing system. Some are ''hard'' disks. There are also soft ''floppy'' disks (also called diskettes). Smaller, less costly. Useful. Okay in clean, dust-free application. Problems in dirty environments.

Software   The ''program''—the way you and I can tell the black box what we want it to do for us. A program typically can record and sort out information on a specific activity (like inventory control). It directs the computer (on your request) to make reports to you. The program normally comes to you on a disk. Often a floppy disk. Which can be transferred to a hard disk.

The computer   The black box with a typewriter keyboard and a TV ''screen.'' It's sort of the traffic center. You use it to call back the information you put on the disk, display it on the TV screen, and change it if you wish. And if you want that TV screen information in writing, just tell it to feed the story over to the printer—part of the package. The computer itself also can store data. Mainly, it temporarily holds the information on which you are working in its limited memory. And, it can compute. Do calculations. It is a ''computer!''

Printer   It's an electric typewriter, capable of typing on endless rolls of paper—anything you want in writing. It's also a word processor. It types so fast!

Remote terminals   Let's say you have the computer (black box), the hard disk for information storage, plus a printer. Now it's spring and you have a heavy load of sales tickets to feed into your system. You need three or four more black boxes for clerks to enter sales tickets. Each extra box is a ''remote terminal.'' They feed data back through your main terminal. They can be ''smart''—that is, computers themselves—or ''dumb''—able to function only when attached to the computer.

Environmental control program   Controls the greenhouse environment. Temperature, humidity, etc.

Megabyte How much information can our computer system store for us? A little can be stored temporarily in the black box—while we are working on it. Most of its permanent storage capacity is on the hard disk—a part of your system. The Ball Technical Services Tandy 16 disk will hold 12 megabytes—which is 12 million characters. A number or a letter (A or B) constitutes a character. Six hundred typewritten pages equal one megabyte of data.

RAM (Random Access Memory) That part of the system's memory that is stored in the black box. One megabyte of RAM is, again, one million characters. Most small computers offer 64,000 to 512,000 characters of RAM. So much for buzzwords.

Here are three of the key messages computers can send to the grower: availability to fill an order, unit cost for a pot mum or a poinsettia, and "do we have any space available for April 15?"

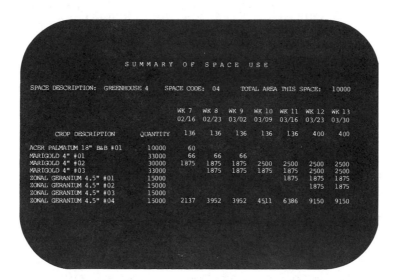

SUMMARY OF SPACE USE

SPACE DESCRIPTION: GREENHOUSE 4   SPACE CODE: 04   TOTAL AREA THIS SPACE: 10000

CROP DESCRIPTION	QUANTITY	WK 7 02/16	WK 8 02/23	WK 9 03/02	WK 10 03/09	WK 11 03/16	WK 12 03/23	WK 13 03/30
		136	136	136	136	136	400	400
ACER PALMATUM 18" B&B #01	10000	60						
MARIGOLD 4" #01	33000	66	66	66				
MARIGOLD 4" #02	30000	1875	1875	1875	2500	2500	2500	2500
MARIGOLD 4" #03	33000		1875	1875	1875	1875	2500	2500
ZONAL GERANIUM 4.5" #01	15000					1875	1875	1875
ZONAL GERANIUM 4.5" #02	15000						1875	1875
ZONAL GERANIUM 4.5" #03	15000							
ZONAL GERANIUM 4.5" #04	15000	2137	3952	3952	4511	6386	9150	9150

One great strength of computerized greenhouse management: You know a week at a time just how many square feet of empty space are lurking around your entire range. It comes to you on a printout (as above). Note "Total area this space: 10,000." That means that this printout reports a space status of 10,000 square feet. Now on the bottom line of the printout note from the left— week seven (February 16), you are using 2,137 square feet of the 10,000 available. And so on, weekly across the whole year.

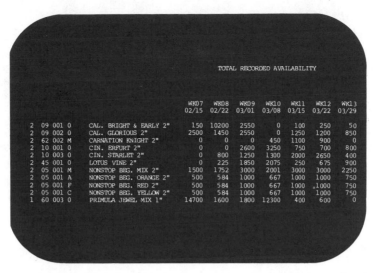

```
                                          TOTAL RECORDED AVAILABILITY


                                     WK07   WK08   WK09   WK10   WK11   WK12   WK13
                                     02/15  02/22  03/01  03/08  03/15  03/22  03/29
  2  09 001 0   CAL. BRIGHT & EARLY 2"   150  10200   2550      0    100    250     50
  2  09 002 0   CAL. GLORIOUS 2"        2500   1450   2550      0   1250   1200    850
  2  62 002 M   CARNATION KNIGHT 2"        0      0      0    450   1100    900      0
  2  10 001 0   CIN. ERFURT 2"             0      0   2600   3250    750    700    800
  2  10 003 0   CIN. STARLET 2"            0    800   1250   1300   2000   2650    400
  2  45 001 0   LOTUS VINE 2"              0    225   1850   2075    250    675    900
  2  05 001 M   NONSTOP BEG. MIX 2"     1500   1752   3000   2001   3000   3000   2250
  2  05 001 A   NONSTOP BEG. ORANGE 2"   500    584   1000    667   1000   1000    750
  2  05 001 F   NONSTOP BEG. RED 2"      500    584   1000    667   1000   1000    750
  2  05 001 C   NONSTOP BEG. YELLOW 2"   500    584   1000    667   1000   1000    750
  1  60 003 0   PRIMULA JEWEL MIX 1"   14700   1600   1800  12300    400    600      0
```

Another real joy of computerized growing: You know at a glance anytime what isn't sold of any crop. It comes in several ways. Example: Note the "Total recorded availability" form; the top line, Calceolaria Bright & Early 2", says that for week seven we have 150 plants unsold, week eight 10,200 unsold plants, etc., weekly across the full year. This report is available constantly on a moment's notice.

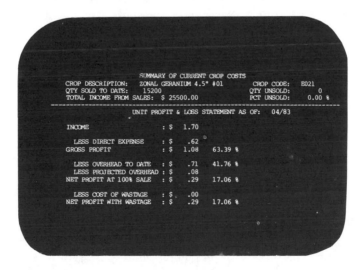

```
                       SUMMARY OF CURRENT CROP COSTS
  CROP DESCRIPTION:   ZONAL GERANIUM 4.5" #01          CROP CODE:   E021
  QTY SOLD TO DATE:   15200                            QTY UNSOLD:      0
  TOTAL INCOME FROM SALES:  $ 25500.00                 PCT UNSOLD:   0.00 %
  ------------------------------------------------------------------------
                    UNIT PROFIT & LOSS STATEMENT AS OF:   04/83

  INCOME                   : $  1.70

     LESS DIRECT EXPENSE   : $   .62
  GROSS PROFIT             : $  1.08     63.39 %

     LESS OVERHEAD TO DATE : $   .71     41.76 %
     LESS PROJECTED OVERHEAD : $  .08
  NET PROFIT AT 100% SALE  : $   .29     17.06 %

     LESS COST OF WASTAGE  : $   .00
  NET PROFIT WITH WASTAGE  : $   .29     17.06 %
```

Clearly the most valuable of all reports is simply unit cost of your major crops. The printout above will tell you that for a crop of 15,200 4½" geraniums, you realize revenue of $25,500 or $1.70 per plant. And that your net profit per plant (since all plants were sold) is 29¢. And that's real cost—based on your labor cost, your fuel, etc.

It's called "Plant Master" by Ball Technical—the group of programs that enable a grower to do crop planning, inventory control, crop cost records. Once you've fed all the details of what you grow into the computer, you can ask (anytime) for:

Cost and selling price   With reasonable accuracy you get *your own* cost per flat of annuals, or per 6" pot mum. Then ask for the average net dollars you received for your pot mums (dollar sales divided by plants actually sold). Plants dumped mean a higher cost per plant sold. All this is on a per plant basis. *At long last, a meaningful reading on profitability of your major crops.* And, an important guide in setting prices. Which are *your* winners?

Any bench space available?   Key question: Will the crops I have planned for the 12 months ahead fill my available bench space? Will there be overflow or crowding? One Eastern grower has already found 5000 square feet of bench space idle during his busy spring months. Costly waste. Typically, it was not 10 empty benches, but a few square feet here, a ¼ bench there. And often, a house of pot geraniums—from which ⅓ of the crop had been sold.

The system tells you months ahead, by week, how many total square feet of bench space are available—and by weeks, how much of it you have filled.

What's the workload look like next week?   Your friendly computer will tell you "we have about 6000 flats of annuals to transplant, 10,000 4" annuals to space, etc. Attention: mobile work crew."

Inventory control!   Can we fill an order for 4500 6" poinsettias? So important to keep track of orders—against the available supply. Per variety, per pot size. And the customer is on the phone! The black box can give you the answer—now. You, the grower, can easily get such answers yourself.

So often we hear of plants dumped—plants which could have been sold if the grower had had good inventory control. Again, wasteful.

Holiday shipping   Always a pressure point. The computer provides your shipping manager with accurate information ahead of time—on how many of what goes where. So he can plan for the necessary trucks and help.

How many petunia seeds will I need and when?   Ask the computer what seed, pots, soil mix, labels, etc., will be needed and when. Seed, by the way, is based on total plants to be grown of each variety. Plus a germination shrink factor.

Budget everything one year ahead   Under this system, you the owner do plan what you will grow a full year ahead. Decisions are made on what to grow and when—informally, by the owner. Based on demand, space available, etc. And your judgment. You feed it into the system. And let's make the point now that management must know what will sell—and at what price. And how to grow it, good quality. And management finally has to face up to such difficult, but vital tasks as collecting old bills. A good computer program can strengthen a good manager who knows and does these things. It won't do them for him.

Anyway, once the grand plan for the year is formed, it can be fitted into the system. From this, the manager can get all sorts of information on the year's operation. If you don't like some parts of it, change them on the screen—*before* the mistake is made in the greenhouse.

And most of all, a projected expense and revenue for the whole year's business—in advance. A profit forecast!

OTHER PROGRAMS AVAILABLE

VisiCalc®   It's a small, but very useful program. Hard to describe. You get it on a floppy disk. With the VisiCalc (visual calculator), you can sketch out ideas, plans, etc., right on the TV screen. It enables you to make an electronic spreadsheet. A good example: You've got 20 greenhouses. You put numbers from 1 to 20 across the top of the screen, then you list your 10 major crops down the left margin. All "typed" onto the screen. Then you can start filling in crops. "Let's fill greenhouses 1 to 10 with Easter pot mums." If it doesn't quite fit, you quickly "rub it out" and start over.

As you get to know it, VisiCalc is a great tool to project a crop "on paper." Rough out costs, returns, net profit. At different spaces or sowing dates. Try it several ways! VisiCalc can multiply, divide, etc. Can divide a whole row of figures by a constant. And, lastly, when you get your "plan" all done, it can be fed directly to your hard disc.

So many people swear by VisiCalc. It is widely used by business. My neighbor keeps his investments portfolio on it.

Grofile   Ball Technical has a program designed for growers who supply plants to brokers. This is of much help in keeping track of prebooking. And responding to constant questions on availability.

Scripsit program   Now you can create a form letter—to go to 500 customers. They will all be typed originals, and the computer can automatically type in each customer's name and address and change a word or two at the bottom of the letter if you wish.

Profile An electronic filing system program. You can put 1000 names and addresses into your "file" (that hard disk again) in any order. You can call back all the Bs or Cs—or all those who live in various nearby towns. Great for keeping your customer list sorted out by groups as you wish. "Let's write a spring promotion letter to all of our homeowner accounts."

All these accessory programs work right through your basic computer, printer, and disk storage.

For the record, all of the "crop programs" dealing with crop planning, crop costs, etc., are proprietary Ball Technical software. Done by Carl Loeb's programming staff. Most of the accounting type programs are "off the shelf." Modified to conform to growers' needs.

WHO DOES WHAT?—IMPORTANT QUESTION

How much should the owner/proprietor be involved in all of this? How about the bookkeeper? How much can be done by lower-cost clerks?

A good starting point: People who work closely with computers in businesses so often urge the proprietor/owner to get very much involved. Especially at first. Really, *this is a whole new approach to planning and managing a business.* If you, the owner, aren't thoroughly familiar with it—and even, more important, thoroughly supportive of it, odds for success go down.

One real plus for Carl Loeb's approach is the one-week training course he has organized. It's aimed at the owner. I took several days of it myself. It leads you slowly (gently!) into all of the strange, new procedures, inevitable buzzwords, etc. You'll work hard, especially the first day or two—but always with a sympathetic staff at your elbow. You spend the first several days just learning how to bring data up from the storage disk onto the screen. You change it, delete something, add something, then send it back. It's sort of the basic skill of working with a computer—which you must have to be able to get answers easily and quickly to your questions later on. And, of course, this equips you, the owner, to make those all important adjustments yourself—as you go along.

No, you don't have to be a typist to make it work or to call up information from the disk storage. But certainly typing skill is needed for a volume of data entry.

The other and more important phase: You learn how Carl's Plant Master program really works. How you feed all that information about your greenhouse into your database. Clerks can actually do it—but you've got to show them— or have Carl's staff train them. (Consultation is available at your office.) How you can constantly and easily monitor—and change—any part of the plan. How you can call for your space availability for the next two years. ("We've got four empty beds in January, February—let's get some 2¼" primulas.")

And so important: Bring up for study the cost projections for your major crop. "My pot mums will cost me $2.96 if I sell 100%. I'm going to need at least $4." And, after the crop is sold, you see how you really did. This has major potential for improving growers' profit pictures.

And, after you get the feel of all this and have a year or two of experience, you can sit there at the computer and "create" a crop on the computer. Let's say one cutting per 6" poinsettia at 14" × 14" final spacing. If the crop looks like a loser at the best price you can get, try it at 12" × 12" (or 9" × 10" like Don Layser does) or try starting with specialist 2¼". See what that does to profitability. Or think about raising the price!

Sort of a "what if" game! Which, by the way, can be done very well with the VisiCalc program.

All of which brings us to one of the key reasons we believe progressive growers should be computerizing their management information systems. Computerizing gives the grower for the first time a close look at his cost—both before growing the crop and after. Which is obviously a key help in building a more profitable operation. Identify your losers!!

This, plus the really telling advantage of accurate planning of space (empty benches are big losers) and planning ahead for labor and supplies. And the great efficiencies of accurate inventory control—knowing what you've got to sell.

EQUIPMENT

Just what equipment is provided for in the Ball Technical package? Essentially the same for the Yoder package. Here it is:

- Computer
- Printer
- Hard disk drive
- Floppy disk

ABOUT YOUR BOOKKEEPER—AND ACCOUNTANT

Assuming you will process all your accounting through your own computer (why not?), you'll probably want your bookkeeper to go through the week of training. He or she must certainly be at home with the black box. Also he must teach clerical help to enter data. To enter sales tickets, bills, etc., into the system. And he must be able to easily and quickly get answers from the black box himself. "How do our receivables look today—especially those past 90 days?" Helpful training tapes are available from Ball Technical.

"How much do *we* owe? Any past 30 days?" And, after a year's experience, a good bookkeeper should be able to forecast cash flow a year ahead. And monitor it as he goes along. Almost never done by growers today—but so terribly important. And helpful. Like everything else in business, seasonal cash is better gotten on a preplanned basis. Your cash flow forecast says you'll need $25,000 through March, April, and May. You'll get it with a lot less sweat (and often cheaper) if you negotiate it *ahead of time*.

How about your accountant? With this equipment, you will create your own monthly operating statement and balance sheet. As we see it, you'll probably use your accountant a lot less—but much more for professional advice. And preparation of tax returns. But mainly as an advisor on financial management. Isn't that his real job?

START AT HALF SPEED?

We talked this with Carl Loeb. There is a case for taking on only part of the job the first year. You and your people getting the hang of it on a limited scale before you go all the way. Especially if you're frankly not at home with computers. (I'm sure not, but I'm learning fast!)

One plan: Take on your one biggest crop the first year. Feed all the database information probably for your whole range, all crops, into the box. Size of all benches, what a 6" pot costs, how many you can fill with a cubic yard of mix, etc., etc. When each propagation of poinsettia cuttings is stuck, potted, spaced, and sold.

But you would do the complete job of crop planning, etc., on only the one big crop.

Carl supports this as a year #1 plan. "It's easier to hire out the accounting function—but not so the Plant Master (crop planning)—part of it."

HOW IS LABOR COST SPREAD?

An important point. Few growers are willing to keep records of what everyone does all day. Yet labor, as we have said so often, is the grower's #1 expense.

Carl's answer is a compromise:

Direct labor Anything chargeable to one crop. Example, transplanting bedding plants. Carl's plan: Make your best estimate of what it costs per flat.

Including break time, welfare, downtime, etc. Be conservative. Then include as a cost of a flat of bedding plants, X¢ per flat transplanting cost. Same to pot mums or lilies. Including moving to the bench.

Overhead labor   All other labor: your night man, cleanup crew, your foreman, yourself. All this is simply lumped together and added to the overhead cost per square foot per month before being distributed to the individual crops. How else could you do it?

ABOUT SECURITY

First, it troubles some growers that "all the facts about my business are there in the black box. Profit, etc. Anyone, computer-wise, can push a few buttons and have it all."

Answer: the obvious need to treat your computer same as you do your written accounting records. Keep it locked. Not available to "anyone."

And, for the record, a firm like Ball Technical, which supplies equipment and training on all of this, has no interest or reason for having access to your own business records. They are your private records.

IF YOU GO ON COMPUTERS TODAY

You'll have an awkward several months getting used to it all. But after all of that, you'll find yourself doing a whale of a lot better, more profitable job of running your railroad. You'll know your losing crops—and your moneymakers. You'll know ahead of time about those four benches that will be empty April 1.

We believe that computers *are* coming into the world of the grower. Soon!

G.V.B.

Chapter 27

ENVIRONMENTAL CONTROL COMPUTERS

CHOICES AVAILABLE

There are today two levels of greenhouse environmental control equipment available to the grower:

- Simple but effective electronic controls—widely used today. Good example: Wadsworth, George Dean, Jr., President.*

- Computerized environmental control equipment—like Oglevee† or Priva‡. And others!

Electronic Controls

The two systems (above) are very much competitive. Wadsworth has been the way to do the job for years—hundreds of ranges depend on it today.

---

*Wadsworth Control Systems, 5541 Marshall St., Arvada, CO 80002. (302) 424–4461.
†Oglevee Computer Systems, 151 Oglevee Lane, Connellsville, PA 15425. (412) 628–8360.
‡Priva Computers USA Inc., 551 SE 8th St., S. 50, Delray, FL 33444. (516) 736–2828. V&V
  Noordland Inc., 16 Commercial Blvd., Medford, NY 11763. (516) 698–2300.

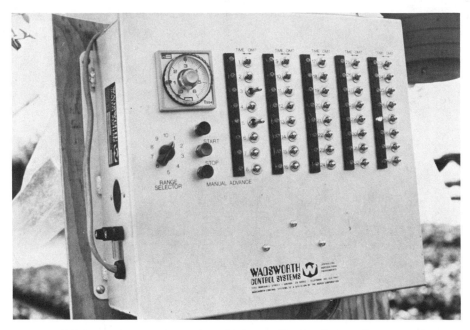

Here's a Wadsworth control panel—widely used in North American greenhouses for environmental control.

Computerized controls are the "new kid on the block." All three suppliers are good, reliable firms. I've listened at length to all three. The question: Where does each type of equipment fit best in today's world? Here from strictly a grower's point of view are my conclusions:

For a start, a new range of a half-acre or so, gutter-connected, all one crop, one temperature requirement—Wadsworth will do this job very well. As house temperature drops from 68° to 67°F, additional unit heaters are turned on. As temperature goes up from 76° to 78°F, more fans will be turned on. CO_2 can be supplied on a timeclock basis. It will be turned on and off at set times. If the air conditioning goes on during an application, Wadsworth will turn off the CO_2.

On humidity, if a set level of humidity is exceeded, Wadsworth will introduce heated outside air and also exhaust some of the moist inside air—simultaneously.

> Given a good hot water system, I can hold temperatures as close to a set point as computerized equipment. Given a situation of bright sun, very cold air, I can open vents just a bit at a time till the inside air temperature is stabilized.—George Dean.

And lastly, we described a small one-crop range as a good "fit" for Wadsworth type equipment. But obviously, a much larger operation with four or five separate ranges, each with a specialized crop, can be handled with Wadsworth equipment—by putting control units in each range. It is much less expensive.

And speaking of expense, to get a very rough idea, George Dean's basic "step 50 control panel" is under $700. His "step 500" is about $1,250. There are some options available at a modest additional cost.

COMPUTERIZED CONTROLS

The section on computerized environmental controls that follows describes Priva equipment. However, in this case we chatted with Bob Oglevee, who also offers competitive equipment.

What's the case for computerized controls?

Bob made several very valid points—which begin to develop the pros and cons of the more sophisticated computerized approach. Examples:

Zones Each unit of Wadsworth equipment (as described above) provides one sensor and one control unit. In effect, it will deal with only one "zone." Computerized equipment, on the other hand, can receive signals from many sensors in different parts of a range, can average them out, and can send back instructions to maintain a desired "climate" based on this average.

And Bob Oglevee makes the point that even given a one-acre range used entirely for one crop, the grower can get a much more precise and more uniform level of environmental control by having at least three or four sensors located across the one-acre area.

And as we get into the ability to hold temperatures more precisely at a desired point, we are avoiding overheating—which means fuel savings. And computerized environmental controls today are in fact making impressive records of fuel economy for growers. Interesting sidelight here: Hundreds of large office buildings have gone to computerized temperature control—with again, very impressive fuel savings.

Flexibility Bob Oglevee makes the point that computers offer much more flexibility. Example: A sunny day in winter: The grower ideally would like a higher temperature—perhaps up to 85° before ventilation—to increase photosynthesis and to hold in CO_2. Computers have this capability of responding to changes in the outside environment.

Bob Oglevee makes a major point here about "plant-oriented controls." Says Bob, "The European computers use outdoor light sensors. I put light sensors in the greenhouse—close to the plant. It's the plant atmosphere I'm trying to improve."

Back to relating light to temperature: Bob makes the point that the "book says that geraniums should be carried at 60° nights. That's great. Fifty years ago someone wrote a book and said geraniums are a 60° crop. They probably are not a 50° or a 70° crop, but especially given ample light in late winter, early spring, *optimum* temperature might well be 65°. Conversely, in dark, winter weather, it might better be 55°." So Bob's point is that with computers sensing and accumulating sunlight data, growing temperatures can and should be related to recent available light. Which only computers can do. If Monday and Tuesday are very cloudy and dark, the optimum night temperature for Wednesday should be lower.

Plant modelling   Says Bob Oglevee: "Plant modelling is the future." And what he means is the example being done at Michigan State to develop optimum levels of temperature, light, CO_2—and nutrients—to get maximum growth for the crop. He cites cases where growth was increased 50% + over "normal levels"—by applying these optimum levels of growing conditions.

Bob sees this plant modelling as the way out of the "art" approach to growing. He sees these model environments being developed for all crops all times of the year—which means that really every crop should be topnotch.

Put a different way: Bob says that if you grow a bangup excellent crop of poinsettias one year, you should be able to go back and recreate the temperature/light and CO_2 levels that turned out that crop—and do that good a job *every year.*

All of which obviously requires computers.

Cost for these computerized environmental control systems generally starts around $10,000, can go $20,000 to $30,000 and more depending on complexity and size of the installation.

There you have it—the Wadsworth good working level environmental control for today. Computers offering important promise for optimum crops and fuel efficiency for the future.

COMPUTERIZED ENVIRONMENTAL CONTROLS

In our opinion, good environmental control (EC) computers can contribute every bit as much—in cost savings, better crop quality, and reduced wear on the owner—as an accounting or crop planning computer. They're widely used in Holland today, only starting to appear in the U.S. and Canada. We look for much more of good EC computers in North America soon.

Priva is a leader among Dutch equipment. Much of this report will deal with Priva equipment—but there are other excellent EC computers available (see list at the end of the chapter). Oglevee is a strong contender for the U.S. market. Bob Oglevee understands this equipment and its potential.

Just what things will computers such as Priva and Oglevee do for the grower? There are many "things"—and what it can do for you depends somewhat on your operation. Examples:

Temperature Control

Less sophisticated (less costly) thermostats will *control* temperature—turn heat off or on as needed.

The more advanced environmental control (EC) stuff will do the job a lot more efficiently. Like 15% or 20% less fuel cost on a typical range of today.

And they do a lot of other important things.

You start to believe that 20% when you see how it works. And you believe the whole EC idea more when you see what this sophisticated climate control does for quality. And again, this quality matter is several things which, when put together, do make a difference. Examples of all this:

Accurate temperature control   Good EC will hold a 60° house at 60°—not 63° or 58°. And many houses we see these days are often several degrees off target. Dutch research demonstrated that each 1°C of overheating raises your total fuel cost 5%. Three degrees overheat means 15% fuel waste. That was done in centigrade—some difference. But the point impresses us as a substantial one.

This accurate temperature control assumes a properly designed heating system—that will, among other things, maintain uniform temperatures end-to-end of the house.

Easy does it   Here's more fuel economy. The new EC computers do the job by gentle nudging, not abrupt off and on changes. Again, fuel efficiency.

And more: If outside temperature goes down suddenly (and sunshine disappears) good EC will anticipate the problem, start the boiler at once. With a hot water system it also starts the circulating pump, starts heating the water in the system. Result: Far less tendency to throw a 100% load on the boiler to catch up. Sudden full loads *are* inefficient.

And all this happens the same way in reverse. The sun comes out, sudden rise in outdoor temperature. A good EC will turn the boiler down, ask for cooler water in the pipes, and soon turn the circulating pump off. EC growers report substantial savings on electric costs with a circulating pump operation.

Temperature fluctuation   Another fine point—but one that saves money on fuel. Thermostats tend to create a fluctuating temperature. Like the accompanying graph. Good EC control *modulates*. Now you've got only a very minimal fluctuation. Obviously more fuel efficient.

Day to night conversion   Every winter in the late afternoon you have to go from day to night temperature. The classic 65° or 68° day, 60° night conversion. And the same thing every morning. Good EC will make that conversion happen *gradually*. Not abruptly. Again, it will anticipate the new load needed in the morning to get up to day temperature. And not throw a 100% load on the boiler—instead it does it gradually.

269

Here is the Priva environmental computer so widely used in Europe today and now coming into the U.S. Jan Prins, president, is pointing to a printout graph— which the equipment can produce. It reports graphically such things as the past 24-hour temperatures, etc. Sorry, no photo of Robert Oglevee and his computer—an excellent U.S. competitor.

Good EC will anticipate adjusting the *time each day* when that day/night conversion occurs. This because of gradual shortening daylength in fall. Maybe you don't get around to responding to the earlier darkness—so crops get day temperature for an hour more at night. Which is a put-down on quality. And a waste of fuel. A small matter? Maybe so—but we get the feeling that again many of these small points put together do add up to quality. And growers using this equipment confirm that.

Another example of little things adding up to big fuel savings—we've all heard of the firms that install advanced EC type controls in larger office buildings. And guarantee maybe 15% or 20% fuel savings. No savings, no paying for the controls. And, typically, they deliver the savings. Priva, by the way, is doing this very thing in office buildings in Holland. Same story.

It's always there 24 hours a day Jan Prins made this point often. And as usual he's right! Good computerized environmental control is working for you every minute, every day—including Sunday! It delivers the most cost-efficient control of your heating/ventilating system every minute of every day—and night.

EC controls unit heaters   For the record, good environmental control equipment can and does control ranges equipped with overhead unit heaters—either open-flame, steam, or hot-water units. And again, some of the refinements—like turning on only part of the units if the load doesn't need them all. Possibly use of the fans alone for air circulation, etc.

Ventilation and Humidity

Same approach—and the result, again, is optimum fuel efficiency and good crop quality due to accurate setting of vents every minute of every day.

EC vent control modulates—up and down just a bit—to maintain the precise temperature desired. We stood in a Priva installation at Lakeshore Produce, St. Catharines, Ontario, recently. You could hear those electric vent controls constantly adjusting. Up a bit, down a bit. No sudden rush of outside air. No overheating (remember how we used to forget to get those vents up on a sunny morning!!).

Next question: Humidity. Obviously of major importance to quality and control of several tough diseases.

Equipment like Priva, again, constantly measures and monitors the percent of relative humidity. And maintains it at precisely the level called for by the grower. Which again, has to be a major help in achieving peak crop quality.

Good EC catches small deviations in humidity from the set point. And at the first sign of trouble it acts. Like the classic late winter afternoon. The sun goes down. The house suddenly cools, and humidity goes up sharply. Perfect conditions for black spot on roses, mildew in Riegers, split carnations, etc. The good, traditional grower is out there, senses this at just the right time, turns on a bit of heat and a bit of air. But typically with good EC, all this is done automatically.

How?

Answer: Again, the computer feeds in the optimum amounts of ventilation and heat if appropriate. Plus in many Dutch ranges today, a Priva air circulating device attacks the humidity problem from a third direction. It may be combined with the CO_2 generator.

Good EC will try to avoid using heat—the computer strives for the most cost-efficient way to control that rise in humidity. If vents and an air circulating fan will do it, don't use heat.

Typically, the grower has options here—in just how he wants the system to respond to this problem. He can limit the use of heat—or he can use it if humidity control on his crop is that critical.

Adjusting Temperature to Light Levels

Good EC equipment can (and normally in Holland does) adjust temperature day and night according to available light. During low-light winter months, a few sunny days mean that more photosynthesis is occurring. And to use this light effectively, higher temperatures are called for. The computer measures light levels constantly—and responds to high light—by boosting temperatures. Again, the grower can preset the response to the situation in the way he feels is best for his crop. How *many* degrees boost in temperature?

Now you begin to get the feeling that the computer does not at all replace the grower's "green thumb sense"—and expertise. In fact, the computer constantly measures what's happening—and will graph it for you. Which you, the grower, use as a basis for decisions on temperatures, humidity, light, etc. You might say, the typical Dutch range is really a sort of team effort between grower and computer. The computer measures and graphs—tell the grower what's happening. The grower decides on response. The grower sets up his desired response in the computer to a variety of situations. Then the computer implements that response.

Twenty-four hours a day, every minute. And as Jan Prins says, "Including Sundays!"

CO_2—Why Did We Give It Up?

A decade ago North American growers had a great burst of interest in CO_2. Most ranges did install burners and use them. Research people documented the gains that CO_2 could provide.

Then we quit!

I'll have to say it, the Dutch didn't. In fact you see CO_2 on the great majority of ranges in Holland today.

And, again, environmental computers. The computer measures the level of CO_2 in the greenhouse atmosphere. And it activates Priva CO_2 generators as they are needed—to maintain the set level. And as CO_2 generators are turned on, ventilators are automatically closed. Again, constantly—24 hours a day. And, again, that "set level" is a grower decision.

Normal outside air contains about 320 ppm of carbon dioxide. During the winter, Dutch growers seem to maintain on the order of 800 to 1,000 ppm. Jan Prins commented on tests by Dutch researchers. Result: Deficient levels of CO_2 resulted in a loss of about 10% of tomato revenue in 100 days. In Holland this will be equal to about $1.60 per square yard.

Another interesting thing turned up this past summer in Holland—somebody left their CO_2 computer sensor on all summer. And, found to their surprise that the level in the greenhouse dropped far below the normal 320 ppm outside level—even with vents wide open. Obviously the high light level in the somewhat restricted area around the plants resulted in rapid growth, heavy draw on the available CO_2—and tomato yields were clearly restricted due to lack of CO_2.

Another interesting point on CO_2 control—this from Kees Huyben of Priva. The point is: If sunlight during a winter day or over a period of several days drops to very low levels, then photosynthesis decreases sharply. Given this situation, less CO_2 is needed. The computer responds to this situation, reduces the level of CO_2—all within guidelines set by the grower. This technology is widely used in Holland. Since CO_2 is normally generated by burning fuel, this means again, notable savings in energy.

Crop Irrigating and Fertilizing

Good environmental computers play a helpful role here, too!

First, the basic application of water (and, normally with it, fertilizer) can be done by the computer. The grower can prescribe per square meter per day. The computer will apply that amount of water each day automatically.

Again, grower judgment: The amount of water and fertilizer applied to a crop is the final, and very critical, decision of the grower. Obviously, larger plants require more water and feed, any plant wants a lot more feed and water in warm sunny weather, etc. However, the computer can be an important help in this decision—in furnishing the grower with accurate data on temperature, accumulated light, etc. Which can be a more intelligent basis for the grower's decision on feeding and watering. In dark weather, we vaguely realize that we've had several cloudy days—but the computer puts it in numbers for you. And if you wish, in a graph—actual vs. normal for this time of year.

Interesting comment: Perhaps a third of the greenhouse vegetable (tomato, cucumber, pepper) crops in Holland are today grown in a rock wool substrate. Which is an inert 4" × 4 " cube of highly porous fiber. And, obviously, nutrients and water are applied to this block regularly. In this situation, the grower can alter the nutrient levels, the quality of nutrients, and the pH with each irrigation. Here the computer does the job very well—in effect, can control the quality of nutrients, the strength of the nutrient solution, and the pH. The computer can measure and again report these numbers to the grower. So, given a highly porous and inert media, the grower can, in effect, adjust the irrigation and nutrient applications really every day. And this is, in fact, done widely among Dutch vegetable growers. Such decisions as ammonia vs. nitrate nitrogen, total concentration of the fertilizer solution, etc.

In fact, most North American pot plants and many bedding crops today are also grown in highly porous and relatively inert mixes. Certainly pine or redwood bark, perlite, styrofoam, etc., are all such materials. And so, to a considerable extent, the U.S. pot plant/bedding grower can also manage his feeding/irrigation program with good EC computers.

All of this sounds like someone invented EC computers, and that's what growers will use from now on. The fact: Firms like Priva and Oglevee started six or seven years ago to design and improve their environmental computers for greenhouses. The "evolving and improving" process has been going on steadily—and is continuing to this day. And certainly the same for other good EC computer manufacturers. As the state of the art advances, newer and more helpful features can be added to existing computers. A proper EC computer installation is very much a dynamic thing. Of course, expansion in the grower's operations, changes in his crops, and heating and ventilating equipment adjustments also mean constant change. And one of the points of good EC computers is that they can respond to such change, and that new state-of-the-art features can be added as they become available.

Another point worth noting: Priva computers, for example, are not "off the shelf" hardware (black box) from computer manufacturers. They are, in fact, engineered and developed specifically for this application.

And, by the way, good EC equipment includes battery backup power—so that data will not be lost in case of a power failure.

Other Chores

Good EC computers do other things—again to relieve the grower. Examples:

Pad/fan cooling controls   EC controls can and do turn on fans and pad water—as needed to control temperature. Again, it's not a mechanical "on/off" kind of thing. Fans can be turned on as needed, a few at first, then gradually more. And of course, ventilators must be closed before pad/fan cooling equipment is activated—one of the many little details EC computers relieve growers of! And if a sudden storm comes along, high winds and heavy rain, the computer turns off the cooling pads and fans, and leaves vents down until the storm passes.

Managing thermal sheets   Thermal sheets are almost universally used in Holland, and today widely used in the U.S. Assuming they are mechanized, a good EC computer will extend the thermal sheets at the correct time each evening, retract them in the morning. And this "correct time" will be adjusted each day as the daylength shortens in fall and extends in spring. Automatically. Every day.

Excess summer light   Assuming installation of the white synthetic fiber thermal sheet, the grower can set his EC computer to extend the cloth sheet anytime during the day when the light exceeds a preset level. Automatically. And the level, of course, is set by the grower.

Daylength control   Assuming now that the thermal sheet is an opaque black poly or black-cloth material, the EC computer can do the "black-cloth" job for the grower. Again, extended at the correct time each evening—and retracted at the correct time in the morning. And now the job can be done at the optimum time for the crop—and not done when there happens to be a crew available to do it. Again, crop quality. Also, by the way, the computer can very easily retract the black-cloth after dark, leave the crop open to the air all night, extend it again before daylight in the morning. Great!

Daylength lighting   Light supplied to provide long days on such crops as mums, kalanchoes, etc., can also be operated by an EC computer. And now, the number of hours of light added per night can be automatically extended each day as the natural daylength shortens in fall and extends in spring. And, of course, the more complex cyclic lighting applications can also be set up on the computer.

About compartments   When computers assume control of the environment in a greenhouse range, the operation must be split into compartments—which are simply closed-in areas with the same temperature, humidity, etc., requirements. Sensing equipment is installed in each compartment and each compartment is regulated as per the grower's requirements. A compartment can be 10,000 square feet or an acre—or much more.

Alarm   Lastly, good EC computers have full capability to alert the grower in case of any deviations from preset levels. If greenhouse temperature falls below a set point—or if steam pressure or if hot water temperature of the boiler falls below a given point—or if any other important aspects of the operation fail, the grower will be alerted. Either by a bell—or if desired, by phone at home. Certainly this could include failure of light on such crops as mums.

Now Hear Some Growers—Users

First, a mid-size (55,000 square foot) rose specialist—A. P. Koole of Langley (Vancouver), British Columbia. The place is nearly all roses (a few pot plants) all glass, hot water heat. Mr. Koole installed Priva environmental control equipment in early July, 1983. Although it's still early to draw a conclusion on fuel savings, for example, Mr. Koole is plainly pleased with the impact of the "good EC" on his roses and his lifestyle.

Fuel savings   Again, it's too early to identify fuel savings—plus the fact that he's added to his range the last few months. But says Mr. Koole, "I'm sure it will reduce my fuel cost."

It's not like a thermostat—it maintains precisely the optimum temperature for a given moment. No overheating. And that's got to save fuel.

I like the fact that it can change from day to night temperatures at a preset point every evening—automatically. I don't have to do it and it corrects each day as the days lengthen.

He also talks about a "night 2 program" which says that somewhere in the late evening before midnight, the plant has used up the carbohydrates manufactured by photosynthesis during the day. Therefore, "growth" slows way down. So the computer responds by lowering temperature a bit the last half of the night—and with no loss in production or quality of roses. And important fuel savings. Then says Mr. Koole, "Just before sunrise the temperature starts up slowly—always slowly—which again means fuel savings."

Crop quality   "Again, we've only operated five or six months—but I'm seeing a lot less problem with mildew and black spot on my roses than I had doing all this by hand. And that does translate into better quality roses. It's the precise humidity control that does it."

Carbon dioxide   The equipment is just being installed—the entire operation will soon be under CO_2, controlled by the computer.

Easier to live with?   Says Mr. Koole, "Definitely! I'm very pleased—it's wonderful—so many things you can do with it. And, I set the limits, the computer makes it happen 24 hours a day after that."

One of the things Mr. Koole talked so much about was the data on temperature, light, etc., both in the greenhouse and outside—made available by the computer. "Every morning I check through the past 24 hours of light, accumulated temperature, also high/low temperatures." He also talks about "calculated temperature." In effect, if the day is bright and sunny, then a higher greenhouse temperature is indicated for the following night period. The computer calculates the increase indicated by the amount of additional light. Then, the next morning it will indicate whether the actual greenhouse temperature matches the "calculated temperature" projection by the computer.

We hear of some growers who in fact installed their computer control equipment in their bedroom! If you have doubts about how things are going on a cold night, just flip on the computer!

Priva computers range from $15,000 to $50,000 + —depending on size of range, number of control options included. Mr. Koole has roughly a $19,000 unit.

Maybe his most telling comment: "It's just a lot easier to live with it. Peace of mind!"

Andy Olsthoorn, Lakeshore Produce, St. Catharine's, Ontario, an hour north of Buffalo. It's perhaps three to five acres of modern Dutch glass, run by Andy Olsthoorn.

Andy installed "quality environmental control" computers recently—again Priva. We visited the place recently along with Jan Prins of Priva.

Why did Andy install this equipment? #1 reason: Fuel saving. And #2: "A lot easier to live with. Less for me to do myself. It does all the ventilating, tight control of humidity, operates thermal curtains (adjusted each day for the lengthening daylight) also it controls the boilers. And it does the CO_2 job very well—maintains the level I set.

"I like the way it maintains the water temperature in the hot water circulating system. Also, it turns the circulating pumps off—they're just on when they're needed—which saves some electricity."

He likes to tell about one evening about 9 p.m. when he was walking through his houses. It was a warm cloudy night. All of a sudden the thermal sheets opened back about a foot or two, and the ventilators opened just a crack. It got just a bit above the set temperature down at the crop level. It was gratifying to know that the computer was always there to respond when anything got out of set limits. And it didn't throw the vents wide open—just a bit. Gradually.

"Humidity is important here: There were several acres of Rieger begonias for one thing. They are a mildew problem. So the computer is set so that when humidity reaches a given level, the vents open a bit, and circulating fans and CO_2 generators turn on. Heat is used only if it's really needed. The computer does it the cheapest way."

Question: "Will the computer extend the thermal sheets in mid-summer if the light level gets too high?" Answer: Yes.

On soil heat: There are a lot of water lines buried in the soil on this range—and they are all computer controlled—to maintain a given soil temperature. Normally 65° for mums or poinsettias. Andy likes the ground benches for these crops.

He also mentioned the graphs that are available every morning to report the light and temperature levels both inside and outdoors for the past 24 hours. What was the temperature in each house through the night—really? Accurately? It's all there on a graph.

On crop quality: "I like the way the air feels—anytime I come in here. You never have that feeling of very high humidity—that steams up your glasses. Which to me is important to quality. I like the way the computer maintains a constant precise climate, and always at the minimum expenditure for fuel. And it's a lot easier to live with than doing all this by hand."

SOURCES

For the record there are several manufacturers of this equipment:

- Hoogendoorn Computers, c/o Jan Kandelaar, Bezwovven Kerf 15, 1424 RM, DeKwakel Z-H, The Netherlands.

- VanVliet Computers, VlieLandse Weg 20, Postbus 65, 2640 AB, Pynacker Z-H, The Netherlands.

- Oglevee (US), 151 Oglevee Lane, Connellsville, PA 15425. (412) 628–8360.

- Priva Computers, Zylweg 3, 2678 LC, de Lier, The Netherlands; and V&V Noordland, Inc., 16 Commercial Blvd., Medford, NY 11763. (516) 698–2300.

- Dansk (Danish) distributed by Grower Technical Systems, 2241 Dunwin Avenue, Mississauga, Ontario, Canada L5L1A3

G.V.B.

SECTION V

Culture by Crops

For convenience, the material on specific crops is arranged alphabetically—crops listed under their common names. Note that several major chapters are included in alphabetical order in the list. Examples:

- Bedding Plants
- Chrysanthemums
- Poinsettias

Germination information listed under each crop heading is largely based on the work done by Dr. Henry M. Cathey of the USDA at Beltsville, Md. "Light" simply refers to the fact that maximum germination is obtained when

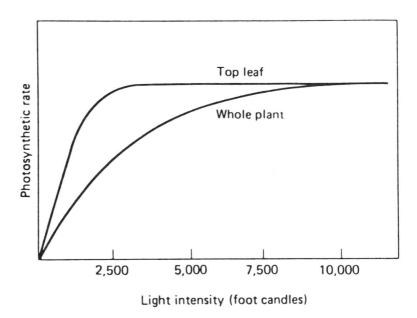

The effect of light intensity on the rate of photosynthesis of a single leaf at the top of a plant and of the whole plant. While the single leaf reaches its maximum rate of photosynthesis at 3,000 foot candles, an intensity of 10,000 foot candles might be required for the whole plant in order to raise the light intensity within the leaf canopy to 3,000 foot candles. The message here: Plants don't need more than 2,500 foot candles for optimum growth! Credit: Paul Nelson, Greenhouse Operation and Management *(Reston, Virginia: Reston Publishing Company, 1981).*

The DuPage Horticultural School greenhouses at West Chicago, Illinois. 38,000 square feet—year-round production of pot plants, bedding plants, foliage, and cut flowers. All grown by students.

the seeds are exposed to light. Conversely, "dark" indicates that for top germination, the seed should *not* be exposed to light. If neither "light" nor "dark" appears, it indicates that the seed will germinate well under either condition, or a combination of the two. "Alt. 70–85°" indicates that this crop should be grown at an alternating temperature of 70° nights and 85° days.

Crop Trends

Basic to anyone planning or already producing ornamentals: Which of the four major crop groups are healthy in expanding, which are less so? Also, what is the outlook for export competition in each?

Our *Ball Red Book* certainly doesn't have final answers on these terribly important questions. But, we are presenting in the following graphs (and others throughout the book) the best available information on recent production of each of the four major crops. Plus, brief comments on each.

We have two sources of crop statistics in the U.S.. Both are presented in these graphs:

281

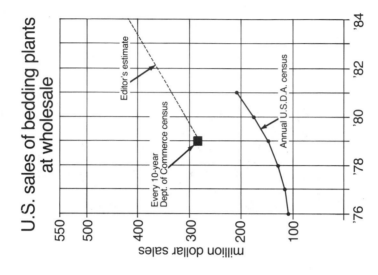

U.S. sales of pot plants
at wholesale

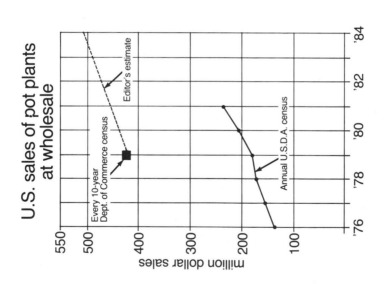

U.S. sales of bedding plants
at wholesale

282

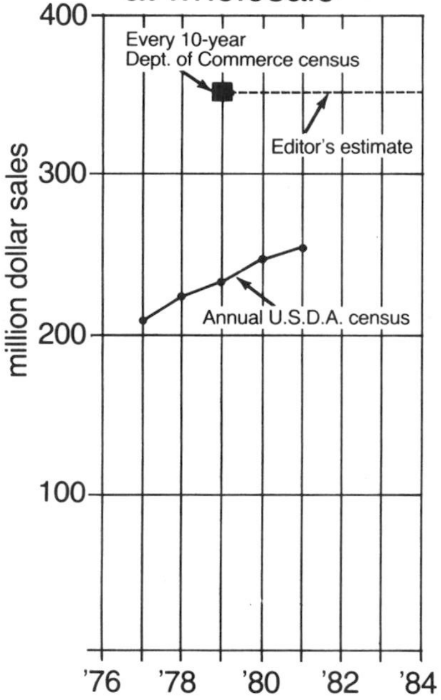

U.S. sales of foliage
at wholesale

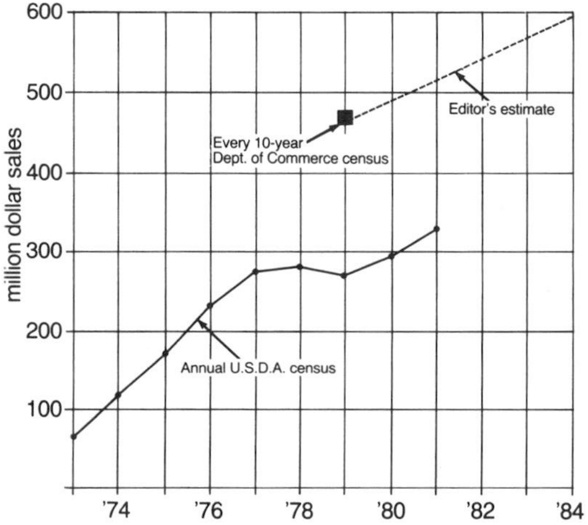

million dollar sales

600
500
400
300
200
100

Every 10-year
Dept. of Commerce census

Editor's estimate

Annual U.S.D.A. census

'74 '76 '78 '80 '82 '84

U.S. sales of cut flowers
at wholesale

million dollar sales

400
300
200
100

Every 10-year
Dept. of Commerce census

Editor's estimate

Annual U.S.D.A. census

'76 '78 '80 '82 '84

283

Statistical Reporting Service   This was published yearly since 1956 by the U.S. Department of Agriculture Crop Reporting Service. It covered only 28 states, only major crops, only growers $10,000 or more in annual sales. It was discontinued after 1981, hopefully will soon be reinstated. While this is only a partial report, its value is that it does show trends.

These USDA figures are shown in the following as *solid* lines.

U.S. Dept. of Commerce Census   Bureau of Census, Census of Agricultural and Horticultural Crops. It reports cut flowers, pot plants, bedding and foliage, vegetable seeds, sod, and cultivated mushrooms. Also, cut greens, nursery products, bulbs, flower seed, and greenhouse vegetables. It reports all growers with over $2,000 per year of sales. It is reasonably accurate, complete—but is only done every ten years. The most recent census was done in 1979.

The total value for the 1979 census at wholesale of the four major crops is shown on these graphs as a large square—on the 1979 lines. We have added *our own estimate* of the growth in value of these crops since the 1979 census—shown as a dotted line extending from the 1979 census square—to the right. Up to 1983. These are strictly our own feel. We have had no USDA census figures since 1981.

V.B.

Here are the classrooms and offices of the DuPage Horticultural School at West Chicago. This plus half an acre of modern greenhouses is where each year a group of young people get intensive training in growing and marketing flowers. The students spend over half of their time "hands on"—in the greenhouse (here and elsewhere) with crops. For details write to the DuPage Horticultural School, PO Box 342, West Chicago, Illinois 60185.

ANNUAL *(A. houstonianum) 200,000 seeds per oz. Germinates in 8 days at 70°. Light.*

Ageratum as a bedding plant.

Because of its habit, so suitable for border usage, and its predominately clear blue color, ageratum continues to hold its place in the bedding plant market.

Uniform and free-flowering, they grow to a height of about 6 to 8".

Ageratum Blue Puffs

Probably the most widely used F_1 hybrid. Vigorous, free-flowering mid-blue, about 6" high, and very uniform in habit.

Other widely used F_1 ageratum hybrids are *Blue Blazer, Adriatic, Blue Surf, North Sea, Spindrift,* and *Blue Angel.*

- *Blue Blazer* is a mid-blue, grows about 6" high.

- *Adriatic* is a mid-blue that grows 8" high and has a uniform plant habit.

- *Blue Surf,* a light blue, grows 6" high, is early flowering, and great for packs.

- *North Sea* is an 8" deep lavender blue. Its buds are of a reddish purple color.

- *Blue Angel* is a mid-blue, grows to a 6" height and is known for its continuous blooming.

- *Spindrift* is a uniform pure white that grows to a 6" height.

285

The alstroemeria is propagated by rhizomes. The tiny "buds" at the tip of the pencil develop under each stem (as it is pulled away in harvesting). They in turn develop a new stem and a new flower spike.

Introduction

The new alstroemeria cultivars that are available from Europe (Table 1) are the result of years of interspecific breeding and irradiation to induce mutations of various cultivars. The majority of the new hybrid cultivars have originated from the van Staavern Company (The Netherlands) and Parigo Seed Company (England). Recently, the Wulfinghoff Company (The Netherlands) has introduced several new and interesting alstroemeria cultivars. Plants are normally leased from the breeder; also, a yearly royalty is assessed on the square footage in production. The Fred Gloeckner Company is the United States representative for the van Staavern Company, whereas the other firms, as far as we know, have no U.S. representative.

Alstroemeria species and hybrids come in many different shades of reds and yellows. The native species are found from the snowline of the high

*Contributed by W.E. Healy and H.F. Wilkins, Dept. of Horticulture, Colorado State University, and Dept. of Horticulture, University of Minnesota, respectively.

286

Table 1   SOME ALSTROEMERIA CULTIVARS BY COLOR

Bronze	**Red**
Harmony (S)	Carmen (P)
	Fanfare (W)
Orange	King Cardinal (S)
Campfire (S)	Red Sunset (S)
Harlequin (W)	Red Surprise (S)
Orange Beauty (S)	Result (W)
Orchid Florin (P)	Valiant (W)
Pink	**Red-Purple**
Capitol (S)	Marina (P)
Mona Lisa (S)	
Pink Perfection (P)	**Yellow**
Regina (S)	Canaria (S)
Rosali Staliro (S)	Orchid (S)
Rosita (S)	White Wings (SD)
Trident (W)	Yellow Tiger (S)
	Zebra (S)

P—Parigo; Spalding, England
S—M.C. van Staavern; Aalsmeer, The Netherlands
W—A. Wulfinghoff; Rijsuiyk, The Netherlands

mountain plateaus of the Andes in South America down through the highland forests to the coastal deserts. The requirements for floral induction in the hybrids can be separated into two groups: the white/yellow, and the red/orange, which originated from several different interspecific crosses. The white/yellows require a shorter cold period, a higher "devernalization" temperature, and a shorter photoperiod for flowering than the red/orange group.

Plant Characteristics

As the leaves on an alstroemeria shoot unfold, they rotate 180° so that the adaxial (upper) surface becomes the abaxial (under) surface. The inflorescence consists of a whorl of flowering cymes with each individual cyme bearing one to five sympodially arranged flower buds.

The alstroemeria plant consists of a white fleshy rhizome from which arises aerial shoots and a root system that is moderately fibrous and can become thickened like a dahlia. The growing point of the rhizome gives rise to aerial shoots. Each new aerial shoot arises from the first node of the rhizome and a lateral rhizome develops in the second node of the aerial shoot.

The aerial shoots can be either vegetative or reproductive. Normally, shoots that have unfolded more than 30 leaves will not flower and are vegetative. Once rhizomes are induced to flower by low temperatures, all shoots that form will flower until plants become "devernalized" by high temperatures.

Flower Induction

The flowering control mechanism for alstroemeria hybrids appears to be of a biphasic nature with a primary cold temperature requirement and a secondary photoperiod requirement. As stated earlier, the temperature effect shows a group specificity with the white/yellow group requiring a shorter cold treatment (2 to 4 weeks of 40°F/4.5°C) for floral induction than the red/orange group, which needs 4 to 6 weeks of 40°F/4.5°C for floral induction.

Once flowering begins, the plants will continue to produce flowering shoots indefinitely until the soil temperature goes above 60°F/15.5°C for extended periods of time. Ten plants were grown at continuous 55°F/12.7°C soil temperature; the plants continued to flower indefinitely regardless of air temperature and regardless of photoperiod. Since the below-ground part of the plant must be kept cool (55°F/12.7°C) for continued flowering, deep soil mulches or misting the mulch to encourage evaporative cooling will help maintain a cool soil temperature along with evaporative air cooling during periods of warm temperature.

The other component that controls flower induction is photoperiod. Once plants have perceived an adequate cold treatment, a 13-hour photoperiod, as obtained by using standard chrysanthemum lighting as a night interruption, hastened floral initiation. Lighting nonvernalized plants will not induce flowering. Photoperiods longer than 13 hours will not promote any earlier flowering, but may decrease flower production. We have found a 4-hour night interruption (incandescent source, 2200 to 0200 hours) adequate. Another method we have used is to add the length of normal existing daylength plus x hours of night interruption in order to equal 13 hours. These night interruptions are effective in promoting earlier flowering without decreasing flower production. Lighting should occur from about September 1 to April 15 at 45° N latitude (St. Paul, Minnesota). Check with your local weather bureau to determine the exact dates when the daylength is less than 13 hours at your latitude.

Light intensity has been shown to affect flower development. In northern Europe where light intensity in the winter is significantly reduced, bud blasting is a problem. In Minnesota we have only occasionally observed bud blasting, and this may have been related to soil temperatures which were too cool. Since the number of cymes per stem is positively correlated with the stem diameter, alstroemeria should be grown with the maximum available light so that a maximum number of cymes per stem can be attained.

Propagation

Alstroemeria plants should be divided every second or third year depending on the cultivar and growth characteristics. About 1 to 2 weeks prior to dividing, plants should be severely pruned leaving only the youngest 6"–8" shoots. The pruning will facilitate handling. When digging well-established plants after flowering decreases in late summer or early fall, care should be taken to dig deep enough to get the growing point as the rhizome can grow 12"–14" deep. Each new division should consist of a single rhizome with an undamaged, blunt growing point, some new aerial shoots, and, most important, some large fleshy storage roots.

The presence of these thickened storage roots is critical for the reestablishment of the plants since the first new roots will arise from these enlarged storage roots. Normally only the youngest 1"–3" of rhizome is kept with the older portion of the rhizome being discarded. These older rhizomes are of no value as the lateral rhizomes that may arise from them are weak and do not appear to regain vigor.

Immediately after the rhizomes are divided or new rhizomes are received, they should be planted. It is essential that pots, soil, or ground beds be ready *before* plants are divided or received. Normally extra plants are potted up to replace plants that die or are not as vigorous as others. It is expected that 5%–25% of the plants will not survive transplanting. To increase the survival rate, a fungicidal drench (8 oz. per 100 gallons of water each of Lesan and Benlate) is recommended at the time of planting and again a month later if vigorous root growth is not observed. Excess watering will quickly rot the rhizomes. After the initial watering with the fungicidal drench, spot water plants as they become dry. Grow the plants at 65°F/18°C until they become well established (4–8 weeks), before lowering the temperatures to 40°F/4.5°C.

When new growth commences, numerous shoots will form. Removing some of the weak vegetative shoots was shown to increase flower production. Shoot removal acts as a "pinch" and encourages growth or lateral branching of the lateral rhizomes. Shoots should be pulled since cutting the stem and not pulling it off the rhizome will decrease flower production. A quick upward pull will cleanly remove the shoot from the rhizome. Stems are harvested when the first group of flowers begins to open. Care should be exercised with young or poorly rooted plants since the rhizome may be uprooted or torn loose from the soil if careless stem removal occurs.

There are currently two methods for marketing alstroemeria. One method simply places 10 to 12 flowers in a bunch. The more desirable method places the stems into three grades. Grade 1 has stems with five or more cymes per 36"+ stem length; grade 2, 3–4 cymes per 24"+ stem length; and grade 3, less than 3 cymes per 12″+ stem length. Stems are downgraded for crooked or damaged stems or poor foliage. A strong 3- to 4-layer support system is recommended. Alstroemeria can produce shoots up to 6′ tall.

Alstroemeria are heavy feeders. We have fed up to 600 ppm N in the form of KNO_3 twice a week to vigorous plants without any adverse effects. Ammoniacal forms of nitrogen fertilizer should be avoided, as at 55° growing temperatures, ammonia is not readily converted to nitrate. Application of minor nutrients may be required to maintain optimum levels within the plant.

Insects and diseases are essentially not a problem on alstroemeria. White-flies and aphids may appear during warm weather. We have observed leaf mottling and verified this as a virus infection.

ALYSSUM

ANNUAL *(Lobularia maritima) 90,000 seeds per oz. Germinates in 8 days at 70°. Light.*

Still widely used for edging purposes (known botanically as *Lobularia*), alyssum *holds up quite well through hot, dry summers. The most popular variety, New Carpet of Snow,* stays quite uniformly down to a height of 3″ to 4″ and withstands the heat quite well. It makes a spread of 10″–12″, and good plants that are produced by sowing around March 15 should be spaced on 12″ centers.

New Carpet of Snow maintains a more compact, uniform habit than the regular widely used strains. In addition to the white forms, a number of purple varieties are available. *Oriental Night* is a compact type. *Royal Carpet,* low and spreading in growth, produces violet-purple flowers on plants 4″ high. *Wonderland* is a cerise rose, very compact and free flowering. It represents an improvement on *Rosie O'Day,* which has been grown for quite a few years. All are at their best in cool temperatures.

All annual alyssums have the same rich, sweet fragrance. The perennial forms are without this rich fragrance. *A. saxatile compactum* is a dwarf-growing variety that forms greyish-green leaves covered by masses of golden-yellow flowers that appear in early spring.

This variety is very hardy and is excellent for edging and rock gardens.

290

Amaryllis, a fine, colorful flowering pot plant for the northern mid-winter.

These indoor spring bulbs are valued for their large, brilliant-colored lily-like flowers borne on barren stems.

While they can be forced into bloom in the greenhouse, most of the bulbs are sold at retail level for forcing in the home.

Bulbs are sold in sizes ranging from 2½″ to 4½″. Generally speaking, the larger the bulb the greater the potential for more flowers. Suggested bulb size for forcing in a 6″ pot is 3¼″ to 3¾″. When potting, the top ⅓ of the bulb should remain exposed. Forcing time is 6 to 8 weeks at 70°F. Temperatures should be lowered to 60°F when plants are coming into flower. Once forcing has started, the soil should not be allowed to dry out. Amaryllis are available in separate varieties ranging in color from pink, red, orange, salmon, scarlet, and white through striped bicolors.

ANEMONES*

PERENNIAL *(Anemone coronarium) 2,000 seeds per gram (clean seed). Germinates in 7–14 days at 15°C (59°F).*

Mona Lisa *anemone.*

Anemone, or "wind flower," as this flower is commonly called, is much more widely known in Europe than in North America. The flowers are commonly used as greenhouse cut flowers in Europe or for perennial garden purposes. Old varieties, such as *St. Brigid* and *DeCaen* mixes, are commonly grown from corms and used both for commercial cut-flower purposes and for home-garden purposes. All the corms originate from seeds planted annually by producers of the corms from open-pollinated seed stocks. These older varieties have a limited color range, mostly blues, reds, whites, orchid, and some bicolors. *DeCaen* types are single-flowered while the *St. Brigid* types have extra petals making them appear more double. Another open-pollinated anemone that has recently been introduced from the Rosewarne Experiment Station in England is called *St. Piran*. This variety does have larger flowers and better stem lengths than either of the older two varieties previously mentioned.

*Contributed by Dr. Scott C. Trees, Pan-American Seed Company.

292

More recently, though, several new F_1 hybrid anemones have been introduced to the market place. Most outstanding among these is a variety called *Mona Lisa,* which has 40 years of breeding in its background. The breeding has resulted in much larger flowers than the traditional corm-type anemones and longer stems. It is not uncommon to get flowers 4"–5" (10–13 cm.) wide and stems 18" (46 cm.) long.

The color range in the new F_1 hybrid *Mona Lisa* is wider than other existing strains and includes good reds, scarlets, pinks, wines, whites, blues, orchids, and many bicolors. *Mona Lisa* anemones are being used by the professional cut-flower grower and are a welcome addition because of the low energy and low labor requirements. Another advantage to *Mona Lisa* is its long vase life (7–10 days). Other F_1 anemones on the market include F_1 *Jerusalem* and F_1 *DaVinci*. For most parts of North America, seed sowing should begin no later than the last week of March or the first week of April. Seed should be sown in a peat-based compost medium like Jiffy-Mix. *Mona Lisa* anemones are "defluffed," which makes them much easier to sow than nondefluffed seed of other F_1 anemones. Seeds should be sown about 1 cm. apart in fairly deep trays (10 cm.) to allow for good root development before transplanting. Anemones have long tap roots that should not be damaged during transplanting, if possible. It is advisable to drench the soil after sowing seeds with a fungicide such as Captan at the rate of 500 grams Captan to 450 liters of water. Cover the seeds lightly ($1/4$–$1/2$ cm. soil) with a sterilized peat-lite medium.

It is critical that during germination temperatures be maintained *no higher* than 15°C. Higher temperatures will definitely reduce germination percentages. High humidity should be maintained during this period of germination, either by misting or covering the flats with clear plastic or newspaper perforated with holes or sterile burlap.

Throughout the entire growing season, it is advisable to keep the pH of the soil medium between 6.8 and 7. Seedlings should be kept heavily shaded and as cool as possible during the warm summer months. Growing them next to pad cooling systems often is an advantage.

Seedlings should be ready for transplanting to either pots or beds about 9–10 weeks after sowing. At this time, seedlings should have 4–6 true leaves. It is recommended that in areas where such plants as dogwood, onion, wild grapes, and other weeds that can carry the disease colletotrichum, appear, weekly sprayings be made using a Ferbam/Benlate® solution (500 grams Ferbam plus 250 grams Benlate® to 450 liters of water).

Captan can also be used to deter "damping off." Good ventilation is a must in preventing the spread of botrytis as is careful watering, which should be done in the morning to allow plants to dry before sundown.

Plants should be spaced about 25 cm. between rows and 10–15 cm. between the plants within the rows. Wider spacings will allow for bigger plants and possibly higher production. As a rule of thumb, we suggest planting about 20 plants per square meter.

After transplanting, lightly mulch between the plants with a clean sterile medium such as straw or rice hulls. Keeping the plants as cool as possible and heavily shaded during the hot summer months is a must if you are to succeed. In transplanting, make sure that the seedlings are placed no deeper than they were in their seedling containers. Never cover the crown since this can cause crown rot or delayed flowering.

In order to stimulate root growth immediately after transplanting, fertilize once with a 9–45–15 (N.P.K.) solution at about 500 grams to 450 liters of water. Once the plants become established, gradually adjust fertilizer levels to a solution of 30–5–25 (N.P.K.) and alternate feedings with clear water.

Soil testing kits are recommended throughout the growing season as well as a pH meter to make sure that your soil nutrient levels and pH are optimal.

Diseases

Anemones are prone to several diseases, especially botrytis. Products such as Botran, Botrilex, and Ornalin are especially useful for control of botrytis. We recommend alternating these different fungicides so that resistance to the disease does not develop. Again, good ventilation helps to cut down on botrytis. Good greenhouse culture (i.e., removing old flowers and leaves) also helps to prevent botrytis. Another disease problem with anemones is anemone leaf curl, colletotrichum sp. As mentioned earlier, this disease can be harbored on wild plants such as dogwood, onions, and grapes and could be controlled and prevented by using a Ferbam/Benlate solution recommended previously. Rhizoctonia can be a problem in poorly drained soils and is controlled with a Terrachlor® drench, while pythium can be controlled using Truban.®

Powdery mildew can be controlled by the use of sulphur dust, and downy mildew can be prevented by using a product known as Alliete.

To keep aphids and white flies under control, we recommend the use of Temik or a Resmethrin aerosol. It is important that thrips also be minimized in the growing area since they can transmit viral diseases such as tomato spotted wilt virus.

Shading

Shading is important in growing anemones. During the hot summer months when plants are being put into the beds, it is extremely important to keep heavy shade on the houses (up to 75% shade) until cooler fall weather arrives, at which time the shading should be removed gradually. During the winter months of October through February, most areas will not require any shading. From late February onwards, growers should monitor the amount of light and temperatures in their greenhouses and apply shade gradually to keep temperatures down into the range of 16° C day temperatures to get maximum production from an anemone. With proper shading, the season can be extended even into April, and possibly May, in some parts of the country.

Growing Temperatures

Anemone is a cool crop and can tolerate temperatures as low as freezing for short periods of time. Ideally, 6–8° C night temperatures are optimal for producing long-stemmed cut flowers. Daytime temperatures, optimally, should be maintained around 16–17° C.

Harvesting

The new F_1 hybrid anemones should be allowed to open and close a couple of times before cutting in order to maximize petalling and flower size. The older anemones such as *St. Brigid* and *DeCaen* types should be cut just prior to opening. The blooms should be cut early in the morning before greenhouse temperatures cause the flowers to open. Always use a sharp knife and sterilize it frequently. The flowers should be cut as close to the crown as possible in order to prevent possible entry of disease organisms such as botrytis into stem material left after cutting.

Stems should be placed in warm water in a cool environment before grading and bunching.

Generally, anemones are sold in mixed bunches of ten. If flowers are to be shipped, the stems should be dried prior to shipping in order to reduce the occurrence of botrytis in the shipping box. If possible, the stems should be shipped upright in order to prevent crooking, but if they must be shipped horizontally, they should be wrapped tightly in newspaper.

If the flowers are to be kept in cold storage prior to shipping, it is recommended that they be held at 1.1° C (34°F) for no longer than 14 days. Final vase life will not be seriously affected under these conditions. It is important that water be changed frequently in the storage containers. Floral preservatives, such as Floralife, are recommended to help extend vase life.

AQUILEGIA (Columbine)

PERENNIAL *(A. species) 15,500 seeds per oz. Germinates in 3–4 wks. at 70–85°.*

Aquilegia—classic perennial.

Under some coarse protection, columbines are dependably hardy with us and rather attractive. They are among the most colorful and easily grown perennials. We have noted them doing fairly well in slightly shaded garden locations, but generally speaking, they enjoy a fully exposed location and rather light or sandy soil. To work up an outdoor supply, sow about February 1 and plant out after hard frosts are over. They will not flower much the first season, but will flower freely the following. For some reason, they drop out after 3 or 4 years with us, so keep additional sowings coming on. While in many areas they are sold as field-grown plants, many bedding-plant growers offer them in packs or Jiffy-Pots right along with their bedding annuals.

An F₁ hybrid, *Spring Song* is the most widely used today along with *McKana's Giant,* which is an excellent strain that has been popular for many years. *Spring Song* grows to a height of about 2½ feet. It is earlier, produces more flowers per stem, as well as more stems per plant. Colors range from bright reds through blue shades to yellows and bronzes.

Dragonfly Mixture is a dwarf strain in a bright range of colors that attains a height of nearly 18″ and is useful toward the front of a perennial border.

ARABIS (Rock Cress)

PERENNIAL *(A. species) 120,000 seeds per oz. Germinates in 3–4 wks. at 65–75°.*

The standard variety is *Alpina Snowcap,* popular for rock-garden work. It is dwarf in habit (6″ to 8″) and produces dense masses of shining, snow-white flowers in very early spring. In full flower, it might be mistaken for a cap of snow. *Alpina Pink* is a delicate pale-pink color. Both are easily grown from seed. They are extremely hardy and make an excellent ground cover.

ASPARAGUS

ANNUAL *(A. species) 400–900 seeds per oz. Germinates in 4–6 wks. at 70–85°.*

Both *Plumosus nanus* and *Sprengeri* are extensively grown as cut greens for flower arrangements. *Plumosus nanus* is the most popular and is widely grown under lath structures in Florida. The main requirements of both are heat, lots of water, and partial shade. Germination of the seed barely holds for a year, so should be sown as soon after it is harvested as possible. New-crop seed is usually harvested in January or February. Sow either kind in a 70°F to 85°F temperature.

These plants are widely used in hanging baskets, urns, and window boxes, and are also sold as specimen plants. Some of them are used strictly for interior landscape purposes. A growing temperature of 60°F is satisfactory. To produce a good 2¼″ pot requires about 4 months time. A heavy 3″ or 4″ pot will require about 6 months growing time, using 3 plants per pot.

Asparagus Falcatus is a slow-growing foliage plant with dark green, wide leaves, useful for hanging baskets and pot plant sales as a houseplant.

Asparagus Meyerii produces gracefully tapered spikes of a bright green color which tend to cascade as they elongate. This variety maintains a neat, unique habit that makes it very attractive as a pot plant. About 12 months is required from seed sowing to a finished 4″ pot.

Asparagus Pyramidalis is an erect form of *Plumosus* with fronds of needle-like leaves borne on a sharp upward angle contrasted to the regular *Plumosus* forms, which produce fronds at right angles.

ASTERS

ANNUAL *(Callistephus chinensis) 12,000 seeds per oz. Germinates in 8–10 days at 70°.*

This versatile flower was one of the favorites of the late Geo. J. Ball, who, over 70 years ago, developed the forebears of some of today's finest varieties. Probably no one series in history was as well known, or has been grown by as many florists as the Ball Florist strain, available as a mix. Despite the inroads of diseases like "fusarium wilt" and the "yellows," they are still grown profitably in some areas, chiefly by specialists.

Additional knowledge concerning off-season culture, based largely on work done at Ohio State University, has also aided growers in producing good greenhouse crops in late winter and early spring—or in any of the 12 months. Details concerning off-season culture will be discussed later in this article.

Cloth-House Culture

The usual handling by retail growers calls for sowing April 15, transplanting to Jiffy-7s or Jiffy-Pots 2–3 weeks later, and planting out to the cloth house about May 20–25, depending on the weather. Space 12" × 12". It's very important that the plants not be allowed to "draw up," either in the seed flats or in the pots.

About Diseases

There are two principal offenders; both can be definitely controlled.

Stem rot (fusarium wilt)   This is a rotting of the plant at the surface of the soil, usually with dark brown lesions extending up the stem. Steaming soil to 180° for ½ hour, 8" deep, will, according to our experience, reduce loss to almost nothing. Next to that, planting asters to soil not used for that crop before usually prevents any serious loss.

Yellows   Part or all of the plant just turns a sickly yellow and stops growing. Flowers on affected plants are also more or less yellowed and do not open properly. Plants are normally a foot or more high before the injury appears. Often, one side of a plant is affected first. Infected plants should be destroyed at first signs of infection.

It's a virus that affects many weeds and common garden annuals. The only way an aster can get yellows is via the aster leafhopper. This little fellow (¼") looks like a small grasshopper. He picks up the yellow virus from weeds, etc. outside the house; then as he feeds on the aster foliage, he infects the clean plant. Aster yellows can be eliminated if plants are grown in a cloth enclosure kept tight enough to exclude the hopper. This calls for cloth that runs 22 threads per inch.

Care of the Crop

A regular spraying program is essential. There are a number of materials that will do a good job. Manufacturers' recommendations should be followed closely. Aster foliage is touchy. Most brands include their own spreader. If aphids aren't kept under strict control early in the summer, they will surely get into the opening blooms—and there's no cure for that. To prevent botrytis, spray every 10 days with Benlate wettable powder at a rate of ½ lb. per 100 gallons of spray.

Asters are usually fed once—several weeks after they are planted out. Any balanced fertilizer, or one of the liquid feedings, is all right.

Disbudding of the sideshoots or "suckers" from the 8–10 lateral stems on each plant is essential to quality flowers. If too many sideshoots develop, some of the lower branches may be removed to prevent overcropping.

Greenhouse Asters—Year-Round

The only important requirements are: 50° night temperature, and additional lighting, which must be supplied continuously from the seedling stage until plants are 20 to 24" tall. The only exception is the period from May 15 to August 1, during which day length is long enough. 60-watt bulbs with reflectors, spaced 5' apart, or the lighting setup you use for mums is satisfactory. Lights must be turned on from sundown to 10 p.m. daily, or for 2 hours in the middle of the night. Spacing is usually 8" × 8".

The following schedule worked out at Ohio State checks closely with our own experience where a 55° night temperature was used.

OFF-SEASON ASTERS (UNDER GLASS)

Sow seed	Pot seedlings	Bench plants	Approx. flwg. date
July 15	Aug. 10	Sept. 15	January
Aug. 15	Sept. 10	Nov. 1	February
Sept. 10	Oct. 1	Dec. 1	March
Oct. 20	Nov. 15	Jan. 1	April
Dec. 20	Jan. 10	Mar. 1	May
Feb. 1	Feb. 20	Apr. 1	June
Mar. 15	Apr. 1	May 15	July
Apr. 20	May 10	June 15	August
May 20	June 10	July 15	September
June 10	July 1	Aug. 1	October
June 20	July 15	Aug. 20	November
July 10	Aug. 1	Sept. 1	December

As in summer, avoid deep planting. Set plants as shallow as possible without exposing roots. Steam sterilizing is very effective in controlling stem rot. Not only the final bench, but also potting soil, germination flats, labels, etc., must all be carefully steamed.

Aster Varieties

Most widely used variety for cut purposes is the *Ball Florist Mixture*, which is a selection of *Perfection* types developed from the original Ball strain.

Pot Plant Asters

An item that may be due more consideration by the pot plant grower who is supplying the mass-market outlet. In addition to their lasting qualities—often as long as 3 weeks in the average home—they offer a variety of colors which can't be had in pot mums. Bright rose, pink, and blue are available, in addition to pure white and red.

Soil Any good mixture will do. Sterilized mum soil is very satisfactory.

Lighting Use 60-watt bulbs with reflectors. Space lights 5' apart, 3' above the bench. Lights-on date is seed emergence date. Lighting is required from August 20 to May 5 and may be done by lighting 4 hours each night throughout this period (from sundown to 10:00 p.m. or, preferably, from 10:00 p.m. to 2:00 a.m.) or controlled lighting (mum schedule):

Number of hours per night	Time
3	Aug. 20–Oct. 31
4	Nov. 1–30
5	Dec. 1–Jan. 31
4	Feb. 1–28
3	Mar. 1–May 5

Shading Plants can be shaded from the time the terminal buds are the size of a dime until the *laterals* show color. This will bring the laterals into flower more nearly the same time as the terminal opens and thereby increase quality. Use *only* Black Sateen Cloth (Mum Black Shade Cloth).

If shading is used, shade between April 1 and Sept. 15. Stop lighting April 1 and start again on Sept. 5 when shade is dropped.

Schedules Summer crops can be produced in 4–4½ months from sowings in February through May.

Spring crops can be produced in 5–5½ months from sowings in November, December, and October. 60° nights during this period will ensure proper heights.

Potting Seedlings can be picked off directly into the finishing pot, but 2¼" Jiffy-Pots® can be used.

While the *Dwarf Queens* have been a widely used variety, *Pixie Princess Mixture,* a recent introduction, shows great promise.

AUBRIETIA

PERENNIAL *(A. deltoidea graeca) 80,000 seeds per oz. Germinates in 2–3 wks. at 60°.*

Excellent perennial for rock garden and edging where sandy soil and a well-drained location are available. Cultivated varieties nearly all fall into the species *deltoidea.*

Aubrietia resembles some of the dwarf "cushion"-type dianthus in general habit of growth. They form dense mats of foliage that are covered with small four-petaled flowers during the spring and early summer. Foliage remains green throughout the season. Most kinds prefer a well-drained location and slightly sandy, light soil for best growth and maximum hardiness. For best results they should be planted in semi-shade. Seed sown during the summer will flower the following spring.

Propagation is customarily by seed or division of clumps. Hybrid seed strains are large-flowered and contain blue, lilac, light blue, purple, and carmine colors. They are about 6" high.

The author, Frank Batson, with production of budded plants in Oregon.

Azaleas are surely one of our major greenhouse pot plants today. The notes that follow describe modern cultural practices of this greenhouse pot azalea—including comments on year-round flowering.

The Main Classes

One of the more confusing aspects of azaleas is the nomenclature of types and varieties. Greenhouse-forcing azaleas generally fall into four main groups.

1. The *Indica* varieties are usually large flowered and come in single-, but most double-flowered types come in a wide range of colors. Our present *Indica* varieties are thought to have originated from species native to India. These were brought to Europe during the past century where considerable hybridizing produced many varieties in use today. The Belgians did a lot of this earlier breeding, and for this reason, the *Indica* varieties are sometimes known as Bel-

*Revised by Frank Batson, Angelwood Nursery, Woodburn, Oregon.

gian azaleas. Such excellent varieties as *Albert and Elizabeth, Jean Haerens, Mme. Petrick, Triomphe,* and *Paul Schame* come under this *Indica* group.

2. *Kurume Azaleas* originally were found in and about the city of Kurume in Japan. This type includes most of the small-flowered single varieties that have small, numerous leaves and dense, shapely plants. Such varieties as *Coral Bells, Hexe, Snow, Hinodegiri* and *Salmon Beauty* are of the *Kurume* group. Incidentally, the *Kurume* class is probably the hardiest for outdoor garden purposes of any of the forcing azaleas. They live over winter with protection along our coast lines beginning with Long Island, down the Southern coast, and throughout the West Coast to Seattle.

3. The *Pericat* group originated in this country in the late 1920s. It is midway between the large-flowered *Indicas* and the small-flowered *Kurumes* in flower size and general habit. The *Pericats* are generally late-flowering and find their best use for Easter forcing. Such varieties as *Marjory Ann, Rival, Sweetheart Supreme* (an excellent early-forcing *Pericat*), *Pericat, Rose Pericat,* and *Pink Pericat* belong in this group.

4. The *Rutherfordianas* were introduced in this country about 1935 and are the most recent group. They resulted from crosses between *Indica* and *Kurume* varieties. *Rutherfordiana* flowers are midway between the two parents in size and are known for their keeping quality. Such varieties as *Dorothy Gish, Rose Queen, Constance, Alaska,* and *Snow Queen* belong in this group.

Many of the above-named varieties are no longer generally available, but have been included here as a matter of historic reference.

Basic Culture

Azaleas are produced either by cuttings or by grafting; however, due to the high labor cost involved in grafting, only a few highly specialized growers are now using this method.

In the past, it was generally observed that own-root plants were the less expensive and were produced in only the smaller sizes, while the grafted plants were the ones that were made up into the larger finishing sizes and specimen plants. Today, with the many new, fast-growing, vigorous varieties, this is no longer true, and almost all azaleas produced are on their own roots.

The only real need for grafting today is to produce the so-called "standard" or tree-form specimen plant.

The general question of varieties, classes, and grafted vs. own-root varies considerably in different sections of the country according to climates and demands.

Propagation of azaleas is generally left to specialists. Cuttings or small grafted plants may be purchased during the winter or spring months. Liners are cuttings that have been grown-on a few months from their cutting stage. Plants larger than liners are usually sold by grades expressed in the inches of diameter of the plant. Thus, a plant with a head between 3″ and 5″ across is known as a ³⁄₅ size. Generally speaking, a flowering azalea, particularly in sizes ⁶⁄₈ and larger, is the result of a minimum of 2 years of growing. Rooted cuttings are normally taken during early spring and are rooted by fall. They become liners by spring and perhaps ³⁄₅s or ⁴⁄₆s by the following fall. These same plants planted indoors during the winter and outdoors during the following summer become flowering plants of at least a size ⁸⁄₈ by the second fall. Very large plants (12″ or larger) usually require a third year to reach their size.

The forcer who buys plants during the winter or spring for flowering the following fall should buy at least a ³⁄₅-size plant (growing-on stock, 3″–5″ top diameter of the plant). These might mature into a ⁶⁄₈ plant by fall. Liners purchased during the winter or spring should normally be grown over the second winter for forcing purposes.

The late 1960s and early 1970s seemed to be the years of the florist azalea. There was more breeding and introduction of new varieties suitable for greenhouse forcing done in that 5-year period than has been done since the late 1920s when the *Pericats* came out, and into the mid-1930s when the *Rutherfordianas* were introduced.

Many of the old familiar names, such as those mentioned at the beginning of this article, are now gone from the lists of available varieties, and whole new groups are on the market.

Of course, there are a few of the old-timers still being grown and these few, having stood the test of time, have been the backbone of the azalea market up to the present time.

These few are: *Chimes, Lentengroot, Erie, Alaska, Sweetheart Supreme, Red-Wing* and *Dorothy Gish,* along with its sports *Gloria* and *White Gish.* These last four, especially, because of their adaptability to year-round flowering. A few others could be added to this list, depending upon what local-market demands are.

One of the most promising new seedlings is a deep red of exceptional lasting qualities, developed by San Gabriel Nursery, called *Mission Bells.* This variety will most likely replace *Chimes* as the No. 1 red for Christmas. Available through Geo. J. Ball, Inc.

Those growers buying rooted cuttings or small liners for growing-on over a 2-year period will usually plant them in flats or benches for the first year, and then transplant them to the finishing-size pot in the spring, moving them outdoors for the summer under either lath or saran, and then moving them back into a frost-free holding area in the late fall.

If one buys a larger-size liner, it can be potted direct and placed under the same environment as described above.

A fine plant of azalea Mission Bells—*such plants are the reason azaleas are still the Cadillac of pot plants.*

Growing Media

Azaleas should be planted in a straight coarse grade of either German or Canadian peat moss having a pH of between 4.0 to 5.5. Such peat will actually contain chunks or lumps of peat up to the size of a golf ball mixed in it along with finer material. These lumps will guarantee that you have well-aerated medium and will ensure a rapid take-off of the roots. This grade of peat is sometimes sold as "chicken litter peat." A mixture of ½ peat and ½ firbark or perlite is also being used by many growers.

There are three common disorders of azalea plants that should be watched for during their growing season. The first and most important is the plant's root

Dick Holmberg, Chicago area grower—who for years has specialized in azaleas. He brings in liners from the South in May, plants them to outdoor frames. Then in September they are dug and potted and put at low temperature—and here they are with Dick Holmberg. (Nelson and Holmberg, Berwyn, Illinois.)

system. Well-grown azaleas should have an extensive ball of glistening-white roots. Azalea roots are prevented from growing or are injured for three chief reasons: (1) too high soluble-salt content, which can be cured by leaching; (2) lack of oxygen in the growing medium, which means too much water and/or insufficient drainage—a reason for growing in straight peat moss; or (3) too little water. Assuming a well-drained medium like peat moss is used, azaleas should be watered heavily and should not be allowed to dry out.

The second symptom is chlorotic foliage. Yellowish or light green foliage with darker green veins indicates a lack of iron. Applications of iron sulfate at the rate of 1 pound per 100 gallons will correct this. Other light, yellowish foliage symptoms are usually associated with alkaline soil, overwatering, and/ or poor drainage or root injury. Chlorotic foliage on azalea plants is a sure sign of trouble and will ultimately lead to loss of leaves and plants. It is unwise to use application of iron as a panacea for all chlorotic azalea troubles. Try to find out first what is causing the chlorosis and then take appropriate remedial action.

Leaf-drop is the third symptom of azalea trouble. Once more, this is indicative of improper growing. Underwatering, overwatering, and/or poor drainage, nitrogen, or general nutrient deficiency, or poor root action will cause leaf-drop. Root injury of bed-grown plants may easily occur during the fall-digging process unless plants are lifted and handled carefully. Azaleas will drop their leaves in cold-temperature storage (temperatures above 40°) unless lighted. Look under "Forcing" for lighting and storage directions.

Azaleas that are grown in greenhouses during the winter or early spring can be planted outdoors as soon as danger of frost has subsided. Outdoor beds should be well-drained and should have ample facilities for watering and overhead syringing. Particularly in our hot, dry, midwestern locations, azalea beds should be shaded with either lath or cloth shading. In some of our coastal regions where summers aren't excessively hot or dry, this shading is not necessary. It is good practice to erect sideboard beds for azaleas outdoors to provide adequate drainage, and these beds should be filled with straight German peat moss. Many growers today are no longer growing in beds but plant directly into the finished size pot and then set the potted plant outside usually on gravel to provide good drainage.

Spacing is important in growing azaleas. At no time should plants be allowed to much more than touch each other. This is particularly important during their summer growing season prior to winter forcing. A crowded plant will not develop into a desirable, bushy plant.

Properly timed pruning or pinching is necessary to assure a well-shaped plant with a uniform setting of buds. Plants should be pruned during their earlier stages of growth, not only to assure well-shaped plants, but to remove any early-formed flower buds, and to keep the plant in soft, vegetative growth. The final pruning of azaleas should be done no later than July 1 in latitudes north of Memphis and earlier for plants and varieties destined for early forcing. Any of the *Indica* varieties for Christmas flowering should be pruned last by late May; *Kurume* varieties for Christmas forcing should be pruned last in early June. All pinching at this time should be "soft" pinching—pinching down into hardwood will not result in shoots that will make buds. Too-late pinching often results in late flowering as well as only one bud to a stem, whereas earlier pinching results in laterals producing buds that will flower along with the central flower.

Bud initiation and development in azaleas are strictly temperature relationships. Generally speaking, buds are initiated in approximately 8 weeks of temperatures above 65° for 8 hours per day. Temperatures below this will continue the plants in vegetative growth. Plants should be well-budded under these conditions by late August or early September. At this time, all shade should be removed from the beds. If grown outdoors, remember that plants are very susceptible to frost damage—they must be dug and/or moved indoors before frost.

Fertilizing

Because azaleas have a rather fine root system, they are subject to root injury if too high a concentration of fertilizer is applied.

There are probably more azaleas lost to overfertilizing (allowing high soluble salts to build up) than to any other single cause. This does not mean, however, that fertilizers should be withheld. A light feed at least once a week, or even twice a week during the period of active growth in the summer, should be the rule. Just prior to feeding, the plants should be given a thorough watering to flush out any salts that might be left over from the preceding feed.

The old method of feeding only two to three times during a growing season will just not make a plant when using the newer varieties. But, by the same token, a grower must use more care in feeding and, if at all possible, a soluble salt test as well as a pH reading should be made just prior to feeding.

An acidifying form of fertilizer should be used such as a soluble 21–7–7 at the rate of 1¼ lbs. per 100 gallons plus 3½ oz. of Iron Chelate, applied once a week. S.T.E.M. (Soluble Trace Element Mix) or equivalent should be added at least every fourth feeding.

Growth Retardants on Azaleas

It has been found that B-Nine (or Alar) growth retardant produces more compact plants and additional buds when applied to azaleas. Each variety reacts differently; some respond better than others.

To produce additional flower buds, spray to run-off condition with a 0.25% concentration approximately 1 month after the final pinch. New growth should be started before application and should be out 1" in length.

To produce compact plants, spray to run-off condition with a concentration of 0.37% in early July. The final pinch should be made in sufficient time so that new growth has started before applying the B-Nine.

B-Nine should not be applied with any other spray materials, and at the time of spraying, the plants must be in a fully turgid condition, as a wilted plant just will not absorb the B-Nine into the foliage. For this reason, it is best to apply B-Nine late in the afternoon so that maximum absorption can occur during the night. The plants should not be syringed for at least 24 hours after applying.

Spraying should be done to just before the point of run-off and need be applied to the upper leaf surface only.

Azaleas that have been treated with B-Nine seem to be more tolerant of early fall frost than those not treated; B-Nine produces a tougher plant.

It has been observed by some growers that treated plants may be slightly delayed in flowering. This delay may actually be beneficial when landscape plants are involved, as it allows the nurseryman additional selling time. Other than slight delay and increased flower buds, normal flowering can be expected; however, on some varieties, a slight decrease in flower size may occur.

A sprayer and the chemicals that are doing the pinching job on azaleas so well.

Chemical Pinching

Off-Shoot-O   Today it is possible to reduce the amount of hand labor involved in the manual pinching of all stages of azalea production.

By using the chemical pinching agent, "Off-Shoot-O," and following the manufacturer's directions to the letter, it is usually possible to produce a larger plant simply because less of the new growth is removed and also, if properly applied, all of the small, shorter shoots in the middle of the plant will be pinched. Often, these shoots are missed if the plant is only given a straight-across shearing-type pinch. It may also allow one to get in an extra pinch during the same growing period by permitting pinching of new shoots after only 8 weeks of growth. This could not be done by hand pruning, as it would mean removing most of the new growth and therefore, no additional size would be gained.

Chemical pinching will not work if a flower bud is present; therefore, it is necessary to start any chemical pinching program from a known vegetative point. This means the grower must manually prune and shape the plant the first time by hand. Thereafter, plants may be chemically pruned at 8–10 week intervals. This does not mean, however, that all hand pruning can be eliminated. Depending upon varieties and amount of growth obtained between pinches, some additional shaping of long shoots must be done. Also, it should be remembered that any plant that is straggly or misshapen to start with *must* first be shaped by hand. Treating poorly shaped plants will definitely not improve their form, it will only exaggerate it. Without uniformity, the results will not be uniform.

Treatment should be made after, not before, the shaping is done. This allows more direct and better coverage of the lower shoots and requires less of the chemical to do the job.

The sooner after hand-shaping the chemical is applied, the better. However, in no case let more than one week elapse, for to do so would mean that any new breaks just starting to swell and push out of the pruned stem would be killed just as the tips of the unpruned shoot are; a chemical-pinching agent is simply a type of contact chemical which kills the tender terminal growing points without injuring the more mature plant growth beneath it.

It is usually safer to treat plants that are outside under lath or saran than in the greenhouse or plastic house. This is because it is absolutely necessary to have some movement of air around the plants that will aid in the rapid drying of the spray material upon the plant foliage. Should the foliage remain wet for more than 15 minutes, excessive foliage damage may occur. The use of fans within the greenhouse is highly recommended.

Under no circumstances should an attempt be made to chemically pinch when a rapid drying of the foliage is not possible such as during a rainy, dark period.

The chemical-pinching process is subject to any number of uncontrollable variables. Each and every variety responds differently depending upon the following conditions:

1. Tightness of spacing.

2. Time of day.

3. Season of the year.

4. Temperature.

5. Humidity.

6. Light intensity.

7. Wind velocity.

8. Configuration of the tip of the plants. Example: The variety *Red Wing* tends to form a natural cup of its uppermost leaves surrounding the tip. This cup will hold the pinching agent in close contact with the tip; therefore, a much lower concentration is needed. The variety *Gloria* does not form this special "cup" and will require a higher amount of the chemical to get the same tip kill.

Spraying in still air at high temperatures (above 85°) and high humidity (over 70%) is not recommended, as incidence of foliar burn is increased.

Trial sprayings of at least three concentrations on ten plants each of every variety to be sprayed *that* day are recommended. A small, plastic trigger-type sprayer (such as a housewife uses to dampen clothes with) is an ideal test sprayer for this purpose. Fill them with a 3, 4, and 5-ounce-per-quart rate and treat ten plants with each. This way, one can "bracket-in" on the proper amount to use on any given variety *for that given day and hour*.

Tip kill will occur within 15 to 30 minutes, but foliage damage, if any, may not show until several hours later; therefore, select the lowest possible rate that shows a definite blackening of *all* of the tips and begin spraying within the hour. If you cannot complete the job within 4 hours, or if the natural conditions show any marked changes, *stop* and retrial again. This may seem like a lot of unnecessary work, but if you've ever seen an entire bed of plants literally "cremated" because of using too high a rate, or not drying off fast enough, you will probably agree that it is time well spent.

However, in order not to paint too black a picture, it is possible that many of these "cremated" plants will actually come back out of it; that is, new shoots will appear from the old leaf axils below the dead branches, etc., but there will be a loss of growing time and size that cannot be made up.

When applying the spray for smaller lots, a 3-gallon hand sprayer may be used to which has been attached a Type TG 0.5 solid-cone-spray nozzle. If much spraying is to be done, a small pressure gauge should be soldered or brazed onto the top of the can so that the recommended pressure of 20–40 pounds may be maintained. The adjustable nozzle commonly found on this type of sprayer should not be used, as it produces too large a droplet size even at its finest setting.

To apply to large areas, a motorized sprayer should be used in connection with a spray boom, either hand-held or tractor-mounted.

One large Southern grower has been said to apply his material through a mist blower.

Atrinal   Atrinal is a chemical that will slowly destroy the apical tip of a shoot when applied as a spray. It may take up to 2 weeks to show evidence that it is taking effect. The tip will turn yellow, and lateral branching will begin. Atrinal is said to increase the number of side breaks that will appear—in comparison to Off-Shoot-O; however, it does not seem to be as widely used by most growers, at least at this time—as is Off-Shoot-O.

In general, chemical pinching is an absolute must for the large azalea growers who can take the time to check each variety each day, and can even afford to lose a few plants now and then. For the small retail grower who only produces a limited number of plants each year, it would seem that chemical pinching may be a luxury that he may well not be able to afford, at least at this date.

Insects and Diseases

Spider mite, aphids, and worms (leaf rollers and leaf miners) are the main pests of azaleas. These can be controlled in the greenhouse by using a Dithio aerosol bomb alternated every third time with an Aramite bomb. To kill the moth stage of leaf rollers, an EPA-approved spray should be used.

Outside, any of the available insecticides that are now legal to use in your particular state may be used; however, it is always best to use the wettable-powder form rather than the emulsion.

By using the systemic fungicide "Benlate," the most serious disease problem of azaleas has at last been brought under control. Cylindrocladium has caused wilting, defoliation, and death of plants, attacking foliage, stems and roots alike, and has caused widespread loss at all stages of growth in all parts of the country.

Apply Benlate as either a spray or a soil drench. Other watermold types of fungus can be controlled by drenching with Lesan or Subdue.

A good sanitation program and cleanliness of operation will aid greatly in reducing loss by disease. Prevention is far better than cure.

Forcing

Most azalea forcers buy plants in the fall, either when they are dug or after a required cool-temperature treatment. Plants fully budded and ready for forcing can be purchased any time from early September on. If you buy plants in the fall for forcing, be sure to ascertain whether or not the plants purchased have been "precooled." Azaleas need a ripening or conditioning period at lower temperatures—40 to 50°—after which they are placed in higher temperatures for forcing. Plants grown in certain sections of our country with cool fall weather are naturally precooled. The states of Oregon and Washington have such conditions. October 1 shipment of certain varieties will bloom in December. Plants from other sections where temperatures do not get as low as 40 to 50° at night must be artificially precooled for proper forcing. A minimum of 4 weeks of this cold storage is required for *Kurume* varieties and 6 weeks for *Indica* varieties. Many forcers place their plants in refrigerated storage chambers to assure uniform temperatures during this cold-storage period. To keep leaves from dropping, artificial lighting (at least 10 foot-candles intensity) for 12 hours each day is required.

During this precooling treatment, uniform temperatures are very necessary. For instance, if plants are stored in a cool greenhouse and temperatures get up to 60° during warm, bright days, the plants will not force uniformly. Plants during this cold-storage treatment should be kept only moderately wet. Excessive watering or excessive dryness of the roots will cause leaf-drop. If you buy plants already budded, their care upon arrival is most important.

Budded dormant azalea production in Oregon. The grower: Lowell Hall and son Steve, Lowell Hall Nursery, Inc., Hubbard, Oregon.

Plants should be immediately unpacked, unless frost damage en route is suspected. Azaleas that arrive in a partially frozen condition stand an excellent chance of recovering by storing the unopened cases in a cool temperature—35° to 40°—for several days, to effect a gradual thawing out. Be sure to notify the transportation company immediately if frost damage is suspected, so you will have the basis of a claim if the plants do not recover.

Plants upon receipt should be watered thoroughly by immersing root balls in water until soil is saturated. Place in a shaded house at forcing temperature—60° to 65°. They can be potted immediately or heeled-in on benches of peat moss. Potting should be done in straight peat moss. Be sure to keep plants amply watered during their first 2 weeks, particularly. Frequent syringing to maintain atmospheric moisture is important, also.

Many Pacific Northwest-produced azaleas are forced for the Christmas holiday. The forcer should obtain only early-blooming varieties if he expects to make Christmas. Some of the better early forcers are *Ambrosia, Alaska, Dorothy Gish, Mission Bells*, Erie, Dogwood*,* variegated *Dogwood*, and Red-Wing.*

Forcing should begin by the first week of November at a night temperature of 60°–65°F.

*Denotes patented varieties.

313

In the North, no shade of any kind should be used over the plants. Southern growers may need a light shade, such as a single layer of tobacco cloth.

Overhead syringing usually hastens flowering, but only up to when color begins to show.

Lighting the plants at night the same as for mums will also help flowering and will tend to even out the flowering.

Watch for aphids, red spider, and whiteflies during this period.

As forcing proceeds, shoot-bypassing of the flower bud may be noticed. These should be removed before they are ½" long, or "blasting" of the bud may occur. Do not pinch them off, but remove the entire shoot, using a quick sideways movement, right down to the base of the bud. On some varieties, it is best to hold onto the bud with one hand as you strip off the bypassing shoots with the other. This is especially true if there are several shoots and they have grown out 1–2" or more and have hardened up at the base; otherwise, the bud may be ripped off along with the shoots.

As the forcing continues, the temperature may be raised or lowered to time the flowering. A plant that is in the "candle" stage, or is just showing color the full length of the bud, may be stored in a 42°–48°F cooler, using 12 hours of light, for a period of 2 weeks, without detrimental effects.

Plants that are going out to a shop or to a customer should be slightly beyond the "candle" stage if they are to open up properly. A plant that is still in tight bud, but showing some color, if placed in a low-light-intensity area, may "stick" and never open as it should.

Again, we stress that to make Christmas, order only early-forcing varieties that have been adequately cooled. To try and force later types, such as *Lentengroot*, will often mean missing the holiday completely. Such varieties, it seems, must go through a longer cold precooling and ripening period or "gestation period," as one broker calls it, and no matter how hard they are forced, they will not flower until this ripening requirement is satisfied.

Any of the previously named varieties, as well as *Gloria, White Gish, Dogwood, Kingfisher, Roadrunner,* or variegated *Dogwood,* may be used for Valentine's Day. At this time of the year, usually 4 to 6 weeks at 60°F will force most varieties quite easily.

Easter is the most difficult holiday to force for, due to the variability of the date, but material obtained anywhere in the country will force readily for it. In fact, if Easter is late, the biggest problem is to hold plants back from flowering prematurely. If one has a cooler, the plants may be held back much better than if only a cool, shaded greenhouse or storage shed is used.

For an early Easter, 2 to 3 weeks at 60°F is all that is required. If it is late, 1 to 2 weeks will be sufficient.

The only way to hold plants for Mother's Day is by storing them in a cooler. They should flower 1 to 2 weeks after being removed from cold storage. The extra work and effort of storing is usually well worth it.

Azalea plants unsold at the end of the forcing season can be kept for forcing the following year. They should be repotted with fresh peat moss and trimmed. Trimming should be confined to soft top growth. Beginning in March or April, they should be grown at a minimum of 60°F so as to start new growth. Thereafter, they are treated the same as younger plants.

Trends of the 1980s

Azaleas have usually been forced in large-size pots, i.e., 6" to 8". The trend of the 1980s seems to be heading toward the smaller sizes of plants, as 5" or even 4" plants are now being offered in many of the chain store outlets as well as by the full service florist shops.

To meet this trend, many of the large West Coast dormant azalea producers are shifting a large part of their production from 6" to smaller sizes. This accommodates the midwestern and eastern forces in two ways. It provides them with a smaller size plant with corresponding size root ball ready to drop into a 4" or 5" pot, and also saves them on freight cost. It is possible to pack 40 to 50 4" plants into the same shipping carton—that will hold only 24 of the standard size dormant plants.

This shift toward more and more smaller sizes will probably continue. The azalea is still ''The Aristocrat of Pot Plants,'' but the price that the retailer is having to charge for a larger well-budded azalea really puts it out of the range of many of today's consumers. Therefore, the only way to overcome this is by offering at least some of the smaller-size finished product.

There is also a very clear trend shaping up: Forcers are no longer aiming most of their flowering azaleas for the Christmas market as was the practice in the past. Today's forcers want a large portion of their dormant azaleas to arrive from the West Coast just a few days before Christmas or right after, just so they have enough time to force for Valentine's Day and later. This has come about partly because of the greatly improved keeping quality of the Christmas poinsettia.

This need to hold an ever-increasing portion of the dormant crop until mid-December instead of shipping it the first part of October for Christmas forcing has stimulated a large expansion of greenhouse facilities on the part of the dormant azalea grower. When they could ship most of their product in October there was no need to provide as much freezing protection for the crop which could be grown outdoors under lath or saran cloth. But now this is no longer the case.

This expansion, of course, shows up in the increased cost of buying dormant plants.

Year-round Production and Flowering

Year-round production of azaleas has been successfully done by a few larger growers in different areas of the country and is, in fact, on the rise as of mid-1980s. The pot grower usually buys budded plants (year-round) from specialists. He then cools them for 6 weeks at 40°F, then forces them for up to 5 weeks at 60° nights. This is done by many growers today.

Much work has been done in development of a year-round program by several of the colleges and also commercial growers in an attempt to make it possible for any grower to set up their own programs. They either start from the cutting stage and do the whole program themselves, or buy pre-started plants at the liner stage and grow them on or buy budded plants that have been artificially cooled—then force them on a monthly schedule.

Because of the high cost of producing year-round azaleas in terms of crop time (14–16 months) plus high energy requirements (i.e., lights, heat, coolers, etc.) the demand for year-round azaleas although still high from the consumer's point of view is, from the grower's viewpoint, not economically feasible in most cases. If anyone is interested in a year-round schedule, it is suggested that they see the 12th or 13th edition of the Ball *Red Book*. Or if interested in more complete details on azaleas, obtain a copy of the University of California's publication #4058, "Growing Azaleas Commercially," by Kofranek and Larson.

"Four-inch" Azaleas*

The versatility of the azalea as a flowering pot plant is evident when one can see them in flower in 4" pots, the more conventional 6" pots, or even in 10" hanging baskets. It is unfortunate, however, that pot size is used as the standard for merchandising, as it is no indication of floriferousness, number of shoots, or other more meaningful plant characteristics. Hopefully azalea plants eventually will be judged by some criteria other than pot size, but at this time growers can visualize the plants when azaleas are referred to as "4"."

In much of our azalea research at North Carolina State University, the term "4"" not only is a poor description but it is actually inaccurate, as we are using 4½" (10 cm.) azalea pots. We found pots that were 4" in diameter to be too small. We primarily use peat moss as our potting medium for azaleas, and it is too difficult to get the peat moss wet again if the medium dries out.

We now grow our small azalea plants in 4½" clay pots (see photo). Comparisons of clay versus plastic pots for small azalea plants prompted us to use clay pots, though we do use plastic pots for the larger sizes. Root systems

*Contributed by Dr. Roy A. Larson, Department of Horticultural Science, North Carolina State University, Raleigh.

316

are very good when 4½" clay pots are used, increasing the likelihood of producing good top growth. We also have found that small plants in clay pots readily withstand the rigors of exposure to 6 weeks in cold storage, a necessity if growers plan to produce flowering azaleas on a year-round schedule. Algae can be troublesome on clay pots, a problem not encountered with plastic pots, but the problem is primarily one of cosmetics. We have used algaecides in efforts to reduce or eliminate algal growth but even the most effective chemicals seem to lose their effectiveness before the plants are sold.

Our original goal with small flowering azaleas was to have plants in bloom one year from the date of propagation. We have come close to achieving that goal, though 14 months frequently is required for the production of satisfactory single plants in 4½" pots. We could shorten crop duration and still attain adequate size and number of flowers if we used two plants per pot, but so far we have concentrated our efforts on single plants.

A sample schedule for production is:

Date	Activity
March 1	propagate
May 1	transplant to 4½" pot and give first pinch
June 15	give second pinch
August 1	give third pinch
September 1	give artificial long days to continue vegetative growth
September 15	give natural short days for flower bud initiation and early development. Keep plants at minimum night temperatures of 60–65°F.
November 15	place plants in cooler to break flower bud dormancy. Temperatures of the cooler can be 35°F, and lights are not needed, or 40° to 50°F, with lights for 12 hours daily at an intensity of only 10 to 20 foot-candles.
January 2	force plants at 60° to 65°F
Mid-February	plants should be in flower

Our pinches are soft pinches, removing about ½" of the shoot tip, unless pruning of longer shoots is needed to give the plants an acceptable shape. A concerted effort is made to remove all shoot tips on a plant, so all shoots will be in a similar physiological state and to assure uniform flower bud initiation and development.

The schedule shown above indicates that flowering occurs within the 12-month period which we set as our original goal. We do make allowances in the schedule, and these allowances almost always lengthen, rather than decrease, the duration of the crop. If cuttings are not as well rooted as we might desire after 8 weeks from the date of sticking, we might still plant them in 4½" clay pots but delay pinching until we are certain vigorous lateral shoots will develop from the pinch. We used to pinch out the shoot apex when we stuck the cuttings but that practice seemed to delay rooting and we abandoned that procedure. Pot size and plant height and diameter must be in balance if

Not yet mature—but an example of the fine azalea plants produced under Roy Larson's experimental project at North Carolina State University. (Photo by Roy Larson.)

a high-quality plant is desired, and that might not be achieved if only 6 weeks elapse between pinches. Eight weeks in the darker periods of the year might be beneficial, and this revised schedule could add 6 weeks to the production of the crop.

Scheduling can be much more precisely predicted after the final pinch, with 6 weeks of long days, 8 weeks of short days, 6 weeks of cold storage treatment, and 5 to 6 weeks to force, totalling 25 to 26 weeks from propagation to flowering. Growers who plan to be on a year-round flowering schedule must have access to daylength control (mum lights from September 1 to March 31 for vegetative growth, black cloth for flower bud initiation and early development from April 1 to August 31); cold storage unit (35°F, dark; 40° to 50°F, lights); greenhouse facilities for forcing.

Small plants respond to temperature and daylength in the same manner as older and larger plants. Disease and insect problems are identical and fertilization programs are similar. Plants can be grown at a spacing of three plants per square foot without adversely affecting quality. Most varieties that are satisfactory for forcing in 6" pots also will be suitable for use in smaller pots. We have had success with many cultivars, such as *Alaska, Dogwood, Gloria, Prize* and *Red Wing.*

A major reason for producing small flowering azalea plants is to make high-quality plants available to a segment of the population not presently considered to be regular purchasers of azaleas in retail florist shops. According to a recent report, 34% of the flowers sold in the Seattle, Washington, area were sold through supermarkets and other grocery stores, approximately 26% through retail florist shops and 15% through chain stores and garden stores. Perhaps those figures are typical. The small flowering azaleas primarily would be directed to the outlets selling about 50% of the merchandise. In 1980 we marketed small azaleas, in flower, at a "cash and carry" outlet in a major shopping center in Raleigh, N.C. The shop charged $3.50 for an azalea with no foil, $4.50 where foil and ribbon was used, and $5.50 if the pot was placed in a straw basket. Plants sold quickly, though the price was higher than I had originally anticipated.

Azalea propagators in some states have seen an increased demand for forcing azaleas in recent years, with special interest centered on small azalea plants. Several of these nurseries are now selling budded-up small plants, indicating the increasing popularity of such an azalea. These plants are not culls or plants that are inferior in any way to larger plants.

Ken Fessler, Fessler Nursery, Woodburn, Oregon, major producer of azalea liners and budded plants—shown with a bench of 4" liners.

BALSAM

ANNUAL *(Impatiens balsamina) 3,300 seeds per oz. Germinates in 8 days at 70°.*

Quite tender, summer-flowering annuals that belong to the impatiens family of plants, producing the same soft, sappy growth that calls for plenty of uniform moisture. Most popular class is the Dwarf-Bush Type. Flowers of this type overcome the shortcomings of the old strains, in that the flowers stand out above the foliage. The *Color Parade Mix* is most widely used.

With an enriched soil and plenty of moisture, they are colorful border plants throughout the summer. The double-bush types grow somewhat taller than the dwarf-bush-flowered, are of good size, and are most commonly used as a color mix.

For bedding-plant sales, they should be handled the same as impatiens. Sow about 8 weeks prior to sale.

BEDDING PLANTS—THE BROAD LOOK

A good starting place: Where have we been, where are we going? Special focus on the five years ahead. What problems on the horizon?

The graph on page 282 tells us that bedding plants are indeed a major crop. Here are Department of Commerce 1979 figures:

	$ Sales/year
Foliage	466.0 million
Bedding	285.5 million
All cut flowers	350.4 million
All pot plants	418.0 million

Trend-wise, bedding plants have shown the most growth in dollar sales and in price the past five years. Our estimate for 1984 bedding sales based on the above totals: $419.4 million. An occasional super wet spring (like spring 1983) probably flattens that growth curve—but clearly the bedding crop is continuing its steady growth up.

A point: We do so very badly need better statistics on our whole business. These figures are unfortunately sketchy and out of date. Based, by the way, on what we get from the USDA and our Census Bureau.

And, like all crops, bedding production and marketing are changing! A clear trend the past five years has been the rise of pot annuals—especially 4". But certainly including 3", 5", and 6" (Long Island). People more and more love that "instant color," hate to wait three to four weeks for pack annuals to be in color. And potted vegetables mature weeks earlier—so they too are rising in demand.

320

We hear knowledgeable growers saying that the U.S. bedding crop will "soon be mainly potted plants." Europe is already.

The plug development is another major change (see the plug chapter elsewhere in this book). Plugs are a real help in mechanization. Plus a 25–30% increase in flats per acre. This could even cause some overproduction until it all settles out. Also, plugs can reduce transplanting labor from the normal 30¢ to 50¢ a flat (72 plants) today—to 10¢ to 12¢ (see the plug chapter).

The other change we see: Much more of other mechanization. Already growers fill flats, irrigate (sometimes), move things (sometimes) mechanically. But there is much more opportunity here. First, in moving flats to the growing area then back to shipping. Self-powered belts, Dutch-style trays are starting to appear. We need much more of them.

In fact, if U.S. growers will really use the mechanical technology available today, bedding plants can become a true low-labor crop. Lower cost means better profits. And even more telling, if the rumblings of cheap foreign bedding plants we hear today come true, the truly mechanized grower can compete very nicely. And not go the way of our carnation crop. It would then become a matter of who is most efficiently mechanized. And that's a battle U.S. growers can win!

One other point: Bedding plants are still today an opportunity for the new entrepreneur (young people or older folks) who have learned growing (as apprentices or in trade schools), who are willing to work hard, and who often have a willing spouse—can and often do set up production in spring annuals, and succeed! We see this often, and welcome these newcomers to our industry. We always urge them to strive for quality, and market aggressively. And remember, you don't have to give it away if it's good! Don't make price your way into the market.

Aart Van Wingerden, a senior in our industry, points out (with pride and joy) that bedding plants are one of the few remaining opportunities for young people to launch themselves into business—without big start-up money.

Marketing and Production Plans—One Every Year

So few bedding growers we know of really do give marketing their product serious thought. They *like* and they *think* growing—then they sell the product "best they can." The following pages are meant to provide a sort of road map—how to study your own marketing opportunities. Steps. Suggestions. Try them.

Basic decision—to be pure wholesale or to retail   You will get $12 a flat at retail (12 packs at $1), maybe $5 to $7 wholesale. But it's a different world. Not all easy. And for the record, either retailing or wholesaling can certainly be profitable.

Do you enjoy dealing with the public? If so, odds for success at retailing go up. Are you a friendly type? Is your present location on a high traffic street—critical to success in retailing. Lots of room for parking? Are you in an affluent neighborhood? These folks want quality and will pay for it. We think of Herman Wallitsch in Louisville, Kentucky, a classic "affluent supplier." Are you well known in your community? Can you breathe life into a newspaper ad—or maybe do a radio or TV talk show? Great for retailing.

Now let's talk the attributes of a good wholesale grower.

First, are you a reasonably good business man? Really basic to either wholesale or retail. Are you a good money manager? Can you collect old bills, buy hard? Can you manage people? Do you really enjoy growing, managing production and help? Are you a quality grower? Important in the tough competitive world of wholesale growing. Are you good with mechanical things? Bedding production is moving steadily toward mechanization. And so often successful wholesale growers we see are good builders—of greenhouses, etc.

Study the competition   Go see their facilities during the spring rush, talk to them. See what parts of your local or regional markets are well serviced today, which are less covered? What areas are flooded with very cheap competition?

Marketing people call it "seeking a niche in the market." Sometimes you'll find a smaller corner, some part of the market that no one else is doing. Reminds us of Curtis Pickens, Orlando, Florida, who came into the growing business several years ago. Small, new, he took a year try at pack annuals, found the competition of very large mechanized producers tough. So, on the advice of his friendly Ball Seed salesman, he dove into the 4" annuals. He's doing great, expanding. A classic niche. By the way, the niche probably won't be there forever—but it's been a great thing for Curtis Pickens.

All of this bears on what marketing people call "market segmentation." What they're saying is that the market for a typical product will have many different "segments." In bedding plants there will be the price-conscious discount outlet, at the other end of the spectrum the garden center appealing to the super affluent buyer—now at top quality and top price. And a wide variety of other special markets. Like the wholesale landscape contractors who want to buy 500 flats for planting a large shopping center. Or a truck load of 4" plants for some big contract thing.

The point of all this: Pick the segment that you can serve most efficiently and most profitably.

The very large wholesale growers, highly mechanized, make tough competition for the wholesale market. With their advanced mechanization, they can produce at a lower price and make a fair profit. The smaller grower quite often at least gets started in retailing. It's a world where being big and mechanized doesn't count much.

By the way, speaking of retailing and competitors—do check out some of the local garden center chains in your local area. They are almost everywhere across the U.S. today and they typically do an excellent job of laying out retail displays, price marking, and other little details of retailing. It's all there for you

*Another niche: Growers in a reasonably affluent area often do Jiffy-Pot an-
nuals—2¼", sometime 3". Here's Joe Altmyer, A & A Growers, Laurel, Mississippi—who grows good plants—and he's going after a special corner of his
market.*

to see and copy where it fits your world. Frank's Nursery chain, Midwest and
East, is a good example of well laid out facilities.

Learn from your successful competitor! Study him. Talk to him, shop his
prices and quality and pack sizes.

Containers—a critical choice   A key way you implement your marketing
strategy is by your choice of growing containers. Back to our friend Herman
Wallitsch of Louisville and his affluent customers. A key item here is a tray
with 12 2¼" Jiffy-Strips® (2 strips of 6 each). The 12 plants in a plastic tray
retail at $4.50 (spring 1983). Perhaps the other extreme would be the very
large wholesale grower producing for K-Mart or Frank's—who as of the mid-
1980s are insisting on 18 packs per 21" flat. Which gives K-Mart or Frank's
the cheapest pack in town. Growers very much don't like this—but these two
giant chains are insisting—as of mid-1980s.

Another affluent area grower: Alden Finch, Chesapeake, Ohio. Here
you'll see 2¼" Jiffy impatiens at 50¢ retail (mid-1980s).

The great majority of petunias, marigolds, etc., are grown either AC 6–
12, 72 cell packs per 21" flat (12 packs of 6 plants)—or increasingly in an AC
4–12—now 12 packs of 4 plants (impatiens—begonias).* Substantial quantities
of especially impatiens and begonias—you'll find in AC 3–12, now 36 plants
per flat.

*What does "AC" mean? Answer: No significance except to identify a cell pack style (see container
 chapter). And, the "6" means 6 cells per pack. The "12" means 12 packs per flat.

Jiffy-Pot annuals continue to be an important part of the crop—especially where there is demand for a better plant. And people love the "plant, pot and all" approach. Here's Gene Young, Auburn, Alabama, grower, who does a volume of them.

Again, Curtis Pickens (Orlando, Florida), grows the same petunias and impatiens now in a 4"-square plastic pot. And again, the container is one of the ways you make your marketing strategy work.

Somehow the industry so often settles on a 3" square or round Jiffy or sometimes plastic pot, for tomatoes and peppers. Especially the better trade. Of course a 6–12 cell pack is a less expensive tomato. The Rahns in Savannah, Georgia, offer 2¼"-square Jiffy pepper/tomatoes at 35¢ retail. At 36 per flat, they get $12.60 a flat.

Another adaptation of the standard AC 6–12 (12 packs of 6 plants) in a 21" flat is the so called mini-flat. It's the same deal all the way through except maybe 20% smaller. The flat dimensions are now 19" by 9¾".

An important point on selecting the right container: So often we see good quality retail grower operators offering a very large pack size at a somewhat higher price. Typically there will be six of these packs to a 21" flat—with maybe 6 or 8 plants in a pack. The grower probably tells you that he gets $1.49 at retail. But look what happens to the return *per flat*:

Pack	Retail price per pack	Pack price times packs per flat
6 packs per 21" flat	$1.49	$ 8.94
18 packs per 21" flat	.59	10.62 K-Mart or Frank's

So now our retail grower friend is getting about 15% less for a flat of his plants than the super-cheap discount store! In fact, he should be getting 50% more. His quality is often a lot better (better care of display). Also, he can offer the customer a wide variety of annuals and other plant material, typically real help on laying out a garden, solving other problems. Also, he typically offers a variety of gardening supplies: peat moss, fertilizer, etc. He has so much to offer compared to the low price chain—but in fact *he ends up getting fewer dollars per flat*. The rationale is always the same: "I want to have a bigger pack than the chain." He too is striving for a niche, but ends up losing the battle.

Speaking of this, we are seeing a clear trend among many growers both retail and wholesale, moving from 6 or 8 packs per flat to 10 or 12. All 22" flats. Reason: Lower cost per pack to the retail outlet whether it be the grower's own garden center or the retailer he is supplying. $5.50 per flat divided by 6 is 92¢ per pack. Same flat divided by 12 cost the retailer only 46¢. And annuals today are sold by the pack, not per dozen.

Other marketing comments   Speaking of marketing—and niches—the food chains (large and small) as of the mid-1980s seem to be an emerging and potentially important market for bedding plants. Oddly enough the big Southern chain such as TG&Y typically displays pack annuals in front of their store in early spring. But less so in the north—where food chains are so very strong in pot plants and cut flowers. Somehow almost the majority of the major Northern and Western chains have simply not gotten into bedding plants yet. One grower (Ivy Acres, Long Island) reported last spring designing and offering a display tray to supermarkets which will handle his plants. The tray is perhaps 5' long by 2' wide (3 or 4 shelves), on wheels, and is made available at no charge to the super. Since there are four or five layers of plants on the tray, this minimizes the floor space tied up in plants. If only there could be some way of mechanically irrigating displays of annuals at supermarkets and discount chains, it would do so much for our whole industry! Dry plants are a chronic and continuous problem.

Watch out, by the way, for high cost of delivering plants to retail outlets. Bart Bernacchi, major LaPorte, Indiana grower, reports that 10 to 12% of his total bedding cost is delivery cost. "We bought some new steel racks—each holds 64 flats, 10 racks to a 40' truck. Now we can load a Hertz truck in 20 minutes. That helps."

Another niche—summer 4"   In a way it's a part of the market separate from all the spring plant business. It's the classic instant color 4" annual offered in June or July. Six or eight of them will make a spot of color in a garden. And the color happens today. The other joy of this is that it's income during the summer months—otherwise slack time for the bedding grower.

Speaking of niches again, we saw a Summerfield, Texas, grower, Bobby Thrash, who specializes in annual vinca. They're hard to germinate, hard to

Here's a classic marketing niche. Growers so often have problems with starting vinca. Plants rot. Somehow Bobby Thrash does them easily and well. So Bobby is the "vinca starter" for a dozen or two bedding growers in the New Summerfield, Texas, area. Here he is with his vinca.

establish after transplanting. He does it well. So his neighbors buy in their semi-finished pack vincas from Bobby.

Watch your dump   One important clue in making your marketing plan for the spring ahead can come from records of the year past. Particularly plants dumped, also what you ran out of and which week it was short. All of which demands good records—more later on this. But it's obviously critical to cover this spring's shortage with a little more production of the same item next spring.

Price—key part of your marketing strategy   In a way, price is the very essence of your marketing plan. So many growers we see just stay with their competition—or often a bit below. Which is a poor basis for setting price.

What's the market?   Clearly the major consideration in setting price should be what the market will pay for what you have to offer. Here again the niche—the new product, the new idea, can often command an extra 10 or 20%. Sometimes a new variety. The first Happipot gerbera brought surprising prices for example. The very essence of good business is sensing when you have something in demand, not offered freely on the market, and which will support a little higher price.

326

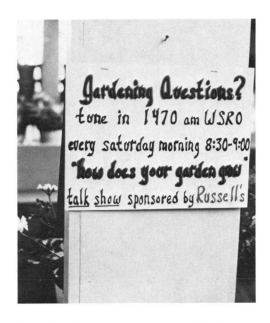

If you have a talent for it, here's a great way to establish your reputation—and your business in any area. Done by Russell's, Boston.

Cost   Again, not many growers really know their cost—but they should! In any case, it's obviously courting disaster to sell at cost or below. If you can't mark up an item substantially above cost, better get out of it. But most of all, know your cost.

Your competitor   No, you can't ignore him—but again certainly don't be tied to his price.

About bundling   It's a buzzword of the marketing profession. What you do is first separate out the components of your price. For example, a pot mum at retail (don't be concerned about the prices—they are only for example):

$10 for the mum

$2 for the wrap/bow

$2 for delivery

$2 for credit

Total $16

The point of all this: If you separate and identify the things you are charging people for, you can price the product at different levels for different parts of the "bundle." For example: The pot mum above at $10 is a cash and carry price. The retailer might offer each of the other three components—at the customer's option. Or various combinations.

Part of the point of all this is to be sure that your competitor is not offering a $10 mum—but not including the wrapping, delivery, and credit—which you may be doing.

Have a production plan   To us, a written plan of the spring's work is a must. It's the way the grower can plan production to fill his range, no more or less. Then his seed, soil and supplies, and help requirements can be tied to that. And—most of all, it's a record of what he sold and what he dumped. Critically important! We recommend for example for *Impatiens Elfins White* the following record:

	To sell week of May 5	To sell week of May 12	To sell week of May 19
Number of flats			
Container used (AC 12 or 4–12?)			
Weight of seed needed			
Sowing date			
Transplant date			
Did we run out?			
Number of flats dumped			

As growers move into plugs, the record of course will change some. But there is the same basic need to plan the operation ahead—and record what happened when we marketed the product.

And lastly, all this presumes a space plan. Square feet available in each house, date space is available, and day it will be needed for other crops. And the number of flats planned had better fill the space available.

Again—enter the computer. A great way to keep such records. See the computer chapter elsewhere in this book.

Have a plan for profit   The very essence of good business is to develop an accurate forecast of your cost, also realistic sales for each part of your spring crop. And from that to forecast your profit. And hopefully hit your profit forecast reasonably well. All this can be done. A few growers today do. And again, this is one of the several things that computers can do for growers.

It can be done—and will be done more and more as growers realize how much better information they get from computers—and how much it simplifies paperwork. And inventory control.

G.V.B.

Ideas on Building Retail Sales

How do the really successful growers build ever-increasing retail sales of bedding annuals? Important clues:

1. Often such successes bear the clear stamp of the owner's personality. Fred Pence, Lawrence, Kansas, gets on a local radio station on Saturday morning, talks gardening. Everyone knows Fred—and a lot of these listeners buy from him. Or David Engh, colorful Salt Lake City veteran—a master at bringing out the crowd—and making them buy. Or big, affable Andy Hauge of Fairmont, West Virginia, who, like hundreds of others, knows and is known personally by most of his customers. People just *love* to be greeted by name. Don't you?

2. They just do a lot of the right things at the right time and do them reasonably well. Let's call it good management.

Use the newspaper!   Newspaper ads are clearly the number one way the winners go. The geat majority use newspaper advertising heavily—generally more so than TV/radio. The number one mission of your advertising program is to get people into your shop—and the local paper seems to do it best.

One problem in using newspapers effectively is just getting the job done—and on time. You really must lay out a plan months ahead. Start hitting readers several weeks before the season. Hit them hard during the peak weeks—and keep after them until it's over. You just can't do such a program on a week-at-a-time basis. Good newspaper ads are a lot less a matter of inspiring copy—and a lot more just getting them in regularly and at the right time. Tell them what you've got to sell. Use pictures.

Push your money-makers! You know the things that earn for you—and what you have in supply. Push good, new items. Push your good service. "Let us help you plan your garden." Things that low-price chain outlets tend not to offer. Important! Most papers have a garden editor. It's a fact of life that good steady advertisers get helpful plugs in these garden columns. "New tomato Better Boy is great, you can get them at Jones' Garden Center." Cultivate your local garden writers. They can help you.

What should your newspaper advertising budget be against your total sales?

Andy Hauge, Fairmont, West Virginia, a successful retail grower, says, "We have both a flower shop and a garden center. Total advertising budget is 6%–8% of sales. Besides newspapers, we are promoting on radio and TV, especially at the height of the spring selling season."

Good colorful newspaper ads are so often the #1 way bedding growers get their message out to the customers. Here's Bob Ench, operator of the Flowertime chain of garden centers and greenhouses on Long Island.

Sam Perino, successful garden-center/bedding-plant outlet, New Orleans, "We use newspaper ads for our publicity. It works. Radio just doesn't seem to get the same results."

Radio/TV Again, newspaper ads generally are number one among retail growers—but in some situations radio and TV do a bang-up job. Our own observation: If the proprietor takes a personal interest in radio and TV, it can really do a job for him. Classic example: the proprietor who knows gardening (growers all really do) and who has a knack for talking about it—on radio or TV. Local stations generally are pleased to have you talk gardening for 10 or 15 minutes weekly in the spring—"What you should be doing in your garden this week." Or, "Here are the new rose and petunia varieties for the season—as I see them for our locality." Or just a troubleshooting program—one fellow keeps a phone hotline open. Folks phone in questions, he fields them as they come (interesting challenge!).

There are "garden writers" in radio/TV, too—important, well worth cultivating. Like Alice Burlingame, Detroit. Bedding growers in the area reported a sell-out of new Early Girl tomato—following some radio comments by Alice!

Price List/Direct Mail—great sales builders Most successful retail-grower garden centers we know do publish a price list. Some represent a major effort

(20–30 pages or more), lots of 4-color. Helpful ideas on gardening, etc. Typically, they go out by mail to the full list of retail customers and prospects—well in advance of the season. The substantial investment made here by successful growers says these lists must be effective sales builders.

Home gardeners love to read, plan, on those cold nights in February! Your message should be there. Some good examples we've seen: Bruce Bordine, Rochester, Michigan (very colorful), also Weall and Cullen Garden Center/Nursery in the Toronto area.

Great opportunity here for helpful ideas for your home gardener customer. Help on the terribly important question of matching shade-loving plants with shady borders. Which plant can stand how much shade? (Did you know that the browallia will flower where shade is too heavy even for fibrous or tuberous begonias and impatiens to bloom?) Also, which of the new varieties this season are really great for *your* particular climate?

Have an open house So often a part of the marketing program of successful retail growers, garden centers. They're done in different ways. Gerhard Siegert, Cristal Springs Florist (Benton Harbor, Michigan) operates an acre of

Planting guide—available in large poster form for garden center outlets.

331

greenhouse, grows pot plants, some cuts—and bedding plants. Early December there are thousands of well-done poinsettias ablaze with color, so they invite the town in for a day. Not to sell, mainly to get new faces into their shop. Builds business.

The Zoerbs, LaCrosse, Wisconsin, grow a lot of fine geraniums each spring. An open house in early May, just before the bedding season begins, brings a lot of new prospective customers into their houses. Again, not much in direct sales that day—but surely good for business.

Have a good sign Good signs cost money, but they are very much a part of success in retailing bedding plants. For an example of a good sign see photo of Carl Padgett's Dogwood Nursery, Gulfport, Mississippi. The sign cost $2,500 plus the maintenance contract.

You often see such signs with provisions for a weekly special below the name of the nursery. "Special this week—pack petunias 89¢."

The emphasis by such retail giants as Holiday Inn and McDonalds must tell us that a good sign is one key weapon in bringing people into your shop. One of the major national motel chain's signs cost around $285 per month per motel—and more than pay their way!

Use of point-of-sale aids! When Mrs. Home Gardener walks up to your display of impatiens plants, for example, it's critically important that several things be instantly apparent to her.

1. That impatiens will flower well in shade—but not dense shade.

2. What actual color she can expect from *Elfin Red* (again, for example).

3. What spacing to allow—and how tall she can expect them to grow.

4. Price per pack or pot.

5. Last, but really most important, sales aids.

Give her a picture in color of what a great show those plants will make in her garden a month or so from now. BPI (Bedding Plants, Inc.) offers such material to members.

How to do all this? Again, here's what some winners we see do:

Color labels are very widely used. We see more of them each season. They give color presentations of the variety—and a label goes out with each pack!

Color labels also relieve much of the pressure to have such annuals as petunias sold in flower. In travels among growers, more than half of all petunias we saw went out green. Comment: "Gardeners are coming to realize that short, bushy, soft green plants will do a far better job in their gardens. And now with Tag-Along® plastic labels, they can plan their color combinations."

332

Good colored picture labels are another basic of marketing bedding plants. The color helps sell; the message answers questions, and saves staff time. Many chains and supers require color labels.

Hascal Collins, Collins, Mississippi: "If we use a color label on each pack, we can sell petunias to our local PGY chain before they flower. It's a better plant, takes less time for us to produce. They don't demand petunias in flower here—but they do want color labels."

Chatty little signs. Here and there we find a grower who makes cardboard signs, puts them up among displays. Just inexpensive white cardboard lettered by hand with a felt-tip pen. The message: practical pointers about the plants you offer. (Impatiens) "Great in that shady spot—but not for dense shade." (Portulaca) "They're happy right in the hottest, driest place you've got." (Vinca) "No good in the shade—need full sun."

Here's a chance for you to use your expertise to help your customers—and serve them better. They'll remember.

Garden books are a sales builder, too! We see people thumbing through these colorful booklets and books. You know they're getting ideas on how they can use annuals around their homes. K-Mart store manager, Oxnard, California, says: "These books sell big here—$1.50 to $1.95. We make money on the books—and they help fire people up about gardening." Three sources for books: Sunset Books, Lane Publishing Co., Menlo Park, CA 94025. Another: Countryside Books, Countryside Publishing, A. B. Morse Co., 2280 U.S. Highway 19 N., Suite 22, Clearwater, FL 33575. Also, Ortho Books, 575 Market Street, Room 3188, San Francisco, CA 94105.

Well-organized self-service builds sales. Virtually all garden centers operate on a "serve-yourself" basis. The point is—if it's organized well so that shopping here is easy and convenient, people buy more. Some points:

Good signs clearly identifying the product and the price are basics of marketing. Even better if there were a suggestion on shade preference, spacing, etc.

1. Display plants at convenient waist height—not down on the ground.

2. Aisles—wide, surfaced (never muddy).

3. Carts—we see all sorts of things, even children's wagons. Just have plenty of them, be sure they're big enough.

4. Ample parking. Eric Schaefer, Montgomery, Illinois, has 60 spaces for roughly a $2,000 turnover of bedding plants per parking space per year.

5. Ample checkout facilities.

6. Have someone around who can answer questions, talk gardening. Good point-of-sale aids (Tag-Alongs, posters) go a long way, but often gardeners like help, especially on "what will grow in that bed just in front of my house?"

7. Boys to help the customer load heavy plants into the car.

Grow quality. There's no sales-builder quite like good plants. Stocky, well-grown cool-finished annuals. Not too crowded—better 72 or 60 to a 21-inch flat. Good varieties—include the new things that gardeners do call for these days. When plants become overgrown, second class, throw 'em out!

334

Just like a good restaurant, the word spreads about good annuals, and most of all, plants that perform well this year will bring that customer back next spring.

Soil Mixes for Bedding

Just 10 to 15 years ago, you'd find most grower's bedding mix was mainly local soil—plus some additives. Today it's mainly "artificial"—and often a little soil. And more each year growers are using mixes from specialists.

First, why the move away from soil—and toward peat, perlite, bark, etc.?

- First, availability. It gets harder every year to find land that can be scraped—for top soil. You've got to buy the land, scrape it, then probably rebuild it. An expensive process. Also, by the way, illegal in some areas.

- More each year farmers are using a variety of weed killers not all of which quickly disappear. We've seen some monstrous problems on this score!

- Bedding plants in straight soil or 3/4 soil are heavy! And labor of moving things around gets more critical each year.

An old cement mixer is a great way to steam and mix soil.

335

- Each lot of soil tends to be a little different—salts, nutrients, disease problems, structure, etc. Once you get used to an artificial formulation, it will be the same each year. Very important!

- More each year growers are learning to rely on specialists for many things—including soil mix (as the Dutch do so well, even in Kalamazoo, Michigan). The grower who uses professionally prepared mixes eliminates an important hand labor job—and since the soil mix specialist uses advanced mechanization, his cost is normally so much lower that even including his profit, the grower will be as well off or better buying from the specialist.

- The advent of bark—both southern pine and western redwood—has brought an important new low price component to our soil mixes. Especially with pine bark we had to learn to use it—but now they are widely and successfully used by bedding and pot growers. In a way the same thing for polystyrene "beads"—the little 1/8" white particles.

What are the mixes of the mid-1980s? Visit 100 growers across the U.S. and you'll find a wide variety of answers to the soil mix question. In some cases, the grower is responding to materials locally available at low cost. Interesting also how many growers use a standard specialist mix—for all crops both pot, bedding, and foliage. But again the question: What are the main types of mixes used by growers today? Some answers we see:

Specialist's mixes Norm White, Chesapeake, Virginia, top-quality large bedding and pot plant specialist, uses specialist mixes. His consistent quality is strong evidence in favor of this approach.

We see also quite often that small- to mid-sized growers lean to specialist mixes—again the high cost for a small grower preparing a small quantity of mixes and the problems of doing it well. Smaller growers can ill afford the costly mixing equipment.

Betty Callahan, Atlanta area grower—all specialist mix—including a wide variety of pot plants, excellent baskets, and bedding plants.

Jim Youngsman, Skagit Gardens in Mt. Vernon, Washington, all specialist mix for 17 years—peat, perlite, and sand.

Here's an interesting example of success with a specialist mix—for a special purpose. The mix: Ball Germinating Mix. We hear many success stories from growers on this one.

What percent of U.S. production is in specialist mixes today? Hard to answer. It must be on the order of at least 1/4 to 1/3—plus a lot of growers who use specialist mixes plus additives.

Specialist mix plus additives A lot of growers go this way. They select a good specialist artificial mix and just to "keep myself out of trouble" they often add 10% to 20% of soil. The word is buffering action—sort of keeps the grower from running into problems on nutritional unbalances, minor elements, etc. It works—and growers, especially until they've had a lot of experience with artificial mixes, often go this way. Perhaps another ¼ or so of the crop is done this way—our guess.

Grower prepared mixes   Here come a wide variety of "home brew" mixes prepared by the grower himself. Principal components we see would be peat, perlite, pine or redwood bark, vermiculite, shredded polyurethane (⅛" white particles), and often some soil. We see endless variations in proportions of these ingredients. Often growers develop a mix that they are comfortable with, use it for years on many crops. Which is a great confidence-building experience. Jack Tomasovic, quality St. Louis grower, is all 1–1–1 soil, sand, and peat. Beardens, major bedding specialist in Alabama: about ⅓ each peat, vermiculite, and pine bark. Again successful and again lots of experience with this mix. Harold Ahner, St. Louis retail grower, uses a mix of peat, perlite, and soil. Rich Malvern, top quality St. Louis pot grower, prepares a mix of one 6' bale of peat, one 4' bag of perlite, two bags of vermiculite, six lbs. of dolomite. The Whites at Godfrey, Illinois (St. Louis), half acre of retail growing, bedding plants mostly, prepare a mix of a quarter each vermiculite and perlite, ⅓ of peat, 15% soil. "I'm afraid to go to zero soil." Billy Powell, Troup, Texas, uses all Cornell mix—and so do most other bedding plant specialists in that area.

Northern Europeans, especially Germans, have been great peat growers for years! Henry Schneider (German trained) and son, Gene, reflecting their German background, are peat growers. The mix here: 85% peat, 10% ground polystyrene, and 5% sand. Says Gene, "We may have to steam the sand—we test every lot."

Suggestions on growing in mixes   It's a different ballgame growing in especially a soil-less mix—compared to the old soil or mostly soil combinations of the recent past—and it's important to know these differences. Here are highlights:

First, on peatlite moisture   Very important that peatlite and in fact all peat in mixes must be thoroughly moistened before planting. A dry spot in a pack of annuals means very high salt levels (no water there to dilute the fertilizer). The plants just don't grow in the dry spot. We often see growers watering two or three times to be sure that the mix is wet clear through.

Again, in peatlite mixes, the nitrate form of nitrogen works a lot better than ammonium nitrogen. And by the way, steaming is generally not necessary in peatlite. In fact, in some cases it will inhibit growth.

A negative point on peatlite: Such pot crops as pot mums, for example, amply fed and watered in a peatlite mix will grow a lush, heavy, fine looking plant with mammoth flowers. But so often these plants just don't have keeping quality. And often can't stand shipping. There is good documentation of this in *Grower Talks,* January 1976, page 1. Actually we see few growers using straight peatlite for general pot plant production. It's great for bedding production (several major growers rely heavily on it). Also, excellent for seed germination. Also, many growers use peatlite as a base—then add soil or bark.

With bark mixes especially, it's very important to start liquid feeding the day you plant. Reason: Bark, even though well composted, does tend to remove nitrogen from the mix. Also, in areas with very hard water it is very important to maintain pH at levels prescribed for the crop. Pine bark tends to drive pH upward and makes iron unavailable.

Interesting point on feeding in artificial mixes   We have noticed many times that where growers combine liquid feed with slow-release fertilizers (Osmocote® or MagAmp®)—they achieve substantially more growth than using either one of the fertilizers separately. No matter how much of the separate ingredient is used, the combination of the two produces surprising results.

Veteran scientist Harry Tayama of Ohio State makes the point that artificial mixes require the grower to importantly increase fertilizer concentration—also to lower pH levels. Certainly these are important points—and are documented in the fertilizer section of this book.

Summary   For a start, we'd recommend using one part each peat, perlite, and soil. A good next step: Jack Van de Wetering's 50% peat, 30% vermiculite, 10% perlite, 10% soil. Once you have gained experience, especially on feeding/watering, then we'd move toward a completely artificial mix—no soil. It's the way of the future for bedding plants and, really, for most flower crops.

Pointers on Culture

Here we talk about the intricacies of good growing and a good starting place: Just what is a good crop of bedding plants?

Our response: In broad sweep, a good crop is a profitable one. This is not a botanic garden. Profit is the goal. So here would be our thoughts on a good crop:

- *First, good quality* is always important! A short stocky petunia with thick stems, strong bottom breaks, buds beginning to show, not a tall lanky plant with flowers out on top.

- *Petunias in color?* Growers are a hung jury on this one. Quite often the quality-oriented good garden center retail grower is proud that most of his petunias go out green. And such a plant will do better in the customer's garden. However, a lot of other growers produce for the major chains—and often they simply insist on color. Since early color is a hard thing to get, we'll talk about that.

- *Minimum weeks from transplant to sell*. Time in the spring is critical. Saving a week on an acre of bedding plants is quite a lot of money. Besides, a week or two saved often permits a second crop. Plugs of course are pivotal in the whole matter of squeezing more crops in during the short spring months. More later on that.

- *Uniformity*. A uniform pack or flat of plants.

- *Maximum shelf life* especially at discount stores is important. Not too soft a plant helps. Also, soil mixes heavy in peat, bark help too.

- A quality plant should be free of insects and disease.

Ways to control growth—hasten flowering There are many! And by the way, much of this is based on tests by Dr. John Seeley, great Cornell scientist/teacher. Here then are the environmental factors that can be controlled by the grower—which affect growth of annuals.

Temperatures. Petunias, and really most annuals, flower earlier at warmer temperatures. Example: *Pink Magic* petunias sown March 9 were 96% in flower grown at 60°F, 4% in flower grown at 50°F. See Table 1. The reason some growers grow annuals at 68°F rather than 60°F or cooler. Warmer temperatures do tend to stretch the plant, discourage bottom breaks—but they do flower earlier.

Soil Moisture. On most annuals, more frequent watering means earlier flowering. Again, John Seeley's classic trials at Penn State: *Comanche* petunias sown March 2 flowered 70% May 21 if watered daily, 7% if run dry. John adds, "The real wet ones (plunged in soil and watered daily) did flower first of all—but they were too tall."

HIGHER TEMPERATURE MEANS EARLIER BLOOM

Tests done by Ball staff at West Chicago

VARIETY	SOWN	PRICKED OFF	% IN BLOOM MAY 21		% IN BLOOM JUNE 1	
			50°	60°	50°	60°
Petunia Allegro	3/9/62	3/27/62	0	5	10	75
Petunia Pink Magic	3/9/62	3/27/62	4	96*	100	100
Marigold Spry	3/9/62	3/14/62	100	100	100	100
Snap Sequoia	3/9/62	3/27/62	0	15*	0	50

REMARKS - the 60° lot was saleable and flowered 2 weeks earlier.

*60° plants, some taller but very saleable.

Watering is so very much a matter of judgement—the reason so many growers hand-water at least up until warm weather. One grower reported, "We water freely for the first week or so to get them started—but then we hold back depending on growth and demand. We have automatic equipment but better done by hand especially in the early stages."

An important point on the conflict between warm wet growing vs. too tall a plant: Use of B-Nine®. To some extent, the grower *can* carry plants warmer and water more, get earlier flowering—and still not have too tall a plant—with generous use of retardant. Says Ken Reeves of Toronto, "I'd rather control height with retardants than with cool temperature which will delay flowering. And B-Nine does not delay color."

Feeding: Same story. More feed on most annuals means earlier flowering. Certainly on petunias. See Table (p. 341): *Allegro* petunias sown March 2, not fed, are 33% in flower May 21. Fed weekly, 90% in flower.

What do growers do about this feeding question? We see a lot of people using fertilizer injectors—but often going back to clear water as the plants become established. Frankly to harden the crop and sometimes to hold it back. Many other growers do use slow-release (MagAmp and Osmocote) only. Often at half the recommended rate. In general, a pot mum crop will probably get liquid fertilizer injection from start to finish. Bedding plants generally are fed a lot less than that. But most of all things in growing annuals, this is a judgement call. Which you get good at only with experience.

```
┌─────────────────────────────────────────┐
│      WARM TEMPERATURE                     │
│      PLUS MORE FEED                        │
│      MEANS EARLIER BLOOM                   │
│   Tests by Dr. John Seeley, Penn State    │
├───────────────────────────────────────────┤
│        PETUNIA ALLEGRO                     │
│   SOWN MARCH 2 - POTTED APRIL 1            │
│        WATERED WEEKLY                      │
└─────────────────────────────────────────┘
```

	50° % in flower May 21	60° % in flower May 21
Fed once	0%	33%
Fed every 3 weeks	0%	86%
Fed weekly	7%	90%

NOTE: 60° plants were not too tall.

Day length control. The giant flowered African marigolds clearly respond to short days. Just spreading a sheet of 1 mil. black poly over a bed of *Moon Shot* 7 a.m. to 5 p.m. will flower the crop several weeks earlier—and perhaps half the height. And the plant stays in flower when it's planted out. It's practical, it's real, and it's done by many growers. Note that the earlier sowings made in January and February often flower just as fast without short day treatment— because of natural short days at that time of the year. Note also that the French marigolds don't respond appreciably to day length control.

Interesting point about petunias: On a short 9-hour day, petunias will be bushy, free breaking, great quality—but delayed flowering. On the other hand, grown warm and under a 12-hour day or longer day they will flower earlier— but tend to be tall and spindly. So Ohio's Tayama says, "Start them on long days at 60°F, apply B-Nine; then as flower buds are visible, stop the lights and cool them down."

Salvias have a complex daylength response. The tall late types are naturally short day plants—flower only in late summer as the daylength shortens. The very short early flowering kinds like *St. John's Fire* will flower short and compact in mid-summer—obviously they are long day plants.

How it's really done Here comes the delicate compromise between high temperature, frequent watering, and feeding that cuts crop time and gives earlier flowers—but which also destroys quality.

Growers we see can be divided into perhaps four groups.

Cool-dry Growers   The fellow who sows very early, soon as seed germinates, he drops the crop back to 50° or even 40°. It can be a 20-week crop from sow to sell. The plants at sale time will be tough, rather hard, good shelf life—but they will take a little time to soften up and grow for the customer.

Start at 60°, drop to 50°   A great many growers across the U.S. do it this way. The crop is kept at 60° nights for a week or 10 days after transplanting then dropped to 50° or even cooler—to harden the plant and improve quality. More bottom breaks. Probably now about a 14-week crop sow to sell. This plan is widely followed.

Straight 60°   Again, a large group of growers follows this plan—60° from transplant to sell. Now down to about 12 weeks sow to sell. Not quite the quality of the fellow who cools down to 50° the later part of the crop. Maybe two more weeks total time sow to sell vs. straight 60°.

Straight 68°–70°   The main practitioners here are the Kalamazoo, Michigan growers. They'll probably cut a week or two off of the straight 60° growers' time sow to sell—important, especially when you're working for a second crop, which many of them do. And for early color on petunias.

Southern growers aim for a peak sales period of April 1 (vs. May 1 in the north). All our records point to perhaps a week or so less time on their April 1 crop vs. the northern May 1 crop. The reports on straight 60°F crops we hear average at about 11 weeks sow to sell. Probably the warmer more favorable spring, especially in the Deep South. Table 1 puts it all together.

Table 1   WEEKS SOW TO SELL

Crop salable	Temperature early	Finishing temperature	Sowing date	Weeks sow to sell	Remarks
March 1	68°–70°F	70°	about 12/1 Nov. 21 to Dec. 10	13–14	Kalamazoo early crop
April 15	68°–70°	70°	1/25	11½	Kalamazoo— "70°F at eye level"
May 1	60°	50°	1/23	14	Average of northern growers
May 1	45°	45°	12/18	19½	The slow, dry, cool, northern grower
May 5	60°	60°	2/6	12–13	Average of northern growers
Southern schedules					
April 1	60°	60°	1/15	11	
April 1	60°	50°	1/2	13	

This heavy-duty forklift can move plants from growing area to the truck—and right up on the endgate. And off they go. The grower: Bo Pinter, Ypsilanti, Michigan. "It costs the price of a Cadillac—but it's worth it!"

An interesting adaptation of all this: Bobby Bearden, a major Plantersville, Alabama bedding specialist. Bobby grows a crop of about 20,000 flats of petunias, sown December 5, transplanted about January 5. Kept at 60° in the greenhouse for a week or 10 days then moved right outdoors. No protection! Result, superb quality, heavy bottom breaks—and a lot of ulcers worrying about a hard freeze. It happened once—he just stacked the flats five high, hauled them into the shipping shed with a forklift. It worked! Total time sow to sell (a green plant), by the way, is now 14 weeks—but most of that time is spent right outdoors in the field. Color appears on petunias about April 1.

HID to hasten bloom   Several growers' experiences clearly confirm that exposing plug annuals, especially petunias, to HID light, for even several weeks, will hasten flowering. It's Marc Cathey's "head start" at work. It does work!

Cutting Labor Cost

We're seeing today (mid-1980s) a classic transition of an industry. The long established neighborhood gardeners transplanting seedlings, the carts, wheelbarrows, moving flats around, etc., are gradually giving way to plugs, to highly mechanized moving of things, etc. And inevitably, the highly mechanized producers, with lower labor costs, are pricing lower—and inevitably taking more share of the market. See separate chapter on plugs.

Mechanizing is certainly available to anyone, and in fact, any producer looking to the future really can hardly escape moving that way. The two requirements we see are reasonable size, and capital for the equipment.

Here's a little more positive facet of mechanizing. We are just hearing the first rumors of bedding production coming from very low labor areas south of our borders. Almost certainly this new production will come onto our market—and as always, at low prices. The good news is that the U.S. producer who really accepts and uses mechanization to the fullest, can compete very effectively with these low labor growers. Using all available mechanization today, the U.S. crop is truly no longer a high labor job—it is in fact capital intensive rather than labor intensive. And by the way, the same thing applies to pot plants. And to a certain extent even to cut flowers.

So here are the basics of mechanizing bedding plant production.

Soil mixing   A fair number of growers still mix their own soil—use a mixer fed either by shovel or with an end-loader. It's an operation that takes quite a bit of time, and certainly a large headhouse with cement floor, good end-loaders, equipment to do a thorough job of mixing, etc. More each year we see growers going over to specialist-produced mixes. Now they simply order in the needed quantities of mix a month or two before the season. And of course the specialist producer is highly mechanized, can do it generally at lower cost than the individual grower—even allowing a profit for his efforts. Again the clear trend seems to be toward specialist-produced mixes—except for the very large growers who are putting in expensive, sophisticated soil blending equipment themselves.

Flat fillers   Widely available equipment to simply fill flats of packs—or for that matter flats of any size pots. Mechanically. For details see "flat fillers" under "Mechanization." Now the grower need only feed soil, empty flats—and remove the filled ones.

Assembling packs, etc.   Most bedding plants are grown in either open packs or cell packs. In either case there is a hand operation in simply inserting a tray of these packs into a flat—just as the flat is fed into the flat filler. It is a hand job—but extremely low cost per flat. We do occasionally see growers assembling loose pots into a flat—or in some cases loose Jiffy-Pots into flats—inefficient, slow, and too costly for the mechanized era. All these growing containers are available in flat size "trays."

Watering—feeding   A variety of nozzles for automatic watering and feeding have been available for years—see the mechanization chapter for full details on them. Bedding growers often use this equipment as warm weather

Assembly line transplanting. Using plugs and predibbled flats, each worker just drops the plugs in one row of holes per flat. Result: 10¢ to 12¢ per flat (72 plants) transplanting cost. The grower, Jim Jeffery, George Jeffery and Son, St. Catharines, Ontario. Jim, front right. A self-powered belt for this is now available from Krieger Industries, Jefferson, Iowa, or from Ball Seed Company.

of late April and May arrives—but typically hand water the first month or so of the crop. The reasoning is that in February and March, there are more hours of time available to hand water—and doing it by hand avoids the very real peril of overwatering. We have to point out though that we see growers of quite respectable quality plants who do use automatics clear through the crop. It can be done—and more and more will be done that way.

Transplanting Digging individual seedlings from a flat, doing the inevitable grading, then digging a hole and planting the seedling, has been the classic way of the industry. It's giving way steadily to plugs, and the grower who organizes his transplanting crew on an assembly line (using a moving belt*) is able to cut transplanting labor cost to a third or a fourth of his former level. Under this system each one of the five or ten transplanters is responsible for dropping let's say six plugs into one tray in each flat as it goes by. The holes are already dibbled; the plugs need only be picked up and dropped into the holes. Result: Cost cut from the old 30¢ to 50¢ a flat (72 plants) down to as little as 10¢ to 12¢. See photo of Jim Jeffery's operation, St. Catharines, Ontario. Result: A major reduction in one of the basic costs of growing annuals.

*Krieger Industries, Jefferson, Iowa (505) 386-8164.

345

The dibble board—another great labor saver. Some growers mechanize them.

Sowing seed Plug growers, of course, mechanize most of the sowing of seed. For details see the chapter on plugs elsewhere in this book.

Moving Things

For either bedding plants or pot plants, clearly the biggest single direct labor cost is moving the flats—from transplanting line to the growing house. Then from the growing house to the shipping room and onto the trucks. And here again, mechanization offers major savings.

Moving belts Using the recently available self-powered moving belts, belt "lines" can be extended from transplanting area to growing house—then back to the shipping room. All done on belts. You just load the flat on in the transplanting room and someone at the other end takes it off and places it on the bench. These moving belts are available in 10' sections (or longer), can turn corners, can go up or down hill, and of course can be tunneled through walls, etc. The largest installation we know of today is at the Aldershot range in Burlington, Ontario. See *Grower Talks,* September, 1983.

These belts, by the way, can also move all sorts of other things. Example: Unloading a truck of peat moss or packs—or bags of soil or fertilizer. And moving all this to the storage area—and up onto a storage pile. Great flexibility. The Aldershots have achieved startling reductions in labor cost on pot mum production using this belt system.

Tray mechanization A different approach to moving things—and again certainly applicable to bedding production. In fact, it's being used for the first time commercially as of mid-1980s. Under the tray system, an aluminum tray perhaps 4' by 8' or 5' by 12' and normally 3" or 4" deep, becomes the bench

346

A very interesting and promising new approach to growing bedding plants. You grow one crop on the ground (above top photo) and another crop on Dutch style trays and rollers—2' or 3' above crop #1. Note the one tray at the rear of the photo. In the bottom photo you see the same roller tracks extending out the end of the greenhouse to the open field. And again one tray for demonstration purposes just rolling out the end of the greenhouse. Soon this whole one- or two-acre outdoor area will be all bedding plants! Here's how the end of the house is opened to accommodate the movement of bedding plants. All the above photos at Ivy Acres, Calverton, Long Island.

top. A row of these trays is set crossways of the house. Normally the house is designed around the trays so that one tray or perhaps two trays set crossways will fill the house leaving only a gutter walk. The key point about the trays: Each row of trays is supported on two lines of pipe—and the almost miracle of them is that thanks to a little Dutch ingenuity, the trays can be moved lengthways of the house with incredibly small pressure. For example, we've seen one man move 1,500 6" pot mums up to the end of the house—by hand. Typically the trays are moved up to the center walk of the greenhouse on these pipes—and are picked up there on either a similar pipe—or several other systems which again are highly mechanized and very low labor. Result of all this: 3000 flats of annuals can now be moved from greenhouse to packing house by one man in one hour. And the same flats can be moved from transplanting room to the growing area in the same length of time. The trays provide extremely low labor moving of growing crops either out to the growing house or back to the headhouse. Again, see the chapter elsewhere in this book detailing these remarkable trays.

The Van de Wetering range at Calverton, Long Island, New York (Jack and Peter Van de Wetering) were pioneers in using trays for this purpose in the U.S. They have major production today built around tray mechanization— and also, by the way, plugs. Typically the Van de Weterings are spring bedding plant producers and do a summer/fall crop of poinsettias or foliage. And of course the trays are just as useful for these pot crops as for bedding.

Automated label inserters   As this edition is published, there are several suppliers who are on the market with automatic label inserters. They have the capability of inserting Tag-a-long type labels into each pack of a flat—or one per flat if desired. The suppliers presently offering such equipment are International Master Products (Master Tag) Corporation, P. O. Box 294, Montague, Michigan 49437 (616) 894-5651. And, Old Mill Company, Savage Industrial Center, Savage, Maryland 20763 (301) 725-8181.

Metal wheeled racks   A sort of intermediate approach to moving things— and widely used today. They are typically wire frame carts perhaps 3' wide and 6' long and maybe 4' or 5' tall—mounted on wheels. They provide variable numbers of shelves from 2 to 3 up to 4 or 5. With adequate cement walks (all mechanized ranges must have them). Growers can load flats from the growing house onto these racks, push them out to the loading dock (often done with a garden tractor to draw them). Then many growers simply load the cart up onto a truck bed with a forklift, roll them back into position in the truck bed. At the delivery point they can be rolled off and lowered with again a hydraulic tail gate and rolled to the desired position in the retail outlet. Very practical and again quite low labor. We think of Bo Pinter, Ypsilanti, Michigan bedding specialist, and the Bernacchis, LaPorte, Indiana, both of whom do this thing so well. See photos.

Monorails rolling above the bench are a great way to move products from bench to shipping area.

Another combination we see so often among bedding growers: a golf cart plus a long string of "trailers." Surprisingly, such a train can be towed around the corner in crowded greenhouse areas very nicely.

Roll-Out Bedding—Great!

Jack and brother Peter Van de Wetering of Ivy Acres, Calverton, Long Island, are bedding plant specialists, operate major production of both bedding plants and fall pot plants. They were one of the first to adopt tray mechanization to moving flats of annuals from transplanting line to growing area and back to shipping room.

In doing this they found themselves with the capability of moving flats of annuals easily up and down the length of the house. Then someone got the idea of opening the end of the house and extending the little pipe rails—so that now a house of well-established annuals could be pushed out into the open air in five minutes of one man's time. They've done that with several acres of their own production—and some surprising things happened.

First, by removing the "raised bench" crop from the pipe rails, they are now able to produce a second crop on the ground—beneath the rails. Result— two crops per house instead of one.

Maybe equally important, the quality of the plants outdoors improves strikingly vs. spring greenhouses. One problem especially with poly grown annuals—it just gets warm on spring days and that softens the plants, impedes quality. On the other hand, these plants, which are put outdoors and left out except on frosty nights (you roll them back in), are far superior in quality.

The Van de Weterings report that when the chains come out to buy, they always head for the outdoor crops first. Says Jack: "They're just better annuals." We're hearing of several other growers across the country doing some of this "roll-out" growing. Really not very much but we'll guess the idea will take hold.

Far better quality—and two crops at once. How can you beat it?

Potted Annuals—Coming Up Steadily

As of this writing, 4" annuals are already a full half of the bedding crop in such areas as California and Florida, and have become a major factor over most of the country. Perhaps in total they might be $1/4$ or more of the total bedding crop . . . in dollars. Billy Powell, veteran North Texas grower, said recently that he fully expects such pot annuals to dominate the bedding market in the near future. The trend is surely that way.

The great case for these pot annuals (always sold in color) is fourfold.

- For bedding, a dozen or two of colorful marigolds or impatiens or petunias can be set out to provide an instant flower bed—in color. How great for the homeowner who forgot to buy pack annuals in May and is having a party mid-June or perhaps early July—and wants some color to show the guests.

- The second great use of 4" annuals is simply as a sort of short-term pot plant. Set them around the house, or on the dining room table or in the kitchen for a touch of color for a few weeks in your home.

- Third, they are great for fast turnover hanging baskets or urns. Several well-developed 4" impatiens planted in a 10" basket will make a colorful salable basket—in weeks!

- Lastly, they are becoming a factor in the landscape contractors' world— major quantities used again to provide instant color flowerbeds around shopping centers, offices, etc.

One of the pluses of these potted annuals is that they have a far better shelf life in discount and supermarket displays. A 6–12 cell pack, 72 per flat, is really a tiny ball of soil, and with a fair size plant will dry out very quickly. A 4" annual especially grown in a fairly fibrous mix, will dry out a whole lot slower.

We also see a variety of other size pot annuals. Long Island for some reason produces acres of 6" annuals—typically for the June market. Other areas do 3" or 3½" plants/pots. Typically, by the way, they are done in sort of an "A-20" multi-pot tray which provides 18 3½" thin-walled plastic pots to a 21" flat. You just set the tray of 18 pots into the flat, run it through the flat filler and plant. Using mature plugs, these 4" can often be salable in a matter of several weeks.

A 4" annual especially grown in a fairly fibrous mix will dry out a whole lot slower.

his flat business is over. Such big chains as Frank's garden centers, and many of the smaller garden center chains and individual garden centers, like to offer quality 4" plants especially through the months of June and July. They, too, like to extend their selling season. George Lucht, Minneapolis grower and retailer, does a volume of them—heavily into 5" and 6" pots, by the way.

Lastly, we see here and there growers trying the winter and early spring market with such 4" color as marigolds, impatiens, pot dahlias, and a variety of other color items. Low cost, fast turnover, they are used of course strictly for home decoration. For sowing dates, see "When to Sow" chapter.

Look for more 4" annuals.

Some Other Points on Bedding

Soil heat annuals   Bill Roberts, ag engineer at Rutgers, New Jersey, has developed a system where warm water pipes are set into a 4" layer of porous concrete providing soil heat for bedding or pot crops. The ground is first leveled; then forms are set up to provide a layer of porous concrete the depth of a two-by-four laid on its edge. The plastic pipes are set in place, the concrete is poured. When dry, the concrete is fully porous; water from a hose pointed right at the floor will quickly dissipate. Excellent drainage! For details write to the Biological & Agricultural Engineering Department, Cook College, Rutgers University, P.O. Box 231, New Brunswick, New Jersey 08903 and ask for their two papers entitled: "Porous Concrete for the Greenhouse Floor and Floor Heating of Greenhouses," January 1979. No charge.

But the real point: Bedding plants and almost any of our ornamental crops for that matter will grow so much faster with warm soil than where the soil is cold. There are weeks difference between the bedding crop grown at 50° soil temperature vs. 70°.

The Swanekamps, Allentown, New Jersey, have several acres of this system. As you would expect, the crop time from transplant to sell is reduced several weeks—which means that sowing and transplanting dates are advanced later into the winter. Result: Three weeks less heating costs during very cold January weather.

Another important payoff of this system vs. overhead unit heaters: Major reduction in fuel cost. The point is, with overhead unit heaters, the "attic" of the greenhouse will be quite warm—let's say 75°–80°. With soil heat, the heat is concentrated down with the plants. And the attic now might be 60°–65°. When you realize that heat loss is calculated on the difference between inside and outside roof temperature, you quickly see that this system can and does provide major savings in fuel cost. We understand there are on the order of 150 acres of this system installed in various ranges across the U.S. today—and more coming in every year. Terry Smith at Bellingham, Washington, has several acres of it. Nick Van Wingerden, Granville, Illinois, has acres of it.

About structures   There is a separate chapter elsewhere in this book dealing with various available structures for growing crops. We'd just like to make the point that the great majority of bedding plants produced in the U.S. are under inflated double poly. The double poly provides about a 1/3 reduction in fuel cost—and the light, especially during the bedding plant growing season, is fully adequate under this roof. Furthermore, the initial cost is low. The only negative: Quality of bedding annuals (especially up into warm days of early and mid-May) tends to deteriorate. Perhaps more capability of rolling sides up with the warm days of spring would help minimize this problem. But that's the U.S. way the crop is grown today!

Open flame heaters—Beware   We keep seeing examples of major losses of bedding—and many other crops—due to problems with open flame heaters especially in plastic greenhouses. The problems most often result when the heat exchange surfaces in the open flame heaters rust out—permitting the flue gasses to escape into the growing area. Growers should be able to detect this by just entering their houses at night during the heating season. You'll smell "smoke." The other problem is lack of a proper "chimney" to again permit escape of the gases of combustion. There must be a chimney—and it must be open. Birds like to nest in them; they develop holes, etc.

Typical of so much North American bedding production—double poly roof, crops on the ground. Those hanging baskets steal a little light—but make good profit. The grower: A. Bernacchi Greenhouses, Inc., LaPorte, Indiana. Well done!

The third problem with these heaters is a lack of a fresh air inlet. Most growers provide a hole maybe 6″ or 8″ in diameter down at ground level and near the heater. This to provide oxygen to support combustion of the heaters. Failure to do so will simply mean that the heater will not burn. There is not enough air. We hear occasionally of the classic grower who simply couldn't get his heaters to stay lit. Problem: Just not enough oxygen. See details on all this in the chapter on air pollution elsewhere in this book.

Retardants—A valuable tool   In the bedding world of today it's mainly B-Nine. Almost all growers we know of do use it—at typically the standard 0.25% dilution. Petunias respond beautifully to B-Nine—it keeps the plants short and stocky and doesn't seem to delay flowering. Many other annuals also respond. 0.25% (2500 ppm) is made up with 0.4 oz. of 85% wettable powder per gallon of water. A 5000 ppm solution requires 0.8 oz. per gallon.

See Table 2 on response of various annuals to B-Nine.

Weed killers—great for summer cleanup   As the last flats roll out of the bedding range in early June, the weeds take over. And good clean operators like to clean those houses up and keep them clean over the summer. There are a variety of weed killers available that can do the job. And there are of course perils in use of these materials on any growing range.

353

For the best of these materials for the bedding grower today we called on Arthur Bing, Long Island extension man, who has specialized in weed control. Says Arthur:

Before the crop is in the greenhouse, either Roundup or Diquat may be used—neither will give off fumes or leave a residue. It is important to remember that Roundup, a systemic that will kill even the most difficult perennial weeds, is only legal to use in *empty* greenhouses. Where there is a growing crop, the contact herbicide Diquat may be used, as long as you avoid getting it on the plants.

Support BPI—the bedding growers' association Bedding growers are fortunate to have a very active and strong trade association. The name: Bedding Plants, Inc. BPI stages a first-class trade fair and seminar each fall. They provide a first-class publication specializing in bedding plants. They support research, provide a variety of point-of-sale materials for the bedding grower, and in other ways serve the bedding grower well. We support BPI and urge growers everywhere to join.

Current scale of dues ('84–'85)

Associate member (all allied trades)	$160
Each additional company member	20
Educator member	20
Student member	10
Active members, growers, retailers, wholesalers:	
Dues based on what they grow per year in sales	
Sales	
$1 million	315
500,000 to 1 million	260
300,000 to 500,000	210
150,000 to 300,000	160
75,000 to 150,000	80
25,000 to 75,000	55
Under 25,000	40

For details either write BPI, Inc., P.O. Box 286, Okemos, Michigan 48864, or phone (517) 349-3924.

Seed geraniums Seed geraniums are widely used as a bedding plant today. A lot of them are grown as 4" or sometimes 3" pots; many more are grown in packs. They have really created a whole new market for geraniums. Plants produce at a price that permits planting of larger flower beds with them.

For full details see the chapter on geraniums elsewhere in this book.

Which are the principal bedding plant annuals? What better answer than to list the major bedding plants from the Department of Commerce Census 1979—and while we're at it, the quantity of each grown in the U.S. that year. Total: A staggering 3.1 billion plants!

About $285 million dollars. Here they are in dollar sales:

Plants	Dollar sales (in millions)
ageratum	$ 6.1
alyssum	$ 5.8
begonias	$ 13.5
coleus	$ 6.9
dusty miller	$ 5.4
geraniums	$ 15.3
impatiens	$ 17.7
marigolds	$ 24.7
pansies	$ 9.3
petunias	$ 31.8
portulaca	$ 4.0
salvia	$ 6.0
snapdragons	$ 4.2
zinnias	$ 6.9
other flowers	$ 15.3
broccoli	$ 5.1
cabbage	$ 10.9
peppers	$ 20.0
tomatoes*	$ 47.8
other vegetables	$ 28.6
Grand total	$285.5 million (quarter of a billion, that is)

*Note that the tomato, again, comes off as number one in dollar sales—and in plants sold.

Timing and retardant table The accompanying table prepared by John Holden gives specific weeks from sow to sell—and response of most bedding plants to the several key retardants.

If you attempt to control habit by lowering temperature after transplanted seedlings are well established and growing in the pack, allow extra weeks depending on the degree of lower temperature.

Many growers use growth retardants such as B-Nine (Alar), Cycocel, or A-Rest to reduce stretching and maintain good compact habit in the pack. This permits them to stay on schedule without having to allow extra time as in the case of using lower temperature.

Please note that this timing schedule is based on our experience at West Chicago for May sales. It will have to be adjusted for other areas of the country.

When in doubt, add a week because it is easier to hold plants back than to push them.

Keep your own records for better scheduling, and for additional information, see the *Ball Bedding Book,* BPI Bedding Plant Chart and *Grower Talks.*

Table 2 TIMING OF BEDDING PLANT CLASSES

Class	Number of weeks from sowing to salable flat†	Temperature‡	Cycocel	A-Rest	B-Nine
				Response to:	
Ageratum	10–12			+	+
Aster*	8–9			+	+
Balsam*	8–10				
Begonia Fibrous Rooted	15–17	60°			
Begonia Tuberous Rooted	18–20	60°	+		
Browallia*	16–17	60°		+	+
Calendula*	6–8				+
Carnation*	10–12		+		
Celosia*	7–9			+	
Centaurea*	6–8			+	+
Cleome*	8–10			+	
Coleus	8–10	60°		+	
Cosmos*	4–6				
Dahlia Dwarf	9–12		+	+	+
Dianthus	10–12		+	+	
Dimorphotheca*	9–12				
Dusty Miller (Cineraria)	9–12	55°			
Dusty Miller (Centaurea & Pyrethrum)	12–14	55°			
Gaillardia*	8–10				
Gazania	9–12				
Geranium	13–18	62°	+	+	+
Gomphrena*	8–10				
Helichrysum*	8–10				
Impatiens	9–10	60°		+	+
Livingstone Daisy	8–10				
Marigold Dwarf	8–10			+	+
Marigold Tall*	5–6		+	+	+
Nemesia	8–12				
Nicotiana*	9–11				
Pansy	14–16				
Petunia Double	12–15				+
Petunia Single	10–15				+
Phlox	8–10				
Portulaca	12–14				
Rudbeckia (Gloriosa Daisy)*	10–12				
Salpiglossis*	10–12				

356

Table 2   (continued)

Salvia Splendens Dwarf	10–12	55°	+	+	+
Salvia Splendens Tall*	8–10	55°	+	+	+
Sanvitalia*	10–12				
Scabiosa*	9–12				
Snapdragon Dwarf	12–14			+	
Snapdragon Tall*	8–10			+	
Statice Sinuata*	8–10				
Stock Dwarf Bedding*	9–11				
Thunbergia*	8–10				
Verbena	8–10	60°		+	+
Vinca Rosea	10–12	60°		+	
Zinnia Dwarf	6–8	55°–60°		+	+
Zinnia Tall*	4–6	55°–60°		+	+
Tomatoes					+

*Generally sold not in bloom.
†Recommended weeks based on experience of midwestern growers and Ball Seed Company for May sales.
‡Temperature—assume 50°–55° unless otherwise noted. When in doubt add a week more. It's easier to hold plants back than to push them ahead.

BEGONIA*

ANNUAL *(B. semperflorens) Approx. 2,000,000 seeds per oz. Germinates in 2–3 wks. at 65° (tuberous) or 70° (fibrous). Light.*

The fibrous begonia class is a major part of the bedding plant crop. One big reason: They are shade-tolerant. Also, they do make a lot of color!

*This chapter based on the *Ball Red Book,* 13th edition, revisions by Heidi Tietz, Ball Seed Company.

357

An almost endless range of beautiful pot and bedding plants comprise the popular begonia clan. From the huge, showy, double tuberous types to the widely used fibrous group, they embrace many desirable forms. The last-named class is a most popular one for combinations, pots and bedding plants, economically grown from seed. Their value as a bedding plant for shady locations, and even in full sun with the new F_1 hybrids, can't be emphasized too strongly.

Fibrous-Rooted

Very few spring bedding annuals have achieved such a rapid rise in popularity in recent years as the perpetually flowering, fibrous-rooted begonia. For many years, they have been grown as pot plants or as specialty items for bedding. Today, with the availability of many excellent F_1 hybrid varieties, most growers offer them in packs just like petunias, marigolds, etc.

They are free-flowering with excellent habit. They are adaptable to a wide range of planting areas. Most important of all, they are "low-care" items, which makes them so well adapted to the American homeowner's yard today.

In sowing, use very light, sandy material with some sifted peat to help maintain uniform moisture without the need of frequent watering. Sow the seed thinly and carefully in shallow rows, and on a well-watered, smooth surface. If gone over with a misty spray, the seed will be washed in enough to make further covering unnecessary, except for a piece of slightly tilted glass, which will maintain moisture without frequent waterings. At 70° media temperature, germination should take place in 10 to 14 days. Because of their extremely fine root system, dilute liquid feedings should be started as soon as the seedlings emerge to prevent post-germination stall. This is the reason so many growers fail with germinating begonias! The tiny plant with so little nutrient in the seed germinates, the nutrients in the top quarter inch of the seed flat are quickly depleted—and the plant just starves. Do start feeding promptly!

When large enough to handle, the seedlings can be potted directly from the seed flat to a 2¼" or 2½" pot. Nice flowering 2½"s can be produced in 3–5 months from sowing, which indicates sowing early February for the main spring supply. While all begonias enjoy a fair amount of heat, some growers, with the coming of warm spring temperatures, run begonias out into frames. Full air and some cool temperature bring out the rich, natural colorings of the foliage, many being rich red, others with red edges and several with dark, metallic-bronze foliage that contrasts strikingly with the flowers. Botanically speaking, the *gracilis* type is a tuberous species, but the term has been applied to several varieties in the semperflorens group by German growers, and usually refers to those with finely fringed leaves.

While fibrous-rooted begonias, by the nature of their growth, divide themselves readily into three groups—tall, intermediate and dwarf—the dwarf class is by far the most popular and widely used. These three groups can be further divided into green-leafed and bronze-leafed varieties. In most areas, the green-leafed will retain a better foliage appearance when planted in full sun (F_1's).

The dwarf class will average 3–5″ in height when grown in pots; 6–8″ in outdoor beds.

Tuberous Begonias

Strong, 4″ flowering plants of both double and single camellia-flowered tuberous-rooted begonias can be grown from seed in 6 months, or an early-December sowing will flower from June on, if grown uniformly warm with a light shade after February, with plenty of humidity. We have repeatedly produced nice summer pot plants in this way, the resultant blooms being fully equal to the finest tuber-grown plants. Night temperature of 65° is an absolute necessity, however, for successful results. Separate colors as well as mixtures are available.

Because of their genetic background, the tuberous types have a tendency to stall or simply stop growing under conditions of extremely low light, and short days, just as we might encounter during the winter months. If a grower has encountered this problem, we suggest that supplemental light for 4 or 5 hours per night be given the plants from germination till about the first of March—which will provide the long day needed to keep the plants from going dormant.

Tuberous begonias can be and are occasionally grown from tubers. Mainly imported from Europe. But probably 90% of all tuberous begonias grown in the U.S. and Canada are from seed. The *Non-Stops*, by the way, aren't a tuberous type and in fact are grown far more than the true tuberous begonias in the U.S. today. *Non-Stop* begonias, by the way, tend to petal drop—which can be effectively controlled by applications of silver nitrate/silver thiosulfate. Same as for geraniums.

Another valuable tuberous-rooted class is known as *Lloydi*. This type is dropping or pendulant in habit, which fits it perfectly for use in hanging baskets or porch boxes. The same plant produces double and single flowers. This strain is offered in a mixture of good colors.

Also popular with retail growers is the ornamental-leafed strain known as *Rex*. The *Changeant* strain makes especially attractive pot plants, and is easily produced from seed.

For Christmas-flowering varieties, the semituberous class is used. While for years the American varieties *Melior*, *Lady Mac*, and *Marjorie Gibbs* have been used extensively for this purpose, the Norwegian or Scandinavian varieties are used because of their sturdiness, flower-holding ability, and better keeping quality in the home. Some of the more popularly grown Norwegian varieties are *Tove*, *Karolina*, *Red Solfheim*, and *Compacta*. Since this type is difficult to propagate, in most cases, it is more profitable to buy 2¼″ pots in June, shift them to 4" pots, and then move them to 5 or 6" pots when well-rooted. This final shift should be made by September 10. Grow them at 60° nights till first flowers appear, then drop temperature to 55°. They do require staking, and although they are self-branching, some pinching should be done to shape them up.

This Christmas flowering type, as of the mid-1980s, is not an important commercial crop in the U.S. and Canada today. This makes one wonder whether this lovely, colorful class of begonias might not find a ready market in today's world—hungry for "new flowering pot plants."

Non-Stops

The *Non-Stop* begonias are really an adaptation of the seed-grown fibrous types. Flowers will not be as large as the occasional giants produced by the fibrous strains from seed or tubers. However, all plants are at least semi-double, they are uniform in habit, and do make shapely, nice, pot plants or hanging baskets. And, most of all, they grow readily from seed. For these reasons, they are finding great popularity in the bedding plant, spring pot plant, and hanging basket trade of the 1980s. They come in a full range of begonia colors.

The *Non-Stops* are also a long day plant. With the coming of short days in late fall, they will go dormant, drop their leaves. This can easily be corrected by simply applying long days, same intensity and duration of light as for mums. Best temperature for rapid growth and flowering: about 70°, minimum night temperature 62°. Extending day length in the marginally long days of February and early March does repress tuber formation and tends to increase plant size and produce more flowers.

Jack Sweet of Earl J. Small reports that silver nitrate/silver thiosulfate as used for geraniums will hold treated blooms and buds for 15 to 18 days—well worth the trouble.

Non-Stop *begonias are fast becoming a favorite for 4" and 5" flowering. Also for baskets. Colorful, easily grown from seed.*

The *Non-Stops* are a fast rising answer to the never ending quest for new flowering pot plants.

Rieger—*and Other* Hiemalis *Types**

Hiemalis begonia is a cross between the winter-flowering bulbous species *Begonia socotrana* and the summer-flowering *Begonia tuberhybrida*. The result of this cross is a winter-flowering begonia with characteristics similar to tuberous begonias. In 1955, Otto Rieger of Germany introduced new varieties that were more floriferous and more resistant to mildew; this was the beginning of the *Rieger®* begonia.

Rieger begonias are immensely popular pot plants in Western Europe. They were introduced to the U.S. by Mikkelsen of Ashtabula, Ohio, and since have enjoyed modest popularity in the U.S. and Canada. Since then, both Mikkelsen and Daehnfeldt of Denmark, as well as Rieger (Mr. Rohde) of Germany, have done breeding work and have introduced additional varieties in this class.

Many basal shoots and asymmetrical leaves are a couple of characteristics of *Hiemalis* begonias. Available colors include shades of red, pink, yellow,

Riegers *are a major crop in Holland. Here's Rinus Bevelander, a major Dutch propagator (highly mechanized/computerized), with a bench of flowering plants.*

*This section is based on a cultural circular by Jim Mikkelsen.

The Aphrodite *group of* Riegers *(above) produces most striking hanging baskets. In the photo: the late Len Shoesmith of the mum breeding family.*

orange, and white. The flower types are single, semi-double, and double. Most cultivars have a green colored leaf, but some of the varieties have deep bronze or mahogany green foliage. Select cultivars have pendulous stems and flowers and are especially appealing in hanging baskets. Other cultivars have more upright growth habits and are better suited for pot production. *Hiemalis* begonias do not have truly tuberous formations, but the fibrous roots are sometimes swollen into tuber-like structures.

Presently starter plants are available as leaf and stem cutttings. The leaf cuttings are available in two forms: multi-stem and single stem. Multi-stem leaf cuttings are started from mother leaves and sprout three or more vegetative shoots. This provides a very full pot plant from one starter. Single-stem leaf cuttings are a by-product of the multi-stem program as they are also started from mother leaves, but only sprout one or possibly two shoots. Starters of this type are fine for 4″ pot productions but when producing 6″ pots, two starters are recommended.

Terminal stem cuttings are commonly called Quickies™*, and are excellent for 4″ pot production. The *Aphrodite* types, varieties for basket use, are produced most successfully as Quickies.

The following cultural information is taken from a culture sheet from Mikkelsen, Inc.

Medium/pH   *Hiemalis (Rieger)* begonias perform best when grown in a fast draining, well-structured medium with sufficient peat moss for water re-

*Quickies™—Mikkelsen, Inc., Ashtabula, Ohio.

362

Rieger *begonias—an important "minor" flowering pot plant. Extremely colorful.*

tention. A mix of 50% peat moss, and 50% aggregate provides an ideal medium for optimal growth. Pasteurize the medium at 180°F for 30 minutes. Supplemental superphosphate and micro-nutrients must be added to avoid any nutrient deficiencies. The pH is adjusted to 5.0–5.5 for a synthetic mix and 5.5–6.0 for a mineral medium by the addition of ground dolomitic limestone. When potting, the top of the young starter plant root ball should be planted ¼" above the surface of the growing mix to aid in prevention of stem rots.

Temperature Optimal temperature for *Hiemalis (Rieger)* begonias to develop lush vegetative growth is 70–72°F with a 14-hour or longer day. After desired size of the plant is reached (approximately 1–4 weeks of long days, dependent on container size and time of year) the temperature should be lowered to 65° with a 12-hour or shorter day. The lower temperature aids in flower initiation and provides deeper bloom color, better bloom production, and an overall sturdier plant. Final development can be delayed by reducing the temperature as low as 62°F. Air-cooled houses may be necessary in warm regions during summer production. Temperatures over 75°F will result in soft, undesirable growth and flower delay.

Carbon dioxide CO_2 benefits plants grown in low light areas by better utilizing the limited daylight, providing faster growth, flowering, and overall plant quality in greenhouses where CO_2 can be contained. CO_2 will increase photosynthesis when used at 1000–1500 ppm during daylight hours. When growing at higher CO_2 levels, greenhouse day temperature should be 5 to 10°F warmer.

363

Growth   *Rieger* begonias are not heavy feeders. For optimal vegetative growth, constant feed at 200 ppm N, 190 ppm P_2O_5, and 200 ppm K_2O is recommended. Continue at this rate through week three of short day treatment. It is essential during the first ten days to keep the medium always moist, not soggy or dry, in order to obtain maximum root growth. Watering should be done in the morning hours to aid in disease prevention, preferably with a tube watering system. This will reduce guttation. Grow on open benches and keep the foliage dry. Be careful to avoid soluble salt buildup; *Hiemalis* begonia roots are very sensitive.

Flower initiation   During the fourth week of short day treatment only clear water should be applied. The fifth week after the start of short day treatment, fertilizer should be resumed but at a rate of 100 ppm N, 190 ppm P_2O_5, and 150 ppm K_2O. Continue to alternate one clear watering to one feed application. Overfed plants with crisp, lush green foliage do not produce as many flowers as plants slightly starved during flower development. Flowering is promoted when moisture and fertility are limited.

Lighting (Long-Day Treatment—L.D.T.)   During the vegetative growth period, interrupted or supplemental lighting of *Hiemalis* begonias may be necessary to maintain a 14-hour day length. Lighting of begonias is basically to encourage growth, not for flower delay, as they are only slightly photoperiodic. Lights should be applied to extend the daylength. In the northern latitudes additional lighting is necessary from September 15 to March 15. Under these poor light conditions *Hiemalis* begonias require additional lighting to prevent growth standstill until short day treatment begins. Interrupted lighting of 50% on and 50% off will fill the plants' needs for added lighting. Light for 3 extra hours daily during months of September and March, 4 hours in October and February, 5 hours daily in November and January, and 6 hours in the month of December. 20–50 foot-candles of incandescent light will give more rapid growth than at 10 foot-candles, which is sufficient to control chrysanthemum flowering.

Be careful not to expose *Rieger* begonias to extremely high daylight intensities. During high light periods apply shade to prevent sun scald (marginal desiccation and burning) and vegetative hardening, causing a reduction of growth. The amount of light intensity that can be tolerated is dependent on temperature. Begonias can be safely exposed to 3000 ft–c at 65°F or below, 2000 ft–c at 70°F, and 1500 ft–c at 80°F.

Short-Day Treatment (S.D.T.)   Short day treatment begins when the desired number of shoots have emerged and sufficient new growth has developed. Since *Hiemalis* begonias are only slightly photoperiodic, short day treatment is basically provided to produce shorter, more compact plants and develop uniform flowering. The older the plant the more readily it will produce flowers, even under long daylengths. The number of flowers and flower buds will be at their peak when the daylength is reduced to 10 hours and the temperature reduced to 64°F. Plants grown in longer daylengths appear to have more vegetative growth at the expense of flower development. Four weeks of short day treatment (maximum 12-hour daylength) is necessary for good flower induction. During periods of high temperatures, black cloth material should be applied at 7:00 p.m. and removed at 9:30 a.m. to prevent heat buildup.

Growth regulators Application of Cycocel® or A-Rest® is needed only when necessary to maintain compact growth. Apply the growth regulator early, 21–28 days after the start of short day treatment for best results. Plants must not be under any physiological stress when applying growth regulators. Apply Cycocel® as a spray at 1500 ppm. Recommended application rate for A-Rest® is 25 ppm. Reduction of water could also be used as a growth regulator during short day treatment.

Non-Stops petal drop can be delayed with silver nitrate/silver thiosulfate—15 to 18 days, according to Jack Sweet.

Pinching Plants should be pinched when young plants show a dominance of one or two shoots overcrowding the other shoots. It is advisable to prune out the stronger growth to allow more uniform bottom growth. A pinch will be necessary on single stem plants to allow the plant to break along the main stem with new shoots emerging at the leaf axis. Pinching helps shape the plant and provides additional flowering shoots.

Insects Cyclamen mites, aphids, thrips, whitefly, and mealybug are the most common insect problems on *Hiemalis* begonias. A regular spray program should be followed to control these insects. Mealybug, whitefly, and thrip can all be controlled with Orthene®. Aphids can be eliminated with the use of Vydate® or Orthene®. Kelthane® WP, Orthene®, or Thiodan® will control cyclamen mite. Emulsifiable concentrates should be avoided on *Hiemalis* begonias.

Diseases

Powdery mildew Powdery mildew is the most frequent disease problem, causing a white fungus growth on the leaf surface. This can be controlled by the use of vaporized sulfur burners or spraying Karathane® WP at 6 oz./100 gals. of water. Karathane® WP, however, when sprayed on open flowers will result in petal burn. A new fungicide, Bayleton® 25% WP, is now labeled for outdoor grown ornamentals. Begonias are listed on the label and the fungicide is effective as both a deterrent to powdery mildew and as a growth regulator. Apply only as a fine mist at the rate of 1–2 oz. in 100 gallons of water (0.8 grams/4 liters of water) after flower initiation. Use of benomyl is not recommended, as it does not provide control in all stages of the life cycle of powdery mildew.

Xanthomonas begoniae (oil spot sickness or bacterial blight)   Discolored spots appear which turn from yellow to brown. Small round greasy spots become evident on the underside of the leaf. The disease affects the stems as well as the leaves. Xanthomonas is intensified by high temperatures and high humidity. To control Xanthomonas: (1) Secure plant material from propagators using cultured index stock; (2) eliminate watering over the foliage—use tube watering systems or capillary mats; (3) complete all watering by noon; (4) lower the relative humidity by using heat and ventilation; and (5) discard *all infected plants!*

Botrytis   Conditions of high humidity and poor air circulation are conducive to botrytis development. It can be controlled by applying Chipco® 26019, Bravo®, Benlate®, and Captan® in rotation. Termil® has also proven effective.

Foliar nematodes   Foliar nematodes (eelworms) are wormlike parasites of plants, infesting stems and leaves with diseases. They cause small yellowish spots that turn the leaf a brownish black, a purple to red on some cultivars. The infected areas take on a water-soaked appearance on the underside of the leaf. Use of the chemical Vydate® will control foliar nematodes. Good sanitary practices are very helpful in prevention.

Xanthomonas, botrytis, powdery mildew, and foliar nematodes can all be controlled through good heating, ventilating, and air movement practices. A Dexon-Benlate drench applied 2–3 days after potting will aid in suppression of root and stem pathogens. When potting, remove all damaged leaves to prevent soft rot from progressing to the new undergrowth. To increase air circulation within the plant the so-called "mother" leaf can be trimmed out.

Spacing   Maintain the plants pot to pot until week four after S.D.T. has begun. Avoid crowding in the finishing stage. Recommended final spacing: 4" pot—4 per square foot; 5" pot—9" × 9"; and 6" pot—11" × 11".

4" multi-stem pot plant program   If started at 70°F and finished at 62°F, it will take 8–12 weeks to produce a crop of 4" pot plants. During the summer a sizable starter plant can go directly into short days. From November to April in low light areas, 1 week of 14 hours or more daylength will be necessary to promote vegetative growth. Pinch if necessary before going into S.D.T. Feed continuously at 200 ppm N, 190 ppm P_2O_5, and 200 ppm K_2O through week three after S.D.T. has begun. Apply clear water during week four of S.D.T., then reduce the amount of feed to 100 ppm N–190 ppm P_2O_5–150 ppm K_2O on week five of S.D.T. and continue to alternate one clear watering to one feed application. Provide 4 weeks of S.D.T. to accelerate flower initiation. From end of S.D.T. to sale will be approximately 5–8 weeks. Application of a growth regulator is necessary only to maintain compact growth and should be used during the second or third week of S.D.T.

4" Quickie™ pot plant production   Provide the plant with 1 to 2 weeks of long day treatment, then pinch to promote sidebreaks. After L.D.T. put the plant into S.D.T. until it is well budded (4 weeks). Upon entering S.D.T. follow the schedule as for the 4" multi-stem program. Total crop time is approximately 7–10 weeks. Quickie™ single stem *Hiemalis* begonias are approximately one-half the cost of a multi-stem and require less production time. This program should be considered especially by mass merchandizers, as it is an economical way of producing 4" plant material.

5" multi-stem pot plant production   Plants should be grown under long days for 1 to 3 weeks and then pinched for uniformity. Proceed with the 4" multi-stem pot plant program starting with the S.D.T. Approximately 9–14 weeks will be needed to produce a 5" pot.

6" multi-stem pot plant program   Provide long day treatment for 2–3 weeks after potting. Pinch and remove the larger leaves to improve light and air circulation and continue with L.D.T. for 2–3 more weeks. Continue with the 4" multi-stem program starting with the S.D.T. It will take 10–16 weeks to produce a 6" pot.

Spring hanging baskets   Hanging baskets are produced by planting three plants per 8" basket or four plants per 10" basket and single-pinching the plants. One multi-stem plant per basket can be used if double-pinching the plant. With single-pinching, 10–20 days of L.D.T. should first be given, then pinched and put into S.D.T. If double-pinching is used, the second pinch should be made about 4 weeks after the first pinch and then put into S.D.T. Production time for a single-pinched *Hiemalis* begonia basket is 10–16 weeks and 14–20 weeks for a double-pinched basket.

Additional uses for *Rieger* begonias   *Hanging baskets* for year-round flowering sales. Avoid *Aphrodite* cultivars in winter because of petal drop. Use double-flowering cultivars for better keeping quality and more color variety. Use for *interior landscaping* because of the excellent keeping qualities. For *outdoor plantings* provide semi-shade; good as bedding plants, borders, and container plants.

BELLIS (English Daisy)

PERENNIAL *(B. perennis var. monstrosa) 170,000 seeds per oz. Germinates in 8 days at alt. 70–85°. Light.*

Though a true perennial, this is commonly grown in America as an annual or biennial. It enjoys cool, moist conditions, such as those which prevail in England, where they are at their best. However, they are much used by our florists because of the attractive way they flower during the cool spring months. They are much like pansies in this respect, the seed being sown in August and the young stock wintered as recommended for that crop. Their compact growth fits them especially for edging as well as bedding and spring plant combinations. They are especially susceptible to aphids, and this pest must be anticipated. While improved varieties are regularly being offered, the *Super Enorma* strain is generally considered the standard variety. Plants grow to a height of 4″–6″ and bear an abundance of 3″ blooms resembling asters with about the same color range.

BELLS of IRELAND

ANNUAL *(Molucella laevis) 4,200 seeds per oz. Germinates in 3 wks. at alt. 60–85°. Light. Prechill at 50° for 5 days.*

Undoubtedly the greatest difficulty involved with growing a crop of *Bells of Ireland* is germinating the seed. However, consistent, reliable results have been obtained by using the above-listed directions.

This rather unique cut-flower item is useful for bouquets and in unusual and striking floral arrangements. The plants are basal-branching with stems 2 feet or more in length, closely set with large bell-like sheaths of translucent green surrounding a tiny white flower. The overall impression is that of a flower spike with green florets. It may be used in the fresh or dried state, and is easily grown in greenhouse benches, in pots or outdoors in summer. Best results are usually had if seed is sown outdoors after danger of frost is past. Germination in hot weather is difficult. If you do sow inside, late March and early April are the best times. If grown single-stem, plants should be spaced 3″ × 6″. Seedlings benched around the first of April will begin to flower in late May grown at 50°.

ANNUAL *(B. speciosa major) 108,000–240,000 seeds per oz. Germinates in 15 days at 70°. Light.*

Browallia make a very showy bright blue basket or pot plant—and are very shade-tolerant.

This native of tropical America will provide an abundance of bright flowers through the summer when grown in the shade. For sales in 3″ to 4″ pots for May, they should be sown in late January; 2¼″ pots can be had from a March 1 sowing. They should be grown at 60°. To get the growth compact and shapely, grow near the glass and do some pinching as needed. Overenriched soil encourages growth at the cost of flowers, just as it does with most plants. They are also excellent for hanging baskets to be placed in a sheltered area. They must be carefully hardened-off before planting outdoors. Most popular variety is *Blue Bells Improved,* with 1″ to 2″ lavender-blue flowers. Also available are the varieties *Silver Bells*, a clear, snow-white; *Sky Bells*, a bright powder blue; *Marine Bells*, a deep indigo blue; and *Jingle Bells* mixture, a formulated mix of all the above.

First, the case for spring bulbs—especially in pots.

1. Esthetically and market-wise, they're colorful and delightful—the very essence of spring. People love them! A fresh breath toward the end of a long winter.

2. In the growers' year-round space plan they offer a profitable, marketable crop to fill January–February benches—after poinsettias. A great Valentine's crop—both cut and pot.

3. To a retail grower a special advantage over the chain. Bulbs have a short shelf-life. Not well adapted to wholesale pot-plant channels, especially chains—but great for the well-planned retail grower.

4. They're not really difficult—just follow the rules.

Plan well. Before you order—plan! Write down how many tulips (or whatever), what varieties, pot size, bulbs per pot, flowering date, and prices. Also, a complete growing schedule. Again, bulbs are not long-lived. Use *The Holland Bulb Forcers Guide* by Gus DeHertogh. It's excellent! See your bulb supplier for a copy.

For his overall plan, Todd divides all bulb crops into an early lot (Group I) for January–February flowering. And, a late lot (Group II) for March–April flowering.

Tulips—The Heart of It

Bachman's flower tulips from early January through Easter. They are clearly number one in the spring bulb crops here.

Ordering/shipping Todd does his annual ordering in February and March—mainly from Holland. "Watch currency exchange gyrations—I'd rather order in dollars, than the Dutch guilder. I know my costs." Shipping needs attention. Bachman's use mainly ocean freight. Shipping dates must relate to planting dates—again in Group I and II. Beware of heat during transit, also delay—and high humidity. Bachman's prefer the plastic container—it's open and porous. "You can order a temperature recording instrument to go with a 40" container of bulbs."

---

*This chapter is partly from several recent Ohio Short Course talks by Todd Bachman, Bachman's, Minneapolis, Minnesota. Bachman's are major retail growers, do a volume of spring bulbs.

Upon arrival, open and ventilate the bulbs. Ethylene builds up, can cause bud blast. "We always check our bulbs, to be sure everything is there. Look for sour smell. We store our bulbs upon arrival at 60°F to 65°F—with air circulation. Cut flower bulbs are immediately put into a 55°F storage to start vernalization.

"Check bulbs for flower bud development. You slice a bulb open, look for complete flower parts, anthers, etc. If they're present, the bulb has reached 'G-Stage'—ready to go. Don't plant bulbs until 'G-Stage' is confirmed."

Pot sizes vs. the market   Bachman's grow a variety of tulip pot sizes:

- six bulbs per 5½" bulb pan—mass market

- eight bulbs per 7" bulb pan—retail shops

- eleven bulbs per 8" or 10 bulbs per 15" bulb pan—again retail

Be sure all pots drain well.

Potting   "We like soil a bit heavier than that for pot mums. Our mix includes sandy loam, Hypnum peat. With too light a mix, bulbs tend to push up and out. We do steam all bulb soils. We fill the pot half-way, set the tulips in (flat side to the outside of the pot), then fill up the pot. Don't push them in—it compacts the soil." There should be at least a quarter inch of soil over the bulb.

Pot tulips—a favorite among the spring bulb pot crops.

371

"Do label each lot carefully. Include plant date, date to remove for forcing, flowering date. If you get two lots of the same variety, mark them Lot A and Lot B—they may not flower quite together.

"Temperature, when bulbs are first placed in the cooler, should be at 48°F. Within several weeks of potting, bulbs should show roots—also shoots. Keep the soil moist. On November 10, tulips should be dropped to 41°F for several weeks at this stage—a more ideal vernalization temperature."

Early January tulips   They can be flowered nicely right about January 5 to 15—a great after-poinsettia crop. To do this bulbs must be artificially pre-cooled. Immediately upon arrival they need six weeks at 48°F—starts vernalization. "We do it in our rooting room. Then to 41°F. Move to the forcing house four weeks before the flowering date."

Group I—the early ones   "Group I should be potted and put in the storage room normally in mid-September. The better pot forcing varieties like *Paul Richter* will want 15 to 16 weeks in the cooler, plus three to four weeks to force. A total of 18 weeks plus from plant to flower. Group I goes into Room 1—Group II into Room 2, so that we can vary temperatures." By the way, the storage rooms have concrete floors, refrigeration, capability of drawing in cool outside air during winter to minimize costly refrigeration. Bulbs are stored on pallets—50 pots per pallet, 12 high—stacked pot on pot. They're moved by forklift. Be sure there is air circulation in the cooler room.

Group II—the later ones   Group II tulips should be ordered to arrive about October 1. Tulips are potted immediately and placed in the Group II cooler room. They are kept at 48°F until December 10, and then dropped to 41°F until they are ready for forcing.

"On all pot tulips, as soon as we see roots and shoots, we apply Benlate and Truban®—8 ounces per 100 gallons of each—as a soil drench. Also, all hyacinth bulbs are sprayed once with Benlate®—8 ounces per 100 gallons. And lastly, we burn Termil in the air as a botrytis preventative—before removing from the cooler."

Forcing   Wants a normally light house, reasonable humidity. It's really very simple—mainly 60°F—or 5°F more or less to time the crop. Later spring crops flower faster, the earlier tulips will take three or four weeks to force. Moisture is again important at this stage. "Never let them dry. Also, we try to water in the morning so as to minimize botrytis." Again, reasonable humidity—avoid the extremes. Feeding is normally not necessary. "Though we often do apply a light nitrate feeding (150 ppm)."

Harvest date   (All harvest dates are for maximum longevity.) Pot tulips should go to the retail display when they are in the green bud stage. "We like slight color at the base of the flower. Again, they're short-lived, so they must be removed at the right time."

372

Varieties for pot forcing For January–February flowering, *Paul Richter* is the clear number-one choice. "We also use *Christmas Marvel, Golden Melody, Prominence.* For March–April flowering, *Arma, Atilla, Orange Wonder, Princess Irene, Yellow Present.*"

Cut Tulips

These are rather important crops at Bachman's—all grown in wood flats 12" by 18" by 3½". They plant ten rows of six plants per flat—60 bulbs. Again, steam the soil.

Cooler room and forcing procedures In general, same procedure used for pot tulips is used with cut tulips. By the way, the St. Valentine's cut tulip crop is big and important at Bachman's. Says Todd, "Good cut flowers tend to be scarce for Valentine's Day. We rely heavily on cut tulips."

Cut tulips are harvested as Todd says, "With slight color—a bit more color than pot tulips." Cut tulips can be stored two or three days at 33°F. Bachman's store them horizontally. Some do pull tulips out bulb and all, but Todd feels they get about the same amount of life cutting them.

"Get them to the point of sale fast—they are beautiful, but short-lived. Give the customer the joy of watching them open."

Varieties for Valentine's Day at Bachman's are mainly *Paul Richter* and *Trance*—"It's a bit short, but a good red color for our use." For late flowering cut tulips, Bachman's use *Golden Melody* and *Oxford*.

Tulips are an important cut flower crop in Holland today—and seem to be coming up in popularity in the U.S.

Crocus

Todd reports strong demand for crocus last spring. "We're doubling our pot crocus this year over last." The principal varieties they use are *Remembrance* and *Purpurea*. "Our crocus are grown mainly five bulbs per 4" pot."

Cooler forcing regime for crocus   A rough schedule used at Bachman's:
For early-flowering (January–February), bulbs are potted and put in a cooler on September 10. Forcing time "often under one week—can be done on carts in any light area."
For late spring (March–April), bulbs are potted and put in a cooler on October 10. Again—a week or less to force.

Harvest date for crocus   Bachman's move them into the retail shop as soon as the buds' sheaths (not the individual buds) are visible. Again, "Let people enjoy watching them develop."

Hyacinths—colorful and extremely fragrant. A great spring bulb crop.

Pot Hyacinths

The normal pot size at Bachman's is one bulb per 3½" geranium pot or three bulbs per 5½" azalea pot for the mass market. For retail shops, five bulbs per 7" pot.

For forcing hyacinths, Bachman's just take them out of the cooler, put them in a warm, sunny area (60°F) on carts—saves greenhouse space. Hyacinths, again, will normally be ready to sell within a week or less of removal from the cooler. Again, keep them watered and ventilated.

Hyacinth varieties *Anna Marie, Carnegie,* and *Ostara Blue* are the main varieties of hyacinths used at Bachman's. "We sell hyacinths with just a little color showing—well before florets open."

Daffodils

Two main pot sizes at Bachman's for daffodils: two bulbs per 4½" pot for the mass market—three bulbs per 6" pot for a retail shop.

Cooler procedure for daffodils For early flowering daffodils at Bachman's, bulbs are potted and put in the cooler on September 10, and for later flowering, bulbs are potted and put into the cooler on October 10.

Forcing Daffodils need more time, normally three or four weeks to force. Temperature should be maintained at 60°F.

Daffodils go to the retail shop when buds are vertical—before they tip. There should be a slight tip of yellow showing.

Main daffodil varieties *Carlton* is the main daffodil variety used by Bachman's.

Retardants

Todd talked A-Rest® mainly for height control of tulips. Also, it helps on stem topple with hyacinths—although "we like to solve this problem with better timing and culture." Bachman's uses ½ mg. with 4 ounces of water on a 6" pot tulip to shorten the plant—hyacinths, the same ½ mg. Be sure the pot is moist, and if the mix includes much of bark or peat, it may take more A-Rest®. Try it on a small scale first. And, best of all, select dwarf varieties.

Problems

Too tall or too short tulips Answer is more or less cold days—more days in the cooler mean taller tulips. Plant one week later if they are too tall. Also, of course, variety selection is important.

Bends or crinkles on tulips This is often the result of overheating during the shipping of bulbs. Over 80°F or 85°F often causes this problem.

Spit on hyacinths The flower stalk separates from the plant. Most often this is the result of freezing of bulbs. This can happen after they are potted if they are outdoors and not covered well enough.

How about prices? Bachman's are normally $5.99 for a 6″ tulip—a $1.99 for a 4″ pot crocus at retail.

Paul Richter pot tulip schedule for Valentine's Day forcing

- October 4: *Plant Date*
- November 10: *Strong Visible Root*—Benlate Truban
- *Shoots Developed*—Chipco 26019 Spray

- January 5: *Drop Temperature to 35°F*
- January 18: *Move to 60°F Forcing Area*
- February 10: *Bud Stage—Ready for Sale!*

Paul Richter—Red   Optimum Cold—15 Weeks   Forcing Time @60°F—23 Days

Paul Richter cut tulip schedule for Valentine's Day

- September 14: *Plant Date*
- October 28: *Strong Visible Root*—Benlate Truban
- *Shoots Developed*—26019 Spray

- January 5: *Drop Temperature to 35°F*
- January 18: *Move to 60°F Forcing Area*
- February 10: *Bud Stage—Ready to Cut!*

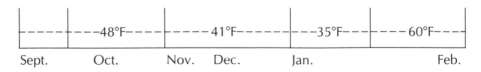

Paul Richter—Red   Optimum Cold—17–18   Weeks   Forcing Time @60°F—23 Days

Table 1 CRITICAL DATES AT A GLANCE

Salable dates	Dates bulbs should arrive	Potting dates[2] Temperature after potting	Temperature, Phase II	Weeks needed to force @60°F
POT TULIPS				
Jan. 5-15	Sept. 1	Pot on arrival (Sept. 1 provided you're at "G stage"). First 6 weeks at 48°.	After 6 weeks move to 41°	4 weeks
Group I—early—to flower Jan.-Feb.	Sept. 1	Pot Sept. 1-Oct. 1. Then 48° until root formation, approx. 4–6 weeks, then to 41°F.	For better vernalization, drop to 41° on Nov. 10.	3–4 weeks for early crops
Group II—later flowering—March-Easter	Oct. 1	Pot on arrival, put in 48° cooler.	Drop to 41° Dec. 10 until forced.	Faster than early crops
TULIPS FOR CUT[1]				
St. Valentine's crop	Sept. 1	Sept. 15		3–4 weeks
Easter crop	Oct. 1	Approx. 20–22 weeks prior to Easter depending on variety.		3–4 weeks
POT CROCUS				
Jan.-Feb. flowering	Sept. 1	Pot Sept. 10, cooler temperature 48°F 4 weeks then to 41°F.		1–2 weeks
March-April	Oct. 1	Pot Oct. 10, move to cooler temperature 48°F 4 weeks then to 41°F.		1–2 weeks
POT HYACINTH				
St. Valentine's crop	Sept. 1	Sept. 15		1 week
Easter crop	Oct. 1	18–20 weeks prior to Easter.		1 week

[1]Store all cut tulips at 55° at once upon arrival.

[2]The above dates assume no precooling. If bulbs have been precooled at 48°F for 6 weeks, they must obviously be planted 6 weeks after the dates that appear here. Precooling is used by growers who do not have refrigerated bulb storage.

Table 2 ROOTING ROOM TEMPERATURE SEQUENCE FOR POT TULIPS

Room 1	Room 2
Early and midseason varieties flowering through February 14. 48°F to November 10 41°F to January 5 35°F to finish	Midseason to late varieties flowering from February 14 to end of season. 48° to December 5 41° to January 5 35° to finish

Table 3 RECOMMENDED VARIETIES

Pot tulips for forcing

Name of variety	Color	Type	Flowering period
Abra	Red-edged yellow	Triumph	Early
Apricot Beauty	Apricot	Mendel	Early
Arma	Red-fringed edge	Single	Midseason
Attila	Purple	Triumph	Midseason
Bellona	Yellow	Single	Midseason
Christmas Gold	Deep yellow	Single	Midseason
Christmas Marvel	Rose pink	Single	Early
Comet	Red-edged yellow	Parrot	Midseason
Couleur Cardinal	Scarlet	Single	Late
Golden Melody	Yellow	Triumph	Midseason
Hibernia	White	Triumph	Midseason
Karel Doorman	Red-edged cream	Parrot	Midseason
Kareol	Yellow	Double	Midseason
Kees Nelis	Red-edged yellow	Triumph	Midseason
Makassar	Yellow	Triumph	Late
Merry Widow	Red-edged white	Triumph	Midseason
Mirjoran	Red-edged white	Triumph	Midseason
Olaf	Red	Triumph	Midseason
Orange Sun	Orange	Darwin	Late
Palestrina	Pink	Single	Late
Paul Richter	Red	Triumph	Early
Preludium	Red & white	Triumph	Midseason
Princess Irene	Orange & purple	Single	Late
Prominence	Red	Triumph	Midseason
Robinea	Red	Triumph	Late
Stockholm	Red	Double	Midseason
Topscore	Red	Triumph	Midseason
Yellow Present	Yellow	Triumph	Late

Cut tulips for forcing

Name of variety	Color	Type	Flowering period
Albury	Red	Triumph	Late
Apricot Beauty	Apricot	Mendel	Early
Bellona	Yellow	Single	Midseason
Golden Melody	Yellow	Triumph	Midseason
Golden Oxford	Yellow	Darwin	Midseason
Hibernia	White	Triumph	Midseason
Kees Nelis	Red-edged yellow	Triumph	Midseason
Orient Express	Red	Triumph	Late
Oxford	Red	Darwin	Midseason
Paul Richter	Red	Triumph	Early
Peerless Pink	Pink	Triumph	Late
Prominence	Red	Triumph	Midseason
Trance	Red	Triumph	Midseason

Table 3   (continued)

Pot hyacinths for forcing

Variety	Color	Flowering period
Amsterdam	Dark pink	Early
Anna Marie	Light pink	Early
Blue Giant	Light blue	Late
Blue Jacket	Deep blue	Midseason
Carnegie	White	Midseason
Delft Blue	Blue	Midseason
Jan Bos	Red	Early
L'Innocence	White	Early
Marconi	Dark pink	Late
Ostara	Dark blue	Early
Pink Pearl	Dark pink	Midsason

Pot crocus for forcing

Variety	Color	Flowering period
Flower Record	Dark purple	Late
Purpurea	Dark purple	Midseason
Remembrance	Purple	Early

Pot daffodils for forcing

Variety	Color	Flowering period
Carlton	Yellow	Midseason
Dutch Master	Yellow	Midseason
Flower Record	White	Late
Tête-a-Tête	Yellow	Midseason

Daffodil Forcing—Pot and Cut*

Daffodils, members of the genus Narcissus, are true bulbs. The bulbs consist of a slender piece of stem tissue surrounded by numerous fleshy leaves. The leaves contain the stored food material; the stem contains the flower inflorescence. The flower buds of this genus form during the spring and summer of the previous year—usually when flowering in the field is nearly over, but just before the bulbs are harvested for next year's sales. In contrast, hyacinths and tulips form their flowers at the end of the growing period or after they have been placed in storage.

Thermoperiodism is the sum of responses of an organism to appropriately fluctuating temperatures. Bulbs which come up every spring in the garden experience an annual thermoperiodism of cool, moist winters followed by dry, warm summers. The greenhouse grower creates these conditions artificially by placing bulbs in a cold treatment area (bulb cooler, cold frames, cold greenhouse), and then forcing them in a warm greenhouse.

Bulbs are cooled to promote stem elongation—not to develop flowers. Cooling temperatures between 35° and 50° F (2° to 10° C) cause many chemical changes within the bulb cells. When temperatures start to rise following cooling periods, bulbs force or grow rapidly. During the cooling period, the starch compounds contained in the bulbs change to sugar. This sugar is utilized in the formation of proteins or other cell-building products needed for growth activity during the warmer forcing temperatures in the greenhouse.

Bulbs can be overcooled; in this case, the bulb will use up all its available stored food and produce poor, unsalable plants. For daffodils, the minimum cold temperature requirement is 13 to 14 weeks; optimum is 18 weeks.

Cool temperatures are not needed for root development. Though temperatures below 35° F (2° C) impair root growth, roots have no dormancy period—they are always growing. If bulbs are being cooled in cold frames, the root development must be complete prior to the onset of freezing weather. Root development should be complete in four to five weeks. To ensure proper development, soil media should be kept moist at all times. In cold frames, keep the bulbs moist with periodic watering if natural rainfall is inadequate.

Upon arrival of the bulbs, open boxes and ventilate. Inspect the bulbs for disease. Most disease disorders occurring on bulb crops are due to diseases present on the bulbs when they arrive. A common disorder of daffodils is Fusarium basal rot. This originates in the production fields. An identifying characteristic is soft tissues—particularly on the bottom of the bulb. If more than 10% of the shipment has this disorder, return the shipment.

*Contributed by Teresa Aimone, Grower Talks managing editor. Here Teresa presents an approach for another important spring bulb crop.

Daffodils—the essence of spring!

Dipping bulbs prior to planting is an easy way to control fungal diseases. Place the bulbs in an open-mesh bag and immerse in a fungicidal solution for 30 minutes, drain, and then plant. Benlate, Terrachlor, Benlate/Terrachlor, or Lesan (Dexon) are all adequate for this purpose. Terrachlor is an effective fungicide, but should not be used more than once due to possible phytotoxicity.

Bulbs should be planted in bulb pans or azalea pots for best results. Pots should be sterilized prior to planting. Either clay or plastic pots can be used. For cut flowers, plant bulbs in wooden flats—14" x 16" x 4". Treat the wood with copper naphthenate. For drainage purposes, the bottom boards of the flat should be placed 1/4" apart.

Soil media should be well-aerated, yet have the capacity to retain sufficient moisture for good growth. The media should also be sterilized prior to planting. Avoid using media which drains too readily such as pure sands, or heavy media such as clay. Loam soils with perlite, vermiculite, or calcined clay in a 1:1:1 ratio work well. Maintain pH of 6.0 to 7.0. Soil temperature at time of planting should be approximately 50° to 65° F (10° to 18° C).

Daffodils should not need to be fertilized during their production cycle since the bulbs themselves contain enough stored food to provide proper nutrient requirements.

Pot daffodils Potting can be done anytime from October 1 to December 1 depending on desired flowering date. For a Christmas flowering, plant on October 1; for Valentine's Day plant mid-October, and for a March and April flowering, plant mid-November. Bulbs which will be forced for earlier flowering dates need to undergo a pre-cooling treatment. Pre-cooled bulbs should arrive at the end of August, and be placed in storage at 48° F (9° C) no later than August 31. Do not plant the bulbs until October 1 for a December flowering date. The sequence for temperatures in the rooting area are the same for all.

But no matter when the bulbs are planted, they should be given temperatures of 48° (9° C) until December 1 to 5; 41° F (5° C) January 1 to 5, then finished at 32° to 35° F (0° to 2° C). The change to different temperatures is dependent on development of the plant. 48° F is for root development—that temperature should be maintained until roots emerge from the bottom of the container. 41° F is necessary for shoot growth. Maintain temperatures at 41° until shoots are approximately 2" long. Temperatures of 32° to 35° F hold the shoot growth until the plants are brought into the greenhouse for forcing.

Forcing temperatures in the greenhouse for potted daffodils are 60° to 62° F (16° to 17° C). Optimum stem length for pot daffodils ranges from 10" to 14". Be sure to check on the response of individual cultivars. A good rule of thumb: When scheduling, always plan your production for seven days prior to the date you want the plants to flower. For example: A grower would schedule his daffodils to flower on February 7 for Valentine's Day sales.

If bulbs must be stored prior to shipment, treat the plants with a fungicide, and place in a 32° to 35° F storage area. Harvest the plants at the "gooseneck" stage of development.

For height control in potted daffodils, the following recommendations are given in the Ohio Florist's Association Bulletin Growth Regulator Chart, No. 651, January 1984. (The original source for the information on the chart concerning daffodils was obtained from the Holland Flower Bulb Technical Services Bulletin 10, *Guidelines for utilization of Florel [ethephon] for reduction of stem topple of potted hyacinths and reduction of total plant height of potted daffodils,* January, 1982, by Dr. A. A. De Hertogh.)

Apply a 1,000 ppm (3.2 ounces per gallon or 25 milliliters per liter) to 2,000 ppm (6.4 ounces per gallon or 52 milliliters per liter) foliar spray of Florel (ethephon) when leaves or floral stalk is 4" to 5" long. Foliage should be dry. If required, use a second application two to three days later. Do not apply if flower bud is visible! The concentration and number of applications varies with cultivars and flowering periods. Bulbs should have received proper cold treatment for given flowering period prior to Florel application. Do not wet foliage for 12 hours after treatment. Florel should be applied in a well-ventilated, 60° to 65° F (15½° to 18° C) greenhouse.

Table 1 CRITICAL DATA SUMMARY

Salable dates	Dates bulbs should arrive	Potting dates and temperatures	Phase II temperatures*	Greenhouse forcing time**
POT DAFFODILS				
Christmas	Late August.	October 1 After bulbs arrive in late August, store at 48° F (9° C) until potting.	41° F (5° C) until November 1, then 32° to 35° F (0° C to 1½° C) until December 1.	Bring into greenhouse three to four weeks prior to sale. Force at 60° to 62° F (15° to 16° C).
St. Valentine's Day	Mid-October	Mid-October 48° F (9° C) until December 1.	48° F (9° C) until December 1, then 41° F (5° C) until January 1, then 32° to 35° F until bulbs are brought into the greenhouse for forcing.	Same as above
March and April flowering	Mid-November	Mid-November 48° F (9° C) until December 1.	Same as for Valentine's Day. Hold at 32° to 35° F until it's time for greenhouse forcing (three to four weeks prior to sale).	Same as above

CUT DAFFODILS
Cut daffodils are difficult to produce commercially for Christmas flowering. However, for St. Valentine's Day and for March and April flowering the sequences are as follows:

St. Valentine's Day	Late September	Late September 48° F (9° C) until December 1.	48° F (9° C) until December 1, then 41° F (5° C) until January 1, then 32° to 35° F (0° to 1½° C) until bulbs are brought into the greenhouse for forcing.	Bring into greenhouse three to four weeks prior to sale. Force at 55° F (10° C).
March and April flowering	October 10 to 30 depending on desired flowering date.	October 10 to 30. Hold at 48° F (9° C) until December 1.	Same as above	Same as above

*These temperatures are the proper temperatures to use; however, the dates listed are approximate. Root and shoot development determine exactly when the temperatures should be lowered. See accompanying copy for determining stages of development, and subsequent temperature changes.

**As a general rule of thumb, plan your flowering date for seven days prior to the date of sale. For example, if daffodils will all be sold on Valentine's Day, plant your flowering date according to the above schedule for seven days prior to the February 14 date.

Cut daffodils Production of cut daffodils is very similar to production of potted daffodils. To hit target holiday dates such as Christmas, Valentine's Day, and Easter or early spring sales, plant at the same time you would plant bulbs for pot daffodil production. Pre-cooling requirements are the same if earlier flowering dates are desired.

Differences lie, first of all, in the containers—as stated earlier, cut daffodils are most easily handled, and, most economically produced, in flats. Allow for approximately four dozen per flat. Another difference in cut daffodil production is the greenhouse forcing temperature. 55° F (13° C) is the optimum temperature. The lower temperature, as opposed to the temperature required for pot daffodil forcing, will induce longer stem length—desirable in cut flowers. Temperatures above 60° F (16° C) should be avoided, as weak stems will result.

A desirable stem length is 14″ for cuts. The flowers should be harvested in the gooseneck stage—no earlier. If the flowers need to be stored before selling—place the flowers dry in an upright position (to avoid stem bending). Store at 32° F to 35° F (0° to 2° C) no longer than one week.

CALADIUM

Caladiums—widely used as a southern bedding plant (the geraniums of the South). They stand heat and are colorful through the long southern summer.

Caladiums are widely grown decorative foliage plants sold mostly as pot plants and, in warmer climates, for outdoor bedding. Caladiums also are used in the central and northern sections of the U.S. in the warm months of June through August for outdoor planting. In those climates where warm weather isn't dependable until mid-June, caladiums must be started in greenhouses.

Plants are grown from tubers produced in Florida. Tubers are sold in grades expressed in inches of diameter. A No. 2 tuber should measure between 1" and 1½" across; a No. 1 should measure between 1½" and 2½"; a Jumbo should measure 2½" to 3½", and a Mammoth should measure 3½" or more. A No. 3 size, measuring ¾" to 1" across, is also available for special purposes. New-crop tubers are usually available in mid-December. Some specialists, however, store bulbs under controlled conditions and can ship at any time during the year. There is some risk involved in maintaining quality for tubers planted after June of each year. Tubers are generally "cured" before shipping from Florida. Tubers which have not been stored for at least 6 weeks at 70°F will sprout slowly.

The caladium is a tropical plant native to the Amazon River district of Brazil. The important environmental conditions that produce fine caladiums are: high temperatures (this includes bulb-storage conditions); ample water and feed combined with loose, well-drained soil; and high humidity.

If tubers cannot be planted as soon as received, they should be unpacked and stored in dry air at 70° temperature with ample air circulation.

There are several ways of starting caladium tubers. They may be planted directly out-of-doors where temperatures don't go below 65° at night; they may be started in flowering-sized pots, or they may be started in Jiffy-(peat) Pots for later transplanting. Most growers start tubers in peat moss beds and transplant either into Jiffy-Pots or other containers as soon as roots are started. From the standpoint of the caladium itself, probably the best way is to plant the tuber in straight peat moss in an 80–85° temperature with high humidity. Bulbs should be planted approximately 1" deep. The peat should be kept not too wet until root action has started; thereafter, the more water, the better. If the peat moss used is a comparatively rough grade, drainage will not be a problem. For small retail growers who don't have 80 or 85° space in which to start caladiums, electric heating cable may be used in a section of bench to provide the necessary temperature. Install the heating cable in a layer of sand or gravel over the necessary bench area, pot tubers in Jiffy-Pots and place the pots on the gravel over the cable. Set the cable thermostat at 80 or 85°, and the caladiums will start to leaf in 4 or 5 weeks. A plastic cover over the caladiums helps to maintain the necessary high humidity and temperature. However, this cover should be removed occasionally to permit air circulation.

Caladium growers are divided over the question of whether to plant the tubers upside-down or right-side-up. The tuber is not unlike a potato tuber in that its growth begins from eyes. If the tuber is planted with eyes on the bottom, generally speaking, more eyes will develop and they will develop more uniformly. However, more time is required for the plant to start. If the eyes are faced up, the plant will emerge and start growing more quickly.

385

Tubers usually have one main eye that is larger than the others. This main eye will produce the largest branch on the finished plant. Many growers ream out this main eye, thus forcing the plant's energy into the other side eyes; this procedure produces a bushier, more branched plant.

If caladium tubers are started in Jiffy-Pots, a No. 2 tuber will fit easily into a 3" pot or a No. 1 tuber will be accommodated in a 3½" pot. The advantage of using Jiffy-Pots is lack of transplanting shock when the plants are moved.

The size tuber to use depends on the size wanted in the finished plant. The larger the tuber, the larger the finished plant. Mammoth-grade tubers produce the large, exhibition plants, whereas No. 2's produce good 4" or 5" pot specimens. Some growers use the No. 3-size tuber for small, 4" pot plants. For most purposes, a No. 1 or Jumbo-size tuber will produce a very satisfactory plant. Some specialist growers even go so far as to cut their tubers into pieces, each piece having at least two, but perhaps three or four eyes. This procedure makes for more uniform-sized finished plants. Generally speaking, each eye produces one branch on the finished plant.

If the plant is ultimately to be sold as a pot plant, as soon as root action is well started (usually 2 or 3 weeks), it should be planted into its final size pot. One plant will fill a 4" to 5" pot and several may be planted in a 6" or 7" pot. A good potting-soil mixture consists of ⅓ each peat moss, soil, and sand. Caladiums grow best in temperatures between 70 and 75°. They should be kept well watered and fed with a balanced fertilizer (not too much nitrogen) every 4 weeks. A cheesecloth shade over the plants as their leaves mature will brighten colors.

Caladiums destined for sale as bedding plants are best started directly in Jiffy-Pots and sold in these pots as soon as top growth is well started—4 to 5 weeks. Some retail growers plant six tubers in a Market-Pak (or a similar container used for bedding plants) and sell them "by the container." Caladiums are tropical plants and lower temperatures can cause discoloration and leaf loss. Temperatures should be maintained near 70°F during shipping of the finished plants and in the selling areas.

Caladiums should not be planted outdoors until night temperatures stay above 65°. If you or your customers use caladiums for outdoor planting, re-member that they do best in partial shade, although some varieties perform well in open sun, and they should be planted in a well-drained location and kept watered and fed. Caladium troubles are usually caused by a too dry soil and/or too much bright sun (foliage has a burned look), or too low temperature (tubers fail to grow or grow slowly and erratically).

Tissue cultured caladiums are now being propagated. Promising results have been seen in some varieties showing uniformity, disease free, and more leaves on each plant. If production can be achieved economically, tissue culture caladiums may be available on a year-round basis producing compact plants.

Varieties

There are hundreds. Probably ¼ to ⅓ of all caladiums used are of the variety *Candidum*—white with green veins. The following list includes only a few of the many fine varieties available, but is representative of the biggest-selling colors.

- *Candidum*. White with green veins.
- *White Christmas*. Another excellent white.
- *Poecile Anglais*. Deep crimson with deep green border.
- *Carolyn Whorton*. Rose, darker veins, green hue. Fine for pots.
- *Freida Hemple*. Dwarf, all-purpose red.
- *Mrs. Arno Nehrling*. Bronze turning white; pink hue, red midribs.
- *Blaze (T. L. Meade)*. Bronze-red leaves; bright red midribs.
- *Fanny Munson (Red Glory)*. Excellent, brilliant pink with deeper veins.
- *Postman Joyner*. Dark red.
- *Candidum Jr*. Dwarf, white.
- *Lord Rosenbury (Rosebud)*. Frosty rose with green edge.
- *Lord Derby*. Transparent rose with dark ribs. Bushy.

The following varieties hold their color well in partial shade or full sun: *Candidum Jr., Seagull, Carolyn Whorton, Rosebud, Mrs. W. B. Haldeman*, and *Firechief*.

Lance-Leaf (Strap) Caladiums

A distinct class, differing from the regular fancy-leafed varieties in leaf appearance. Strap-leafed varieties have heavier textured, leathery leaves than other varieties. Leaves are usually narrow and plants grow shorter. Because of their heavier textured leaves, strap-leafed varieties are generally better for open-sun planting, since their leaves and coloring do not fade or burn as easily. Strap-leafed varieties produce smaller tubers than fancy leafed varieties and are usually priced 1 grade above their actual size, as compared to prices for the fancy-leaved varieties. Leaves of the strap-leafed varieties hold up well when cut. Culture of this class is identical to that of the fancy leaved varieties.

Following is a representative list of varieties suitable for pot plant or bedding purposes:

- *Rosalee*. Shiny red leaves with green border.

- *White Wings*. White-green background with crimson outline.

- *Lance Wharton*. Pink.

- *Pink Gem*. Pink.

CALCEOLARIA (Pocketbook Plant)*

ANNUAL *(C. herbeohybrida) 500,000–1,150,000 seeds per oz. Germinates in 16 days at 65°–70°. Light.*

Calceolarias—ever popular among the cool pot plant group.

Traditionally grown at low temperatures to flower from late January through April, this member of the cool pot crop clan has become more versatile insofar as it can now be flowered at other times of the year without the 4–6 weeks of temperatures below 55°F thought to be necessary for bud initiation. This is dependent upon individual varieties and is a result of research work and the introduction of new, improved varieties. Most of the production currently lies with F_1 hybrids. While the 6" pot size is still used in some areas, the majority of calceolaria is now being flowered in a 4" to 5½" pot size.

*Contributed by Ed Harthun, Ball Seed staff.

The seed of calceolaria is extremely small and should be sown directly on top of the germinating medium with exposure to light. As soon as seedlings emerge, they should be exposed to good air circulation and not exposed to direct sunlight. Four to five weeks after sowing, the seedlings should be ready to transplant to a 2" to 2¼" cell or pot. After 5–6 weeks they are ready for shifting into the finishing pot.

Calceolaria will tolerate quite a range of growing media as long as these media have good drainage and aeration. They are subject to chlorosis caused by overwatering. The first week or two following a move up are critical. Stem rot can also be a problem, which in many cases can be avoided by not planting too deep. Sensitive to high salts, care should be taken when watering and feeding. Calceolaria are not heavy feeders. Fertilization with a complete analysis at the rate of 100 ppm is adequate. Frequency of application would largely be dependent on the medium. If a soil mix, apply every 10 days to 2 weeks. If peat-lite, use once a week. The pH should be maintained between 5.5 and 6.

Some shade must be provided to prevent foliage burn when days start getting longer and brighter (usually about mid-February in the Midwest).

Traditional schedules using standard varieties for spring flowering call for an August 1 to September 1 sowing for flowering from early January into March. Crop time averages from 20–22 weeks using a 60°F night temperature until plants are well established in the finishing pots. Then temperatures are lowered to 55°F nights for 5–6 weeks for bud initiation. At this point, temperatures can be raised or lowered 5° to control flowering. After bud initiation, mum lights can be used to hasten flowering. Varieties generally used for this scheduling include F_1 *Brite 'N Early Mix* and F_1 *Glorious Mix*.

The *Anytime* F_1 hybrid series of calceolaria is probably first in its class of so-called fast crop types that do not require the cold treatment period, but are grown at 60°F nights and can be flowered, as its name implies, nearly anytime of the year except for the high temperature months of July and August. Crop time for this type runs from 16–18 weeks. Another variety in this class is the F_1 *Melodie*.

CALENDULA (Pot Marigold)

ANNUAL *(C. officinalis) 3,000 seeds per oz. Germinates in 10 days at 70°. Dark.*

Hardly used anymore at all as a cut flower, this cold temperature item is an important bedding plant particularly in some areas. Certain varieties also perform well as 4" pot plants. Where climates are mild in the winter, they are sold in the fall for winter and spring blooming. They are also well used in areas where the summers are cool.

For pack sales sow 7–8 weeks prior to selling season. Good 4" pots can be produced in 8 to 10 weeks from sow date. They grow at their best at a temperature range of 45°–50°F.

The newer, more dwarf forms (12") are those being more widely used. The orange and yellow *Coronets* are popular. More recently introduced is a dwarf, very compact series, *Fiesta Gitana*. The series includes a yellow, orange, and mixture. They respond to B-Nine and are good for 4" pots.

Family Circle is a mixture, 12"–15" tall with 2"–3" flowers.

CALLA

Callas may be grown either as a year-round bench crop (or in pots) for cut flowers (usually the large white *Aethiopica*), or as pot plants for flowering during the spring months. There are three principal species of callas. *Aethiopica* is the common large white calla; *Godfreyana* (listed commercially as *Godfrey*) is a dwarf, smaller-flowered variety of *Aethiopica* grown chiefly as a pot plant. *Calla Elliottiana* is the common yellow calla. It is grown either as a pot plant or for cutting.

Calla Rehmanii Superba, known as the "Pink Calla," is a dwarf plant with flowers mostly white with a rose tint.

Callas are propagated by division of parent rhizomes or by "offsets" from the original rhizome. "Bulbs" are commonly produced in California and are available during the fall months. Callas may be planted as soon as received in a loose loam soil. They are native to shady locations near streams or ponds, which gives an indication of their requirements. Callas do best in a loose peat loam with plenty of water and frequent liquid fertilizing during their growing period. When planting in benches for cutting, space the plants liberally—2 feet between plants is ample. Many growers grow their cut-flower crop in large pots instead of in open benches. Callas are subject to fast-spreading root and rhizome rots that are kept from spreading if all plants are grown in pots. Callas do best in full sunlight during the winter months and in partial shade during the bright summer season. *Aethiopica* enjoys a minimum night temperature of 55°, while *Elliottiana* and *Rehmanii* do best at 60°.

The yellow calla may be forced as a pot plant for Easter flowering. At 65°F night temperature, 12 to 14 weeks forcing time is required. Soil in pots should be loose with perhaps 1 part in 3 of peat added. They should be fertilized regularly during their growing season. Although callas grow best at 65°, lowering the temperature to 55° at flowering time will help the plants and flowers to last longer.

Calla bulbs are sold by sizes expressed in inches of diameter. Bulbs sold as 1½" to 2" for instance will be between 1½" and 2" in diameter. Commercially available bulbs of the different varieties vary in size from 1¼" to 3". Generally speaking, the larger sized bulbs produce the largest flowers and the most flowers per bulb.

The most common trouble with callas is with one or more fungus rots that affect the roots or the rhizome. Rhizomes should be inspected at the time of planting for soft, rotted areas. These areas should be cut down to living tissue and the rhizome treated with a fungicide. A 1 hour soaking in a solution of commercial formaldehyde of 1 quart to 12 gallons of water will clean up any infections on the rhizome. Nonmetal containers should be used, and the bulbs should be planted while wet. The use of Temik will keep common insect infestations under control. Aphids, mealybugs, or red spider are the most common offenders.

CAMPANULA (Bell Flower)

PERENNIAL *(C. species) 120,000 seeds per oz. Germinates in 15 days at 70°.*

Most popular and valuable of the wide variety of plants under this heading is *C. Medium Calycanthema,* the cup-and-saucer type, available in separate colors, but most widely used as a mix. Actually a biennial, it will reach a height of 30″. Its chief usage is in the perennial border and garden. *C. Carpatica* series is a dwarf type. It's a slow growing (8″) vigorous type with a 10″ spread. Available in separate colors and a mixture, they produce 1½″ cup-shaped flowers. Ideal for borders.

Campanula can be sown from July to September. They should be transplanted to small containers and overwintered in cold frames or cold plastic houses where they can be mulched with straw or a similar material.

CANDYTUFT (Iberis)

PERENNIAL *(I. species) 11,500 seeds per oz. Germinates in 3 weeks at 60–65°.*

While iberis has both annual and perennial forms, the annual form, especially the hyacinth type, formerly used as a greenhouse cut flower, is seldom seen now.

There are several hardy perennial iberis or candytuft in general use. *Sempervirens,* the most popular, is 12″ tall with clear, pure white flowers; it blooms heavily in April and May. Its foliage is evergreen, and even with us it is extremely hardy. Don't plant candytuft where it can't be kept uniformly wet. It is an excellent border or rockery plant.

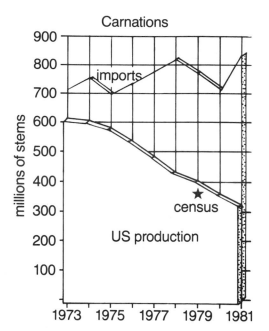

Carnations—nine years of US production plus imports. US figures are from the USDA. The Department of Commerce census is posted for 1979. As indicated, total US and import production for 1981 was 840 million stems.

Carnations are still one of the mainstays of the cut flower industry. Unfortunately, heavy competition from imports has reduced U.S. production now centered in Colorado and coastal California. While it is estimated that Colorado production will continue to drop, California production looks rather stable in the coastal California area from San Diego to Salinas.

Structures

Today, most new carnations are planted in ground beds in double-poly structures. Fiberglass is also widely used, especially on structures built several years ago. They were basically inexpensive structures—good enough, though, to produce quality crops.

*Contributed by Ed Rose, Ball Seed Company.

Soil Preparation

Much of the California carnation-belt area is blessed with naturally sandy soil to which little, if any, organic matter needs to be added. If soils are heavier, addition of fir bark to loosen the soil is beneficial. Drainage is most important. If good natural drainage is not available, mounding up of ground beds 8"–10" and/or installation of drain tile under the beds is a must. Carnations don't like wet feet!

Most growers use methyl bromide on the soil before planting to prevent diseases. Steam, while great if available, is just not available to most carnation growers as most carnations are grown with little or no heat—especially from the Nipoma Mesa Santa Maria area south to San Diego.

Planting

Rooted cuttings from a specialist propagator are planted on a two-year rotation April through August. Standard 36" wire mesh, 6" x 8" spacing (two layers) are placed on the beds with one cutting planted in each space. Wire supports are moved upwards as plants grow.

Rooted cuttings are almost always planted directly into soil. One wonders, though, if established plants in cell packs or Jiffy-Pots wouldn't reduce time to first bloom.

Watering/Nutrition

Once planted, some growers *temporarily* water overhead until plants are established, then use the drip tube method of watering for the duration of the crop. The temporary overhead sprinklers ensure uniform moisture and cutting turgidity prior to establishment.

Fertilizers such as super phosphate and lime are sometimes incorporated into beds before planting. Water-soluble fertilizers with micro nutrients are injected into the drip tube irrigation system with all irrigations. Soil and plant tissue tests should determine the amount and type of fertilizer used by the grower. Generally a 200 ppm NPK balance is a good starting point—then follow the soil test recommendations.

Temperature/Light/Ventilation

In California, as mentioned earlier, many growers don't heat—others very little. Carnations can withstand almost freezing temperatures—but they

The miniature carnation—a major crop in the U.S. Low labor!

just won't grow. Ideally, 50°F nights and 75°F days with the usual high light (no shade except for the hottest summer weather) of California will produce great quality carnations. Yes, carnations like high light. Fan cooling is almost dead! Energy costs are too high for the crop's return—natural coastal breezes cool houses with roll-down side walls and/or roof vents. Wide open doors help too!

Timing/Culture

Most growers pinch young cuttings after carnations are well established in beds—3–4 weeks after planting. An interesting variation on pinching is to again pinch half of the new secondary shoots. This spreads out the bloom date on new producing plants—important for startup operations. Normally new plants will begin blooming 12–15 weeks after planting. Many growers cut back almost to the original break, leaving a node or two for new breaks to develop. This method provides for even production year round—practical for California because of year-round, near-perfect weather for carnations.

Varieties/Types

Many California growers are producing more miniatures and less standard varieties. Labor is the big factor as standards need disbudding and taping of

394

the flower bud to prevent splits. Some growers tell us, "leave the standards to the Colombians." Your sales representative can tell you the varieties best suited for your area. This is partially dependent on the grower's market—local or shipped. Novelties are becoming more important as these varieties are not as readily available from foreign growers. White is still the most popular, followed by various shades of pink. Red, while popular for Valentine's Day, Christmas, and other holidays, is not what it used to be. Here again, plant what your market dictates.

Some popular varieties:

Standards	*Color*
Scania	Red
Improved White Sim	White
Nora	Dark pink
Baranna Soana	Light pink
Peter's New Pink Sim	Light pink
S. Arthur Peterson	Red & white stripe novelty
Pink Ice Novelty	Scarlet/white novelty

Miniatures	
White Elegance	White
Dad's Crimson	Red
Star Five	Red
Tinkerbell	Pink
Barbi	Pink
Goldilocks	Yellow
Elegance	Pink/white novelty
Orange Picotee	Orange novelty
Maj. Britt	Purple/yellow novelty

Insects/Diseases

Aphids and spider mites are the most prevalent insect pests. Cygon controls aphids. Pentac or Vendex controls the spider mites. Carnations are bothered less by insects if good sanitation and preventative maintenance are maintained. Subdue controls root rot diseases and Exotherm Termil controls botrytis in flowers. An interesting point: Silver thiosulfate will improve keeping quality of cut carnations; also, it significantly prevents botrytis. While oversimplified, these are two of the potentially serious disease problems. Here again, good sanitation, chemically sterilized soil prior to planting, plus good nutrition and watering practices will reduce diseases to a minimum. Plus, of course, planting disease-free cuttings.

Carnation root rot (fusarium oxysporum) is a common, and increasing, problem among growers the world over. It is common among California growers. No one seems to really know why. Most growers plant cultured cleaned

Typical West Coast carnation production, Silver Terrace Nursery, South San Francisco.

cuttings into beds of methyl bromide-treated soil—and still we see occasional loss of plants. Obviously either there is a leak in the clean stock procedure—or the grower is not doing a thorough enough job of soil pasteurizing. Ground beds (often used) offer the possibility of the disease rising up from the lower soil.

Dutch growers recently acknowledged the presence of the problem—"world wide" per a major propagator.

Summary

For coastal California growers, carnations can be a good crop. Low operating costs make it possible to compete with low priced imports. Really, carnations aren't that difficult to grow. The big problem is often sales—it's sometimes easier to grow a crop than sell it! Also, are you labor efficient? The really labor-efficient grower who knows how to market has a *big* headstart in successful carnation growing.

CELOSIA

ANNUAL *(C. argentea cristata and plumosa)* 28,000 seeds per oz. Germinates in 8–10 days at 70°.

One of the showiest and most dependable of annuals for cutting, garden decorations, bedding, borders, or pot plants. Currently, they are showing increased usage, for they are exceedingly attractive from late summer until frost. Celosias are easy to grow if a few simple rules are observed. They are heat-loving plants, and no attempt should be made to handle small plants for bedding unless a night temperature of at least 60° (preferably 65°) can be maintained. Even under these conditions, seed should not be sown earlier than 7 weeks before time for selling and planting out (after all frost danger has passed and nights are dependably warm). If their growth is checked in any way, either by cold temperatures, or by remaining too long in their growing containers, they will produce small flowers prematurely, and will probably not reach their full potential.

The two main types of classes are the *cristata* or *coxcomb,* producing the large, curiously shaped heads, and the *plumosa* or "feathered" type flower. The *cristata* may be had in both tall (2–3') and uniformly dwarf strains (10–12"), that make showy, 4" pot plants, as well as bedding plants. Dwarf strains of *cristata* in colors come quite true in every way. *Imp. Kardinal* is a popular bright red. Dwarfest of all is *Jewel Box* (4–5"). It has large combs in a color mix from white and light yellow to pink, red, and purple. It's our top choice for 4" pots. Figure 12 weeks from sow to sell. The taller *cristatas* are used where appropriate colors are wanted in fall decorative work. Outstanding in this class is the variety *Toreador* (18–20") which has extremely large combs of a bright red color.

The *plumosa* class is also available in tall semi-dwarf and dwarf strains. Most popular tall one is *Golden Triumph.* Reaching a height of 2½', it has golden-yellow plumes and bright green foliage. *Forest Fire* (2½') has been very popular for some time with its fiery, orange-scarlet plumes contrasted with bronze foliage. A semi-dwarf class (10–12") is also now available. Called the *Geisha* series, this strain represents an improvement over *Fairy Fountains.* It's available in a mix and separate color shades of carmine, orange, scarlet, and yellow. A good 4" pot item.

Still a popular dwarf one is *Fiery Feather,* bright red (1'), which makes a good pot plant or can be used for edging. *Golden Feather* is a deep yellow of similar habit.

CENTAUREA (Cornflower)

ANNUAL *(C. species) 7,000 seeds per oz. Germinates in 10 days at 65°.*

A brightly colored summer annual—fine for cut flower beds.

A cool-temperature, hardy annual useful for cutting both in and outdoors. Also, several dwarf Dusty Millers come under this heading. Most valuable for cutting is *Centaurea cyanus* or Bachelor Button. A September sowing on a raised bed in a 50° house can be flowered in February, but the more natural and better time to flower all the Centaureas is the spring months. This is done through planting from November to January, or even February, if well-started pot plants are used. While a late or spring-flowering crop can go on ground beds, we prefer raised or shallow beds especially for the cyanus class because of the heavy, almost unmanageable growth they make in deep, rich soil. They should be spaced at least 12" x 12". In the early stages of their growth, a low temperature will naturally be good for them, because it permits building up a strong root system that responds better to higher temperatures later.

After the centaureas get well-started, 50° nights suit them very well.

By far, the best color is blue. *Blue Diadem* is a good improved strain. The standard for many years has been *Blue Boy*, which normally grows to a height of 3'. *Pinkie* is a bright pink. There is also a formula mixture available that contains *Blue Boy, Pinkie*, and white and red shades.

Taken together, chrysanthemums are a big, important, and growing part of U.S. flower production. The dollar sales total $169.5 million (1979 U.S. Dept. of Commerce Census)—not including garden mums. It breaks down as follows.

Type	Dollar sales (in millions)
Pot mums (trend up a bit)	$ 93.7
Pompons (trend steady)	$ 47.5
Standards (trend down some)	$ 28.3
No figures available for garden mums (trend up)	
Total	$169.5

Another clue to the importance of mums: Specialist propagators across the world supply an estimated one billion plus cuttings (author's estimate) to growers—per year. And, these propagators also support their industry with substantial and steady breeding programs. And with major pathology especially aimed at virus problems. Result: Cuttings generally free of disease and insects. And true to type.

Mums can surely be called a basic crop, shifting constantly in detail but in the overall, for a generation or more, clearly a major part of ornamentals. And all signs as of the mid-1980s point to a continued steady growth of them.

Basics of Controlled Flowering

Underlining the major success of mums the past 20 or 30 years is the fact of controlled flowering. Any mum crop can be forced to flower at any target date anywhere—if the rules are followed. The marketing implications of this are weighty and obvious.

All this is based on the fact that mums are a "short day" crop. Simply stated, they will set bud and flower if exposed to a short day. Which of course reflects the way "natural" season or fall mums have been grown for hundreds of years. Here the formation of buds and flowers occurs precisely because the days do naturally shorten in fall. For the record, the researchers who discovered this most important phenomenon were two USDA scientists, Allard and Brown. The year: 1937. Since then many other crops have been found to be either short day responsive or, in some cases, will flower on long days.

So, in the late 1940s, growers began to force mum crops into flower early by early summer application of black cloth over the beds, typically from 5 p.m. to 8 a.m. Result: An artificial short day (9 hours long), and November

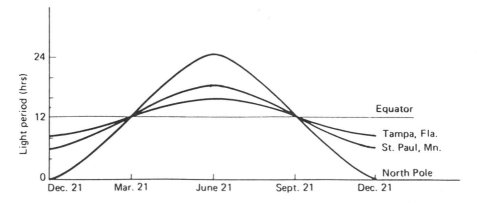

The length of the light period throughout the year, different latitudes of the northern hemisphere. Which is basic to controlled flowering of mums at various latitudes. Drawing courtesy of Paul Nelson, Greenhouse Operation and Management *(Reston, Virginia: Reston Publishing Company, 1981).*

varieties now flowered in September. And brought better prices! All of which gradually led to flowering mums, both pot and cut, 52 weeks a year. All by simply controlling length of day.

Early in the game, several refinements became apparent:

Need for a long day period If short days were applied immediately upon planting the new cutting, the crop would immediately go into bud and flower. Result: A pot mum perhaps 6" or 8" tall and a cut mum much the same. Obviously there was a need for more or less several weeks of long days immediately upon planting the cutting—to allow the plant time to develop enough stem length before flowering.

Response periods Again, early in the game, growers and researchers were able to sort out mum varieties according to "response period." Which means simply the number of weeks from the beginning of short day or black cloth application until the crop flowered. So now a typical crop would be planted, given 2 or 3 weeks of long days, then perhaps 10 weeks of response period. Result: A crop that took roughly 12 weeks from plant to flower.

Varieties varied in response period from as little as 7 and 8 weeks to as long as 14 to 15 weeks. In general, the very early responding varieties (7 and 8 week) are the garden varieties that flower normally outdoors in September, early October. The great majority of commercial pot and cut mum varieties are 9 week and 10 week responders. These are varieties that naturally flower in early November. There is also a group of 13 to 14 week responders which are varieties that naturally flower in December. Mainly they were a group of pompons and formerly they were used importantly for winter flowering con-

400

trolled crops in northern greenhouses. Because of certain unreliabilities, they have been replaced largely by new and improved 10 and 11 week varieties for the northern winter pompon crop.

Schedules for northern vs. southern growers We've talked mostly scheduling crops for the northern greenhouse (latitude 40° to 45° north). Typically northern *winter* crops might need 3 or even 4 weeks of long days—to develop enough stem and substance during the low light, slow growing, winter crop. A grower in the same northern greenhouse now flowering a crop in summer or fall would reduce the number of long days to a week or two— since the crop grows so much faster in the higher light intensities and the longer days of summer and fall.

Another adaptation of this: Deep South growers (and south of the border crop) experience in effect high light and longer days year round. Therefore, schedules for these southern crops tend to follow very closely the schedules and even selection of varieties used by northern growers in summer and early fall.

Once all this basic know-how was in place, propagators soon developed very complete schedules prescribing a precise number of weeks of long days and short days for crops to flower each week of the year. And schedules were

Ice Cap—Nova Scotia mid-winter. Not heavy production here but good quality.

developed for varying degrees of latitude from north to south. And typically these schedules also prescribed certain varieties for each of these crops in each latitude. Such schedules are available in fact to this day—from major propagators. It's all a very striking example of technology descending upon our industry.

Exactly What Makes the Mum Flower?

We've talked generalities up to now. Next question, precisely what are the conditions of daylength and other environmental factors—that will cause the chrysanthemum to set bud and flower—or to prevent flowering?

The answer unfortunately is not really precise—since varieties differ substantially in their response. But, some fairly safe ground rules can be laid down. Let's start with the conditions to make the typical chrysanthemum variety set bud and flower.

Daylength 12 hours or less of daylength will cause most varieties to set bud and flower. A few varieties will flower with 12½ hours of daylength per day. In fact, early researchers such as Kenneth Post pointed out that it's the long night, not the short day, that does it. But the answer comes out the same.

Temperature Another clear requirement to cause the mum to set bud and flower is temperature—normally stated at 60°F. Again, varieties differ; some will set bud and flower at 55°, some require even a "warm" 60°— perhaps 62°. But for most commercial crops of pot plants or cut flowers, growers do maintain 60° at least until buds are set.

The very early 7–8 week sorts Some of the earliest of our garden varieties (normally flowering in late August) and many of the English so called "early mums" which again flower outdoors naturally in late summer seem to flower more in response to temperature than they do to daylength. If grown quite cool, 50° or 45° nights, they will remain vegetative. If grown warm, 60° or 65°, they tend to set bud and flower. In fact, some of the most "responsive" of these varieties will set bud no matter what you do! The Japanese also have a race of mums which are widely used for April and May flowering—without daylength control—again which seem to flower more on temperature than on daylength.

How to Prevent Flowering

Now let's describe the conditions that will keep the mum plant vegetative—nonflowering. The heart of it is to maintain a long day. Which of course occurs naturally in summer but during the short-day fall and winter months it is necessary to supplement natural daylight with artificial light. The rules to remember: Buds will not form as long as the periods of uninterrupted darkness are not over 7 hours long. Example: In mid-winter assume natural light is from 8 a.m. to 4 p.m. Lights provided from 10 p.m. to 2 a.m. will produce two six-hour periods of darkness, 4 p.m. to 10 p.m. and 2 a.m. to 8 a.m. No buds will occur.

Intermittent Light

Can save a lot of electricity and will do the job. Use the same number of hours per night as with continuous light. But now during the hours of light, turn lights on only six minutes out of each 30 minute period. In other words, 6 on, 24 off, then 6 on, then 24 off, etc. Some growers, to be sure, use 12 minutes on, 18 minutes off.

How to Light

	Watt	Spacing	Height above soil
One 4' bed	60	Every 4'	60"
Two 4' beds (One row of lights)	100	Every 6'	60"
Three 4' beds (One row of lights)	150	Every 6'	60"

Reflectors must be held up off the bulb. For a 20' wide house, a single row of 300 watt reflector bulbs facing down at a 45° angle, spaced every 10', will do it. Bulbs should be staggered on alternate sides of ventilators—not directly under because of rain damage to bulbs. Figure about 1½ watts per square foot of ground covered. Use flood, not spot bulbs. It takes 10 foot-candles to prevent bud formation.

On large installations, half the area may be lighted before midnight, half after. This halves the demand cost. 230-volt lines reduce main sizes greatly.

Hours of light per night

Latitude 35–40°		Latitude 25–30°	
North of Charlotte, N.C.; Memphis, Tenn.; Bakersfield, Calif.			
June 15–July 15	No	Dec. 1–Mar. 31	4
July 15–July 30	2	April 1–May 31	3
Aug. 1–31	3	June 1–July 31	2
Sept. 1–Mar. 31	4	Aug. 1–Sept. 30	3
April 1–May 15	3	Oct. 1–Nov. 30	4
May 15–June 15	2		

Light leakage   There have been cases where light "leaking" onto the crop by accident from some nearby source in effect delayed flowering of a crop. Effect is like heat delay. The tipoff nearly always is the area affected. Plants nearest to a window of a nearby home—light shining out at night—or in some cases, lights used on main walks by night men.

It is obviously important in year-round flowering to carefully "cage in" light being applied to a bench of young plants. If a bench is being lighted and the benches on either side are not being lighted, then the light must be confined to the one bench by means of sateen curtains, etc. Light that "leaks" to other benches will cause blindness—failure to flower.

Daylength Varies with Latitude

As you get near the equator, winter days are longer, and fewer hours of light are needed. In fact, growers in Bogota, Colombia, very close to the equator, can actually prevent bud formation on some varieties without lights in mid-winter. Same in Hawaii—on certain varieties. Of course, the natural daylength at the equator is 12 hours year round; at the North Pole, it's zero hours in mid-winter and 24 hours in mid-summer. See accompanying graph.

Another Point

Speaking of preventing mum flowering, there is one other factor. A mum's proclivity to set bud and flower increases as the stem elongates. Propagators learn from experience that stock plants (mother blocks) allowed to grow older and flower tend to set buds regardless of daylength. Conversely, the first flush of cuttings from a healthy, soft, succulent, stock plant will nearly always be free of buds.

A mum stem, physiologically tending toward buds and flowering, will first display "strap" leaves—long narrow leaves without notches—up near the growth tip. It is an early warning sign!

Schedules

Here are samples of typical commercial pot plant growing schedules. Most of them are based on flowerings once a week year round.

9-week variety	10-week variety	11-week variety	Pot	Pinch	Lighting periods	Shade
	Tall treatment				Jan. 28–	
April 8	April 15	April 22	Jan. 28	Feb. 11	Feb. 3	Mar. 15
	Medium treatment				Jan. 28–	
April 15	April 22	April 29	Jan. 28	Feb. 11	Feb. 10	Mar. 15
	Short treatment				Jan. 28–	
April 22	April 29	May 6	Jan. 28	Feb. 11	Feb. 17	Mar. 15

Note that all varieties of the "tall treatment" group—potted January 28 and handled the same. Note that the 9-week variety flowers April 8, the 10-week variety (one week longer response) flowers April 15 and the 11-week, of course, April 22. All these flowering dates are from a short-day date of February 3. Shading in this case does not start until March 15—because days are naturally short enough up until March 15.

Now let's go down to the bottom—"short treatment." This is a naturally short growing variety. As mentioned above, these naturally short varieties need several weeks more time to develop strength and substance compared to a naturally tall variety. Therefore, from the same potting date (January 28), the short treatment varieties have a later short-day date (February 17 vs. February 3). This is done to allow an extra two weeks from plant until short days—again, to allow the plant to develop more substance.

Therefore, the short treatment, 10-week variety will *flower* two weeks later than the 10-week tall treatment (April 15 vs. April 29).

It's easy to see now why growers try very hard to plant a whole week's pot mums up with the same response group and the same "tall treatment—short treatment" group. It makes life a lot simpler.

For the record, all catalogs designate the pot varieties as tall, medium, or short treatment.

Two essential conclusions here: Varieties that naturally grow short need several weeks more long-day time from plant to short days. And in the same way, crops grown during northern, dark, mid-winter weather also need several more weeks of long days compared to summer or fall crops with high light.

Year-round Cut Flower Schedules

Same basic idea—schedules designed to flower crops at predictable dates. And, again, they are adjusted for dark winter weather vs. bright, summer, fall

Plant date[1]	Pinch date	Modified date[2]	Lighting period	Start shade	Stop shade[3]	Response group	Flowering date
Jan. 7	Jan. 28	Feb. 4	Jan. 7–Mar. 3	Mar. 15	Note 1	10	May 13
Jan. 21	Feb. 11	Feb. 18	Jan. 21–Mar. 10	Mar. 15	Note 1	10	May 20
Jan. 28	Feb. 18	Feb. 25	Jan. 28–Mar. 17	Mar. 18	Note 1	10	May 27
Feb. 11	Mar. 4	Mar. 11	Feb. 11–Mar. 24	Mar. 25	Note 1	10	June 3
Feb. 18	Mar. 11	Mar. 18	Feb. 18–Mar. 31	Apr. 1	Note 1	10	June 10

[1]For single-stem crops, plant cuttings on pinch date.
[2]For crops produced in CO_2 environment or for retail production, use dates in this column.
[3]Stop shade on pompons when buds show color; stop shade on October through May standards when bud is size of a nickel; stop shade on June through September standards when bud is taken.

weather. Also, typically cut flower schedules are done on a year-round basis—successive crops that flower one week apart.

Note the table above.

Schedules for cut flower growers are available for each of the four or five "zones" across the U.S. Example, Zone 1 from Chicago to the Canadian border; Zone 4 will be southern Florida and the Brownsville, Texas area. Schedules between Zones 1 and 4 will be roughly comparable in August/September—but for January/February flowering, several more weeks of long-day time is required in the North.

Again, detailed tables for both pot plants and cut flower crops are available from propagators and seed firms.

All About Pot Mums

The broad look Pot mums in the 1980s are not booming—but they are expanding a bit, and are a big and steady part of the U.S. and Canadian pot plant business. Growers consistently complain about depressed prices and profits—but they are the backbone crop on most pot ranges today.

Production the past decade has shown steady growth (see accompanying graph) and the past year or two there seems probably modest continuing growth. It will probably continue that way in the near future. Part of the success of pot mums is the dramatic rise in supermarket sales of pot plants generally. The pot mum with its long shelf life, bright colors, and wide varieties of flower types is #1 among their flowering pot plants. Certainly the nonflorist outlets in total are selling the big half of U.S. pot mums today.

Market the crop first! It makes so much sense to thoroughly study your market—before you commit to any production. And a good starting point is to realize the wide variety of pot sizes and spacings available to the pot mum grower. All the way from 3½" up to 7" and 8". Including pinch crops and single stem. Another very important variable is simply your crop spacing. More and more we hear growers talking about growing a crop of pot mums or

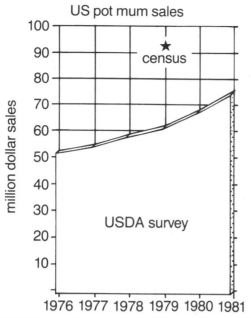

US pot mum sales ★ census

US pot mum sales. The solid area is the USDA survey. The star posts the 1979 Department of Commerce sales totals.

Most U.S. mum cuttings today are produced by specialists—mainly in southern Florida. Here is part of Pan American Plant's operation at Cortez, Florida. From the left, Carl Ball, chairman of the Ball Company; Robert Danielson, vice president; and William Hubbard, president of Pan American Plant Company. And on the right, Alfred Horn.

407

A point on marketing: Here's Jim Leider, M. Leider & Sons, Prairie View, Illinois, with an interesting corrugated tray that holds 4" pot mums. It is inserted into the larger corrugated box. At the point of sale, the larger box is removed and the tray remains for display purposes.

poinsettias to the "specifications of the buyer." If it's a quality retail shop, a 6" mum may get 14" or 15". For a super or discount store wanting lower price, the spacing will be crowded down—and the pot will often go down from 6" to 5" or even 4". And fewer cuttings.

Suggestion #1: Go talk to several of your most promising prospective customers (or present ones); see what they are looking for and what sort of price they are willing to pay. Offer them a variety of alternatives—with your pricing. Many or most will welcome this. Talk also with experienced seasoned seed house salesmen. They have a good grasp of the market, other producers, etc.

We are in fact seeing more each year of a break from the standard pot 6" mum. Some major producers are moving importantly toward 5". Also, the 4" and 4½" mums are clearly coming up. Europe is almost entirely 12cm (4¾"). Interesting clue: One major West Coast grower, fall 1983, has gone almost entirely to 4" poinsettias.

Next suggestion: "Grow" the crop on paper first! A simplified cost forecasting is not that big a job—see the chapter elsewhere in this book for a practical plan. The objective of course: To be sure that for the crop you are planning, for the spacing planned, and for your price, that you will produce a fair profit. Including packing cost, selling cost, all overhead items, and shrink. As this edition goes to print, computers are just coming into this planning process—see the computer chapter elsewhere in this book. The goal: To be able with computers to try different spacings and different prices and quickly compute a net profit on each variable. *Before* you grow the crop.

The typical result of such a thorough market study as this will be production of several different sizes and spacings—plus perhaps some special crops grown for a major holiday. And always basic to success in any size or price range is quality and reliability. Reliability to keep your commitments to your customers.

About expansion: Often existing growers plan and build new greenhouse areas—without really serious study of where the new product will be sold. Result is often a scramble, selling the product at least at first at distressed prices, and, so often, strained credit relations with suppliers.

Important point: The pot mum crop is potentially 52 crops a year—one each week. Poinsettias, lilies are one crop a year—and that's a big difference. The original uniform production 52-weeks-a-year programs have given way in many cases to considerable peaking for major holidays. And, in some cases,

Certainly over half of the U.S. pot mum crop is sold in various supermarkets and other nonflorist outlets. Here is an example of a display in a West Coast food chain.

pot mum production only in season when space availability or the market make them profitable. A typical year-round grower will often "bump" his weekly average production by 3 to 5 times for Easter and Mother's Day.

Now a production plan Having decided what you can produce—and at a profit—the next and very important step is to put in writing your production plan in detail. How many pots, what varieties, how many cuttings, and what spacing for each phase of the crop. Most pot mums are grown in a starting climate (70° and long days) for the first several weeks. Then they are moved to final spacing. Some growers practice three spacings, not two. And of course all this spacing problem must be carefully coordinated with available space. Again, starting to be done by computer.

Important! All this production planning really must be in writing a minimum of 6 months ahead of plant date. Several reasons:

- The plan is the basis for ordering of cuttings from suppliers. Substantial discounts are offered for early ordering—and late orders often don't get the desired varieties, especially for holidays.

- The quality profitable growers we talk to normally have a definite commitment from their major customers well in advance of even planting the cuttings.

- With 6 months planning you are in a much better position to plan other crops around space needed for the pot mums.

Such a plan must include varieties, complete schedules, pot size, spacing, date to pot, pinch date (some judgement here), short date, and flowering date. Propagators' catalogs have tables providing suggested dates for all of this, also varieties. As you gain experience you'll of course adjust to your own circumstances.

Variety selection is a critical part of planning the crop. It's a point which requires constant communication with your customers. There is a constant stream of new varieties coming onto the market, most of which must be evaluated and some put in your program on a trial basis at least.

Sorting out varieties so that all pots in a planting are in the same response group is very helpful. Propagators classify pot mums as short, medium, or tall varieties. The short ones are those which tend to grow short; the tall ones of course tend to grow tall. As you would expect, the short varieties are generally given a week or two more of long days, especially for winter flowering—to provide adequate stem length. The tall ones are given a minimum of long days. Commercial growers try very hard to include varieties of the same response group in a given week's flowering—and if at all possible, the same height group. Height of individual varieties can be controlled somewhat by more frequent retardant spray.

It's a lot less work, a lot less detail to watch, if a whole week's crop of pot mums can be grown on the same schedule all the way through! Simpler!

Finally, a crop well planned is a whole lot more apt to succeed than one thrown together the last minute. We hear growers saying "tell my supermarket buyer about that." Major crops of pot mums, especially for big holidays, are sometimes a last-minute decision—and often do succeed, but usually at a real penalty. Cuttings cost more; space is hard for the grower to find, so plants get crowded; you often take whatever varieties are available—and 3 or 4 different ones with different scheduling requirements, all of which cost more.

It seems that as the better growers develop a reputation for quality and reliable delivery they seem to find supers and good retailers willing to commit ahead. But you've really got to push for it.

Growing the crop   Now some of the highlights of growing quality pot mums:

Soil mixes: See chapter on soil mixes.

Irrigation and feeding: Almost universally, pot mums in the U.S. and Canada are fed and irrigated with a small tube leading to each pot. The grower can "water" a bench by just turning a valve for a couple of minutes—or even more frequently today, it's done by computerized controls. Dutch growers seem to generally use mat irrigation—with a thin sheet of perforated poly on top of the mats to prevent algae. It's often tied in with aluminum trays. They seem to use an "ebb and flow" system where the tray is actually flooded. And, they often use the irrigation water over and over. A word on feeding: Commercial pot mums are nearly always fed with tubes, and with each irrigation. The fertilizer is injected into the irrigation water line with a fertilizer injector. It's simple, nearly labor free. See fertilizer chapter for details. Normal injection level will be 200 ppm of nitrogen and potash, 300 or more on the northern winter crop. See John Peterson's notes on this point under fertilizers. See the separate chapter in this book on automatic irrigation.

Last point on watering: Water quality. Very hard high salt water can and often does detract importantly from the quality, flower size, etc., of a mum—or any crop.

Typically the problem creeps up gradually; the grower really isn't aware of it. One interesting way to put your finger on it: Grow a few plants with distilled water from a filling station—on the same schedule, etc., as your tap water. The difference might surprise you. A Solubridge will give you a definite reading on salt content of your water supply. See fertilizer chapter. Another point on water: Temperature. We are seeing growers beginning to realize the major impact on all pot crops of soil temperature. And that cold water will drop soil temperature 20° in a minute or less. So water heaters are appearing. See *Grower Talks,* April 1984.

Temperatures: Most year-round pot mum specialists carry a 63° typical night temperature, 65° cloudy days, maybe 70° sunny days. Growers who have a separate area for starting their crops will typically maintain a warmer night temperature—often 70° for this first several weeks.

Where possible, a cooling down at the finish can do wonders for color and quality. Maybe gradually dropping off to 55° or 50°. Before year-round flowering, the mum was always considered a 50° crop.

Toning: Cloy Miller, a key figure in the early days of year-round flowering, was a great exponent of toning pot mum crops. Just as buds are starting to form, carry them on the dry side for a week or so. Just let them dry at the edges a bit, not severely. You'll end up with a bit less flower size—but a lot more keeping quality and substance.

Plant a good cutting: A quality crop must be done the quality way right from the beginning—including starting with a good cutting. Wherever it comes from, it should be a reasonably heavy stem, free of insects and diseases. Uniform in caliper and length. Also, very important—it must be succulent, not hard and woody. Rooted cuttings should have several ½″ to 1″ bristly white roots, not a mass of 2″ to 3″ roots. Roots should be solid, not hollow and tubular.

Heat delay: Mums subjected to temperatures well into the 90s for a week or two or three will typically flower late. In aggravated cases of a month or more of very high temperatures, this can result in a delay of 7 or 10 days or even more in flowering. The clues are, of course, first simply a delay in flowering beyond the scheduled date. Also, you'll see "heat delay buds"; the little sepals coming up the side of the buds are curled inward in a very distinctive way. Look for it.

The answer of course in most cases is evaporative pad cooling. In fact, most production of mums across the U.S. and Canada today is under pad and fan cooling. Some moderate summer areas such as the Northwest and New England may not need this.

One point here: Some varieties are clearly more tolerant of high temperature than others. If you are in a high temperature prone area, be sure to lean on the heat tolerant sorts. Your propagator will know them.

Low winter light problems: In areas such as northern U.S. and Ontario, winter quality of the pot mum depreciates seriously. Even worse in areas like Seattle or Cleveland, Ohio. Depending on the number of cloudy days, we've seen a marked drop in quality as early as late November and December. The late December noon sun, when you can see it at all, rises only a bit above the southern horizon. By early February, as daylength increases, the sun rises higher each noon, and cold clear days occur more often; quality starts up again. What to do about it?

First, be sure that the roof is clean and clear. In fact, a double poly roof so often used today allows perhaps 8% or 10% less light to get to the crop vs. good clean glass. Glass itself should be kept clean—we so often see summer shade still on the glass in November and December! Fiberglass ranges which have been allowed to deteriorate to a point of serious light loss are not great for winter mums in the North. Or anywhere for that matter. A light meter will often provide shocking news of light loss from even seven- or eight-year-old fiberglass.

Part of the answer to the problem is to space the plants out a bit further (more light to each leaf), allow an extra week or 10 days of long days to develop more substance. Another critical point: Again variety selection. Some varieties perform much better under marginal winter light than others. Again, talk to your propagator, your salesman.

Some growers have set up supplemental light programs—high intensity discharge (HID) lights. They deliver on the order of 500 foot-candles, are most often used during the first several weeks of the crop when many plants can be influenced at low cost. (A light meter is a valuable ally in appraising this sort of problem.) You'll see that 12,000 foot-candles (mid-day in July) shrink to 1200 or even 300 foot-candles on a cloudy December day. And now it's light only 6 to 7 hours vs. 13 or 14 in July.

Retardants: On pot mums, mainly B-Nine. Very widely used and effective in controlling height of pot mums, especially some varieties in some seasons. For taller varieties flowered in August and September (highest light and tallest plant), growers often make several applications. Dilution:

- 2,500 ppm: 0.4 oz. of 85% wettable powder per gallon of water

- 5,000 ppm: 0.8 oz. of 85% wettable powder per gallon of water

Most important point about B-Nine: Be sure not to water the foliage immediately after application—you'll just wash it off. Application on wet foliage is OK. The first application is made normally 10 to 15 days after pinching—or with a minimum of 1" to 1½" new growth on new shoots. Applications are often repeated every three weeks and sometimes more often than that. One of the few penalties is the tendency for white varieties to turn cream.

B-Nine is a great helper!

To get some idea of how much B-Nine can be applied without problems, we were surprised to find a grower producing single stem *Bright Golden Anne* in late summer—thanks to heavy B-Nine application. In fact, he seemed to apply B-Nine every Wednesday to the crop from 2 weeks after pinch until near flowering date. The only casualty was that *Cream Yellow Princess Anne* would turn a heavy cream yellow. The flowers were huge, the stems short and sturdy. The plants lovely.

Pot mums too tall? A common problem. Things that can be done about it:

- Reduce the long day period—although most growers like to allow a minimum of one week.

- More applications of B-Nine—3 or 4 times not uncommon.

- Select shorter growing varieties.

- Less water/fertilizer.

- More light—is the roof glass clean?

- A little more space.

A remarkable specimen plant of Bright Golden Anne. *It's grown single stem and "B-Nined every Wednesday" from shortly after pinching until several weeks before sale. The grower (above right), Clarence Sturm, and on the left, Tom Aykens, owner of Memorial Drive Flowers, Appleton, Wisconsin.*

Now, what if plants are too short? Usually a much simpler problem. Mostly add some long days to the schedule; also select medium/tall varieties. Also, less B-Nine. Feed/water more. Are roots OK?

Question: What is the optimum height for pot mums? We've always used the rule of thumb of 12–12. The plant should be 12″ high from the pot rim, 12 open flowers on a plant. Supermarkets, recently though, are wanting plants more like 11″ or 10″ from the pot rim.

Crowd plants carefully—for profit: The point here: The more space you give a plant the better the quality—and the lower the profit tends to be. Space costs a lot of money; therefore the pressure is on the grower to crowd plants down. The traditional 14″ by 14″ spacing for 4 or 5 cuttings per 6″ mum is giving way a lot these days to 12″ by 13″ or even 12″ by 12″. Or less!

The effect on profit in moving from 14″ by 14″ to 12″ by 12″ is monstrous. In fact, you get 27% more plants on a bench at 12″ by 12″. So pressure is on the grower to be able to crowd the plant down—still produce quality. Same thing, by the way, for poinsettias. So how do you do it?

To restrict height, more use of B-Nine is one obvious answer. Another more difficult response is less water and fertilizer. Another helpful answer is to select varieties which tend to grow more upright—*Torch* and, somewhat, the *Anne*s.

Partly it's just a matter of being a good grower—it does take real skill to crowd plants down and still maintain quality. Not a deluxe plant, but a somewhat more restricted plant, fewer flowers—but still quality. That's an important distinction.

414

These plants demonstrate the impact of B-Nine on pot mums—plus the importance of timing the application. Series was done at Ohio State. Cuttings potted October 8, pinched October 22. Plant on the left was treated with B-Nine three weeks after pinch. Next right, two weeks after pinch. Next right was treated at time of pinch. And the plant on the extreme right was the untreated check. In the photo: Howard Jones, then undergraduate at Ohio State, now production manager for Alexander Masson, Linwood, Kansas.

Direct Stick? A few growers today are sticking unrooted cuttings directly into the flowering pot. They are rooted in the pot and of course flower and are sold in the same pot. The saving in time and labor is obvious. The problem: To maintain quality. For one thing, it's much more difficult to grade cuttings effectively at the unrooted stage. Result: Inevitably less uniformity with direct stick. Also, direct stick means that the entire house of direct stuck pot mums must be handled as a rooting area. That means in winter, 70° or more soil temperature, usually mist or an equivalent is needed to keep cuttings turgid until they start to root. Also, a lot more grower skill in gradually withdrawing heat and mist at the right time—to prevent softening of the plant.

For all these reasons, the great majority of pot mum specialists today either buy rooted cuttings or buy unrooted and root them separately. Cuttings are again graded but just before potting. If there is any trend here, it would seem really to be away from direct stick.

The successful pot mum specialists really have to be quite dedicated to quality—and direct stick makes it tougher to do a really top quality job.

About disbudding: Traditionally, pot mums are disbudded. Each one of the 8 or 10 or 12 stems is disbudded down leaving only top buds to flower. It's costly! We hear 25¢ and more a plant. With the immense pressure on labor cost, growers are looking hard for ways out of this cost. And there seems

415

Biotherm used for bottom heat on direct rooting of mums at Sandyland, Las Cruces, New Mexico.

increasing evidence that the lady who buys the pot mum may not always really want the disbudded plant! For example, daisy pot mums sold today are virtually all not disbudded—and they seem to sell more each year. Removal of the center bud is practiced—but no lateral disbudding.

Growers frequently put this job on a piecework basis, but that requires careful followup inspection of the work.

One helpful answer again is variety selection—some varieties will require twice as much or even more time per pot to disbud. The *Annes* are very fast to disbud, the white *Puritan* is very slow. The obvious answer: Select varieties which are faster to disbud.

You have to wonder too about the possibility of carefully selecting varieties which present themselves best with center bud removal only—and trying them on *your* customers. The *Mandalay's* are a good starting point. We've seen them done with only center bud removal and they're really a very colorful plant. The *Annes* are a good example of a variety that must be disbudded.

Many quality growers are looking very hard for ways to get out from under this expensive hand job. We have to wonder if it really is necessary.

Single stem pot mums: Some growers consistently produce perhaps 5% or 10% or 15% of their crop single stem, typically 7" pots with 7 cuttings each. Each cutting is disbudded, grown up to a single flower; there is no pinch. Result if well done is of course a very showy plant—for which there does seem to be demand especially among the better retail shops. One of the problems involved is height control—and inevitably more B-Nine applications are used,

Disbudding pot mums is an expensive job and especially hard to manage for big holidays. Here Norm White, White's Nursery and Greenhouses, Inc., Chesapeake, Virginia, makes a case for center bud removal (above left) vs. normal disbud (right) and no disbud (center).

A well-grown specimen of Pan American Plant's Independence.

417

shorter varieties are often selected. The *May Shoesmith* group, white and yellow, are favorites for both their very large flowers and tendency to compact growth.

The question here again is whether your market will pay the additional premium in space and cutting required to produce such a plant—and still yield a fair level of profit.

An adaptation of this plan is the one cutting per 4″ pot. For years growers have done this, often using *Nob Hill* varieties. Again, the *May Shoesmith* family do well in this situation. Somehow it seems to be a favorite ploy of super and discount stores to contract for quantities of white flowers at such holidays as Christmas, then spray them with all sorts of colors and apply gimmick decorations. Hearts for Valentine's, Santas for Christmas.

Mechanize—specialize! As our 14th edition goes to press, the pot plant and especially the pot mum industry is involved in some sort of conversion. Principally this involves mechanization and specialization. The highly mechanized and specialized grower seems in general to reduce cost substantially— but against the traditional grower, he has a strong marketing disadvantage. The pattern among U.S. pot plant growers for many years has been to produce a diversity of crops, perhaps a dozen or two throughout the year—with which he can provide his outlets with a complete line.

The specialist/mechanized grower's answer to this is that with his much lower labor cost he is able to compete very effectively with the more traditional grower.

Pan American Plant's Bright Light—*an extremely free-flowering yellow daisy.*

The Dutch as of today are a classic example of both mechanization and specialization—see *Grower Talks,* December 1983 issue, for details on such operations as Boekestijn, de Lier, Holland.

The controversy and competition between several Canadian specialists and the U.S. growers is thoroughly confused by the seriously distorted currency values across our borders—a 20% break to the Canadian grower as of early 1984. And the high dollar problem is even more pronounced in relating U.S. cost to those of Dutch growers.

Altogether, a tough problem for the traditional U.S. grower.

G.V.B.

Pompons—An Opportunity!

Outlook for the crop Basic fact: Unlike the standard mum (total U.S. *use* is down sharply), total U.S. *use* of pompons is *up* sharply. Note the accompanying graphs for dramatic evidence of this.

The public loves pompons! They fit so well into smaller arrangements; they're widely used in the very popular mixed bouquets, both retail shops and supers. And again, there is that wide range of colors and flower forms. Daisy pompons are big and climbing importantly in popularity. And spider pompons dominate the European market.

U.S. *production* of pompons, as of the mid-1980s, seems to be steady, perhaps up a bit. Heavily in California, by the way. But—imports continue to expand strongly, mostly from Colombia. Some Central America, some from Holland. As of 1981 (last figures available), well over half of pompons used in the U.S. were imported—and the trend of imports as a percent of pomps used, is up steadily.

Pomps have traditionally been a high labor crop. The big question we see today: Can the U.S. grower through advanced mechanization and careful management cut their labor cost in half or less—and move the crop down to the low labor column? The Dutch seem to have done just that. Example: The Middelburgs in the Westland area, 6 acres of year-round pomps all grown and harvested by four men. See *Grower Talks,* November 1983.

It *can* be done. Will North American growers do it?

Marketing the crop As with any crop, a good marketing strategy is basic to profit. How will the crop be sold? Through what channels? And, having resolved that, what flower types, what colors, what stem length, etc., does your market want? Many West Coast growers today deal through local "shippers" who forward the crop typically to an eastern wholesaler, then to the retailer. Some growers more recently are dealing directly with eastern wholesalers. And now the giant chains are sometimes buying directly for themselves. Smaller and even medium sized chains typically buy through local wholesalers.

419

Pompons in the Deep South: the grower, Robert Davis, Dewyrose, Georgia. Typical of many growers, he reports that his customers really appreciate the better quality and condition of locally grown pompons.

Spraying, like everything else, is done so efficiently in Holland. The grower draws the hose down the walk, then sends a radio signal back to the center walk. Now the hose automatically retracts. The grower: Leen Middelburg.

420

Typical Dutch pompon production. Note: only one rather narrow aisle in the house. Plus a still narrower foot path on either side of the center walk.

Plowing beds is done quickly and easily with this tractor/tiller.

421

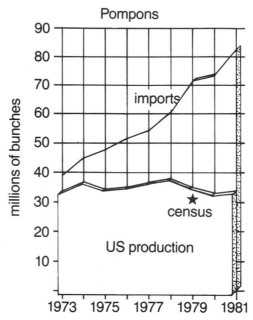

Pompons

millions of bunches

90
80
70
60
50
40
30
20
10

imports

★
census

US production

1973 1975 1977 1979 1981

Pompons—nine years of US pompon production plus imports. US figures are from the USDA. The Department of Commerce Census is posted for 1979. As indicated, total US and import production for 1981 was 84 million bunches.

Eastern and northern greenhouse growers often serve several dozen retailers within a hundred miles or so radius. Also, many of them serve especially the smaller food chains. Five to 10 or 20 store chains.

Kurt Laubinger, Cleveland area, grows pompons at times, buys on the market at times, mass produces mixed bouquets, etc., for small food chains; he does very well. Willard Hartzell, and son, Tom, Dayton area, are mass producing short stem pompons on a special arrangement with the giant Kroger supermarket chain. Leiders, Prairie View, Illinois, major pot growers, also operate several dozen consumer flower outlets, contract with local area growers for pompons for mixed cut flower bouquets for this trade. They go very well.

The Colombian crop enters the U.S. through major "reshipping facilities" mainly in Miami. We hear of some production, by the way, starting in the Encinitas area, 100 miles or so south of San Diego on the Baja Peninsula in Mexico. This production enters the U.S. through San Diego. Also, some developments in pompon production in central Mexico.

Then there is the classic northern retail grower—who in many cases continues to grow pompons, especially in the summer and fall months, for his own retail shop. The great point here: They are strictly fresh.

Important: It's important to get a fair price! Which reminds us of a Minnesota grower who had been growing half an acre of year-round greenhouse pompons. He did his cost forecasting well—and found that at the present going price he was just not making a profit. He called on a dozen of his key retail accounts, told them frankly he was going to $2.50 a bunch for his pompons

422

and if they wouldn't support that price he would give them up. To his surprise, they almost unanimously supported the higher price. The price, by the way, was $2.50—as of 1980. Probably $3.50 today. And he's still growing the pompons!

The bottom line of all this: Before production is committed, there must be a plan to market the crop. Including certainly some commitment to handle at least most of the crop—and certainly with a close feel for likely prices.

And again from all this, there is the importance of projecting all cost—and sales. And from this, ensuring a profit—before the commitment is made.

Plan ahead   It's really critical to plan. We've always felt that a crop planned well in advance of planting time is a lot more apt to be profitable than one thrown together the last minute. The plan (based on a marketing study) must include exactly what varieties and quantities will flower on what dates. And from that, specific planting, pinch (if any), short day dates for each planting. Certainly to include spacing—and to include total cuttings needed. Again, published tables (from propagators and brokers) giving suggested schedules for crops in various latitudes are available. Typically they include recommended varieties for each season. Variety selection is so important!

Where specialist cuttings are to be used, propagators typically offer substantial discounts for cuttings ordered 6 months or more in advance of shipment. And most of all, the grower gets the varieties he wants if he orders well in advance—otherwise you get what nobody else wants.

All of this planning of mum crops is gradually beginning to move to computers.

A bit on response groups   Most commercial pomps are 9- and 10-week varieties, occasionally 8-week, and a few northern winter crops use a few 11-week varieties.

Several other points here:

- It simplifies the growing operation so much if a crop can be planned to include all the same response group. All 9-week varieties or all 10-week varieties. Again, that's 10 weeks from start of short days to flowering.

- Commercial growers are always pushing for faster responding varieties—which will still make a quality pompon. A 9-week variety means one week less time on the bench than a 10-week. That means 10% less overhead cost for the crop. And that can be the profit! Breeders are striving for these faster responding varieties—still being sure that it will be a quality crop.

- In grouping varieties, growers also strive to combine varieties which take roughly the same number of long day weeks. A tall, rapid growing variety may well produce a quality crop with one week less of long

423

days than a naturally shorter growing variety. The idea is not to mix the two—and wherever possible, use the naturally taller variety that will make a crop in a week's less time.

- Again, the summer and fall crop in the northern greenhouse will be typically 8- and 9-week varieties, the winter crop will be 10- and 11-week varieties, often 3 to 5 weeks more time plant to sell. In Florida or southern California, the 8-, 9-, and 10-week varieties are used year-round (it's really eternal spring in the South and West!).

Pinch vs. single-stem crops It's done both ways. Typically the quality greenhouse crop is single-stem. All Dutch production is done this way, much of California. The point is: Overhead costs are so high under glass that the several weeks' time saved on the crop more than offsets the added cost of cuttings for single-stem growing. On the other hand, most of Central and South American crops are pinched, and most of Florida crops (cloth house) are pinched. But not all. Always the grower striving for quality tends toward single-stem crop. And the quality grower gets the price. On a soft market, quality pomps sell; the others don't.

Here's the case again for projecting cost. If you know your overhead cost per week, and you know the additional total crop time for a pinched crop, and you add the cost of the pinch, you can quickly make a decision—based on cost. But there is also the very important element of quality involved. The single-stem crop is typically heavier and better spray.

Where crops are to be pinched (tip pinched out several weeks after planting), the propagators' schedules normally include a pinch date. And the pinch, by the way, should be a soft one, always allowing several new leaf axles (in new soft growth) to provide breaks for the crop.

For the record, a typical "bunch" of pompons for most markets will include a minimum of five stems, weigh about 10 ounces. Some retail outlets do like more than five stems. Also, all outlets, retail or supermarkets, do very much want long peduncles—the little stems that connect the flowers to the main stems. They want these because they can pull them off and use them individually in small arrangements. For tricks to produce longer peduncles—see "culture." The opposite of long peduncles is a tight and "clubby" spray—with peduncles now only perhaps an inch or two or three long. Not good. This can be partly a varietal problem, by the way.

Growing the crop Highlights of good culture:
Soil: Pompons will grow in a wide variety of soil types! Excellent quality crops are grown in the rather hard clay like northern California field soils. And equally good crops can be done in peat-lite (peat and vermiculite), which is very light and very porous. The essentials: The soil must drain reasonably well (mums just won't grow in a heavy, wet, poorly drained soil). Soluble salt levels must be within reasonable limits, also pH. And the soil must be free of path-

ogens and soil-borne insects. Hundreds of acres of pomps are grown in Florida—the typical mix of sand and some humus, often peat. The typical northern greenhouse crop will be in local soil with perhaps once a year additions of peat moss or other additives to provide better structure.

A warning: In using any field soils, always be on the lookout for weed killers used recently by the farmer. We've seen some fine crops destroyed this way.

About sterilizing soil (pasteurizing). The typical northern greenhouse practice has been to steam soil between each crop—three times a year.

High fuel cost plus the availability of clean cuttings from specialist propagators has resulted in cutting this sterilizing typically to once a year. The Dutch practice is to use chemical sterilizing once a year. It's a judgement call. Sterilizing costs labor and fuel. But, insect and disease losses can be devastating.

Speaking of soils, we've seen quite often especially the small to midsized northern retail grower do pompons in pots. So often the grower produces spring pot crops (pot mums, lilies), follows this with summer and fall cut pompons. And since the benches and Chapin tubes are all in place and pots are available, these growers often just grow the cut flower crop in pots. Especially with fertilizer injection, and easy mechanical irrigation, it works quite well. Often the mechanized black cloth equipment is already in place from a spring pot mum crop.

Irrigation/feeding: Nearly always mechanized today. You see it done with overhead nozzles, in Florida with "rainbird nozzles" which slowly rotate around a 360° radius. Many of the greenhouse crops are irrigated with plastic lines around the periphery of the bench—nozzles directing the spray toward the crop and not toward the walk. The big thing is to be sure that the job is automated. See mechanization chapter for Roy Larson's notes on mechanical irrigation of bench crops.

Typically, fertilizer is injected with each irrigation. A normal rate of application would be 200 ppm of nitrogen and potash, which might be raised somewhat higher in winter. And also tends to be higher with very porous nonsoil mixes. See John Peterson's comments on this elsewhere in this book.

Insects: There is a tabulation of the main greenhouse insects—and sprays for them—also elsewhere in this book.

Commercial growers generally rely on specialist propagators for disease- and insect-free cuttings. Major propagators invest heavily in special graft indexing procedures to be sure diseases are held under control on cuttings which they supply to the grower. And they also maintain rigid insect control programs in their stock areas. If the grower plants these clean cuttings in a pathogen-free soil, and maintains a good insect control program, these problems are generally held to a minimum. Typically, some signs of insects and disease will appear occasionally—but if both propagator and grower do their job well, they do not normally damage the crop economically. Exception in recent years: leaf miner.

Temperature for the crop: The standard rule for pompons is 60° night temperature (5° more cloudy day) at least from planting cuttings until buds appear. The temperature may be and often is lowered gradually to 55° or 50° as color appears—both to conserve fuel and to improve quality and color. Sunny day temperature perhaps 10° higher. Nearly all commercial varieties will set buds uniformly at 60° minimum night temperature. A few prefer warm side (perhaps 62° or 63°). Some will set buds at 57° or even 55°. Not many of the good ones. The plant will "rosette"—make short clusters of leaves down near the ground. Crops grown much above this (especially under low winter light conditions) will be drawn, thin, poor quality.

In areas where mid-summer temperatures can go to 90° or 95°F, heat delay may be encountered. Buds will form but will fail to develop. Again, you'll see the little "heat bud"—a bud surrounded by stipules or little ridges that curl up around the bud. They will be concave-shaped. The only answer: Pad/fan cooling, which is in fact widely used by mum growers in most areas where summer temperatures soar.

Somewhat, the crop "remembers." Example: Higher day temperatures up to 75° and 80° may offset night temperatures below 60°. Even cuttings grown under high temperature tend to flower better at marginally cool temperatures. Ken Post, the great Cornell scientist, used to say, "The mum remembers."

Lastly, it's interesting to remember that the mum was originally a natural season crop. Which meant planting and "long day" periods occurred during mid-summer (warm temperatures and long days). Then as fall approached, day length shortened and temperatures were typically maintained at 50° until flowering. But normally buds have been set during August/September during warm temperature and shortening days.

Winter crops—low light: Substantial commercial crops of pomps are grown under northern winter conditions. And that typically means low light. Best example: The Dutch crop, grown at 53° north latitude, equal to our Hudson Bay. There a winter day is short, and lots of cloudy weather. A truly low light crop. Which demands important changes in handling the crop.

First, certainly be sure that all possible available light gets to the crop. No place here for dirty glass or glass with summer shade still on the roof. Next point, careful selection of varieties—some will do better during dark mid-winter weather than others. Third point: Extend the long day period, in effect giving the crop several weeks more total time from plant to flower. This allows time to develop a quality pompon even though light is sharply reduced. And lastly, wider spacing is commonly practiced under such conditions. And by the way, crop irrigation must be carefully controlled—don't overwater under such conditions especially on the ground. It may be weeks between waterings in mid-winter in Cleveland!

As mentioned before, these winter crops are typically done with 10- and 11-week varieties.

On selection of varieties: Since varieties change so rapidly, we aren't recommending specific varieties for each period of the year. Again, major propagators and broker catalog recommendations are updated annually and are the best source of information for the grower. (Pan—American Plant, Yoder Bros., Cal—Florida.)

In general, varietal selection is critically important. There are constantly new varieties being offered, some of which may fit your crop; many probably won't. The big thing is to sort them over carefully, try the ones that look promising.

Other cultural points

Retardants on pompons: Especially the Dutch growers commonly use B-Nine on pompons. The application is made mostly on winter crops.

Clubby spray: Again, the problem of short peduncles. Perhaps 1" or 2" long rather than the 8" or 10" which retailers love.

It's partly a matter of variety, and is certainly always aggravated by cold, dark winter weather. However, there is also a daylength manipulation that can help. In effect, you inject a 10-day, long day period into the crop. Let's say the normal day to start short days would be February 1. You would start short days actually 10 days earlier (January 20), continue short days for 10 days. Then inject a 10-day long day period into the crop schedule. After that (February 10) go back to short days to flower.

Crop too tall/too short? If a pompon crop flowers out normally, good quality, more than 3½' to 4', it's a good sign that for the conditions of that crop, the long day period was excessive. In other words, the same crop grown next year could be cut down to correct total height by reducing a week or perhaps two weeks of long days—and with an important economy in cost. Of course, crops where bud development is delayed by excessive heat—or by air pollution—may stretch in height and perhaps never will flower. That's a different story.

Pompon crops that flower too short and still good quality indicate an insufficient long day period. For the same crop next year, add another week of long days. If there are obvious quality problems in the crop, it may be an excessively wet heavy soil, nematode or other soil-borne insect problems, high salts, etc. And of course variety selection influences the height of the crop importantly!

Recommended spacing: Will vary with the season, especially in northern areas. Winter pompons in the Midwest are typically grown (single stem) at 5" by 6". The same crop now flowered in August or September will be grown at 4" by 5". Pinched crops are adjusted accordingly. The pinched crops are often pruned to several stems per plant, typically one extra stem on the outside row. We often see growers completely omit the center row on a bench of northern winter pompons or mums. The quality problems are worse in the center—by removing this row, it gives the several center rows a lot more light.

Spacing is one way growers can adapt their crop to a market that frankly wants a little less quality—or conversely a quality retail shop that does want better pompons.

427

Direct stick—pro and con: A few growers here and there practice direct sticking—which means that unrooted cuttings are stuck directly into the bench where they are to be flowered. This requires that a soil temperature of at least 65° or 70° or better be maintained during the rooting period. Also, mist is really needed in some form to minimize wilting the first few days. Some growers direct-stick during the summer months when high temperatures occur naturally—and supply the mist with overhead irrigation. The same grower will plant rooted cuttings during the fall and winter months. Generally speaking, the better quality growers plant rooted cuttings. It permits a more uniform grade, eases problems of maintaining high temperatures during rooting, genrally simplifies the grower's job. Some growers buy unrooted cuttings and set up their own rooting operation—which is okay if careful attention is paid to the rooting operation. It is exacting.

Peduncle problems: We talked earlier about the little stem that connects the flower on a pompon spray to the main stem. If it's too short (2" or 3") that's a clubby spray which retailers and consumers don't like. A longer peduncle (5" to 6") is an "open spray"—which permits the retailer to remove and use the individual flowers in arrangements. Which he likes very much! Question: How to produce sprays with long peduncles?

First, variety selection is important. Some varieties are inherently good; some are bad. Also, some varieties which produce a good open spray most of the year will develop a tight clubby spray under northern winter conditions.

Peduncle length can be importantly influenced by manipulation of the transition of daylength. See pot mum section on this.

Plant a good cutting: As with the bedding grower using good seed, starting with a good cutting is one of the basics to producing a good crop. And of course good cuttings aren't cheap. But planting a crop with cuttings that are hard, uneven, tending to bud prematurely, etc., is starting the job with a penalty. And worst of all, insect and disease problems.

As always, there are few bargains here.

Standard Mums

This is the football mum!

Showy, large 5" and 6" blooms, great for large basket designs, wearing to football games, etc. But unfortunately, the demand picture, at least in the U.S., is clearly down. (See accompanying graph.) And, as of the last information available (1981), that trend is still continuing. However, there are still roughly 100 million stems grown and used in the U.S.—and most of them are U.S. produced. So it's still a big crop. The #1 production area in the U.S. would be clearly California, especially northern California. Some are grown in Florida, and many northern greenhouse growers across the U.S. continue them as a year-round crop. Colombia is producing some—but again the great majority are domestic production.

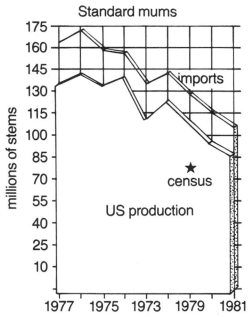

Standard mums

millions of stems

175
160
145
130
115
100
85
70
55
40
25
10

imports

★ census

US production

1977   1975   1973   1979   1981

Standard mums—nine years of US standard mum production plus imports. US figures are from the USDA. The Department of Commerce Census is posted for 1979. As indicated, total US and import production for 1981 was 108 million stems.

Study the market Again, with standard mums, there are options available to the grower—depending on the sort of market he can develop for his crop. Examples:

For the carriage trade, full-spaced single-stem standards producing 5" plus flowers can be produced year-round reliably. If, on the other hand, the market wants not so large a bloom at a lower price, the crop can be grown pinched, maybe ⅓ more flowers per square foot. And, of course, lower cost which permits lower prices to the buyer.

Disbuds: A crop that has hung off in the wings for a decade or more. You plant a standard mum crop the normal way, but now pinch and allow 3 or even 4 or more stems per plant. Result will be a shorter stem, not so large flowered—but a very nice maybe 3"-plus disbud mum on perhaps an 18" stem. For which in certain markets there may be demand.

One major market for standard mums is the funeral basket or spray. We see lots of them used this way. Retail outlets in the southern states have consistently wanted a smaller, perhaps 4" or so, mum for this trade—at lower than the 5" and 6" mum price.

Plan the crop Just as with pompons (preceding chapter) so much can be gained by planning a crop well in advance of planting date. At least 6 months. You gain so much in so many ways. Perhaps most of all in planning of your own space requirements. Fitting the mums into other crop rotations. And certainly, do a cost forecast before you commit the crop.

Standard mums in the northern greenhouse—a fine crop! Photo taken at Frank Clesen & Sons, South Elgin, Illinois.

Growing the crop   Again, much of the cultural details will be identical to the preceding section on pompons. Several comments special to standards:

Northern winter crop—tough! Standard mums perhaps even more than pompons suffer in quality with the very short days and cloudy weather of the northern winter. How do you maintain reasonable quality under these conditions?

On varieties: There are relatively few that are used by the major commercial producers. The California summer crop is still mainly *Albatross.* It's 40 years old, getting a bit smaller each year—but it does ship well. The *Dignities* are making some inroads. *May Shoesmith* and its sports are the backbone of the winter crop in California.

Regional crops   Just a bit on the way the crop is done in the principal producing areas:

Northern California: Here it's almost entirely a greenhouse crop, often under poly, sometimes fiberglass or glass. There has been and still is a little of cloth house standards and pompons in summer and early-fall in the West.

Florida crop: Good-looking standard mums are grown year-round under saran mesh (outdoors) in Florida. You typically see heavy fungicide spray on the crop—but with any sort of luck, growers seem to do quite well with them. The flower tends to be a bit soft, doesn't stand shipping to the northern market. Used mostly locally, whereas California is mainly a "ship back East" crop.

430

Standard production in the Midwest. In the photo, from the left, Robert Hartman, president of Hartman's, Inc., Palmdale, Florida, and Arthur Maton. An excellent crop.

Northern greenhouse crop: Here it's under glass, sometimes wholesale specialists, sometimes retail growers or smaller—mid-size growers supplying directly a local group of retailers.

Bogotá: It's nearly all under poly here. Interestingly, some varieties really don't need black cloth shading—the natural daylength is so near the short day requirement that some varieties even in summer will make it without black

Shows the remarkable effect of CO_2 on northern winter standards. Variety is Indianapolis Bronze.

cloth shade. The Bogotá crop is of course shipped almost entirely to the U.S. market—and with apparently mixed success. The standard mum doesn't ship as well as the pompon, and having to go through several "forwarding points" doesn't help the quality either. Result, locally grown standards often have an important advantage over the South American crop.

Garden Mums (Hardy Mums)*

The term *garden mums* applies to mum varieties which will flower naturally in most parts of the United States early enough in the fall to be showy before the first heavy frost. This contrasts with most commercial varieties which bloom naturally late in October and early November and hence would be nipped long before flowering in most parts of the U.S. The term *hardy* has been abandoned by most suppliers—not many pot flowering and cut flower varieties are indeed very "hardy"—the hardiness of garden mum varieties may vary significantly from one part of the country to another and from season to season.

Garden mums are selected for plant habit and flower characteristics second to earliness. The term *cushion* indicates plant habit forming a rounded 180° mound when the plant is grown in an uncrowded full-sun location. Read

Garden mums are much used for early May flowering—plant March 1, no light, no shade. Colorful!

*Contributed by Bill Hamilton, Ball Seed staff.

432

variety descriptions thoroughly; on occasion the word cushion is part of the variety name, of a variety which has quite another habit. The contrast to cushion habit is *upright* habit, describing a plant that displays a stiff vertical character. Semi-upright describes varieties which appear less formal in habit but marked vertical character. The growers variety lists have completely eliminated varieties with tall heights in all habits. If grown in the open, garden mums are selected to be self-supporting.

Flower color, type, and size are important aspects of garden mum variety selections. Mostly small, ¾"–2" flowers are the rule; a few varieties bear flowers up to 5" in diameter—generally these large flowers are not as durable in the outdoor environment. A full range of flower types is available but the varieties with a hard texture—heavier, fleshier, stiff petals—are more durable and survive the breeder's selection process. Vivid colors dominate the scene, ranging from pure white through the full range of mum colors to the darkest, nearly black red shades. Resistance to fading is seen in many of the more recent garden mum introductions.

For the grower, garden mums offer two main growing seasons—spring and fall. For spring sales, one cutting per 3" to 4½" pot is flowered for sale from early February in the South and West through May. This crop may be grown under one of two production techniques.

No lights/no shade   For flowering up until Mother's Day. Cuttings are planted, pinched 7–10 days after planting and require no more than general growing care until maturity. A selection of 15–20 varieties will flower over a 2–3 week period, not all precisely on one date. This growing technique can be practiced from about September 15 planting through March 15 planting in the North. Not all varieties listed are suitable for this type of production—read variety descriptions carefully. The classic crop is potted March 1, no shade no light, 60°—to flower early May.

Light and shade   Garden mums can be flowered any week of the year using this technique—just as are other chrysanthemums. Four hours of light in the middle of the night are provided beginning when the plants are potted. The following schedule is suggested for mid-late winter growing:

- Short treatment varieties: 3 weeks light—pinch 2 weeks after potting

- Medium treatment varieties: 2 weeks of light—pinch 2 weeks after potting

- Tall treatment varieties: 1 week of light—pinch 2 weeks after potting

Most all varieties accommodate this type of production—again, read variety descriptions. The ultimate retail customer takes home a flowering plant to use for decoration indoors or out. This plant, when past its prime, can be planted in the garden—cut back to just lower foliage—and it will produce a full-sized garden mum for natural fall flowering. The advantage to flowered sales is that the customer sees "in the flesh" the variety purchased.

Also for spring sales, vegetative plants sold with a color variety label are growing in popularity. This crop is timed to be marketed with the big push of the bedding plant season—with tomatoes, impatiens, begonias, and the like. Cuttings are planted in single plastic pots, A/18s or A/24s; the larger size cell packs; AC 4–8s or AC 2–12s; or equivalent containers. For best results these plants should be placed where they will receive 3 hours of light in the middle of each night from planting until sale—they are ready for sale when breaks are ¾" long or longer. If sales are slow, a second pinch can be made 2–3 weeks after the first. B-Nine will be helpful to control growth.

Fall sales These plants are in flower or at least showing color when sold. In some areas fall sales begin the first of August and run until frost. In the most favored climate areas, flowered garden mums are still selling in December for quick color effect.

August flowering plants are grown in containers, one plant per 4½" on the small end to several plants double-pinched in an 8" nursery container at the larger end. This crop can be precisely timed using the variety response information to develop a schedule (see general mum chapter elsewhere in this book) and black cloth. For example, a crop of 7-week medium treatment varieties to flower for August 10 should go under black cloth 6/20. Production scheduling prior to black cloth can vary depending on type of crop desired. See Table 1 for guidelines and comparisons.

Table 1   7-WEEK VARIETIES FOR FLOWERING AUGUST 10

Type of plant	Black cloth shade	Last pinch	First pinch	Plant date
4½"—1 plant/pot	6/22	6/22	—	6/8
6–6½"—1 plant/pot	6/22	6/22	6/1–6/8	5/18–5/25
7–8"—1 plant/pot	6/22	6/22	6/1–6/8	5/18–5/25
7–8"—3–5 plants/pot	6/22	6/22	—	6/8
7–8"—3 plants/pot	6/22	6/22	6/1	5/18

This schedule can move easily forward and backward in the calendar. Shade one week later for 6-week varieties—i.e., 6/29, and 1 week earlier for 8-week varieties—i.e., 6/15.

A second method of production for fall sales steps around the use of black cloth shade and employs natural season techniques. Field grown plants fall in this category and should be spaced at least 24", preferably 30" in the row, with rows 3' apart. These plants are dug when color shows and placed into containers or balled in burlap. This is probably the least used and least effective method for growing and marketing of garden mums today. Vastly more popular, container grown natural season plants may not be as large as field grown, but without a doubt give the ultimate customer the greatest satisfaction and, at the retail sales point, much less grief. Container plants should be pinched the last time 7/15–7/20. This can be the only pinch if multiple plants per container are used, 3–5 plants per 7½"–8" container. For two-pinch plants, allow 2–3 weeks from first pinch to last pinch and in either case receive cuttings and start plants 2 weeks before first pinch.

	Last pinch	First pinch	Plant
1 plant/container—double pinch	7/15–20	6/22–6/29	6/8
3 plants/container—single pinch	7/15–20	6/29	6/15

Another natural season method for smaller pot plants in terms of height and spread is known as "fast crop." Cuttings are planted 7/20–7/25 and allowed to grow without pinch, shade cloth, lights, or other manipulation. The result is a free-breaking plant flowering 6–8 weeks from plant date and ideal for quick-sale, spot-of-color markets in late September and October. Not all varieties respond well; avoid taller ones and 8-week varieties.

About culture   Some general garden mum cultural comments that apply to all techniques suggested above. Garden mums in the first 3–4 weeks of production should always enjoy a minimum 60° night temperature. When the season allows for cooler finish it will enhance flower color and shelf life. Avoid below 40° to keep foliage color green. Garden mums respond to well-drained production media and a regular, balanced fertilizer program. They should be fertilized until they are sold as long as some crop toning is practiced the last two weeks of the crop.

Generally, garden mums don't require any bud removal to improve habit. Neither are there important varieties in the trade that require disbudding.

The first 2–3 weeks after planting are very important to the crop. Warm growing temperatures, full sun, CO_2 if available, thorough irrigation practices, and regular liquid fertilization are all important. We suggest for crops that are to be grown single plants in 6" or larger containers that the cuttings be established in Jiffy-Pots or 32 cell packs, pinched there and grown until breaks are ¾"–1" long, then placed in the finished container. This provides a much easier-to-maintain starting environment and may double the number of breaks on your crop. Depending on your work schedule, it may allow the more labor intensive part of the job at an easier scheduled time.

If a garden mum crop numbers more than a few plants, mechanical watering is important. Mechanical watering will do a consistently good job plant to plant, minimize labor, and enhance crop management. Fertilizer should be a minimum of 200 ppm nitrogen and potassium each watering, with one leaching per week in media with mineral soils. Rates can range as high as 250 ppm nitrogen and potash in mixes of mostly peat, bark, or peat and bark combinations.

435

B-Nine is an effective growth retardant for garden mums and contributes to growing a well-tailored crop. Standard rate of 2500 ppm is minimum strength. Experience may dictate that 3750 ppm or even 5000 ppm may be necessary in your growing environment. First application may be 3–5 days after planting or after first breaks are ¾" long. A second application two weeks later is suggested for all but field grown crops, and a third application may be appropriate where growth seems too vigorous, here 3750 or 5000 ppm is probably appropriate (see page 414 for general B-Nine comments).

Sales aids are effective with garden mums—especially the green vegetative ones in spring. Major suppliers ship Tag-Alongs or similar color variety labels for a small additional charge at the time the cuttings are shipped. Insert the labels as you plant and make one job of it.

A word about garden mum sources—the major mum propagators produce garden mums on a year-round basis for orders received 19 weeks before ship date. Their stock management techniques strive to produce soft vegetative cuttings for weekly harvesting. The variety list of these producers ranges from 50–60 varieties selected for their adaptability to this type of cutting production and to the two main garden mum production seasons we have addressed here. In addition, there are a number of garden mum propagators who address a narrower segment of the wholesale growing industry and often address retail customers. These producers may rely more heavily on seasonal climatic variations for stock management, may carry a much longer and broader list of varieties, and deal in smaller quantities.

CINERARIA

ANNUAL *(Senecio cruentus) 150,000 seeds per oz. Germinates in 10 days at 70°.*

The cineraria is a star of the cool house spring pot plant group: Here is the variety Improved Festival.

Cineraries are very colorful, inexpensive pot plants to produce, and are still much in demand from January through April.

For midwinter and Easter plants in 5" or 6" pots, most seed is sown during August and September. Nice 4"–5" pot plants are made from a sowing about October 1. Just when they will come in from any sowing depends, of course, on winter temperatures. A night temperature of 48–50° will keep them in good shape. Cinerarias are cool-temperature plants and will not set buds at night temperatures above 60°. Normally it takes 3 to 4 weeks at temperatures of 55° or lower to set buds. These will then develop and mature regardless of lower or higher temperatures.

To avoid damping off, transplant the seedlings as soon as they can be handled. We prefer to plant them into 2¼" Jiffy-Pots or similar containers in light soil with little or no fertilizer in this stage. When they begin to crowd, pot direct into 5"s or 6"s. B-Nine at .25% applied as soon as they are established will help prevent stretch and promote uniformity. We find that while this method calls for a little care in preventing overwatering until they make new roots, it produces better results with less labor. When they become pot-bound, the main point to watch is the watering. They dry out fast, and on bright days, might easily wilt. Also, they should be protected from strong sun, but during the short days, they can stand all we usually get. Since cinerarias are subject to verticillium, all pots, flats and soil should be sterilized. Light feedings of liquid commercial fertilizer, after buds show, will also be beneficial.

Varieties

Probably the most widely used variety for 5"- or 6"-pots is *Ball Florist Select*. It combines compact, well-rounded habit with large heads of medium-sized flowers. It is 2 to 3 weeks earlier than *Improved Festival,* which has been widely used for many years.

Varieties in the multiflora Nana class, better suited for smaller pots and mass market sales, include *Scarlet,* an extra dwarf compact grower with a wide range of flashy colored flowers, and *Tourette,* which has a high percentage of bicolors.

Two of the finest of the Dusty Millers also belong to the cineraria clan. *C. maritima Diamond Candicans* is an excellent bedding plant along with *C. maritima-Silver Dust.*

CLEOME *(Spider Plant)*

ANNUAL *(C. spinoso) 15,000 seeds per oz. Germinates in 12 days at alt. 70–85°.*

Widely grown years ago in old-fashioned gardens, spider plants, as cleomes are commonly known, still seem to have a place in American gardens. This is due principally to the popular, large-flowered variety, *Rose Queen,* and the equally large, pure *White Queen.* With their 6" to 7" heads of attractive flowers, and heavy hedgelike growth reaching a height and width of 4', they are well suited for planting along walls or to hide unsightly spots. They are easily grown and bloom throughout the summer until frost. Seed should be sown indoors in March or April for May bedding-plant sales. Other varieties are available, but the two named are by far the best and most widely used.

COLEUS

ANNUAL *(Coleus x hybridus) 100,000 seeds per oz. Germinates in 10 days at 65–75°. Light.*

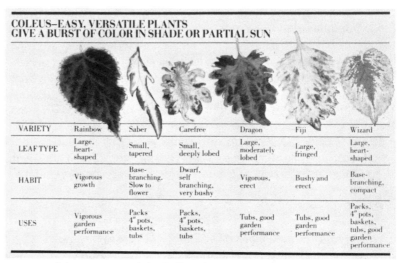

COLEUS–EASY, VERSATILE PLANTS GIVE A BURST OF COLOR IN SHADE OR PARTIAL SUN

VARIETY	Rainbow	Saber	Carefree	Dragon	Fiji	Wizard
LEAF TYPE	Large, heart-shaped	Small, tapered	Small, deeply lobed	Large, moderately lobed	Large, fringed	Large, heart-shaped
HABIT	Vigorous growth	Base-branching. Slow to flower	Dwarf, self branching, very bushy	Vigorous, erect	Bushy and erect	Base-branching, compact
USES	Vigorous garden performance	Packs 4" pots, baskets, tubs	Packs, 4" pots, baskets, tubs	Tubs, good garden performance	Tubs, good garden performance	Packs, 4" pots, baskets, tubs, good garden performance

This is one of the most useful of all colored foliage plants, suited for growing in shaded and semishaded areas. There are several classes, their distinction largely based on the size of their leaves. There are numerous small-leafed named varieties that are still propagated from cuttings; however, the majority of coleus now being produced are grown from seed. The *Carefree* series strain is outstanding in the small-leafed type. It is self-branching and bushy with small leaves deeply lobed. It is a multi-use strain available in a full range of coleus separate colors as well as a mix. Another small-leafed type widely used is the *Saber* series. Unique because of its long sabre-like leaves, it is very compact and slow to flower with excellent shelf life. Available in nine separate colors and a mix.

In the large-leafed class, the *Rainbow* strain dominated sales for many years. With its heart-shaped leaves and vigorous growth habit it is an excellent garden performer. Recently a mostly improved strain called the *Wizard* series has nearly taken over *Rainbow* sales. Better basal branching, reluctance to flower, and slow stretch have made this series the #1 coleus performer. It's available in 11 rich colors and a mix.

438

Other types or classes currently being used include *Exhibition* type, a large-leafed strain typified by the variety *Red Monarch*.

Fringed type coleus are sold as *Fiji* series and *Magic Lace* 90% true to type, whose color shades are largely rose, bronze, green, and salmon.

Scarlet Poncho, with deep scarlet leaves edged with chartreuse, is specifically bred for hanging baskets. Its elongated stems create a cascading effect in baskets.

Coleus, being of tropical origin, will grow freely only in a warm house, and this requirement, of course, very much extends to the germination of its seed. If grown in a 60°F house, a January sowing should make good 3"–4" pot plants in 10–12 weeks. An early March sowing is about right for early May bedding-plant sales.

CROSSANDRA

ANNUAL *(C. infundibuliformis) 4,000 seeds per oz. Germinates in 3–4 wks. at 70–85°.*

Crossandra—an interesting member of the "other flowering pot plant" group.

This is an unusual and attractive pot plant and came originally from India. Introduced to the American trade by our firm many years ago, it had declined in popularity until a few years ago when it started to make a rapid comeback. It is popular today as a 4"–5" spring and summer flowering pot plant. The

439

plants have glossy, gardenia-like foliage with flower spikes of overlapped, clear salmon-orange florets. A minimum temperature of 75 to 80°F will be necessary for satisfactory germination with a minimum of 65°F nights for growing on. It needs rather rich, well-drained soil and will flower in 7 to 8 months after it is sown. Germination usually starts 10 to 14 days after sowing and will continue slowly and irregularly over a period of a month. Transplanting, therefore, must be done at intervals as the plants appear and when they are large enough to handle. Use care in transplanting so that the ungerminated seeds will not be disturbed. Light should be between 2,000–3,000 foot-candles for an average daylength. Summer growing will require about a 30% shade. They are an average feeder requiring about 200 ppm of N, P, and K with each irrigation. Crossandra will send up flower spikes blooming over a period of time.

CYCLAMEN—FASTER CROPS ARE HERE

Cyclamen.

The traditional 15–16 months cyclamen crop is history. Sow September, flower January, a year later.

The fine work at University of Minnesota by Dr. Richard Widmer developed a cookbook formula for an eight–ten month crop. Seed is now sown early April 1 to flower a full 6" plant for Christmas—early January. Through a combination of higher temperature, carefully selected varieties, and otherwise optimum culture, Dr. Widmer did cut the crop-timing potentially almost in half! This was also demonstrated by crops grown at Cornell under John Seeley.

The big question: How is the crop grown by the real commercial world—as of the mid-1980s? There are several answers.

Smaller Retail/Wholesale Growers

In most cases today, such growers will order in well-established specialist-grown 3" plants—normally received from June until September. They are carried at 55–62° nights. Well grown, such plants will produce quality 6" plants in flower for Christmas–January sales. Only six months later! The savings in bench time and labor are obvious. Another big plus—the grower avoids the germination and care of these plants through the busy spring months. These specialist-produced plants can come from the East, some Midwest, some from California.

Southern growers prefer to receive these 3" plants after mid-September. Midsummer heat in the South is very tough on cyclamen! One St. Louis grower reports that 108° temperature, August 1983, "really destroyed our cyclamen crops."

Why 3"? Several years ago there was much traffic in 4" prefinished cyclamen. The shift to 3" seems mainly a matter of major savings in freight cost.

Larger Growers—Sow Your Own

An interesting compromise has developed between Dick Widmer's 8-month crop vs. the traditional 15–16 month way. In fact, the commercial trade growing the crop from seed typically is growing a 10–12 month crop. About midway between the old and new. Several Iowa growers report sowings in December, January to flower 12 months later.

Dick Widmer, of the University of Minnesota, cyclamen researcher, reports that many Minnesota growers are producing 6" cyclamen on schedules varying from 10 to 12 months sow to sell. One grower (Johnson Wholesale) is actually doing 4½"–5" plants in about 8 months. With good culture, 12 months tend to produce really too big a plant.

Applications of gibberellic acid is becoming fairly common practice among commercial growers. Conclusion: Cutting the crop time from 15–16 to 11–12 months means a full 4 months less time on the bench. And that's a lot of economy.

Widmer Basic Rules

What are the key cultural points in reducing all this crop time? Says Dick Widmer:

- *Carry correct temperature:* From seed sowing (March to early April) until the 5- or 6-week stage (130 days) an honest 68°. Then after the 5- or 6-week stage (now late summer) carry 62° until flowering. Note that the 68° temperature occurs mainly in spring, summer—little fuel expense.

- *Use the right varieties:* Some adapt well to faster crops, some don't. Important! The F_1s are more consistent in flower, earlier, seed more costly. *Tosca* is fine.

- *Media:* Also critical. I like peat. It's consistent.

- *Feed:* Follow the rules. Too much feed will produce cabbage leaves, few and late flowers. Too little produces a weak plant.

How about outdoor culture in summer? Dick Widmer is not in favor. "Too much exposure to disease. If you do go outdoors, plants should be protected from rain by a solid poly sheet to prevent disease. Also, reduce light to a maximum of 4,000 foot-candles. And spray."

"We had severe heat early in this area, summer of '83—terribly hot. Growers got big plants, big leaves, late and fewer flowers."

How about miniature cyclamens?

"The Iowa growers use mostly standards. Lots of F_1s."

St. Louis area "mostly standards. The miniatures do make a nice 4½"–5" plant. Trend seems to be up on them. Those 4" miniatures fit in nicely after poinsettias—with primula, calceolaria, etc."

Gibberellic Acid

Gib can do a lot to improve cyclamen. Examples:

- Tends to make a crop flower all at once. You'll see 8 to 10 flowers on a plant all at one time vs. 3 or 4 flowers over a longer period of time. Hastens flower of the whole crop.

- Improves uniformity of the crop.

Important: Don't overdo! Insert spray nozzle below the leaf canopy, wet only the crown—once. Not "spray to run-off." Excess spray will stretch and weaken the flower stems and the foliage.

Try a few plants the first year and be sure the gib spray is fresh here. Needs refrigeration. Normal application: 150 days after sowing. See Widmer paper later in this section for details.

G.V.B.

Seven Months Cyclamen*

Schedule for Christmas cyclamen

May1: Sow seed about May 1 if you have good bright greenhouses. If you are growing in double polyethylene-covered houses or for late winter bloom, plant production may require a few extra weeks. Germinate the seed in nutrient enriched moss peat (Table 1) or a peat-lite mix at an air temperature of 68°F in the dark.

Table 1 RECOMMENDED CHEMICAL ADDITIONS TO
SPHAGNUM MOSS PEAT FOR USE IN CYCLAMEN
PRODUCTION

Fertilizer	Grams*/bushel	/Cubic yard
Ground Limestone	200	9.7 lb.
Magnesium Sulfate	20	1.0 lb.
Potassium Nitrate	7	5.5 oz.
Superphosphate	12	10.0 oz.
Osmocote (14-14-14)	16	12.5 oz.
Peters Fritted Trace Element Mix	1	0.75 oz.

*28.35 grams/ounce

Cover the seeds with ¼" to ⅛" of medium and use a Benlate drench (1 oz./12 gal.) if any mold develops. Strive to obtain fresh seed (no more than 1 year old) for best germination. Keep the medium surface moist during germination. The containers of germinating seeds are moved from the dark to a humid (80–90% R.H.), shaded greenhouse when about half the seeds have

*Contributed by R. E. Widmer, M. C. Stuart, and R. E. Lyons, University of Minnesota, taken from a paper on cyclamens in the University of Minnesota State Bulletin, April, 1983.

443

germinated. This must be done promptly to avoid excessive stretching of the cotyledon hypocotyls. With good conditions, the move may be made about 28–30 days after seeding. Excessive light and/or low humidity levels at this time can result in shriveling and dying of the hypocotyl near the cotyledon. Loss of or delay of plant growth by a month usually follows. Germination of 80–90% is usually expected. No one cultivar is consistently highest. Sometimes a higher or lower percentage is noted. Remember that seed quality and freshness is not the only factor influencing germination.

A less humid (60–70% R.H.) atmosphere is satisfactory after several weeks. Continue at a 68°F night temperature with a maximum light level of 4000 foot-candles.

September 1: About 120 days after seeding when the plants average 5–6 unfolded leaves they are transferred to 4" pots. Plant in nutrient enriched moss peat as was used for seeding. We plant with the top of the "corm" flush with the surface. This practice provides more firmly "anchored" plants and sometimes results in wider spreading plants. Recently, a report from another geographic area noted significant plant loss when "corms" were so planted. Obviously, if plant loss follows planting at this depth and raising the corm is helpful in such circumstances, the latter should be practiced. We have never experienced significant cyclamen plant losses at the University or in commercial greenhouses in Minnesota in over 10 years of cyclamen studies.

Following potting, the night temperature should be lowered to 62°F to encourage earlier flowering. Temperatures below 60–62°F will slow vegetative plant development.

October 1: Flowering is advanced 2 to 5 weeks (varying by cultivar) if treated with gibberellic acid (GA$_3$) at this stage. Plants should average 10 unfolded leaves at this time. Recent findings indicate that an application of 8 ml of a 15 ppm GA$_3$ spray to the crown of the plant can now be recommended for most cultivars. Earlier application may be ineffective and later application may cause undesirable side effects on some cultivars. Growers who have not used the GA$_3$ treatment before would be wise to use it on a limited scale for the first time or when growing a new cultivar. If GA$_3$ is not applied, half or more of the crop may not flower in time for Christmas. When the additional production cost of 1 extra month in the greenhouse is considered, the benefit of using GA$_3$ is most apparent. In addition to inducing earlier flowering, a much larger number of flowers open within the first 2–4 weeks of flowering.

Fertilization-watering Fertilization should begin within 60 days after sowing the seed and 30 days after potting in the nutrient enriched moss peat. Quantity required increases with plant size. A constant flow of nutrients is necessary for optimum growth of good quality plants in the minimum time. Leaf size and plant habit can be controlled by the supply of nitrogen and potassium. Monitor soil analysis readings and combine with plant appearance in order to determine appropriate fertilizer application rates which will encourage sturdy compact plant development. Insufficient nutrients will result in

444

smaller plants and delayed maturity. An excess of nitrogen or potassium or both will result in rank plants with soft large leaves that lack substance. Insufficient light and crowding of plants are also common causes of stretched out, poor quality plants. Phosphorus should also be applied at regular intervals. Phosphorus is not retained as long in soilless media as it is in mineral soils. An application of microelements 60 days after transplanting into 4" pots is also recommended.

We grow our plants on capillary mats covered with black polyethylene film with $1/4$" holes at about 1" intervals. Less leaching occurs so fertilizer applications must be lowered accordingly, in contrast to top irrigated plants. Occasional watering from above may be desirable to prevent salt buildup in the medium. Mat watering saves time, lowers the frequency of watering required and lessens the likelihood of the development of botrytis crown rot.

Cyclamen sales are increasing on a national scale. Capitalize on this trend by producing quality plants on a fast schedule. Don't limit sales to the Christmas season. Depending on your geographic area, the plants should find a receptive market from early fall to late spring. In some areas, summer sales are also practical.

The schedule provided herein can be modified for year-round production purposes. Providing proper culture makes good plant production relatively easy. Careless culture, neglect, or significant modifications of cultural practices will void the advantages of recommendations provided.

Cultivars Fast crop production requires early flowering cultivars. Cultivars with compact plant habit and small- to medium-sized leaves are also required. We have found that large, medium and small flowered cyclamen are all suitable for culture in 4" pots, if they meet the other prerequisites. We have grown a large number of cultivars in our studies over the years. Those that proved most appropriate are as follows:

Nonhybrid medium and large flowered

Albadonna	early, large, white flowers; fast grower
Improved Bonfire	early, red
Cardinal	very early, rich red
Hallo	early, compact, scarlet
Rosa von Zehlendorf TAS	early, vigorous
Dark Salmon Red TAS	early, vigorous
Pure White TAS	early, vigorous

Hybrid medium and large flowered

Boheme	compact, fuchsia red
Carmen	very early, scarlet red
Finlandia	early white, prolific bloomer
Gypsy	salmon red

445

Manon	about 2 weeks later than Finlandia; compact plants; large, rich pink
Pastourelle	early, large white; vigorous
Rosamunde	early, rose pink
Swan Lake	early white, dark stems
Tosca	early lilac

Minis—small flowered

Annelie	small, white with violet red eye with many flowers
Beautiful Helena	white, pink and red flowers
Brigette	pure white,* larger flowers than Annelie
Collette	medium early, good red, stocky
Mini-red	rich pink to light red, stocky
Mini-white	pure white, some variation in flower size
Steffo	pink to violet red with dark eyes, good flower count, crinkly leaf margins

*Also listed as deep salmon in catalogs.

A great many mini-flowered cultivars have appeared on the market. Most of the early cultivars lacked substance, were too variable, had poor plant form, extra long flower peduncles or other faults. Cultivars we listed were among the best in our studies and worth growing. Despite a great deal of publicity, mini-flowered cultivars are not as popular as the larger flowered cultivars. Mini-flowered cultivars are quite attractive, but the larger flowered specimens usually sell first when displayed together. Attention directed to "minis" has apparently served to increase interest in cyclamen in general. If "minis" are more popular in your sales area, do not ignore them.

Cyclamen Notes From Ball Red Book, *XIII Edition**

Cut flower sales In Europe, nearly 40% of the production is for cut flowers. Growers there make a practice of pulling the first several flowers from each plant and slitting the end of the stem for this purpose, later selling the blooming plants. With 12" stems, cyclamen are as attractive as sweet peas in table arrangements and hold up much better—and their use doesn't hinder the sale of the plant later.

Seed germination Germination, in our experience, is best done in a neutral peat. The peat used for this purpose (and for soil mixtures for later

*Editor's note: Here are some very practical pointers on growing and marketing the crop from our last edition—which we felt should be included. G.V.B.

446

shifts) is about pH 6.8. Some soil may be added, but it isn't necessary for sprouting, in our experience. Best practice: make a "dibble board" that will punch holes in the soil surface spaced 1" x 1". Drop a seed into each hole—it shouldn't be more than ¼" to ½" deep. Carry flats at 60° till they sprout, then drop back to 55°.

Summertime—hard on cyclamen   Cyclamen are lovers of cool, moist climates, so the summer—particularly in our Midwest and in the South—is a trying period at best. Much can be done, though, by keeping the plants in a well-shaded and ventilated area frames—and by spraying them overhead on all hot afternoons to keep up humidity. This spraying is a real help in control of mites—they hate moisture. Problem here: There is a tendency for disease to appear on outdoor grown plants not protected from the rain. Crown rot of plants. We see it often.

Getting them to flower   In the fall, feeding program should be held off unless plants absolutely need it—and until plants are definitely setting buds. Heavy feeding and watering encourages leafy, rank growth and no buds. Plants need full sun during budding and blooming and again, plenty of space.

Demand for cyclamen continues brisk through late November, Christmas, and through Valentine's Day. From then on they seem to be less wanted. Hence, the importance of getting them to bloom early.

Clues on getting cyclamen to flower early:

- Cyclamen to a considerable extent flower when they get pot-bound, which is governed by final shift date.

- During the fall, carry them a bit dry, and avoid nitrate feeding as much as possible.

- Temperature affects flowering—50° nights is best in our experience. 55° may flower them a bit sooner, but certainly with no better quality.

- Strains will vary in their earliness. In evaluating our flowering trails and selecting the best source, we keep an eye on the strains that are first to bloom.

Insects/diseases   Mites are a headache. You have to fight them from the very start—a mite-infested plant is so deformed that it won't sell. Even a light infestation severely reduces the keeping quality of the plant. They aren't easy to keep out, but good growers do it. They are almost too small to see without a hand lens, but you'll know their presence by the twisting and deforming of growth tips. They cause flowers to be deformed and streaked.

Crown rot is probably the most troublesome disease. This can be largely eliminated by allowing good air circulation around the plants at all times, by being careful not to overwater, and by placing the top of the bulb or corm above the surface of the soil when shifting to the finishing pot.

Comments from John Seeley of Cornell "Too much GA can be disastrous because a heavy application or spray to run-off will cause weakening of the flower stem so they will not support the flowers. Practice with plain water before applying the GA solution. Some cultivars are more responsive than others so record the results obtained under your specific growing conditions."

DAHLIA

ANNUAL (D. hybrida) 2,800 seeds per oz. Germinates in 10 days at 70°.

In certain limited areas of the country, the taller growing, large-flowered varieties are used for cut-flower purposes by some florists. If used for cutting, the ends of the stems must be seared to avoid "bleeding" and consequent wilting.

The most profitable part of the dahlia business lies in the growing of the dwarf varieties for sale in the spring, either as potted or bedding plants in packs. These are best and easiest grown from seed, usually sown as a mix.

For Mother's Day in 4" pots, we suggest an early February sowing. An early January sowing will provide 4" pots for April. Sow in late February and early March for pack sales in May. If well fed and amply spaced, they require no pinching.

The dwarf strains grow to a height of from 10"–24" and produce an abundance of brightly colored flowers in a range of 2" to 3" across. Flowers are single, semidouble, and double. *Figaro* and *Rigoletto* have approached the "most popular" status. This is because of their dwarf habit (12"–15"), and high percentage of double blooms. Outstanding for dwarfness (10") and free flowering is *Dahl Face*. It's super in 4" pots.

A relative newcomer to the spring flowering pot plant line are the Dutch-grown tuberous rooted dahlias. Forced singly in a 6" standard pot from tubers, crop time runs from 10–13 weeks when grown at 62°–65°F night temperature. Key to quality production lies in the use of A-Rest, which must be applied as a drench when shoots are only ¼" long. Currently 12 varieties are available ranging in color from yellow to orange through red to purple and lavender.

DAISY

PERENNIAL (Chrysanthemum maximum) 21,000 seeds per oz. Germinates in 12 days at 60–65°.

While many varieties of plants are loosely referred to under this heading, what most of us have in mind by this term is *Chrysanthemum maximum*, commonly known as *Shasta daisy*. This is the largest and best of the perennial daisies for cutting and is easily grown from seed, after which particularly good specimens may be propagated by divisions. If sown February 1, planted outdoors in enriched soil, a few late-summer flowers will be produced with the best crop coming the following season; with us, this is usually the last one. Our winters are too severe, without enough snow protection to carry them beyond two seasons.

Sown in January and February, excellent plants are produced for spring sales along with annuals in packs or pots.

Widely used is the variety *G. Marconi,* which produces double and semi-double flowers of a large size with long stems. *Alaska,* the standard for single flowers, is still used along with *Dieners Double* (36"), which produces double, semidouble, and a few single flowers.

DELPHINIUM

PERENNIAL *(D. elatum) 10,000 seeds per oz. Germinates in 18 days at alt. 70–85°.*

Delphinium—a spectacular perennial, especially in cooler summer climates.

Today's stately delphinium is an excellent garden perennial and has some commercial importance. While delphinium are admittedly one of the most valuable hardy perennials for outdoor cutting, they also respond well to forcing. Outdoors, they seem to be profitable from Canada to Florida, though the finest flowers are produced where summer temperatures are moderate. In Florida, they are largely grown as an annual. Some southern growers find it best to use well-established seedlings that are started farther north.

449

While they seem to do well in all types of soil, if a choice is available, we prefer a moderately heavy loam for all perennials. Such material retains fertility as well as moisture better than soil largely made up of sand. In Florida, where sandy soil prevails, growers overcome the leaching tendency from such soil by top-dressing lightly but frequently with balanced fertilizer.

We find the best plan for producing strong plants to set out in spring is to sow about September 1 in finely prepared soil in a cold frame. Be sure the soil is perfectly level and well-watered, and don't spread the seed too thickly unless you plan to transplant (which we find unnecessary). After the soil is frozen, remove the sash and cover with any coarse material to prevent too much thawing and freezing. Ordinary straw, we find, is inclined to pack and rot what it is supposed to protect. Cornstalks are ideal for protection. As it warms up in spring, remove this material and replace the sash, but don't soften them through lack of air; let them come slowly and be hardened off. Set out as soon as they are well in growth. Plant out in deeply prepared, fairly enriched, drained soil. Avoid using the same soil over, for they are susceptible to various rots that are carried over in the soil. Another commonly used method of starting this crop is to sow indoors in January. With seed well-matured and temperatures cool at that time, germination should be at its best. Seedlings can be transplanted about 3" apart in flats, grown cool, and set out early to harden before planting in the open. Some growers sow the seed direct into the open ground as early as it can be handled; and this, too, is a good plan, for it combines a minimum of labor with an unchecked start that promptly gets into rapid growth.

For forcing, the *Giant Pacific* strains are best. Sow the seed not later than August 1 in flats set in the coolest spot available and later, transplant the seedlings into frames. In late November, after they have had a short rest, they are taken up and planted in a cold house, spacing 6" x 8". About February 1, they are started into growth by a minimum temperature of 40–45°; as spring advances, this is increased to 50° nights. This schedule gets them into full crop by Mother's Day and they continue producing nice stock well into July, after which they are discarded to be followed by other crops. If the *Belladonna* type is used, and they are excellent, space them 6" x 6".

There are two distinct types of delphinium—the species *elatum,* to which most of the *Giant Pacifics* belong, and *cheilanthum,* which includes the *belladonna* types. The latter are not so strong in growth or as long-stemmed as the hybrids, but are more free-flowering. *Belladonna Imp.* is a very choice light blue. But little of the dark *Bellamosum* is wanted. *Connecticut Yankees,* an All-America Selection, produces bushy well-branched plants with very large florets in shades of lavender and blue. Decidedly, the best strain of giants is known as the *Giant Pacific Court* series, which was developed from, and offers the same fine quality as, the original *Giant Pacific* strain (no longer available) originated by Frank Reinelt. They are available in a fine line of colors from light to the darkest blues, lavenders, mauve, and white. The best varieties in the leading colors are *Galahad,* white; *Guinevere,* lavender; *Summer Skies,* light blue; *King Arthur,* royal violet; and *Blue Bird,* a mid-blue. *Astolat* contains lavender-rose shades, some of which are near pink. Most of them have a conspicuous center or "bee," as it is called. Nearly all come remarkably true to color. Also, they are quite mildew-resistant. While this strain is at its best under the ideal climate of its native state, it does remarkably well in the middle states. There are two varieties of *Dwarf Giant Pacifics* available: *Blue Fountains,* which consists of blue shades blended with white, and *Blue Springs* in shades of blue and lavender. In some areas these might be preferred for landscape and garden purposes because of their reduced height, 30"–36".

DIANTHUS

ANNUAL *(D. chinensis) 25,000 seeds per oz. Germinates in 7 days at 70°.*
PERENNIAL *(D. species) 28,000 seeds per oz. Germinates in 10 days at 70–80°.*

Dianthus, Queen of Hearts—*a promising bedding plant.*

Dianthus or pinks, as they have been called for generations, comprise quite a large and very useful genus. Altogether something over 250 species are recognized, but not more than 2 or 3 dozen are of any commercial importance. Varieties under *D. caryophyllus* comprise our popular greenhouse carnations; aside from this group, nearly all dianthus are grown outdoors as garden plants for cutting, borders or edging work, etc. Many dianthus species used today are perennial and, if not wintered-over in too-wet ground, are very hardy. Any good, fairly light garden soil will suit them; they lean to alkaline rather than acidic soil. Most of the perennial dianthus are easily propagated from seed that

451

produces flowers the second season from sowing. Division by cuttings or roots is practiced in the case of some large double forms that don't propagate true from seed.

The annual form of dianthus (*D. chinensis*) is very slow, and interest in its usage has quickened in recent years. Intensive breeding efforts have produced improved varieties with better habit, flower form, and vigor. The majority of the varieties bloom throughout the summer, and for bedding-plant sales, should be handled the same as petunias (50°–55°F). Generally, they grow to a height of 6"–12", although the variety *Wee Willie* (annual Sweet William) grows to only a height of 3" or 4", and makes a fine display of color in packs just 6–8 weeks from spring. Outstanding is the F$_1$ *Charm* series. Plants are 6" high, bushy and uniform. Five separate colors available as well as a mix. Twelve weeks from sowing to blooming paks. Another outstanding F$_1$ is *Snowfire*. Compact 6"–8" plants are covered with many fringed 1½" white flowers with cherry red centers. *Queen of Hearts* is another F$_1$ that produces scarlet red flowers. *Princess Scarlet* is a dwarf compact scarlet red well suited for 4" production.

D. barbatus, or Sweet William, is one of the best known of the "old-fashioned" garden flowers. The double mixture grows 18" high and is propagated most commonly and easily from seed. Sweet Williams are, strictly speaking, biennials, but are commonly used as perennials. They enjoy a fully exposed location and are shown to best advantage in massed plantings. The most commonly used varieties are double-flowered and sold as mixed colors, ranging from red through pink and white. An extra-dwarf (6"–8") is available and sold as *Double Midget Mix*. Another single dwarf is *Indian Carpet Mix*.

There are many other attractive dianthus species and varieties that space doesn't permit describing. The outdoor carnations (*Chabaud, Enfant de Nice*, etc.) and the hardy *Grenadin* types are treated under carnations.

EUPHORBIA

PERENNIAL *(E. species) 6,500 seeds per oz. Germinates in 4–5 wks. at alt. 70–85°.*

The euphorbia family consists of a great number of plants varying widely in form, habit, and use. There are, however, only a few euphorbias that are of importance to the commercial grower. *E. pulcherrima*, poinsettia, is a major pot plant crop.

The annual *Snow-on-the-mountain* is *E. variegata*, also known as *Marginata*, and is of some use to retail growers for summer cutting. *E. heterophylla* is sometimes referred to as annual poinsettia or Mexican fire plant because of the red shading on the upper bracts. *E. polychroma* is an attractive perennial rock garden plant. Bushy plants 15"–18" high produce bracts of a bright yellow color changing to rosy-bronze.

452

(Exacum affine) Persian Violet.

Exacum Blue Champion. *A much used spring/summer flowering pot plant—and more recently for winter flowering. Photo by Jack Sweet, Earl J. Small, Pinellas Park, Florida.*

This beautiful blue-flowered plant has exploded into popularity as a pot plant in just a few years. The myriads of dime-sized flowers—blue with bright yellow pollen masses in the center—tend to cover the whole plant when grown well. Plant and pot size vary with the grower and his market. Most seem to be grown as 6" or 6½" pots but with the advent of some of the newer, faster growing, compact varieties, we should see a lot more grown in 4" or 5" pots. Some growers have a white exacum to add a little variety.

Most exacum are purchased from specialty growers as small plants ready for potting into 4", 5", or 6" pots. These plantlets may be from cuttings or from seed depending on method of propagation.

Seed is available, but it is quite tiny—even smaller than begonia seed—and must be handled very carefully. Exacum seed are slow to germinate—2 to 3 weeks—and should be planted in a lightweight starting media with little

*Contributed by Jack S. Sweet and Paul Crimmiskey, Earl J. Small Growers, Inc.

or no covering. The seedlings will be ready to transplant in about 6 weeks into 2" pots. Then about 7 weeks later can be put into the final pots for flowering.

The cultural procedures that follow are based on using plants ready for final transplant from 1½" to 2" pots generally produced by specialty growers.

Potting   Use a very light, well-drained potting soil, which is loose and has plenty of soil amendments, such as perlite, calcine clay or styrofoam, and peat to allow good root aeration. One plant per pot is sufficient and should be placed deep enough in the soil to stabilize the plant as it grows larger. Initial watering and for the first ten days should be very light to encourage root action.

Temperature   Exacum grow best at 60–65°F nights and 75–80°F days.

Light   Plants should be grown under full sunlight in winter months. During the summer months a light shade should be applied (4500–6000 foot-candles). During the spring and early fall, plants should be grown in full sun, and light shade applied when plants start to flower. Shading at this time will produce darker colored blooms. Excessive light and heat will cause flowers to be faded.

Media   Exacum grow best in a loose well-balanced soil mixture that has plenty of peat and perlite in it for good aeration.

Fertilization   Exacum are moderate feeders. We have found it grows best by alternate use of fertilizers such as 15–16–17 Peatlite Special and calcium nitrate at the rate of 2 pounds per 100 gallons every third watering. If desired, Osmocote 14–14–14 may be incorporated in the growing media at the rate of ¼ to ½ teaspoon per 6" pot of soil.

Some growers have experienced an excessive leaf curl or crinkle. This seems to be related to excessive light and possibly a low copper level in the leaf structure. A foliar spray using Tri-Basic Copper at one pound per 100 gallons applied two weeks after potting has been very successful in reducing crinkle on exacum—soil applications of copper on exacum have not been too useful.

Winter growing   Winter seems to produce more growing problems than summer. Apparently the lower light levels and shorter days make a softer plant that can be easily injured and attacked by disease. This must be compensated by lower fertilizer levels and reduced watering to make a "harder" plant. Starting around October pots should thoroughly dry out between waterings. Water early in the morning so foliage is dry by late afternoon. Provide good air circulation around plants, and reduce fertilizer levels by ½. Overwatering and high nutrient levels, besides promoting disease, *cause delayed flowering.*

In additon, exacum requires much less fertilizer and soil moisture than pot mums, lilies, or poinsettias, and responds poorly if fed with high levels of fertilizer on constant feed, with every watering, such as other crops may require. Again, remember, to accelerate winter flowering of exacum one should lower fertilizer levels and make sure plants dry out between waterings. Light at normal mum intensity will force winter plants into bud and bloom.

Production time Timing of the crop is seasonably variable with a marketable 6" flowering plant being produced in 7–8 weeks in the summer and up to 12–14 weeks in mid-winter. Smaller plants grown in 4½" or 5" pots for mass market sales can be produced in less time and on less bench space, as exacum can be forced to flower at an early stage. No pinching is necessary as they are self-branching plants. In case of premature bedding of small exacum, larger plants can be produced by removing the earliest flowers.

Disease We have minimized disease problems with exacum by the following procedures. Using Banrot as a light drench at 8 oz. per 100 gallons of water applied right after potting and at 3 to 4 week intervals. Chipco 26019 at 16 oz. per 100 gals., Daconil at 6 oz. per 100 gals., or Ornalin at 12–16 oz. per 100 gals. also work well. We have also used Benlate at 6 oz. plus Subdue 2-E at 1½ oz. per 100 gallons. Subdue is very effective against Pythium and Phytophthora. Gray mold (botrytis cinerea) can be a problem in the winter and early spring. It can be controlled by using Daconil 75 WP at one pound per 100 gallons or Benlate at 4 oz. plus Daconil at 10 oz. per 100 gallons.

Insects The most damaging insect to exacum is the broad mite. They are usually found on the upper parts of the plant and cause the leaves and growing tips to become yellow and distorted, and buds will fail to open. Broad mite can be controlled by various miticides such as Pentac, Kelthane, Vendex. All three can cause flower injury so caution is advised on mature flowering plants. Worms can be controlled with Thuricide or Resmethrin aerosol. Thrips may attack growing tips. They can be controlled by using Lindane or Orthene.

Height control Height of exacum can be controlled by using B-Nine at regular mum strength (.25% solution) applied one week after potting and, if needed, a second application can be given 2 to 3 weeks later for plants that are being grown under lower light conditions. Height can also be controlled by regulating the amount of water they receive. If small plants are desired they should be allowed to dry out more between waterings.

Post-greenhouse care Exacum should be placed next to a window or some artificial light source for long-lasting quality. Low light conditions will cause flowers to fade. Exacum may also be placed outside in a semi-shaded area or on a patio. They are hardy to 32°F.

FOLIAGE PLANTS*

Section I: Tropical

Although the foliage industry has been identifiable in the United States since the early 1900s, it is only within the last 20 years that it has become a major industry. In southern parts of Florida, Texas, and California, the industry developed initially outdoors and under slat sheds, but in recent years, has moved into polypropylene shadehouses and fiberglass and glass greenhouses. In northern areas, production has been centered in Ohio, Pennsylvania, New York, and nearby states in glass and double-layer polyethylene greenhouses. Since 1969, a number of companies have developed stock production units in the Caribbean region for shipment of propagative units to the United States and Europe. In 1981, it was estimated that at least 25 million dollars of propagative material was shipped into Florida for finishing.

Major production areas within the United States are listed in Table 1. Concentration of the foliage industry in Florida, Texas, and California is primarily because of reduced production costs associated with moderate winter temperatures and high light-intensity year round. Production in northern areas is facilitated by access to local markets and a product mix that stresses easy to grow, rapid turnover of smaller pot-sized foliage crops and hanging baskets.

Table 1 MAJOR UNITED STATES FOLIAGE
PLANT PRODUCTION AREAS AND ESTIMATED
SALES (USDA 1982)

State	1977 wholesale value (millions of dollars)
Florida	162
California	77
Texas	29
Ohio	14
United States—16 state total	329

Foliage crops were not of major economic significance in relation to other floriculture crops until the late 1960s. As late as 1970, foliage accounted for only 15 million dollars at wholesale in Florida. The most recent USDA data (1981) indicates that the total United States foliage market at wholesale was nearly 330 million dollars in 1981. Thus, foliage crops have become of major economic importance in a relatively short span of time.

*Contributed by Charles A. Conover, University of Florida, Agricultural Research Center, Apopka.

456

Many definitions exist for foliage plants; however, they are so diverse in habit and use, it is difficult to develop one that is inclusive. One definition that addresses itself to both form and use and is commonly used is: "Any plant grown primarily for its foliage and utilized for interior decoration or interior landscape purposes. While it may have flowers, these will be secondary compared to foliage features."

Detailed information on the national foliage plant product mix has been unavailable since 1970, but it has been compiled for Florida, which accounts for 49.3% of national production. The data in Table 2 is not listed by genera throughout, since many diverse genera may be included in plants sold as hanging baskets and thus, individual genera may be responsible for very minor segments of the industry. On a national basis, this information is probably low in hanging baskets and terrarium plants, which are often grown for local markets in northern areas of the United States. Also, larger foliage types would be listed at higher percentages than they actually are nationally because Florida is responsible for well over 75% of plants grown in 10", or larger containers.

Table 2   FOLIAGE PLANT PRODUCT MIX IN FLORIDA, 1975

Product	%	Product	%
Philodendron spp.	20	Combinations	2
Dracaena spp.	11	Hanging baskets	2
Palms	7	*Aphelandra* spp.	2
Ficus spp.	6	*Aglaonema* spp.	2
Dieffenbachia spp.	5	Aralias	2
Brassaia actinophylla	5	*Hoya* spp.	2
Maranta spp.	3	Terrarium plants	1
Epipremnum spp.	3	Crotons	1
Totem pole plants	3	Cacti	1
Ferns	3	*Ardisia* spp.	1
Peperomia spp.	3	*Spathiphyllum* spp.	1
Sansevieria spp.	3	Other	9
Syngonium spp.	2		

Stock plant culture—field   Growth of foliage stock plants in the field (outdoors) is restricted to southern Florida and California and the tropics. Only a few stock plants can be grown in full sun. For the most part, stock plants are grown under polypropylene shade cloth that provides the required light levels or in full sun.

Land selected for stock production should have good internal drainage as well as sufficient slope to allow surface water to drain off rapidly when excessive rainfall occurs. Temperature ranges should preferably be between 65°F minimum at night and 95°F maximum day for best quality and yield. Infrequent lows of 50°F and highs below 105°F will not damage plants, but will reduce yields. Farm location should also be considered in relation to wind speed and frequency, since it may affect structural design as well as types of crops grown. Wind-induced tipburn and foliar abrasion reduce crop quality and salability.

Structures used to support shade cloth can be constructed of treated lumber or of concrete or steel with cable stringers supporting shade cloth. Height of the structure and size is important because it influences temperature at plant height. Because heat rises and air movement is slow through shade cloth, it is wise to provide a minimum of 8' and preferably 10' clearance. Erection of 1- to 5-acre units with spaces between units will help prevent excessive temperature buildup.

Foliage stock plants grown outdoors or under shade cloth are usually watered with impulse or spinning sprinklers, which are also used for fertilization. Therefore, it is very important to have a properly engineered system so that good coverage will be obtained. Use of low-angle trajectory sprinklers will be necessary to prevent contact of water with shade cloth. Normally, foliage plants grown under shade cloth require 1" to 2" of water a week. Soils in tropical and subtropical areas are rarely satisfactory for foliage stock production when used in their native state. Thus, sandy soils usually require organic components such as peat moss to improve water and nutrient holding capacities while heavy tropical soils require peat moss, bark, coarse sawdust, or rice hulls to improve internal aeration.

Stock plant culture—greenhouse Although most foliage stock plants grown for cuttings or divisions may be grown in greenhouses, economics of production limit the final selection. Size of plants in relation to yield of cuttings per square foot and need of specific types to be grown under cover for pest protection govern selection. Foliage stock plants can be grown in any type of greenhouse that provides sufficient light and required temperatures. Stock plants should be grown in raised benches or pots that provide sufficient medium volume for good root growth, drainage, and adequate aeration. Benches with 6" sides and wire bottoms serve this purpose best, but some smaller plants will grow well where 4" sides are used. Growing media selection depends on local availability, cost, and personal preference. Some excellent media for foliage stock plants include: (1) 50% peat moss/50% pine bark; (2) 75% peat moss/25% pine bark; (3) 75% peat moss/25% sharp mason sand; and (4) 75% peat moss/25% perlite.

Selection of watering systems for stock plants grown in greenhouses is important, since foliar disease control is reduced where folige is kept dry. Another advantage to keeping foliage dry and reducing pesticide usage is the reduction of foliar residues.

Temperatures needed for maximum yield from stock plants are 65°F minimum and 95°F maximum. Maintenance of the minimum temperature is expensive during winter months; and if heat conservation is a problem, it is better to keep soil temperatures at 65°F minimum and allow air temperatures to drop slightly lower.

Growth of foliage stock plants in greenhouses is limited only by economics; valuable and costly space devoted to stock plant production may be better used for potted plant production and propagation of purchased cuttings. It is generally conceded that bench space in northern greenhouses costs at least $10 a year per square foot, while in warmer areas this may range between $5 and $10. Only a few fast-growing foliage plants yield sufficient cuttings to make them profitable where heating costs are high. Therefore, before establishment of a stock production area, it is wise to compare purchase costs per cutting versus those expected from a stock production area.

Propagation of foliage plants   Propagation methods used for foliage plants include cuttings, seed, air layers, spores, division, and tissue culture. Using cuttings is one of the most popular propagation methods; cuttings can be tip, single- and double-eye leaf bud, leaf, or cane. Selection of a specific method depends on plant form (upright, vining, etc.) and availability of propagative material. Seed propagation is increasing in popularity because costs are lower than for vegetative propagation. However, seeds of many foliage plants are not available, or plant type is not stable from seed. Some of the more popular foliage plants grown from seed include *Araucaria, Brassaia Coffea, Dizygotheca, Podocarpus* and nearly all of the palms. Seed of tropical foliage plants should be planted soon after harvest because germination percentage decreases rapidly with increased time between harvest and planting. Air layering is decreasing in importance as a propagation method because of high costs and need for large stock plant areas. Plants most commonly air-layered include *Codiaeum, Ficus* and *Monstera.* One of the problems with air layers is that their large size makes them difficult to ship without mechanical damage occurring. Division is the only method of propagation for crops like *Calathea* and *Sansevieria.* This is a high-labor method and presents problems of carrying disease, insect, or nematode pests to new plantings. Spores are commonly used to propagate a number of fern genera, although many ferns are grown from divisions or offsets.

Tissue culture is becoming an important system of propagation for foliage producers. Rapid multiplication of new cultivars is an important advantage of tissue culture, but some old cultivars such as the Boston fern are commonly propagated by this system. At the present time, about 20 cultivars of foliage plants are being propagated by tissue culture. Two major advantages of tissue culture are change in plant form and disease control. Genera such as *Dieffenbachia, Nephrolepis, Spathiphyllum,* and *Syngonium* produce multiple crown breaks when grown from tissue culture and yield plants with more compact form and fuller appearance. Tissue culture has been successful in reducing disease problems with several genera since disease-free stocks can often be maintained free of disease when grown in enclosed greenhouses. Two major foliage crops *(Dieffenbachia* and *Spathiphyllum)* are grown from disease-free stocks and yield high quality potted plants. The future for tissue culture is excellent, but it will be years before special media for all foliage plant genera are defined.

Propagative systems   The usual propagation system is a mist bed where cuttings are misted for 15 to 30 seconds each 30 to 60 minutes. Cuttings are stuck in the bed and then rooted, pulled, and potted. During the last ten years, many producers have shifted to direct stick propagation where cuttings are placed directly in the growing pot, rooted, and finished without being moved. This system is especially adapted to plants such as *philodendron,* where three to five single-eye cuttings may be placed in each pot. The frequency of misting depends on light intensity and temperature, and should be set to keep some moisture on foliage at most times. In cooler climates, growers often use tents over the propagation bench to provide 100% humidity and eliminate misting. Mist application is very useful in lowering temperatures in summer months, but can prolong rooting during periods where medium temperature drops below 65°F. For this reason, propagation beds or benches should be maintained at 70° to 75°F at all times within the medium.

Numerous media have been used for foliage plant propagation, with sphagnum peat moss most commonly used either singly or when amended with perlite, styrofoam, pine bark, or other organic components.

Production   Cultural variability between foliage plants prevents development of a detailed crop production guide, but factors influencing most foliage crops are discussed so that logical decisions can be made.

Potting medium used to grow foliage plants can range from 100% organic to approximately 50% organic and 50% inorganic. Key factors to consider in selection of potting media include aeration (measured as capillary and non-capillary pore space), moisture retention (water holding capacity) and nutrient retention (cation exchange capacity). Several other factors that must be considered when selecting potting media include: consistency, availability, weight, and cost. Examples of potting media utilized by commercial foliage growers are shown in the lower portion of Table 3, although many of the commercially prepared media are excellent.

Normally, pH is adjusted at the time potting mixtures are developed. The best range for most foliage plants is between 5.5 and 6.5, but several genera, including *Maranta* and most ferns, grow best with a range between 5.0 and 6.0. Dolomite is suggested for pH correction, but any calcium-containing material can also be used. Superphosphate should not be incorporated into potting media unless foliage plants not sensitive to fluorides are being grown. Where fluoride sensitive crops are being grown, the best pH range is 6.0 to 7.0. Micronutrients are normally included in the fertilizer program, although they may also be included in the potting medium.

Potting methods and systems fall into two main categories: hand potting and pot fillers. Hand potting is still used by the majority of producers with small or medium sized operations. Systems vary, but potting media are usually delivered to a central site where potting occurs, and potted plants are then moved to growing areas. Most pot filling machines are stationary—potting takes place in a central location; however, smaller portable pot fillers are also utilized.

Table 3 PHYSICAL AND CHEMICAL CHARACTERISTICS OF POTTING

Table 3 PHYSICAL AND CHEMICAL CHARACTERISTICS OF POTTING MEDIA COMPONENTS COMMONLY USED TO GROW FOLIAGE PLANTS AND SELECTED COMBINATIONS

Medium	Aeration	Water holding capacity	Cation exchange capacity	Weight
Sphagnum peat moss	M*	H	H	L
Composted pine bark	H	M	M	M
Perlite	H	L	L	L
Sand	M	L	L	H
Shavings	H	M	M	L
Peat:Perlite (2:1)	H	M	M	L
Peat:Bark (1:1)	H	H	H	L
Peat:Sand (3:1)	M	H	H	M
Peat:Bark:Shavings (2:1:1)	H	H	H	L

*H = high, M = average, and L = low.

Spacing of foliage plants directly controls final plant quality. Plants that will be finished within 3 months are usually placed at their final spacing when placed on the bench with spacing distance varying from 0 (pot to pot) to 3 times pot diameter. Plants grown in container sizes of 6″ or larger may take 6 months to 2 years to reach maturity. Such plants are often placed pot to pot until they become crowded and then spaced to their final spacing. Depending on type of growth, spacing varies from 1 to 6 times the container diameter. Crowding of plants reduces light reaching lower foliage and may cause it to abscise, or may cause plants to grow tall without proportionate spread which reduces value.

Light intensity. Information has been included in Table 4 for many foliage crops. Light intensity is one of the most important factors to consider in culture because it influences quality factors such as internode length, foliage color, carbohydrate level, growth rate, and acclimatization. Light green foliage or faded colors such as in the case of *Codiaeum* are indicative of excessive light and reduced chlorophyll levels. This can be corrected in most cases by increasing fertilization or reducing light intensity. Because increases in fertilizer often cause excessive soluble salts levels, the proper corrective method is to reduce light intensity.

Fertilization directly influences growth rate, and thus profitability, but because fertilizer levels provided also influence longevity indoors, it is important to be sure excessive levels are not used. Maximum growth rate of acclimatized foliage plants can be obtained with moderate levels of soluble, organic or slow release fertilizers applied constantly or periodically. Suggested levels of fertilizer provided in Table 4 are for plants grown under light intensities recommended for production of acclimatized high-quality plants.

461

Table 4 SUGGESTED LIGHT AND NUTRITIONAL LEVELS FOR PRODUCTION OF SOME POTTED ACCLIMATIZED FOLIAGE PLANTS

Botanical name	Light intensity (foot-candles)	Fertilizer requirement lbs/1000 sq. ft./yr.[1]		
		N	P_2O_5	K_2O
Aeschynanthus pulcher	2000–4000	34	11	23
Aglaonema spp.	1000–2500	28	9	19
Aphelandra squarrosa	1000–1500	34	11	23
Araucaria heterophylla	4000–8000	28	9	19
Asparagus spp.	2500–4500	20	7	13
Brassaia spp.	4000–6000	41	14	27
Calathea spp.	1000–2000	28	9	19
Chamaedorea elegans	1500–3000	28	9	19
Chamaedorea erumpens	3000–6000	34	11	23
Chlorophytum comosum	1000–2500	34	11	23
Chrysalidocarpus lutescens	4000–6000	34	11	23
Cissus rhombifolia	1500–2500	28	9	19
Codiaeum variegatum	5000–8000	41	14	27
Coffea arabica	1000–2500	34	11	23
Cordyline terminalis	2500–4500	28	9	19
Dizygotheca elegantissima	4000–6000	28	9	19
Dieffenbachia spp.	1500–3000	28	9	19
Dracaena deremensis (cultivars)	2000–3500	28	9	19
Dracaena fragrans (cultivars)	2000–3500	28	9	19
Dracaena marginata	4000–6000	41	14	27
Dracaena - other species	1500–3500	28	9	19
Epipremnum aureum	1500–4000	34	11	23
Ficus benjamina	3000–6000	41	14	27
Ficus elastica (cultivars)	6000–8000	41	14	27
Ficus lyrata	5000–6000	41	14	27
Fittonia verschaffeltii	1000–2500	20	7	13
Gynura aurantiaca	1500–3000	34	11	23
Hedera helix	1500–2500	28	9	19
Hoya carnosa	2000–3000	28	9	19
Maranta spp.	1000–2500	20	7	13
Monstera deliciosa	2500–4500	34	11	23
Nephrolepis exaltata (cultivars)	1500–3500	28	9	19
Peperomia spp.	1500–3500	14	5	9
Philodendron selloum	3000–6000	41	14	27
Philodendron spp.	2000–3500	34	11	23
Pilea spp.	1500–3000	14	5	9
Polyscias spp.	1500–4500	41	14	27
Sansevieria spp.	3500–6000	14	5	9
Schlumbergera truncata	2000–3000	28	9	19
Spathiphyllum spp.	1500–2500	28	9	19
Syngonium podophyllum	1500–3500	34	11	23
Yucca elephantipes	3500–4500	28	9	19

[1]Based on a 3–1–2 ratio fertilizer source—if growing medium is known to fix phosphorus and potassium, they should be added at the same rate as nitrogen—i.e., use a 1–1–1 ratio fertilizer source.

Fertilizer ratios for foliage plants need to be approximately 3–1–2 when potting mixtures listed are utilized. A ratio of 1–1–1 is also acceptable, but because nitrogen is the key element in growth of foliage plants, this ratio will result in higher fertilizer costs to obtain the desired nitrogen level. Rates listed can be calculated on a periodic basis and applied weekly, or every other week. Periodic fertilization less often than every 2 weeks often results in growth decreases. Where a constant feed program is desired, the suggested level of nutrients at each application is 150–200 ppm nitrogen, 50–75 ppm phosphorus, and 100–150 ppm potassium. Potting media used for foliage plant production are normally very low in micronutrients, and thus, most fertilizers used should contain at least the minimal micronutrient levels suggested in Table 5.

Acclimatization of foliage plants utilized for interior use is necessary to ensure that they perform well indoors. Acclimatization is the adaptation of a plant to a new environment—in this instance, preparation for growth in building interiors under low light and humidity conditions. One of the most important aspects of acclimatization is development of shade foliage, which is characterized by large, thin leaves with high chlorophyll levels. A second important factor is nutritional level, which should be as low as possible while still producing a quality plant. The major objective of acclimatization is to produce plants with low light compensation points. Such plants are able to make the transition from production to interior environments without serious loss of quality. The most highly acclimatized plants are those grown under recommended light and fertilizer programs for their entire production cycle (Table 4), for only with this system are leaves of all ages acclimatized. Also, plants grown under recommended light levels for full term will have a more open appearance, which is an adaptation to reduced light intensity.

Foliage plants such as *Brassaia, Chrysalidocarpus,* and *Ficus* are often grown in full sun and then acclimatized by placing them under suggested shade and lowering fertilizer levels for 2 to 6 months. Although chloroplasts and grana are capable of reorientation within sun-grown foliage, the leaf anatomy—small size and thick cross-section—prevents them from being as efficient after acclimatization as shade leaves. Therefore, such plants are less tolerant of low

Table 5 AVERAGE LEVELS OF SEVERAL MICRONUTRIENTS REQUIRED FOR FOLIAGE CROPS

Element*	Spray application lbs./100 gal.	Soil drench oz./1000 ft.	Soil incorporated oz./yd.
B	0.01	0.03	0.010
Cu	0.10	0.30	0.100
Fe	1.00	3.00	1.000
Mn	0.50	1.50	0.500
Mo	0.01	0.01	0.001
Zn	0.30	1.00	0.300

*One application is often sufficient for short-term crops, while reapplications are usually necessary for crops grown 6 months or more.

or medium light levels indoors than plants acclimatized during the entire production period.

Temperature control is very important, since most foliage plants are tropical and require high night temperatures in the range of 65°F minimum. Soil temperatures are also important, and if they can be maintained at 65° to 70°F, the air temperature may drop as low as 60°F at night without significant crop response. Best temperature range for production of a wide variety of foliage genera is 65°F minimum night and 75°F minimum day. Night temperatures of as high as 80°F and day temperatures as high as 95°F will not be damaging; however, it is often uneconomical to maintain these in temperate climates.

Watering levels should be established that ensure that foliage plants receive sufficient water to remain turgid at all times. Water requirements during winter, when temperatures are low and growth slowed, may be less than once a week; in spring or summer, daily application may be necessary.

Use of watering systems that water the potting medium without wetting foliage is desirable because this reduces foliar disease and residue problems. Leader tubes provide best watering control and provision for leaching. Mat irrigation can also be used to produce foliage plants, but when using them, fertilizer should be incorporated into the potting medium for best results. Fertilizer application to mats may cause soluble salts excesses at the surface of the container and also contributes to excessive algae growth on mats.

CO_2 application to foliage plants is uncommon, although growth responses of up to 25% have occurred with several foliage plants. However, it appears that temperature is the key to increased growth during periods when greenhouses are closed, and unless a range of 65° to 75°F minimum is maintained, the injection of CO_2 will probably not be beneficial.

Humidity requirements of foliage plants during production are not verified by research, but maintenance of 50% or higher relative humidity appears to be desirable. In areas where humidity falls below 25%, it is desirable to install mist lines or otherwise raise humidity.

Control of insects and diseases

Insects and mites: Factors that affect pest populations include temperature, humidity, irrigation method, potting medium, and access to the structure. Temperatures above 80°F can cause rapid increases in mite populations, especially if humidity is low. Under such conditions, heavy dependence on chemical control is necessary to produce mite-free plants. Cold or cool temperatures reduce pest problems in unheated production areas, while in greenhouses, they present year-round problems. Fungus gnats are much more of a problem in greenhouses than outdoors, especially where organic potting media are kept too wet. When a particular pest such as scale becomes a problem, cultural procedures must be checked carefully to see if stock plants are infested and if crawlers or adults have been carried through propagation to potted plant production areas. It is imperative that stock be kept as free of pests as possible to lower need for spraying of potted materials for sale. Frequent and continued spraying is undesirable because it increases potential for phytotoxicity and leaves hard-to-remove residues on foliage.

Control outdoors and under shade cloth in areas open to pest movement, requires spraying or drenching with pesticides as primary methods of control. Mites present most problems in spring, summer, and fall when temperatures are high, while caterpillars and thrips are heaviest in spring and fall. Use of high pressure sprayers and careful application to both sides of foliage provides the best assurance of control. Air blast sprayers, while providing high pressure and wide dispersal, often do not properly coat both sides of foliage with pesticides.

Table 6 lists the major pests of foliage plants and some of the hosts they are most commonly found feeding upon. Chemicals registered for control of specific pests are subject to change, and thus for up-to-date recommendations on chemical pest control procedures on foliage plants, check with your co-operative agricultural extension agent.

Table 6   MAJOR FOLIAGE PLANT INSECT AND MITE PESTS AND CROPS COMMONLY SERVING AS HOSTS

Pest	Hosts
Aphids	*Aphelandra, Brassaia, Gynura, Hoya, Dieffenbachia*
Broad Mites	*Hedera, Aphelandra, Pilea*
Caterpillars	*Philodendron, Dracaena, Brassaia, Maranta, Aglaonema*
Fungus Gnats	*Schlumbergera,* Palms, *Peperomia*
Mealybugs	*Aphelandra, Ardisia, Dieffenbachia, Gynura, Asparagus, Maranta, Dracaena, Dizygotheca*
Spider Mites	*Brassaia, Codiaeum,* Palms, *Cordyline, Calathea, Dieffenbachia, Maranta*
Scales	*Aphelandra,* Bromeliads, *Ficus,* Palms
Thrips	*Brassaia, Ficus, Philodendron, Ctenanthe, Syngonium*

Control in greenhouses is somewhat easier, since producers can use many chemicals used outdoors or under shade structures, as well as smoke bombs or thermal fogs and biological control agents. However, smoke bombs or thermal fogs only work where greenhouses can be entirely closed for several hours or more. Because many greenhouses in warm climates are open on the pad side of the greenhouse for 6 months or more a year, this system is best used in cooler climates. Another problem in hot climates is the problem of phytotoxicity which may occur if fogs or smoke bombs are applied when temperatures are above 85°F.

Diseases (fungi, bacteria and viruses): Fungal and bacterial diseases are more troublesome where wet foliage is combined with high temperatures and humidity. Therefore, these diseases are most prevalent in tropical and sub-tropical areas with high rainfall. Even in these areas, however, growing plants under cover and irrigating without wetting foliage will nearly prevent their occurrence. Soil-borne fungal diseases become more severe where poor quality growing media without good aeration and drainage exist, or where plants are constantly overwatered. Several bacterial diseases become more severe where plants are grown with excessive nitrogen fertilization or are stressed through high-soluble salts, excessive temperatures, or high light intensity. Virus diseases are disseminated by insects in nonenclosed areas, but many foliage plants already contain at least one known virus, and thus insect exclusion may not be beneficial.

Control outdoors and under shade cloth is usually necessary in subtropical and tropical areas with high rainfall, and is difficult except with preventative spray programs. Depending on disease pressure and during periods of frequent rainfall, it may be necessary to spray weekly or more often; however, during dry seasons little, if any, pesticide application may be necessary. Irrigation application to the soil or overhead application should be made during the middle of the day when rapid drying can occur, and plants should be properly spaced to reduce humidity. Directed high pressure sprays rather than air-blast sprayers provide best control of disease pests and are usually worth the extra cost of application. Table 7 provides a listing of some of the major disease pests and primary hosts. As with insecticides and miticides, most up-to-date control information can be obtained from the local cooperative agricultural extension agent.

Control in greenhouses of foliar fungal and bacterial diseases is easiest if foliage can be kept dry. Where this is impossible, fairly good control can be obtained with chemical sprays to the foliage. Soil drenches for control of most of the soil-borne diseases are fairly successful in raised benches and in containers off the ground. No control procedures are presently recommended for plants with virus except to rogue infected plants and use virus-free stocks.

Packaging systems The two main packaging systems are boxing and shipping loose in specially constructed racks and trucks. When boxing, boxes must meet interstate shipping regulations concerning weight of corrugated cardboard and either be waxed or moisture resistant. This is necessary to prevent deterioration of boxes in transit because of moisture in containers. Plants in containers up through 6″ are usually placed in a waxed tray, and the tray slid into a box of the proper height. Such boxes usually do not contain dividers or other restraints, although some producers have designed boxes with dividers and other restraints that hold the pot in position and the potting medium in the container. Plants in 6″ or larger pots are usually sleeved and placed directly in containers of the proper height or shipped loose in specially designed trucks.

In recent years, some producers and shippers have designed adjustable racks to accommodate various sized plants which they wheel directly into trucks. Usually, no dividers or restraints are necessary with this system, and physical damage is minimal.

*Table 7 MAJOR FOLIAGE PLANT DISEASE ORGANISMS AND CROPS
COMMONLY SERVING AS HOSTS*

Organism	Area affected	Common hosts
Fungal pathogens		
Alternaria	Leaves, stems	*Brassaia, Schefflera, Polyscias Fatsia, Calathea*
Fusarium	Leaves	*Dracaena*
Fusarium	Stems, leaves, roots	*Dieffenbachia*
Leptosphaeria	Leaves	*Dieffenbachia*
Myrothecium	Leaves	*Aglaonema, Dieffenbachia, Spathiphyllum, Begonia, Syngonium, Episcia, Aphelandra, Peperomia, Aeschynanthus*
Drechslera, Bipolaris	Leaves	Palms, *Maranta, Calathea*
Colletotrichum	Leaves	*Dieffenbachia, Hedera*
Rhizoctonia	Leaves, stems, roots	Many plants, especially ferns, *Hedera, Philodendron, Epipremnum*
Pythium	Stems, roots	Many plants, especially ferns, *Epipremnum, Philodendron, Peperomia*
Phytophthora	Leaves, stems, roots	Many plants, especially *Brassaia, Spathiphyllum, Dieffenbachia, Aphelandra, Philodendron, Saintpaulia*
Sclerotium	Stems	Most plants grown on the ground are susceptible
Corynespora	Leaves	*Ficus, Aeschynanthus, Aphelandra*
Cylindrocladium	Stems, roots	*Spathiphyllum*
Bacterial pathogens		
Erwinia	Stems, leaves	*Dieffenbachia, Aglaonema, Philodendron, Syngonium, Dracanea, Saintpaulia,* and many others
Pseudomonas	Leaves	*Caryota, Philodendron, Syngonium,* ferns, *Dracaena, Schefflera*
Xanthomonas	Leaves	*Philodendron, Dieffenbachia, Hedera, Aglaonema*
Viral pathogens		
Cucumber mosaic	Leaves	*Maranta*
Dasheen mosaic	Leaves	*Dieffenbachia, Aglaonema, Spathiphyllum, Philodendron*

Storage and shipping   Storage of foliage plants is not a normal practice, but with increased sales in mass market outlets that use central distribution points, there has been increased interest in how long plants can be held without significant decrease in quality. In actuality, storage and shipping are very similar in nature, and environmental conditions for both are similar. However, plant

467

preparation for storage and/or shipping does not start at the time of the intended practice, but during the production period. Research has shown that many foliage plants can be shipped for 2 to 4 weeks in darkness provided they were acclimatized and given proper environmental conditions during the storage/shipping period.

Preshipment factors affecting plant quality

Light: Preshipment light levels have a strong effect on postshipment plant quality. Plants grown under high light will not ship as well because they are not properly acclimatized. This results in excessive leaf drop or other loss of quality either in shipment or after placement in an interior environment. Also, plants grown in higher light are not as likely to tolerate lower shipping temperatures without sustaining chilling injury.

Nutrition: Preshipment fertilizer levels also affect acclimatization and, in turn, subsequent interior quality, but this is not often expressed during shipment. Foliage plants grown on higher than recommended nutritional regimes will not be well acclimatized and will ultimately lose more leaves and be of lower quality than those properly acclimatized. However, serious reduction in plant quality during the shipping phase will only be noticeable if the fertilizer level is more than twice the recommended level.

Soil moisture: Low soil moisture during shipping periods increases desiccation of plant tissues and raises potential for leaf drop or injury. Plants should be thoroughly watered approximately 24 hours prior to shipment and allowed to drain before packing.

Season: Foliage plants grown during high light and high temperature periods are less tolerant of the shipping environment and are more likely to decline in quality during shipment. This may be due to lower levels of acclimatization or inability to tolerate lowered shipping temperatures. It appears that plants grown in summer and shipped then or in early fall will require warmer shipping temperatures than plants grown and shipped in winter or spring.

Shipping environment factors

Light: All shipments to date have been made in darkness. Addition of light during the shipping period might be beneficial, but incorporation into storage and/or shipping environments would be difficult.

Temperature: Controlled temperature at a level specified for the crop can be a major factor in maintenance of plant quality. Shipping at low temperatures, 45° to 60°F versus 65° to 70°F, can be beneficial in maintaining quality, provided plants are not chill-damaged. However, the best shipping temperature for specific plants changes with the season, and is lower in winter and higher in summer. Duration of exposure to a specific temperature can also strongly affect plant quality, since a temperature that might be optimum for 2-week shipments might cause damage when plants are exposed for 3 to 4 weeks (see Table 8).

Table 8 SUGGESTED SHIPPING TEMPERATURES (°F) FOR ACCLIMATIZED FOLIAGE PLANTS

Plant name	Shipping duration	
	1–15 days	16–30 days
Acoelorrhaphe wrightii	50–55	—z
Aglaonema "Fransher"	55–60	60–65
Aglaonema "Silver Queen"	60–65	60–65
Ardisia crispa	50–55	—
Aspidistra elatior	50–55	—
Brassaia actinophylla	50–55	50–55
Chamaedorea elegans	55–60	—
Chamaedorea seifrizii	55–60	—
Chrysalidocarpus lutescens	55–65	60–65y
Codiaeum variegatum "Norma"	60–65	60–65
Cordyline terminalis "Dragon Tongue"	60–65	—
Dracaena deremensis "Janet Craig"	60–65	—
Dracaena deremensis "Warneckii"	60–65	—
Dracaena fragrans "Massangeana"	60–65	—
Dracaena marginata	55–65	60–65y
Ficus benjamina	55–60	55–60
Ficus nitida	55–60	—
Howea forsterana	50–65	50–65
Philodendron selloum	55–60	—
Phoenix roebelenii	50–55	—
Pleomele reflexa	60–65	—
Rhapis excelsa	50–55	—
Schefflera arboricola	50–55	50–55
Spathiphyllum "Mauna Loa"	50–55	55–60
Yucca elephantipes	50–55	50–55

zData not available, and it is not known how they will tolerate shipment beyond 15 days.
yPlants observed to lose quality beyond 15 days shipping duration.

Humidity: Although all plants need to be thoroughly watered prior to shipment, this will not prevent them from desiccating if humidity is too low. A relative humidity level of around 85% to 90% is necessary for maintenance of foliage plants stored or shipped for long durations. This level can be obtained with boxed plants or when air exchange controls on the shipping container are set in the closed position with sleeved or open shipped plants.

Gases: Research on foliage plants has shown that ethylene is probably the only contaminant that may occur in a cooler, unless it receives pollution from an outside source. However, foliage plants require fairly high levels of ethylene (1 to 2 ppm) and relatively high temperatures (65°F or higher) for long durations before any damage will occur. Experience has shown that ethylene does not seem to be a major problem when plants are shipped at cooler (65°F or lower) temperatures.

469

Selected References

1. Chase, A. R. 1981. Common diseases of foliage plants. Florida Foliage 7(9):39–56.
2. Conover, C. A. 1980. Foliage Plants. In: *Floriculture*. R. A. Larson, N. C. State Univ., Ed., Academic Press, NY.
3. Conover, C. A. and R. T. Poole. 1981. Basic fertilization guide for acclimatized foliage plants. *Florists' Review* 168(4360):10–11, 29–32.
4. Hamlen, R. A., D. E. Short, and R. W. Henley. 1978. Detection and identification of insects and related pests of the commercial foliage industry. Fla. Coop. Ext. Serv. Circular 432.
5. Joiner, J. N. 1981. *Foliage Plant Production*. Prentice-Hall, Inc., Englewood Cliffs, NJ.
6. Short, D. E. and R. W. Henley. 1981. Insect, mite and related pest control on commercial foliage crops—1981. *Foliage Digest* 4(12):3–7.
7. Simone, G. W. 1982. Available disease control pesticides for foliage production—1982. *Foliage Digest* 5(8):7–16.

Section II: A Close Look at Thirteen Major Foliage Plants*

Aglaonema (Chinese Evergreen) One of our most satisfactory house plants because of its low-light-intensity requirements. Should be grown under 50 to 500 foot-candles and can tolerate down to 10 foot-candles under home conditions. Can be grown in shallow water gardens. Propagated either from single-node stem divisions or tip cuttings. Commercially available in propagating canes (stems), rooted or unrooted cuttings, or potted plants. Cuttings are usually sold in grades by inches of height and number of leaves. *Simplex* is the common, all-green Chinese evergreen. *Commutatum* is similar, except that leaves are mottled with silvery grey.

Roebelini is a large-leafed, extremely tough species with silvery-grey patches on dark green foliage.

There are several new selections now available: *Silver King, Silver Queen, Fransher,* and *Pseudo-Bracteatum*. All are very tough as well as attractive. Use aglaonemas for those dark spots.

*Editor's note: The late Robert McColley of Bamboo Nurseries, Orlando, Florida, knew foliage so very well. He was a practical man, got his grasp of foliage by simply working with the crop for a lifetime. He also did major breeding. We thought it would be a valuable addition to the excellent basic foliage information by Charles Conover (Section I of this chapter) to include this closer look at some of the leading foliage plants as seen by Bob McColley.

Foliage production is heavily tray-mechanized in Holland. These Yucca canes (just received from Central America) are on trays—to permit easy moving to the headhouse for transplanting, etc. Photo at Boekestijn's, de Lier, Holland.

Foliage produced for retail shops and other outlets is important business for Masson's, Linwood, Kansas. This display is simply samples—used by retail shop buyers to make up orders.

Asparagus meyersii—*a soft, different, and very attractive pot fern.*

Boston fern—so very widely used as a hanging basket or in a fern stand.

Chinese evergreen Aglaonema simplex.

Aphelandra (Zebra Plant)   A compact-growing plant of the *Acanthaceae* family. Its leaves are shiny, emerald-green, elliptical, and of medium size with prominent white veins and midrib. Most species and varieties have bright yellow flowers.

The aphelandras require more water than most plants, with about 30% shade. If the plants should wilt, water frequently until growth is revived. Fertilize lightly about every 2 months, unless plant is in rapid growth, and then fertilize lightly every 2 to 4 weeks.

Dieffenbachia   A very handsome, large, decorative plant. Commonly propagated by cutting stems into sections containing one or more eyes or by rooting tips under mist. Commercially available in propagating canes, unrooted cuttings, rooted cuttings, or established pot plants. *Amoena* has large, broad, and pointed leaves, deep green with cream-white bands and blotches, and is most widely used. *Bausei* has a large pointed leaf, yellowish-green with dark green and white spots and a dark green edge. *Hoffmannii,* a comparatively new variety, has pointed leaves. Deep green with leaves and petioles marbled and spotted white. White midrib. *Picta* has light green, oval leaves with ivory-white marbling and blotching. Petioles dotted pale green. *Rudolph Roehrs* (Roehrsi), a variety of *Picta,* has leaves yellow and ivory with white blotches; midrib and borders dark green.

473

Aphelandra squarrosa.

Dracaena   Dracaena constitutes a large family of attractive houseplants. The Hawaiian ti plant is a close relative. *D. indivisa* is propagated from seed. Propagated mostly by rooting tip cuttings, although a few of the lesser-used kinds such as *Massangeana Tricolor, Eugene Andre,* and *Fire Brand* are propagated by cutting up old canes that root at each leaf axil. Unrooted canes of these varieties are also available, in addition to rooted plants. Catalogs usually list small cuttings or plants by number of leaves, number of tiers of leaves, or inches of height. Their growing medium should be kept quite wet.

    Godseffiana usually has several wiry spreading stems. Thick, leathery leaves grow in pairs or whorls and are liberally spotted yellow or white. *Sanderiana* is a particularly nice plant in small sizes. It grows upright and has long, narrow leaves that are sometimes twisted slightly. Leaf color is deep green with prominent marginal white band. *Warnecki* is a particularly good plant for dark locations. It has large, sword-shaped, leathery leaves. Each leaf has a milky-white streak down the center and another translucent white band on each side, bordered by a narrow, bright green edge.

    Ficus (Rubber Plant)   Most attractive as comparatively large specimens. They are propagated by specialists, mostly by the air-layering method, in which a layer of moist peat moss is wrapped around a section of stem from which part of the outer "bark" has been removed. Roots result in several weeks and the stem is then cut just below the roots to produce a "tip cutting." Ficus is occasionally propagated by tip cuttings, but this method is much more expensive. Small plants are available as "air layers" or "mossed rooted cuttings," and most catalogs specify number of leaves per plant. *Elastica* is the original and very durable rubber plant. It grows into a 100-ft.-high tree in its native Malaya or India. Its close relatives supply the world with natural rubber. *Elastica* has deep, glossy leaves with a rosy sheath enclosing newly formed leaves.

474

Dracaena sanderiana.

*Weeping Fig (*Ficus benjamina*). Very widely used and excellent in containers as an indoor plant.*

*Red-veined Prayer Plant (*Maranta*)—so called because its leaves assume a vertical position in darkness resembling hands in prayer.*

There are several newer and superior varieties of *Elastica*. One is *Decora,* an *Elastica* seedling with broader heads and heavier leaves. New leaves are borne in red sheaths. This is by far the most popular variety in use today. *Doescheri* is a variegated variety of *Elastica* that originated in New Orleans. Leaves are variegated with gray, creamy yellow, or white. *Pandurata* is sometimes known as the "fiddle-leaf plant" because of its fiddle-shaped leaf. Leaves are quilted and wavy with attractive yellow-green veins. Grows more upright than the *Elastica* family.

Do not allow any of the ficus to become dry, or the plants will drop a number of their lower leaves.

Maranta Marantas and their close relatives, the calatheas, are an attractive group of small, low-growing, decorative foliage plants. Their one drawback is that they require conditions of quite-high humidity—higher than is found in the average home. They make excellent subjects for glass terrariums or home greenhouses, however. Commercially available as unrooted cuttings, rooted cuttings, or established pot plants. Catalogs usually specify number of leaves

476

Nephthytis Green Gold.

per plant. *Kerchoveana* is probably the most common of the marantas . . . popularly known as the "prayer plant" because its leaves point down
toward the ground and fold up at night. Leaves are a pale, grayish-green with
prominent chocolate or dark green blotches. *Makoyana,* properly listed under
calathea, is a bushy plant with beautiful feathery designs on both sides of its
oval leaves. Colors are opaque olive-green lines and ovals in a field of pale
yellow-green. Leaves are purplish-red beneath.

Nephthytis Properly listed as *Syngonium,* nephthytis are climbers in
their native habitat. They are attractive plants in small sizes before they begin
to creep or climb. Older plants are used on poles. An excellent house plant
because it seems capable of withstanding no end of abuse. One of the common
troubles in growing nephthytis is that its leaf colors don't develop properly.
This is usually due to insufficient light and/or temperature. Nephthytis should
be grown in a 75° temperature and comparatively high light intensities. Propagated commonly by single-node stem cuttings. Commercially available as
rooted cuttings (catalogs usually specify number of leaves) or established pot
plants. Propagating vines are also available for those growers wishing to root
their own cuttings. *Emerald Gem* is the commonly grown, all-green variety,
with arrow-shaped leaves. This variety can be grown from seed which is highly
perishable, and thus available only at crop-harvest time. *Green Gold* has leaves
marked with whitish centers. *Imperial White* is a mutant of *Green Gold* and
improves its parent with better coloring and a more compact habit. *Imperial
White* is more bushy and doesn't begin to climb as quickly as other varieties.

Palm One of the more miniature palms represents its large family in the
decorative foliage-plant field. *Neantha bella* is a comparatively inexpensive

miniature palm tree, very attractive even in small sizes. Usually grown by specialists from seed. Approximately 5 months is required to produce a 2¼″ pot at 70°. Plants are available as seedlings in sizes measured by number of leaves (usually 2 or 3) or transplants that usually have 5 to 10 leaves. Also available as established pot plants.

Peperomia One of the outstanding exceptions to the "constant-water" rule. One of the main troubles encountered in growing these plants is a root or stem rot that is encouraged by overwatering. Allow soil to become moderately dry before watering. Propagation is by leaf, stem, or tip cuttings. The overwatering problem also extends to the propagating bench. Most specialists propagate peperomia cuttings in sharp sand because of the extra drainage thus afforded. Commercially available as unrooted tip cuttings, usually with 3 to 5 leaves, rooted cuttings, or established pot plants. *Obtusifolia* is the standard all-green kind. *Variegata,* a creamy-white variegated form of *Obtusifolia,* makes a most attractive pot plant even in small sizes. The amount of coloring in variegated peperomias varies considerably. Most specialist producers carry on a constant process of selection to improve their stock. In some cases, these selected plants are marketed under special names. *Emerald Ripple* is a sturdy and very useful little plant from Brazil. Leaves are heart-shaped and attractively rippled. Produces upright-flowering stalks of greenish-white flowers. Available as rooted cuttings or established pot plants.

Philodendron Undoubtedly our most important tropical decorative plant family. Grow at their best under typical tropical conditions as described earlier. However, most philodendrons are very tolerant of dry air and low light intensities found in most homes. Most philodendrons are strong climbers in their native habitat, which makes them ideally suited to totem-pole work.

There are over 100 kinds being grown today, and there are many more species, mutants, and hybrids that are making their way into the marketplace.

Cordatum is probably the most important single decorative foliage plant in the trade. Estimates run to a hundred million or more grown each year. They are propagated by rooting sections of stem with the roots coming from leaf axils. They are commercially available as propagating vines which are cut up and rooted; started eyes that are callused cuttings just beginning to root; rooted cuttings with 2–4 or 3–5 leaves each; or as established pot plants— sometimes with 2 or 3 plants in a pot. *Cordatum* is sold to retail customers in all sizes, from the familiar "rooted cuttings in a plastic pot" in dime stores to mature specimens on large totem poles, or in hanging baskets.

Hastatum is one of the many large-leafed, climbing species. Leaves are arrow-shaped. Propagation is by tip cuttings, rooting of stem sections, or by cutting up stems that throw aerial roots. Commercially, they are available most commonly as 3″ and 4″ pot plants, but also as rooted and unrooted cuttings. Very salable in smaller sizes.

Philodendron cordatum, *best known of this outstanding indoor plant family.
One of the most versatile and adaptable houseplants for interior design.*

Philodendron panduraeforme.

Propagated and available same as *hastatum, panduraeforme* has large, fiddle-shaped leaves. A good climber and a very durable houseplant. Propagated and available same as *hastatum, pertusum* is probably the most widely sold of the large-leafed philodendrons. It is a fast climber for totem-pole work. Its first leaves are almost solid, but as the plant develops, "character leaves" with typical indentations begin to develop. *Monstera deliciosa* is a *pertusum* plant that has grown to maturity with deeply cut leaves. *Selloum* is one of the best arborescent or "tree-like" philodendrons, which means it is not a climber. These nonclimbing types make large plants, suitable only for large, roomy locations. Leaves are deeply lobed and cut. *Selloum* likes higher light intensities and slightly cooler temperatures than most other philodendrons.

Some of the new hybrids that have already proven they are excellent houseplants are *Emerald Queen, Red Emerald,* and *Florida. Emerald Queen* is a bright green with arrow-shaped leaves. *Red Emerald* is similar in shape and growth, but has darker green leaves with red stems and petioles. *Florida* has anchor-shaped leaves with red petioles.

Red Princess is a new patented hybrid that is outstanding as a keeper in the home. It has heart-shaped, undulating leaves of medium size with red stems and petioles.

All of the varieties listed above with the exception of *pertusum* and *selloum* can be used in dish gardens and small planters, if grown from single-eye cuttings. The cane of an overgrown plant can be cut up: Use about 2 inches of cane with a leaf attached, and plunge in peat with 70° temperature. In 10 to 12 weeks, one has a compact rooted cutting that makes an excellent small pot or dish-garden plant.

Pothos aureus   Sometimes listed as *Scindapsus aureus.* A very satisfactory and easily grown climber. Similar in general habit and growing to philodendron *cordatum,* but somewhat coarser in form. Sometimes, Northern growers have trouble establishing rooted cuttings received from Florida during the winter. Maintaining high humidity and watering with warm water will help. During the first week or two, rooted cuttings should be watered sparingly until new roots are established. Cold drafts during these first few days should be avoided. Sold extensively, both as small potted plants and in more mature forms on totem poles. A "giant-leaf" offering of *pothos* means that the plant has been held until the leaves are large—6" to 8"—as compared to the normal 2" or 3". In its native habitat in the Solomon Islands, *pothos* leaves are 2' or more wide. Commercially available as propagating vines for growers who root their own cuttings. Vines should be cut up into "eye" sections and rooted. Be careful to keep the leaf axil or leaf stem of each eye above the soil or sand level. Also available as rooted cuttings, unrooted cuttings, or established pot plants. Started eyes are callused cuttings that have just started to root; they are a particularly good buy for large growers. *Wilcoxi* or *Golden* have leaves marked with yellow blotches or streaks. *Marble Queen, Orange Queen,* and

Pothos aureas, *Devil's Ivy.*

Silver Marble are marked with white instead of yellow. Specialists are constantly selecting their stock for better colored markings and some improved strains are marketed under special names.

   Sansevieria   One of our most common and durable houseplants. Will stand almost no end of abuse *except* (1) overwatering, or (2) sudden chilling. Should be grown a bit on the dry side, and this is particularly true under home conditions. There are a dozen or more attractive species and varieties. The most common fall into three main headings. *Zeylonica* is the one with light green to grayish-white cross-bands on its leaves. Normally propagated by root (rhizome) divisions or by cutting leaves into 2" or 3" sections and rooting them as cuttings. *Laurentii* has yellow bands across its leaves. In order to maintain its yellow markings, *Laurentii* must be propagated by root (rhizome) divisions. Leaf cuttings as outlined for *Zeylonica* will revert back to the green-and-white *Zeylonica* coloring. Both this and *Zeylonica* are commercially available in grades expressed by the length of leaves. The normal range is from 4" to 6" to 18" to 24". These are bare-root plants. These grades are available in plants having 2 leaves, 2 to 4 leaves, or 3 to 5 leaves. Also available as established pot plants. Miniature plants are very small and suitable for small dish-garden planting. *Hahni,* the third type, is a comparatively small plant, growing only

481

in a rosette form with no long, sword-like leaves such as has *Zeylonica* or *Laurentii. Hahni* is a sport of *Laurentii* and has light green cross bands on its leaves. *Silver Hahni*, a sport of *Hahni*, has leaves almost entirely pale, silvery-green. *Golden Hahni*, another sport of *Hahni*, has broad cream-to-golden-yellow bands across its leaves. The *Hahni* types are commercially available as bare-root plants listed as small, medium, or large, and also as established pot plants.

Schefflera actinophylla   Attractive, fast-growing plants, and salable in either small or large sizes. Large, compound leaves with 6 to 9 leaflets. Usually propagated from seed. Available either as seedlings, transplants, or established pot plants.

FREESIAS*

Freesia, a native of South Africa, is a colorful, fragrant, high-yielding commercial cut flower crop with good keeping quality and suitable for low temperature forcing. In the Netherlands it is the fourth most valuable cut flower crop and second only to carnations in the number of cut stems sold. Freesias can produce 300–400 cut flower stems per square meter (10.56 sq. ft.).

There are 19 naturally occurring species of which *Freesia refracta* is the primary forcing species. In its native habitat, freesia sprouts in the warm autumn and flowers during the cool (8–10°C) (40–50°F) moist winters. Temperatures below 15.5°C (60°F) are necessary for floral initiation. The corms go through a dormancy period during the hot (31°C) (88°F), dry summer months. This hot treatment is required for "ripening" or breaking of dormancy.

Freesias can be grown from either corms or seeds. Seed-raised freesias require 7–8 months from seed to flowering; corms require about 5 months from planting to flowering. While corms traditionally are planted from September through October for flowering in January through April, they can be flowered at any time provided proper temperatures are maintained. Continuous

*Contributed by Terry Gilbertson-Ferriss and H. F. Wilkins, Graduate Research Assistant and Professor, respectively, Department of Horticulture, University of Minnesota.

planting every 7–10 days can help stagger flower production; however, proper growing temperatures must be maintained. Plant the corm with the apex slightly above the soil line. Maintain temperatures above 15.5°C (60°F) until 3–4 leaves are visible, then lower the temperature to continuous 13°C (55°F).

Freesia corms can be held over for the next year's production. After flowering, *gradually* withhold water and fertilizer. Generally the plants die down in 4–8 weeks. After digging, a storage temperature sequence of 13 weeks at 31°C (88°F) followed by 2–4 weeks at 13°C (55°F) should be followed. An inadequate heat treatment can cause pupation. When a corm pupates, a new corm is formed at the apex of the old corm, which prevents normal sprouting when planted. Currently some American growers are using the warm summer temperatures to "naturally" fulfill these requirements. At this time we believe freesia growers should consider definite, regulated storage temperature regimes for obtaining earliness and a more efficient timing schedule.

Phaseolus virus and freesia virus in freesia corms can decrease production. English growers have consequently started growing freesias from seed as the seed are virus free. University of Minnesota germination studies have shown 15°–18.5°C (60°–65°F) to be optimum for rapid, uniform germination. Drop seed on soil in flats or packs, cover with 3/4″ vermiculite and water. Keep seed evenly moist. Germination under a mist system works well. Seed will germinate in about 21 days. Four to five weeks after seeding, when seedlings are about 5–6 cm (2″ tall), transplant them into deep flats, pots, or benches for forcing. Grow at 21°C (70°F) or warmer and 18.5°C (65°F) nights until the plants have seven visible leaves, then lower the temperature to continuous 13°C (55°F) for floral initiation and flowering. Some European growers have grown freesias with night temperatures down to 7.5°C (45°F).

Production studies at the University of Minnesota have shown the highest yields and quality to come from April and May seedlings which flowered from late December through early February. June, July, and August seedlings flowered from January through early April with slightly lower but still acceptable quality. May and June seedlings can be grown for a Valentine's crop. Timing freesia crops is very temperature dependent. Warm autumn weather may delay flowering if 13°C (55°F) greenhouse temperatures cannot be maintained. Grow freesias under normal photoperiods since photoperiodic manipulations are not commercially beneficial.

We do not recommend the use of superphosphate or treblesuperphosphate in soil for freesia production. University of Minnesota experiments have confirmed that these materials cause tip burn on freesia leaves. Symptoms suggest the fluoride contaminants in superphosphate and treblesuperphosphate were the cause of tip burn. This was shown to be the cause of tip burn in gladiolus, which is closely related to freesia.

At this time of high fuel costs, energy conservation, and consumer interest for "something new," we believe freesia has great commercial potential.

A Grower's Experience

Tod Bachman, Minneapolis retail grower, comments that the corms will produce flowers in several months less time than seed. Here is his schedule in brief:

Freesia production schedule—from seed and corms*

- June 10: *Seed Date*
- July 20: *Transplant Seedling*
- October 5: *Plant Corms*
- February 10: *Plants in Flower*

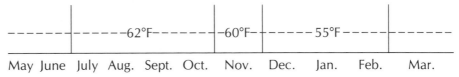

May June July Aug. Sept. Oct. Nov. Dec. Jan. Feb. Mar.

*We recommend corms because you save 4 months of time. Corms are readily available from suppliers.

FUCHSIA

ANNUAL *(F. hybrida) 20,000 seeds per oz. Germinates in 4–6 wks. at 65–75°.*

Largely propagated from tip cuttings, fuchsias are only occasionally grown from seed. These cool-temperature plants enjoy a rather light soil with some organic material. The trailing varieties are fittingly used in hanging baskets or porch boxes; and the more upright varieties are used for pot plants and bedding, but when summers are hot, they must have considerable protection from the sun. This gives them special value for use in boxes and baskets that are usually in at least partial shade. Tip cuttings that are 2" to 3" in length will root in two or three weeks. Once they are rooted they can be planted direct in pots or hanging baskets. Usually one cutting per pot is used. For hanging baskets use one plant in January, three plants in February, and five in March.

After six pairs of leaves have developed, pinch to leave four pairs of leaves. In order to produce stocky, well-branched plants, two or three pinches will be necessary. Allow 7 to 8 weeks from last pinch to sale.

The important fact to keep in mind when it comes to flowering fuchsias is that they are long-day plants and that they will flower when the daylength is more than 12 hours. A total of about 25 successive long days is required to assure flower development. Lighting with mum lights from 10 p.m. to 2 a.m. will do the job.

The more popular varieties include *Dollar Princess* and *Winston Church-ill*. Varieties especially suited for hanging baskets include *Marinka*, *Dark Eyes*, *Swingtime*, and *Southgate*. In a climate such as is enjoyed in California, they grow into fine, large specimens in the open and sometimes withstand some frost.

GAILLARDIA

PERENNIAL *(G. grandiflorum) 9,500 seeds per oz. Germinates in 20 days at 70–75°.*

There is an annual form of gaillardia, but the perennial is very much the better for cutting, and when well grown, is profitable for this purpose. They need plenty of water, and will suffer if they have to endure much hot, dry weather. Under Midwestern conditions, they rarely last more than two seasons, so must be treated as a biennial. By sowing seed early in February, strong plants can be planted out after hard frosts are over. Such a planting should flower some late in summer and be in heavy the following season. Plant in well-enriched, deep soil and space at least 12" in the row.

Of the available varieties or strains, the *Monarch* strain is largely called for and grown. However, it is really a large-flowered mixture of red and yellow in varying proportions. Another variety quite popular is *Goblin*. Fourteen inches tall, it produces abundant flowers of deep rich red with yellow borders.

GERANIUMS

The Cutting Geranium*

During the late 1950s and early 1960s, the commercial production of gera-niums declined because slow crop turnovers and major losses due to systemic diseases made the crop unprofitable to grow. Today, however, the situation has changed dramatically. In 1980, geranium sales totalled 42 million dollars, a 30% increase from 1976. The change is due to an increase in consumer demand for better performing flowering crops and an increase in the supply of clean plants for propagation.

As the popularity for bedding plants has increased, the consumer has been looking for plants that will grow and flower in all types of climate and soil conditions. The consumer also wants a plant that is relatively labor free, requiring little or no pinching, watering, fertilizing, or spraying. The geranium seems to have these qualifications. According to a recent BPI survey, cutting

*Contributed by Richard C. Oglevee, Oglevee Associates, Inc., Connellsville, PA.

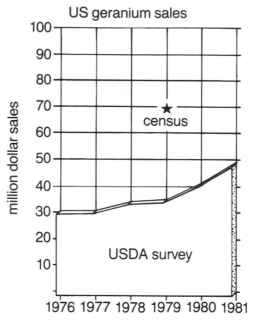

US geranium sales. The solid area is the USDA survey. The star posts the 1979 Department of Commerce sales totals.

geraniums account for approximately 10% of the total bedding plant production with the future potential looking very bright. At the same time the crop has become more profitable for the grower as turnovers and plant quality have been increased and crop losses minimized through the use of clean stock.

As the total market for geraniums grew, so did the variety of uses for geraniums. Previously, consumers usually purchased red geraniums for the cemetery to be planted on Memorial Day. Today, consumers want geraniums in a variety of colors, both flowers and foliage, that perform in either full sun or full shade. They also want varieties that suit large open gardens, planter boxes, window sills, and hanging baskets of various sizes. The increase in demand for geraniums along with the Culture-Virusing-Indexing (CVI) program, which includes breeding and selection, has resulted in a dramatic increase in the number of good, clean cultivars now available.

The ivy geraniums, for example, have greatly improved flowering ability, plant habit, and cultural adaptability. The ivies are ideally suited for a sheltered area of a garden, used as a bedding plant or in a hanging basket. For areas receiving high light and warmer temperatures, a group of ivy geraniums called the Alpine Series is recommended. There are also dwarf ivy geraniums available, such as *Sugar Baby*, that are well suited to small hanging baskets.

The Brocade Series, known as "fancy leaf" or "variegated-leaf" zonal geraniums, flower more freely and have more plant vigor, thanks to the CVI program. The grower now has a choice of plants such as *Wilhelm Langguth* or *Mrs. Parker*, that have green and white foliage and red or pink flowers. *Velma Cox* has multicolored leaves with a small salmon bloom. Other multicolored foliage varieties with different bloom colors are scheduled to appear on the market within the next two years. These newer varieties will have better vigor and improved blooming ability. These varieties should be as successful as the introduction of the green- and yellow-leafed variety, *Happy Thoughts*.

Recently, varieties have been bred with different regions of the country in mind. The Sunbelt Series™ are zonal varieties which have been bred by Dr. Griffith Buck of Iowa State University for outdoor performance in high light and high heat areas such as the South and the Midwest. The Glacier™ Series will finish well in low light areas that have cool night conditions. This Series is especially suited for the northwestern states such as Oregon and Washington.

Finally for the home there is the Regal geranium *(Pelargonium domesticum)*. This flowering plant, which has attracted many customers, has not always been finished reliably. Recommendations for precision finishing have been vague at best and more often than not, inaccurate. Moreover, Regal flowers were prone to heavy shattering. However, the Regals now available will bloom consistently on a timed schedule with less shattering. Varieties are being investigated and developed for use in the garden as well as indoors.

Culture indexing   The major crop losses, common 20 years ago, were due to various bacterial and fungal diseases—especially bacterial blight (Xanthomonas pelargonii) and Verticillium wilt (Verticillium albo-atrum)—that plug the conductive tissues and make the translocation of water and nutrients nearly impossible. Because there are no chemical protectants or cures for these diseases, once the crop is infected the disease cannot be eradicated. Hence the losses became a part of growing. Growing plants infected with these bacteria and fungi meant managing the disease instead of the plant, through low temperature, fertility, and water which in turn slowed crop turnovers.

With the advent of culture-indexing, these bacterial and fungal diseases have been controlled. Briefly, culture-indexed geraniums are the product of a laboratory procedure which allows trained personnel to visually check for the presence of systemic diseases, and select cuttings which do not have the diseases. To ensure that bacterial and fungal diseases do not escape detection, the indexing or testing procedure is repeated for three consecutive generations. The plant is then placed in a specialized greenhouse called the "nucleus house." As a further check, the nucleus stock is periodically culture-indexed, and no plants are held for longer than one year.

It should be noted that culture-indexing is a procedure that allows for the selection of those cuttings not infected and does not alter the genetic structure of the geranium. Therefore, culture-indexed plants have no change in their resistance or susceptibility to fungal or bacterial diseases. If any of these diseases are introduced during production, the plants will become infected. Indexed stock should never be mixed with nonindexed stock, and plants should not be held over from year to year. It is critical to realize that no matter how well a crop is managed, there is always the possibility of reinfection. If this happens, all the advantages of using culture-indexed stock will be lost. For the best results, growers must follow the strict sanitation procedures discussed below.

Before planting stock plants, the greenhouse should be clean and free from weeds, pests, and diseased plant material. If the house was used previously, the entire greenhouse should be sterilized. Steam sterilization should be used as a priority treatment. On items that cannot be steamed, chemicals such as a hospital disinfectant or commercial bleach should be used. Any debris such as dead plant material, especially under raised benches, should be removed.

All soil should be treated with either steam or chemicals. The chance of recontamination will be reduced if all the soil in a given greenhouse area is treated. The floors should be sterilized with a formaldehyde solution before dumping treated soil on them. Containers need to be new, steam-sterilized, or soaked in a disinfectant (1 hour soak in a 10% hospital disinfectant solution or ½ hour in a 10% Chlorox solution).

Ground or raised pot benches need to be steam-sterilized or chemically treated. Wooden benches can be sprayed or painted with a brand of copper naphthenate such as "Cuprinol." Creosote should never be used in the greenhouse due to its toxicity to plants.

Any tool or material that comes directly or indirectly in contact with the geraniums should be sterilized. Automatic watering systems and growing implements (i.e., shovels) should be soaked in a disinfectant as described above. All watering hoses should be soaked in a disinfectant. These hoses should be hung up so the nozzles never touch the ground. The use of knives in taking cuttings should be avoided. When knives must be used, keep several soaking in a disinfectant. The cutting knife should be changed every ten minutes for a "clean" knife that has been soaking in the disinfectant.

The "clean" geranium has given the grower the ability to manage the growth of the plant as opposed to managing the disease, which results in faster crop turnovers. No longer is it acceptable for a grower to lose 20% or more of a crop. A careful grower should not lose any geraniums. The use of culture-indexed plants in conjunction with advanced cultural practices has provided the industry with better performing plants that are more profitable to grow.

Virus problems—and answers With the fungal and bacterial diseases under control, it was apparent the next major limiting factor was viral diseases. Viral diseases are much different from bacterial and fungal diseases, due to the nature of viruses. Fungal and bacterial diseases are characterized by severe crop losses, but viral diseases usually affect the quality and the overall performance of the plant. Chlorotic spots and vein clearing may indicate the presence of virus, while other symptoms, not as obvious, are reduced plant vigor, fewer and smaller flower heads, stunting, poor plant habit and poor rooting. Unless a plant without virus is grown beside the plant with virus for comparison, these "symptoms" can go unnoticed. Plants may not show any of these symptoms and still carry a virus which may lead to further infection in the greenhouse.

As in the case of bacterial and fungal diseases, there are no chemical treatments to control or eliminate a virus. Virus can only be controlled using a systematic approach of heat treatment, meristem-tip culture and virus-indexing. Like culture-indexing, virus-indexing is a laboratory procedure to test for the presence of virus. Briefly, the process starts with a culture-indexed geranium which is heat-treated for three weeks at 100°F during a 16-hour day and 95°F during the night. This helps to reduce virus levels in the plant. The meristem-tip, a small 0.5–1.0 mm cutting, is removed and propagated in test tubes in the laboratory under sterile conditions. The resulting plant must then be virus-indexed or tested for the presence of specific viruses. Heat treatment and meristem-tip culture do *not* guarantee virus removal but only aid in removing virus.

The differences between virus-indexed material and material not indexed is dramatic. Plants are more vigorous and break more freely. They have more blooms because there are more florets per bloom and the bloom lasts longer. These plants tend to bloom sooner and are more uniform in blooming time, size, and overall quality. This increases the percentage of high quality plants which command a higher price and leads to faster crop turnovers. It all adds up to higher profits for the grower.

It is important to note that virus-indexed plants are not immune to virus. Again strict sanitation is an important step in preventing reinfection. Moreover, many viral diseases are transmitted by insects, such as aphids. It is extremely important to follow a preventative maintenance program for these pests.

As mentioned previously, these CVI geraniums have a tremendous built-in potential. Through sanitation and good growing techniques the grower can take advantage of this performance potential in stock production, propagation, and finishing. The rest of the article will show the grower how to optimize the factors of production.

Geranium stock production   There are many growers today who still find it profitable to propagate cuttings for their own use or for sale to other growers. Each grower must determine whether stock production and cutting propagation fit into his crop rotation. Although there are several factors which make geranium stock production more profitable, the key is to use "clean" geranium stock, preferably "culture-virus-indexed" material, in a sanitary environment. We do not wish to belabor these points, but even with excellent cultural practices, a stock program has a high probability of not only being unprofitable but also of failing completely at some point in time, if these two critical factors are ignored.

There are various methods that a grower can use to provide the necessary quantity of cuttings for a finished crop or for sale to other growers. The tree geranium has been receiving attention recently as a stock production method. The tree geranium utilizes the vertical area of the greenhouse and also allows the grower to store the cuttings on the stock plant, for the time when they are required. The entire plant can be used to produce various types of cuttings. Research at the University of Missouri has shown that 80 terminal cuttings plus other type cuttings can be harvested to produce 214 4″ geraniums from one stock plant. However, this method of production has proven to be costly due to the high labor intensity. Tree geraniums require staking, pruning, and cleaning on a weekly basis to permit light penetration to the lower part of the plant. Trialing this method of production is the only way for the grower to determine if this program is an economical way to produce geranium cuttings.

The grower can also choose from one of the many detailed buildup programs outlined in the Penn State Geranium Manual. These programs vary in the number of cuttings taken per plant with the time of year the cuttings are planted. Depending on the particular buildup program, the grower can finish other crops for holidays and still finish a geranium crop for spring. These programs usually involve planting the cuttings in a small container. However, the grower must pay very close attention to the irrigation and fertilization of the plant. The small volume of media has a reduced margin of error, which can quickly lead to fertility, soluble salts and/or pH problems, especially over an extended period of time. If one of these variables is out of line, production can be reduced.

Another method of producing geranium cuttings is the conventional stock production program in which the stock is planted in the summer in at least an 8″ pot. All of the programs mentioned require similar types of media, fertility regimes, and pest control procedures. The information provided in this article can be applied to any of the production methods, but the conventional stock production program will be addressed more specifically.

The most critical element for successful geranium production is light. Geraniums are high-light-requiring plants. Therefore, the more light they receive the greater the number and quality of the cuttings. The difference in annual cutting production between a June 1 planting and an August 1 planting has been estimated to be 30%. Knowing that light is a critical factor for geranium stock production, the grower should allocate the greenhouse area that allows the greatest amount of light to be transmitted to the stock plant. Generally, geranium stock should be grown under glass, due to its ability to transmit more light than other types of glazing materials.

Another important environmental factor in geranium production is carbon dioxide. Carbon dioxide, one of the elements required for photosynthesis in plants, is normally 300 ppm or 0.03% of the atmosphere. However, when the greenhouse is closed during the colder months of the year, the plants may deplete the supply of carbon dioxide. This lack of carbon dioxide is a limiting factor in plant growth on sunny days. Various studies have shown that enriching the greenhouse environment with carbon dioxide at levels of 1000–1500 ppm will develop a better branching plant and will improve the quality and the size of the cuttings. However, carbon dioxide enrichment also increases the leaf size, resulting in the shading of potential cuttings. This increased leaf size also

490

reduces airflow around the plants, which contributes to a higher incidence of botrytis blight (refer to section on botrytis). The larger leaves should be removed periodically to minimize these problems.

The key to a successful growing program is to minimize the variation throughout the growing cycle. Variation can be greatly reduced by standardizing the media and fertility programs. The media should be high in organic matter, preferably long-fibered sphagnum peat moss, for good drainage and aeration. Although mineral soil can be included, it should only account for a maximum of 25% of the media. The mineral soil acts to increase the buffering capacity of the media and provides a reservoir of trace elements. Pulverized limestone should be added to the media to raise the pH to the range of 6.0–6.5. Many growers use dolomitic limestone because it is a good source of magnesium and calcium. Magnesium, calcium and phosphorous should be added to the media, not only because geraniums respond well to these elements, but these elements are much cheaper in granular form than in a soluble form. Moreover, the pH can be adjusted and maintained more efficiently when these elements are mixed into the media, because magnesium and calcium dramatically raise media pH.

The selection of the media is an important part of growing productive plants, but the quantity of media used is equally as important. Choosing the best container involves an analysis comparing the added cost of a large container with more soil and the extra production gained by using the larger container. It is strongly recommended that the grower use a container larger than a 6" pot. The added soil in the larger container provides an excellent margin of error against changes in pH, fertilizer, and soluble salt levels. These larger amounts of soil require less frequent irrigations, which allows a grower to take care of a larger area. It is for these reasons that the larger container should easily pay for itself over the growing season.

Fertilizer program   The successful fertility program is one in which the grower makes *minor* adjustments over the growing cycle to maximize the growth of the plant and minimize the error. Large doses of fertilizer or excessive environmental changes to correct low fertility levels are as dangerous as the low fertility condition and can result in further damage to the plant. The key to successful fertility management is plant observation along with the use of monthly soil tests to determine media pH and salinity, and foliar analysis to determine the nutrient status of the plant. These tests will help to determine the various fertility trends in the media and the plant. Remember, these tools are excellent for the management of a successful fertility program but a poor solution for "fire-fighting" major fertility shortcomings.

It is important that the grower not only use these analyses but also use the same institution to ensure that comparable results are obtained. The institutions that conduct these soil and foliar analyses can use different laboratory procedures. This may lead to variability of results from one institution to another, even when the same soil or tissue sample is analyzed. It is important that the grower use one particular institution to ensure meaningful and comparable results. Knowing the particular shortcomings of the soil and foliar analyses will allow the grower to find the relationship between the test results and the growing crop.

Growing is not an exact science. There are many situations in growing when the observation and judgement skills of the grower are necessary to make a decision. For example, the plant appears to be growing vigorously, but the soil test indicates the nitrate levels are below the recommended levels. This requires a judgement by the grower to determine if there is a testing error or if a problem does, in fact, exist. This does not mean the grower should rely on observation to make a decision. The art of good growing is to quantify whenever possible, using all the tools at the grower's disposal to make an educated decision.

To obtain reliable soil and foliar analyses, close attention must be paid to the sampling method. To collect soil for testing, the top $\frac{1}{2}''$ of the media should be removed and a core sample should be obtained from the entire pot. Several core samples should be randomly taken from a bench until one quart of soil is obtained. The cores should be mixed thoroughly, dried, and sent to the laboratory. When collecting samples for foliar analysis, it is necessary to remember that nutrient levels vary with the age and the location of the leaves. The grower should select the tissue that has a representative balance of the nutrients. For geraniums, the leaves that are expanded to about the size of a fifty-cent piece, but not fully mature, should be used. Again, a random sample of a particular variety is required to ensure that valid results are obtained.

These two particular tests should be done in conjunction with each other to ensure that the proper diagnosis is made. Using only one of these tests may lead to an improper diagnosis of a particular problem. For example, through foliar analysis it is determined that a crop is deficient in iron. Without a soil test a grower might add iron to the media to correct the deficiency. However, a soil test for the crop may reveal adequate iron levels which are unavailable to be absorbed by the plant because of a high media pH. In this instance, the pH should be manipulated and not the iron level in the media.

Soluble salt levels are very important and should be checked regularly to ensure maximum plant growth. Soluble salts are the sum of all dissolved minerals in a soil or a solution. The total concentration of soluble salts in a solution can be estimated by measuring the electrical conductivity of the solution with an instrument called a "Solu Bridge." Under the proper irrigation practices the leachate solution should have a conductivity reading very close to that of the fertilizer solution. If the conductivity of the leachate is higher than the applied solution, the grower is probably not irrigating with enough solution each time. If the conductivity of the leachate is lower than the applied solution, the plants may be using the fertilizer faster than it is being applied. Various experimental work has shown that as soluble salts increase beyond a threshold level, plant growth for the geranium decreases. Certain geranium cultivars, such as *Sincerity*, are more tolerant of high soluble salt levels than others, such as the pink and ivy varieties. The grower should try to maintain total salts as low as possible without causing deficiency problems. To ensure that the proper soluble salt levels are maintained, the grower should follow the media and fertility recommendations and allow 15% of the fertilizer solution to pass through the container. If the soil test indicates the soluble salts are too high, the grower should leach the media (irrigate with clear water three times at one-hour intervals).

It is difficult to recommend a general fertility program suited for all growers. Fertility programs vary with environmental factors, media selection, availability of fertilizers, etc. However, a liquid fertilizer program using a solution of 250–350 ppm nitrogen would be a good beginning. The grower should use this solution for three out of every four irrigations, making sure there is a 15% leachate to control excessive soluble salts. A commercial 15–15–15 fertilizer, which has a lower potential acidity, can be used alone or alternated with a 20–20–20 fertilizer. However, it is important to monitor the pH levels closely because the triple 20 is more acidic than the triple 15. Magnesium sulphate (2 lbs./100 gal.) can be added on a bimonthly basis. Trace elements such as iron, copper, manganese, and boron should be monitored using soil and foliar analysis. For optimal nutrient levels, consult the laboratory conducting the soil and foliar analysis or the local extension agent.

Care of the crop   The optimal day temperature depends on the temperature that will economically maximize photosynthesis. On dull days, the optimum temperature is 65°F, while on sunny days it should be 68°–75°F. Night temperatures should vary with the amount of sunlight received during the day. It is during the night that the greatest amount of plant growth occurs because the sugar which was photosynthesized during the day is converted into energy and growth products. After a dull day, because there has been little photosynthetic activity in the plant and therefore little sugar to convert, night temperatures can be set to 55°–60°F. However, after a sunny day the night temperatures should be kept at 60°–62°F, to maximize plant growth.

In geranium stock production, the first week is critical to maximizing cutting potential. The stock will never recover to its full potential if injured in the first week. The stress on the plant can be minimized by watering three times the first day with a 15% leachate. This improves the root-soil contact, raises the relative humidity, lowers the temperature around the plant, and reduces water stress. The plants should be watered once a day for the next three days. By the seventh day, new white roots should be seen on top of the soil. If 8″ pots are used, white roots should be to the edge of at least 10% of the pots after seven days. Ten days after planting, the stock plants should be leached to reduce the soluble salt level.

Once the plant is established and checked for trueness to type, the plants must be shaped to maximize the number of breaks. The grower should aim for a stock plant that has a height of 8″ to 10″. This is done by taking the first cutting approximately one month after planting, leaving at least four leaf nodes behind. Four to six weeks later, the scaffold branches are pruned to leave two or more leaf nodes behind. From this time on, all available cuttings should be taken to allow more light to reach the breaks and thus promote cutting development.

Florel, a chemical which promotes more rapid development of axillary shoots, has been found to be effective in geranium stock production. The use of Florel can improve overall cutting production by causing more breaks to develop. A side benefit of Florel use is that it aborts flower buds, removing blooms for about 4–6 weeks, which can help in the control of botrytis. However, the results of the commercial use of Florel have been variable. The particular program a grower uses depends on many factors including geographic location, water quality, nutrition, climate, cultivar, and the frequency of the applications. It is because of these variables that each grower must design his or her own system for using Florel. Before using Florel on a large scale, it is suggested the grower consult the studies done by Cornell University and Ohio State University, and begin a trial using a very small block of plants.

Geranium stock plants should be spaced to maximize the amount of light the plant receives while maintaining good airflow through and around the plants. Good airflow reduces the relative humidity around the plants. This lower relative humidity helps to reduce the incidence of airborne diseases such as botrytis blight. There is an obvious tradeoff between spacing for cultural reasons and spacing for economic reasons. The stock can be spaced pot-to-pot in the early stages of plant growth, but must be spaced further apart when the plants reach the edge of their pots. Summer and fall plantings should be spaced at 1.3 plants per square foot, while winter stock plantings can be spaced at 2.0 plants per square foot.

Insects and diseases   There are several pest and disease problems that the grower must be aware of in order to manage the environment. Botrytis blight, a disease caused by an airborne fungus called botrytis cinerea, lives on aging tissue such as old leaves, blooms, and debris. Under the right environmental conditions, botrytis can attack and damage young, soft, succulent tissue. The fungus produces spores which are carried through the air, on splashing water, and on cuttings. Once on the tissue the spores will attack the plant if the conditions of high humidity and free water are found in the greenhouse. When the cutting stubs are infected, the disease can progress several inches down the previously healthy stem.

Botrytis is always present in the greenhouse environment. The best way to control botrytis is to make conditions less favorable for its growth and development. Flowers should be removed while in the bud stage. All dead and infected plants, parts, leaves, and blooms must be cleaned up and removed from around the plants and under the benches. This reduces the sources of infection and therefore the load of spores present in the greenhouse. Because botrytis spores require moisture to germinate, holding the relative humidity below dew point will reduce the number of infections. The relative humidity can be lowered by venting on dry days or venting while heating on very humid days. Weekly applications of Exotherm Termil, Daconil 2787, Chipco 26019, Ornalin, or Benlate are good preventative measures. However, Benlate should be used with caution; prolonged use of Benlate at recommended rates has been shown to inhibit the rooting of cuttings in certain cultivars such as *Pink Camelia*, *Pink Fiat*, and *Springtime Irene*.

Geraniums are attacked by a number of greenhouse pests. Pests which are particularly bothersome to geraniums include aphids, whiteflies, and spider mites. These pests are a problem because of the damage they cause and their potential to carry and reinfect plants with various bacterial, fungal, and viral pathogens. The most effective method to control insect damage is to follow a regular preventative maintenance program. Weeds must be controlled throughout the greenhouse because they serve as an ideal reservoir for spider mites and aphids. During the warmer months of the year the grower should also screen the side vents of the greenhouse to prevent the entry of insects such as aphids and whiteflies.

Aphids injure plants by piercing and sucking the sap from the plant, which causes the leaves to curl. This affects the appearance and the performance of the plant. Aphids are commonly found in groups on the stems and leaves. The female aphid is capable of producing 50 daughters, each maturing within a week under average conditions! Aphids can also introduce certain viruses to geraniums.

Whiteflies can be a problem on geraniums, particularly Regal geraniums. The adult whitefly is a tiny, white moth-like insect which can fly short distances in the greenhouse. The whitefly adults and nymphs feed by piercing and sucking on the underside of the plant's leaves. Damage due to whitefly can be in the form of a stunted and yellow plant. The whitefly completes one generation from egg to larvae to adult in about 30 days. Many recommended chemicals are aimed at only one phase of the insect's life cycle, and spraying schedules must be planned accordingly for effective control.

Two-spotted spider mites, nearly invisible to the naked eye, are persistent pests with geraniums. The adults and nymphs suck the sap from the plant, resulting in mottled, bleached-appearing foliage. If a plant is heavily infested, its photosynthetic rate is decreased, resulting in minimal new growth. Under average greenhouse conditions, the spider mite requires about 11 days to develop from egg to adult. As with whitefly, the recommended chemicals for spider mite attack only certain stages of the insect's life cycle. This must be taken into consideration when setting up spray schedules to control this pest. The varieties that are susceptible to spider mites include *Red Perfection*, *Cardinal*, and most of the ivy geraniums, especially *Sybil Holmes*.

Because chemical registration varies between states and countries, it is impossible to recommend a general spray program suited for growers across the United States and Canada. This information can be easily obtained from the local extension agent.

Another disease problem in geraniums is oedema (or edema). Oedema is a physiological problem caused by environmental conditions. On a cloudy day when the soil is warm and moist but the air is cool and moist, the plant will absorb water rapidly, but it will lose very little water through its leaves. The cells of the plant, especially on the undersides of the leaves, swell with the excess water and form blisters that eventually burst. These broken cells later harden and turn brown with a corky appearance. Generally, ivy geraniums and the *Irene* cultivars are particularly susceptible to oedema. Among the ivies, *Yale*, *Cornell*, *Beauty of Eastbourne*, and *Amethyst* are very susceptible to oedema. Cultivars such as *Double Lilac White*, *Sugar Baby*, and *Galilee* are the more resistant varieties. Although oedema is not caused by an insect, spider mite damage can resemble oedema. The grower must be careful in the identification of the problem.

In order to control oedema, there are several steps that must be followed. Soil pH should be 5.2–5.7 for zonals and 5.0–5.5 for ivies, and a peat-lite medium such as the one described previously must be used. High levels of nitrogen and iron must be maintained in this type of medium. The temperature during the day must be kept cooler, and the light levels should be held at less than 3,500 foot-candles. Proper irrigation is very important: Water plants only in the morning and remove all saucers from hanging baskets.

Propagation   The key to the successful propagation of geraniums is to use cuttings from healthy, well-grown stock plants. The old saying "garbage in, garbage out" is very appropriate. Poorly grown stock plants produce poor

The Jiffy-7—widely used for rooting geraniums both in Europe and the U.S. Here's a newly stuck cutting.

496

quality cuttings, which are difficult to root and propagate. These in turn produce a poor finished crop. Strict sanitation procedures mentioned in geranium stock production must follow through to propagation to prevent any reinfection.

The ideal cutting for propagation is a 2″ to 3″ terminal with a good active growing tip and no physical damage. Terminal cuttings are preferred because they finish two weeks earlier than the eye or heel cuttings. For disease control, cuttings should be broken off whenever possible. When breaking, it is important to break cuttings cleanly, leaving no jagged edges. When clean breaks are not possible and knives must be used, they should be soaked in a disinfectant and changed frequently. Before sticking the cuttings, the bottom inch of the cuttings should be cleaned. There should never be any petioles or stipules below the soil line, because this is a source of rot. Only those petioles and stipules which will be below the soil level need to be removed.

Some researchers recommend the use of rooting hormones while others point out that rooting hormones provide little value to cutting propagation. Rooting hormones are probably unnecessary on fast rooting varieties without fertility imbalances. However, if there is a fertility imbalance or if a slow rooting cultivar is being propagated, the rooting hormone seems to be of value. The use of rooting hormones, such as Indolebutyric Acid (IBA), have been shown to improve the uniformity of root development and to speed up the root initiation, especially on slow rooting cultivars such as *Pink Camelia*, *Wendy Ann*, and most of the ivy geraniums.

IBA can be applied by using commercial dust or solution. If the liquid form of IBA is used, care must be taken not to use more than a 0.10% solution or damage will result. A fungicide such as Benlate (10%) or Captan (7%) can be added to the rooting duster or solution to help control basal rots caused by various bacteria and fungi. There are unpublished reports that Captan has also been shown to increase rooting. Rooting mixtures should always be dusted or sprayed on to the basal end of the cuttings. For disease control purposes, *never* dip the cuttings into a powder or solution.

The fungi pythium and rhizoctonia are eliminated by proper sterilization. However, these fungi can be left in small cool pockets of the media if not properly sterilized. Treating cuttings with fungicides should give some protection from these and other fungi. Pythium can be controlled with a Truban drench (30% wettable powder 8 oz./100 gal.) Rhizoctonia can be controlled by using a Benlate drench (50% wettable powder 1 lb./100 gal.).

Media have three functions in propagation: (1) to hold the cuttings in place, (2) to retain moisture for the cuttings, and (3) to provide good drainage and aeration. There are various media from which a grower can choose, including peat-lite, peat-perlite or vermiculite (no soil), Jiffy-Pots, and Oasis Rootcubes. The media must be sterile to prevent the introduction of pathogens. Contrary to popular belief, peat has been found to contain bacteria and fungi and therefore must be sterilized. The propagation media should be watered thoroughly before the cuttings are stuck to protect them from drying. A prepunched 1″ hole in the media to support the cutting is imperative to reduce

497

damage to the cutting. The cutting will bruise if pushed directly into any media, regardless of how light the medium is.

There are two stages in the propagation of geranium cuttings: (1) root initiation and development, and (2) a growth stage. Both stages are important in development of high-quality cuttings, but root initiation and development is probably the most critical.

The objective of propagation is to quickly put roots on a cutting to relieve the dehydration of the cutting. When a cutting is taken, the natural water supply to the leaves from the roots is eliminated, but the leaves continue to lose water or transpire. The transpiration rate must be reduced to keep the cutting alive. This is usually accomplished by raising the relative humidity around the leaves or through the use of mist. The use of mist allows the grower to use soft, succulent cuttings, which root faster, but tend to lose water more rapidly, than hard cuttings.

Mist is an effective propagation tool which lowers the transpiration rate of the cuttings by raising the relative humidity around the leaves. Mist also lowers the leaf and air temperatures. The cooling is so effective that leaf temperature is often 10°–15° lower than air temperature. The net effect is that geraniums can be propagated under relatively high levels of light to increase the growth rate of the cutting. This higher light intensity increases the photosynthetic rate, ensuring that the cutting has the necessary carbohydrates for root initiation and development. A cutting propagated under heavy shade without mist may lack the food necessary for rapid growth because the cutting's respiration rate is higher than the photosynthetic rate.

The optimum mist program will depend on light, humidity, temperature, cultivar, and the cutting's age. Ideally, the grower should try to maintain a thin layer of moisture on the leaves during the day. During the night, the cutting should be misted periodically to relieve the water stress caused by evaporation. Care must be taken not to overmist as this may leach the nutrients from the foliage, especially after the cutting is rooted.

Another key factor to initiating root development is proper temperature control. The grower should provide bottom or soil heating, to maintain a soil temperature of 65°–70°F. Air temperature should be 70°F during the day with night temperatures maintained at 62°F. Air temperatures above or below these recommended levels will have a negative effect on the cutting's development. Air temperature above 75°F promotes bud development in advance of root development, which increases the transpiration rate. Air temperature below the recommended level lowers the cutting's growth rate.

Under ideal conditions and depending on the cultivar, a callus should form on the basal end of the cutting after 5 days. Roots should be developed within 10 to 14 days after sticking the cutting. At this stage, those cuttings for finishing should be placed in 4″ pots. Using lightly rooted cuttings will minimize transplant shock. More vegetative growth will be required if these cuttings are to be shipped.

The objective of the growth stage of propagation is to promote the development of vegetative growth. Cuttings at this stage are self-sufficient and should not require mist. Temperature is an important variable in the growth stage, and the temperature in the propagating area should remain above the temperature in the stock area. Day temperature should be at least 70°F, and recommended night temperature is 65°F or higher. These rooted cuttings should be spaced at 20–25 per square foot, and placed on a constant feed program of 200–300 ppm nitrogen. Carbon dioxide can be used to increase the vegetative growth of the cuttings. The growth stage should take approximately 3 weeks in order to prepare the cuttings for sale.

Fast cropping 4″ geraniums   To profitably finish geraniums, one must turn over as many geraniums as possible from a given area in the shortest time possible. The use of the culture-virus-indexed geranium with new fast cropping techniques has allowed the grower to finish a 4″ product in less than 6 weeks. Furthermore, breeding and selection have produced varieties that finish pot-to-pot, maximizing the utilization of the bench area. These pot-to-pot varieties in the red category include *Irene, Stadtbern, Improved Matador, Hildegaard, Glacier Crimson, Glacier Scarlet, Glacier Carmen,* and possibly *Yours Truly.* The pink cultivars that can be grown this way are *Pink Camelia, Didden's Improved Picardy, Cherry Blossom, Salmon Irene,* and *Veronica.* Of the fancy leaf cultivars (Brocade Series), *Wilhelm Langguth, Mrs. Parker,* and *Velma Cox* do well pot-to-pot, and so do many of the ivy geraniums.

The fast cropping technique involves the same media mix and pest management programs as geranium stock production. The medium must be tested and adjusted to proper pH, salts, and fertility levels before the crop is planted, because there is no time to adjust afterwards and still grow a good crop. A slightly higher fertility regime of 350 ppm nitrogen should be used at three out of every four irrigations. This higher fertility promotes more compact plant growth with short internodes and dark green foliage. High nitrogen and soft growth do *not* delay flowering of geraniums.

The plant should be pushed in order to maximize its potential. Plants should not be pinched because this delays flowering. Plant height can be regulated with Cycocel, A-Rest, or B-Nine. Cycocel is recommended over A-Rest and B-Nine because it provides more uniform results over a broad range of cultivars. Florel should *never* be used to manage the height of a finished crop because it aborts flower buds for 4–6 weeks, thus delaying the crop. Water should not be withheld to control plant height because this slows plant growth and lengthens finishing time.

Before spraying with Cycocel, be sure the geraniums are moist and are well fertilized to prevent plant damage. The geraniums should be sprayed on a cloudy, cool day or early in the morning. When spraying with Cycocel, a 1500 ppm solution should be used. This is equivalent to a 1:80 dilution. Do *not* use a spreader sticker with the Cycocel solution.

Cycocel should be applied 17–21 days after planting, when the axillary shoots are ¼" to ½" in length. At this time there should be approximately seven sets of leaves on the plant. The leaves should only be sprayed to glisten without any run-off. A 1500 ppm Cycocel spray of ¼ to ⅓ of a gallon should cover 100 square feet. If at the time of the application you see Cycocel running to the center of the leaf, the foliage can be syringed. This will reduce but not completely eliminate damage to the plant. If sprayed properly, yellowing may appear on the leaves in 7 days, but should disappear in 3 weeks, with the possible exception of one or two bottom leaves. If too much Cycocel was applied, or if the conditions were not right for spraying, yellowing of the leaves will appear in 3 to 4 days, with physical damage to the plant being the end result. The grower who is unfamiliar with using Cycocel, or wants to be cautious, can use a Cycocel spray of half strength (750 ppm) with two applications 7 days apart.

Some varieties may require two 1500 ppm applications of Cycocel to control plant height. The second application should be made 10 days after the first application. The following cultivars could be included: *Sincerity*, *Yours Truly*, *Irene*, *Toreador*, *Cardinal*, *Wendy Ann*, *Penny Irene*, *Rockford*, *Springfield Violet*, *Pascal*, and the Sunbelt varieties.

Gibberellic acid has been reported to increase flower size and life on geraniums. Treated blooms have been reported to last 7 to 10 days longer than blooms of nontreated plants. A grower wishing to try gibberellic acid should begin with a 1 to 2 ppm solution. Plants should be sprayed to glisten after two or three florets have opened. Because little work has been done with gibberellic acid, a small trial should be conducted before deciding to use the gibberellic acid on a large block of plants.

Ivy geraniums As previously mentioned, ivy geraniums require more attention than zonal geraniums with respect to oedema. This holds true for finishing as well, and the steps to prevent and control oedema must be followed in finishing. Zonal geraniums can receive up to 5000 foot-candles of light before the foliage and flowers start to burn. However, ivy geraniums must be grown in a greenhouse with only 2500 foot-candles of light. If the light is higher, the plants will be small with tiny, cupped leaves and small blooms and some burning. The grower may notice aborted buds and florets. This is due not so much to high light, but to high air and leaf temperatures. If the leaf and air temperatures could be kept below 80° F, the high light would not affect the ivy geraniums. Because leaf temperature is so important, ivy geraniums should never be hung close to the glass as this only multiplies the problem of high leaf temperature.

Ivy cultivars can be separated into three categories depending upon their light tolerance capacity. Those cultivars which must be grown under very low light of 2000–2500 foot-candles are *Sybil Holmes* and *Sugar Baby*. Other cultivars such as *Beauty of Eastbourne*, *Balcon Imperial*, *Double Lilac White* and *Balcon Royale* can be grown with 2500–3000 foot-candles of light. The third category is the most light tolerant and can be grown with light levels of 3000–3500 foot-candles. This category includes such cultivars as *Pascal, Galilee, Yale, Princess Balcon, Cornell, Amethyst,* and *King of Balcon.*

Hybrid or Seed Geraniums*

Geraniums of all kinds are seeing good times!

The USDA census figures show roughly a doubling of sales ($12 million to $25 million) from 1976 through 1981. Most of this probably was 4" *from cuttings.* The Department of Commerce census 1979 shows sales of *"bedding plant* geraniums" at $15 million—a major item. Impatiens, for comparison, total about $17 million. Probably most of this $15 million was from seed geraniums sold in packs and smaller 2½" to 3" pots. Some certainly in 4". This bedding geranium crop or seed crop, whichever you call it, is almost certainly expanding across North America. The two must total $40 million per year plus.

We have such poor census figures on our industry!

The fascinating point about all this is that both seed and cutting geraniums seem in recent years to be holding their own; in fact, both are expanding steadily. The quality 4" geranium trade generally wants a cutting geranium—they just look a lot nicer at the point of sale. The bedding grower, selling 18 or 24 smaller potted plants in a 21" flat, will usually grow from seed. Same for those who produce 3 or 4 plants in a pack.

Growers tell us three things about all this:

- Cuttings do make a lot more salable, showy plant in May.

- Seed plants outdoors (except in cool summer areas) will look a lot better by September–early October.

- So often I hear, "I make more money growing seed geraniums."

If we are seeing any trend at all, it might be a bit in favor of seed.

Surely the excellent work done by Oglevee on virus and disease control has been a major factor of cuttings. The ever troublesome xanthomonas pelargonni (bacterial blight) would be a disaster without Oglevee. It doesn't seem to appear much on seed crops.

Seed germination   Geraniums germinate promptly and easily if the media itself (not air temperature) is kept at 75° and uniformly moist. The germinating mix must be porous, screened, sterile, and free of excess salts.

Some cultivars may produce one "flush" of seedlings 7 to 10 days after sowing. Then a second flush may appear a week or so later. Simply remove

*Based on a story in *Grower Talks,* by Vic Ball, February, 1983.

and transplant seedlings as they are ready. Seedlings are fairly good size—better not aim for over 500 seedlings per 21″ flat.

Transplant stage   Most growers producing 4″ pot hybrid geraniums transplant seedlings first to a 1½″ to 2″ pot, or cell pack, or to a Jiffy-7. Recently, we're seeing well-established plug plants move directly to a 4″ pot—with good results. It's best if this plug is quite mature before going to the 4″. A very few growers do transplant bare root seedlings directly to a 4″ pot—or even direct seed to the pot. But far more of costly spring bench space is used that way.

Crops to be sold in packs or smaller pots (A-18, 18 pots per 21″ flat, etc.) are normally set directly into the final pot or pack—as seedlings.

Growing containers   We see hybrid (seed) geraniums offered for sale in a wide variety of containers:

1. 4″ pot market—will vary from 3″ to often 4½″ or even 6″ pots. All this depending on the grower's market. One eastern grower reported 25% more dollars per square foot using 3″ plastic pots joined together. He spaces freely, gets top price. Mainly they are grown in plastic—but occasionally in clay.

2. Packs/smaller pots—a wide variety of containers are used here. Some are grown in A-18s (18 3″ pots per 21″ flat). Some in A-24s, some A-32s. Many are done in cell packs, 8 packs of 4 plants each per flat. Some in open packs, 6 or 10 per flat, 4 or 6 plants per pack. Again, all depending on the market.

Soil mix   Again, a wide variety of mixes is used. Most common, and our recommendation, is 1-1-1 peat, perlite, and soil. Sterilized. Commercial mixes are widely used—actually the majority of growers probably go this way today, mainly to save labor. Good commercial mixes for geraniums would include Ball Choice. In using mixes with heavy bark content, be sure to start feeding as soon as plants are potted.

Peat lite, peat/vermiculite, such as the Cornell mix, will grow good geraniums, much used by research workers working with geraniums. Actually any mix that's open, porous, free of excess salts, and sterilized will do the job.

Feeding   Best practice is to start liquid feeding with all irrigations the day plants are potted from the seed flat. A 20-20-20 mix at 100 ppm is recommended.

Retardants   Mainly Cycocel, will mean shorter, more compact plants and often 7 to 10 days earlier flowering. Cycocel is very widely used by commercial growers and is certainly recommended.

Normal practice is one application at 1500 ppm 40 days after sowing. That should be a plant well established in the cell-pack or Jiffy-7, etc. 1500

Seed geraniums have become an important bedding plant! Here Bill Stoffregen, Raleigh, North Carolina, retail grower, shows his pack—that retails for $3.

ppm will mean 1¾ ounces Cycocel per gallon of water. Spray until leaves are wet. The second application should be made 1 to 2 weeks after the first. Many growers do—and depending on the crop, it, also, is recommended. Leaves will yellow for several weeks after application of Cycocel—but it goes away quickly.

Insects—diseases   No especially troublesome insect problems seem to appear. Most growers maintain a preventative program on all crops. An occasional grower will apply a fungicide drench after transplanting from 2¼"s to 4"s.

Supplemental light   HID light will hasten flowering on geraniums. Occasionally growers apply it to seed flats, in some cases, on up to the 2¼" stage. John Tomasovic, St. Louis grower, applies HID lights to his seedling flats of geraniums (see p. 505). He reports 10 days earlier flowering as a result. Jim Tsjuita, Guelph, Ontario, reports that 630 foot-candles from sowing to flowering will save 4 weeks time.

When to sow   Fortunately, there is ample data available to growers. Providing correct temperatures, light levels, etc., are maintained, a crop of hybrid geraniums should be easily timed for the grower's market demand. You may occasionally lose 3 to 5 days in case of an abnormally dark February or March.

503

The tables that follow are based on our own experience at West Chicago plus reports from growers everywhere and several university research projects, which also help bracket these critical dates. Of course, a grower's own experience under his own culture is the real key to accurate timing. If he keeps good records!

Table 1   RECOMMENDED SOWING DATES

The North—Chicago–New York Latitude

4" pots To flower*	Sow seed	Weeks sow-to-sell
April 15	Dec.13	17½
May 5	Jan. 6	17
May 25	Jan. 26	17
Packs or small pots†		
May 5‡	Jan. 20	15
May 15	Feb. 2	14½
June 1	Feb. 22	14

The South—Atlanta–Oklahoma City Latitude

4" pots*		
April 1	Dec. 6	16½
April 15	Dec. 24	16
May 5	Jan. 13	16
Packs or small pots†		
April 15‡	Jan. 7	14
May 1	Jan. 26	13½
May 15	Feb. 13	13

*"To flower" here means 75% of all plants showing a minimum of several open florets. Allow 1 to 2 weeks more to have a minimum of one fully open flower head per plant and second head well on the way—or showing color.
†For 2" to 3" pot size—or 4 plants per 5" to 6" open pack.
‡"To flower" here means about 25% of plants at least showing some color. Two Cycocel applications were used—one week apart.

Many growers today are relying on Florida-grown small 2" or so started plants of hybrid geraniums. It's a very fast turnover crop for the northern grower—at a time when space is so valuable. Typically, it will be 6 to 8 weeks from potting of these Florida-started plants to flowering a 4". And under especially favorable sunlight and growing conditions, as little as 5 to 6 weeks. The high sunlight in Florida does give them a great start. And now hybrid geraniums are available in small plugs. A ⅝" potted plant, a mature well-grown plug, will grow into a 4" in remarkably short order. Example: *Spark Plugs.*

504

Seed geraniums two different ways. The grower: Jack Tomasovic, St. Louis. Plant on the right was a 1" Florida plug, potted March 1. Plant on the left was Jack's own home-grown plug (with HID light), potted several weeks earlier. Florida plug plant flowered earlier than Jack's plug, even though it was planted later.

The Mast brothers, Jack on the left and Hank, Grand Rapids, Michigan, do about one million 4" seed geraniums a year. The crop comes up as Florida-started plugs, is out the door as 4" pots in flower in 5 weeks. Highly mechanized.

HYBRID GERANIUMS FOR PERFORMANCE IN PACK OR POT

	Red	Salmon	Pink/Rose	White	Bicolor
PACKS: 32, 36 OR 48 PER FLAT	Hollywood Red Smash Hit Red Ringo Scarlet	Hollywood Salmon Smash Hit Salmon Ringo Salmon	Smash Hit Rose Pink Ringo Rose	Hollywood Star Snowdon*	Razzmatazz* Ringo Dolly
PACKS: 18 OR 24 PER FLAT	Hollywood Red Smash Hit Red Ringo Scarlet	Hollywood Salmon Smash Hit Salmon Ringo Salmon Cameo	Smash Hit Rose Pink Ringo Rose	Hollywood Star Snowdon Ice Queen	Razzmatazz
4½-INCH POTS FOR A STRONG, FULL PLANT, GOOD HEADS	Hollywood Red Smash Hit Red Mustang Ringo Scarlet	Hollywood Salmon Smash Hit Salmon Cameo	Smash Hit Rose Pink	Hollywood Star Ice Queen	Razzmatazz
4-INCH POTS, GROWN TIGHT	Hollywood Red Smash Hit Red Ringo Scarlet Mustang	Hollywood Salmon Smash Hit Salmon Ringo Salmon Cameo	Smash Hit Rose Pink Ringo Rose	Hollywood Star Ice Queen	Razzmatazz
GREAT OUTDOOR PERFORMERS	Hollywood Red Smash Hit Red Red Express	Hollywood Salmon Smash Hit Salmon Cameo	Smash Hit Rose Pink Deep Rose Flash	Hollywood Star Ice Queen	Razzmatazz

One more point on timing: What are the peak demand weeks for 4″ geraniums?

1. In the North, most growers' peak shipping is mid-April to mid-May. Mother's Day is big. Growers aim to be sold out by May 30.

2. In the South, the peak is April 15 to 25 or April 30. And the goal is to be sold out by Mother's Day.

Varieties—which are best?   There are so many. But typical of these situations, it quickly boils down to two to three top-notch proven ones for each purpose.

A point: The major effort that had been made to improve hybrid geraniums by leaders the world over is a clue on what happens when breeders are given assurance of exclusive use of their winners. Which is the case in hybrid geraniums (being F_1 hybrids). In contrast, look at the restricted breeding effort and money being spent on such nonhybrid species as carnations, poinsettias, foliage plants (almost zero breeding to support our number one dollar crop)!

Back to "all the best" in hybrid geraniums. See Table 2 on varieties.

Petal shatter on hybrids   A vexing problem. The grower works for months to produce quality plants, then just as they are set out on a garden center display rack, petals start falling. Messy!

A spray has been developed in Holland, perfected at Michigan State University, which does control this shatter very well. Here are details from an Ohio State University publication.

506

Table 2 RECOMMENDED HYBRID GERANIUM VARIETIES

Variety	Color	Zoning	Multiple or single flower heads	Flower head size	Outdoor performance	Pack performance	Sow to flower in packs (# of weeks)	Pot performance	Sow to flower in pots (# of weeks)	Overall rating
Mustang	Strong Red	Good	Single	Medium	Excellent	Good	16	Excellent	17	A+
Red Elite	Strong Red	None	Multiple	Medium	Excellent	Excellent	14 to 15	Good	16 to 17	A+
Ringo Scarlet	Soft Red	Excellent	Multiple	Medium	Good	Excellent	15	Good	16	A+
Smash Hit Scarlet	Bright Red	Very Good	Multiple	Medium	Good	Excellent	15	Excellent	16	A+
Hollywood Red	Bright Red	Very Good	Multiple	Medium to Large	Good	Excellent	14 to 15	Good	16	A+
Ringo Salmon	Light Salmon	Good	Multiple	Medium to Small	Good to Fair	Excellent	15	Fair to Good	16	B
Smash Hit Salmon	Deep Salmon	Very Good	Multiple	Medium	Good	Excellent	15	Good	16	A
Hollywood Salmon	Deep Salmon	Very Good	Multiple	Medium to Large	Good	Excellent	14 to 15	Good	16	A+
Smash Hit Rose Pink	Deep Pink	Good	Multiple	Medium to Large	Very Good	Good	15	Very Good	16	A
Ringo Rose	Light Pink	Very Good	Multiple	Medium	Good	Good	15	Good	16	A

507

Table 2 *(continued)*

Variety	Color	Zoning	Multiple or single flower heads	Flower head size	Outdoor performance	Pack performance	Sow to flower in packs (# of weeks)	Pot performance	Sow to flower in pots (# of weeks)	Overall rating
Ice Queen	Pure White	None	Multiple	Medium to Large	Good	Good	15	Excellent	16	A
Hollywood White	Pure White	None	Multiple	Medium to Large	Good	Excellent	14	Good	15	A+
Smash Hit White	Pure White	None	Multiple	Medium	Good	Good	15	Excellent	16	A+
Hollywood Star	Rose & White	None	Multiple	Medium to Large	Good	Good	14	Very Good	15	A+
Razzma-tazz	Salmon Red & White	None	Multiple	Medium to Large	Good	Good	15	Very Good	16	A
Cameo	Deep Coral Salmon	None	Multiple	Medium to Large	Very Good	Good	15	Excellent	16	A+
Picasso	Violet Red (Purple)	None	Multiple	Medium to Large	Good	Good	16	Excellent	17	A

Ways to ease the problem:

1. If at all possible, ship plants out just as they show color. Shatter won't be a problem.

2. Be sure plants are watered before shipping. Avoid tight boxes, tight truck bodies. Ethylene builds up, aggravates petal drop.

3. During growing of the crop, provide ample ventilation. Somehow, plants from low, humid, poorly ventilated, dark houses shatter worst.

Guidelines for trial use of silver thiosulfate sprays to reduce seed geranium petal shattering and holiday cactus flower drop*†

Direct spray method

1. Weigh 380 milligrams silver nitrate and dissolve in 1 gallon distilled water.

2. Weigh 2.2 grams sodium thiosulfate (prismatic) and dissolve in a separate gallon of distilled water.

3. Pour the silver nitrate solution slowly into the sodium thiosulfate solution and stir rapidly to mix.

4. You will have 2 gallons of final spray solution. Spray 10 milliliters per plant. You will have enough solution to treat 750 plants.

5. *For seed geraniums:* Apply when florets just show color. No spreader/sticker should be used.

6. *For holiday cactus:* Repeat steps 1–3 above, but use 1.52 grams silver nitrate and 8.8 grams sodium thiosulfate instead. Apply at tight bud stage. Use a spreader/sticker.

7. Wear protective clothing and a respirator when applying solutions.

Concentrate method

1. Weigh 20 grams (¾ ounce) silver nitrate and dissolve in 1 pint distilled water.

2. Weigh 120 grams (4½ ounces) sodium thiosulfate (prismatic) and dissolve in a separate pint of distilled water.

*Willie Faber, Extension Floriculturist, Department of Horticulture, The Ohio State University.
†Note: Above guidelines were adapted from research at Michigan State University and the University of California. This compound is not a registered use product and, therefore, the Cooperative Extension Service of The Ohio State University cannot recommend its use. Responsibility of its use lies solely with the user.

3. Pour the silver nitrate solution slowly into the sodium thiosulfate solution and stir rapidly to mix.

4. This will give you 1 quart of stock solution.

5. *For seed geraniums:* Use 2 teaspoons (¹/₃ ounce) of this stock solution to one gallon of water for a direct spray solution. Spray 10 ml per plant, just as florets show color. This amount of stock solution will prepare 96 gallons of spray, which is enough to treat 36,000 plants.

6. *For holiday cactus:* Use 2 ounces of this stock solution to one gallon of water for a direct spray solution. Spray 10 ml per plant at tight bud stage. This amount of stock solution will prepare 16 gallons of spray which is enough to treat 6,000 plants.

GERBERA (Transvaal Daisy)*

ANNUAL *(G. jamesoni) 6,000–7,000 seeds per oz. Germinates in 10 days at 70–75°.*

Happipot gerbera *has become an important spring flowering pot plant. Sown in January, it will produce several flowers by mid-May. Colorful and highly salable. Many are grown from Florida-started plugs.*

*Contributed by Mike Behnke, pot plant grower, Wahneta, Florida.

Gerbera, already an important crop in Europe, is becoming popular in the United States as a potted plant indoors, in landscapes, and as a cut flower. It is among crops such as syngonium, spathiphyllum, and fern which have benefited so much from tissue culture in the last few years.

Cultivars are now bred for either pot or cut flower production. More recent introductions are improvements over older seed and vegetatively propagated varieties grown in the past. Most have better growth habit, stronger flower stems, and increased vase life along with enhanced productivity.

Gerbera may be categorized by flower form: singles, doubles, crested doubles, full-crested doubles, and quilled types. Of the American tissue culture varieties, some better selections for pots are *Friendship*, *Tropic Gold*, *Tropic Holiday*, *Tropic Breeze*, and *Tropic Princess*. A few Dutch types for pots are *Appleblossom*, *Peach*, *Rosemarie*, and *Snowball*. Top American cuts are *Tropic Tiger*, *Tropic Lady*, and other *Sunshine State* hybrids. *Fleur*, *Clementine*, *Veronica*, *Terramix*, *Marleen*, *Elfe*, and *Martinbijl* are a very small number of the Dutch varieties presently grown.

Breeding work in Holland is advancing at such a pace that lists of cultivars are quickly outdated. The five top European gerberas, for example, were not on the market five years ago.

Several good seed varieties are available: the *Jongenelen* strain, *Mardigras*, *Florist Strain*, *Parks Mix*, *Fantasia*, and *Happipot*. *Happipot* is the most significant development in seed varieties for pot production. Its numerous shorter flower stems and compact foliage make it ideal for smaller pots and for annual planting into flower beds.

Propagation

Although tissue culture has become the method of choice for propagating gerbera, both seed and divisions are used and each has its advantage. Plants from labs are often sold at what is called Stage III of their growth, e.g. rooted plantlets. They may come still in culture jars or in plastic bags. If the plants are shipped in jars, the agar medium must be thoroughly washed away with water. They are immediately planted into cell-packs, 2¼" (5.6 cm) pots or Jiffy-Strips. Soil should be clean and well drained. Several of the soilless plug mixes do a good job and are easy to handle. After transplanting, plantlets are put under 50% shade with intermittent mist and drenched with Banrot, Truban plus Benlate, or Subdue plus Benlate. Mist cycles will depend on the stage of growth of plant material and individual conditions at each operation. Mist can be gradually reduced and most will be ready for planting in six weeks. Temperature is 77°F (25°C) during the day and minimum 60°F (15.6°C) at night. Feeding may begin at the rate of 100 ppm N and K in 2 to 3 weeks or when plants become established. Since tender new growth is easily burned, rinse soluble fertilizers from foliage.

A mix of 60% perlite and 40% peat is good for germinating gerbera. Approximately 1000 seeds may be broadcast in a 14" x 18" (35 cm x 45 cm) flat and covered with a thin layer of vermiculite. Bottom heat is used to maintain a soil temperature of 68°F (20°C). Direct sunlight ought to be avoided, and seeds must be kept moist at all times or germination is uneven. Emergence will be in 7 to 14 days. In about 4 weeks when two true leaves develop, seedlings are transplanted in cell-paks, 2¼" (5.6 cm) pots or Jiffy-Strips.

Division is a method of propagation that is still used. June is a good time to divide one- or two-year-old clumps so that size is reached for flowering in the fall. Each division should have two or more growing points. These are planted into beds or benches on 12" (30 cm) centers with crowns slightly above the soil.

Growers choose one method of propagation over another for various reasons. Tissue-cultured plants are generally free from disease and are uniform in color and growth habit. Seed, however, is easily stored for use at any time and can be less expensive. Plants from seed, though, are often variable in color and habit. Flowers from divided clumps are larger than those from tissue culture, but production is somewhat less.

Pot Production

When five true leaves have developed, liners are planted in a well-drained mix with a pH close to 6.5. Some research indicates that gerbera grows best in mixes with less than 20% bark. Crowns should not be buried. As heavy feeders, 200 ppm N and K at each watering will provide adequate nutrition. In some programs Osmocote 14-14-14 at 8 pounds per cubic yard is the only source of fertilizer. During warm weather in Florida, 14-14-14 releases too rapidly and slower 18-6-12 is used at the same rate.

Space requirements are dependent upon light quality and market demands. For the first month plants may be spaced pot-to-pot. Final spacing for 6" (15 cm) pots is typically 12" (30 cm). In northern areas 14" or 15" may be needed in winter. Final spacing for 4" (10 cm) pots can be as close as 7" (17.5 cm) apart for *Happipot*, to 10" (25 cm) for the larger varieties. A-Rest is helpful in situations where pots must be spaced tightly. A drench at the rate of 0.125 to 0.25 mg. a.i. per 6" (15 cm) pot no later than 2 to 4 weeks after transplant makes leaves greener and reduces flower stem and leaf petiole length.

Gerbera grows best under maximum light intensity. Northern greenhouses should not be shaded at all during fall, winter, and spring. Temperature is not as critical as with some other greenhouse crops. Day temperatures of 70° to 80°F (21.1° to 26.7°C) are optimum. For pot production most growers are holding night temperature near 60°F (15.6°C), but some in Florida run regularly at 48°F (8.9°C).

Production time from 2¼" (5.6 cm) liners to flower is approximately 10 weeks. Unless an entire bench is one uniform tissue-cultured color, gerbera will not bloom all at once. The first few flowers appear about 8 weeks after transplanting and the last plants begin blooming about 4 weeks later.

Cut Flower Production

Ground beds are usually between 2.5' to 3.5' (75 cm to 105 cm) wide. Either two or three rows are common with plants spaced on 10" (25 cm) or 12" (30 cm) centers. Growers generally mound beds or use side boards. Beds are replanted annually and should be amended with peat or other organic matter to improve fertilizer retention and water-holding capacity. Soil testing also is done, and if calcium, magnesium, or phosphorus are needed then dolomite or superphosphate is incorporated.

Raised benches are sometimes used, and several large growers are planting in two or three gallon nursery containers instead of beds. Yield is slightly less, but containers help isolate soil-borne fungus that can be very damaging. Unthrifty plants may be immediately replaced, and at the end of the season the plants are sold for landscape use.

Trickle irrigation is the most common means of applying water and fertilizer. In Florida, beds receive two to three pounds of slow release 18-6-12 per 100 square feet along with an additional 100 to 200 ppm N and K at each watering. If supplemental soluble fertilizer cannot be applied, four or five pounds may be mixed into the first 6" of soil before transplanting. First bloom is 10 or 11 weeks after transplanting from 2¼" (5.6 cm) liners, somewhat more for northern locations.

Most Florida gerbera for cut flowers are grown in sawtooth or saran houses. In Florida these are usually unheated, but in-bench or bottom heat appears to be a trend of the future. As long as the soil remains warm, air temperature at night may be set 10°F (5.6°C) lower than normal. Northern growers, who seem to require higher night temperatures to keep plants active, set thermostats near 60°F (15.6°C).

For beds, average production of flower stems in a season is around 20 per square foot, but 25 to 30 is considered very good. Blooms are harvested by pulling sideways when the first row of outer staminate flowers show pollen. Early harvesting may result in wilting or closing at night. Preservatives are useful but flowers should be shipped as soon as possible. Do not store cold. Delivery upright in water prevents bending of flower stems, but most growers box and ship dry.

Pest Control

Pythium, fusarium, verticillium, phytophthora, and rhizoctonia are soil-borne diseases that cause serious losses. Beds and benches should be steamed or treated with methyl bromide prior to planting. Soil must be allowed to dry

513

somewhat between irrigations. Along with strict sanitation and clean stock, drainage is an absolute requirement. Some beds are mounded as much as 10" or 12" above walks. Field soils and ground beds are often ditched or tiled so that excess water can be moved away rapidly. Banrot, Truban, Benlate and Subdue® are all useful at times.

Foliar diseases are alternaria, phytophthora, botrytis and powdery mildew. Presence of these organisms suggests improper watering practices or inadequate ventilation. Daconil or Manzate are effective chemical controls.

Principal insects are leaf miner, mite, whitefly, and thrip. Pencap-M, Monitor, and Ambush are presently being used for serpentine leaf miner, the most difficult insect to control. Trigard, a promising new chemical, will be registered soon for leaf miner. Pentac and Kelthane are two effective miticides.

GEUM

PERENNIAL *(G. varieties) 7,000 seeds per oz. Germinates in 3 wks. at alt. 70–85°.*

Species and varieties of geum are quite widely used for decorative garden work in borders, beds and in the rock garden. They are of comparatively easy culture and most varieties flower from early May or June throughout the season. Their clear scarlet, orange and yellow shades are hard to beat in our common selection of summer-flowering decorative plants. The double varieties, like *Mrs. Bradshaw,* are suitable as cut-flower subjects.

For garden decorative work, geum should be spaced 20" apart and established in a fairly loose, well-drained location, although ample moisture is desirable during the summer-growing months. Partial shade is desirable for most varieties. Geum are perfectly winter-hardy if some protection is provided. Propagation can be effected by root division and several varieties, as noted, reproduce quite readily and with fair certainty from seed in a soil temperature of 70° to 85°.

There are over 50 species of geum described; most are native to our temperate and northern climates. Only a very few, however, are in common use. Most of the common taller garden varieties are, botanically speaking, varieties of *G. chiloense (G. atrosanguineum).* These varieties grow to about 2' tall. *Mrs. Bradshaw Imp.,* double fiery scarlet, is perhaps the most popular.

514

Gloxinia trials—Ball Seed Company. The gloxinia is a widely used spring, summer, and fall pot plant—always at its best at high temperature and high light. And so colorful!

Gloxinias *(Sinningia speciosa)* have increased in popularity to the extent that many growers consider them to be a major crop. The wide variety of colors and types include double and single varieties, standard solid colors that run predominately red, pink, deep purple lavender, or white as well as many shades of two-tones with white centers or white rims and a few new spotted types are now appearing.

Gloxinias can be grown from tubers or seed; however, tubers are only available in mid-winter so this limits their flowering period to the early spring months, whereas seedlings are available all year long. Gloxinias from seed are also much more economical, because the tubers are mostly imported from Belgium and have increased in cost in recent years. Most growers purchase gloxinias as seedlings from specialty growers instead of planting seed.

For those who wish to start with seed they must use much care and have a warm moist house with 65°–70°F nights. The seed is very fine, 800,000 seed per ounce, and should be planted in a light media with very little if any covering

*Contributed by Jack Sweet and Paul Cummiskey, Earl J. Small Growers, Inc., St. Petersburg, Florida.

over the seed. The tiny seed takes 2–3 weeks to germinate and will be ready for first transplanting in about 6 weeks. Second transplanting goes directly into 6" pots about 4 weeks later making total crop time from seed to spring flowering about 6 months.

Gloxinia seedlings in small pots can be purchased any week of the year from specialty growers and have proven to be a very profitable crop. Many growers raise them as a year-round crop without any special requirements. They do require a reasonable warm night temperature of 65°F with at least 75°F days to grow properly, but no night lighting, black shade, pinching, or disbudding is needed for normal growth.

There are several strains available such as fast-growing compact types for 4" to 5" pots, the regular gloxinia for 6" to 6½" pots and the double-flowered strains. Your trade can help you determine which is best for your own sales.

Seedlings purchased in small pots should be unpacked as soon as received and placed in trays in a warm greenhouse, watered lightly to help acclimate them, and potted when convenient in a few days. Do not leave gloxinia seedlings too long in a small pot as they become stunted rapidly and will flower prematurely with a much smaller plant and only a few buds. In fact any type of shock during the first few weeks after receiving gloxinia seedlings can produce stunted inferior plants that bloom early with only a few flowers. Too much fertilizer, high light, high temperature, or loss of root system causes premature flowering of gloxinias.

Starting with small gloxinia seedlings, the following procedures will produce good finished plants in 10 to 14 weeks depending on the season. They grow much faster in the long warm days of summer.

Potting

Plants should be potted deep, ¼" to ½" from crown of plant in a loose potting soil containing plenty of peat and some soil amendments such as perlite, vermiculite, calcine clay, or coarse sand for good aeration. Better grades of peat-lite mixes can also be used. Heavy soil mixes with poor aeration will result in poor root development and stunted foliage. Use a loose, well-balanced soil media that has plenty of peat and perlite for good aeration. Set the seedling well down into the soil to stabilize the plant, leaving only the four uppermost leaves above the level of soil. Gently tap the pot to level the soil but do not pack around the plant as gloxinias like a very loose open soil mix. Next, the plant should be watered in lightly with a good dual-purpose fungicide such as Banrot, Benlate and Dexon, or Benlate and Subdue. This will eliminate most disease problems that might show up much later in the crop.

Fertilizer

Gloxinias are moderate feeders and cannot use as much fertilizer as other flowering pots such as mums, poinsettias, or lilies. Excellent results can be had using weekly feedings with two pounds per 100 gallons of a 15-16-17 peat-lite formula alternated with plain calcium nitrate at the same strength. If desired, slow-release fertilizers such as Osmocote 14-14-14 may be incorporated in the potting soil but must be used at $1/4$ recommended strength. Be careful not to use any fertilizer with excessive amounts of phosphate or urea (ammonia) as gloxinias react poorly to both. Remember 20-20-20 has a very high amount of both and is not recommended.

Temperature

Greenhouse temperatures should range from 65°F nights to 75°F days for best results. In northern climates, tempered water is recommended for gloxinias. Water below 50°F can cause injury to foliage and root systems.

Light

Optimum light intensity for gloxinias is intermediate between African violets and pot mums—about 2,000 to 2,500 foot-candles. Excessive light above 3,000 foot-candles will cause yellow blotched foliage, hard growth, or small irregular light brown spots on leaves.

Height Control

To produce a choice gloxinia, B-Nine can be used 12–16 days after potting. This will shorten the main stem and leaf petioles—producing a sturdy well-shaped plant. The suggested rate on gloxinias is only $1/3$ that used on mums— approximately 0.10%. This can be made by dissolving B-Nine SP at the rate of 2 teaspoons per gallon of water. A second application may be used 7–10 days later for plants grown under low-light conditions—under 2,000 foot-candles.

Disease

Immediately after potting, a good fungicide drench should be applied. Use either Banrot at 8 oz. per 100 gallons of water, Benlate at 6 oz. plus Dexon

(Lesan) 6 oz. per 100 gallons of water, or Benlate at 6 oz. plus Subdue 2E (Ridomil) at 1½ oz. per 100 gallons of water. A second application may be applied 4 weeks later for complete disease control to last the entire production time.

CROP PRODUCTION TIME

WINTER—December through March	13–14 weeks
SPRING—April and May	12 weeks
SUMMER—June through September	10 weeks
FALL—October and November	11–12 weeks

For growing temperatures below 65° F add two weeks to the above schedules. Do not allow temperatures to fall below 60°F. Gloxinias are delayed by low day or night temperatures and dark overcast winter days. Auxiliary lights such as fluorescent or HID lights which produce 200 or more foot-candles at bench level used in the daylight periods and extended into the night (8:00 a.m. to 10:00 p.m.) will speed up winter growth by several weeks.

Insects

Spider or cyclamen mites can be controlled by Pentac, Vendex, or Kelthane. Cyclamen mites are usually too small to see but may be detected by discolored reddish brown center leaves that are stiff. Army worms or loopers can be controlled with Thuricide or Resmethrin aerosol. Thrips can attack the young growing tips or flower buds. First indication of thrips is usually some leaf injury. As the leaves start to grow they show elongated holes, slits in the leaves, or distorted edges. Later the stem and lower leaf petioles will show a definite brown discoloration that may extend to part of the underside of the leaves. Thrips can be controlled by using Lindane or Orthene.

GOMPHRENA (Globe Amaranth)

ANNUAL *(G. globosa) 5,500 seeds per oz. Germinates in 2 wks. at 70–75°. Dark.*

Easily grown and quite heat-resistant border annuals, the "everlasting" gomphrena clan is seen quite often, especially in the South and Midwest. Seed is sown in March, and the plants transplanted out to the border in late May. A fair check on drought resistance was a spell of 100° weather at our West Chicago trials, and gomphrena continued to look as well as even the vinca after such abuse. The dwarf variety, *Buddy*, a bright reddish-purple, growing to a height of 9″, makes a fine, dwarf, uniform plant for bedding.

To aid in germinating the seed, soak in water for 3 or 4 days, and then spread the wet, cottony seed mass over the top of the soil thinly.

The taller forms (18") are not nearly as widely used. They are usually sold as mixtures in shades of purple, white, pink, and red, and can be used for cutting and drying.

GYPSOPHILA (Baby's Breath)

PERENNIAL *(G. paniculata) 34,000 seeds per oz. Germinates in 10 days at 70°–80°.*

The hardy perennial form is of considerable commercial importance. It calls for completely drained and not over-enriched soil. The traditional method of grafting has been replaced by vegetative cuttings. Plants can be grown from seed, but the commercial cut type is seldom started this way. Most of the gypsophila crop is produced outdoors in Florida. The perennial varieties do best in rather gravelly or coarse material. The dry, calcareous soil of cool Colorado is where it seems to do best, though some eastern nurserymen make out very well with it. Good drainage is required along with a pH of 6.5 to 7.5.

Repens is a very compact grower with white or light pink flowers that make an excellent ground cover for sunny areas.

HANGING BASKETS—FOLIAGE

Foliage as a hanging basket crop has never been more popular than it is today. For a modern grower, baskets are one of the best ways to effectively maximize the usage of both space and heat in a greenhouse.

Today's most popular hanging basket foliage varieties:

Asparagus sprengeri	Asparagus Fern
Begonia sp.	Rex Begonia
	Iron Cross Begonia
	Angel Wing Begonia
Cacti and Succulents	Peanut Cactus
	Dogtail Cactus
	String of Pearls
	Jelly Beans
	Burro's Tail
Chlorophytum sp.	Spider Plant
	Variegated Spider Plant
Cissus rhombifolia	Grape Ivy
	"Ellen Danica"—Oak-leaf Ivy
Ficus repens	Creeping Fig

Three interesting ways to get a lot of hanging baskets in a little space.

Fittonia sp.	Nerve Plant
*Hedera helix	Needlepoint Ivy
	Manda's Crested Ivy
	Glacier Ivy
	Gold Dust Ivy
Hoya carnosa	Hindu Rope Plant
	Wax Plant
Maranta leuconeura	Prayer Plant
*Nephrolepis exaltata	Boston Fern
	Roosevelt
	Whitmanii
*Nephthytis podophyllum	Emerald Gem
(Synogonium)	White Butterfly
	Cream
*Philodendron oxycar-	Heartleaf
diam (cordatum)	
Pilea sp.	Scandens—Philodendron Peperomia
	Glabella—Wax privet
Plectranthus australis	Swedish Ivy
*Scindapsus aureus	Golden Pothos
	Marble Queen Pothos
Tolmiea menziesii	Piggyback Plant

*Top 5 in popularity.

Getting Started

With a few exceptions, most of these foliage plants can be self-propagated from cuttings, under mist. But because of the need to "turn" that space, most growers find it more profitable in the long run to buy starters from a specialist propagator. Rooted material can be purchased in many different forms, each more developed than the previous form.

Rooted cuttings Rooted cuttings are just what the name implies. They are the simplest form, and the cheapest, in which to buy basket material. Cuttings are usually bench or flat-rooted, pulled and shipped bare-root. Most propagators wrap several cuttings together in paper to retain as much moisture as possible around the roots during shipping. An extremely large number of rooted cuttings can be packed in a box, thus reducing the *per-cutting* freight charge.

Cell-pack foliage The biggest difference here is that the cell-pack cutting is shipped with a *root ball* instead of bare-root. This gives the buyer less damage during shipping, less transplant shock, a quicker takeoff, and a greater ease of

521

handling. Most propagators direct-stick into cells; most are using 96-, 72-, or 50-celled trays, depending on the variety. Though sometimes pulled from the trays and shipped alone, we mostly see the cuttings being shipped right in the trays for protection during shipping. Shipping charges are slightly higher than for bare-root cuttings.

Potted plants   Plants in pot sizes from 2¼" all the way up to 6" can be used as liner material for hanging baskets. The larger the pot, the shorter the time to finish. Pots are usually planted with several cuttings. Shipping charges for potted plants, especially the larger sizes, can be quite high and to some areas of the country may be prohibitive. You, as the grower, must weigh the quicker finish time versus higher plant and freight costs.

	ROOTED CUTTINGS		CELL-PACKS		3" POTS	
Baskets	Plants per pot	Weeks to finish	Plants per pot	Weeks to finish	Plants per pot	Weeks to finish
6"	3–5	8–10	2–3	4–6	2	4–6
8"	5–7	8–10	3–5	7–9	3	6–8
10"	7–9	10–12	5–7	9–11	5	6–8

Based on average Midwestern greenhouse. Add more plants for fuller appearance and/or faster finish.

HANGING BASKETS—FLOWER/VEGETABLE/HERB

Flowering hanging baskets are playing a more important role in greenhouse products. One great joy: They usually don't take precious spring bench space. One suggesion: Do them well. For a few weeks of additional growing time or some additional handling, considerably more profit can be realized. Here are some varieties and appropriate handlings.

Tuberous-rooted begonias   Very popular in hanging baskets with showy 2½" camellia-like flowers. *Non-Stops* are excellent for baskets. Recommended handling:

- Sow seed early December for mid-May flowering. Allow approximately 4 weeks in seedling flat. Shift to AC ⁴/₈ cell packs or A-18s and grow on until root system is well developed, approximately 14–15 weeks. Shift into baskets, putting 3 in an 8" or 5 in a 10" basket. Four weeks to finish in baskets at 60°.

- Obtain ⁵/₈" plug and shift immediately into AC ⁴/₈ or A-18 cell pack, grow on for 10–12 weeks and shift into 8" or 10" baskets. Finish in 4–6 weeks.

- Obtain 1½" or 2¼" plug and shift immediately into hanging baskets. Will finish in 12–15 weeks depending on size of plug.

522

Meet a hanging basket specialist. His name, Robert Mann. Location, just north of Atlanta, Georgia. Perhaps an acre—and most of the flower baskets here are grown from specialist plugs.

Browallia   One of the few classes where blue flowers can be obtained—beautiful habit in baskets and they love shady areas. Any of the Bell varieties perform well. Recommended handling:

- Sow seed mid-January for mid-May flowering. Allow 2–3 weeks in seedling flat. Shift to AC ⁴/₈ cell packs and grow on at 50–55°F for 6–8 weeks or until roots are well developed. Shift into baskets, 3–5 plants per 8″ and 5–7 plants per 10″ basket. Grow on 4–5 weeks or until baskets are full and in flower.

Coleus   Very colorful and easy to grow. Best varieties for baskets are *Wizard, Saber*, and *Poncho*. Recommended handling:

- Sow seed; allow 10–14 days in seed flat. Shift into AC ⁴/₈ or ⁶/₁₂ cell packs and grow on for approximately 6 weeks. Shift into baskets—5 plants per 8″ and 7 plants per 10″ basket. Finish in 4–6 weeks.

Fuchsia   A very important hanging basket item with an eye-catching beauty. *Swingtime* is the most popular variety. Recommended handling:

- Obtain rooted cuttings, cell packs, or 2¹/₂″ material. Shift to 4″ pots or plant directly to hanging baskets—use 1 plant per pot if purchased in

523

December or early January; 3 plants in February; and 5 or more plants for an early March planting. Fuchsias are long-day plants and will flower when daylength is greater than 12 hours. Once the plants have been established and start to grow, pinch back to fourth node to encourage the development of well-branched plants. If baskets are for late May sales, make the final pinch 7–8 weeks before the sale. If the plants are for Mother's Day (mid-May), allow 8–9 weeks from last pinch to sale.

- In order to develop full, showy plants, 2–3 pinches are needed. This will result in well-branched plants in full flower.

- Obtain dormant fuchsias—3" dormant fuchsias have 1–2 cuttings per pot with multiple branches. 4" dormant plants have 3 cuttings per pot with multiple branches. They are shipped bare-root with few or no leaves.

- Cut the bottom of soil ball for better initial growth or pull roots outward for better plant takeoff. Dormant fuchsias have "year-old wood," which produces earlier flowering plants. They flower 2–4 weeks earlier than rooted cuttings or cell-pack material. As a result, baskets can be in flower for mid-April in the North and earlier in the South.

- An initial shaping pinch when the plants are received is the only pinching necessary. After 3–4 weeks, another shaping pinch may be applied. Salable plants are ready 6–8 weeks after last pinch.

- One plant per 8" or 10" basket is recommended. Dormant plants are available December through February.

Gazania   Gazanias are very hardy, being both heat- and drought-tolerant. This makes them ideal for those areas on the patio where other items won't survive. *Sundance Series* is excellent for baskets. Recommended handling:

- Sow seed late January or early February to flower baskets in mid-May. Transplant seedlings 10–14 days after seeding into AC ⁴/₈ or ⁶/₁₂ cell packs. Grow on at 65°F night temperatures until well rooted, approximately 6–8 weeks. Shift to baskets using 5 per 8" and 7 per 10" basket.

Geraniums   Ivy-leafed geraniums have long been popular with gardeners. Now there are Ivy-zonal crosses and Alpine types that are very attractive for spring sales in baskets. Popular varieties are: *Yale, Double Lilac White, Sugar Baby, Cornell, Sybil Holmes, Gretchen* and the *Balcon* series. Recommended handling:

- Obtain rooted cuttings, usually planted direct. For Mother's Day sales in 10" baskets use 1 cutting planted December 1, and pinch when ready 'til mid-March; plant February 1, use 3 cuttings per basket and

524

pinch 2–3 times; plant March 1, use 5 cuttings and don't pinch. For late May sales, delay planting for 2 weeks. Pinch cuttings about 2–3 weeks later or after well established. Cycocel with 1500 ppm solution when new growth after the pinch is 1½–2" long. Extra dwarf varieties like *Sugar Daddy* do not need Cycocel.

Impatiens Tops all annuals in increasing popularity and usage. Excellent varieties such as *Showstopper*, *Blitz*, and the *Super Elfin Series* helped promote the use of impatiens in hanging baskets. Recommended handling:

- Sow seed in late January, early February, for mid-May flowering. Transplant when seedlings are large enough to be handled, approximately 3–4 weeks. Shift into AC ⁴⁄₈ or ⁶⁄₁₂ cell packs. Grow on 60°F night temperatures until plants are well established, approximately 6–8 weeks. Shift to baskets and finish in 4–5 weeks.

- Obtain plugs and transplant into cell packs. By obtaining plugs, crop time is shortened greatly. Baskets can be finished in 5–6 weeks from receipt. Careful growers are successfully transplanting plugs direct to the finish basket.

Petunias Although not as popular as they once were, petunias are still grown extensively in hanging baskets. Cascades are very popular as well as

Impatiens, perhaps next to petunias, are probably the favorite flower for baskets.

the newer varieties—*Flashes, Fulcons, Crockett's Victory White*, and *Summer Madness*.

Recommended handling:

- Sow seed late January–early February for mid-May bloom.

- The procedure is almost the reverse of pack or flat petunia culture. The objective is to keep plants growing with no checks to produce a soft growth. Sow seeds in well-drained soil. Transplant into cell packs and grow on at 65°F until plants are 8″ tall. Give them a soft pinch and move into final sales container. Put 5 into a 10″ basket.

- Reduce feed to once a week and continue to give adequate water and temperature to promote unchecked soft growth. Plants should start to "cascade" before selling.

Portulaca   Very colorful in hanging baskets. There are two types grown for baskets, the typical annual or grandiflora type and the oleracea type available from cuttings or seed. Recommended handling:

- When growing seed varieties, sow seed direct to finishing basket. Provide temperature to maintain 70° soil temperature. Grow on at 60–65° night temperatures. Baskets should be salable in 16 weeks from sowing.

- The oleracea type can be grown from cuttings or seed. If grown from cuttings, place 5 cuttings per 8″ and 7 cuttings per 10″ basket.

Poinsettias   Versatility is becoming very popular in producing poinsettias. Consumers are demanding something different and hanging baskets fit this need. Recommended handling:

- Obtain cuttings, callused or 2¼″ plants, in late August. Shift to 3″ pots and give plants a soft pinch around September 15. Grow on until mid- to late-October. Transplant into Belden hanging baskets, placing 6 plants around the side and 3 in the middle, no sooner than October 15. Grow on at 65° night temperatures. Plants will cascade down but will not turn back up if you have waited until after October 15 to pot into baskets. See poinsettia chapter for complete details on culture.

Ornamental peppers   Ornamental peppers are excellent for fall sales. Their brightly colored fruit and excellent habit make them very attractive in hanging baskets. They have long lasting qualities for the home. *Fireworks, Holiday Cheer* and *Red Missile* are excellent varieties in baskets. Recommended handling:

- Sow mid-May for fall color on fruit. Transplant seed approximately 3 weeks from sowing. Shift into cell packs and grow on for about 6 weeks. Shift to baskets and finish 10–13 weeks.

Thunbergia Thunbergia, or Black-Eyed Susan Vine, is very, very attractive in hanging baskets. The solid colors such as orange, white, or yellow with black eye are especially eye-catching. The Susie series from seed are the best varieties. Recommended handling:

- Sow seed, maintaining a good 70° soil temperature. Transplant into cell packs or small 2¼–3″ pots in 2–3 weeks. Grow on until roots are well established or approximately 5–6 weeks. Use 5 plants per 8″ basket or 7 in a 10″ basket. They will be salable in 3–4 weeks. Thunbergia grows well in partial shade or full sun.

Vinca (Periwinkle) Many new creeping or prostrate varieties of vinca make excellent hanging baskets. The new *Carpet* series spreads 24″ and flowers well all summer. Recommended handling:

- Sow seeds in flats allowing for warm 75°F soil temperature. Apply water sparingly as vinca likes it hot and dry. Transplant seedlings and maintain a minimum 60°F night temperature for at least the first 3–4 weeks.

Annual vinca makes a fine basket—and Pink Carpet *is a good new one. Photo: Pat Bellrose, Glencoe, Missouri.*

When plants are well established, shift to baskets, 5 plants to an 8″ and 7 plants to a 10″ basket. Sow seeds in January for May sales.

Strawberries Strawberries are not only used as an edible crop but are also very attractive and used for decorative purposes in hanging baskets. Dormant plants or seed-grown plants can be used for this purpose.

- When growing *Strawberry Sweetheart* from seed, sow seed on sterile media maintaining 65°F soil temperature. Seedlings should be up in 21–28 days. Transplant approximately 2 weeks after germination at the 3–4 true leaf stage. Grow in good light at 60°F night temperature. Four weeks after transplanting, plants can be kept cool for growing on but avoid subfreezing temperatures. Sow seed in early December for May sales. Use 5 plants per 8″ basket and 7 in a 10″. Plants with runners and fruit make a very acceptable basket.

- Obtain dormant plants and plant directly in finished basket. Put 9 plants in a 10″ basket. Plants will be filled out and fruited within 8 weeks for a salable basket. Obtain plants mid-March for mid-May sales.

Vegetables As garden size decreases and apartment dwellers need vegetables, varieties in hanging baskets are increasing in popularity. These vegetables are very easy to grow and extremely profitable.

- Cucumbers—*Bush Crop* and *Pot Luck* have excellent habits for hanging baskets. Sow seed directly in baskets, approximately 10 seeds per 10″ basket. Plants will be fruited and salable in 8–10 weeks from sowing.

- Tomatoes—Plants grown cool (58–62°F), with the minimum fertilization and moisture will be the most attractive. Sow seeds 10–12 weeks prior to selling season. Transplant to Jiffy-Pots or cell packs. Two weeks after transplanting, spray with Alar® to control height and darken foliage. Transplant with 3 plants to an 8″ or 10″ basket. *Florida Basket* is the best hanging basket variety available.

Herbs Sow both annual and perennial herbs in flats and transplant to cell packs or small pots. After 6–8 weeks of plant growth, transplant to baskets. Plant a substantial amount of plants to fill basket well. Grow on and finish in 3–4 weeks.

- Chives—Perform beautifully in baskets. Sow seed directly in baskets, maintaining 70°F soil temperature. Once seedlings are up, grow on at 60°F night greenhouse temperature. If plants get too tall, cut back halfway to promote dense, stocky plants.

528

Table 1   HANGING BASKETS FOR MID-MAY SALES—VARIETIES FROM SEED (Based on West Chicago Conditions)*

Class	Sow	Transplant to small pack or pot	Plant basket	Plants per 8"	Plants per 10"	Pinch	Growth retardant	Recommended varieties
T.R. Begonias	Dec.12	Jan. 15	Apr. 1	3	5	No	No	Non-Stop Series
Browallia	Jan. 15	Feb. 10	Mar. 23	3–5	5–7	No	No	Bell Series
Coleus	Jan. 15	Feb. 7	Mar. 20	5	7	Yes/Rainbows No/Others	No	Rainbows, Wizard, Saber, Ponchos
Gazania	Jan. 25	Feb. 12	Mar. 25	5	7	No	No	Sundance, Mini-star
Impatiens	Jan. 25	Feb. 15	Mar. 28	3	5	No	No	Super Elfin, Novette, Blitz, Showstopper,
Petunias	Jan. 20	Feb. 10	Mar. 23	3	5	Yes	No	Crockett's Victory White, Summer Madness, Cascades, Flashes, Fulcons
Thunbergia	Jan. 15	Feb. 15	Mar. 21	5	7	No	No	Susie Series
Vinca	Jan. 1	Jan. 22	Mar. 12	5	7	No	No	Carpet Series, Polka Dot
Strawberries	Dec. 5	Jan. 16	Feb. 14	5	7	No	No	Sweetheart
Cucumbers	Sow direct Mar. 21			Sow 8 seeds— Thin tc 5	Sow 10 seeds— Thin to 7	No	No	Pot Luck, Bush Crop
Chives	Sow direct Mar. 7			Sow 8 seeds— Thin tc 5	Sow 10 seeds— Thin to 7	Cut back	No	
Herbs:								
Annual	Mar. 7	Mar. 28	Apr. 25	5	7	If necessary	No	Dill, Marjoram, Mints, Rosemary, Thyme
Perennial	Feb. 22	Mar. 14	Apr. 11	5	7	If necessary	No	
Parsley	Feb. 15	Mar. 7	Apr. 1	5	7	No	No	Extra Triple Curled
Tomatoes	Feb. 22	Mar. 12	Apr. 5	3	3	No	Yes	Florida Basket

*For Southern growers: subtract 2–3 weeks from each date.

529

- Parsley—Sow in flats, cover seeds, and germinate at 80°F soil temperature. Transplant to packs or pots 3 weeks after germination. Grow on at 60°F night temperature. Plants salable in 12–15 weeks.

HIBISCUS—A POT PLANT*

For many years hibiscus has been popular in the homes of northern Europe, illustrating it can be acclimatized to the home environment. In recent years growers in the United States and Canada have slowly become interested in the hibiscus. This plant has become a specialty item in the North for home use as well as in the South, where it survives in the landscape under frost-free conditions. Regardless, this plant is tolerant to high temperatures and full sun in the South as well as being an excellent patio plant in the North.

The genus *Hibiscus*, a member of the *Malvaceae* family, has been so commonly grown in gardens that its site of origin is lost. However it is believed to have originated in China and Cochin China (Vietnam) and is extremely common in the East Indies as well. In China, some varieties have indeed been cultivated since the dawn of history as recorded in ancient art and writings. Women have used the sap from the flowers to color their hair black and the juice can also be used to stain shoes black.

There are about 250 species which are widely diffused geographically, but they are particularly abundant in the tropics. The name hibiscus probably derives from ibis, a bird that was believed to live off certain hibiscus plants. In fact, many species of hibiscus are naturalized in marshy localities where such birds abound.

We do not not know for sure how many varieties have been developed during the past centuries, or how many have been lost since *H. rosa-sinensis* was first introduced into Europe in 1731. This species is certainly the most beautiful of all the hibiscus and there are numerous magnificent hybrids, each more attractive than the next.

Hibiscus is a shrub whose leaves are a shiny dark green, can be variegated, and are usually simple and palmately veined. The flowers are mostly solitary in the leaf axils consisting of five petals with a bell-shaped calyx; the stamens are united into a tubular column which is frequently longer than the petals. The style usually has a five-branched stigma which can be quite proliferated and ornamental. The ovary is a five-celled structure with three or more seed per cell. Colors of the blossoms range from vivid red to white to various shades of yellow and orange. Flowers can be single or double. Contrary to the situation some years ago, single-flower types are common. Flowers last but a day; however, selections do exist whose flowers last somewhat longer. The

*Contributed by H. F. Wilkins and Don Kotecki, University of Minnesota. From University of Minnesota State Florist Bulletin, August 1982.

senior author was amazed to observe in Hawaii that flowers can be harvested in the morning, placed on a table, and they will remain turgid and open for 20 or so hours without water.

Propagation of hibiscus can be achieved by seed, cuttings, grafting, or layering. However, hybrids of *H. rosa-sinensis* must be propagated from cuttings because they do not come true from seed. Four to 5" cuttings with two or three leaves are taken from stock plants every 2 weeks. Karl Wikesjö states that in Sweden stock plants are grown in beds or in large containers for 5 to 7 years. In Florida, they are commonly placed in a medium of 50% Canadian peat/50% coarse perlite and placed under a mist. Wikesjö reports that rooting takes place in 35–40 days under milk white plastic tents in the summer or under clean plastic in the winter without mist. Little air is allowed under the tent until rooting commences; then, the center is opened 1 cm and afterwards gradually enlarged. Other literature shows maximum rooting was achieved in a sand/moss mixture (1:2 by volume).

No rooting hormone is required. However, rooting hormone hastens the process and may be desirable on some cultivars. Various concentrations have been recommended: 3,000 ppm IBA in talc or Hormodin #1. Bottom heat of 22°C to 24°C is beneficial and will speed rooting. Air temperatures for rooting and production are maintained at 13° to 16°C nights and 16° to 18°C days (minimum). A 20°C day is best, but do not go above 30°C days. Under these conditions, rooting takes 4 to 6 weeks and sometimes up to 2 months.

Cuttings can be stuck directly into small pots, Jiffy-7s, or a rooting bed. After rooting, cuttings can be transplanted, two or three cuttings per pot, in a well-drained and well-aerated medium consisting of loam, sand, and peat or similar media combinations. When cuttings are first stuck, a Banrot drench can be used. Dead leaves should be continuously removed. Captan can be dusted on plants every second week under the tents during rooting.

Production of hibiscus may be a profitable summer fill-in crop. With the economics of energy as they are, winter production could be questioned. However, with the rapidity of crop turnover when compared to other crops, this may not be true.

Growth and flowering time of *H. rosa-sinensis* is greatest in the summer. It has been established that flowering of *H. rosa-sinensis* is not photoperiodic. High light and long photoperiods result in maximum flowering. Professors von Hentig and Heimann have illustrated that the plants respond to high light conditions (100 to 150 w/m^2).

Nutrition: *H. rosa-sinensis* is considered to be a moderate feeder. Recommendations for nutrition have varied. If regular or treble superphosphate is used, frequently only the N and K supply must be of concern. Osmocote (17-7-12) and micromix can be incorporated into the medium. A pH of 6.0 to 6.5 should be maintained. Criley, working in 1:1 volcanic ash:wood shavings, incorporated 4 oz. Osmocote (14-14-14), 2 oz. treble superphosphate, and 6 oz. dolomite per cubic yard of medium. Plants were also fed two times daily with 200 ppm N & K. Never allow plants to dry.

Height of out-of-doors plants in China can be up to 30'. In Florida and California it seldom reaches 15'. Pinching in the greenhouse can be used to control the growth and shape of the hibiscus plant. Von Hentig and Heimann report that when new shoots reach 3 to 5 cm in length they should be pinched. As many pinches as deemed necessary to achieve the desired shape and form can be used.

In commerce for houseplant and patio specimens, growth regulators are commonly used. Sprays of CCC or chloromequat not only induce shorter plant internodes and darker green leaves, but also more flowers sooner during the summer months. Initial sprays are applied 2 or so weeks after plants are pinched and active growth has commenced. Shanks used single aqueous sprays of CCC (1000 to 4000 ppm active ingredient); Criley used 3000 ppm to control growth of hedges in Hawaii. However, an application of two to three individual sprays spaced 3 to 4 weeks apart have evolved as commercial recommendations. Criley recommends 75 ppm (0.016% active ingredient); Wikesjö recommends 95 to 140 ppm (0.02–0.03% active ingredient). The different levels could be relative between amount applied per plant, location (Hawaii vs. Sweden) and cultivars. Criley used 0.05% Tween-20 as a wetting agent. A-rest (ancymidol) has also been reported to retard growth on several cultivars.

Dwarfing of *Hibiscus rosa-sinensis* by the use of CCC has also been reported by Bhattacharjee et al., Bose et al., Hore and Bose. Bhattacharjee et al. report that a soil drench of CCC at 2500 and 5000 ppm suppressed growth on some 10 cultivars. With CCC drenches some cultivars produced fewer flowers, all produced larger flowers, and the effect persisted for over 360 days for most cultivars. Reduced flower numbers and persistent activity were also reported by Criley when drenches were used.

Common insects of hibiscus are red spider, aphid, and white fly. Temik, Pentac, and Plictran are used as preventatives. Olson used Temik and Pentac year-round, but during the summer he alternated Pentac with Plictran.

Applications of Captan, Benlate, Terrachlor, or Daconil can be used for any respective disease problems. A common disease is angular leaf spot. The best control for this is to keep a close watch over temperature, moisture, and humidity levels. Many times this disease cannot be controlled and infested plants should be discarded.

Hibiscus rosa-sinensis is very beautiful and useful as a garden, terrace, or balcony plant, or as a houseplant in the North or South. Cultivars reported to be used in greenhouse culture are: *Abricot, Brilliantissima, Cooperi, Double Red, Flamingo, Freidsdorf, Holiday, Kona, Lagos, Laterita, Miami, Moonlight, Odense, Weekend,* and *Yellow Koniger.*

Table 1 SCHEMATIC GROWING PROGRAM FOR HIBISCUS ROSA-SINENSIS (DIPLOID CULTIVARS TYPE, MOESIANA)
(WIKESJÖ 1981)

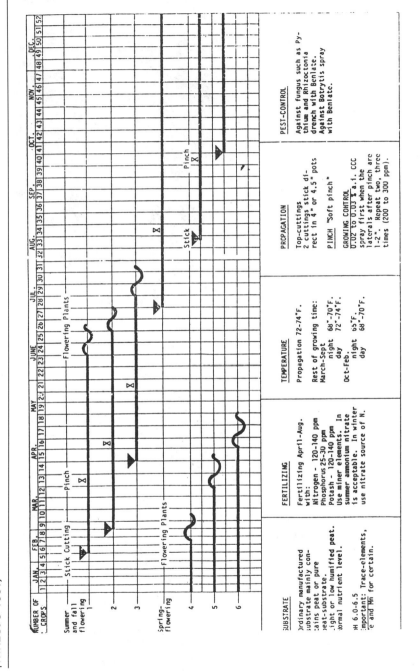

HOLLYHOCK

PERENNIAL *(Althea rosea) 3,000–6,000 seeds per oz. Germinates in 2–3 wks. at 60°.*

Ever popular hollyhock.

This old-fashioned garden favorite has been greatly improved and modernized with double flowers and an array of rich colors. They are usually sown in April, potted as soon as they can be handled, and either planted out or sold as pot plants. They can also be sown out in the open in May and if kept thoroughly cultivated, will grow into strong plants by fall. An early March sowing will usually flower some in following late summer. Hollyhocks are usually rather short-lived perennials, so must occasionally be replanted. This may not be true of old varieties, but we find it so of the finer strains. Under our trying winter conditions—temperature extremes and irregular snowfall—hollyhocks should be given the protection of any rough loose material. If growth is vigorous and free, as it will be in deep, well-drained soil, little will be noted of the rust that sometimes overwhelms them. When transplanting, care should be taken to see that the roots go straight down into the soil with the crown about 2 inches below the soil level. This will assist the plant in obtaining good anchorage and prevent wind damage. The double colors or varieties are by far the most popular and their color range is complete.

For years the only perennial double Hollyhock available has been *Chater's*, which is still widely used. *Powderpuffs* mixture is a large double-flowered strain that is more bushy and compact than *Chater's*.

Introduction

Native to Japan, the florist hydrangea, or pink-blue hyudrangea as it is sometimes called, belongs to the *Saxifrage* family and is known bontanically as *Hydrangea macrophylla* (Thunb.). Varieties designated as suitable for outdoor use may be bud hardy in zone 6, but greenhouse forcing varieties are usually bud hardy only into the lower part of zone 7. Outdoor plants grow vigorously even though winter-killed to the ground, and early budding varieties may still develop flowers by late summer.

The inflorescence of the hortensia types used for greenhouse forcing is a globular cyme with perfect flowers capable of forming seed only in the inner regions while the flowers making up the outer portions of the inflorescence are staminate. All flowers have a reduced corolla, but the staminate flowers have large petaloid sepals which make up the showy portion of the inflorescence. Thus, the hydrangea, like the poinsettia, has the capability of being a long-lasting, flowering plant as the showy parts are not petals which rapidly fade and fall. The outdoor types with flat cymes and staminate flowers only at the outer edge are known as lacecaps.

Hydrangeas growing out of doors make vegetative growth in July and August with the initiation of terminal flowers in September and October, after which the flower buds are in a resting state and resume growth after normal winter chilling and leaf shedding. Overwintering flower buds are usually in flower by late June. The usual method of greenhouse forcing simply mimics the natural sequence with propagation in May or June and the substitution of a controlled cold period of 6–8 weeks for winter chilling, followed by 12–14 weeks forcing in the greenhouse. The period of availability as blooming pot plants extends from early March to early May.

The resting flower bud of hydrangea contains six to eight sets of leaves for, being a deciduous plant, the flowering shoot must develop a new set of leaves by flowering time. A relatively long forcing period is thus required for the development of leaves and flowers. The hydrangea, unlike the lily, also requires a great deal of bench space in forcing so that the hydrangea becomes an expensive plant to produce. Hydrangea production has declined in recent years because of the inability of the greenhouse operator to sell the product at a profit. Table 1 (p. 536) illustrates this decline in the relative importance of the hydrangea in the U.S.

*Contributed by James B. Shanks, University of Maryland at College Park.

Table 1   HYDRANGEA FORCING IN THE U.S., 1959–1980

	1959[1]	1970[1]	1976[2]	1980[2]
Number of forcers	1,528	883	448	446
Number of pots	3,173,013	2,035,681	2,225,000	2,680,000
Sq. ft. in production	—	—	2,950,000	2,926,000
Wholesale value	$4,159,390	$3,795,393	$5,032,000	$6,842,000
Average value per pot	$1.31	$1.86	$2.26	$2.55
% value of 5 pot[3] crops	8.8%	4.6%	3.7%	3.4%

[1]U.S. Bureau of Census figures.
[2]Data for 28 selected states by USDA Crop Reporting Service.
[3]Data available included chrysanthemum, geranium, hydrangea, lily, and poinsettia.

On the positive side of hydrangea production, the plant fulfills a need for a very showy and long-lasting plant which can be accurately timed for a holiday market. There is need for variety in flowering pot plants, and a well-grown hydrangea fulfills the demand for a distinctive, high-class, flowering plant for all occasions.

Some means of improving the position of the hydrangea in the market would be:

1. Production of uniform quality in the greenhouse with consideration for lasting in the home.

2. Education and promotion of the hydrangea as a plant of distinction for which a price commensurate with the cost of production could be charged.

3. Reduction of the cost of production by research into means of streamlining growing procedures, reducing heat and space requirements, and perhaps extending the period of availability to other periods than the early spring months.

In our present period of specialization, fewer hydrangea growers are performing all phases of growth, and specialists are performing the separate operations of cutting production and propagation, summer growing and cold storage, and the greenhouse forcing of blooming plants.

Growth Characteristics and Cultural Requirements

Root media   Hydrangea growers have gradually changed to media containing little or no soil for many reasons including availability, uniformity, and ease of handling. In addition, watering is easier, a more vigorous root system

536

Standard hydrangea in 7" pot grown in equal parts of sludge compost, pine bark, and vermiculite.

is possible, and, where plenty of peat moss is included, the all-important water supply to the hydrangea plant is provided. Soil-less mixes contain little aluminum and maintaining pink sepals becomes easier.

Field soil, where used, should not constitute more than ⅓ of the total bulk of the medium with other ingredients being peat moss and perlite, vermiculite, pine bark, composted hardwood bark, etc. In a soil-less mix the medium should have at least ⅓ peat moss for moisture-holding capacity. With peat moss becoming scarcer, other forms of organic matter, particularly composted materials, can be substituted. Hydrangea growth in composted sewage sludge containing wood chips has been satisfactory; and a mixture of compost, pine bark, and vermiculite has given excellent results, both in summer growth and at forcing.

All media should have ground limestone added to attain pH 6.5, a source of slowly available minor elements, and a wetting agent. Media with composted sludge need no further addition of minor elements. Steaming or methyl bromide fumigation can eliminate weeds and pathogens. In the shift to a larger size pot at forcing, a soil-less mix containing peat moss or peat moss alone can be packed around the original soil ball.

Fertilization and color control Some understanding of the effects of fertilization on the color change in pink-blue hydrangeas is essential to good fertilization practice. The sepals of these hydrangeas contain a red anthocyanin pigment that becomes blue upon complexing with certain metals including

537

aluminum, which is abundant in most soils. The relative availability of aluminum is thus the principal factor in determining the color of the pink-blue florist hydrangea. Unless steps are taken to prevent aluminum uptake, the otherwise pink sepals gradually become blue; and unless enough aluminum is present to complex completely all the anthocyanin, an intermediate color will be produced instead of a clear blue color where the color change is desired. Intermediate colors are not attractive in most varieties.

Aluminum becomes more available to plant roots as soil acidity increases (pH values are lower), and liming to pH 6.5 is usually practiced in the production of pink hydrangeas and acidification to pH 5.5 for the production of blue flowers.

Phosphorus will also render soil aluminum unavailable, and high phosphorus and high nitrogen during flower development promote clear pink sepals; whereas lower phosphorus and nitrogen but an abundant supply of potassium promote clear blue sepals where the soil contains plenty of aluminum.

Growth of hydrangeas in both plant production and forcing requires a relatively high nitrogen ratio so that a 2-1-1 or 3-1-1 ratio is adequate. The object of summer growth is to provide a base for flower formation without excessive height, and a moderate program of fertilization with a 25-10-10 or similar analysis at 340 ppm of nitrogen each week or a biweekly application at 700 ppm nitrogen should suffice.

Plants are not fertilized in cold storage, but an application of 25-10-10 at 700 ppm should be made upon removal from storage. For the production of pink sepals this is continued at weekly intervals except that ammonium phosphate (either mono- or di-ammonium) at 700 ppm nitrogen is used on alternate weeks after flower buds are visible. Fertilization is reduced when sepals are in full color and plants are hardening.

In the production of blue flowering plants, it is best to make an application of aluminum sulphate in September at the rate of 15 pounds in 100 gallons of water. Fertilization for plants being forced for blue sepals is lighter than for pink sepals, and low phosphorus and high potassium levels should be used for the clearest blue color. Biweekly applications of 25-5-20 at 700 ppm should be adequate. Additional applications of aluminum sulphate made on several alternate weeks after flower buds are visible should assure complete bluing of the sepals. Additional applications may be required if the soil or water is alkaline.

Constant fertilization during the summer, and in forcing of plants for blue sepals, is done with 100 ppm nitrogen while constant fertilization in the forcing of pink sepals is done with 200 ppm nitrogen. Levels must be higher if clear water leaching is practiced. White varieties are best fertilized on the pink sepal program for best plant appearance.

Growth pattern and effects of environment With the longer nights and cooler temperatures of late summer and early fall, the vigorous summer growth becomes slower, and internode elongation gradually ceases with the formation of the large, terminal resting bud. The stem apex within the bud begins the formation of the branches of the cyme, upon which the first flowers formed are the inner perfect flowers followed by the formation of pistillate flowers. The buds may be in various stages of development as temperatures become too cold for further growth. While some development will take place during storage, such growth becomes very slow, and without internode elongation; we say that the flower buds are in a state of rest.

The resting stage gradually disappears as leaves are shed and the buds are subjected to a period of cold temperatures. This is followed by the ability of the buds to again make vigorous growth indicating that the resting stage is terminated. Development is rapid, internodes long, leaves large, and cymes and flowers become maximum size. The more completely rest is terminated, the faster the rate of development, the larger the growth, and the cooler the temperature at which growth will take place. Efficient hydrangea forcing is thus possible only if rest has been completely terminated. An additional 1 or 2 weeks of storage may be more advantageous in making an early flowering date than the early removal from storage.

Minimal storage requirements vary with plant maturity and natural exposure. In the Midwest, plants stored in September need 8 weeks of cold while by late October a 6-week storage may be adequate under constant temperature conditions. Under natural storage conditions of a shed, cold frame, or greenhouse where temperature fluctuates, the periods of time below the critical temperature are approximately additive, and a longer period is required for the accumulation of the 1000 to 1200 hours required.

The resting condition is alleviated by temperatures below 55°F, and for early forcing, a temperature of 52°F has been superior to colder temperatures. There will be bud development during the storage period and leaf abscission is more rapid at the warmer temperature. This is true only for a dark, controlled temperature storage. Any light reaching the plants stored in a greenhouse or cold frame situation will favor leaf retention and raise the bud temperature. In holding plants for late forcing, a colder temperature (to 35°F depending upon duration) is necessary to conserve plant strength and to prevent bud and stem elongation as rest is terminated.

All axillary or nonflowering terminal buds will be intensely vegetative following the termination of rest. The tendency to initiate flowers becomes stronger with the continuation of growth and passage of time. Unpinched shoots may initiate flowers in mid-summer and continue development to full bloom in August. Such shoots are lost for commercial use. In normal flowering procedures, all early propagated plants must be pinched and cuttings for single-stem plants must be taken from pinched shoots or from leaf-bud cuttings.

Continued pinching or the removal of cuttings helps maintain stock plants in a vegetative condition. By late summer, the use of low intensity (10 ft-c from 10:00 p.m.-2:00 a.m.) incandescent light will also aid in maintaining vegetative growth. Cuttings can be removed at 8-week intervals in late summer and fall whereas only 6 weeks may be required for a crop of cuttings following termination of rest. Stock plants have been maintained in a vegetative condition

539

Single-bloom plants given natural short days in a 60°F greenhouse to flower under continuous growing procedures. Left to right: Continuous long days from propagation or 4, 6, or 8 weeks of short days before returning to long days. Production time, 5 months.

for long periods of time with the use of all-night lighting and a temperature of 68–75°F, but cuttings must be removed or stems pinched every 8 weeks followed by an application of gibberellin at 25 ppm.

The flowering process is not only favored by aging, or growth after rest, but is also promoted by cool temperatures, particularly night temperatures between 50° and 65°F. Photoperiod also is involved in flower formation as long nights tend to promote flowering by the restriction of vegetative growth. The primary effect of long nights, however, would seem to be that of initiating terminal buds and inducing rest. Other requirements for the rapid induction of flowering are adequate sunlight for photosynthesis and adequate fertility. It is doubtful that a phosphorus level higher than that provided by normal fertilization practices promotes flowering.

A growing period of 2 weeks following propagation is usually adequate for establishment, but 4 weeks should be allowed for pinched plants before young plants are fully responsive to flower inductive conditions. A 6-week flower induction period is required early in the season, but as stock plants become further removed from rest a 4-week period will be adequate. By late summer a 4-week cool period coupled with the longer nights of September will assure complete flower initiation.

Plants are pinched from mid-June to early July to prevent excessive summer growth in normal plant production, and flower and inflorescence primordia are present in the Midwest by early October. If pinched in late May, the initiation of flowers will have taken place by early September.

Temperature, photoperiod, and forcing Photoperiod may affect rate of development and type of growth during forcing. Plants placed in cold storage early and forced under the long nights of November, December, and January, or which have not had an adequate storage period, will be benefited by a night break with 10 ft-c incandescent light. Additional light will have little effect on plants forced late in the season as these plants had a longer bud development and rest period.

The mistake of removing plants from cold storage too soon. The plant on the left was removed December 9; plant on the right removed December 23. Both forced at 62°F nights. At least 6 weeks of temperature below 50° are necessary to force hydrangeas efficiently.

There may be slightly greater promotion as the lighting period is increased to 8 hours or all-night lighting, but a light break from 10:00 p.m. to 2:00 a.m. appears to have near maximum promotion during forcing in increasing the rate of development, height, and flower size.

Hydrangeas force more rapidly at a warm temperature (plant on left), but stems and flowers will be small. The plant on the right, grown at a cool temperature, will be much taller and have larger flowers.

Flower buds are visible and the size of a pea 8 weeks before full bloom, the size of a nickel 6 weeks, and the size of a 50¢ piece 4 weeks before flowering at a temperature of 62°F.

A commercial crop grown in Vancouver, British Columbia. Excellent!

The temperature at forcing regulates not only the rate of development but the ultimate height, size of cyme, intensity of sepal color, and quality of the finished plant. Basically, the hydrangea is a cool temperature plant, making its best growth at night temperatures below 60°F, although the rate of development will be faster at a higher temperature. Night temperatures in the mid-50's will produce taller stems, larger leaves, and larger flower heads than plants growing at 62–65°F. Representative forcing periods at different night temperatures are 16 weeks at 54°, 12 weeks at 60°, and 10 weeks at 66°F. At a temperature of 60–62°F buds are visible 8 weeks before bloom, ¾" at 6 weeks, and ½" in diameter at 4 weeks before flowering.

Split-night temperatures have been proposed as a means of reducing the energy requirement by reducing the night temperature after the plants have had their most efficient growth, which with hydrangea is immediately following daylight and the production of food by photosynthesis. This reduction in temperature will also be during the period of lowest outside temperature. Some representative data for forcing at split-night temperatures for early varieties are shown in Table 2. Hydrangeas respond well to split-night temperatures, combining the features of maintaining a good rate of development with vigorous plant growth and production of large flower heads.

Table 2   FORCING HYDRANGEAS AT SPLIT-NIGHT TEMPERATURES (SUNNY DAY RISE PERMITTED TO 75°F)

Thermostat settings	Means ± standard error		
	Time to force	*Stem length*	*Inflorescence diameter*
	days	centimeters	centimeters
63°F	85 ± 0.6	20 ± 0.7	17 ± 0.3
63°F with 48°F from 2 a.m.–8 a.m.	85 ± 0.2	22 ± 0.7	18 ± 0.2
63°F with 48°F from 11 p.m.–8 a.m.	92 ± 0.6	22 ± 0.7	18 ± 0.3
63°F with 48°F from 8 p.m.–8 a.m.	95 ± 0.8	23 ± 0.7	17 ± 0.3

Varieties and sizes   Most hydrangea varieties have originated in the European countries of Germany, France, Belgium, and Switzerland. Some have retained their original names while others have been renamed by the introducers and are known by different names in the U.S. Only one currently popular variety, *Rose Supreme,* is of U.S. origin, although Merritt has recently concluded an intensive breeding program and is offering several new introductions.

The varieties currently most popular in the U.S. have quite large, distinctive flower heads or cymes which are usually grown as single flowers or with two to three flowering stems to the finished plants. Many newer varieties which branch freely but have smaller cymes are grown with five or more flowering stems per plant. We will refer to this latter type as "multiflowering" and to the former as "standard" hydrangeas. Multiflowering hydrangeas are more popular in Europe and to some extent in Canada. They offer some advantages in handling and shipping.

The plant characteristics of branching, stem length, size of flower head, and most especially the time required to force depend upon climate and culture, so it is difficult to characterize varieties accurately.

Multiflowering plant in 8" pot.

Single-bloom plants typically have larger flowers than plants of the same variety grown with two, three, or more inflorescences. Usually, only those varieties capable of producing large flower heads are used for single-bloom culture. Single-bloom plants are becoming more popular as they are easily produced, take less space at forcing, and are more suitable for merchandising. They possibly could represent the most profitable hydrangea of the future. On the other hand, the two- or three-bloom standard plants, and the multiflowering plants, should be grown for the better trade with the emphasis on top quality and top price.

Early varieties are expected to force in 12 weeks, mid-season varieties in 13 weeks, and late varieties should force in 14 weeks under usual forcing conditions. Sepal colors are always more intense when forced at a cooler temperature. In the interest of plant quality, water relations, and lasting in the home, it is suggested that the following schedule of pot sizes be adopted for finishing plants in forcing.

No. blooms	Rose supreme	Standard varieties	Multiflowering plants
1	6"	5½"	—
2	7"	6"	5½"
3–4	8"	7"	6"
5	—	—	7"
7 or more	—	—	8"

544

Varieties

The following varieties are listed approximately in their relative order of importance.

- *Merritts Supreme:* The most popular variety in North America. Can be forced for deep pink or blue sepal color. Has medium-size flower heads borne on medium-height plants which branch freely. Early in flower initiation and early in forcing, it is forced in both northern and southern areas.

- *Rose Supreme:* Pleasing clear, light pink, or light blue sepal color. Plant has heat tolerance and thus is popular with southern growers. This has become the most popular variety for single-bloom production. Flower heads are quite large with single inflorescences up to 12″ in diameter and borne on tall stems which may need staking. Growth retardants can keep height to a minimum by use on both summer growth and at forcing. A late variety, suitable for Mother's Day forcing in the Midwest or Easter forcing in the South.

- *Todi:* An important variety in northern states and in Canada with large flower heads and deep pink sepals; a little too dark when blue. Early in forcing.

- *Kasteln:* A variety of increasing importance which can be forced later in the season as it withstands heat better than Todi. Deep pink sepals. Plant is suitable for multiflowering with a tendency to smaller flower heads. Ships well without injury to flowers. Mid-season in forcing.

- *Mathilda Gutges:* Sepals are medium pink and can be readily grown for blue. The plant branches readily and can be grown as multiflowering but may need treatment with a growth retardant as the variety tends to be tall. Mid-season in forcing.

- *Kuhnert:* The only currently grown variety of the old group of *Europa, Gertrude Glahn,* and *Hamburg* is valuable for producing clear blue sepals. Mid-season in forcing.

- *Red Star:* A vigorous variety with large flower heads and brilliant pink or blue sepals. Mid-season in forcing.

- *Merveille (Merritts Improved selection):* A versatile variety because it is equally satisfactory as bright pink, mauve, or medium blue with medium-size flower heads. Stems are inclined to be tall. It has declined in popularity partially due to susceptibility to diseases.

- *Strafford:* A dark pink variety of medium habit and good quality flower heads. Decline in popularity may be due partially to difficulties in production and to incidence of green sepal disorder. Mid-season to late in forcing.

- *Bottstein:* A newer variety which may become more popular. Growth habit is definitely dwarf; it has red sepals and could be grown as a multiflowering plant. Flowering plant ships well and is long lasting. Early to mid-season in forcing.

- *Royal:* A new dark pink variety tending to remain short and branching well. Mid-season in forcing.

- *Sister Therese* and *Regula:* These are the two standard white varieties but each constitutes only 1–2% of total sales and only a small number are usually forced. Both are mid-season in time to force.

- *Rosa Rita:* Deep pink sepals with medium-size flower heads. Plant branches well and can be grown for multiflowering but tends to be tall and may need to be retarded.

- *Dr. Steiniger:* Red sepals and medium-size flower heads with tendency to be tall. Branches fairly well.

Plant Production

Propagation   Cuttings may be obtained from (1) forcing plants at about the time flower buds are visible and excess shoots are pruned, (2) from greenhouse-grown stock plants, and (3) from field-grown stock plants. The first source results in a long growth period in the greenhouse but could be valuable in the production of plants for early forcing or for emergency buildup of stock for flowering. The second source is in use by some hydrangea specialists, but most propagated material currently comes from field-grown stock plants in coastal California and Oregon. Cuttings are available for shipment from April to mid-July.

Three types of cuttings can be made from leafy, vegetative propagation material. A tip cutting is made from the upper $3^{1}/_{2}$–4" of stem. Leaves may be trimmed lightly to reduce the space requirement in the propagation bed, but this is not necessary. The lower nodes of the stem can be made into two-eye (butterfly) cuttings or into single-eye (leaf-bud) cuttings by splitting the main stem. Many growers depend upon the two-eye cuttings to produce a two-bloom plant, but both shoots may not be the same height or one shoot may not develop or may fail to form a flower bud. Single-eye cuttings can be selected for uniformity for pinching at different dates or grown for single blooms. The large number of nodes concentrated at the base of single-eye cuttings provides for more branches, although they require several weeks longer than terminal

Field of hydrangeas for cutting production in Oregon.

cuttings to attain the same size for pinching. It is important that stock plants, propagation material, and young plants be continuously rogued to eliminate growth abnormalities which may appear under periods of stress.

Hydrangea cuttings root readily under intermittent mist at 68–70°F but take 3–4 weeks for good rooting depending upon variety, time of year, and type of cutting. Tip cuttings root fastest and butterfly cuttings probably slower than single-eye cuttings. A rooting hormone treatment such as $1/10$% IBA or NAA in talc should hasten rooting. The medium should be well drained and loose with cuttings watered in by heavy misting. Cuttings can be rooted directly in growing medium in small pots for ease in transplanting later. Adequate mist to prevent wilting is essential and some reduction of sunlight in late spring and summer may be necessary, particularly in southern areas.

Terminal cuttings made in early May can be potted under protective shade in the middle and southern states and remain outside until taken to cold storage in the fall. Pinching can be in mid-June for larger size plants and late June for two- to three-bloom plants. Single-eye cuttings from the same material in early May would be suitable for smaller sizes for single-bloom plants. Terminal cuttings made in July are flowered as single-bloom plants. Rooted cuttings or established plants in small pots are grown over summer in 4″, 5″, or 6″ pots, depending upon size of plant and whether grown for local forcing or shipping to other forcers.

547

Vegetative shoots for propagation can be made into one tip cuttings plus several single-eye or two-eye cuttings, as shown on the right.

Saran shade for starting young plants, getting better breaks, and increasing summer growth. In the photo, the author of this chapter, Professor James B. Shanks, University of Maryland.

Summer care Summer growth of plants for Easter–Mother's Day forcing is normally out of doors in the middle and northern states and in Canada. Plants are established under partial shade—then they can be in full sun to maintain short growth. In warmer areas it may be necessary to provide partial shade until the side shoots on pinched plants are well established to protect from heat injury. Farther south, the protection from a shade house may be necessary. More protection is required in the low humidity areas of the Sun Belt from central Texas to the high plains. Here, summer growth must be under glass or plastic with reduced light, but the efficiency of air-conditioning is an invaluable asset in these areas.

Fertilization should be adequate to maintain good leaf color but not to encourage large leaves or excessive height. Regular applications should be continued until plants are placed in storage, letting them "ripen" from cooler temperature and short days rather than lack of nitrogen. Continuous inspection for insects and mites with appropriate insecticidal sprays and roguing of any malformed plants should be done during outdoor growth. A mildicide can be applied in early fall and one or more applications of Benlate made before storage.

Flower initiation is earlier in northern areas because of cooler night temperatures, although shorter photoperiods do not occur until after the autumnal equinox. An ever-recurring problem in the outdoor production of plants is the possibility of frost injury before plants have adequate flower initiation to be placed in cold storage. Some growers have solved this by taking plants to glass-

Plant production in air-conditioned greenhouse in Texas.

549

Butyne diol as a defoliant, control plant on left. Picture taken one week following sprays of (left to right) ¹/₂, 1 and 1¹/₂% of butyne diol.

or plastic-covered areas before danger of frost where they remain for their dormant period. This is efficient in some respects, but lack of early defoliation may create disease problems, and daytime warming will delay the termination of rest. Hydrangeas gradually acquire more frost tolerance after flower initiation, and controlled frost is sometimes permitted to induce defoliation.

It would be desirable from the standpoint of savings in handling and better disease control in storage to induce defoliation before placing plants into storage. In some areas this may be possible if temporary frost protection is available or frost is not a problem, as there will be a week's delay in moving into storage.

The most effective spray defoliant has been butynediol (2-butyne-1,4-diol), a brown crystalline substance soluble in water. It is available in small lots from chemical supply houses but is manufactured by GAF Corporation. A foliar spray of 1¹/₂ to 2 pounds of butynediol in 12 gallons of water (no spreader required) should cause abscission in one week. The ethylene-producing chemical ethephon (Ethrel or Florel) can initiate defoliation, but a concentration higher than the relatively low dosage rate of 1000 ppm will retard growth at forcing. The addition of 50 ppm gibberellin (GA_3 from Pro-Gibb, Gibbrel, Gib-Tabs, etc.) should be used with ethephon to hasten defoliation and promote forcing.

Plants in an enclosed area or storage room can be defoliated with ethylene or the vapors from Vapam®. Apples produce ethylene and an old recommendation by Dr. Post of Cornell was the use of 1 bushel of apples to 400 cubic feet of storage. Ethylene gas can be purchased in small cylinders and emitted slowly, bubbling through water, to maintain ethylene for a period of up to a week for defoliation. The concentration is not critical, and 1 cubic foot of ethylene in 1000 cubic feet of storage as used in banana ripening would be adequate. Constant replacement would be required in most hydrangea storages.

Defoliation by Vapam must be done carefully as vapors can injure plants, and the operator must remember that this is not an approved use of the material although it is used in soil fumigation. Fifty milliliters (1/5 cup or 10 teaspoons) mixed in water and sprinkled on the walkways for each 1000 cubic feet of storage is usually an adequate treatment. A second treatment, 3–4 days later, may be required if the storage is not tight.

Fumigation by either ethylene or Vapam is more difficult in a greenhouse situation because of the greater volume and likelihood of air exchange. Defoliation by any method should be done only after flower bud initiation has been assured. The temperature during the treatment and for at least a week should be 60°F as abscission is actually a phase of growth. Variety and maturity are important factors in ease of defoliation. The use of gibberellin will accelerate defoliation by any means. The pre-storage use of 50 ppm gibberellin can be recommended where early forcing is to be attempted, as a more desirable type of stimulation is produced by application before defoliation than when applied after storage.

Forcing   Dormant plants are placed in the greenhouse at forcing temperatures of 60–64°F immediately upon removal from storage. Spacing closely for the first 2–4 weeks will save on heat and space. Plants received with bare-root balls can be placed together on a solid bottom bed for up to 2 weeks. It is best to start forcing in the same size pot as for summer growth. The shift to final pot size is made after 2–4 weeks of forcing depending upon the size of the original pot. Root growth will have resumed by this time, and it will not be necessary to break the old root ball as is done when repotting is done before growth has started. Final spacing can be made at this time and a lower forcing temperature selected if desired.

Every effort should be made during forcing to prevent plant growth from becoming soft and subject to excessive water loss or desiccation injury upon removal from the greenhouse. Maximum sunlight, adequate space, and low humidity are important, and any wetting of leaves should be avoided. Tube watering is practical during the forcing period, but mat or capillary watering can be done. Growth will be more vigorous with a constant supply of moisture to the roots.

Growth regulators are frequently used to prevent excessive height in forcing as well as in summer plant production and to reduce the space requirement. The use of such growth-retarding chemicals must be anticipated, and an application of a retardant in mid-September is an excellent means of reducing stem stretch at forcing without severely reducing the inflorescence size. Plants forced for Mother's Day particularly need an application of a retardant. Application of a retardant in the forcing season is made during the third week of forcing and usually at a lower rate than on summer growth. B-Nine at 2500 ppm or A-Rest at 50 ppm is satisfactory as a foliar spray at forcing. PP333, a new chemical from ICI Americas, is also effective as a foliar spray at 50 ppm.

Application of B-Nine made during the summer can have a desirable shortening effect on the plant at forcing (plant on the right).

Should plants show signs of insufficient storage as evidenced by slow development, short internodes, small leaves, or a general rosetted appearance, an application of gibberellin should be considered. GA_3 at 2–5 ppm is used in the forcing period. A single foliar application may be adequate, but weekly applications may be made if plants do not respond. Careful observation is the only means of determining the number of applications necessary to restore growth.

As sepals enlarge and become pigmented it may be necessary to reduce the light intensity to prevent fading and injury to sepals from excessive transpiration. Plants should be hardened as the sepals approach maturity by giving cooler night temperatures and ample ventilation. If the plant growth has been restricted by environmental care and growth retardants, the staking and tying of flower heads should not be required. Multiflowering plants usually need no support. Mature hydrangea plants can be held under refrigeration at 35–40°F for several weeks if necessary.

Out-of-season forcing Extending the period of availability would increase the market potential, add variety to available potted flowering plants, and reduce production costs by growing hydrangeas at other than the coldest period of the year. Some of the principles involved in early flower initiation could be of value to southern growers who lack the cool fall temperatures for flower initiation.

Forcing hydrangeas for sales later than Mother's Day has always been possible by holding plants in artificial cold storage. Much of the heat cost of winter forcing would be avoided, but a market potential would need to be developed as for any out-of-season production. A means of shortening the growing period, or simplifying production for the spring period, would of course have important advantages.

Forcing for late January and the Valentine's Day market has been demonstrated in our work. One method for earlier forcing is to obtain flower initiation in the summer by the use of early propagation and pinching followed by a controlled temperature storage period and forcing with an incandescent light break to provide long photoperiods. Leaf-bud cuttings made in late February from the excess wood of forcing plants and rooted and handled in 3" peat pots in greenhouse flats holding 35 plants each are suitable. These are potted to 6" in early May in a protected frame and pinched May 25. Plant height is controlled by foliar applications of B-Nine at 5000 ppm on June 15, July 15, and August 15. Plants are placed in dark storage at 52°F in early September for 8 weeks and forced at 62°F with a 4- to 8-hour night break of 10 foot-candles of incandescent light. Early varieties can be salable by January 20.

The other alternative to early forcing involves continuous growth without defoliation or a dormant period. Plants are initiated by either a 4-week pre-cooling period in a 52°F storage with 12 hours/day 100 ft-c fluorescent light during the summer months or 4 weeks in the greenhouse at 54–64°F with 16-hour dark periods provided by black cloth shading if necessary. Plants are then placed immediately under long photoperiods at a temperature of 62°F for flower development. For single-bloom plants in 4" to 5" pots, tip cuttings must be established for a minimum of 2 weeks and leaf-bud cuttings for a minimum of 4 weeks. Select both for uniformity. Multiple bloom plants must have been pinched at least 4 weeks prior to the flower initiation treatment.

Attempts at a year-round program of forcing hydrangeas by these continuous growing procedures should be initiated on a small scale because of differences in local environmental conditions. The greatest potential would seem to be in the production of small, single-bloom plants. Quality has been excellent with leaves down to the pot rim. The traditional storage of hydrangeas assures uniformity and predictability in forcing. Plants flowered by continuous growth are more variable in time of forcing and not as suitable for a holiday market.

Summary of Hydrangea Production

The following suggestions are based on Maryland conditions. Adjustments may be necessary for other areas.

Easter to Mother's Day flowering

Propagation: Single blooms   —Tip cuttings June 10
                                        —Single-eye cuttings May 10
               Two blooms   —Butterfly cuttings May 10
               Multiple blooms —Tip cuttings May 10; pinch July 1
                                          —Single-eye cuttings April 10; pinch July 1

Outside culture (May-October):   Full sun to light shade, moderate fertility. Retard tall varieties Aug. 10 with ½% B-Nine.

Rest period: Controlled temperature of 52°F in dark for 8 weeks minimum with careful watering and humidity control. For longer storage periods use 45°F. Defoliation with butynediol, ethylene, or Vapam is possible.

Forcing period: First 3 weeks at 65°F and close spacing, then 58°F or split-night temperature of 62°F until 2:00 a.m., then 48°F until 8:00 a.m. for final 9–10 weeks. Full sunlight until color, then light shade. Retard tall varieties and plants in small pots at final spacing with ¼% B-Nine and shift to final pot size in peat or peat-lite mix. Fertilize heavily with high N and high P. Bloom 85–100 days.

Valentine's and early flowering

Propagation: Single blooms   —Tip cuttings May 10
                                        —Single-eye cuttings April 10
               Two blooms   —Butterfly cuttings April 10
               Multiple blooms —Tip cuttings April 10; pinch May 25
                                          —Single-eye cuttings March 10; pinch May 25

Outside culture (May-August):   As above but retard according to variety with ½–¾% B-Nine on June 15, July 15, and August 15.

Rest period: Controlled temperature of 52°F in dark from September 10 to November 10 with natural defoliation.

Forcing period: Use 10 ft-c incandescent light from 10:00 p.m. to 2:00 a.m. at 62°F immediately upon removal from storage. Bloom 100–110 days. Retard tall varieties at 3 weeks with ¼% B-Nine.

Mini-pots by continuous growing procedures

Stock plants: Six months after a cold storage treatment, begin the use of continuous night lighting with 10 ft-c of incandescent light at 62°F to maintain continuous growth. Cuttings must be taken at 6- to 8-week intervals or else all shoots pinched to prevent flower initiation. A foliar spray of 25 ppm GA_3 should be applied after each crop of cuttings.

Propagation: Tip cuttings are rooted at 68°F under lights (not needed May, June, July) and lighting continued for 2 weeks growth at 62°F after rooting. Single-eye cuttings are rooted as above but maintained at 62°F under lights (not needed in May, June, July) for up to 6 weeks to beginning of bud growth. Apply a foliar spray of GA_3 at 25 ppm in winter months if terminal buds have begun to form during this initial period.

Flower initiation: From September 15 to May 15 grow plants at 52–62°F for 4–6 weeks under 8-hour photoperiods using black cloth from 4:00 p.m. to 8:00 a.m. if required. Where cool summer temperatures prevail, as in northern states, coastal areas, or high elevations, this may be continued during the summer months. Otherwise, from May 15 to September 15 in Maryland and similar areas, plants are placed in a cooled room at 52°F under 100 ft-c fluorescent light for 12 hours and 12 hours of darkness for a 4-week period.

Forcing period: In June and July, simply use natural conditions in the greenhouse. From August through May use 10 ft-c incandescent light from 10:00 p.m. to 2:00 a.m. at 62°F. Use GA_3 at 25 ppm at beginning of forcing from September through April.

Average production time for terminal cuttings:

Propagation—	4 weeks
Growth	— 2 weeks
Initiation	— 4 weeks
Forcing	— 8 weeks summer
	16 weeks winter
Total	18 to 26 weeks

Troubles

Cultural problems Failure to initiate flower buds or evidence of crippled buds during forcing may be due to poor culture during summer growth, frost injury, drying in storage, or bud rot (gray mold) in storage. The initiation of flowers early in the summer may result in fewer than normal leaves at forcing, causing poor flower development because of lack of leaf area. Cymes containing leaves are also associated with early initiation. Removal of leaves in early forcing usually permits the cyme to develop normally.

Single-bloom hydrangeas in 5" pots flowering in August after 6 weeks of pre-cooling under lights with no defoliation.

Iron chlorosis (interveinal yellowing) is frequent in rapid forcing without adequate root development or is due to alkaline soil, overfertilization, or overwatering during summer growth. The young growth of hydrangea leaves and flowers at forcing is very susceptible to injury from insecticides, fungicides, and growth regulators. Caution is advised in using any chemical spray and dosages should be confined to the lower rates recommended for use.

Insects The usual run of insects may be found on hydrangeas, but the most common problems are aphids during the forcing period and two-spotted spider mites during summer growth. Plants should undergo continuous inspection and appropriate insecticides or miticides used to bring the infestation under control. The use of a soil-applied systemic insecticide may not always be satisfactory, particularly during forcing after the plant has developed a woody stem. Slugs and snails may be present on plants as they are brought from storage and can be particularly troublesome where plants are forced on soil or on solid-bottom beds.

Diseases Hydrangeas are not often subject to root and stem rots provided usual sanitation and good cultural practices are followed. Propagation benches, all media, as well as pots, flats, etc., should be disinfected by steam or fumigation to eliminate pathogens and weeds. Good drainage is important as is the avoidance of overwatering.

Botrytis causing gray mold on leaves and stems in propagation or bud rot in storage occurs in high humidity and high moisture situations, frequently

556

starting on injured or dead tissue. Injured leaves should not be permitted on cuttings, and fallen leaves should be removed from plants in storage. Ventilation, air circulation, and avoidance of overhead watering greatly reduce the incidence of gray mold. The systemic fungicide Benlate is used on plants and cuttings before placing in a high-humidity environment to reduce susceptibility. Other fungicidal sprays may be used.

Powdery mildew is most prevalent on outdoor plants in the fall and in the greenhouse under conditions of high humidity and crowding. Older leaves are most susceptible. A protective mildicide can be used in the fall while humidity control is usually adequate to prevent serious infection in the greenhouse.

There is a wide range of variety susceptibility to both gray mold and powdery mildew, and susceptible varieties should not be grown where an environment conducive to disease cannot be avoided.

Viral agents The hydrangea ring-spot virus has been found in most present-day commercial varieties. Typical symptoms show only during winter growth, and the effect on susceptible varieties is generally weakened or smaller growth. Roguing is difficult, and virus-free plants of commercial varieties are not currently available.

Virescence, or the green sepal mycoplasma complex, has been responsible for a series of problems and is divided into three distinctly different but related groups:

1. *Severe*. Extreme stunting, small leaves with vein yellowing, and dwarf, green cymes followed by death of the plant.

2. *Intermediate*. Reduction in vegetative growth but with normal leaf expansion and continued vein yellowing. Cymes contain both green or bronzed sepals and normal-colored sepals.

3. *Mild*. Stock plants gradually decline in vigor. Forcing plants retain normal pattern of growth with green leaves, but cymes contain large, green sepals and reproductive parts may revert to a vegetative type of growth.

The severe form of virescence can readily be eliminated by roguing as the symptoms appear at any stage of growth. Careful observation and continued roguing can eliminate the intermediate type. The mild form is the most dangerous as symptoms appear only at forcing, so greenhouse-grown material or other flowering stock must be used to replace all plants used in cutting production. Hydrangea virescence has been virtually eliminated by most hydrangea specialists by careful roguing. Since *Stafford* and *Rose Supreme* currently appear to be most susceptible, the mild form of virescence would most likely appear in these varieties.

Useful Chemicals for Hydrangeas

A-Rest (ancymidol): A growth-retarding chemical effective, but not registered for use, on hydrangea. Spray application is suggested as for chrysanthemum.

Benlate (benomyl): A general fungicidal protectant with systemic action for stock plant treatment before taking cuttings or for application before cold storage. Registered for use on flowers and ornamentals.

B-Nine (daminozide): A growth-retarding chemical registered for use with hydrangea on summer growth and at forcing.

Daconil 2787 (chlorothalonil): A spray for protection against gray mold and mildew. Registered uses include a number of flowering and foliage plants.

Enstar (kinoprene): Juvenile hormone which controls aphids. Registered for use on general ornamental plants.

Karathane® (dinocap): Labelled as both a fungicide and miticide for control of powdery mildew and two-spotted spider mites on hydrangeas.

Malathion: Registered for control of aphids and many other insects on general ornamental plants.

Metasystox R (oxydemeton-methyl): A systemic control for aphids and many other insects and mites. Registered for general use on flowers, including greenhouse crops.

Orthene (acephate): Controls many insects and is registered for use on greenhouse and outdoor floral crops.

Pentac: Control for resistant two-spotted spider mites and registered for use on many ornamental plants and flowers.

Pro-Gibb and other trade names (gibberellin GA_3): Powerful growth stimulant registered for general stimulation of blooms. Used at 2–5 ppm on young growth out of cold storage, 25 ppm on rosetted plants in full leaf, and 50 ppm before defoliation and storage.

Truban (ethazol): Soil drench for control of pythium and phytophthora root rots. Registered for use on many types of flowers and ornamentals.

Vendex—also *Orthomite* (hexakis): Control for two-spotted spider mites and registered for use on greenhouse and outdoor ornamentals.

Acknowledgements

The author acknowledges and expresses appreciation to the following individuals for providing current information through personal communication:

Roger Lawson—USDA, Beltsville, Maryland

Joseph S. Merritt—Dundalk, Maryland

John Valk—Grimsby, Ontario

Norman Yock—Brookings, Oregon

ANNUAL *(I. wallerana hooker f) 40–60,000 seeds per oz. Germinates in 18 days at 70°. Light.*

IMPATIENS—NOTHING BEATS THESE POPULAR PLANTS FOR SUMMER-TO-FALL BLOOMS IN SHADE!

GARDEN HEIGHT*	8-10"	10-12"	12-14"
VARIETY	Super-Elfin® Sherbet Mixture	Fantasia Ripple Futura Twinkles Novette ShowStopper	Blitz Series Duet Mixture Grandé Rosette Mixture
SPACING	12"	14"	18"
FLOWER SIZE—TYPE	1½-2" flowers, solid and "eyed" types	1½-2" flowers, solid, eyed and bicolors—see descriptions	2-2½" flowers, Rosette has double flowers
HABIT	Very compact and spreading	Compact	Mounded
BLOOM PERIOD	Early summer till frost	Early summer till frost	Early summer till frost
USE	Packs, 4" pots, tubs, baskets, garden beds	Packs, 4" pots, tubs, baskets, garden beds	Tubs, baskets, garden beds. Doubles, best in 4" pots.

Here we're talking the seed-grown bedding annual. Well known for many years largely because of its ability to produce flowers under poor light conditions, the impatiens has really come into its own as a popular bedding and pot plant, filling the need for a plant that will continue to thrive and flower under conditions of partial to heavy shade. Another reason for its rise to prominence has been the development of new and vastly improved dwarf F_1 hybrid forms. As an annual for shaded spots, it has surpassed the begonia.

Impatiens are quite easy to grow from seed; however, they should be germinated at a minimum temperature of 70°F under full-light conditions. Sown around February 15, packs will be ready for May 1 sales if grown at 60°F. For 4" pots in the North allow 12 weeks from sowing (2–3 weeks less in the South). To obtain plants with maximum number of flowers and limited vegetative growth, we suggest leaving the seedlings in the germination flat as long as possible, and restricting the amount of feed and water given to the plants. Both A-Rest and B-Nine are effective on impatiens.

As mentioned above, the prime reason for the vastly increased usage of impatiens as bedding plants has been the development of the F_1 strains. Briefly, here are the advantages:

1. Better seed germination

2. Increased vigor

3. Produce more flowers

4. Have better habit (dwarf)

559

Here's Elfins—*one of the bedding plant impatiens group. The outstanding success of this class is clearly and simply because it produces color in the home gardener's shady corners.*

Heading the list of these F_1 hybrids is the *Super Elfin®* series (8–10"). Compact, free-flowering and available in the 11 separate clear colors listed as well as a mixture, it is in the No. 1 spot. Currently available are *Elfin Orchid, Fuchsia, Orange, Pink, Rose, Salmon, Scarlet, Blue, Blush, Lipstick,* and *White.* Also being widely grown is the F_1 *Fantasia* series. Free-flowering, basal branching with large flowers, it comes in about the same range of separate colors as the *Elfin* series except that it contains an orange-white and a red-white bicolor. The *Futura* and *Novette* series, both F_1s, are similar in color range and grow to a height of 10–12". Best of the bicolor series are the F_1 *Twinkles* because of their consistent bicolor pattern, earliness and abundance of blooms. Best for hanging baskets are the F_1 *Blitz's*, orange and violet. These are the largest flowered so far with 2" to 2½" blooms. *ShowStopper* F_1 produces masses of bright pink blooms with deep rose eyes. Extremely free flowering, making it a great choice for hanging baskets. *Super Elfin Blush* F_1 is also a winner in baskets. In some areas the *Dwarf Baby* mixture is still used, along with an F_2 *Dwarf Mixture.*

Gaining in interest and use each year are the so-called New Guinea hybrids. Available only as rooted cuttings or small plants presently, they represent a radical departure from common, widely used strains in that many of them have variegated or multicolored foliage. Original stock was released by

560

A new family of New Guinea impatiens—the Vistas. *Very large-flowered, very colorful. Here's one of them in a basket.*

the USDA. The flowers are large (1" to 2½" across) and make excellent specimens when planted to the garden. They are usually sold in 3"–4" pots or hanging baskets along with bedding plants. They require a coarse porous soil, maximum light intensity, and a 65°F night temperature. Using 150 ppm of N and K for each irrigation should supply adequate fertilization. From a small cell to a finished 4" pot requires about 12 weeks time.

Most prominent are the *Sunshine*™ series, consisting of 20 to 30 varieties. More recently introduced is the *Vista*® series, consisting of 12 varieties.

New Guinea Impatiens

An exciting, colorful, and very promising new class of impatiens. First, a very basic and important point: The New Guineas are an entirely different species vs. the "Elfin common bedding plant impatiens." Their light needs, propagation methods, etc., are totally different. One problem in launching this new class is getting the public to understand its different requirements for growth. But the gorgeous, large, colorful flowers will sell the public.

First, the New Guineas, unlike the Elfins, want at least ⅔ or more sunlight. They will flower sparsely or not at all in heavy shade. What we've seen of them so far indicates that they are happy in full sun—but very unhappy in full shade. The Elfins type, of course, will flower so very well in even moderately heavy shade—but they are not happy in full sun.

Difference #2: The New Guineas, at least in most cases, are quite a lot larger flowered (commonly up to 3"). And among them are some gorgeous tropical colors; and in some cases very attractive leaf colors and variegations.

561

The New Guineas that we've seen so far have been most exciting as an 8" or 10" hanging basket, in 5" and 6" pots. Also, we've seen some excellent flower beds planted with them.

Another major difference: The New Guineas are nearly all propagated vegetatively up to this point. Almost none of them are grown from seed.

Culturally, they enjoy a porous soil mix with ample organics—peat and perlite.

Cuttings are generally first potted to a cell-pack or small pot, then moved to a 4" or larger if needed. Three 4" make a fine 10" hanging basket. They are not too happy if overpotted—like putting three rooted cuttings in a 10" basket.

They are native to the jungles of New Guinea—which means lots of moisture, some light, and lots of humus in the soil mix.

Available classes As of this edition, there are four classes available commercially.

- *The Astrological series* and *The Mikkel Sunshine series* propagated by Mikkelsens, Inc., Ashtabula, Ohio (216) 998–2070.

- *The Indian series* from California-Florida Plant Corp., Freemont, California (415) 656–1424.

- *The New Vistas* available from Pan-American Plant Company, Parrish, Florida (813) 776–1291.

The first three classes are typically rather free blooming, compact, and even in habit. Many varieties have colorful foliage. Flowers are generally colorful—only medium large but larger than the Elfins type.

The fourth class is quite different from the others. Many varieties feature very large flowers, again, up to 3" and more. And very lovely, tropical flower colors. And again, in many cases, colorful foliage. The Vistas are not quite as even or compact as the first two groups—but on balance are reasonably even and of good habit. The *Vistas* make a spectacular 8" or 10" hanging basket. They do beautifully under half or 3/4 sun in a midwestern or eastern patio or porch situation.

All four classes are patented—propagation is restricted. Plants from all groups, by the way, are available from brokers.

One last point: The New Guineas were brought to the U.S. by plant hunters (Longwood Gardens—USDA team) some years ago. They have been made available to flower breeders across the U.S. Perhaps 10 to 15 years of effort has produced, from these original native species, a colorful and very promising array of the New Guineas we see today.

We need more plant hunters!

G.V.B.

562

Iris—great for winter color.

Forcing

Many growers, both retail and wholesale, find it profitable and not too difficult to force iris during the winter months. Here, we refer strictly to forcing varieties classed generally as Dutch iris. These bulbs are grown in Holland as well as in our Pacific Northwest. However, with the excellent quality produced in this section of our country, it is wise for a grower to limit his purchases to the American-grown bulbs.

Bulbs should be planted in deep flats (4–5") or into a bench. The top of the bulb should be level with the surface of the soil. Iris must be kept moist and should never be allowed to dry out. Since, in flats, iris form a thin matted layer of roots on the bottom, thorough watering is a must. Placing of the flats too near the heating pipes will cause rapid drying out and subsequent bud blasting. A spacing of 3" x 3" is recommended. Some growers mark the flat or bench at this spacing after thoroughly watering the soil, and then push the bulbs into the soil, covering them with an inch layer of peat which is again watered. If placing flats on a bench, it is a good idea to allow a 1" air space between them. Iris need plenty of light and ample ventilation with uniform temperatures. The bulbs should be planted in an ordinary loose, well-drained soil without any special fertilizer added.

Due to the excellent work which has been done by the USDA and other experiment stations, fairly accurate schedules are available today which allow the grower to plan his crop by selecting the proper variety, size, temperature, and treatment to force a crop from mid-December through May.

Bulbs are usually dug in July and immediately given a 10-day curing period at 90°, which accelerates the formation of flower buds. Immediately upon arrival at warehouses, all iris that are to be shipped to customers for planting after mid-November are put into a heat-retarding chamber at 70°–80°. They are left in this chamber until they go into precooling, which is approximately 6 weeks before planting, depending on variety and size. Those bulbs that are to be planted before mid-November can be left in open storage for about 30 days until they go into precooling. By precooling, the bulbs force more quickly and uniformly. Bulbs are placed in a 50° precooling storage at the proper time so that they can be removed at planting time. Precooled bulbs must be planted immediately, since a delay will nullify the precooling effect. Some growers have facilities to do their own precooling, and thus use regular or heat-treated bulbs, depending on the intended planting date. Generally, these are shipped 6 weeks prior to planting. However, the time of precooling varies from 4 to 8 weeks, depending upon the time of the season, variety and size of bulbs. If a grower is in doubt about this, he should consult those firms where scheduling services are available.

The most widely used varieties are *Wedgewood,* a light blue; *Ideal,* a lobelia blue sport of *Wedgewood; Blue Ribbon,* a dark blue; *Golden Harvest,* a deep yellow; and *White Wedgewood,* a creamy white.

Iris come in sizes measured in centimeters of diameter: $6/7$, $7/8$, $8/9$, $9/10$, $10/11$, and $11 +$. Iris can be forced in a wide range of temperatures (from 45–60°) and the forcing temperatures are dependent upon the size and variety of bulb used. Higher temperatures (55–58°) are used for forcing $10/11$ bulbs which are used for early forcing. Smaller size bulbs are used for later forcing.

Regular iris cannot be timed accurately, so only the grower with pre-cooling facilities will be interested in the regular bulbs.

There are two principal troubles encountered in the forcing of iris. *Bud-blasting* is generally caused by too-high temperatures in forcing (about 60°), overcrowding in the bench, or not enough water or light. An aphid infestation on the bulbs can also cause blasting. If bulbs are infested with aphids at time of planting, a methyl bromide treatment before planting will solve the problem unless the bulbs are already damaged. Blasting is more common in the early-forced crop than in later plantings. *Blindness* is generally caused by too-early digging of the bulbs and too-early precooling and planting. Blindness should not be excessive if bulbs are dug and cured by August 15, precooled September 1 to October 15, and planted on October 15. Although it is possible to harvest flowers from 95 to 100% of the bulbs planted, percentages of 80 to 90 should be considered satisfactory for the earliest crop.

When iris flowers are destined for long-distance shipping, they should be cut in the bud stage just as their true color begins to show. For local selling, flowers should be cut nearly wide open.

KALANCHOE*

ANNUAL *(K. blossfeldiana) From seed: 1,000,000–2,500,000 seeds per oz. Germination in 10 days at 70°. Light.*

The kalanchoe is a member of the Crassulaceae family, and species of it originated in the arid regions of Madagascar, Africa, and Asia. Many brightly colored hybrids are available in shades of pink, orange, red, and yellow. Where photoperiod and temperature can be controlled, this versatile plant may be forced year round in 4" to 6½" pots and finished in 10–16 weeks.

From Cuttings

By far the easiest and quickest method of growing is to buy rooted plants (usually 2½") from specialist propagators. These may be purchased pre-pinched with breaks or unpinched and should be handled as follows:

Boxes should be opened immediately upon entering the greenhouse and the plants allowed to adjust to the greenhouse temperature. A highly organic, well-drained soil mix should be used with a pH of 6.0–6.5. When setting the plants, make sure they are not set too deeply, but at about the same depth as in the original propagation container. Stem rots can be a problem but usually only if good soil sterilization is not practiced. A soil drench with fungicide is optional.

Unpinched plants are usually finished in 4½" pots and need one to two weeks of long days before blackout. Pre-pinched varieties such as the SUPER-START® 6, AZTEC® series from Pan-American Plant Company will have three or more breaks upon arrival and can be shaded immediately upon planting to finish in 10–12 weeks in 4½" pots. For 5½" or 6½" pots, extra long days need to be given to increase the height of the finished product. Also, for these larger sizes, an extra pinch is recommended at the start of short days, but may not be necessary under some conditions or for very free-branching cultivars. The number of long days given will also vary depending on the temperature and amount of light. A typical schedule might look like this (long days):

Container	Summer	Spring/Fall	Winter
4½"	0	1 week	2 weeks
5½"	1 week	2 weeks	3 weeks
6½"	2 weeks	3 weeks	4 weeks

*Contributed by Peter Hesse, Pan-American Plant Company.

565

One of the Aztec *kalanchoe group. The kalanchoe is quite a popular winter-spring flowering pot plant.*

Most cultivars require 5 weeks of short days to initiate flowers and this means 14 hours of darkness *seven days a week*. Darkness may be provided by black cloth between March 15 and September 15, but extreme care must be used to prevent excessive heat buildup under the cloth. Night temperatures between 60–70° are optimum while lower or higher temperatures can cause delay in flowering and extremely high temperatures can cause complete flower abortion.

Most varieties grow best under high intensity, but in the summer in very sunny locations as much as 60 percent shade may be necessary.

Kalanchoes are succulents, but should never be allowed to wilt. Water should be applied thoroughly when the surface of the pot is slightly dry.

A constant liquid fertilizer of 250–400 ppm nitrogen and potassium is recommended, and varieties vary in their fertilizer requirements. The keeping quality of the very floriferous and early AZTEC® series is improved by the higher feed levels. A moderate amount of phosphorous should be included in the soil or supplied for the first couple of waterings by a 20–20–20 liquid feed. Excessively high phosphorous levels may cause flattened stems (fasciation) due to zinc imbalance in some varieties. Calcium is also very important and may be supplied as calcium nitrate or as dolomitic limestone in the soil.

Kalanchoes respond to growth regulation, and applications of B-Nine improve the appearance of the finished product. Apply 2500–5000 ppm after a couple of weeks of growth, but especially right when the flower buds begin to show. The number of applications may vary depending on the temperature and light intensity, but excessive applications can cause delay in flowering.

Ancymidol may also be applied for tall varieties. Sixty ml per 4" pot applied as a drench at a concentration that allows ¼ to ½ mg of Ancymidal to be applied is adequate. This method does not delay flowering.

One mistake that is commonly made and really can hurt sales is to ship a kalanchoe too green to the market. Kalanchoes will not finish opening under low light like a chrysanthemum will, and should be allowed to fully open on the bench. Even shipped fully open, a well-grown kalanchoe will keep in the home up to six weeks.

Kalanchoes are rather pest-free, with aphids and mealybugs being the major problems. These insects can be controlled with many insecticides. Never apply Kelthane EC or any xylene-based pesticide to kalanchoes. They will quickly be defoliated. Powdery mildew can be a problem, especially on older varieties. This can be controlled by fungicides, burning sulfur, or by heating and venting.

Varieties from Cuttings

There are two groups of varieties available from cuttings. Already mentioned is the early response (10–12 weeks) very floriferous type. The other type has a response 12–16 weeks with some cultivars having fewer, but larger flowers. Both include many excellent varieties.

Varieties from Seed

Kalanchoes may also be propagated from seed. *Vulcan* is a bright red variety to be sown carefully in a well-drained soil. Keep the temperature at 70°F and expose the seed to full sun. Transplant into 2¼" pots and grow at 60°F and then move these plants up to a 6" pot to make a good display. For a November flowering, give short days from late August to late September and for Christmas, shade for four weeks starting about September 10. Once in bud, no shading is required.

LANTANA

ANNUAL *(L. camara). 1,300 seeds per ounce. Germinates in 6–7 weeks at 65–75°.*

Very useful for spring bedding sales. These colorful, free-flowering plants will perform well under many varying soil conditions. They do, however, like warm temperatures.

While a mixture of colors and habit can be had from seed, uniformity in these important characteristics can only be had from cuttings. Thus, the wide majority grown are vegetatively propagated. They are easily rooted in September if taken from outdoor plants. Perhaps a better plan is to lift such plants and plant them in a 55° house. If the old plants are trimmed back some and not watered much till they get into growth, plenty of cuttings will become available as spring approaches. If strong, 4″ pot plants are wanted, fall cuttings should be used. Lantanas will not do well without some heat—this is why they flourish during the heat of summer and make such an attractive showing in the South. In the greenhouse, they should be grown at a minimum of 60°. A wide range of varieties and colors are available from propagating specialists.

LARKSPUR

ANNUAL *(Delphinium ajacis) 8,000 seeds per oz. Germinates in 20 days at 55°. Dark.*

Larkspur—a fine annual spring-summer cut flower.

The half-hardy nature of the larkspur can be taken advantage of by outdoor growers in the near South. If a sowing is made in the open in this section 6–7 weeks before the ground freezes, plants well enough established to winter-over should be produced. An exceptionally severe winter will sometimes destroy them, but usually they come through very well. Most growers find that a covering of even coarse material tends to rot them. With perfect drainage and some coarse covering, a fall sowing outdoors does usually come through nicely if made late enough to avoid germination before the ground freezes.

The advantage of such a sowing lies in the promptness with which it germinates in early spring. Such a sowing will flower at least 2–3 weeks earlier than if sown out after the ground dries in the spring. In figuring seed requirements for an extensive planting, do so on the basis of 25 ounces of seed covering an acre; this is figured on double 8" rows spaced 3' apart. Spacing plants in the rows is not so important. They will fill out the row if spaced 10–14", but will do so more promptly if allowed half that distance. Some growers plant out March 1-sown seedlings, usually getting good results, but we believe that if the fall sowing comes through, it will be more profitable because of the cost of greenhouse plants and transplanting. If you are depending on spring sowings, two should be made 2–3 weeks apart. By all means, get the first one in as early as possible and use deep, fairly well-enriched soil, and it will pay to irrigate during dry weather if it can be done.

LILIES—ASIATICS AND ORIENTALS

Hybrid pot lily Enchantment. *A colorful, showy, much-used pot plant—on the way up, by the way.*

Here are two important groups of lilies—beyond the traditional Easter crop. Both supply lots of bright strong colors—and both are having an important impact on North American pot and cut flower growers. They are both relatively short-term crops, and not difficult to grow. And both are relatively long life—either as a pot plant or a cut flower. The Asiatics, for example, are reported to last up to two weeks as a pot plant. Understandably, both groups are enjoying substantial increases in North American production.

The Asiatics*

Perhaps the biggest single impact is from the bright colorful Asiatics—as a cut flower. They come in strong bright shades of gold, yellow, orange, rose, pink, and white. They are already an important cut flower crop, both in North America and Holland—and the trend is clearly up! California and Colorado are the primary producers of cut flowers, but eastern growers are showing important interest (as they are in many cut flower crops, by the way).

As a pot plant, Asiatics are grown substantially—but a bit less than as a cut flower. And the present trend here is steady. As a class, the Asiatics are perhaps four or five times more important than the Orientals (Sans Souci)—as of the mid-1980s.

Asiatic individual blooms are 3″ to 4″—vs. 6″ to 8″ for the Orientals. Also, the Asiatics are a relatively short-term crop—65 to 90 days, plant to sell (pot or cut) vs. 120 days for the Orientals (Sans Souci).

Availability of Asiatic bulbs (mainly Oregon, some Dutch) is now almost year-round—and this adds an important year-round capability to the crop. Any quality new pot or cut flower with year-round availability will go further than a one-time seasonal crop. A grower can today turn out five crops a year. The Mother's Day crop is perhaps shortest of all—roughly a 60-day crop, plant to sell. They do flower uniformly.

Asiatic Pot Culture

A few highlights based on recommendations for the variety *Enchantment:*

Bulb preparation   Proper precooling prior to forcing is critically important. Essentially it's vernalization—and to do it, it needs 6 weeks at 34°F— immediately after harvest. Bulbs become available the end of the year—and by the way, the majority of forcing both pot plants and cut flowers today is for the spring holidays. However, they can be stored for forcing virtually year-round—by freezing the bulbs. Starting January 15 hold them at 28° until ready to force. Normally bulbs supplied by the major bulb producers will be precooled prior to shipment—and ready to plant. If you must hold the bulbs prior to forcing, additional precooling will not be harmful. They should be stored at 34° to 40°F.

Soils   A wide variety of soils will do the trick—they should be open and porous, sterilized, free of pests and disease. Especially recommended: 2 parts sandy loam, 1 part sphagnum peat, 1 part sharp sand. A pH of 6 to 6.5 is recommended.

*Cultural notes here are based on Oregon Bulb Farm's (Ron Beck's) recommendations.

Planting   Tips of bulbs should be covered with a minimum of 1½" to 2" soil for adequate rooting. Bulbs should be potted and stored at 40° to 50° for 2 to 4 weeks prior to being placed in the greenhouse.

Here is the spacing recommended for the variety *Enchantment*:

Pot density*	Bulb size (inches) circumference	# Bulbs/ pot	Pot size	#Pots/ ft.²
(Finish space)	⁴/₅	3	6½"	1.6
	⁵/₆	1	5½"	3.3

*Pot densities are dependent upon owner's greenhouse, light intensity, and geographical location. Pot densities should be increased or decreased slightly depending upon greenhouse conditions.

Fertilizer   The bulb itself is a food reservoir so light feeding is recommended especially at first—and especially where the original mix included fertilizer. After plants show bud, a well-balanced liquid fertilizer is recommended.

Forcing temperatures   Night temperatures of 50°F to 55°F and 65° to 70° daytime are recommended. They just aren't happy being included with 60° or 63° mums—it's too warm. However, as the crop comes into color, flowering dates can be controlled somewhat by temperature—it can be dropped to 40° or a maximum of 60° to 65° toward the end of the crop.

Watering   Uniform moisture important. And especially during the first few weeks, water sparingly. The stem roots are usually well formed when the growth tip appears and water can then be increased. Until shoot is 4", water sparingly.

Bulb size   Bulb sizes from 4" to 9" in circumference will force well. The larger the bulb, the higher the bud count. 4" to 7" bulbs are usually recommended for pot culture. For cut flowers, all sizes are used. Bulbs over 9" are not generally satisfactory.

Forcing time   At 55° nights and 70° days:

Planting dates	Forcing times*
12/15	82 days
1/15	77 days
2/15	72 days

*Forcing times are approximate and will vary according to each grower's greenhouse environment.

Retardants   They are needed especially for *Enchantment, Connecticut Lemon Glow,* and *Love Song.* Good height control can be obtained with A-Rest concentrations of 0.50 mg per pot—applied at shoot emergence, 1" to 2". Single applications of A-Rest have been successful. Note that A-Rest is not effective in growing media containing bark. Also note that in a pot with three bulbs, if two shoots are at the 1" stage, go ahead with the retardant application.

Photoperiod   In low light intensity areas, a 16-hour photoperiod is required in the months of December, January, and early February to prevent bud abortion.

When to ship   When three buds show color, the plants are ready to ship and buds will open in 5 to 7 days.

The above data are based mainly on Oregon Bulb Farm culture.

Asiatic Cut Flower Forcing

Planting   Asiatics (again based on *Enchantment*) can be forced in ground beds, benches, deep flats, or pots. Tips of the bulbs should be covered with a minimum of 1½" to 2" of soil. Recommended spacing, as a cut flower:

	Planting densities*		
Planting date	4/5 bulbs per ft²	5/6 bulbs per ft²	6/7 bulbs per ft²
November	6.0	5.0	4.0
December	6.6	5.5	4.5
January	7.5	6.5	5.0
February	8.0	7.0	5.5
March	8.5	7.5	6.0
April	8.5	8.0	6.5
May	8.5	8.0	6.5
June–August	8.5	8.0	6.5

*Planting densities are dependent upon greenhouse, light intensity, geographical location, and greenhouse type. Planting densities should be increased or decreased depending on local greenhouse conditions.

Approximate forcing times @ 55°F night and 70°F day

Dates	Forcing times*
12/15	82 days
1/15	77 days
2/15	72 days

*Forcing times are approximate and will vary according to each grower's greenhouse environment.

Photoperiod lighting   In northern climates or low light intensity areas, a 16-hour plus photoperiod is required in the months of December, January, and early February to prevent bud abortion. In most other respects, cut flower culture will follow the basic rules of pot plant growing.

Orientals (Sans Souci)

The heart of the Oriental class in North American production is the variety Sans Souci. Its flowers are huge (6" to 8"), colorful (pink and white, and very fragrant). These flowers make a real show. We see them mainly as pot plants— but some are grown as cuts. It's a substantial crop today—and the trend especially as a Mother's Day pot plant is definitely up.

There are other varieties, all shades of pink and white. *Speciosum rubrum* is mainly a pot plant. Other promising new pot varieties are coming. Keep in touch with your supplier.

The Orientals need 60° to 65° nights vs. 55° for the Asiatics. Again, they are flowered mainly as a Mother's Day pot plant. This is roughly a 120-day crop plant to sell.

Sans Souci Culture

The following details are for Mother's Day forcing:

Potting date   For example, Mother's Day on May 13, 1984 requires a potting date of January 14. Subsequent years can be based on this.

Soil   Must be coarse and well drained; recommended is 3 parts soil, 2 parts coarse perlite or coarse sand, 1 part coarse peat. A pH of 6.7 to 7.0. Soil should be sterilized.

Fertilizer   General recommendation: 16–4–12 or 15–0–15 at 100 to 200 ppm each watering. Slow release fertilizer may be used in the soil just prior to potting. Feed with all irrigations after plant is 1" high; continue until buds turn down.

Potting   Pot bulbs immediately upon receipt. Place them deep in the pot. Fill the pot with soil mix and firm. Water thoroughly. Drench with Lesan 35% WP (8 oz.), and Benlate 50% WP (8 oz.) and 100 gallons of water. Lesan drenching every 3 or 4 weeks is recommended. If bulbs are received prior to the desired starting date, place potted bulbs in a 50° to 55° house.

Temperature   Night temperature recommended is 62° to 65°F.

Growth regulator   2 oz. of A-Rest per 3 gallons of water (0.25 mg per pot recommended). Use 6 oz. of the above mix per 6" pot twice: First application at emergence of shoot tip. Second application at 3" to 6" stage.

Sans Souci *lily.*

Crop uniformity Sans Souci will emerge at an irregular rate. Adjust uniformity of development by moving slower plants to a warmer area and vice versa.

Days to flower Using precooled bulbs, it will take about 112 days from potting to flowering.

Keys to Sans Souci Success

- Bulbs will emerge over a period of time. Plants will even up in height during the first 6 to 8 weeks. Adjusting temperature will hasten time to uniformity. Be patient.

- Leaves will gradually change in color from yellowish to green to dark green. Leaves also will broaden considerably during the growing period.

- From bud visible stage until opening will be 30 to 40 days. Sans Souci open much slower than Easter lilies. Do not slow development by lowering night temperatures at this stage.

- From visible bud stage, avoid high daytime temperatures (over 80°F). This condition tends to cause a heat check on bud development.

- Buds open from the bottom to top of the plant.

G.V.B.

574

A fine example of an Easter lily—ready to go. The grower: Gene Schneider of G&E Greenhouses, Batavia, Illinois.

Cultivars

Lilium longiflorum Thurnberg, the Easter lily, belongs to the sub-genus *Eulerion,* the true lilies. The Easter lily with a white trumpet is the most popular lily for greenhouse pot lily production. Asiatic and Oriental hybrid lilies are gaining in popularity. *Nellie White* replaced *Ace* as the most popular variety, probably in 1980. Additional varieties resulting from Oregon State University-Pacific Bulb Growers Association-sponsored breeding programs are being introduced. Best known to date is *Harbor.* Characteristics of the Oregon introductions are earlier flowering and shorter plants. Field performance has yet to be determined.

Georgia lilies, either from the southern United States or from Japan, are used less and less. Problems are height, virus content, and especially the overall plant appearance and lasting quality of individual flowers. Frequently flower splitting occurs, and unsatisfactory plants result.

*Contributed by Robert O. Miller, chairman/CEO, Dahlstrom & Watt Bulb Farms, Inc., Smith River, California.

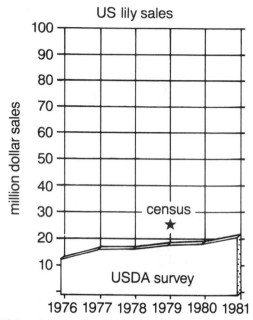

US lily sales. The solid area is the USDA survey. The star posts the 1979 Department of Commerce sales totals.

A comparison of the major varieties, *Ace* and *Nellie White,* follows:

- Height. *Nellie White* is shorter than *Ace.*

- A-Rest tolerance. *Nellie White* is more apt to suffer leaf yellowing from growth retardant application than *Ace.*

- Bud count. *Nellie White* will usually have ½ to 1 fewer buds for a given size bulb. This is why most growers force larger size bulbs of *Nellie White.*

- Flower size. *Nellie White* is generally credited with having larger flowers than *Ace.* The newer introductions have even larger flowers.

- Forcing time. There is no difference. In most years *Nellie White* is slower to emerge than *Ace,* but from emergence to flowering, it is faster.

- Leaf number. *Nellie White*—for a given size bulb vernalized in the same way—usually has fewer leaves than *Ace.* In some years 10–20 fewer leaves have been recorded. This is why *Nellie White* flowers in the same time as *Ace* even when it emerges later.

- General toughness. *Nellie White* is not generally as "tough" as *Ace.* *Ace* is more tolerant of temperature extremes, A-Rest, root rot, fertilizer excess and deficiency, etc.

- Precooling temperature. *Nellie White* is best vernalized (precooled) at near 45°F while the optimum for *Ace* is 40°F (4.4°C).

- Scorch. *Nellie White* is more resistant to true leaf scorch than *Ace*. *Ace* is much more resistant than the older variety *Croft,* no longer grown. *Ace* is not troubled by scorch if a few rules are followed (see fertilizer).

- Space. *Nellie White* and *Ace* have the same space requirements.

- Fertilizer requirements. *Nellie White* and *Ace* require essentially the same fertilizer. *Nellie White* may show higher leaf nitrogen content than *Ace* under similar regimes.

- Timing from visible bud. *Nellie White* and *Ace* have the same time of development from visible flowers until flower opening. The same "bud stick" may be used.

- General plant picture. *Nellie White* generally is given credit for having broader foliage and a more pleasing picture. It is difficult, however, to distinguish between well-grown *Ace* and *Nellie White*.

What Cultivar to Grow

Grower preference is the single determining factor. Larger growers, especially, should be familiar with the forcing characteristics of both varieties and be prepared to utilize either. *Nellie White* is more prone to summer sprouting in the field than *Ace*. Since summer sprouting can on occasion affect 10–50% of the crop, summer sprouting could affect the supply of *Nellie White* in a given year.

It is also true that weather conditions on the West Coast can affect bulb size of the cultivars differently. There are *Ace* "years" and *Nellie White* "years." The ability to handle either variety is an advantage for a particular grower.

Height is perhaps the singlemost important consideration. The fact that *Nellie White* is the shorter of the two varieties is balanced in many instances by the fact that *Ace* is less likely to suffer leaf yellowing and thus can tolerate higher A-Rest rates and be held as short as *Nellie White*. The cost of A-Rest may be offset by the higher bud count obtained with *Ace*.

Field Culture

Most Easter lilies are produced on the West Coast on the Oregon-California border (many fields overlooking the ocean) between Harbor, Oregon and Smith River, California. Production requires 2 to 4 years growth in the field, depending on size and whether scale production is utilized or plants are started from bulblets (small bulbs formed around the below-ground stem above the bulb). Bulbs from scales (modified leaves broken from "mother bulbs"), called scalets, can be produced in one year. Scaling, combined with tissue culture, offers a means of rapid buildup of desirable stocks. Other factors being equal, scalets produce more uniform crops than bulblets.

Bulblets or scalets are graded and planted to produce 4" to 8" bulbs called "yearlings" the first year. These yearlings are harvested, graded, treated, and replanted to produce "commercials." Because of demand for larger sized bulbs, some smaller commercials are replanted for still another year.

Packing and Size

Bulbs are harvested in late September and October, usually being completely packed by October 20. Rain is a determining factor in some years. The rainy season can begin on the coast about September 15; thus, rain can hold up the harvest. Forcers should be aware of this and be prepared to adjust their procedures should delayed harvesting result.

Long standard lily packs are presented below. Changes are being considered to allow smaller cases for ease of handling and shipping.

Bulb circumference (inches)	Number per case
6½–7 (16.5–17.75 cm.)	300
7–8 (17.75–20.3 cm.)	350
8–9 (20.3–22.9 cm.)	200
9–10 (22.9–25.4 cm.)	150
10–11 (25.4–27.9 cm.)	100

Bulbs are packed in peat moss of a standardized moisture content. It is probable that the ratio of bulbs, peat moss, and moisture is of critical importance. Bulbs must not dry out during the vernalization period or afterward.

Vernalization (Precooling)

Easter lily bulbs of presently grown cultivars have similar though not exact vernalization or precooling optima. Vernalization is the proper term to describe the cold treatment associated with the initiation of flower buds several weeks after exposure to low temperatures. While vernalization is the proper word, the process is often referred to as precooling, cooling, chilling, cold treatment, etc. It is important to remember that not only is the cold treatment critical but it must be given under moist conditions. Cold received in late October, November, and December is "remembered" by the stem, causing flowers to be initiated in January. If plants are not exposed to cold (or long days) the stem will eventually grow—perhaps indefinitely—and not initiate flowers. Stems with over 300 leaves have been recorded. Cold thus causes leaf-making to cease and flowers to form.

Methods of Vernalization

Before specifics, the several methods of precooling should be broadly explained. Case precooling bulbs are precooled in the packing case, wherever it takes place. Pot cooling is a broad term also and means that plants are precooled after potting. Pot cooling has many variations such as "cold framing," which refers to early potting and placing in cold frame or other location which will prevent freezing but otherwise is not temperature controlled. Outdoor cooling refers to potting and placing outside with perhaps a straw cover to prevent drying, protection from heat during the day, and frost at night. CTF or controlled temperature forcing is a popular and preferred system of pot cooling. The CTF system or variations of it allow more definite control of vernalization. When the investment in bulbs, soil, pots, and labor is considered, we believe it prudent that all pot cooling be done under controlled conditions.

Case cooling   Bulbs are shipped from the production area to either commercial cold storage facilities or to greenhouse growers who place them into refrigerators in the cases in which they have been shipped. It is important that temperature and time be carefully controlled. Table 1, though reflecting some variation in the data, illustrates the effect of too little or too much vernalization or precooling.

Table 1

Weeks of storage	Days to flower	Number of flowers
0	196	10.0
1	176	9.7
2	160	9.1
3	135	7.1
4	123	6.4
5	114	6.5
6	109	5.6
7	112	5.6
8	110	5.2
9	103	5.0
10	100	4.9
11	98	4.4
14	103	4.5

Source: *Lilies,* edited by D. C. Kiplinger and Robert W. Langhans, New York State Extension Service. February 1967.

Almost always, vernalization times of 6 weeks are recommended. With 5–6 weeks, expected forcing times of 110–115 days usually result. Longer vernalization results in faster forcing but lower bud count. This is a tradeoff. *Nellie White* has an optimum vernalization temperature of 45°F (7.2°C) and

An example of what can happen if precooled bulbs received in the fall are not placed in cold storage or potted immediately upon arrival. The bulb on the right was held at room temperature for two weeks before potting.

Ace at 40°F (4.4°C). Times of longer than 6 weeks are not suggested. Bulbs probably vary from year to year either in the amount of cold they have accumulated in the field or in the time requirement for vernalization and perhaps temperature optima as a result of seasonal changes. It has not been necessary to vernalize longer than 6 weeks nor less than 4 weeks. For practical purposes less than 5 weeks is never recommended and only feasible in some years.

CTF cooling   Immediately after potting, many schedules call for 3 weeks of 63°F (17.2°C) for root growth, and 6 weeks at 40°F (4.4°C) or 45°F (7.2°C) for vernalization. This is a total of 63 days. When bulbs are received early and Easter is relatively late this is no problem. When Easter is early and/or bulbs are received late there is just not time to accommodate the entire CTF 9-week schedule. More on this later.

Many texts have placed the forcing time for *Nellie White* and *Ace* lilies at 120 days. The 13th edition of the *Ball Red Book,* for example, says "timing of lilies for Easter centers around a basic rule that the bulb requires approximately 120 days from potting to flowering." Table 1 shows (after 6 weeks vernalization) 109 days. The point is, no less than 110 days should be allowed from bringing bulbs to the heated greenhouse until shipping, depending on when this is. Usually ⅓ of the crop is shipped up to 2 weeks before Easter. Many growers in recent years have not allowed enough time for forcing.

Consider the following:

Easter date	Description	Days from Dec. 7	Days from Dec. 15	Days from Dec. 21
March 26	Early	110	102	95
April 7	Early-Mid	122	114	107
April 14	Late-Mid	129	121	115
April 21	Late	136	128	121

For early or early mid-Easter dates, plants must be brought to the greenhouse by December 7–15 or earlier to allow time for forcing. On the latest dates, enough time is available from a December 15 to 21 date.

Most practically, whatever the date of Easter, we strongly suggest that plants be in the greenhouse no later than December 15. On a very early date, December 7 is much preferred. This allows the plant time to develop. If December 15 is used as a date to begin forcing (no matter what the Easter date) then either the schedule before forcing or the forcing time must be adjusted or both. See the suggested schedule below.

SUGGESTED CONTROLLED POT COOLING SCHEDULE

Easter date	Begin forcing date	Days to Easter	Days of vernalization	Date to start vernalization
March 26	Dec. 7	102	42	Oct. 26
April 7	Dec. 15	114	42	Nov. 3
April 14	Dec. 15	121	42	Nov. 3
April 21	Dec. 15	128	42	Nov. 3

Note that for the earliest Easter a vernalization date of October 26 is suggested and earlier is better. If bulbs are shipped from the West Coast October 10 and require 5 days in transit and require 3 days to get potted, it is obvious that it's October 18 or thereabouts and that at most there are only 7–8 days for 63°F (17.2°C) rooting treatment. The movement to the greenhouse at the proper time and a full vernalization treatment are more important than 3 weeks at 63°F (17.2°C); therefore the rooting period should be cut short. Note also in many cases, weather and other factors prevent bulb shipments as early. Also, as more and more forcers elect pot cooling, more and more early shipments are requested; it is obvious that all shipments cannot be made at once. Further, bulbs are not always out of the ground to honor all these early shipments.

In summarizing pot cooling techniques, remember that Easter lilies need 110–120 days from the start of forcing to flowering. Many troubles in forcing result from bringing bulbs to the greenhouse too late and "starting from behind." Pot cooling is to be recommended for those who can use it and understand it. The 63°F (17.2°C) rooting period should be adjusted (eliminated if necessary) to allow for a full 6 weeks of vernalization and moving to the forcing greenhouse in time. It is also critical that forcers understand that they must keep pots moist to ensure that the bulbs can perceive the proper cold temperatures. Many problems are blamed on bulbs which have dried out during pot cooling.

With today's poinsettia shipping schedules, lilies can be brought in at the proper time. While this may require some special management, the extra trouble will be more than repaid by the crop quality which results. Raising the temperature of the storage after precooling prior to moving the pots to the greenhouse is a method used to start forcing at the proper time if some problem prevents moving to the greenhouse on schedule. Growth in storage is probably slower than in the greenhouse, however, because of no "sun heat," and this should be considered. There is also danger of sprouting in the dark in storage.

Modifications of Pot and Case Cooling

In the past, some growers have requested that bulbs be shipped to them early, prior to the finish of case cooling, so as to be potted in late November. They then run cool temperatures near 50–55°F (10–12.8°C) until late December when they raise temperatures to 60–65°F (15.5–18.3°C) to start forcing. This is a workable system. The cool temperatures during December allow for some rooting and also some vernalization. The 4 weeks at 50°F (10°C) equates to near 2 weeks at 40°F (4.4°C). This is a system that was in widespread use before the long-lasting poinsettia varieties became common.

In some warm areas such as inland valleys of California and in the South, a modified pot cooling program works although controlled conditions are to be preferred. Some forcers allow bulbs to have 2–4 weeks of vernalization in the case, then pot them allowing the balance of the vernalization to proceed under natural conditions. This procedure, too, allows some rooting to occur.

Lighting

Long days can substitute for cold on a day-for-day basis. Long days also have the same effect on reducing bud count as does increased vernalization. From a practical view, use of lights can be very beneficial if combined with sorting. Lighting of 10 foot-candles (mum lighting) 4 hours nightly is used. If a new installation is put in just for lilies, installation costs can be reduced by use of an intermittent lighting system. Lights should be applied immediately on emergence (have lights on 1–2 days prior to emergence) and left on for the number of days desired. There is one problem. Early emerging plants receive more long days than they need and late emerging plants not enough unless early emergers are moved to an unlighted area. Remember, lighting for too long a period can cause reduced bud count.

Bud Count and Bulb Size

Bud count is controlled by bulb size, vernalization, and growing factors. Bulb size affects bud count. Table 2 is idealized but gives a rough idea of the number of flowers to be expected from a given size bulb treated properly. Note that "pot" cooling can increase bud count. Bud count is probably controlled by meristem area at the start of the flower initiation period near January 15 through February 7. Thus, larger bulbs—which have larger meristems—have more flowers. Similarly, anything which promotes vigorous growth of the new stem can increase flower count. Most recognized of these growth factors is temperature.

Forcers who use smaller bulbs such as 6½–7" *Ace* or ⅞" *Nellie White* must bear in mind that should any difficulties arise during the forcing period, where they lose a bud or two, they may end up with an undesirable, nonsalable plant.

Table 2

Bulb circumference (inches)	Case vernalized		Pot vernalized*	
	Ace	*Nellie White*	*Ace*	*Nellie White*
6½–7	3	2	4	3
7–8	4	3	5	4
8–9	5	4	6	5
9–10	6	5	7	6
10–11	7	6	8	7

*Note: Pot cooling in many of its variations will usually produce an additional 1 or more buds.

Temperature Dip

By reducing the night temperature during the flower initiation period, growth slows and the meristem apparently expands, allowing more area for flowers to form. Reducing temperature to 55–58°F (12.5–14.5°C) for 7–14 days can increase bud count appreciably. Perhaps more importantly, it must be emphasized that raising the temperature during this period can cause a severe loss of flowers. It must be emphasized that in no case is it suggested to use a temperature dip unless the leaf count method of timing is being used to monitor crop development.

Other factors such as sunlight, good fertilizer, high carbon dioxide levels, good roots, proper watering, etc., all have a definite effect on bud count.

The bad effects of over-vernalization have already been covered. The most beneficial effect of pot cooling is that roots are established when flower initiation occurs. This allows lots of water and nutrients to be absorbed to promote vigorous growth. Much as a pot mum cutting fattens after planting, a lily stem also expands. The better the growth, the more the bud count.

Bulb Drying and Vernalization

Vernalization is a process that takes place under cool moist conditions. Drying during vernalization either in the case or in the pot can prevent the bulb from receiving the cold and result in uneven and non- or partially-vernalized bulbs. After vernalization, especially if vernalization is not complete, exposure to temperatures of near 70°F (21°C) or higher can erase the cold treatment and can cause growth anomalies.

Potting

Bulbs should be potted upon receipt or upon completion of cooling. Delay in potting is a serious potential problem.

Bulbs should be planted deep in standard pots (6" × 6", 15 cm., for example) to protect against early emergence in controlled storage and to allow adequate room for the development of stem roots above the bulb. Two inches of soil over the bulb is preferred.

A few bulbs may sprout in the case. Sprouted bulbs are not hurt. The critical factor is to bury the entire etiolated (white) stem below soil level. Sometimes planting the bulb on its side can accomplish this. If the entire stem is covered, growth will be normal on emergence. If a portion of etiolated stem remains above ground, leaves will not elongate and small stem bulblets will form.

Some forcers still prefer gravel in the bottom of pots, mostly for weight to prevent tipping. Gravel probably serves no drainage purpose; in fact, it probably shortens soil, water columns, and contributes to a wetter root area.

With more height specifications by large buyers, more ³/₄"-deep pans (6" X 5") are being seen. This 1" shorter pan may make a difference between 3 and 4 layers in a truck. In any case, deep potting is beneficial and should be a goal.

Soils

Good lily soils are soils with water-holding capacity but good drainage and especially good fertilizer-holding capacity. It is unlikely that the keeping quality of lilies grown in lightweight peat mixes is as good as that of lilies grown in heavier soil base mixes. Further, lily soils should have enough weight to prevent tipping should lilies get taller than desired.

Depending on physical characteristics, a medium with $1/4$–$1/2$ soil is the best mix. Vermiculite is excellent to increase nutrient exchange capacity. Peat moss at $1/4$ or more and bark (be sure to add nitrogen to correct for bark decomposition) is suitable. Remember that, on a volume basis, peat moss has very little fertilizer-holding capacity. A useful mix has been:

$1/3$ soil

$1/3$ peat moss (or peat-bark, $1/2$ each)

$1/6$ vermiculite

$1/6$ coarse sand

The pH is adjusted to 6.5–7.0 with calcium carbonate using 2 lbs. per yard as a basis. Certain limestone deposits have apparently high fluoride content and known sources of this material should be avoided.

A complete fertilizer, 12–12–12 for example, can be added at the rate of 1 lb. per yard. *Do not* use superphosphate (see leaf scorch). If bark is added to the mix, we suggest an extra $1/2$ lb. of urea formaldehyde fertilizer per yard be added to compensate for nitrogen tieup in bark decomposition. If soil is to be stored, organic nitrogen should not be used. Trace elements are probably best added in liquid form.

Easter lilies need fertility early in their development to produce vigorous stem expansion and a large leaf canopy. For this reason, soils should contain enough fertility to allow liquid applications to maintain a high fertility level. Good nutrition starts with a soil of high initial fertility but one not exceptionally high in total soluble salts. High soluble salts can cause erratic sprouting and in extreme cases can prevent sprouting completely.

Fertilization

Ace is more susceptible to leaf scorch than *Nellie White* but *Nellie White* can show scorch symptoms. Leaf scorch is a serious disease and many younger growers have not seen the extreme loss that can result. Fertilization of lilies should be based on elimination of leaf scorch as a problem in addition to other considerations. Leaf scorch can be controlled—whatever its true cause—by high calcium levels, high nitrate nitrogen levels, and low phosphorus levels. This is the reason for lime for pH control, and no superphosphate in the initial mix. After potting, calcium nitrate at 200–750 ppm actual nitrogen, coupled with soluble trace elements and potassium at 200 ppm, is satisfactory depending on soil mixes and irrigation schedules.

Use of phosphorus at 20 ppm in irrigation water is not likely to induce scorch and certainly provides adequate phosphorus.

One of the most important cultural considerations is to provide adequate nitrogen to prevent lower leaf yellowing and subsequent leaf loss. Experiments removing the lower $1/3$ of leaves induces tall lilies. Lower leaf loss by nitrogen starvation also can cause stretch. The time nitrogen is most likely to be limiting is at bud initiation. A high nitrogen requirement at this time plus a possible deficiency because of organic matter decay can result in an incipient nitrogen deficiency. Often, also, it is difficult to make adequate liquid fertilizer applications at this time because of constantly wet soils due to dark weather, and other liquid applications. Often the yellowing of a few lower leaves is attributed to root loss or drying and nothing is done. Nitrogen deficiency then becomes progressively more pronounced until it is too late to correct it. The best method to prevent this and to ensure a dark green shiny healthy leaf surface is to top-dress with a dry, long-lasting nitrogen source such as urea formaldehyde nitrogen—nitroform, for example. One teaspoon per 6" pot at mid-January to February 1 is adequate. Application costs are more than repaid.

Soluble salts should be kept below 2.0 micro per cu. cm.

For best keeping quality, plants should be well fertilized during the growing season so that the fertility level can be reduced in the greenhouse during the last two weeks. Clear water applications will leach out any excess salts. Lilies, like foliage plants, use much less fertilizer and are more susceptible to fertilizer injury when they are moved from the growing environment to a nongrowing environment. This is especially true when lilies are boxed and cold-stored prior to shipping.

Watering

Lilies should not be automatically watered by mat or drip tube systems. Excess height almost always results unless special conditions prevail. Overhead sprinkling, however, is satisfactory. As with all crops, water management is tied up with soil management.

Heavier soils are harder to manage with respect to water relations than lighter soils, but the better customer satisfaction resulting from soil-based mixes makes the extra effort worthwhile.

Excessive watering can encourage root rot problems. It is probable that currently available fungicide drenches have allowed growers much more latitude in watering. Careful watch should be maintained on the root system should wet rot symptoms appear. Careful assessment of water level, soluble salt level, and fungicide drench timing must be made.

Early in the life of the crop in the dark days of December and January, it is difficult to time fungicide drenches, liquid fertilizer applications, and liquid growth regulator applications.

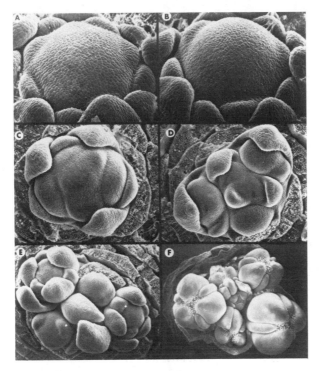

Six pictures of a lily growing point as seen under a binocular microscope or powerful hand lens. Development from A to D is a vegetative growing point to a stage of flower development just before buds would be visible.

A. *Lily meristem in October. No floral development.*

B. *Early January. No floral development evident.*

C. *Mid-January. This is a reproductive meristem. This would be difficult to distinguish without lot of experience.*

D. *Late January. A reproductive meristem with four or five buds formed. This is about the earliest stage that growers can verify bud set.*

E. *Further advancement of flower development. Four buds with either a flower bud or a secondary vegetative meristem in the lower center (covered by two leaf primordia).*

F. *Further advancement. Six flower buds evident.*

Timing

Until Dr. A. N. Roberts of Oregon State University devised the leaf counting method of timing lilies, most growers relied on height to time the crop until flower buds were visible. From visible flower buds, timing was aided by "bud sticks." The photo shows a pattern. This pattern can be traced onto a pot label

587

to make a "bud stick." The pointed end is sharpened and then aligned with the base of the small developing bud (where the peduncle ends and the petals and sepals begin). This tip of the flower is then aligned with three numbers showing the number of days at three temperatures required to bring that bud into flower. Note that a bud near $\frac{1}{2}$" long—about the visible stage—can be brought to flower in as little as 20 days by "hard forcing" at near 70°F (21°C) night temperature (day temperature 10–20°F higher) or as many as 36 days at 54°F (12.2°C).

Time of emergence and height are still useful guides for early development. Such detailed schedules were published by many colleges in the past. Few are now available. Below is an approximate schedule based on an early, mid-, and late Easter.

	Date of Easter		
	Early	Mid	Late
Emergence	Dec. 28	Jan. 1	Jan. 7
Plant 1"*			
Plant 3"*			
Plant 6"*			
Plant 8"*			
Buds visible	Feb. 11	Feb. 25	Mar. 11
Buds 1" long	Feb. 25	Mar. 11	Mar. 25
Buds bent and 2½" long	Mar. 11	Mar. 25	Apr. 8
Flowers open	Mar. 25	Apr. 8	Apr. 22

*Varies with cultural practices and weather conditions.

Note that the essential fact of these height schedules is that they entirely fail to take growth factors into account which influence height. They are rigidly fixed in allowing 6 weeks for development from buds visible and also relatively rigid upon emergence. The only flexibility is the "middle of the schedule." Since they allow absolutely no method of determining how fast development should be in the middle of the schedule, they really are quite useless. If buds are not seen by a particular time, temperatures can be raised but it would obviously be advantageous if an earlier measure were available. Such a system was devised by Oregon State University research and has been widely publicized and refined by Dr. Harold Wilkins of the University of Minnesota. If the leaf counting procedure is followed, a grower can determine by mid- to late January exactly how many leaves the crop has (remember, the number of leaves varies with the amount of cooling). Since the rate of leaf unfolding is determined by temperature, the temperature to force can be determined as early as leaf count is determined. By monitoring the rate of leaf unfolding, development can be continuously monitored. The number of leaves the crop has must be determined after flower initiation has occurred. To count leaves use the following procedure:

1. Jan. 15th to 20th select 3–5 representative plants of each major lot to be monitored.

588

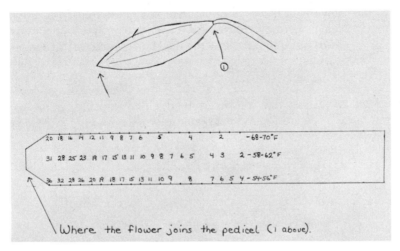

The famous lily "bud stick." Example: If you're growing at 68° to 70° and if the bud reaches out from circle one above to the number five on the top scale (68° to 70°), then that bud will be open in 5 days. Only qualification: A lot of bright sun will hasten the process.

2. With a felt tip pen or by notching a leaf, select the uppermost "unfolded" leaf.

3. Start at the bottom and count all leaves which have unfolded up to the notched or marked leaf (in #2 above). Write this number down.

4. Start with the notched or marked leaf and remove and count leaves toward the growing point. This is easy until the leaves get to be 1/4" to 1/2" long; then a mounted hand lens and needle will be necessary. Count the leaves right into the growing point—buds should be visible. Write down the number of leaves. The numbers written down would appear—for example—as follows:

   • Leaves unfolded   50

   • Leaves not unfolded   45

   • Total leaves   95

5. Average or look at the figures for 3 to 5 plants. If, for example, this count was made January 15th and 45 leaves were left to unfold, compute as outlined below the number of leaves per day to unfold.

   a. Count back from Easter the number of days before Easter that buds should be visible. Usually 6 weeks is used (but less can suffice). So, for an Easter on April 19 less 6 weeks equals March 8. Now from January 15 to March 8 there are 52 days.

589

b. Divide 45 leaves not unfolded by 52 days to unfold, equaling .87 leaves per day. So .87 leaves per day need to be unfolded to see buds on March 8. Now the question is, how many leaves per day can be unfolded?

After leaves per day are determined, the following can be used as a starting place to pick a forcing temperature:

Night temperature	Small bulbs	Large bulbs
60°F (15.5°C)	.75	1.00
65°F (19.0°C)	1.25	1.50
70°F (21.0°C)	1.75	2.00*

*Under certain conditions more than two leaves per day can be attained.

Assume in our example that we have a large 8"–9" bulb. We can change temperatures to 60°F (15.5°C) because we can expect to unfold near one leaf per day.

It's nice to read in a book that for a "large bulb" 60°F will cause the unfolding of one leaf a day. It's even better to actually measure the average number of leaves unfolding per day. To accomplish this, follow the procedure below:

1. Select another three to five plants from each major lot. Put a pot label in each pot and use a tall flagged stake to mark it to make it easy to find.

2. Write the date on the label and notch or mark a leaf in the same relative position as in step 2 of the previous procedure (p. 589).

3. Wait 4–5 days and again mark a leaf in the same relative position as in step 2.

4. Then count the number of leaves that have actually unfolded from the most recently marked leaf down to the earlier marked leaf. Write this down on the label with the new date.

5. Compute the leaves per day as follows:

5 = number of leaves unfolded
4 = number of days
1.25 = number of leaves per day

Computation in step 5 of the leaf counting procedure showed a need to unfold .87 leaves per day. This computation showed that 1.25

A fine house of lilies just breaking color.

leaves per day are unfolding. Temperatures need to be slowly lowered to decrease the rate of unfolding to .9 to 1 leaves per day.

6. By counting each 4–5 days, crop progress can be followed. This is a workable system. All lily growers should use it. Remember, leaf counting allows timing to start January 15 rather than when buds are visible. Growers have 4 to 6 weeks longer to manipulate temperature using this system.

Leaf counting also allows more reasoned decisions regarding temperatures and thus allows fuel savings. If consistent records of the rate of leaf unfolding are kept along with major cultural events—periods of high or low light intensity, irrigations and fertilization, carbon dioxide additions, temperature changes, root loss, fungicide applications—it is possible to determine the effect of these changes on growth rate. It thus builds a body of knowledge which can be used to judge the effect of future cultural changes.

Chemical Growth Retardants

At this writing, A-Rest is the only practical chemical to reduce the height of pot lilies. While expensive, its use often is necessary if height is to be controlled.

591

The material may either be applied as a drench, a spray, or as a combination. Soil application may be made early before leaf surface is expanded to absorb a spray and may have a more lasting effect. Shredded bark—especially pine bark—absorbs A-Rest, thus reducing its effectiveness. More material must be used to counter this loss. Greater expense is incurred and this may offset the advantage of soil application. Rates of near 0.5 mg. per pot as a soil application or 33 ppm as a spray (see A-Rest label) are effective in some bark soils under conditions of low light. In higher light areas, or if bark is not used, it is probable that lower rates should be used.

Some thought persists that A-Rest reduces flower count; however, it is unlikely that this is true unless it is applied excessively early at excessive rates.

A-Rest is to be avoided if possible. The known effect of rapid senescence (leaf yellowing from the bottom to the top) has been associated with A-Rest applications, particularly on *Nellie White*. Most yellowing has occurred under conditions of "carbohydrate shortage." Prolonged high temperature forcing, long shipping distances, and long storage of boxed plants have been associated with yellowing. It is also expensive.

Growth retardant should be applied in relation to leaf number in order to have more predictable response from year to year. First spray applications can be readily made when 25–30 leaves have unfolded. Sprays much earlier have less dwarfing effect apparently because of lack of leaf surface. Usually two applications are necessary, the second 7–10 days after the first. There may be some advantage to a first spray application to have a rapid effect followed by a drench which seems to be slower to take effect but is more long lasting.

Diseases

Root rots Root rots are probably the most serious diseases of lilies in greenhouses. Well-drained soils and attention to good irrigation practices are of importance. The wide array of soil drenches available, however, are of prime importance in control. Pythium, rhizoctonia and to a lesser extent fusarium appear to cause the most problems. The drench schedule below has proven effective:

Case-cooled bulbs	Benlate 1 lb./100 gal.	Lesan 8 oz./100 gal.	Terrachlor 4 oz./100 gal.
At potting		X	X
January 15	X	X	
February 15	X	X	
March 15	X	X	
Pot-cooled bulbs			
At potting		X	X
Start of forcing	X	X	
January 15	X	X	
February 15	X	X	
March 15	X	X	

Roots should be monitored and the drench schedule adjusted as needed. One Terrachlor application is important because of its effectiveness in rhizoctonia control. Rhizoctonia infections may be associated with bulb mite infestations and Terrachlor is most effective in preventing this.

Viruses Two major viruses affect lilies. When cucumber mosaic and lily symptomless virus are at high levels, "fleck" symptoms appear. This virus can be crippling. The fleck spots on the leaves and sometimes distorted plants can cause economic loss. All lilies in commercial production have lily "symptomless" virus. Clones made free of this virus grow much taller than infected clones. Flower count and other characteristics are apparently not much affected.

Poor growing conditions can magnify virus symptoms. Low temperature starting, low humidity, and no doubt other conditions can cause more symptom expression. Due to rogueing and aphid control in the field, viruses are usually not a problem.

Botrytis Under low light, high humidity conditions, botrytis can be a problem on unopened buds and flowers. Best control is by adding heat while venting to reduce relative humidity. Daconil sprays (1 lb. wettable powder/ 100 gallons with a recommended spreader) over the bulbs are also used. Botrytis is seldom a problem on foliage in greenhouses, although it is the most important disease in field production. Under severe humidity and free water situations, botrytis on leaves can occur.

Insects

Mites There has been much publicity recently about mites. Mites have long been associated with bulbs and are responsible for consuming the sloughed-off outer scales of the bulbs as they grow from inside out. Mites have been seen tunneling in stems apparently entering between the bulb and the soil surface. It is debated whether the mites are primary, causing the lesion themselves, or secondary, entering a lesion caused, perhaps, by rhizoctonia. It is to protect against the latter that Terrachlor is specified as a drench at potting. Most severe mite-type damage has been seen in pot-cooled lilies. Plants are often bent because the lesions on one side of the stem stop growth while the opposite side elongates. Dwarfed, stunted growth with thickened leaves and crippled growing points has been attributed to mites but this has not been established.

Bulb dips in Kelthane can be effective in elimination of mite populations. Rates are 1⅓ lb. of Kelthane 35% wettable powder per 100 gallons of water and immersing the bulbs for 30 minutes. Planting should be done immediately to prevent drying.

Aphids Aphids transmit viruses in lilies and should be controlled in greenhouses rigorously. A few aphids early in the crop can cause considerable damage. Distorted foliage, honeydew secretions with subsequent black mold, as well as virus buildup, can result from aphid infestations. Controls are as follows:

- Piramor at 6 oz./100 gallons

- Malathion WP, 25%, at 2 lbs./100 gallons

- Malathion Emulsion, 55%, at 1 pt./100 gallons

Three preventative sprays are suggested beginning in early January and ending two weeks prior to shipping.

Fungus gnats can build up on lilies kept especially moist or when much algae is present. It is not known if direct charge can result; however, their presence is not a good sign.

Other Troubles

Leaf scorch was discussed under fertilization. Symptoms are very characteristic, half-moon-shaped areas, often with concentric rings of varying colors of brown. These scorched areas are almost never located at the tip of the leaf but are usually ¼" or more from the tip. Uniformly brown "dieback" of leaves is not true leaf scorch and while occasionally seen, the cause of this problem is not known. Often such symptoms are seen after a period of clear weather following a long period of dark weather.

"Greenhouse twist"   The cause of greenhouse twist is debated. Some believe an organism—perhaps a bacterium—is the cause. Whatever its cause, twist can be serious in limited situations. Symptoms are sickle-shaped leaves appearing at the growing point, often with brown necrotic areas bordering the inside of the sickle. The plant may only produce one or two such leaves and usually outgrows the problem, with the plant being salable.

No-shows   Lily bulbs are a field crop and by the very nature of production, all bulbs are not perfect. It is to be expected that yearly a percentage of the crop may not emerge. There are several causes of this phenomenon although some nonemergence cannot be explained. The most common causes are:

Broken sprouts   If lily bulbs "summer sprout" in the field, that is, if the stem that normally emerges in the greenhouse emerges in the field, the sprout may be broken off during the harvest operation. Bulbs are inspected prior to packing but the broken sprout may not be detected. A bulb with a broken sprout will make good roots and will eventually sprout but the plant will be "off cycle" and will not bloom for Easter.

"Die back"   Phytophthora and perhaps other soil-borne diseases can cause a dying back of the flowering stem in the bulb. This can occur on a

prematurely sprouted bulb in the field or in a sprouting bulb after potting. Such bulbs make good roots and eventually sprout but they, too, will be off cycle.

Broken bulbs   During the harvesting process some bulbs are broken. This is evidenced by bulbs which do not emerge and when dug up, and scaled down, show excessive amounts of bulblet formation.

Unexplained nonemergence   Some bulbs while making roots do not sprout. This is seldom a problem but can be observed. Some bulbs do not sprout or make roots. The causes of nonemerging bulbs of this kind can arise either in the field during vernalization, or in the greenhouse. Severe drying, anaerobic conditions from soils high in readily decomposable organic matter, and/or water and probably other factors can cause rest in the bulb. That is, even though the current environment is favorable, internal factors prevent sprouting and growth.

Bud abortion and bud blasting   There are three phenomena which pertain to loss of flower buds.

Blasting   Buds that have blasted are evident on the plant. The first sign of blasting is a stoppage of growth of the bud followed by shriveling starting at the base of the bud. This is followed by further browning of the bud. Causes are most often high temperature forcing especially if humidity has been allowed to be low. Lack of water is also critical. This situation is made possibly worse by root rot at this time.

Abortion   This bud loss occurred just after bud initiation. Signs of buds show that they were present but were lost. Again high temperatures during and just after the bud initiation set period are most often responsible. Drying or any other growth factor can affect this. Small scars, small "pimples," and bractlike leaves (which always are present below a bud) are all signs that buds were there or were potentially there but lost.

Loss of potential   In severe situations, buds may be lost but leave no telltale signs. This phenomenon is best observed in comparing bulbs from the same case grown under different conditions, pot and case cooling for example. Again high temperature during the bud set period is most frequently responsible, but also poor growing conditions from potting through the bud initiation period is often at fault.

In most cases excessively low bud count is caused by greenhouse forcing problems. So many factors affect bud count that simple answers are often not possible. Most problems, however, relate to temperatures during the bud initiation period.

Shipping

Lilies are sold through retail florists or mass merchandisers. Most retail florists are delivered unboxed plants. Most mass markets are delivered in boxes. It is the practice in many instances to pack plants as they reach the "white puffy" stage and place them in the cooler. This is the proper stage for packing;

Robert Miller, D&W Bulb Farms, Inc., author of our lily chapter. The occasion, by the way: May pack trials at Ball Seed Company.

however, early packing is being abused. Packing too early can result in reduced quality in stores and ultimately for the customers. Good quality means good future sales. Efforts should be made to reduce box time in all instances. Lack of keeping quality in stores and in the home is potentially the most severe problem in the industry. Long box time, high temperature forcing from late potting, soils with no soil base, high A-Rest rates, and other factors must all be considered.

LOBELIA

ANNUAL *(L. erinus) 1,000,000+ seeds per oz. Germinates in 20 days at 70° (Exception: Variety Heavenly best at 50°).*

Although more at home in a moderate climate such as England's, lobelias are used throughout the U.S. for their brilliant blue effects in combination boxes, pots, and hanging baskets. With the development of many delicate-toned varieties, lobelias have gained in popularity and are highly valued plants in shady or semishady areas.

Culturally, they are not difficult. Being a bit slow-growing, they should be started not later than February 1, if flowering pot plants are wanted for Memorial Day. The seed is very fine; don't cover. A moderate temperature, say 55°–60°, will keep them moving without undue softening. They stand transplanting satisfactorily, and do well in any ordinary garden soil. If you can give them some shade, they will stand heat much better. They do not tolerate high temperatures and high humidity.

596

Most popular is *Crystal Palace* . . . a very dwarf, deep blue with dark, bronze-green foliage. *White Lady* is clear and showy. *Heavenly* is a deep sky-blue with large flowers and compact habit. All of the above varieties will stay below 8".

There is a trailing class known as *pendula* that works out well for trailing over porch boxes and for hanging baskets. Outstanding is *Sapphire,* deep blue with white eye and light green foliage.

LUPINE

PERENNIAL *(L. polyphyllus) 1,000 seeds per oz. Germinates in 30 days at alt. 70–85°.*

At one time, the annual form of lupine *(L. hartwegii)* was used as a cut flower crop under glass. Today, however, it is seldom used for this purpose, and the perennial form has greater commercial value.

The perennial species generally grown is known as *polyphyllus* and is not dependably hardy under our climatic conditions, though they will come through if covered with coarse material. Like the entire lupine family, the *polyphyllus* class resents such high temperatures as we occasionally meet with during June, their flowering season. They reach their highest state of perfection in England. There are favored locations here—mild winters and moderate summers—and under such conditions, they should be used. They delight in a loose, rather sandy soil that must be well drained. By far, the best class of hardy lupines is the *Russell* strain. All garden forms grown previous to the introduction of this strain were superseded by its development. Producing large blossoms and shapely spikes in an extensive range of color, they provide a brilliant display in the early perennial border.

MARIGOLD

ANNUAL *(Tagetes patula and erecta) 8,000–11,000 seeds per oz. Germinates in 7 days at 70–75°.*

One of the most showy and easily grown annuals, useful for bedding, pots, and cutting purposes, the marigold continues to grow rapidly in popularity. Responsible to a great degree for this continued rise in popularity is the development of new and improved varieties to such an extent that there are types and varieties available today that would fit nearly every gardening need (see photo). While they are native to warmer countries they do not perform at their best during periods of extreme heat such as we often experience here in July and August.

With the wide selection of types and sizes available today for general bedding plant purposes, the most feasible descriptive type of classification is simply to group them according to height: Dwarf, short, medium, intermediate, and tall.

597

MARIGOLDS—BRED FOR AN ARRAY OF FLOWER FORMS IN BRIGHT, CHEERY COLORS

GARDEN HEIGHT*	6-10″	10-12″	12-16″	16-18″	24-36″
VARIETY	Bonanza Series Boy Series Janie Series	Encore Honeycomb Queen Series Royal Crested Mixture Sparky Types Red Cherry	Solar Gold Space Age Series Sunshot Inca Series	Galore Series Lady Series	Gold Coin Series Jubilees
FLOWER SIZE—TYPE**	1-2″ double	1½″-2″ double	2-3″ double	3-3½″ double	3-4″ double
SPACE	10-12″	12″	12″	18″	18″
HABIT	Ball-shaped compact	Bushy, compact	Basal branching	Hedge type	Tall, bushy
USE	Border	Foreground	Foreground	Background	Background

Dwarf Marigolds (6″–10″)

Most useful for pots and bedding plant sales. For 2¼″ pots for Mother's Day, sow about February 15. For blooming plants in packs for May sales, sow 8 to 10 weeks before selling season and grow warm. Following is a listing of those varieties that are time-tested and have proven to be most popular in their class, along with a few new ones showing great promise.

The *Boy Series* is a dwarf strain (8″) used in a mixture as well as separate colors, with the yellow being most popular. The *Bonanza Series* is rapidly coming into prominence. Currently in three separate varieties, *Flame* has light maroon petals with a gold border, *Harmony* has a deep orange center with a maroon collar, and *Yellow* is very bright. Also fitting into this dwarf class is the *Janie Series* consisting of an orange, a yellow, and a red/gold bicolor called *Flame*. *Lemon Drop* (lemon yellow) is a long-time favorite.

Short Marigolds (10″–12″)

Encore, a primrose yellow triploid, produces large 2″ flowers. It has excellent shelf life and flowers all summer long. A very dependable performer in both pack and field is *Honeycomb*, which has crested flowers with light maroon petals with gold borders. Unique because of its broad, flattened petals, the *Queen Series,* a French type, produces 2″ blooms on ball-shaped compact plants. They're great for borders and 4″ pots. Included in the *Queen Series* are *Honey Sophia,* russet red-edged with golden bronze; *Scarlet Sophia,*

598

rich scarlet; *Queen Victoria*, a deeper gold version of *Queen Beatrix;* and the *Queen Mixture,* composed of the above separate colors. Still fairly popular after many years of usage is *Sparky Type Mixture,* a semi-double French type also sold as *Bonita Mix.* The *Crush Series* produces 3"–4" semi-double carnation type flowers on short, compact plants. Colors are gold, yellow, and orange; a mixture *Red Cherry* has bright mahogany red-crested blooms.

Medium Marigolds (12"–16")

The *Space Age Series* F_1 has been popular for many years and continues to be a good seller. They are very early and produce 3" semi-double flowers. Comprising this series are *Apollo* F_1, bright golden orange; *Moonshot* F_1, brilliant yellow; *Viking* F_1, gleaming gold; and a formula mixture of the above. *Sunshot* F_1 is an excellent large flowered yellow that is very uniform and superior to *Moonshot* F_1. The *Inca Series* are rapidly becoming well known because of their large flowers, freely borne on very compact plants. They're available in gold, orange, and yellow. *Solar Gold* and *Showboat* are two triploids in this bright class. The former produces bright gold 2³/₄" flowers. *Showboat* has consistently higher germination than most triploids and produces 2¹/₂" golden yellow blooms.

Intermediate Marigolds (16"–18")

A significant development produced by intensive breeding efforts has been the introduction of the "hedge type" F_1 hybrid group. Densely branched with a very compact habit, intermediate marigolds produce large flowers in abundance all over the plants. They have the ability to stand upright throughout the growing season without staking. Included in this type are the *Galores*, gold and yellow; also the *Lady Series—First Lady* is yellow, *Gold Lady, Orange Lady, Primrose Lady* (light yellow), and a mixture called *Gay Ladies.*

Tall Marigolds (24"–36")

Probably the best of the tall-growing F_1 hybrids is the *Gold Coin Series,* which in addition to a mixture consists of *Double Eagle,* a pleasing light orange; *Doubloon,* a bright yellow; and *Sovereign,* pure gold. These vigorous hybrids produce large double flowers. Second to the *Gold Coins* in popularity is the F_1 *Jubilee Series: Diamond, Golden, Orange,* and a mix.

Crackerjack Mix is an excellent inbred, fully double, carnation-flowered variety. Flowers are 100% double and produced in shades of orange, yellow, and gold.

Two single-flowered types still widely used are *Cinnabar* (12"–14"), a deep mahogany red; and *Dainty Marietta* (12"–14"), golden yellow with a red fleck at the base of each petal.

Crop time in packs runs from 8–12 weeks. The *Space Age Series, Dolly, Lady Galores, Sunshot* and the *Inca* types are sensitive to daylength and should be sown prior to February 15. If sown after that date use black cloth to restrict the light to 9 hours per 24-hour period. They should be black clothed from transplant time to bud stage. Light can be restricted to 9 hours for 2 weeks after sowing.

De-tailed seed of a number of varieties of marigolds is now available. De-tailing makes it possible to make sowings with an automatic seeder.

MORNING GLORY

ANNUAL *Morning Glory (convolvulus species) 650 seeds per oz. Germinates in 7 days at 68°.*

Popular as these showy vines are, we occasionally get complaints about "all vines and no flowers." There are two reasons why this sometimes happens: too much moisture or excessive soil fertility. For bedding plants, use in a 4" Jiffy-Pot with a stake in the center. Sow 4 or 5 weeks before time to sell. *Heavenly Blue* is, in our opinion, the showiest and the best seller.

NASTURTIUM

ANNUAL *(Tropaeolum majus) 175 seeds per oz. Germinates in 10 days at 65°.*

While the ordinary kind is sometimes very effectively used for bedding, it is not, on the whole, much of a florist item. But it is popular with the gardening public who buys tons of seed for outdoor planting. Of much more interest and value is the *Double Gleam* type. Of a trailing or climbing habit, it produces fragrant, double, long-stemmed flowers in rich colors. It is well suited for outdoor use.

More suitable for outdoor bedding purposes because of its dwarf, rounded, compact habit, *Jewel Mixture* is widely used. It produces large, double flowers of the *Gleam* type in a brilliant assortment of colors.

ANNUAL *(N. strumosa suttonii) 125,000 seeds per oz. Germinates in 10 days at alt. 55–60°. Dark.*

There are two distinct classes of this showy annual. *Grandiflora* is the name of the taller strain that will draw up to a height of about 2 feet.

Of much greater value is the *Nana Compacta* type. Its dwarf habit, 10" in the greenhouse, makes it popular to use in combinations. For this purpose, it should be sown in January and February for April and May flowering in 2¼" or 3" pots. While available in separate colors, it is chiefly used as a mixture. The *Carnival Mixture* is a most excellent strain, which is more heat resistant and will remain in flower several weeks longer.

Decorticated or cleaned seed is available on nemesia. This allows for many more seeds per ounce and much improved germination.

NICOTIANA (Flowering Tobacco)

ANNUAL *(N. affinis) 300,000 seeds per oz. Germinates in 10–12 days at 70°. Light.*

Several ornamental species of the tobacco family have been improved to the point where they are quite attractive for garden decoration. They are a taller-growing annual and adaptable to a wide variety of planting compositions. In sunny areas, they will give a continuous display of color over a fairly long season. Easily grown from seed, they should be sown about the middle of April for late-May pack sales. The F_1 hybrid *Nicki Series*, 16" to 18" tall, self-branching, free flowering with fine fragrance, represents a great improvement over existing strains. It's currently available in five separate colors: pink, rose, white, red, yellow, and a mixture. After transplanting, they should be grown-on at 60°. Responding well to B-Nine, they should not be sown before March 1 for flowering plants, since they require long days to bloom.

ORNAMENTAL PEPPER* AND CHRISTMAS CHERRY‡
(Jerusalem Cherry)

ANNUAL *(capsicum species) 9,000 seeds per oz. Germinates in 12 days at 70–80°. ‡(Solanum pseudo-capsicum) 12,000 seeds per oz. Germinates in 15 days at 70°.*

Ornamental peppers were formerly better known as Christmas Peppers. In some areas of the country they are still referred to as Christmas Peppers. However, currently there are many more of these colorful plants grown for sale during the months of September, October, and November than for Christmas sales.

The majority of this item is sold in 4" or 4½" pots. A possible variation to this would be to pan three or four 2" established plants to a 6" pot sometime in late summer.

Ornamental peppers.

Sowings are usually made from April until mid-July for sales from September until Christmas. Seedlings can be transplanted into cells (2"–2¼" size) or directly into 4" pots, using one plant per pot. Care should be taken to see that seedlings do not become crowded or stretched.

Most varieties benefit from a single or double pinch. The exceptions to this are *Holiday Time* and *Fireworks*. These two varieties are suitable for use in hanging baskets because of their growth habits.

A standard feeding program would require the application of 200 ppm nitrogen and potassium at each irrigation. This should be continued until fruit is set and then be reduced along with water.

Peppers require high light, good air movement, and temperatures between 65° and 70°F for maximum fruit set. As they reach maturity, temperatures can be lowered to 60°F. Peppers are best produced in a greenhouse. Most popular varieties include *Holiday Flame F₁*, which produces an abundance of slender, tapered fruit which turns from yellow to red; *Red Missile F₁*, whose red fruit is 2" long and tapered, and *Fireworks,* which has a semispreading habit and produces early cone-shaped fruit.

Mostly finished in 6" standard pots, well-fruited Christmas Cherries do find a ready market during the Christmas holiday season. Sow in mid-February, transplant seedlings into 2¼" pots or equivalent cells and then go directly to the finishing 6" pots. Plants should be pinched first when they develop three to four nodes of growth. They can be further pinched then from July 1 until July 15, dependent on geographic location. Christmas Cherries are grown at 50°F night temperature, and during the summer should be grown outdoors for best pollination and maximum fruit set. Care should be taken not to allow the roots to penetrate the soil that they might be set on. Injury to the roots results in both foliage and fruit drop. In the fall before frost the plants are brought back into the greenhouse and grown at 50°F nights. Feed and water must be closely monitored at this stage of growth. Most widely used varieties are the *Ball Christmas Cherry* and *Red Giant,* which has somewhat larger fruit.

PANSY

ANNUAL *(Viola tricolor) 20,000 seeds per oz. Germinates in 10 days at 65–70°. Dark.*

Pansies—heart of the April-May home garden display in the North—and year-round in the Deep South. Lovely!

Pansies continue to rate high on the list of American gardeners' favorite bedding plants. Coming into bloom early in the spring in a wide and interesting color range, a quality pack or flat of pansies in flower is hard for the home gardener to resist. Adapted to a wide variety of planting uses, they are a most consistent performer, even under conditions of high pollution. With the advent of F_1 hybrids, showing apparent ability to flower in the heat of summer, their future potential appears well ensured.

When to Sow

Midsummer has long been the traditional sowing time, generally late July or early August in the North. But any pansy plants which must grow from

603

August 1 to April or May before being sold—about 9 months in all—encounter many conditions that can reduce quality. Their worst testing time is usually during winter, when exposure to weather can harden and damage outside leaves, even though the heart of the plant comes through in good shape. Good-looking pansies can be grown from summer sowings, though, by keeping the plants well watered and fertilized during their growth and giving thorough winter protection. One other point: This system usually produces the heaviest plants.

The method being used by more growers each year calls for a December or early January sowing. Pansies can be grown steadily straight through to selling time with no dormant period. There is no hot-weather trouble during seed sowing and no damage from winter injury. Plants are either taken straight through in a 50° greenhouse, or else shifted to frames when weather permits, usually early March. The greenhouse growing is often on shelves and racks or in little-used cold houses; heated frames also work well. This minimizes use of expensive greenhouse space.

Seedlings started in November or early December and carried around 40° or 45° make good, heavy plants, which often bring more than enough to justify the added time and expense. At the other end of the scale are late sowings made up to March 1. These produce young stock for sale with annual bedding plants, and can increase your overall pansy business. Southern growers frequently purchase seedlings shipped down from the North instead of trying to grow their own, since pansy seed can be difficult to germinate in extremely hot weather. August sowings are the most common, whether for spring sales in the mid-South or midwinter sales in the Deep South.

Containers

Consider for a moment the labor it takes to sell pansy plants. Making up baskets is a time-consuming job that must be done when you can least afford the time. A good many growers are shifting over to the bedding plant method of handling—growing them in the selling container. They find that top-quality plants can be grown in their own choice of the many pack sizes and types available. Widely used today is the multiple-unit type, where the seedlings are grown as individual plants, separated from each other, and yet handled as one unit. The Jiffy-Strip is an example of this type. Another widely used type is the cell-pak, a vacuum-formed plastic unit that is available in a wide range of configurations. Four to six-plant units are becoming more common. In these size units, ample space is provided to finish extra-heavy plants.

Customer satisfaction should reach new highs when they discover that there is no transplanting shock, and each plant has a large intact root system. Pansies, it is being found, will bloom well into summer with this treatment. With either of these containers, beds or benches should have a root-discouraging surface, such as a layer of polyethylene or pea gravel. This keeps the pack clean and attractive, and easily restrains the root system.

Seed Starting

Pansy germination requirements include:

- Temperature: 65°–70°.

- Medium: Something sterile, well drained and low in fertility, that will not pack.

- Covering: Enough to hide the seed.

- Moisture: Constant. Intermittent-mist systems work well, as do plastic sleeves over the seed flats.

- Air and light: Little at first, to retard drying; plenty as soon as seedlings are up.

In the greenhouse, these requirements are met much the same as for snaps, and you may wish to check the snap story for some of the details.

Night temperatures of 65° to 70° are best until seed is up, when you can begin dropping to 50° by a week or so after germination.

A fine, friable soil mixture is suitable for a germinating medium. You can use sand-peat, perlite, leaf mold and other ingredients as well, just so you come up with a mix that meets the physical and chemical requirements.

Whatever means you employ to keep the seeds moist while sprouting, they should not dry out at all. After they are up, they do need plenty of air and light, and the soil surface can get quite dry between waterings.

Germinating pansy seed outside in frames is quite an art, practiced successfully by many careful growers. Sowings are made right in the frame where the seed bed has been carefully prepared and leveled. After thoroughly soaking the soil, about ½" of screened neutral peat is added. Beds are then steamed or treated with chemical sterilants. Steam is best. Seed is broadcast *thinly*, one ounce to 75 square feet. A very thin layer of sterilized neutral peat, or a mixture of 2 parts peat and 1 part soil (sifted), is used to cover the seed lightly. Constant moisture must be retained after sowing. Any period of dryness during germination is usually fatal. Germinating time is usually 10 to 14 days, depending on weather conditions.

Frames are covered with burlap and a double layer of lath to preserve moisture, which means that usually no watering is needed before sprouting. As soon as seed is well sprouted, the cover starts coming off, and within a week or so, they are receiving full light and air.

General Growing

Pansies can get too soft. Watering, feeding, temperatures, light, ventilation, soil, spacing, all are influenced by this fact. Fifty degrees is usually considered the maximum night temperature, and this during good weather. In dark, cloudy periods, growers may favor dropping the temperature below 50°.

At these cool temperatures, water requirements will be modest. Letting the plants dry to the point of slight wilting before giving water promotes the deep green foliage customers like to see. Feeding is usually light or nonexistent during winter. Summer-started plants, or those sown in the greenhouse later on, should get enough feed from the original planting soil until bright spring weather arrives, when one or more applications of 25–0–25 at 1 ounce to 3 gallons of water will help in finishing them.

Pansy soil should be loose, with plenty of organic matter—1 part peat to 3 parts soil, or a 2″ layer worked into the top 6″ of soil in frames or beds. Twenty % superphosphate is usually added, 5 pounds per 100 square feet, or 2 pounds per cubic yard.

Full light develops the best pansies. In fact, some growers use the sash all winter with frame-grown stock, even when plants are dormant and frozen. More conventional protection is loose straw or salt marsh hay applied only after freeze-up. Along with plenty of light, they like plenty of air. Except for frost protection, sash should be left off altogether once plants are in active growth. In greenhouses, pansies need maximum ventilation to keep from getting too soft.

In outdoor beds or frames, pansy spacing varies from 4″ × 4″ to 9″ × 9″ —6″ × 6″ is a rough average. Flat and pack growers generally space them much closer, since they are growing smaller, younger plants. They find that as soon as a few flowers pop, the packs are salable, and thus it is not necessary to grow the plants to an extra-large size.

Varieties

Based on our yearly flowering trials at West Chicago, here is the way pansy varieties stack up.

- F_1 *Majestic Giants*. This most popular large-flowered, early-blooming giant blooms well throughout the summer. Flowers have conspicuous blotches.

- F_1 *Universal Series*. Produces masses of multiflora blooms under extremes in temperature.

- F_1 *Crystal Bowl Series*. A more recent introduction of bright, clear colors with no dark blotches.

- F_1 *Color Carnival*. A large flowered *Swiss* giant type similar to *Roggli*.

- F_1 *Viking Series*. Produces extra large *Swiss* type flowers.

- *Color Festival*. An F_2 with a wide range of colors of large flowered *Swiss* types. Of the open pollinated strains, *Ball Giant Mixture* is our most popular dwarf bedding strain. Contains principally a *Swiss Giant* mixture, with separate colors added to ensure a well-rounded balance of all bright pansy shades.

- *Roggli Giant Elite Mixed* has a color richness not equalled by any other strain. This original *Swiss* strain also excels in dwarf habit and large flowers with excellent substance.

- *Steele's Jumbo Mixture*. Large flowers; early, vigorous grower. Always popular. Does well in the South.

- *Four Aces Formula Mixture*. Combines by formula blend these best sellers: *Ball Giant Mixture, Roggli Giant Elite Mixed,* and *Steele's Jumbo Mixture*.

There is considerable demand for pansies in separate colors, and many growers offer them this way to give a distinction to their line. While they are available in many separate colors, demand is greatest for white, yellow, and blue. Most popular in the F_1 separate colors are: *Azure Blue,* a rich azure color with lighter petals at the top; *Golden Champion,* the largest flowered clear golden yellow; *Imperial Giant Blue* (AAS), a light lavender-blue with yellow eye; and *Imperial Giant Orange,* bright orange. Widely used inbreds include *Pay Dirt,* large yellow with black lines; *True Blue,* light mid-blue shades; and *Paper White,* pure white with a yellow eye.

PETUNIA

ANNUAL *(P. hybrida) 285,000 seeds per oz. Germinates in 10–12 days at 70–80°.*

VERSATILE F₁ HYBRID PETUNIAS FOR EVERY TYPE OF CONTAINER OR GARDEN ARRANGEMENT

TYPE	Single Grandiflora		Double Grandiflora	Single Floribunda	Single Multiflora	Double Multiflora
VARIETY	Cascade Series	Flash Series Happiness Improved Magic Series Old Glory Series Penny Candy Sugar Daddy	Ball All-Double Mixture Bouquet Series Circus Fanfare Mixture Sonata	Summer Madness	Comanche Joy Series Sugar Plum Summer Sun	Sweet Tarts
FLOWER SIZE	3½-5"	3-4"	3-4"	3-4"	1½-2"	2"
SPACING	10"	10"	10"	10"	10"	10"
USE	Bedding, tubs, hanging baskets	Mass plantings, bedding	Porch boxes, tubs	Mass plantings, bedding	Mass plantings, bedding	Porch boxes
COMMENTS	The largest-selling type		Unique double types	Most disease/weather tolerant	Prolific bloomer	Popular novelty

The many and important cultural aspects of petunias are covered in some detail in the bedding-plant section of this book.

Not covered in that section, though, is the very important question of what's best in classes and varieties of petunias. The following is a resume of "best in class" for each of the various colors and types as of today:

Classes and Their Uses

Grandiflora doubles Well known for their value as pot plants, the grandiflora double petunias do very well as bedding plants, too. Varieties with 3" flowers provide an ever-widening range of solid colors and two-tone combinations for every taste. "Best in class"—*Nocturne Improved,* dark blue; *Pink Bouquet,* rose-pink; *Salmon Bouquet,* light salmon-pink; *Sonata,* white; *Valentine,* red; and *Circus,* a salmon-red and white bicolor.

Good doubles in 4" pots for early April are best produced from a late-December sowing, growing them at about 45°. For later May flowering, 3" pots are usually preferred. A January sowing will bring these along for Mother's Day or Memorial Day gifts or combinations. The grandiflora doubles require a little more attention than the other petunia classes. They cannot develop to their full potential if grown half starved or too cold. Growing them under these conditions will often produce semidouble or poorly developed flowers.

Multiflora doubles Free-flowering and showy, they bloom more freely than the grandiflora doubles, when planted outdoors. Compact in growth, they produce many miniature carnation-like flowers in a good color range, and provide an outstanding show of color, even under the difficult conditions of the midwestern summer. "Best in class"—*Cherry Tart,* #1 multiflora double, rose-pink and white bicolor; *Plum Tart,* penciled bright orchid; *Apple Tart,* coral; *Snowberry Tart,* pure white; and *Red and White Delight,* white and strawberry red.

As with grandiflora doubles, these should be sown earlier than the other types to sell at the same time.

California giants Recommended mainly for spring pots. The variety *Ball Dwarf Giant #1* is noted for extra early flowering on dwarf, compact plants. Flowers often reach 5" to 6" in diameter. While declining each year in popularity, there still is some demand for this class. However, these appear to be giving way to new and larger-flowered single grandifloras. Sowing dates: same as for all doubles.

Single grandifloras This class, with its large and attractive individual flowers, continues to lead in popularity and includes all the "fancy" single types—petals are ruffled or fringed or both; flower size is medium or large. Virtually all the key varieties are F$_1$ hybrids, which are available in every petunia color, with many bicolors and other unusual flower forms. Certain grandifloras are best suited for pots, with a dwarf, early-blooming type of growth. Others, having a more vigorous growth habit, find their best use in beds. A good many varieties, including *Pink Magic* and *White Magic,* give top performance either way. "Best in class"—*Penny Candy,* variegated scarlet and white; *Royal Cascade,* a deep blue; *Red Cascade,* a large, early bright red; *Red Flash,* a close #2 in reds; *Pink Cascade,* a smooth bright pink; *Coral Cascade,* coral-rose; *White Cascade,* giant, pure white; *Yellow Magic,* ruffled light yellow; and *Sugar Daddy,* bright orchid with deep red veins.

The Cascades are an outstanding series in the F₁ single grandiflora class. While with their vigorous growth habit and extra-large flowers they are ideal for bed planting and pots, their most popular usage is for hanging baskets, window boxes, etc., where their cascading habit is a "natural."

Single multifloras   Here is the traditional bedding class of petunias. F₁ hybrids provide vigorous plants of excellent, compact habit in all major petunia shades, with starred and striped varieties as well. An early March sowing means salable plants in flats or packs by about mid-May.

"Best in class"—*Starfire,* scarlet and white; *Sugar Plum,* orchid with wine-red veins; *Paleface,* white with small creamy eye; *Pink Satin,* rose-pink; *Comanche,* scarlet-red; *Coral Satin,* coral-rose; and *Summer Sun,* rich deep yellow.

Single floribundas   A new class just recently introduced, with the flower size being a cross between the grandifloras and multifloras. The flowering habit is extremely prolific. Tolerance to disease and weather is excellent.

At this writing, the variety that introduced the class, *Summer Madness F₁,* is the only one available. It is a bright, rosy-red color with deep red veins and flowers "like mad."

PHLOX

ANNUAL *(P. drummondi)* 14,000 seeds per oz. Germinates in 10 days at 60°. Dark.
PERENNIAL *(P. paniculata)* 2,500 seeds per oz. Germinates in 3–4 wks. at 65–75°.

A very showy, colorful annual that probably requires a little more attention than common annuals, such as petunias, when planted to outdoor beds. Phlox will easily make satisfactory-sized bedding plants for spring sales by sowing about the middle of March.

There are both a tall and a dwarf class of phlox, known as *Grandiflora* (15″–18″) and *Nana Compacta* (6″–8″), respectively. The former is not as widely used as the dwarf form, which is most popular and of greatest commercial value.

The most widely used dwarf forms are *Globe Mix* and *Twinkle.* The former has an almost perfectly rounded ball-like growth habit and an exceptionally

609

free-flowering characteristic. It branches out beautifully from the base of the plant in marked contrast to the other types of annual phlox, and has a good range of showy colors. *Twinkle,* an early bloomer, produces an abundant amount of dainty starred flowers with pointed petals.

Then there is the whole class of perennial phlox, about which a separate *Red Book* might be written. Briefly, though, the most important group is the summer phlox (*P. decussata, P. paniculata, P. maculata,* etc.). There are dozens of brilliant reds, purples, salmons, and varicolored varieties propagated by divisions and root cuttings in this group. They like a fairly well-enriched soil and should be kept fairly moist. Let each clump have 4 or 5 square feet to develop. Their normal flowering season is mid-July to September. *Beltsville Beauty* is a blend of *P. paniculata* types under the name of *Beltsville Beauty.* Seed should be exposed to freezing weather for several weeks for best germination.

For rock-garden work, the dwarf perennial *Phlox subulata,* variety *Nelsonii,* makes a brilliant showing. It is division-propagated, flowers in May and June, and makes a mat of bright green foliage clear through the season. In addition to *Nelsonii,* there are a dozen or so other choice varieties varying from white through bright pink, red, and crimson. All of this *subulata* group are procumbent, under 3", and are used for carpet plantings, rockeries, etc.

POINSETTIA CULTURE*

General Requirements and Characteristics

Cultural programs have changed substantially in poinsettia production over the past decade due to the differences in growth habit of the new varieties. Fortunately, most of the changes in variety characteristics have made it easier to produce a quality plant.

As new varieties are developed, tested, and introduced into the trade, there will undoubtedly be new approaches employed in their handling. However, certain basic characteristics of poinsettias will prevail, regardless of developments, and it is the purpose of this section to provide both background and practical-application information on handling this crop in particular. The information presented should be considered as guidelines only, since conditions differ from Northeast to South to Midwest to West. Therefore, schedules and programs must be adjusted to correspond to local conditions of daylength, temperature, light intensity, humidity, and markets.

*Contributed by Paul Ecke, Jr., Paul Ecke Poinsettias.

Paul Ecke, Jr., author of this chapter, and Paul Ecke, Sr., holding a new white seedling poinsettia.

The poinsettia is a short-day plant that is grown in greenhouses to produce colored leaves called "bracts." The flower itself is a relatively inconspicuous yellow organ. It has been demonstrated that in the northern hemisphere, flower-bud initiation occurs in early October, and under favorable temperature conditions results in flowering during late November and December. Some of the varieties may flower faster and others slower than the average. One of the attractive features of poinsettias for Christmas production is that there is little or no need for daylength control. For other blooming periods, daylength must be artificially controlled. In general, it can be assumed that the bract development will be completed 2 to 3 months after initiation.

611

Commercial poinsettia production.

Although all aspects of the mechanism have not been clearly demonstrated, it appears that there is a certain minimum daylength requirement for the first stage of initiation. If this critical daylength remains constant, the plant may tend to split as if it had been pinched, and proceed to produce three vegetative branches. However, if the daylength is gradually reduced from time of initiation, the tendency then is to produce a single stem terminating in bract and flower. Thus, under normal conditions, initiation occurs when days are just short enough to stimulate this reaction, and as days gradually become shorter, they automatically satisfy the second requirement.

Poinsettias have been and currently are being grown in a wide variety of media. There is little question that best root development and subsequent growth occur in growing media of high porosity. It has further been demonstrated that poinsettias thrive under conditions of high fertility and high moisture supply. The tendency has been to use very high fertility programs, but it is questionable whether they actually need to be any higher than for many other common pot plant crops, such as pot mums and Easter lilies.

The growing medium should be in the pH range of 5.0 to 6.5. Nutrients are thought to be most available if soil pH is in the range of 6.0 to 6.5. However, recent research indicates that for soilless or peat-lite mixes nutrients are most readily available if the pH range is 5.0 to 6.0. High pH results in reduced availability of metallic elements—iron, manganese, and zinc—causing upper foliage chlorosis. Low pH results in reduced molybdenum solubility. This leads

612

Not a controlled experiment—but the plant on the left was grown in the low 60°s, plant on the right, mid-50°s. Poinsettias are a tropical plant—like it warm! Photo at Cornell University.

to solubility of metallic elements such as copper, zinc, manganese, iron, and aluminum, causing toxicity.

Susceptibility to unfavorable conditions of salinity, high boron, and high sodium are no greater than for other pot plant crops, and if anything, they're somewhat less susceptible. Domestic water containing chlorine and/or fluoride is not harmful to poinsettias.

Disease prevention deserves constant and persistent attention if successful production is to be attained. For most growers, the primary problems of disease are those which result in root deterioration during the development stages and botrytis during the finishing stages. The latter becomes particularly important when temperatures are reduced. Normal botrytis precautions exercised for any other flowering pot plant crops are applicable to poinsettia production. Propagation is a particularly sensitive stage and is frequently the source of problems for the grower who does his own rooting.

Facilities required for pot plant production of poinsettias include an ability to supply heat with minimum temperatures of no lower than 60°F and preferably capability for higher minimum temperature. The facilities should also include means of controlling excessive temperatures, though this condition usually occurs only in the earlier forcing stages. Optimum daytime temperature is 80°–

85°F, though the plants will tolerate considerably higher temperature. Extremely low temperatures will tend to retard growth and incite chlorosis, while extremely high temperatures with limited light encourage stretching and thin growth. It is desirable to keep different varieties in separate houses so they can be exposed to their own optimum temperatures.

Temperature Control Is Important

Rising fuel prices have encouraged some poinsettia growers to conserve fuel and reduce costs by operating their greenhouses below recommended temperatures. There are guaranteed risks when cheating on temperatures. Low temperatures affect timing, quality, and disease control of poinsettias.

Depending on local light conditions, schedules may have to be advanced under low temperatures to ensure maturity by time of Christmas sales. Low temperatures adversely affect root activity. Common symptoms of low temperature are poor uptake of nutrients and chlorotic plant leaves. Root rot diseases and botrytis are more prevalent and more difficult to control at lower temperatures.

Growth regulators are often used to restrict stem elongation, though this has become unnecessary or nearly so for some of the new varieties. The use of growth regulator is sometimes employed for "toning" the plant. Leaf color is darkened by this treatment. Another toning practice is that of reducing temperatures in final stages of development, particularly for purposes of creating deeper bract color.

The typical Christmas crop is grown either as a single-stem plant terminating in bract and flower, or as a multiflowered plant with each branch resulting from the pinch producing its own bract and flower head. New varieties make the multiflowered plant highly attractive, both physically and economically. A properly grown modern variety will have a large bract and heavy stems, requiring no staking. *Eckespoint® C-1* will long be remembered as a first in demonstrating these desirable characteristics.

Varieties

Standards Within this group the principal series is the beautiful *Eckespoint® C-1* which is available in red, pink, white, and Jingle Bells, a red and pink novelty. The culture of this entire group is the same. These medium-height growers are considered 11-week varieties and must be grown at 65°F night temperatures to ensure early to mid-December blooming, unless they are black-clothed starting September 15 for 3 weeks for December 1st blooming.

Gutbier™ V-14 Glory, a red variety, is a short grower which seems to do very well without any growth regulator treatment. It makes an excellent branched plant and definitely must *not* be finished warm. This variety should also be grown at 64°F night temperatures but finished at 62°F from mid-November on.

Color sports of this exciting poinsettia are *Gutbier™ V-14 White, Gutbier™ V-14 Pink,* a flesh pink color, and *Gutbier™ V-14 Jingle Bells 2,* a red and pink novelty. *Gutbier™ V-14 Glory* and its sports are outstanding varieties for poinsettia trees.

Multiflowering varieties The most important group in this category is the Norwegian introduction, *Annette Hegg™,* and its many sports. The varieties of this family are medium-short growers and branch readily. The red varieties are *Annette Hegg™ Dark Red, Annette Hegg™ Brilliant Diamond, Annette Hegg™ Lady,* and *Annette Hegg™ Diva.* The other varieties in this group are *Annette Hegg™ Topwhite, Annette Hegg™ Pink,* and *Annette Hegg™ Marble,* a white and pink novelty.

The *Annette Hegg™* varieties should be grown at 62°F night temperatures and therefore can be produced with considerably less heat requirement. In fact, *Annette Hegg™ Dark Red,* considered a 9-week variety, must be finished near 60°F during November and December to ensure the best color in the bracts.

Annette Hegg™ Brilliant Diamond has a brilliant red color that shines through even when displayed under poor quality fluorescent lights. *Annette Hegg™ Lady* is the earliest blooming of all the Annette Hegg™ varieties. When grown under the same light and temperature conditions, *Annette Hegg™ Lady* will bloom about 10 days earlier than *Annette Hegg™ Dark Red.*

The *Annette Hegg™* family of poinsettias has a particularly strong root system and can generally withstand a lot of abuse before and after blooming.

Gutbier™ V-10 Amy is a light red, short growing variety which blooms very early and makes excellent branched plants. It stays short in Florida and other parts of the South which have high night temperatures. This variety should be grown at Hegg temperatures and definitely finished cool to retain intense color. Other color sports are *Gutbier™ V-10 White, Gutbier™ V-10 Pink,* a flesh pink, and *Gutbier™ V-10 Marble,* a white and pink novelty. Varieties of the V-10 group may drop their foliage prematurely if not watered and properly cared for after production.

Other multiflowering varieties within this classification are *Mikkel® Super Rochford* and *Mikkel® Fantastic.*

Stock Plants

To produce flowering plants true to variety, poinsettias are vegetatively propagated using stock plants of selected quality. The use of seedlings is confined to breeding in the constant search for plants of better color, better structure, greater vigor, and overall improved quality. Fortunately, the climatic conditions in southern California are particularly favorable for year-round growing and breeding of poinsettias. The bulk of the plants used in commerce originate from this area.

Growers often set large specimen pots up on stands this way. We see them often above benches of azaleas.

Not all growers produce their own cuttings. Many purchase rooted, callused, or unrooted cuttings directly from a specialist propagator, who, in turn, grows the stock plants. Specialists produce greenhouse-grown cuttings where controlled environment ensures high production at periods of maximum requirement and also availability of vegetative plants the year round.

Where cutting production is to be carried out by the local grower, the procedure of developing stock plants starts with purchased liners—usually 2¼" pot-size plants—from a specialist propagator in March, April, May, or June. The specialist propagator, by virtue of controlled environment, including artificial lighting for his own stock plants, can provide vegetative plants whenever the grower might want them.

Liners received for stock-plant production should be planted as soon as possible into beds or containers in which they will be grown throughout their period of production. Placing a small liner in a large container will result in greater total growth than shifting it up from one size pot to another. Growing medium and feeding program should be the same as for Christmas crop production. Night temperatures of 65°F and day temperatures between 80°F and 90°F will favor healthy development.

Spacing of plants placed in beds must be determined at the time of planting as opposed to container planting, where later spacing can be provided according to need. The earlier the stock is planted into beds, the wider the spacing should be. The earlier the stock is planted into containers, the larger the container should be. Since cultural practices as well as varietal character-istics will determine optimum handling in any given situation, only guideline approximations can be suggested (see Table 1).

Table 1   STOCK PLANT BED SPACING/CONTAINER–SIZE GUIDELINES

Month planted	Beds		Containers	
	Min. spacing	Sq. ft./plant	Min. diameter	Final spacing
March	18" × 18"	2.25	12"	18" × 18"
April	15" × 15"	1.55	10"	15" × 15"
May	12" × 12"	1.0	8"	12" × 12"
June	8" × 8"	0.44	6"	8" × 8"

There are many different and potentially successful approaches to the use of liners as a source of stock plants, but for purposes of illustration, a typical program is outlined.

1. Upon receipt, liners should be immediately potted into sterile con-tainers of pasteurized or otherwise disinfected soil of high porosity. Soil-less lightweight mixes have been very successful. At this time, and throughout the life of the stock plants, it is important to maintain high humidity in order to encourage maximum growth and maximum number of breaks.

2. Upon planting, drench with fungicide using the following:

   Amount per 100 gallons water

   4 ozs. Lesan® 35
   4 ozs. Terrachlor 75% W.P. *or* Benlate 50% W.P.

3. Maintain high fertility as for forcing of pot plants, using constant liquid feed or one of the other alternatives.

4. Provide medium shade (2500–3500 ft-c) during establishment with 65°F to 70°F night temperatures, continuing to maintain high humidity during daylight hours. After plants are well established, the shading may be reduced slightly. Day temperatures should be 80°F to 85°F, if possible to control.

5. As soon as liners are established, make a soft pinch (remove tip, including one fully expanded leaf). Depending on variety, three or more breaks should arise from nodes below the pinch.

6. When new growths have attained a mature state (leaves fully expanded as opposed to being paper-thin and light-colored), and when there is a minimum of four fully-developed leaves on the shoot, it can again be pinched in the same manner as above. This will leave three mature

617

The Van de Wetering brothers, Ivy Acres, Calverton, Long Island—and examples of the poinsettia sizes they grow.

leaves and respective nodes from which additional breaks can arise. Frequently, only two breaks arise from the second and later pinches.

7. To avoid possible flower-bud initiation, use night lighting (10 p.m.- 2 a.m.) at 10 ft-c until May 15.

8. Harvesting and propagation of cuttings can start about July 15 and proceed through the last of September. Many growers finish propagation by mid-September. Earliest propagations should be designated for branched plants of specimen plants and may require growth-regulator treatment, depending on variety. The early propagations are more subject to "splitting" unless they, in turn, are pinched.

9. The grower who wishes to produce his own cuttings from stock plants will first want to estimate the number of stock plants required to produce the desired number of cuttings. There is no substitute for experience in this regard, since so many factors enter into the calculation of production potential. Such items as time of planting, growing conditions, efficiency of pinching, efficiency of harvesting, success in propagation and, above all, the characteristics of the variety, must be considered. A table of procedure and production based on strictly theoretical considerations of a typical variety is provided (Table 2) for illustration. Free branching varieties of *Annette Hegg*™ may show 25% to 50% additional production.

618

Table 2 THEORETICAL STOCK PLANT PRODUCTION

Plant Liners	March 15	April 15	May 15	June 15
1st pinch (at 2 weeks) 3 breaks	March 30	April 30	May 30	June 30
2nd pinch (at 6 weeks) 6 breaks	April 30	May 30	June 30	July 30
3rd pinch (at 10 weeks) 12 breaks	May 25	June 25		
4th pinch (at 14 weeks) 24 breaks	June 25			
Harvest 1st cuttings, Aug. 13				
Number:	24	12	6	3
Harvest 2nd cuttings, Sept. 17				
Number:	48	24	12	6
Total cuttings/stock plant	72	36	18	9

In practice, it is generally found that the first pinch and the second pinch can be fairly accurately predicted. However, growth rates of some branches will be different from others. Also, it is not uncommon to obtain more than the theoretical number of breaks. For this reason, after the second pinch, it becomes necessary to examine the stock plants at about weekly intervals and pinch those stems that have matured sufficiently in the interim. The result is that stems ready for harvesting of cuttings will reach this stage at different times after any theoretical starting point. From the time that cuttings are harvested for propagation, it is usually desirable to repeat the cutting harvest at weekly intervals until the deadline date, which is frequently established as September 15.

Propagation of Softwood Cuttings

The term "softwood cuttings" applies to vegetative branch tips carrying one or more mature leaves. This is different from hardwood cuttings, which are taken from mature stems with or without leaves, and usually stripped of leaves if they exist.

There are basic criteria which must be satisfied if success in propagation is to be assured. These include:

1. Absolute freedom from disease.

2. Elimination of moisture stress once cuttings have been removed from the stock plant.

3. Adequate bottom heat (70°F–72°F) during rooting.

Conditions during propagation are highly favorable to spread of and infection by disease organisms. The program of sanitation must be directed toward *eliminating* disease rather than attempting to suppress it. This program must start before cuttings are taken from the stock plants.

In the outline to follow, one or more of the three criteria listed above are involved in each step. Normally, cuttings can be considered internally clean when removed from the plant. Surface-carried, inactive fungal spores may be a source of contamination if not eliminated. Procedures listed below have given excellent results in propagation. This does not mean that deviations and alterations of these procedures will not also be successful. Common sense and constant attention to sanitation are primary requisites for success.

1. Use a spray program on stock plants at one-week intervals occurring 1 or 2 days before the cuttings are to be taken. The objective is to provide protection against possible surface contamination being carried into the propagation bed. The following combination has been successfully employed as a fine-mist coverage:

   Amount per 100 gallons water

   16 ozs. Captan 50% W.P.
   8 ozs. Benlate 50% W.P.
   1 fl. oz. wetting agent

   Ornalin is a relatively new fungicide which also seems to control botrytis gray mold. It is of interest that wetting agents materially improve the ability of subsequent mist to wet leaf surfaces thoroughly. There is some variability with varieties. Also, it appears that the improved wetting results in improved color retention.

2. Rooting medium can be any clean and well-drained combination of sand, peat, perlite, vermiculite, or other available materials of similar properties suitable for soil mix composition. Preformed foam media are also available and can be used. The medium should have a pH of 5.0 to 6.5 for best results, since excessive acidity slows rooting and excessive alkalinity contributes to chlorosis. Fertilizers as used in regular potting media incorporated into the rooting medium do not seem to inhibit rooting. Cuttings can be rooted in the containers in which they will be finished, thus saving one or two steps in handling and avoiding additional opportunity for contamination. This procedure is termed "direct rooting" and is rapidly attaining popularity for starting plants. The procedure saves approximately 1 week in the forcing schedule and will produce uniform pots if carefully

managed. The procedure is fairly simple but does require special care in handling cuttings. Uniformity is most important. Cuttings should be of the same age (taken from the shoots of equal length). They should be similar in length, caliper, and color and should be stuck to the same depth. Finally, uniform mist coverage is required to produce plants of equal size and growth rate.

3. Cuttings 2"–3½" in length should be removed from stock plants by means of a clean, sharp knife, making the cut anywhere between the third and fourth fully expanded leaves on a mature shoot. Ideally, the cut will leave at least two mature leaves on the stock plant stem as a source of new growth and subsequent cuttings. Leaves should be removed from the base of cuttings *only* when they interfere with sticking. Leaf removal reduces the stored food reserve and provides additional injury for possible infection.

4. Collect cuttings in sterile containers. Plastic containers prerinsed with diluted bleach are ideal (1 gallon 5% household bleach diluted to 10 gallons with water is satisfactory).

5. Avoid any moisture stress by undue exposure to dry air during period of collection. Ideally, though not always practical, cuttings should be taken in the evening, at night, or very early in the morning when moisture stress is minimal and cuttings are turgid.

6. For efficient and rapid handling, do not collect too many cuttings at any one time. Transport each batch under sanitary and moist conditions to the propagation area. Stick cuttings as soon as possible in steamed or otherwise decontaminated rooting media. Start mist as soon as possible to minimize moisture stress.

7. All personnel handling cuttings should thoroughly wash hands with soap and water followed by a rinse with a hospital or dairy-type disinfectant. Other materials are equally satisfactory and nonirritating. Shallow tubs or basins of disinfectant should be kept handy for frequent rinsing of hands and/or tools and changed as needed.

8. If cuttings are to be spread out on any surface for handling, be sure that such surfaces are sanitary. Film plastic covering is desirable and can be disinfected easily by washing with one of the hospital disinfectants or with bleach. Any cuttings which accidentally fall to the floor or contact nonsterile surfaces should be discarded.

9. Cuttings should be stuck by placing in preformed holes or by simply pushing into soft media. Do not flood them in after sticking, but do commence mist or other humidity supply immediately upon sticking. Flooding causes rooting medium to compact around the stem, increasing the moisture and reducing the air in this zone. This condition

is highly conducive to bacterial soft-rot infection, which can occur within the first 2 or 3 days after sticking.

10. Mist frequency and duration should be such that leaves always have a film of moisture covering them. A satisfactory program in California has been 5 seconds of mist at 5-minute intervals on bright, sunny days. Should drying conditions occur at night, it may be necessary to use mist during this period. In very bright weather, moderate to heavy shading is required to protect against rapid drying and high-light-intensity bleaching of the foliage.

11. At the end of one week, there should be evidence of callus formation. At this time, fertilizer plus fungicide can be employed as a protective drench and a means of setting the medium around the cutting. Callus formation seems to occur best when there is a large amount of air surrounding the cutting, but root initiation occurs most rapidly under slightly less open conditions. Choices of fungicide and/or fertilizer are numerous, with the following having been satisfactorily employed:

Amount per 100 gallons water applied

4 ozs. Terrachlor 75% W.P. *or* 8 ozs. Benlate 50% W.P.
1 lb. Captan 50% W.P.
8 ozs. ammonium nitrate

12. At 14 to 21 days, root initiation should be at a stage which permits reduction or elimination of mist. If day temperatures can be controlled adequately, mist should be turned off, since surface-applied water does have a bleaching and nutrient-leaching effect on the foliage. All effort should be exercised to maintain good fertility in the rooting medium as soon as callus and root initials appear. If stretching and bleaching are problems, spray with Cycocel at 1500 ppm to reduce stretch and hold color.

13. Transplanting should occur as soon as practical after roots are established in order to minimize shock due to root disturbance. Use of fertilizer in mist is practiced by many growers and has been advocated by numerous researchers. Experience to date indicates considerable variation in results due to materials and methods employed. Unless previous experience has provided the necessary background, the grower is advised to approach this program on a trial basis. Elements most rapidly leached from the foliage by mist are nitrogen and potassium. Phosphorus seems to encourage stretching. As a guide for initial trials, the following mist-water composition is suggested.

622

4 lbs. ammonium nitrate
2 lbs. potassium nitrate
1½ fl. oz. sodium molybdenum stock solution (use 1 lb./5 gal to prepare stock solution)

Rooting can take place in a variety of media and containers. Preformed rooting media are being successfully used. Any new approach should be given adequate trial before being used on a large scale. Rooting in beds is common, but care must be exercised in lifting cuttings to avoid injury to roots.

Where rooting media are shallow, there is frequently an interface effect which results in waterlogging in the zone occupied by the base of the cutting. Such a condition will cause darkening and deterioration of the stem and give the appearance of disease, even though disease organisms may not be present. The reaction is actually due to lack of oxygen. Where direct rooting in shallow containers is practiced, the containers should preferably be placed on sterilized sand, perlite, or vermiculite to increase effectively the soil column height. Good contact with a wood surface can also provide a certain amount of "blotter" effect causing free water to move out of the bottom of the pot.

Excessive crowding of cuttings in the propagation bed should be avoided in order to reduce soft growth, stretch, and slower rooting. In bed-rooting, allow at least 12 inches (2" × 6") per cutting. For rooting in 2¼" pots, Jiffy-7s and 9s or Oasis Rootcubes, allow 15 square inches (3" × 5") per cutting. Units should be spaced so that the leaves barely touch to allow air movement around the cuttings. Tips should not be covered by other cutting leaves.

Although rooting hormones are not used by all propagators and are not essential to root initiation of poinsettia cuttings, experience has indicated that they do speed up the rate of rooting and improve uniformity. Normal acceleration is several days.

One of the most convenient methods of hormone treatment is to provide a quick dip of cutting base in liquid solution. Indolebutyric acid has been successfully employed at 2500 ppm strength. A calculated risk in employing this treatment is the possibility of spreading disease from one infected cutting to all other cuttings dipped in the same solution. An insurance practice which has been shown to be beneficial is to add 10 drops of household bleach per pint of hormone solution. The use of hormone powders reduces the chance of cross-contamination, particularly if some Captan is mixed with the powder. Dusting the powder on the base of the cutting is less apt to spread disease than dipping the cutting in powder. However, the use of powder provides less uniform treatment than the liquid quick dip.

Some growers use fan and pad cooling in their propagation areas. This is hardly necessary where frequent mist cycles are in use, but may be helpful under some circumstances. Ideally, the foliage of the cuttings should be kept cool and humid while the stem in the rooting medium should be kept warm, but not waterlogged. The ideal mist system would maintain air humidity at near 100%, but would supply little or no free water to the rooting medium. Some compromise is commonly necessary in practical procedure.

Producing a Christmas-Season Crop

Although detailed discussion of specific phases of plant handling is provided in sections to follow, it may be helpful to have a generalized program in mind and at hand when reviewing subsequent sections, if only for use as a point of departure. There can be many successful alterations to any outlined program including that to follow.

The first step in planning the Christmas crop is to determine the desired final product in terms of:

1. Pot size

2. Varieties

3. Blooms per pot
   a. Single-stem
   b. Branched

4. Date ready for sale

A production plan can then be drawn up and compared with space available in order to make final decisions on the intended inventory. It is quite important to be certain that there will be sufficient space at each stage of production, since crowding will definitely reduce quality. Table 3 provides a typical worksheet for this purpose.

Following the preparation of the plan, a "deadline" log should be prepared to indicate exact dates for completion of action for each phase of production. Since growing conditions are variable as to both location and facilities, this portion of the planning should be carefully reviewed by experienced personnel and adjusted to suit the particular conditions anticipated.

All plants for the Christmas crop should be established in their final containers by September 25. A possible exception would be the 4" pot or smaller size where direct rooting can be started as late as September 25, in some parts of the country, in order to assure short plants. Earlier propagations are required for large-size containers to attain desired height at time of maturity.

Where single-stem multiple-plant pots are to be produced by direct rooting, it is essential that all cuttings be uniform if a uniform finished plant is to be produced. Cuttings should be selected from *stems* of equal length to ensure equal stage of maturity and should be equal in length, stem size, leaf number, and color. Finally, they should be stuck in the rooting medium to the same depth.

Table 3 POINSETTIA PRODUCTION PLAN FOR _____ (Variety)

Container size	4"	5"	6"	7"	——
SINGLE STEM					
Total Pots					
Plants/Pot					
Cuttings Required					
Final Space (sq. ft.)*					
Sales Price/Pot					
Theoretical Gross					
BRANCHED					
Total Pots					
Plants/Pot					
Cuttings Required					
Final Space (sq. ft.)*					
Sales Price/Pot					
Theoretical Gross					

Total cuttings required _____

Total bench space required _____ sq. ft.

Total theoretical gross $_____

*See Table 7. Select 2 or 3 flowers/sq. ft. spacing. For branched plants, program pinch to produce 3 or 4 flowers/plant.

Table 4 CUTTING PROPAGATION AND PINCHING DATE GUIDELINES

Pot size and form	Direct rooting in finishing pot	2¼" unit rooting	Pinch
7" SS 5–7 plants	Sept. 1	Aug. 25	
7" Br 1–3 plants	Aug. 15	Aug. 10	Sept. 5
6" SS 3–5 plants	Sept. 1	Aug. 25	
6" Br 1–2 plants	Aug. 20	Aug. 15	Sept. 15
5" Same as 6"			
4" SS 1 plant	Sept. 20	Sept. 15	
4" Br 1 plant	Sept. 5	Sept. 1	Sept. 20
Smaller pot sizes—same as 4"			

SS = Single Stem, typical *Eckespoint® C-1*

Br = Branched, typical *Annette Hegg™ Dark Red*

Branched plants can be programmed to produce a desired number of flowering stems, particularly in the case of the free-branching Hegg varieties. This is accomplished by removing the top of the plant at a point which leaves the desired number of nodes above the soil line. Each node will generally produce a flowering stem. Where this procedure is used, earlier propagation or transplanting can be employed since height will be controlled by removal of more of the top of the plant, should it be excessively tall.

Where cuttings are rooted in 2¼" pots or preformed rooting media, panning should be scheduled for 21–28 days from time of sticking. By this time, roots should be well established and yet not root-bound.

In order to avoid stretch, all finished containers should be placed at final spacing as early as possible and no later than October 1.

Feeding should be carried out, preferably as constant liquid feed, from the earliest date possible after roots appear. At each stage of transplanting, the new pots should be drenched wih a fungicide solution as a matter of precaution against accidental contamination. Subsequent drenches with Lesan should occur at minimum 30-day intervals. The first drench should include Terrachlor or Benlate, but these materials can be omitted in subsequent drenches unless a particular problem arises, requiring their use.

In producing branched plants, the shoot tip should be removed at an early enough date to provide sufficient growing time to produce the length of stem required for the pot size. Immediately following the pinch, it is very important to maintain high humidity by frequent misting until branches have started to develop (approximately 1 week). Temperatures should be about 80°F in the daytime and no lower than 65°F at night. Moderate shade will help in maintaining humidity. Care should be taken to avoid excessive water application to the roots, since plants will use less moisture due to fewer transpiring leaves. Waterlogged soil will cause new leaves to be yellow.

The period of flower initiation will start between September 23 and October 10. High temperatures seem to counteract the stimulus to initiate flowers, so temperatures during this period should be reduced. Night temperatures of 64°F or lower are considered satisfactory for normal development with day temperatures not exceeding 80°F. Lowering temperatures below recommended levels causes longer production schedules.

Since some varieties flower earlier than others, consideration must be given to providing proper temperatures and/or special treatment, depending on variety and desired date of maturity. Typical examples are Annette Hegg™ Brilliant Diamond as an early-flowering type and Gutbier™ V-14 Glory as a mid-season flowering type.

If the early-flowering type is being grown, a night temperature of 64°F after initiation will usually bring it in for Thanksgiving (November 23–November 27). If early flowering types are used for near Christmas flowering, night temperature should be no higher than 62°F until November 1 and then reduced to 60°F. Another method of delaying the crop is to provide long-day lighting from September 15 to October 10 using appropriate temperatures thereafter.

About May 1-15 plant established cutting into 8" or 10" pot. To ensure height, grow warm and humid until first pinch.

From May 15 until July 1 remove the very lowest side shoots when they become 1" long. Leave the top 10 shoots.

First Pinch: Remove ½" of growing tip, a regular soft pinch. Leave 8-10 side shoots at the top of the plant. Remove lower remaining shoots.

Three weeks after first pinch, use a sharp knife and remove all foliage below the branches.

Second Pinch: Shape the plant—generally leave 2-3 mature leaves on upper branches and 3-4 leaves on lower branches. This will ensure a short, strong stem for the heavy bracts. Remove stake, carefully.

Coming into full bloom with 25-30 blooms. Notice the shape developing. Adequate spacing at all times during production gives a better finished product.

627

Table 5 ANNETTE HEGG® BRILLIANT DIAMOND
(MULTIFLOWERED, 5" or 6" PAN)
*A TYPICAL PRODUCTION PROGRAM GUIDELINE**

Date	Temperature °F		Cultural procedure
	Night	Day	
Aug. 10	72	80	Direct-stick uniform unrooted cutting in center of pot. Rooting is slower below 70°F soil temperature. Use automatic mist during daylight hours. Use medium shade. Do not water in.
Aug. 20	72	80	Water in with 8 ozs. ammonium nitrate per 100 gallons of water.
Sept. 1	68	80	Commence constant liquid feed (CLF). Drench with 1 oz. Subdue/100 gals plus 4 oz. Benlate/100 gals.
Sept. 5	68	80	Program pinch to leave 4 or 5 nodes above the soil, depending on how many flowers are desired. Maintain high humidity. Avoid waterlogging. CLF.
Sept. 23	64	80	Lower temperatures for uniform bud initiation.
Oct. 1	64	80	Breaks should be about 1" long. Space to 14" × 14". Drench with 1 oz. Subdue/100 gals plus 4 oz. Benlate/100 gals. CLF. Spray or drench with Cycocel.
Nov. 1	62	75	Color development well underway. Use Termil once each week until sale to protect from botrytis. If possible, ventilate and heat at night to reduce humidity. Use internal air circulation. CLF. Drench with 1 oz. Subdue/100 gals. plus 4 oz. Benlate/100 gals.
Nov. 25	60	75	Ready for sale.

NOTE: If direct-rooting of unrooted cuttings is not used, then plant 2¼" liners or rooted cuttings into 5" or 6" pans on August 20; drench with Subdue, Benlate, and ammonium nitrate. Then follow the schedule.

*Based on Ohio conditions. Northern areas may require earlier programming, with later programming for southern areas.

Where a mid-season flowering type is being grown, it will be necessary to use black-cloth shading from September 15 to October 10 to obtain *earlier* initiation for a Thanksgiving crop. After initiation, night temperature should be approximately 65°F with day temperature about 80°F. Obviously, it will be necessary to advance the propagation and planting schedules where normal season varieties are being shaded for early flowering.

Table 6   GUTBIER™ V-14 GLORY
(3-BLOOM, SINGLE STEM 6" PAN)
A TYPICAL PRODUCTION PROGRAM GUIDELINE

Date	Temperature (°F)		Cultural procedure
	Night	Day	
Sept. 1	72	80	Direct-stick uniform unrooted cuttings close to pot edge. Rooting is slower below 70°F soil temperature. Use automatic mist during daylight hours. Use medium shade. Do not water in.
Sept. 7	72	80	Water in with 8 ozs. ammonium nitrate per 100 gallons of water. Continue mist.
Sept. 15	68	80	Reduce mist. Start constant liquid feed (CLF). Drench with 1 oz. Subdue/100 gals plus 4 oz. Benlate/100 gals.
Sept. 23	62–64	80	Space 14" × 14". Avoid water-logging. CLF. Lower temperature for uniform bud initiation.
Oct. 1			Spray with Cycocel @ 2000 ppm.
Oct. 10	65	80	Start of forcing period. CLF.
Oct. 15	65	80	Spray with Cycocel @ 1500 ppm. Drench with 1 oz. Subdue/100 gals plus 4 oz. Benlate/100 gals. CLF.
Nov. 7	65	75	Color showing in upper leaves. Use Termil once each week until sale to protect from botrytis. If possible, ventilate and heat at night to reduce humidity. Use internal circulation of air. CLF.
Nov. 15	65	75	Drench with 1 oz. Subdue/100 gals plus 4 oz. Benlate/100 gals. CLF.
Dec. 1	60	70	Terminate fertilization.
Dec. 5	60	70	Bracts approaching maximum size. Lower night temperatures will enhance color. Reduce light intensity if weather is bright.
Dec. 10	60	70	Ready for sale. Can be held in good condition for at least 2 weeks.

NOTE: If direct-rooting of unrooted cuttings is not used, then plant 2¼" liners or rooted cuttings in 6" pans on Sept. 15; drench with Subdue, Benlate, and ammonium nitrate. Then follow the schedule.

Some temperature manipulation may be required as plants reach maturity to ensure their being in prime condition when sold. Lower temperatures during the final 1 to 2 weeks of forcing will enhance bract color. The one adverse feature of lower temperatures is the risk of botrytis infection. Protection can be afforded by providing good air circulation at night along with some heat

Two good examples of how growers adjust spacing, pot size, number of cuttings, etc., to the customer's pocketbook. On the left is Don Laser, Meyerstown, Pennsylvania, grower, who does several acres of poinsettias. One important block (an acre or more) is finished at 10" × 10" spacing. And here's the plant. Not a blue ribbon winner at a flower show—but, yes, a winner when it comes to profitability. On the right, Hank Mast, another major pot specialist at Grand Rapids, Michigan. Hank also varies spacing of his 6" poinsettias—again, depending on the customer's wishes.

and ventilation to dry out the air. Also, certain thermal dust fungicides can be used at regular intervals (usually once per week) to present a barrier against botrytis infection.

Fan and pad cooling can be used during periods of extremely high temperatures and will, under these conditions, have a very beneficial effect. However, it is important that day temperatures be in the range of 80°F for best plant performance. If the crop should appear to be ahead of schedule, air conditioning can be used to drop the temperature to 70° or 75°F and hold the crop back. Usually, this is not practiced until fairly late in the production cycle. If temperatures are too low during the bract-maturation period, size may be adversely affected.

Spacing for Flowering Plants

For best quality, plants should be spaced early in their growing period to final location on the bench. This avoids temporary periods of crowding, reduces labor, and permits use of automatic irrigation for maximum periods of time.

As a rule of thumb, maximum density for a high-quality product of the large bract type should be figured as two flowers per square foot with square patterns most commonly employed. Depending on variety, method of handling, and market acceptance, up to three flowers per square foot can be produced.

A guide for spacing distance (Table 7) is provided as a convenient means of determining the number of plants that can be grown in a given area. This approach assumes that pinched plants have three flowers per plant and that planting into the final container size will have occurred by September 30. Where quality is less important than quantity, later planting and closer spacing can possibly be employed. Growth-regulator sprays and drenches can be used to minimize stretch, which does occur under close spacing conditions. Usually, the flower head is smaller and plants are less vigorous with weaker stems when spacing has been reduced.

Table 7   SPACING GUIDE FOR POINSETTIAS

Pot size (inches)	Plants/ pot	Pinching treatment	2 Flowers/sq. ft.		3 Flowers/sq. ft.	
			spacing (inches)*	*sq. ft./pot*	*Spacing (inches)**	*sq. ft./pot*
4	1	none	9 × 9	0.56	7 × 7	0.34
4	1	pinched	15 × 15	1.56	12 × 12	1.00
5	2	none	12 × 12	1.00	10 × 10	0.67
5	3	none	15 × 15	1.56	12 × 12	1.00
5	1	pinched	15 × 15	1.56	12 × 12	1.00
6	3	none	15 × 15	1.56	12 × 12	1.00
6	4	none	17 × 17	2.00	14 × 14	1.35
6	1	pinched	15 × 15	1.56	12 × 12	1.00
6	2	pinched	21 × 21	3.05	17 × 17	2.00
7	4	none	17 × 17	2.00	14 × 14	1.35
7	5	none	19 × 19	2.51	15 × 16	1.67
7	7	none	22 × 23	3.50	18 × 18	2.25
7	2	pinched	21 × 21	3.05	17 × 17	2.00
7	3	pinched	25 × 25	4.33	21 × 21	2.90

*Approximate—rounded off to nearest inch.

Accidental Bud-Set Delay

Each year, more and more growers are having trouble getting poinsettias to set bud properly in the autumn because of unnoticed extraneous lights shining into the greenhouses at night. The proximity of well-traveled highways, new and improved street lighting, and large, well-lighted shopping centers near poinsettia-producing greenhouses impose new threats. If it is impossible to eliminate the unwanted light source, it is necessary that black cloth be pulled starting October 1 to ensure a 14-hour dark period until plants are ready for sale. Black clothing will ensure bud set if the temperature is not above 65°F at night.

Fertility Maintenance

Poinsettias in particular seem to require a substantial rate of nitrogen application with modest phosphorus and modest potassium rates. It has been observed that very low soil potassium is still sufficient to supply the requirement of poinsettias. Apparently, this plant is capable of extracting potassium with greater efficiency than many other crops. In order to provide a simple and straightforward selection of liquid-fertilizer programs, an outline of several approaches (Table 8) has been provided. Molybdenum has been included in several of the formulas, since this element has been found to be quite important in poinsettia nutrition, particularly in soilless mixes.

Table 8   POINSETTIA LIQUID FEED PROGRAMS

	Amt./1000 gals. water applied	PPM in water N P K
CONSTANT LIQUID FEED		
Make your own:	3 lbs. ammonium nitrate	263 – 30 – 135
	5 lbs. calcium nitrate	+0.1 ppm Mo
	3 lbs. potassium nitrate	
	10 fl. ozs. 75% food-grade phosphoric acid	
	1½ fl. ozs. molybdenum stock solution*	
Prepared Mixes	13 lbs. 16–4–12	250 – 27 – 158
	or	
	8.5 lbs. 25–10–10	250 – 44 – 85
INTERMITTENT LIQUID FEED		
(Every 2nd or 3rd irrigation)		
Make your own:	6 lbs. ammonium nitrate	526 – 60 – 270
	10 lbs. calcium nitrate	+0/2 ppm Mo
	6 lbs. potassium nitrate	
	20 fl. ozs. 75% food-grade phosphoric acid	
	3 fl. ozs. molybdenum stock solution*	
Prepared Mixes	26 lbs. 16–4–12	500 – 54 – 316
	or	
	17 lbs. 25–10–10	500 – 88 – 170

*Molybdenum stock solution: Dissolve 1 lb. sodium or ammonium molybdate in 5 gallons water.

Methods of supplying fertilizer to plants vary greatly. All possible combinations and types of programs cannot possibly be covered, but the principal approaches are listed below. The best program is, of course, one which requires the least amount of labor and permits the least opportunity for error. Also, economics is a factor, though fertilizer cost is usually not considered a major part of production costs. A number of typical approaches follow.

Liquid fertilizer at every irrigation   In recent years, this has become the most popular of programs and is probably the most foolproof as well as most economic. It automatically limits the quantity of fertilizer applied in case of underwatering and prevents excessive buildup, even under conditions of overwatering. If all irrigation water contains fertilizer of desired concentration, there are no problems in administration of the feeding program. When water is required, fertilizer is automatically supplied. A single formula can be satisfactorily employed for the entire production period under most circumstances. A good poinsettia program is like a good Easter lily and/or pot mum program. Prepared fertilizer formulations are available for use with soilless growing media.

In making small quantities of fertilizer solution, it may be helpful to have some idea of quantities to use (Table 9). Since quantities less than an ounce are difficult to weigh; volume measure is more commonly used for this range, but is subject to greater error.

Table 9   *AMOUNT OF FERTILIZER TO MAKE A SOLUTION OF 250 PPM NITROGEN*

Fertilizer formula	Final volume of solution (gallons)				
	1000	100	50	5	1*
25–10–10	8 lbs. 5 ozs.	13 ozs.	6½ ozs.	4t	1 − t
16–4–12	13 lbs.	21 ozs.	10½ ozs.	2T	1 + t
34–0–0 (ammonium nitrate)	6 lbs. 4 ozs.	10 ozs.	5 ozs.	4t	1 − t
15.5–0–0 (calcium nitrate)	13 lbs. 6 ozs.	22 ozs.	11 ozs.	2T	1 + t

*1 − t = slightly less than level full
1 + t = slightly more than level full
t = teaspoon
T = Tablespoon

Liquid fertilizer at fixed intervals   A popular approach that varies from the above is to inject fertilizer at weekly or other fixed periods, using higher concentrations than for the constant liquid program in order that levels will not be depleted too much during the interim when clear water is being applied. This type program may require adjustment of concentration at different stages of growth due to increasing frequency of interim irrigation as plants attain large size and utilize more water. The intensity of watering can have a substantial effect on the average fertility level.

Top dress with dry fertilizer   Where liquid-feeding facilities are not available, many growers may wish to use dry fertilizer. Rates should be relatively high for poinsettias compared to many other crops. A program which has proved successful should not be replaced by a new program without appropriate trial.

This approach requires care and experience where fertilizer is fast-acting or highly soluble, but may have much the same effect as constant liquid feed where slow-release fertilizers are employed. Again, differences in irrigation intensity can greatly affect the levels attained. Also, temperatures are sometimes a factor in rate of release. Higher temperatures can increase the rate of nutrient release.

Incorporation of slow-release fertilizer in mix   This procedure has gained some favor and prominence as better products have become available. Again, it is similar in effect to the constant-liquid-feed program except that the control over fertilizer availability is subject to such factors as rate of application, temperature of soil, and intensity of irrigation. In some instances, the addition of the slow-release fertilizer must be made after steaming to avoid excessive release at the outset. Soil with slow-release fertilizer salt buildup can occur during storage.

Where a grower wishes to try one of the slow-release fertilizers, experience to date suggests that Osmocote 19–6–12 or 14–14–14 are suitable formulas for poinsettias. For top dressing after planting into pans or pots, 1 level tablespoon per 6" pot is a reasonable rate, if the soil is well drained and if irrigations are thorough. Lower quantities should be used where light irrigations are practiced, or where soil textures include substantial silt and clay. Addition of slow-release fertilizer to the soil mix prior to planting can again utilize the same material at a rate of 7 to 10 lbs. per cubic yard. Slow-release Osmocote should not be added until soil has cooled after steaming. Rates most appropriate for a particular condition will have to be determined by trial and error, and will be affected by soil temperature as well as irrigation frequency and intensity. Osmocote seems to provide continuous nutrition for about 12 weeks. It will, therefore, usually carry the crop through the entire forcing period when added about mid-September.

Incorporation of a slow-release product subjects the grower to a set of conditions over which he has less control. It would seem that if liquid-feeding capability is available, this would be chosen as the system for maintaining fertility. If it is not available, it would seem wise to consider a slow-release fertilizer system which would approach constant liquid feeding in its effect.

Chemical Height Control of Poinsettias

With the advent of new naturally short-growing varieties, the importance of growth regulators and their effect on height control have been somewhat

A demonstration of different rates of the growth regulator Cycocel.

reduced. However, in the period following flower initiation, it may be desirable to apply growth regulators as a spray or drench. This practice seems to improve plant quality by darkening foliage and strengthening stems, even though varieties being grown may be naturally short. Varieties which tend to grow tall may need several applications.

Factors affecting the action of growth regulators include concentration of active ingredient, quantity applied, time of application in relation to flowering date, stage of root development at time of application, temperature and humidity prior to and after treatment, plant moisture content, interaction of other spray materials, and method of treatment, whether by spray or drench. In general, growth regulators are less effective when temperatures are high, humidity is high, light is reduced as from crowding, and when nitrogen supply is largely ammonium or urea.

There are possible undesirable side effects from treatment. These include reduced bract size, crinkling of bracts, blotchy yellowing of leaves, marginal leaf burn, and delayed flowering. By early application under favorable environmental conditions, the yellow blotching which sometimes occurs will gradually disappear. Soil application seldom produces these undesirable reactions. However, foliar application permits the best opportunity to even up the height of the plants.

Cycocel is applied either as a soil drench or foliar spray. The soil drench application will usually provide greater height control than spray application per treatment. Cost of material and labor of application are higher with the soil-drench procedure.

Solutions of desired strength (Table 10) should be made by measuring the appropriate quantity of growth regulator into an empty container and then adding enough water to make the desired final volume.

Table 10   CYCOCEL GROWTH REGULATOR SOLUTION PREPARATION (BASED ON 11.8% CONCENTRATE)

Desired concentration		Fluid ounces to make:		Dilution ratio
%	ppm	1 gallon	10 gallons	
0.1	1000	1	11	1:116
0.15	1500	1½	16	1:80
0.2	2000	2	22	1:58
0.25	2500	3	28	1:46
0.3	3000	3½	32	1:40
0.5	5000	5½	54	1:24
0.6	6000	6½	64	1:20
0.75	7500	8	82	1:16
1.0	10000	11	108	1:12

NOTE: Fluid ounces rounded off to nearest ½ ounce.

8 fl. ozs./cup	32 fl. ozs./quart
16 fl. ozs./pint	128 fl. ozs./gallon

Soil-drench application should be made as early as practical after plants are well rooted in the container. Late applications affect bract size and form. In northern areas, it is not recommended that application be made later than October 15. In southern areas, applications have been successful as late as November 1. Treatment of branched plants should occur approximately 2 weeks after pinching when new shoots are 1½″ long.

Treatment by foliar spray normally should be completed by October 15 or earlier. Spray should be applied to the top side of all foliage of the plants for maximum benefit. Some growers make a practice of treating individual plants in multiplant containers in order to equalize the height. Applications late in the day when temperatures are lower will decrease chances of leaf yellowing. Spray treatment should be given only when soil is well supplied with moisture. Further moistening of foliage should be avoided for at least 24 hours. This permits maximum absorption.

Rates (Table 11) are usually higher in strength for early applications than for late. Numerous variations on treatment have been tried by researchers and growers with results equal to those advocated here. When a program is providing desired results, no changes should be made except by comparative trial. Since the spray approach is most apt to cause leaf yellowing or burn, it is desirable to test-spray a few plants one week ahead of the intended general treatment as a check on possible damage. Even this precaution is not foolproof.

Another effective growth regulator is A-Rest. Used as a drench, one pint of A-Rest should be mixed in 16 gallons of water; then apply 4 ounces of this solution per 6″ pot, 2 times, 1 week apart. It should be applied to the *Heggs* and *Rochfords* no later than October 15, unless the plants are lighted. Although not labeled for use as a spray, some growers have experimented using A-Rest

Table 11 TYPICAL RATES FOR GROWTH REGULATOR APPLICATION

	August	September	October
Cycocel Soil Drench*	3000 ppm	3000 ppm	3000 ppm
Cycocel Foliar Spray	2000 ppm	2000 ppm	1500 ppm

*2 fluid ozs./3″ pot; 3 fluid ozs./4″ pot; 4 fluid ozs./5″ pot; 6 fluid ozs./6″ pot; 8 fluid ozs./8″ pot.

successfully this way. Their recommendation is to mix one pint A-Rest to 3 pints of water and apply this solution to 100 square feet, 2 times, one week apart.

New Forms of Poinsettias

Pixie poinsettias Pixie poinsettias are usually grown in 4″ pots (see photograph). The objective is to produce a very short branched plant that is less than 12″ total height. *Annette Hegg*™ *Brilliant Diamond* and *Gutbier*™ *V-10 Amy* both make excellent pixie-type poinsettias.

Arrangement Pack poinsettias The Arrangement Pack poinsettias grown in cell-paks,″® is a convenient way to grow very short-branched plants which can be popped out of their containers and used in an unlimited number of ways for dish gardens and flower arrangements. Guidelines for the production of these exciting forms of small poinsettias are given on the next page.

Poinsettias as a pixie in a 4″ pot; one plant branched in a 6″ pot; a standard tree in an 8″ pot; a 12″ tub display plant, and a 10″ basket.

637

A GUIDELINE FOR PRODUCING ANNETTE HEGG® BRILLIANT DIAMOND 4" PIXIE TYPE POINSETTIA AND ARRANGEMENT PACK POINSETTIAS

Bloom date	Direct stick into 4" pot or arrangement packs	Temperature at plant level	Day	Night	Lights on	Pinch	Lights off start black cloth	Stop black cloth	CCC spray @ 2000 ppm 1:60 2 oz./gal.	Bloom date
Nov. 25	Aug. 15	Aug. 15–Sept. 15	75	70	Sept. 7	Sept. 7	Sept. 23	Oct. 21	Sept. 1	Nov. 25
		Sept. 15–Nov. 7	70	64					Sept. 23	
		Nov. 7–Nov. 25	65	58–60					Oct. 5 (if needed)	
Dec. 8	Aug. 25	Aug. 25–Sept. 25	75	70	Sept. 7	Sept. 17	Oct. 1	Oct. 21	Sept. 7	Dec. 8
		Sept. 25–Nov. 17	70	64					Oct. 1	
		Nov. 17–Dec. 8	65	58–60					Oct. 10 (if needed)	

NOTE: If lower temperatures are used in October and November, naturally the schedules for sticking and pinching will have to be advanced accordingly. Remember that *light intensity* and *light duration* in the fall will also have a great influence on any schedule.

NOTE: This schedule, prepared for central Ohio, does allow enough time to produce a good plant with three perfect blooms—of course *local* conditions will require certain adjustments to the schedule. Be sure the plants are not exposed to *any* unwanted lights from such sources as other crops being lighted, streetlights, floodlights, or freeways—if in any doubt, shade.

An arrangement pack poinsettia rooted in a cell.

Poinsettia hanging baskets   These attractive baskets make a handsome display of poinsettias which can be hung on a fern stand. The smaller sizes can also be used as centerpieces.

INSTRUCTIONS FOR MAKING POINSETTIA HANGING BASKETS

This technique uses 9–10-week response one-plant pinched *Annette Hegg*™ poinsettias in 3″ square pots properly treated with a growth regulator. This three piece 10″ Belden Hanging Pot is made up approximately 30 days *before* being in full bloom and ready for sale.

1. Start with a 3″ pixie-type poinsettia and a 10″ Belden hanging pot.

2. Carefully place plant with all branches outside of the pot.

639

3. Carefully select uniform plants and make sure the stem does *not* rub the side of the hole and become bruised.

4. Place ring lid on top of pot.

5. Carefully snap ring lid in place.

6. Place three or four short plants on top— add soil, but leave enough space for watering.

7. Place 3-wire hanger in lid holes. Follow regular growing procedures, including watering, fertilizing, and temperature.

8. This handsome plant can be displayed as a hanging basket or placed on a fern stand.

Poinsettia trees Poinsettia trees (see photograph) can be grown in two sizes: 40"–48" in overall height and 25"–30" in height. The latter size is also referred to as a mini-poinsettia tree. The taller tree begins with a rooted cutting approximately May 1, and the mini-tree about June 10.

PRODUCTION GUIDELINES FOR A POINSETTIA STANDARD TREE "SCHEDULE" USING GUTBIER™ V-14 GLORY

	California/Florida	Ohio/Wisconsin
Pan rooted cutting	May 1	May 1
1st Pinch	Aug. 5	Aug. 1
2nd Pinch	Sept. 10	Sept. 5
Full bloom	Dec. 7	Dec. 7 (approx.)

GUIDELINE FOR PRODUCING A MINI-POINSETTIA TREE USING GUTBIER™ V-14 GLORY (2 PINCH PROGRAM)

Pan up established rooted cutting	June 10
1st Pinch	Aug. 10
2nd Pinch	Sept. 10
Full bloom	Dec. 10

- Pot size—7" azalea pot has good soil volume and good appearance.

- At the beginning, it is very important to grow the plant under warm, humid conditions to get height on the stem.

- Staking from time of potting until October 10 will ensure a much straighter stem.

- Starting about July 10, remove the volunteer side shoots that will normally develop near the lower part of the plant.

- Leave 8–10 shoots at the top of the plant.

- Pinching. *First Pinch*—Remove ½" of the growing tip (soft pinch). Remove lower leaves on stem 3 weeks after first pinch. Use a sharp knife to cut the leaves off, so the stem will not be injured. *Second Pinch*—Should be done so there will be two or three nodes left after pinching. This will allow two to three blooms per shoot.

- Temperature—use V-14 schedule.

- Feeding should be on a constant basis.

- CCC drench at 1:40 October 5–10.

- This mini-tree should be about 25"–30" in height, including the pot.

A mini tree poinsettia.

Physiological Characteristics of Poinsettia

Available forms of nitrogen Nitrogen can be utilized by plants directly as urea, ammonium nitrogen, or as nitrate nitrogen. The poinsettia reacts unfavorably to excessive quantities of ammonium or urea. Poor root development, yellowing of foliage, leaf drop, and stunting have been observed in commercial and university trials. As a rule of thumb, no more than half of the nitrogen supplied to poinsettias should be in the form of ammonium, and urea is preferably omitted completely.

Another effect of nitrogen that has repeatedly been observed is a difference in height when ammonium nitrate is compared wih calcium nitrate as the sole source of the element. Plants supplied ammonium nitrate are consistently taller.

Molybdenum deficiency With the use of soilless mixes, fertilizers of high purity, plastic pipes, and intensively grown stock plants, there have been numerous occurrences of molybdenum deficiency. The characteristic symptoms observed in many parts of the U.S. and Europe have been those of young, mature leaf yellowing, sometimes confused with nitrogen deficiency or iron deficiency. The symptoms may progress to include some leaf-edge burn. The

642

leaves characteristically curl upward in just the opposite manner from moisture stress. Since molybdenum deficiency results in nitrate accumulation in leaves, a test for nitrate nitrogen in dried leaf tissue is an indirect method of assessing the molybdenum status. No symptoms have been observed when nitrate nitrogen was less than 3000 ppm in dry leaf tissue. Severe symptoms have been associated with values of 6000 to 14,000 ppm nitrate nitrogen.

Leaf crippling, distortion, puckering   For many years, leaf deformity has been seen in some stock plants, and sometimes appearing on pot plants in greenhouses. The observed symptoms are extremely variable. In some cases, damage has occurred only at the tip of the immature leaf, and it will give the appearance of having been chopped off at a later stage of development. Where the entire margin of the leaf has been affected in earlier stages, later growth of all except the margin causes a "puckered" appearance, as if a drawstring around the leaf margin had been pulled up tight.

Many plants, including poinsettias, have leaf structures that include hydathodes or vein endings opening along the edges, tips, and sometimes leaf surfaces. Under cool, humid conditions, with ample soil moisture supply and elevated soil temperature, the pressure of fluids in the conducting system may cause guttation (the formation of small drops of liquid along the leaf edges, tips, or surfaces). If a rapid rise in temperature and drop in humidity occur simultaneously, as frequently does happen in the mornings of bright days, the liquid droplets will rapidly dry. Dissolved contents will become more concentrated. Sudden use of air-conditioning fans or natural movement of air from wind can cause much the same effect. This concentrated solution may be strong enough to cause cell damage, and when sudden stress on the plant occurs simultaneously, the concentrated fluid may be drawn back into the vein endings and cause damage to cells in and around this area. Since the phenomenon occurs only on immature leaves still undergoing expansion, subsequent growth in areas of cell injury will be inhibited and developing leaves will be distorted.

A complicating factor is frequently that of infection of injured tissue by botrytis when temperatures at night are sufficiently low.

Control of this leaf-edge damage can best be attained by maintaining low humidity at night and avoiding conditions of rapid drying in the morning. Syringing of foliage in the early morning may also aid by removing the droplets before drying commences.

Latex eruption   Plants belonging to the *Euphorbia* family contain latex, which is exuded upon cell injury. This became a problem in poinsettia production when Paul Mikkelsen and its sports first became popular. The malady is termed "crud." The mechanism is one of bursting cells resulting from high turgor pressure with latex spilling over the tissue and, upon drying, the creation of a growth-restricting layer. When this occurs at developing stem tips, distortion or stunting of growth results. The exuding of latex has also been observed on fully expanded leaves, sometimes giving the appearance of mealybug infestation due to the white splotches scattered over the leaf surface.

All contributing factors have not been clearly defined, but several obvious ones include high moisture availability and high humidity, both of which result in high fluid pressure within the cells. Low temperature is an important contributing factor. Mechanical injury from rough handling or from excessively vigorous air movement may also increase injury to cells. High rates of photosynthesis may contribute by building up a high osmotic pressure in cells from carbohydrate accumulation.

Control is best attained by using growing media which dry out in a reasonable length of time and avoiding extremes of high humidity, particularly during the night. Moderate shading in extremely bright weather may also aid. Sudden lowering of temperature can trigger the reaction. Fortunately, most varieties are not highly sensitive to this problem.

Stem splitting   Under certain conditions, poinsettias which do not normally branch unless pinched will suddenly produce stem branches at the growing tip. Careful examination will reveal that the true stem tip has stopped growth or aborted. This first became a prominent factor in 1964 when the Paul Mikkelsen variety was being heavily propagated. Many growers encountered splits and splayed flower heads. The phenomenon is not peculiar to Paul Mikkelsen, but was brought about by a major change in cultural practice at that time. Propagators soon learned the reason for splitting and have taken steps to eliminate it.

Splitting is actually a first step in flower initiation. The stimulus to flower increases with age of stem, with lengthening of night, and with low temperatures. Even with short nights and normal temperatures, splitting can be expected if the stem is permitted to grow until 20–30 leaves are present. Stem tips which are continuously propagated carry an increasing tendency to flower. To ensure against this, lights should be supplied to stock plants until May 15. Propagations prior to July 15 should be grown as multi-flowered or branched plants with tips discarded. Probably no hard and fast rules can be laid down, since new varieties may exhibit new tendencies. It is always good insurance to discard early pinches instead of trying to propagate them. Also, stems which are heavily shaded by a canopy of higher foliage may be subjected to enough reduced light to cause them to split even in periods when daylength would be considered adequate.

Leaf drop   The older varieties were much more prone to sudden loss of leaves than are modern varieties. There are several indirect causes of leaf drop. Under conditions of moderate to severe stress, it is not uncommon for older leaves to form an abscission layer at the juncture of the petiole and the supporting stem. This is believed due to loss of auxin from the leaf blade under the stress conditions. Once started, the reaction is irreversible, and the leaf petiole is virtually severed from the stem. Also when plants are kept under very low light intensity for a period of several days, lower leaves will yellow and drop.

Many of the older varieties were very susceptible to leaf drop. Before better sanitation reduced or eliminated disease problems, leaves would frequently drop in the greenhouse as root disease reduced the ability to supply water to the top of the plant. A parallel contributing factor was also the deliberate attempt of growers to carry the soil dry in an effort to restrict disease activity. Even with healthy roots, many of the varieties would drop leaves within a day or two after being moved from the humid glass house to a warm and dry living room. The change in environment induced more water stress than the leaves could tolerate. The moisture loss exceeded the ability of the roots to supply water.

Modern varieties are far more resistant to leaf abscission, though not completely immune. Modern methods of sanitation should make it unnecessary to impose dry soil conditions in the greenhouse or the home. Healthy poinsettias thrive under high moisture availability and moderate to high light. Waterlogging should be avoided, however.

Bract burn Although botrytis causes an injury which is typically observed as a burn, all such injury is not necessarily due to the fungal disease. Severe bract burn has been encountered where extreme rates of fertilizer, particularly slow release, have been used. Under these conditions, the leaves may show no damage. It is theorized that during growth, there is a diluting effect of plant-absorbed fertilizer, but at flowering, new tissue development has virtually ceased and the fertilizer salts accumulate in the youngest mature and most sensitive tissue—the bract. This accumulation causes cell damage usually starting on the bract edges.

Where slow-release fertilizers are used, the rate should be modest and application should be early enough to ensure almost complete depletion at time of flowering. It may also help to increase intensity of irrigation in the finishing stages to ensure adequate leaching and removal of accumulated salts.

Bract burn may also be triggered by environmental factors. Research is currently underway to study the effects of water stress, temperature, light intensity and humidity on bract burn, which typically occurs on transitional bracts (those structures which are usually colored, but are between the green leaves and true bracts). Changes in the environment, such as large temperature fluctuations, may be conducive to this malady.

Insects

With the present emphasis on ecology and the effects of pollution, it becomes necessary to know what greenhouse pests are infesting the poinsettia and how best to control these infestations. The present federal regulations governing the use of pesticides make it doubly difficult to know what material can be used.

One of the most important practices is that of keeping the greenhouse immaculately clean. Experience has shown that growers with the fewest problems are those with the cleanest operations.

Poinsettias are subject to attack by various pests under greenhouse conditions. Where warm, humid conditions prevail, plants are always under constant threat of being infested.

Biological control   This is the use of parasites, predators, and diseases of insect pests. Unfortunately, the "good" insects are sometimes more susceptible to the insecticides. Many of them are host-specific. They do not necessarily eradicate the undesirable pests and may only reduce the population.

Chemical control   With new federal regulations and the ever-changing list of pesticides, treatment control as outlined here can only serve as a temporary guide. Always consult the local and state rules and regulations governing pesticide applications.

Table 12   POINSETTIA PEST CONTROL CHART 1982

Pests	Materials	Form.	Dose/100 gal.	General remarks
Ants	Temik	10G		Follow directions on label.
Aphids	Orthene	75SP	8 oz.	Use as a foliar spray. Also available as aerosol.
RootAphids	Temik	10G		Follow directions on label.
	Vapona	fog		Follow directions on label. Effective at cooler greenhouse temperatures.
Fungus gnats	Resmethrin	2EC	1 pint	Foliar spray. Best results if greenhouse temperatures are cool (50–72°F). Also available as fog and aerosol formulations.
	Temik	10G		Follow directions on label.
Mealy-bugs	Orthene	75SP	8 oz.	Use as a foliar spray. Also available as an aerosol.
	Temik	10G		Follow directions on label.
	Vapona	fog		Follow directions on label. Effective at cooler greenhouse temperatures.
Oligochaets	Temik	10G		Follow directions on label.
Scale	Orthene	75SP	8 oz.	Use as a foliar spray. Also available as an aerosol.
Slugs	Temik	10G		Follow directions on label.
	Metaldehyde			Several formulations. Follow directions on label.
Snails	Mesurol	2% bait	1 lb./ 1000 sq. ft.	Scatter pelletized bait on soil surface.
Spider mites	Kelthane	18.5 EC	1 pint	Foliar spray. Some spider mites resistant to this material.

Table 12   (continued)

Pests	Materials	Form.	Dose/100 gal.	General remarks
	Pentac	50WP	8 oz.	Foliar spray. May not be effective at high temperatures.
	Temik	10G		Follow directions on label.
	Vapona	fog		Follow directions on label. Effective at cooler greenhouse temperatures.
	Vendex	50WP	8 oz.	Foliar spray best used in a preventative control program.
White flies	Resmethrin (SBP-1382)	2E	1 pint	Foliar spray. Best results if greenhouse temperatures are cool (50–72°F). Also available as fog and aerosol formulations.
	Temik	10G		Follow directions on label.
	Vapona	fog		Follow directions on label. Effective at cooler temperatures.
Worms & Tortrix (leaf roller)	Orthene	75SP	8 oz.	Use as a foliar spray. Also available as an aerosol.
	Lannate			Follow directions on label.

Caution

- It is always wise to ask local university extension personnel for any locally preferred recommendations.

- When using unfamiliar materials, trial a small portion of crop. When practical, allow 3–4 weeks for possible plant damage to show up before treating entire crop.

- All pest control should be completed by November 1 before bracts show color, if at all possible. Following this procedure will avoid the possibility of fading or injury to the bracts.

- After color shows, only thermal dusts are advisable.
        E.C. = Emulsifiable concentrate
        WP = Wettable powder

- *Spray* means apply material with full coverage to top and bottom side of foliage. When using wettable powder, it is good to fog off the accumulated material on the upper side of the leaves immediately after application. This will eliminate the residue problem that may develop when the material dries.

- *Drench* means apply material as a thorough watering to the soil. Soil should be moist before drench is applied. Plants should not be under water stress. Apply at a maximum rate of 8 oz. of mixture per 6" pot.

Certain resistant strains of any pest may develop which will require different materials from those mentioned above.

Greenhouse Poinsettia Diseases

Pathogens of primary importance include fungi and bacteria. For disease to occur, the organism and the host plant must be in close proximity. Fungi infect plants through wounds, natural openings such as stomates, and intact epidermal surfaces. Bacteria infect primarily through wounds or natural openings including stomates, lenticels, nectaries, hydathodes, and glandular hairs. Under favorable conditions, wounded tissue is quickly covered by a suberin film, which protects against bacterial infection.

Disease control can only be attained by using clean plants, clean growing media, and complete sanitation, and providing appropriate environment. All other procedures must be considered as suppression—*not control!* The use of chemicals anticipates that the control measures will not be, or have not been, properly executed.

The diseases described include pertinent information on the ecology of the pathogen. This background often provides the most important basis for planning control measures and preventing infection.

Where chemicals are to be used, limited trials should be employed before treating an entire crop, unless there has been adequate prior experience.

Rhizoctonia solani (stem and root rot)

Plant symptoms: Brown rot of stem at soil line; roots may have brown lesions and leaves can become infected under mist propagation where they touch soil. Infected plants are stunted with leaves yellowing from the bottom and sometimes dropping. Complete plant collapse under severe conditions.

Organism characteristics: A fungus which carries over in the growing medium or on infected plants. Easily spread by water. No airborne spores. Favored by moderately high available moisture, high temperature and factors which weaken the host, such as salinity.

Suppression: Rogue infected plants and avoid scattering debris from infected plants. Drench with fungicides such as Terrachlor 75%WP (PCNB) at 4 ozs. per 100 gallons, or Benlate at 4 ozs. per 100 gallons, *or* Banrot 40WP at 8 ozs. per 100 gallons. Keep growing medium on dry side.

Pythium spp. (water mold root rot)

Plant symptoms: Root tips and cortex rotted. May advance up stem. Plants stunted. Lower leaves yellow and drop. Entire plant may collapse. Growing medium tends to stay wet, since roots are incapable of removing moisture leading to the erroneous diagnosis—"too much water."

Organism characteristics: Carries over in growing medium or infected plants and is spread in water. No airborne spores. Requires high moisture availability. Active at cool temperatures. Inactive spores may live in dry growing medium for several months.

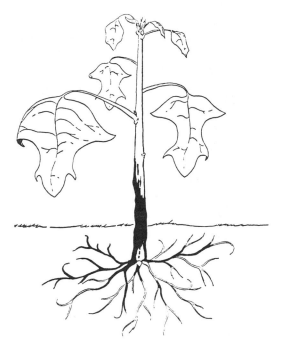

Rhizoctonia: stem and root rot.

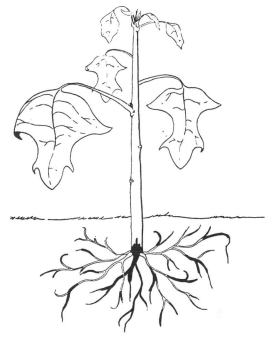

Pythium: water mold root rot.

649

Suppression: Rogue obviously infected plants, taking care not to spread debris to healthy plant areas. Maintain low growing medium moisture. Drench with fungicides such as Lesan 25WP at 4 ozs. per 100 gallons, or Truban 30WP at 4 ozs. per 100 gallons, or Subdue 2E at .5–1.5 ozs. per 100 gallons.

Thielaviopsis basicola (black root rot)

Plant symptoms: Roots develop black rotted areas. Stem may accumulate black sclerotia, which form in the pith area. Plants show lack of vigor, leaf yellowing, leaf drop, and sometimes sudden collapse, particularly after temperatures have been lowered below 60°F.

Organism characteristics: A fungus having long life in growing media as sclerotia resting stage. Favored by cool, moist environment. Slow growth at elevated temperatures and in acid growing media (pH below 5.5). No airborne spores.

Suppression: Rogue infected plants, avoid low temperatures, use acid growing media and acidifying fertilizers. Drench with Benlate at 8–12 ozs. per 100 gallons or Banrot 40WP at 8 ozs. per 100 gallons.

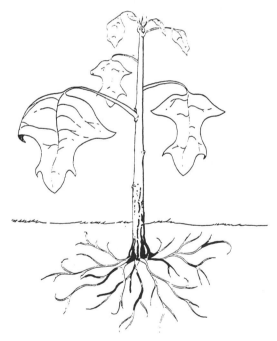

Thielaviopsis: black rot.

Rhizopus sp. (rhizopus rot)

Plant symptoms: Poinsettia plants growing under high humidity, high temperatures (80–90° F) and poor aeration are subject to a soft, wet rot of foliage and stems caused by rhizopus. Cuttings in propagation during hot weather are attacked especially when they are placed too close together. The stems, leaves, and/or leaf petioles become very soft, brown, and mushy. When rhizopus attacks the stem of poinsettia cuttings the resulting rot can resemble bacterial soft rot.

Organism characteristics: The spores can be carried by air currents, and the organism can live over in plant debris. It requires high temperatures (80–90° F), high humidity, and wounded or weakened host tissue for activity. It grows rapidly, forming abundant and visible surface mycelium. The mode of attack is similar to bacterial soft rot with an enzyme being released to cause cell deterioration.

Suppression: Improving environmental conditions for the plants or cuttings such as lowering the temperature and humidity should help control this relatively uncommon but potentially destructive disease. Suppression is best attained by sanitation, careful handling of the cuttings to avoid injury, and possibly applying a fungicide such as Captan 50W at 2 lbs./100 gallons of water.

Phytophthora parasitica (phytophthora crown and stem rot)

Plant symptoms: This fungus is closely related to pythium, but the pattern of symptoms that develops on the plant is quite different. Poinsettias infected by phytophthora may have no root rot at all. A characteristic sign is a brown canker just above the soil line about ¾" long. The canker often shows a black rim around it. Under more humid conditions gray, wet lesions develop at the soil line. As the disease progresses the affected stem or the entire plant may wilt and die.

Organism characteristics: Phytophthora is an organism which historically has not been as prevalent or damaging as pythium root rot or rhizoctonia stem rot. Phytophthora crown and stem rot is caused by a water mold as is pythium root and stem rot. The organism is able to invade tissue very rapidly through wounds. This fungus often attacks plants at the soil line where optimum levels of humidity exist. A lesion or brown canker is formed just above the soil line. Additionally, a black streak may run up the stem from the canker. The shoots above the stem discoloration eventually become brown; stems may become extensively brown and shrivel. Any or all of these symptoms may be on a given plant. The disease affects the vascular system so that wilting may precede the externally visible black discoloration.

Suppression: This problem can be overcome with strict sanitation. All plants with symptoms must be discarded, and healthy plants must not be handled after touching diseased plants. Splashing during watering is very likely to spread the contamination. This organism can be carried over in soil, and contaminated soil or pots should be disinfected before reusing. Chemicals which suppress other water molds such as pythium root rot are also usually effective against phytophthora. Drench plants with fungicides such as Lesan 25WP at 4 oz./100 gallons or Truban 30WP at 4 oz./100 gallons or Subdue 2E at .5–1 oz./100 gallons of water.

Botrytis cinerea (gray mold)

Plant symptoms: Rotting of tissue, frequently starting on young leaf edges or other immature tissue. Sometimes causes damping-off symptoms at or near the soil line. Red varieties develop purplish color on infected bracts. Difficult to distinguish from edge burn due to chemicals or salts when bracts are affected.

Organism characteristics: A fungus whose spores are airborne and can be assumed to be present everywhere at all times. Not an aggressive parasite unless favored by injured, aging, or succulent tissue, moderately low temperature, and 100% humidity at site of infection. Thrives on plant debris on floor of greenhouse.

Control: First line of defense is control of environment. Avoid physical injury to plants, maintain air circulation at night, use night heat plus ventilation to lower humidity, keep temperatures above 60°F if at all possible. Remove all dead plant material. The dense habit of multiflowered types presents a special problem of leaf and bract overlap.

Suppression: Numerous fungicides are effective as inhibitors to germination of spores and growth of mycelium. New developing plant tissue must be repeatedly covered to provide continuous protection. Materials which leave no residue are preferred to maintain salability. Fungicides employed include Exotherm Termil thermal dust at 3.5 ozs. per 1000 sq. ft., Captan 50%WP at 1 lb. per 100 gallons, and Benlate 50%WP spray at 8 ozs. per 100 gallons. Exotherm Termil programs have been widely used with little or no reported damage on blooming plants.

Rhizopus Although not a virulent parasite, this member of the phycomycete family can be a destructive fungus under favorable conditions in propagation. *Rhizopus nigricans* is noted for causing sweet potato storage rot. *Rhizopus stolonifera* (causes rot of lily bulbs) has been associated with poinsettia problems.

The spores can be carried by air currents, and the organism can live over in plant debris. It requires high temperature (70–85°F), high humidity (min. 75%), and wounded or weakened host tissue for activity. It grows rapidly, forming abundant and visible surface mycelium. The mode of attack is similar to bacterial soft rot with an enzyme being released to cause cell deterioration.

When wounds callus or heal rapidly, rhizopus is not able to establish. It is a sort of "high temperature botrytis."

Suppression is best attained by sanitation, careful handling of cuttings to avoid injury, and possibly applying a fungicide such as Captan 50W at 2 lbs./ 100 gallons water.

Erwinia carotovora (bacterial soft rot)

Plant symptoms: Rot of covered stem in propagation. Occurs within three days after sticking cuttings. Callus and rooting sometimes occur above rot. Rot usually stops at or near the soil line.

Organism characteristics: This bacterium is not particularly aggressive except under highly favorable conditions. Wounded tissue, waterlogging, and high temperatures are very favorable. The organism is prevalent on dead plant material and can be carried on wind-blown dust, nonsterilized tools, and unwashed hands. Readily spreads in water.

Control: Grow stock plants under glass or other controlled environment. Avoid waterlogging of rooting medium. Add bactericide to rooting hormone, particularly if liquid. Use extreme sanitation throughout harvest and propagation of cuttings.

Suppression: If other sanitary precautions are not taken, dip cuttings in chlorine (500 ppm) and drench rooting medium with chlorine (50 ppm) immediately prior to and after sticking of cuttings. Streptomycin is not too effective and does tend to bleach the foliage.

Corynebacterium poinsettiae (bacterial canker)

Plant symptoms: Black, elongated, and watersoaked streaks occur on green stems. Stem tips abort or bend over. Spots or blotches occur on leaves. In a favorable (warm, humid) environment, disease progresses rapidly, resulting in death of stem above infection and/or entire plant. Not a common disease except during hot humid weather, such as found in summer climate of Midwest, East, and South U.S. It has shown up in other areas where inoculum was present and environment favorable.

Organism characteristics: A bacterium transported in water, soil, on contaminated tools and on the hands of workers. Enters plant through stomates or wounds. Spreads in plant through thin-walled parenchyma cells.

Suppression: Severe roguing should be practiced and all overhead irrigation or syringing avoided. Humidity should be kept as low as practical and excessive temperatures should be avoided. Plants should be protected from wind and/or rain. If stock plant infection is suspected, sterile knives should be used in removing each cutting to avoid spread.

Note: A number of additional diseases are reported as occurring on poinsettias, but these are primarily of concern in outdoor or landscape plantings. The following is a brief listing of the principal ones.

- *Sphaceloma poinsettiae* (scab)—a fungus disease of stem and leaf.

- *Phymatotricum omnivorum* (Texas root rot)—a fungus disease of roots.

- *Uromyces euphorbiae* (rust)—a fungus disease of leaves.

Sanitation Hints

1. Hose end off floor.

2. Hand rinse before handling plants.

3. Copper naphthenate on all wood, metal, or composition surfaces.

4. Presteam all soil or sand benches.

5. Steam or fumigate all soil mixes.

6. Avoid inoculation from dust.

7. Use a tool dip to decontaminate.

8. Never pick up cuttings or tools from the floor where they may have fallen. Discard cuttings, rinse tools.

9. Remove soil from tools, pots, benches before treating with Clorox or other disinfectant.

10. Eliminate weeds and debris—they harbor disease and insects.

11. Think "clean."

*Poinsettia Production Costs 1982**

Profitable production is very dependent on knowledge and control of production costs. Costs are normally subdivided into four categories: overhead, labor, materials, and marketing costs.

Overhead A less obvious component of production costs is overhead since it remains an indirect cost. It is frequently referred to as greenhouse space cost. Overhead varies by geographic area as well as by the level of investment. Overhead expenses or fixed costs include such items as depreciation, fuel, insurance, interest on the capital investment, maintenance, and taxes. Many growers have used a poinsettia marketing/pricing strategy of pricing at a level

*Excerpts from *1982 Poinsettia Production Costs,* Jerry L. Robertson and Laura Chatfield. Ohio Florists Association Bulletin No. 634, August 1982.

that would allow them to recover material, labor, and marketing costs, but not all the overhead expense. This strategy can only be justified if some other crop carries more than its share of overhead, or as a short-run strategy as profits are not earned to provide a return-on-investment and risk. Many firms have witnessed serious problems with these marketing methods as it takes precise knowledge of production costs. To generate a profit, pricing in such a manner to recover all expenses, including overhead, is the only prudent long-run strategy.

Labor Direct labor includes the potting, pot moving, pinching, daily maintenance, and harvesting activities of poinsettia production. Poinsettia production is not considered to be a labor intensive crop compared to crops such as pot mums. The most labor-intensive activity is the potting and moving of the plants as well as the daily watering and spraying maintenance activities.

Materials Production materials account for a major component of poinsettia production.

Marketing costs The marketing charges such as sleeving, boxing, and subsequent labor, and transportation charges are a cost for poinsettia producers.

Total Production Costs

An average production cost for a 6″ poinsettia is about $2.60–$3.41 per finished plant as overhead, labor, materials and marketing costs account for 40%, 17%, 25%, and 18% respectively.

TOTAL COSTS OF PRODUCTION OF 4″, 5″, AND 6″ FANCY GRADE
POINSETTIA PLANTS

	4″ Plant ($/plant)	5″ Plant ($/plant)	6″ Plant ($/plant)
Overhead	.532	.832	1.371
Labor	.390	.475	.579
Materials	.634	.764	.861
Marketing costs	.302	.390	.601
Total	$1.858	$2.461	$3.412

Assumption: High energy use area, high investment facility.

COMPARISON OF THE COSTS OF PRODUCTION OF FANCY GRADE POINSETTIAS UNDER GLASS AND POLY

LOW ENERGY USE AREA (inflated double poly)—SUNBELT

	4" Plant ($/plant)	5" Plant ($/plant)	6" Plant ($/plant)
Overhead*	$.216–.312	$.388–.488	$.556–.804
Labor	.390	.475	.579
Materials	.634	.764	.861
Marketing costs	.302	.390	.601
Total	$1.542–1.638	$2.017–2.117	$2.597–2.845

*The difference is due to the use of a glass or poly greenhouse.

HIGH ENERGY USE AREA (glass)—NORTHERN U.S. AND CANADA

	4" Plant ($/plant)	5" Plant ($/plant)	6" Plant ($/plant)
Overhead*	$.417–.532	$.648–.832	$1.076–1.371
Labor	.390	.475	.579
Materials	.634	.764	.861
Marketing costs	.302	.390	.601
Total	$1.743–1.858	$2.277–2.461	$3.117–3.412

*The difference is due to the use of a glass or poly greenhouse.

Energy use Production costs are about 14%–16% less in a low energy use area compared to a high energy use area. The difference is due to differences in fuel use and investment requirements. If greater space efficiency through close spacing can be employed in a low energy use, high light area, a greater difference could be realized. While low energy use areas can realize substantially lower unit production costs, frequently market prices are correspondingly lower.

Productivity The most important factor influencing production costs is the productivity of the greenhouse space. In recent years, the productivity capacity of floral production operations has increased due to more efficient use of greenhouse facilities. For poinsettias, many growers have reduced poinsettia production costs through space efficiency gains. However, in many cases, these productivity advantages such as closer spacing may be offset by reduced quality, which reduces market price. Price has been more important than productivity in influencing margins and profitable floral crop production. As a result, producers must carefully evaluate these tradeoffs.

Pricing After the production cost has been calculated, careful consideration should be given to pricing. Pricing has to first take into consideration the number of plants that are dumped or reduced in price. A $3.41 poinsettia production cost increases to $3.79 with a 10% shrinkage [($3.41 ÷ .90) = $3.79]. Thus, shrinkage, if not considered, could easily eliminate all profits.

Secondly, with a desired return on inventory, greenhouse, equipment, and other assets, an annual revenue of $10/sq.ft. results in a sales/asset productivity of 1 ($10 in sales ÷ $10 in assets). Thus, a 25% markup on poinsettias would result in a 25% return on sales as well as assets. For a 25% return, a $3.41 poinsettia with a 10% shrinkage should be priced at $5.04 [(3.41 ÷ .90) × 1.33 = $5.04]. The following table provides the multipliers that should be used to obtain the desired net profit margin.

Desired net profit margin (%)	Multiplier
10	1.11
15	1.18
20	1.25
25	1.33
30	1.43
35	1.54

Marketing

Historically, poinsettias have been marketed through flower shops and, in some sections of the country, garden shops. With the introduction of the long-lasting varieties, poinsettias are being marketed in other sales outlets and it appears that this trend will continue. Because many of the longer-lasting varieties bloom earlier than the older varieties, sales are starting at Thanksgiving time. It is possible to ensure end-of-November flowering by black-clothing from September 15 for 3 weeks. Naturally early-blooming varieties will not require this treatment.

The pricing of poinsettias varies greatly, depending on many factors. In New England, where the investment in greenhouses is high and where the fuel bill is a factor, it is obvious that these producers must get more for their plants than those in Florida growing in the field under saran covering. Many growers have tried to sell their crop by the bloom, particularly when plants were grown as single-stem. Now that there are good varieties producing excellent multi-flowered plants, most growers are marketing the plants "by the pot." In either case, it would seem that the producer should determine the cost of production and then attempt to sell the plants based on cost and reasonable return. Many wholesale growers are now planning to gross at least $4.00 per sq. ft. of finished bench space on their Christmas crop. A rule of thumb used by some growers is to figure a minimum return of $1.00/sq. ft./month for bench space. Spacing and time to produce a salable crop then become the deciding factors in establishing the sales price.

657

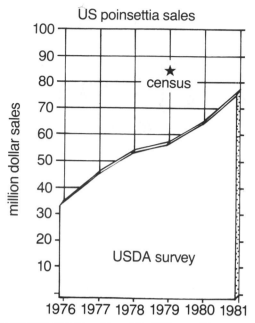

US poinsettia sales. The solid area is the USDA survey. The star posts the 1979 Department of Commerce sales totals.

Shop care All varieties must be handled carefully when being wrapped and packaged in the greenhouse for delivery to retail outlets. The use of paper sleeves is common practice and is recommended. Cellophane sleeves, if used, should be perforated to avoid possible condensation of moisture on the inner side and subsequent botrytis infection of the bracts.

Prompt and proper care will extend the useful life of poinsettia plants. After receiving your plants they should be unpacked and unsleeved *immediately*. If poinsettias are left in unopened containers or sleeves too long, bending of the petioles (the structure connecting the leaf blade to the stem) may occur, or the leaves may turn yellow and fall off prematurely. Poinsettias should then be placed in a 65° to 75°F room with enough light so one could easily read a newspaper. Do not expose the plants to drafts or have hot air blowing on them. Higher humidity is much better than low humidity; of course the ideal place is a greenhouse environment.

Poinsettias must be kept moist at all times, not too wet, not too dry. It is best to water thoroughly until water seeps through the drain holes. Never allow poinsettias to sit in water. Check the plants daily and water when the soil feels dry to the touch.

Poinsettia bracts are sensitive to bruising and must be handled carefully. The appropriate care-tag should be attached to the plants so that the retailer as well as the consumer can follow the care-tag instructions. A typical care-tag is shown here. With proper care poinsettia plants can give a great deal of satisfaction for you and your customers; but they must be cared for properly, at all times.

658

Watering by the consumer, which is certainly key to customer satisfaction.

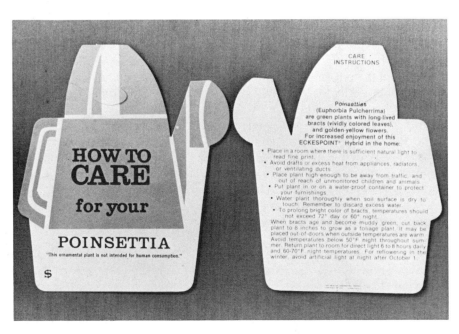

Poinsettia care tag.

659

Do not use fluorescent lamps for displaying plants, as this light source distorts the true color of bracts and leaves. Most homes are lighted with incandescent filament lamps. Light your plants with the same kind of lamp—the consumer will see what he or she is getting.

Poinsettias are not poisonous   For years, there has been adverse publicity during holiday time concerning the *alleged* poisonous nature of poinsettia plants. Past research at The Ohio State University has disclosed that laboratory rats are not subject to any ill effects from eating leaves and bracts. This research indicates that the poinsettias are not harmful to humans and animals, though, of course, it is not recommended that they should be taken internally.

POPPY (Papaver)

PERENNIAL *(P. nudicaule) 275,000 seeds per oz. Germinates in 10–14 days at 70°. (P. orientale) 108,000 seeds per oz. Germinates in 10–14 days at 70°.*

It is interesting to reflect that from the same genus can come the flaming *Oriental* poppy in springtime perennial gardens and the charming little *Iceland* species that fairly covers acres with color. These and over a hundred more species come under the head of *Papaver*, but only the *Oriental, P. orientale* and the *Iceland, P. nudicaule,* are important in horticulture.

The *Icelands (P. nudicaule)*, native to Arctic regions, are perennials, but can be grown as annuals. They might well answer the quest for "something different" in spring-forcing annuals. Sow in January, either directly into pots or into the bench where they are to flower; if allowed to flower in 4" pots right where they are, they will come in earlier as a result of the check. A 50° temperature and ordinary garden soil are OK. Flowers cut full-blown during the day will drop their petals in an hour; if cut early in the morning in the bud stage, and if the cut ends are burned, they will keep several days; in fact, they are even shipped in this loose bud stage. Several named varieties are available in this group, but mixtures are by far the most popular. *Iceland* mix and F_1 *Champagne Bubbles* are two of the best.

Most popular is *Champagne Bubbles*. Far superior in the inbreds, it produces flowers two to three times larger than other inbreds on bushier, more compact plants (1'), and flowers over a much longer period of time. It has an extremely wide color range, including bicolors.

Once a year, in early June, we are treated to the large, gaudy, scarlet blooms of the Orientals (*P. orientale*). What they lack in extended flowering season is made up many times by the brilliance of their flowers. Their use is primarily for perennial borders: flowers just aren't satisfactory for cutting. Sow almost any time during open weather, but figure on two seasons for established flowering clumps. They have no special cultural requirements beyond a good loam; usual height about 3 feet. Named varieties from seed other than red are inclined to vary in color. There are many other named varieties from both seed and divisions.

PORTULACA (Moss Rose)

ANNUAL *(P. grandiflora) 280,000 seeds per oz. Germinates in 10 days at 70°.*

Here's a champion for hot, dry, full sun locations.

One of the most popular and colorful annuals, moss roses are widely used today because of their ability to thrive under adverse conditions. They are truly procumbent and quite spreading, so a few plants cover a good bit of ground. While portulaca can be sown directly where they are to flower, as early as the ground is warm in early May, your customers will eagerly buy started young plants, and it's here where the profit lies. They flower in a month or 6 weeks from sowing date, and require no special care beyond fairly moist soil during germination. They have also become a popular hanging basket item.

Many growers will either sow the seed direct into the selling container, or transplant several seedlings to one spot in the pack to allow for better color balance in a mixture. Sowings are commonly made for mid-February through March.

Most popular is the *Double Mixture,* a showy blend of white, primrose-yellow shades, orange, red, lilac, and mauve. Single strains are still available and used on a limited scale, but these are rapidly being replaced by the more showy doubles. The *Sunglo* series, eight separate colors and a mix, is the first F_1 on the market. *Sunnyside Mixed* is a large flowered double strain. *Calypso* mix is an F_2 double-flowered variety.

Primula malacoides—*a delicate, fragrant, and pleasant cool-temperature pot plant.*

Malacoides

ANNUAL *(P. malacoides) 385,000 seeds per oz. Germinates in 3–4 wks. at 60°–65°. Light.*

This baby class of primula is much more easily and quickly grown than the *obconica* and is not irritating to the skin. With the advent of new and vastly improved varieties, interest in their production and sales has quickened. From our trials here in West Chicago, they would seem to be particularly well adapted to mass-market outlets.

First sowings are usually made in July for flowering in 5" pots shortly after the first of the year. The majority of this crop is produced in 4" or 4¼" pots. Crop time runs about 22 weeks. Sowings made after October 15 will come blind unless grown at 50°.

Preferring cool temperatures (40°–45°) for greenhouse growing, they do suffer during the midsummer heat and often are very difficult to germinate at this time. Thus, it is advisable to get them started before the heat, or wait till September. Seed can be sown in a mixture of equal parts of leaf mold, sand, and soil or in a mix of equal parts of peat, soil, and vermiculite. Keep the seed flat in the coolest spot possible. When the seedlings are large enough to be transplanted, they can be spaced out (1" each way) in another flat, or shifted directly to 2¼" Jiffy-Pots or cells. Primulas like a light, well-drained soil with a good percentage of humus added to it. However, stay away from ingredients with an acid reaction, sinch chlorosis caused by acidity can be troublesome.

Many growers have found it advantageous to buy-in young plants ($2^1/_4$") from a specialist grower, rather than attempt to start them from seed.

From $2^1/_4$" size, the plants can be shifted directly to finishing pots. Frequently, fertilization is necessary to keep the plants in active growth. When shifting to larger pots, care should be taken to see that the crowns are set just above the soil line. If set too low, rot can result; if too high, the plants will topple over. If grown under glass during the summer, shading is required. Also, the application of a light shade during late winter can intensify the flower color.

One of the common ailments of primula is yellowing of the foliage. This can be caused by the soil being too acid, too wet, or poorly drained. It can also be caused by deficiencies of nitrogen and/or potash, or spraying with certain insecticides.

Snow Cone and Pink Ice are separate colors widely used today. Compact, basal-branching, with flowers borne close to the foliage, they have good lasting qualities. The King Series is an excellent one and consists of four separate colors and a mixture. Another widely used mixture is Magic Pearls, with bright colors in lavender, rose, and pink shades.

Hardy Primula

PERENNIAL *28,000–35,000 seeds per oz. Germinates in 3–4 wks. at 60–65°.*

There are many, many species of hardy primulas, but only a few which are of importance to the grower today. These varieties and strains belong to the *veris (polyanthus)* and *Acaulis* groups. When given a sheltered position in a shaded spot with light winter protection, they will overwinter in this part of the country. Of much greater importance is the fact that they make excellent pot plants for early spring sales. An August sowing, wintered in frames, or grown in a cold greenhouse, will make attractive flowering 4" pots for sales from February through April. They must not be exposed, though, to high temperatures; as with other species of primulas, they do their best in a light, well-drained soil, high in organic matter. When in the greenhouse, they should be lightly shaded.

Renewed interest in perennial primulas for winter and spring pot sales is, to a great extent, due to the *Pacific Giant* strain; with beautiful, clear, large flowers on longer stems, they make excellent pot plants. While the *Blue Shades* are most popular, they are available in *Pink, Rose, Red, White* and *Yellow Apricot* as well as a *Mixture*. Representing an improvement in uniformity of color, habit, and performance is the *Laser* series. Available in seven separate brilliant colors and a mix, it probably has the greatest potential. Other mixtures in this same class are *Jewel Mix, Casino Mix,* and *Colossea* which is hardier than most strains.

In recent years there has been a great deal of breeding activity in the *Acaulis* group, resulting in a proliferation of new varieties and types. Top performers are the F_1 *Pageant Series*, which is very free flowering with large

Primula veris *are widely used for January/February flowering in the northern greenhouse—and are a major garden favorite in such cool summer areas as the Northwest. Here's a crop at Meiring's, Carlton, Michigan.*

blooms. Each of these has five or six separate colors plus a mix. *Ducat F₁ Mix* is an improvement over the *Aalsmeer Giants.*

The *Acaulis* group could be further divided into *Julian* types or miniatures. The varieties in this class have smaller flowers, 1"–1½", and generally are better suited for 3½" pot production. In general they are 10 days to 2 weeks earlier. *Julian Mix* and *Julian Bicolor Mix* are excellent F₁ strains. *Cherriette* is a unique type with a flower form similar to a cherry blossom. *Goldridge Mix* is unique with a silver or gold edge on many flowers. It flowers later than the other *Julian* types.

Caution Some people, if exposed by contact to Primula *obconica*, develop severe skin rash. For this reason, these plants are, in some cases, not allowed in hospitals, etc. On the other hand, they still seem to be widely grown and enjoyed by many people. If you grow a crop, be sure to have this in mind.

PYRETHRUM (Painted Daisy)

PERENNIAL *(P. roseum) 18,000 seeds per oz. Germinates in 2–3 wks. at 60–70°.*

Among the most valuable and best known of these easily grown perennials is *P. roseum* or "painted daisy." It includes a number of useful, long-stemmed, cut flower varieties which bloom heavily in June with a few scattering flowers during summer. In England, named varieties that are propagated by divisions are very popular, the climate there enabling them to be marketed on heavy 2' to 3' stems. We have tried some of this division-propagated stock, but found they die out shortly, while seed-grown plants will do well for 3 to 4 years. Double strains of pyrethrum have been developed and they improve upon the single form, but the strength of at least 2-year-old plants is necessary to produce double flowers. The first year, nearly all will be singles. While there are separate-color varieties available, the *Double Mix* strain is most popular. Another English strain known as *Robinson's Mixture* produces large, single, attractive flowers.

ROSES*

Cut roses—for so many years the Cadillac of all cut flowers.

*Contributed by Robert Danielson, Pan-American Plant Company.

665

The Cut Crop

Rose growing has long been assigned to the specialist, for it does adapt itself to a large operation with many thousands of plants. Producers of cut roses need a constant supply of blooms during all seasons of the year. In order to do this, you need a large number of plants to produce enough roses to grade out fancy, long, medium, and short lengths for the various needs of the retail outlets. As a producer, you need a selection of varieties that will give you types (hybrid teas and sweethearts), as well as the color classes (red, yellow, pink, white, and bi-colors). It is obvious, then, that 1,000 or 2,000, or even 5,000 plants will hardly carry on all the needs of one flower shop. However, one grower and five employees can profitably supply the roses required within a limited market area with 20 or 30 thousand plants, one acre of roses.

With the application of new technology in heat shields, high energy lighting, drip irrigation and fertilizer application, high pressure mist for cooling and humidity control, and CO_2 enrichment, high quality roses can be produced in many areas from which they had disappeared in recent years. The market for these locally grown roses in the midwestern and eastern areas of the United States and Canada has been good. These growers using this new technology are very satisfied with the results both in quality and profitability.

Rose plants are very specific in their requirements and therefore should be more or less isolated in one house or area where this can be achieved. They are more exacting in their light, temperature, and humidity requirements than are most other crops. It would be very difficult to control disease and insect problems if they were not restricted to a given area.

Structures for growing roses   The most practical type of structure is one that will give full sunlight to all plants in the house. There should be no shading from other greenhouses, buildings, or trees. Preferably, the greenhouse should have adequate ventilation so it can be ventilated during all seasons of the year without cold drafts. The house should have at least 7' gutters so that the roses will not touch the glass when they are at their highest level of production.

Whether roses are grown in ground beds or raised benches makes little difference as long as good drainage is supplied. Those grown in ground beds are generally easier to manage and generally give more long-stemmed flowers.

Roses are generally planted four plants across a 42" bench with a 12" spacing down the bench. This planting gives you approximately 1 square foot of area for each plant.

The heating of a rose house should be adequate to supply 60°F in the coldest weather. The source of heat should be from the floor of the house, which creates rising air currents that will give you the maximum circulation. You should also have pipes around the perimeter of the house, which can be left on at all times to keep plants dry at night. Roses grown in ground beds may have the pipes around the perimeter of the beds, thereby giving even heat

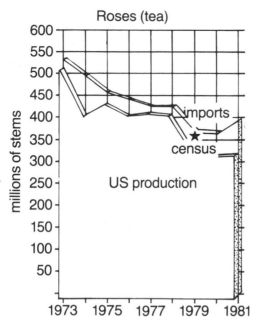

Roses(tea)—nine years of US rose production plus imports. US figures are from the USDA. The Department of Commerce Census is posted for 1979. As indicated, US and import production for 1981 totalled 400 million stems.

HID here coupled with double poly roof. The supplemental light overcomes the light deficiency of the poly roof—and heat from the HID lights means major fuel savings.

to the house. Controlling the temperature is a very important part of rose culture, especially on timing and quality. The rose structure should supply warm, humid atmosphere with high light intensity during the daytime, and at night a lower humidity with an even, warm 60°F. Good quality roses can be grown with a cooler night temperature, but production will be reduced.

When roses are grown in double poly structures, they must be equipped properly to provide even distribution of heating, ventilation, and air circulation, and other necessary environmental conditions. Humidity will remain higher in a poly house and air can become stagnant if proper circulation is not provided.

Gas-fired unit heaters can be used with poly convection tubes for distribution as an alternate source of heating, but some provision should be made to increase the soil temperature to 65°F for winter production.

Also, all gas-fired unit heaters should be provided with outside outlets both for intake and exhaust requirements.

Environmental controls

Cooling and humidity The rose plant requires a specific environment in order to control quality and productivity. The past 10 years has seen the use of new technology in environmental controls for greenhouse production.

Computer control of greenhouse environments based on outside environment and crop requirements has enabled the grower to fine-tune the growing environment.

Fan and pad cooling has been used for many years to reduce stress on plants during high temperature periods; as an alternative, roses require a high humidity environment and this can be accomplished by installing a high pressure mist system in the structures to provide summer cooling and year-round humidity control.

Supplemental light During the shorter-day period of the year, supplemental light for photosynthesis can be supplied with high energy lighting (HID) high pressure sodium vapor.

Research today has determined that supplemental light at a minimum of 350 ft-c and up to 500 ft-c for 16 hours per day between September 15 and March 1 will increase production of quality roses by 25%. Producers should cut seven to nine more roses during the peak demand season.

The optimum installation of high pressure sodium fixtures would use 1000-watt bulbs with a density of 250 units per acre (167 sq. ft. per fixture) and up to 300 units per acre (125 sq. ft. per fixture).

In some areas off-peak demand electrical rate can be attained, reducing the cost of lighting. Spacing for even distribution of light is important depending on the width of the structure.

It is necessary to increase the use of CO_2 and fertilizer with HID lighting. The CO_2 level should be established between 600 and 800 ppm during sunlight hours.

HID light—already widely used across Canada and coming into U.S. ranges more recently. It provides a major boost in winter production and quality—especially for the critical St. Valentine's and Easter markets.

The fertilizer level should be raised to compensate for the increased growth rate with HID lighting. You may need to double the rate of application in the feeding program and monitor the minor elements by soil testing. Deficiencies of minors can show up under lights.

J. R. Johnson, Minneapolis rose grower, has several acres under HID light as of the mid-1980s. Some interesting details:

Most of the lighting is done with 400-watt fixtures—smaller fixtures make more shade but require less maintenance. They're spaced on 9' centers; a 35' house has two rows of lights. "You need 500 foot-candles to make any important difference." Lighting schedule: September from sunset to sunup, 12 hours a night. October through February: 24 hours a day. Three years is average length of life for fixtures, some go up to 5 years.

Planting stock   The time to plant roses is usually between January 1 and June 15. It is generally believed a better practice to plant in January or February and bring the plants into production in the early summer. This gives you time to build a large plant to go through the following winter.

Budded plants are the most widely used at the present time. The rose variety is budded on a root stock of superior type for vigorous root growth. The budding usually takes place on the West Coast during May and June. Some of the buds take earlier than others, and these usually become your started-eye plants. The buds which do not begin to grow the first year become dormant-

669

eye plants. Actually, the new growth the plant makes from the eye is vigorous and strong, and the individual grower's ability to get dormant-eyes to break with strong canes determines his success with a new crop. On started-eye plants, this new-growth budding already has taken place and they usually break out from this growth a little earlier than dormant-eye plants. The object of any rose planting is to produce three to five working canes per plant that will give you maximum production per square foot.

Rose plants should be ordered from the producer at least 6 months to a year ahead of time of delivery. This usually amounts to a substantial reduction of price and assures you the best quality plants.

The plants will arrive in large cases and should be opened for inspection on arrival. If the plants are dry, water thoroughly and cover up with plastic to put moisture back in them. If you leave the plants set in a warm room (70°–80°F) for 3 or 4 days, the buds will swell and the roots will begin to make feeder roots. The roses are now ready to plant.

When planting, the soil should be moist, but not to the point that it packs. The plants should be taken out of the box and roots pruned back about 1" from the root tip. The canes of started-eyes are pruned back to about 6"; dormant-eye plants are planted without pruning. Some started-eye plants may be branched, and all weaker growth should be removed and the canes trimmed back to 6" or 8".

The bud graft on a plant is very noticeable, and the plants should be set in the soil with this union about 1" or 2" out of the soil. This will allow the root system good aeration near the soil surface. It will also allow room for a mulch as the plants come into production.

When planting, a trench may be dug across the bench and the root system spread out across the bench. The soil is then packed in around the roots. This system gives maximum root development and is much easier than planting individually.

Starting the new crop   The soil used for roses should meet drainage, moisture-holding, and fertilizer-retention requirements. It has also been found that roses will grow in a wide range of soils, but this will depend on the grower's ability. In general, a good loam soil with plenty of organic matter will give them their best year-round growth. Remember these plants are going to be in this soil for a minimum of up to 4 years, and because of this, the soil must be able to hold its properties. Before the soil is put in the bench, drainage capacity must be supplied through tile or naturally. In concrete benches, drainage capacity should be supplied through a "V" bottom with coarse gravel to cover the tile laid down the center. In wooden benches, the boards should have ½" between them. Soil that will not or cannot drain will soon destroy the plants placed in it.

Roses are very heavy feeders, and as they grow and produce, the soil should have a good supply of the necessary elements. When soil is placed in the bench, room at the top should be left for a mulch that can be applied later as the plants begin to grow. The bench should be filled to a depth of at least 6". Leaving room for 1" or 2" or more of mulch on the bench is always necessary. At this time, 5 pounds of 20% superphosphate per 100 square feet should be applied to the soil. If possible, the pH should be adjusted to 6.5. This may be done by adding flowers of sulfur to the soil. As the plants begin to grow and become fertilized, the pH can be controlled by the addition of fertilizers that will control the soil reaction.

The first 6 weeks of the new rose planting is very important to your success. The plants should be watered thoroughly several times and then they should not be watered until the soil has dried out thoroughly, or there is sufficient top growth. Instead of watering plants, the top should be syringed four or five times a day during this period. This practice will induce top growth. Rose plants at this time are not losing water to transpiration, and any water tends to reduce the amount of air in the soil. The grower should strive to get maximum root growth to drive new vegetative growth out of the new eyes breaking above on the plant. A rose plant that develops top growth without root growth will soon die.

It is very important that all of the plants on the bench break at one time so that the bench can be watered and fed as the new growth begins to mature. Any plants that hold back will soon be lost because the bench needs are that of growing plants. Slow-breaking plants should be covered with a plastic bag to control humidity around them. To build up a plant for production of cut flowers, all new growth must be pinched when buds appear. This soft pinching is usually practiced at this time. Pinch all new growth back to the second 5-leaflet leaf. The new growth resulting from this pinch will be pinched, and so on, until a high level of production is reached. If plants are started in January, a partial crop may be had for Mother's Day by selecting a few of the stronger canes to flower at this time. At no time should a heavy crop be taken from young plants. Rose plants should be at their maximum growth during September and October in order to produce during the winter months. The recommended practice is to build plants up during the summer and fall and cut down on the wood during January through May.

Supporting the plants   The usual method of supporting rose plants is to string layers of wire down the bench and cross them with bamboo canes tied to the wire. This makes a maze to support new breaks on the plants.

Watering   Watering of a rose crop is very important, and a number of factors enter into the amount of water they need at any one time. If the plants have a lot of top growth and are coming into crop, water requirements are high. The bench dries out quickly, and watering should be adequate to prevent checking of the growth. In general, a rose crop should be watered thoroughly and then allowed to dry. If roses are cut back or if a crop is taken off, the water requirements will be less than a full-production crop. Rose plants should require considerably less water in winter than in the summer months. Mulching will tend to reduce the amount of water necessary during the summer months. It will also tend to keep the soil open and aerated. A soil that is not mulched soon becomes compacted from the great amount of water applied. Mulches or corncobs, hulls, peat, or other similar material can be applied at almost any time. Cattle-manure mulches must be applied at a time when the houses can be ventilated adequately, from early March through September. Care shuld be taken not to put much manure in the house at one time, or an ammonia buildup will occur that will burn the foliage and leaves and give your plants a real setback. When mulch is applied, or even manure, an application of nitrogen is needed to offset the reaction caused by the decomposition of the mulch. A good practice is to apply 1 pound of ammonium sulfate per 100 square feet. Then go ahead with your regular feeding program.

Occasionally a heavy hand watering with a full flow breaker will be required to even out the moisture within the bench or for leaching purposes.

Either a drip system or spray nozzles should be installed for feeding and watering. The new drip systems with individually spaced drip at 1' intervals are ideal for rose watering.

Feeding   Feeding roses is again based largely on the time of the year and amount of top growth. You may follow an injector feeding program based on soil tests and supplement this with special applications of lime, sulfur, or gypsum to adjust the pH and calcium levels of the soil (see p. 673).

Feeding is usually discontinued during the darker months of winter and again during the warmer months if roses stop growing. A very good practice is to discontinue feeding during December and January, and test your rose soils regularly.

All roses should maintain 40–60 ppm nitrates, 5–10 ppm phosphorus, 25–50 ppm potassium—Spurway. The pH of the soil should be on the acid side—6.5. When watering roses, you should water thoroughly at all times to eliminate soluble-salt problems. If soluble-salts do become a problem through overfeeding, leaching several times with large amounts of water will bring the soil back to normal.

If HID lighting is applied, be sure to evaluate your feeding program and increase the use of fertilizer based on soil tests and foliar analysis.

Disease and insect control   The health of rose plants depends largely on success in controlling diseases and insect pests in your plantings. In contrast, we should say that all these factors work hand in hand. Red spider must be controlled, since roses simply will not produce on starved and spider-infested plants. You must have a regularly scheduled program of *prevention* to control insects and diseases. Spraying is generally preferred to eliminate spiders.

The second most important pest is powdery mildew, and the spores occur when environmental conditions are optimum for the spread of the disease when moisture condenses on the leaf surface. Mildew can ruin a rose crop

	Fertilizer used	1:100 injector	1:200 injector
	20–20–20	42	84
	20– 0–30	42	84
	25– 5–20	34	68
potassium nitrate	13– 0–44	18	37
ammonium nitrate	33– 0– 0	25	50
muriate of potash	0– 0–60	14	28
ammonium sulfate	20– 0– 0	28	56
potassium nitrate	13– 0–44	18	37

Dry feed applications

Reaction	Fertilizer	Analysis	Rate
neutral	ammonium nitrate	33– 0– 0	1 lb./100 sq. ft.
acidic	ammonium sulfate	20– 0– 0	1 lb./100 sq. ft.
alkaline	sodium nitrate	16– 0– 0	1 lb./100 sq. ft.
alkaline	calcium nitrate	16– 0– 0	1 lb./100 sq. ft.
neutral	muriate of potash	0– 0–60	1 lb./100 sq. ft.
neutral	potassium nitrate	13– 0–44	1 lb./100 sq. ft.
acidic	sulfur flour		1–3 lbs./100 sq. ft.
alkaline	limestone dolomite		5 lbs./100 sq. ft.
neutral	gypsum		5 lbs./100 sq. ft.
	10–10–10		3 lbs./100 sq. ft.
	10– 6– 4		3 lbs./100 sq. ft.

unless checked. Watch for cold drafts from ventilation or broken glass during the heating season. Avoid sudden drops in temperature.

Black spot of roses has been a problem in the past, but largely disappeared when the practice of syringing roses was discontinued.

Rose plants will often lose mature leaves if sprayed or fogged when the soil moisture is low. Leaves will ripen and fall when the soil is allowed to dry out too much between waterings. When applying insecticides, the condition of the plants should be watched carefully. Never use a spray that you have not carefully tested before subjecting the crop to it.

Flora fog systems, pulse fog, solo dusters, and hydraulic sprayers can be used for insect application.

Common materials used for pest control:

Red Spider	Pentac (Liquid)	Aphids	Orthene
	Kelthane	Thrip	Metasystox-R
	Morestan	Nematode	Vydate drench
Mildew	Milban	Symphilids	Lindane drench
	Pipron		
	Morestan vaporized		

Rose cutting Rose cutting is a very important part of rose production. Where you remove the rose from the plant largely determines the ability of your plant to produce. Many systems of cutting have been used, the most common being to cut to the second 5-leaflet leaf on the new wood. This will assure you of another rose within 7 weeks (42–45 days) from this cut. This type of cutting in the summer and fall will tend to build your plants up. The hooks produced by this type of cutting can be removed by cutting below the hooks in the late winter and spring months. Another method is to soft-pinch all breaks as they appear and cut the rose back below the pinch. With this method of cutting, you will have a long stem and better quality, but production will be reduced.

During the spring and summer, knuckle cuts may be practiced on older wood, where cuts are made just above the branch and adventitious buds appear and develop; later these knuckles can be removed with the next cut.

Roses must be cut twice a day to assure that none will open on the plant and be lost. It is also important that benches be cut at the same time every day since 1 or 2 hours will result in a lot of blasting. These roses cannot be held, but must be used immediately. A new method recently practiced is cropping roses by pinching specific benches in rotation.

Roses cut at the right stage of development will last 5 to 7 days under refrigeration at a 32°–35°F temperature, 80% humidity. Sweetheart roses and some hybrid teas will last well over a week.

As the roses are cut, they should be placed in water as soon as possible. The water should be room temperature and deep enough to immerse all the stems in 8″ to 10″ of water. They can then be placed in a cooler at 32°–35°F for a few hours to take up water. The roses should be graded by length and quality. Water for cut roses should be "relatively salt free and soft. Deionized water is recommended. Soft water is not recommended—too much sodium." All this per Harry Tayama of Ohio State.

The number of roses per pack varies by markets, but usually 25 roses of equal length and quality are rolled into a pack with parchment, wax-coated paper, or similar waterproof paper.

About preservatives: Any preservative containing 1% to 3% sucrose, citric acid, and 8 HQC can be used. The solution temperature should be 110°F. Aluminum sulfate is not recommended in the preservative. It results in poor flower opening and shorter vase life.

Resting roses It can be very desirable at times to rest roses. This will give you an opportunity to clean out the old wood and bring a more vigorous plant into production. The first practice is to dry the soil until it cracks and the plants seem to be almost dormant. You would then cut back all the plants to between 18″ and 24″ above the soil; also, be sure to remove all the dead wood from the plants. It usually takes about one month to dry rose plants back for pruning. Immediately after pruning, give plants several very good waterings, soaking the soil thoroughly. Once the soil is absolutely soaked, you may return to normal watering. Rose plants will break out in new growth at once, and again, these shoots have to be pinched to bring the wood up to a new productive level. You will be back in production in September if you dry plants back in June.

Once planted in the bench, plants can very well last for 4 years or longer with good growing practices. They should be gone over regularly to pinch out blind shoots, remove the dead wood, and die back, and return long, irregular growth to a good production level. If this is done, rose plants may never have to be rested, but can be kept in steady production.

A common practice is to cut up on roses in fall and early winter and reverse the process and cut down in spring and early summer, thereby maintaining an optimum level of production.

Timing of the rose crop   There is always an increased demand for roses for Christmas, Valentine's Day, Easter, and Mother's Day. To meet this demand you must pinch off enough of your crop prior to the holiday. Count the number of pinches to control the crop. This is done by determining when you wish to start cutting, probably 7 to 10 days before the holiday. Soft pinches are generally several days later than hard pinches. It is a good practice to soft-pinch earlier and hard-pinch later when timing a crop.

The Christmas pinch date is based on 49 days for most varieties. You would then pinch your roses on the last 2 days of October and the first 2 days of November for the Christmas cut.

Valentine's Day would largely depend on the return crop from what you cut at Christmas since only 7 weeks separate the two holidays.

Both the Easter and Mother's Day crops would result from a pinch 45 days before the cut date.

Weather has a very definite effect on the timing of roses. Cold and cloudy weather will slow the crop down considerably. Likewise, warm and balmy weather will speed it up. As the case may be, you may have to raise or lower your night temperature to offset weather conditions. You must watch and study your crop to see how far along the buds are, and determine what you can do to bring them in on time. Rose buds should be the size of a pea 3 weeks before the cut date.

The use of HID lighting has made it possible to cut a bearing crop for both Christmas and Valentine's Day peaks.

Summary   The rose grower must not neglect the planting at any time. Work must be scheduled so that there is time to fit all the needs of the rose crop into the daily routine.

The night temperature should be 62°F for most varieties. This temperature should be adjusted as soon as possible at the close of the day. In mild weather, some air circulation should be maintained in the houses at all times. Under no condition should the houses be closed without at least some heat being given. This can be accomplished by having at least one heating pipe in each house on at all times. The heat from this pipe keeps the foliage dry and the air movement optimum for rose growing. Bright and sunny days call for the ventilators to be cracked or open. Mildew is always present in rose houses where cold drafts are not avoided. The temperature of the houses on sunny days should run about 8° to 10° over night temperature. On cloudy days, the day temperature should only be raised about 5° over night temperature.

In the daytime, the humidity of the house should be raised by wetting the walks and with normal watering of the mulched beds. This should not be done too late in the day, because low humidity is desired at night to control mildew.

The cutting of roses should be one of the first and last jobs of the day. Never cut so tight a bud that it will not open or take up water. Secondly, do not let buds open too far on the plant. As a grower, let the people who use roses tell you how far open to cut the buds. The stage at which the bud is cut is very important to the life and usability of the rose.

It is good practice to carry a light shade on rose houses during late May through August. Shading of the house will keep the temperature to where the flowers will not be burned by the sun's rays.

The foliage of roses can become very tender during periods of dark weather, and because of this, plants should always be watered on the first sunny day. If you have a large number of buds almost ready to cut, you must watch to see that they are not injured by changing weather conditions. The people cutting these roses must always be careful not to injure the buds and foliage when cutting.

The rose grower must continually have a planned control program for aphids, spiders, and mildew to grow quality roses.

It is very important to stay abreast of the new technology.

- *HID lighting* has been proven a profitable practice

- *High pressure mist* for cooling and humidity control

- *Drip irrigation* for improved fertilization and soil environment for root action

- *CO_2 enrichment* for improved productivity and quality using the above technology.

Popular varieties for the mid-1980s Stay up with new varieties from your specialty companies—Jackson and Perkins, Carlton Rose Nursery, Amling DeVor, and Conrad Pyle—which bring you the best from all world breeders. New varieties can provide increased productivity, quality, shelf life, and disease and pest resistance.

676

Hybrid teas

Red	*Forever Yours*
	Samantha (using HID lights)
	Cara Mia
	Royalty
Yellow	*Golden Fantasie*
	Emblem
	Golden Emblem
White	*Bridal White*
	White Butterfly
Pink	*Pink Sensation*
	Sonia

Sweethearts and floribundas

Red	*Mary DeVor*
	Sassay
	Red Garnette
Yellow	*Coed*
	Golden Garnette
Pink	*Bridal Pink*
	Junior Bridesmaid
White	*Jack Frost*

The Spring Pot Crop*

A well-done spring pot rose.

*Contributed by Ian MacKay, DeVor Nurseries.

Roses suited for pot forcing have been sold to the greenhouse trade for many years. Originally, sales of the plants were limited to Easter and Mother's Day but new and improved varieties together with the aid of HID lighting are extending this selling season to include Christmas. Indeed, there is no reason why certain varieties may not be sold year-round. Being hardy they can also be planted in the home garden provided that they are not allowed to freeze; if planted in active growth, or if sold in the summer, they have sufficient time to acclimatize to the outdoors before fall frosts occur. No other pot plant offers such versatility and value.

Pot forcing roses may be divided into roughly three classes:

1. The *Koster* and *Garnette* varieties and their sports together with a few of the more compact growing cut flower sweethearts. These established and long-grown varieties are the present-day mainstay for the industry.

2. The hardy miniatures, composed of varieties which form floriferous, repeat-blooming, compact plants of up to 15" in height, with flowers of about the size of a quarter.

3. A new class, which may be called intermediates for lack of a better name, and which fall in size between the *Kosters* and the miniatures. Only recently introduced in the United States, they have established themselves in Europe as serious competitors to the more commonly grown flowering pot plants. Their outstanding characteristic is their flower longevity of up to 3 weeks without color deterioration. They form symmetrical, well-branched plants with stiff growth. *Orange Sun Blaze* and *Scarlet Sun Blaze* are two varieties presently available with other colors being introduced in the near future. They represent a breakthrough in rose plant breeding for the greenhouse trade.

The *Koster* and sweetheart varieties are normally sold by the plant producer as 2-year-old, field grown, dormant, bare root plants. These are dug in the late fall and held in refrigerated storage until shipment is requested by the greenhouse forcer. Storage is best left to the supplier, as precise temperatures and humidity are necessary for extended periods. These plants are sold in three grades according to size and maturity and are priced accordingly. All will produce good salable plants, but the smaller grades will require one or two pinches to finish out well-branched plants.

The miniature and intermediate classes, while they may be sold by the producer as budded plants, are more generally dormant rooted cuttings in 3" or 4" pots. Again they are shipped to the grower when requested at the proper time for forcing.

Care upon arrival   As soon as plants are received, the boxes should be opened and the plants examined for possible damage in transit. If there is any evidence of freezing, the boxes should be closed and placed in 35° to 40° to slowly thaw out. Do not water them! Also, the transportation company should be notified so that a claim may be filed if it is found that on thawing, injury has been received by the plants. Actually, bare-root roses will tolerate freezing to some extent without detriment, if they are slowly thawed out. Provided the shipment is in good condition, bare-root plants will benefit from being left in the box in a temperature of 50° to 55°, but not in the sun, for up to 3 days to induce root hair and bud development, a process that the cut flower growers call *sweating*.

Culture   Regardless of class, all pot-forcing roses require much the same handling and culture. Budded plants will perform best in 6" or 7" pots, while the intermediate and miniature classes will be satisfactory in 4" pots or larger. All plants should be pruned to promote strong vigorous shoots. The bare-root sweethearts should be reduced to within 6" to 8" of the scion union with the understock, and any weak or broken canes removed. Also, these plants should have any excessively long roots cut back but only so that they can be placed in pots without breaking. The smaller classes, received in pots, should be cut back to within 3" of the soil level, and any very weak or spindly canes removed.

Roses should be potted in a good well-drained soil mixture. The soil around the roots should be firm to ensure that no air pockets are left around the roots. They should never be allowed to dry out in the air during the potting operation. Keep them moist at all times. As soon as the pots are placed on the bench they should be heavily watered at least twice.

Roses initiate growth best in an atmosphere of high humidity. This can be achieved by covering the plants with white opaque polyethylene, damp burlap, or repeated misting. These measures should be discontinued as soon as the first leaves open fully. Ideally, roses should be kept in a temperature of 45° to 50° for the first week or 10 days, which reduces stress to the plant and encourages further breaks. Once the plants are growing the heat can be raised to 58°.

The question of whether or not to pinch pot roses varies with growers. Some growers do not pinch at all. Others use pinching not only to develop more flowers, but also to help time their crop. For instance, if an April 1 Easter crop is planted January 1 and given a soft pinch February 1, the plants should be in flower by April 1—8 weeks after pinching. A Mother's Day crop should be pinched 7 weeks before flowering. Control of flowering time is also possible by adjusting temperatures. The basic forcing temperature should be 58°, but the crop can be advanced with a higher temperature (62°) or retarded with a lower temperature (55°). Bear in mind, however, that temperatures above 58°

are apt to result in loss of quality in the finished plant. For instance, flowers grown on plants forced at too-high temperatures are much more apt to shatter than those grown at lower temperatures.

A crop of pot roses for Mother's Day should be potted the first week in February. Otherwise, the same cultural practices apply as for the Easter crop. Plants unsold for Easter may be pinched back for a later crop. A pinched-back plant should flower in about 6 weeks from an Easter pinch.

Feeding will be dictated by soil testing, but fertilizer should *not* be applied until growth has started. At the time of potting, rose roots are dormant and salt levels which would not affect a rooted mum cutting are sufficient to inhibit root hair development in the rose plant.

Intermediate and miniature varieties are handled in the same manner. They can be grown on as received from the propagator without repotting, or, for a larger, better finished product, they can be repotted and pinched at the grower's discretion. However, they must have 4 weeks of dormancy before forcing.

For Valentine's Day sales, they will need 7 weeks of forcing at 60° and for Mother's Day 6 weeks. If pinched, the crop will require 4 weeks longer and should only be done with the plants in 6" pots.

The chief insect pest of roses is spider mite but this can be controlled by an application of Temik immediately after planting. Mildew, a fungus disease, is the only other problem which may be seen, and this can be well taken care of by fuming sulfur in electrically heated pots which are sold for this purpose.

Varieties While the *Kosters* and *Garnettes* still predominate in the pot rose business, new varieties are making their mark. This is where your supplier's salesman should be your guide. He is up to date with what is new and the market response to it. The new intermediates especially warrant close scrutiny, if their success in Europe is any measure.

All in all pot roses offer a quick, easy-to-grow crop. In addition, the newer varieties, with their long-lasting flowers, offer considerable flexibility in marketing.

The Summer Garden Flower*

Garden roses remain the most popular, hardy, flowering ornamental plants. Their wide adaptability to climate, ease of culture, and wide range of types and colors make their reputation well deserved. There is no other hardy flowering plant that has so long a season or can provide so many bouquets of cut flowers for the home.

*Contributed by Ian MacKay, DeVor Nurseries.

While rose plants were formerly sold exclusively by mail order nurseries and garden centers, they later became available in grocery and other chain outlets, being sold dormant with the roots enclosed in foil or polyethylene bags. Unfortunately, many of the latter sources allowed the plants to languish in locations unsuited to perishable products resulting in high mortality and disappointed customers. Today's buyer is more discriminating in how he spends his money and wants some assurance that he will receive satisfaction for his purchase.

This is where the retail florist and garden center with growing facilities enters the picture. By potting and growing on a good selection of garden roses, they will find that they can attract a much larger clientele than is possible with bedding plants and run-of-the-mill nursery stock alone. Potted roses growing and well maintained are a drawing card that inevitably leads to increased sales of all other materials handled. Garden rose growers are an enthusiastic group who provide much word-of-mouth advertising when they find a good source of plants. A further advantage of handling potted roses is that they can be sold throughout the summer to provide quick and colorful additions to the home garden.

Culture There is no problem in starting potted roses, providing a few rules are followed exactly. In our business of selling dormant, bare-root garden-rose plants to florists, we have found a considerable lack of basic information concerning their requirements. From our own experience, the following rules are applicable for starting potted roses.

Cherish *(left) and* Brandy—*two recent All-America Selections rose winners.*

1. Order your bare-root dormant plants for delivery at least 2 months before you want to sell them as started growing plants. For your own convenience, you can order your plants delivered in more than one shipment to spread out your workload and to give you a succession of plants to sell throughout the spring and summer. We will discuss the question of varieties later in this article. Rose plants do not have to be sold as soon as they are started. A plant properly started will remain in salable shape for several months.

2. When your rose plants arrive, you will find them packed in containers and in material which protects them from frost and drying out. If the shipment arrives damaged, be sure to file a claim with the trucking company immediately. If your plants arrive frozen, it is wise to file a claim, even though there is a good chance of thawing them out with no loss. If, when you open the shipment (and it should be opened immediately upon arrival), you find the plants frozen, pack them up again and store the shipment in a cool (temperatures between 34° and 40° are ideal), dark place for 2 or 3 days, especially if frozen hard. This will give the plants a chance to thaw out gradually, which is the secret in salvaging frozen rose plants. Dormant rose plants can stand considerable frost, *if* they are thawed out gradually.

    The most important, basic point in handling rose plants is to be sure the plant is *never* allowed to dry out—either its roots or canes. As soon as roses are dug in the growing field, they are pruned, graded, and packed in moist packing material immediately and put into cold-temperature, high-humidity storage. If, when you receive them, they are allowed to stand out in the open sun and wind for a few hours, all this careful handling will have been for nothing and the plants may die. Even if they do not die, they will be sufficiently injured to cause slow starting and poor subsequent growth. It is a good idea to soak the plants in water for an hour or two as they are unpacked. In case the plants have dried out a little in transit, this dip will replenish their supply of moisture.

3. Rose plants should be pruned and potted *immediately* upon receipt. If you can't get to them immediately, leave the plants in their shipping containers until you are ready to pot them. However, don't leave them packed any longer than necessary—a day or two at most.

    Pruning rose plants is a second important fundamental. At the time of potting, the plants should be cut off to within 6" or 8" of the crown of the plants. This should leave 2 to 4 "eyes" from which growth will start. Don't be afraid to cut most of the cane off. Long canes produce weak new growth and small blooms. Also, the plant will be more subject to injury from desiccation. Remember that until new root hairs are produced, the plants have no way of compensating for moisture lost from the canes, and the longer the canes, the greater the loss. Grading by the American Nurserymen's Association requires, among other things, canes of a certain length, which is the reason canes are left long when shipped to you. Also, trim off any damaged roots or any roots that are excessively long. The finer roots are the important ones—heavy, thick ones do not produce the all-important white roots that the plants need to start growing.

This pruning procedure applies to all varieties and types of roses, including the climbing varieties.

4. There are several types of rose pots available. They should be at least 6" or 8" wide at the top and 8" or 10" deep, and should have holes in their bottoms to ensure good drainage. Soil used for potting should be of a loose consistency to provide aeration and drainage. Peat moss incorporated into a heavy soil will help. Add *no* fertilizer to the potting soil except superphosphate, if it is needed. Apply nitrogen and potassium only after the plant has started into active growth and can make use of it. Water, not fertilizer, is the "mother's milk" of a starting rose. Rose plants should be potted to a depth so as to just barely cover the bud union. This is the thickened part of the stem from which the canes grow.

Firming the soil around the roots of the plant during potting is important. Place a handful of soil in the bottom of the pot and then put the plant in the pot. Fill up the pot with soil, frequently firming the soil as the pot is being filled. If the soil isn't firmly tamped around the plant roots, air pockets may dry out the roots before they have had a chance to get into the soil. Fill pot to within an inch of the top.

5. *Immediately after potting*, the pots should be thoroughly soaked with water. This can be done by repeated hose waterings until the soil in the pot is completely saturated. The pots should be placed on a surface that allows drainage out of the bottoms of the pots. Gravel, for instance, is a good material to place pots on. Newly potted rose plants must be protected from wind and sun until root action starts. The best method of getting strong initial growth is by using white opaque polyethylene. Cover the plants completely and tuck the plastic under the outer pots. When growth starts and the first leaves have appeared, the sides of the poly can be folded back to allow the plants to become adjusted to a lower humidity gradually, and then removed completely after a couple of days. Caution: Where air temperatures are likely to exceed 80°, do not use clear polyethylene unless you spray it with shading compound. Should high temperatures follow within 48 hours of potting, heat buildup under clear poly will sometimes result in the plants being killed outright. Once the roots are active, they can tolerate any temperature to be experienced in a greenhouse. Roses started outdoors under plastic should present no problems.

During the growing period, the soil and the pot should be kept wet and not allowed to dry out at any time. Varieties vary in the time required to start growth. Some will begin to break within a few days.

Others may take a week or more. Slow-starters may be aided by being separated and covered with polyethylene until growth starts.

You can sell a started rose pot plant to your retail customer with every confidence that it will continue to grow when planted out in the garden. Just caution the customer not to break up the root ball when removing the pot. Nothing helps rose sales more than to have one or two plants showing color, and if you have the facilities, it is worthwhile starting plants early so that their flowering coincides with your peak selling period. If these are kept on display, they will be found to be a real assistance in selling roses that are not yet in bloom. You should also not be afraid to charge extra for a potted growing plant over and above the dormant bare-root price. You have put your skill, time and effort into producing a growing plant and the customer will not object to paying extra for this service. Most homeowners have had sufficient experience in trying to start dormant roses to be only too glad to leave that job to you, the professional.

6. Once the rose plants are growing, the only care they need are an occasional spraying and feeding. Blackspot and mildew are the principal diseases of roses, both of which can be easily controlled with modern fungicides. Blackspot is a defoliating disease which does not often occur in a sales lot, but it is well to be on the safe side and practice prevention. Mildew, on the other hand, under certain weather conditions, can appear and will be disfiguring to the foliage. Both mildew and blackspot can be controlled by spraying at 14-day intervals with Benlate, or a combination of Folpet and Actidione.

Rose plants which remain on the sales lot after midsummer may become infested with aphids or spider mites. Tedion is one of the most effective outdoor miticides. Malathion or Diazinon are two materials which will control aphids and also nonresistant mites. At the first signs of either of these pests, a spray application should be made, as it takes very little time for them to build up into a major problem. Occasionally, carpenter bees may make their home in rose canes by boring in from the cut end. Dabbing tree paint or cane sealer on the cut ends will stop their activities, as will the use of the more prosaic thumbtack.

Once your plants are actively growing, they can be fed either by an application of soluble 20–20–20 during your normal greenhouse feeding, or they can be top-dressed with one of the many rose fertilizers or plain agricultural 10–10–10.

Feeding and spraying will help to keep your roses looking in their best shape over a long selling season, and it should not be necessary to have to cut prices because of their poor appearance.

The choice of varieties will be dictated to a degree by your location and climate. AARS Award winners are usually satisfactory nationwide, but some introductions by rose nurseries may be of regional adaptability. This is where your salesman should be helpful in providing such information.

An average rose order should consist of at least 50% patented varieties. Hybridists are steadily improving the breed, and the newer patented varieties are generally quite a bit superior to those of 20 years ago. It is to these newer roses that your type of customer will gravitate.

Today, roses come in almost every color range. In making your variety selection, you should take into account customer preferences. As an example, last year, our customers ordered their roses by color in these percentages— Red 33%; Pink 32%; Yellow 14%; Orange 10%; Multicolor 07%; Lavender 02%; White 02%. It is wise to bear in mind that preferences change from year to year, albeit slowly, and it is always hard to predict exactly what will sell in colors.

RUDBECKIA (Gloriosa Daisy)

PERENNIAL *(R. hirta burpeii) 45,000 seeds per oz. Germinates in 3 wks. at 70°.*

Often called "coneflowers," rudbeckias are easy to grow and will produce long-stemmed flowers excellent for cutting. Easily grown from seed and an excellent perennial for spring plant sales to go with annual plant offerings, the *Gloriosa Daisies* make a fine bedding display and are also excellent for cutting. They will flower the first summer from a February or March sowing. The *Single Mix* is a *tetraploid,* producing large single flowers in shades of yellow and mahogany-red. Producing large (4") and many fully double flowers of golden yellow, the *Double Gloriosa Daisy* fits well into the hardy border.

SAINTPAULIA (African Violet)*

ANNUAL *(S. ionantha) 1,000,000 seeds per oz. Germinates in 25 days at 70°. Light.*

Since their discovery in East Africa in 1896, African violets have become a favorite in many homes across the country. Whether grown on windowsills or under fluorescent light, African violet hybrids are extremely rewarding. They flower freely year round and tolerate home conditions well.

Propagation is by both seed and leaf-petiole cuttings. The fine seed should be germinated on a screened, well-prepared medium at 70°F. Germination takes approximately 25 days. The petioles on leaf-petiole cuttings should be ½" long. These are inserted into the rooting medium, usually of ½ peat and ½ sand or vermiculite. Cuttings are rooted in flats at 65°F minimum with no mist, heavy shade, and infrequent watering. After 10–14 weeks, plantlets are

*Contributed by Wendy Spelman.

ready for transfer from the mother leaf to a 2"–2½" container. It is another 10–12 weeks until the plantlet is ready to be transplanted to a 4" pot.

The African violet requires a highly organic, well-drained medium with a pH of 6.0–6.5. Seventy-five percent peat moss and 25% perlite or styrene is excellent. Young plants do well if fertilized on a regular basis with 100 ppm 20–20–20 liquid feed. Halfway through the crop the nitrogen should be cut in half, and a 12–36–14 type fertilizer can be used to finish.

Optimum growing temperature is 68–70°F nights and 70–75°F days. Water temperature is equally important. Water must be no more than 5° cooler than air temperature and no warmer than 80°F. Cold water will cause ring spots on the foliage.

Flowering of the African violet is controlled by light intensity. An intensity of 900–1200 ft-c is ideal. Less than 500 ft-c and *plants will remain vegetative.* Cool-white fluorescent lamp lighting at 600 foot-candles for 15–18 hours a day also produces quality plants.

The major pests are cyclamen mites and thrips. Cyclamen mites can be controlled with Kelthane and other miticides. Orthene is effective on thrips. Botrytis can become a problem with high humidity and cool temperatures. Heating and venting in the evening can help control botrytis.

To ensure that the beautiful finished plants, cuttings, or 2¼"s arrive in the same excellent condition, shipping temperatures should be kept ideally at 65°–75°F. The further below 60° the greater the chance of cold damage. Over 75° in a closed box almost guarantees heat damage. Close attention to the temperatures will help sales considerably.

Propagated by specialists and sold as 2¼" transplants, growers can finish a crop in 10–14 weeks in a 4" pot. The plants should be sold with a full head of flowers. Nothing is more eye-catching on the shelf than *Fairy Queen* in full bloom, which is one of 38 outstanding violets in the *Fischer BALLET*® series. The series features large showy flowers, upright habit, and a large selection of colors and flower forms including *Camelot, Don Juan, Big Star,* and *Dark Prince,* an unusual dark cranberry-red ruffed double. Also widely used are the *Optimara, Rhapsody,* and *Melodie* series.

The other important family of violets in the U.S. today is *Holtkamps Optimara.* All groups include some excellent varieties.

SALVIA

ANNUAL *(S. species) 7,500 seeds per oz. Germinates in 12–15 days at 70°. Light.*

The immense popularity enjoyed by this brilliant red "scarlet sage" for many years shows no signs of declining. They are of special interest to the florist because, while they are seed-propagated, few home gardeners have the heat to sprout the seed—so they buy plants.

686

Biggest call is for bedding-size stock in packs or 2¼" pots for planting out during May. An early March sowing should have no trouble making this size by mid-May if carried at 55°. An early February sowing should easily make 3"s or 4"s for May sales—and there is call for these from folks who want to make more showing in a hurry. Salvias are also useful in combination pots. Our trial-ground salvia that makes a fine showing for us is not actually sown until early April.

Seed Germination

Certainly not hard, but salvia germination failures are more frequent than average—because their requirements are not understood. We never have trouble sprouting good salvia seed if:

1. Seed flats are soaked thoroughly at time of sowing, covered with paper or glass to hold moisture, and not watered till seed sprouts, unless surface of soil is absolutely dry (it shouldn't get dry before seed comes through). Excellent results can also be had by germinating under a mist system.

2. Seed flats are kept in a minimum of 70° till seed sprouts. It just won't come through at 50°—and that's likely the biggest reason for failure.

3. Seeds are not covered.

Note: Salvia seed is sensitive to methyl bromide-treated soil.

Lastly, we move the flats to a cooler house (55°) as soon as seed is well germinated. This helps prevent damp-off that can wreck seedlings in a hurry if conditions are right.

Cultural needs beyond this are simple—an average, good garden soil lightened with peat, or a peat-lite mix, as you would do for any annual, and the usual routine spray program to control spiders that are especially fond of them. They like full sun all the way, but we have seen them make a fine showing outdoors where they had sun only till noon.

About Varieties

There are quite a few of them, and obviously a lot of misunderstanding as to exactly what each one is supposed to look like. After many seasons of flowering the best domestic and foreign strains in our trial grounds, we have developed the following classification. Note that the more dwarf sorts are the earliest. The midseason kinds have more vigorous growth, and may look somewhat better than the earlies late in the season.

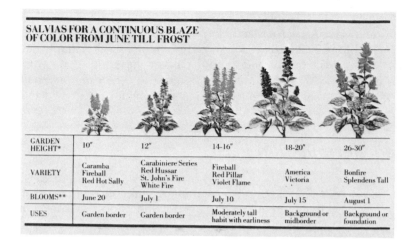

SALVIAS FOR A CONTINUOUS BLAZE OF COLOR FROM JUNE TILL FROST					
GARDEN HEIGHT*	10"	12"	14-16"	18-20"	26-30"
VARIETY	Caramba Fireball Red Hot Sally	Carabiniere Series Red Hussar St. John's Fire White Fire	Fireball Red Pillar Violet Flame	America Victoria	Bonfire Splendens Tall
BLOOMS**	June 20	July 1	July 10	July 15	August 1
USES	Garden border	Garden border	Moderately tall habit with earliness	Background or midborder	Background or foundation

Earliest and most dwarf are *Red Hot Sally*, about 10"; *Fireball*, 10"; and *Caramba* at the same height. In the 12" height class are the *Carabiniere Series*; *St. John's Fire*, a long-time favorite; *Red Hussar*; and *White Fire*, a creamy white. Next comes *Red Pillar*, top in the medium class with well-formed spikes, excellent habit, and dark green foliage. It flowers about July 10 at a height of 14". *Violet Flame*, a dark violet purple, flowers at a 14"–16" height. *America* flowers about mid-July at a height of 18"–20".

In the tall class, *Bonfire* grows up to about 26" and flowers very uniformly. *Splendens Tall* will go up over 30" and flowers around the first of August.

Leading the scarlet-red varieties in popularity and usage are *Red Hot Sally* and *Carabiniere Red*. These are followed by *St. John's Fire* and *America*. *Carabiniere* Orange and White are used to a much lesser extent, with the white being most popular in its color class. *Carbiniere Blue*, a blue violet, is best in its class.

Salvia farinacea (blue and white salvia) is still widely used for border work and cutting. *Victoria* is a deep violet blue with a compact growth habit that grows to 18" tall.

SCABIOSA (Pincushion Flower)

ANNUAL *(S. atropurpurea) 4,500 seeds per oz. Germinates in 12 days at 70°.*
PERENNIAL *(S. caucasica) 2,400 seeds per oz. Germinates in 18 days at 60°.*

Often called "pincushion-flower," the annual form of scabiosa is another outdoor summer-cutting item that produces reasonably long stems under trying outdoor conditions. Scabiosa should be placed out as early as soil will permit. Fall sowing under favorable conditions is even better. Annual scabiosa also does well forced for spring flowering a cool house (50°), but in a warm house or during warm weather, the naturally slender stems draw up rather weak. For May flowering, the seed should be sown in March and benched in April. For cutting purposes on a small scale, the *Giant Imperial Mix* is a good strain.

The perennial form, like the annual, is a cool-temperature plant. While both suffer in excessive summer heat, the perennials are inclined to die out if it gets too trying. Probably for this reason, they are not widely used in the Midwest, but are very choice where summers are more moderate. The variety known as *House Mixture* is very popular. Flower size is 3″ with colors ranging from white to deep blue.

*SNAPDRAGON**

ANNUAL *(Antirrhinum majus) 180,000 seeds per oz. Germinates in 1–2 weeks at 65–70°F (18–21°C).*

Greenhouse snaps are still widely grown in northern greenhouses. They provide a delightful, colorful, fragrant, "spiky" vertical effect to arrangements. Market price as of the mid-1980s—$4.50 to $4.60 for 10 spikes.

In 1938 the first F_1 hybrid greenhouse-forcing snapdragon was introduced. Its name was *Christmas Cheer* and was followed in the 1940s by many other important cultivars. Since that time Yoder Brothers Inc. and George J. Ball Inc. have bred and introduced most varieties still in the trade.

*Contributed by Michael Behnke, a commercial grower at Wahneta, Florida.

Snapdragons as a bedding plant.

Following a peak in popularity around 1959, when snapdragons were listed as the seventh most valuable cut flower, there has been a slow decline in importance. Much of the decline has been due to problems shipping blooms over long distances.

Despite difficulties shipping the snapdragon, it remains a cut flower worthy of strong consideration by growers throughout the country. An absence of foreign and regional competition, the crop's low energy requirements and its "programmability" are attractive features in its favor.

Propagation

One-half a trade packet (1000 seed) may be sown uncovered in a 14" × 22" (36 × 56 cm.) seed tray. Sowing seed in rows restricts the spread of pythium and rhizoctonia, which are often present. Until emergence, trays are placed under mist or enclosed in plastic. Soil temperature during germination is 70°F (21°C). After germination, temperature is reduced slowly to 60°F (16°C) to help harden plants prior to transplant.

Time from sowing to transplant will vary from as little as 18 days in summer to 30 days in winter. HID lighting during November, December, and January will improve seedling quality and shorten time to benching.

During August, when light intensity in the North is falling, sowings should be made 5 to 7 days apart to cut every other week in December and early February. Seed sown every 3 weeks during spring will finish 2 weeks apart in the summer.

690

Certain problems, such as these, associated with propagation and scheduling of snapdragons may be avoided by purchasing ⅝" (1.5 cm.) plugs. Details should be worked out with individual seed houses providing the plants.

Production

Snapdragons are planted at the same depth as in the seed flat when seedlings reach 1" (2.5 cm.) in height. Some growers transplant into small plastic or peat pots and later plant into beds. This results in earlier flowering and saves approximately 3 weeks of bench time but reduces flower quality.

Snapdragons may be grown successfully in a variety of soils. Mixes that are well-drained, loose, and with a pH around 6.5 perform best. Beds are soil-tested between crops. This is particularly important following chrysanthemums since soluble salts may be too high.

Nylon mesh and welded wire are used for support and serve as guides during planting. For single-stem crops two tiers of wires are adequate. These move up as plants grow taller. Pinched crops may need four or more. Spacing in the South is generally 4" × 4" (10 × 10 cm) for single-stem crops and 4" × 6" (10 × 15 cm) for pinched crops with four breaks. For single-stem, northern growers use 4" × 5" (10 × 13 cm) or 4" × 6" (10 × 15 cm) in winter and 4" × 4" (10 × 10 cm) in summer. Pinched crops require a spacing of 8" × 8" (20 × 20 cm) in winter and 4" × 6" (4 × 15 cm) during the summer. The number of plants may be greater in the two outer rows of each bed since outside rows receive more light.

A temperature of 62°–64°F (17°–18°C) for the first 10 days will help get plants growing. Temperatures thereafter are slowly reduced to between 50°F and 55°F (10°–13°C).

Upon benching, most growers begin a program of constant feed at 75–150 ppm N. In the vegetative stage of growth plants prefer fertilizers higher

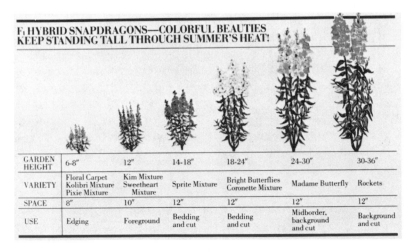

F₁ HYBRID SNAPDRAGONS—COLORFUL BEAUTIES KEEP STANDING TALL THROUGH SUMMER'S HEAT!

GARDEN HEIGHT	6-8"	12"	14-18"	18-24"	24-30"	30-36"
VARIETY	Floral Carpet Kolibri Mixture Pixie Mixture	Kim Mixture Sweetheart Mixture	Sprite Mixture	Bright Butterflies Coronette Mixture	Madame Butterfly	Rockets
SPACE	8"	10"	12"	12"	12"	12"
USE	Edging	Foreground	Bedding and cut	Bedding and cut	Midborder, background and cut	Background and cut

691

in nitrate rather than ammoniacal forms of nitrogen. As plants reach visible bud stage, fertilizer should be switched entirely to potassium nitrate. At first color, fertilization stops. Often a result of overliming, snapdragons occasionally require additional Boron. Borax may be applied at the rate of $1/2$ oz. per 100 sq. ft. (14 g. per 9 m²) a maximum of two times a year.

Watering is an important aspect of snapdragon culture. Overwatering produces soft weak growth and is an invitation to losses from root rots. Low volume or twin-wall polyethylene tubing is the most common means of applying water. Overwatering during early stages can be particularly harmful. Often, beds become dry along the edges but remain moist in the middle. Spot watering by hand is required when this happens.

Scheduling

Classification of snapdragons is determined by response to temperature and daylength. Group I cultivars flower well in winter when temperatures are cool and days are short. Group IV flowers well at higher temperature, higher light intensity, and longer days. Group II and Group III are intermediate in response and are appropriate for northern flowering late fall, early spring and late spring, and early fall, respectively.

Classification of a variety is not always absolute. Performance and response vary from one part of the country to another. In Table 1 are approximate dates for cutting and sowing of response groups in the North and South. Group I cultivars are not generally used in the South. Some care should be given to selecting colors that flower together (Tables 2 and 3). Among varieties in Group II, for example, *California, West Virginia,* and *New Jersey* flower together.

Although most snapdragons today are grown single-stem, pinched crops and second cuttings (from the same plant) are not uncommon. They are not recommended in the very deep South and should not be flowered in the North from June 15 through November 1. Pinching adds 3 to 4 weeks to schedules. Although timing for pinched crops and second cuttings is less exact, some growers report that smaller stems from pinched crops are used in greater numbers by their customers. Highest grade spikes as established by the Society of American Florists seem to be too large for many table arrangements.

A number of other factors can also affect crop time. Snapdragons are 1 to 2 weeks slower in ground beds than benches. Greenhouses which are darker than usual delay flowering while carbon dioxide enrichment at 1200 ppm will hasten maturity in northern latitudes by 2 to 4 weeks. HID lighting of seed flats also shortens crop time. Most schedules used today are for average conditions and under better circumstances allow too much time.

Pests

Soil-borne diseases which attack snapdragons are rhizoctonia, pythium, phytopthora, verticillium, thielaviopsis, and fusarium. Sanitation and steam

692

Table 1 SNAPDRAGON GROWING SCHEDULE

| Group | North | | South | |
	Sow	Flower	Sow	Flower
I	Aug. 15–Aug. 31	Dec. 10–Feb. 15		
II	Sept.11–Dec. 10	Feb. 15–May 10	Aug.22–Dec.20	Dec. 1–May 1
	July 24–Aug. 9	Oct. 25–Dec. 10		
III	Dec. 10–Mar. 21	May 10–June 30	July 6–Aug. 16	Oct. 1–Dec. 1
	June 18–July 16	Sept.10–Oct. 25	Jan. 7–Mar. 8	May 1–June 15
IV	Mar. 28–June 10	July 1–Sept. 10	Mar. 15–July 2	June 15–Oct. 1

Table 2 SNAPDRAGONS FOR NORTHERN CULTURE

Color	Group I Dec. 15–Apr. 1	Group II Nov. 15–Dec.1 Mar. 1–May 1	Group III Oct. 1–Nov. 15 Apr. 15–June 1	Group IV June 1–Oct. 1
White	Oakland E	Oakland E Snowman E California M	San Francisco E Virginia E Panama ME	Panama E Potomac Wt. M Texas M Houston L
Pink	Bismark E Washington M	New Jersey ME Christina L Debutante L	Colombia E Baltimore M	Winchester E
Yellow	Cheyenne E Doubloon ME	Peoria E W. Virginia M	Missouri E St. Louis E Tampico F	Tampico M Potomac Yel. M Oklahoma L
Other	Michigan E	Montezuma ME Montana M	New Mexico E Tennessee E	Potomac Red E Rockets

Table 3 SNAPDRAGONS FOR SOUTHERN CULTURE

Color	Group II Dec. 15–Apr. 1	Group III Apr. 1–June 1	Group IV May 15–Nov. 1
White	San Francisco E Virginia E California M	San Francisco Virginia E Panama E	Houston E Panama E Potomac WT. M
Pink	New Jersey ME Christina L	Colombia E Baltimore M PA Summer PK. M Winchester L	Winchester E Florida L
Yellow	Peoria E W. Virginia M	Missouri E St. Louis EM Tampico E Potomac Yel. L	Tampico ME Potomac Yel. M Tampico M
Other	Montana ME	New Mexico E Tennessee E	Potomac Red E Tennessee E Rockets

pasteurization are the best preventatives. The chemicals Subdue, Lesan, and Truban along with Terrachlor are useful on occasion.

Principal foliar diseases are rust, botrytis, mildew, anthracnose, and phyllosticta. Proper ventilation and application of such fungicides as Zineb, Benlate, Daconil, Mancozeb, and Karathane will control most foliar problems.

Major insect pests of snapdragon are aphids, spider mites, thrips, whiteflies, and loopers. Malathion, Diazinon, Metasystox-R, Temik, Dipel, Thuricide, Kelthane, Omite, and Pentac are among those chemicals commonly used on snapdragons.

Harvest and Care

Snapdragons require light for continued flower development but are harvested when the florets on the lower third of the spike are open. Snapdragons respond favorably to floral preservatives. Typical vase life in distilled water is one week, but may be extended to as long as 3 weeks. Storing upright in clean, well-ventilated coolers at 40°F (5°C) will maximize keeping quality and prevent crooked flower tips. If snapdragons are delivered the same day as harvested, they may be shipped dry in boxes.

Shatter and tip breakage are sometimes problems. Although promising work has been done with silver thiosulfate sprays to prevent shattering, selection of varieties which are more shatterproof and less prone to tip breakage is the best solution.

Snaps are very popular as a summer cut flower in the home garden—and we're hearing increasing reports of commercial cut flower crops grown outdoors in the North. People love these fresh, colorful garden flowers!

Table 4   SNAPDRAGON SCHEDULE AND CO_2 EFFECT*

Flowering group number	Without CO_2		Date of last cut	With CO_2		Decrease in growing time
	Sow	Plant		Sow	Plant	
3	Mar. 25	Apr. 19	July 1	Mar. 25	Apr. 19	0
4	Apr. 8	Apr. 31	July 11	Apr. 8	Apr. 31	0
4	Apr. 20	May 10	July 21	Apr. 20	May 10	0
4	May 1	May 21	Aug. 1	May 1	May 21	0
4	May 12	May 31	Aug. 11	May 12	May 31	0
4	May 23	June 10	Aug. 21	May 23	June 10	0
4	June 3	June 21	Sept. 1	June 3	June 21	0
4	June 13	July 1	Sept. 11	June 13	July 1	0
3	June 24	July 11	Sept. 21	June 24	July 11	0
3	July 2	July 19	Oct. 1	July 2	July 19	0
3	July 9	July 26	Oct. 11	July 9	July 26	0
3	July 14	July 31	Oct. 21	July 15	Aug. 1	1 day
2	July 21	Aug. 8	Nov. 1	July 24	Aug. 11	3
2	July 27	Aug. 14	Nov. 11	July 31	Aug. 18	4
2	July 31	Aug. 18	Nov. 21	Aug. 8	Aug. 24	6
2	Aug. 3	Aug. 21	Dec. 1	Aug. 11	Aug. 27	8
2	Aug. 6	Aug. 24	Dec. 11	Aug. 17	Sept. 7	11
1	Aug. 10	Aug. 28	Dec. 21	Aug. 23	Sept. 11	14
1	Aug. 14	Sept. 2	Jan. 1	Aug. 30	Sept. 18	16
1	Aug. 18	Sept. 6	Jan. 11	Sept. 5	Sept. 24	18
1	Aug. 22	Sept. 10	Jan. 21	Sept. 11	Sept. 30	20
1	Aug. 26	Sept. 14	Jan. 31	Sept. 18	Oct. 7	23
1	Aug. 29	Sept. 17	Feb. 11	Sept. 24	Oct. 12	25
2	Sept. 2	Sept. 22	Feb. 21	Sept. 29	Oct. 19	27
2	Sept. 7	Sept. 27	Mar. 2	Oct. 5	Oct. 26	29
2	Sept. 15	Oct. 6	Mar. 12	Oct. 14	Nov. 5	30
2	Sept. 23	Oct. 15	Mar. 22	Oct. 22	Nov. 14	30
2	Oct. 3	Oct. 26	Apr. 1	Nov. 2	Nov. 25	30
2	Oct. 12	Nov. 6	Apr. 11	Nov. 9	Dec. 4	28
2	Oct. 24	Nov. 19	Apr. 21	Nov. 16	Dec. 12	23
2	Nov. 5	Dec. 3	May 1	Nov. 21	Dec. 20	17
2	Nov. 26	Dec. 26	May 11	Dec. 5	Jan. 5	8
3	Dec. 26	Jan. 26	May 21	Dec. 29	Jan. 29	3
3	Jan. 21	Feb. 21	June 1	Jan. 21	Feb. 21	0
3	Feb. 16	Mar. 18	June 11	Feb. 16	Mar. 18	0
3	Mar. 7	Apr. 4	June 21	Mar. 7	Apr. 4	0

*This table was prepared by Jay S. Koths, and originally appeared in his "Snapdragons in the Greenhouse," University of Connecticut Extension Service.

Not a great picture—but a fascinating point. These snaps are grown within a mile or two of the Pacific Ocean at Ashne Farms, near Santa Maria, California. Excellent quality—and no fuel cost ever!

Snapdragons for Bedding

Snapdragons continue to be a bedding plant of some importance, especially with the coming of the very dwarf *Floral Carpet* class—which is widely grown in packs along with other bedding plants. It will produce lots of color at roughly 6" to 8" height.

Also, we're beginning to see the first of bedding plant growers offering various summer annuals for cut flowers. And here snapdragons are superb. The tall *Rocket* class is recommended. Besides the normal snapdragon flower type there is a *Butterfly* class, an open tubular flower resembling a pentstemon. There is also a medium high class, F, *Sprites*—14" to 18" high. Attractive either for cutting or bedding.

STATICE (Sea Lavender)

ANNUAL OR PERENNIAL *(Limonium species) 13,000 seeds per oz. Germinates in 15–20 days at 70°.*

Botanically, the genus *Statice* is no longer recognized, the various species now belonging to the genus *Limonium*. However, the term "statice" has been used so long that we shall continue to refer to them under this name. Principal use of statice is to furnish dried material for winter bouquets, wreaths, etc. The annual type, *S. sinuata*, is grown by the acre in Florida, while the perennial types are found all over this country and Europe, and are handled as hardy perennials.

Sinuatum is sown in Florida during the midsummer, usually in late July or early August. This crop will flower during midwinter—January and February—right outdoors. The flowers are used both for the tourist trade and for shipping to northern markets. Later sowings keep a succession of bloom until spring. Incidentally, it requires about 3 pounds of annual statice seed to plant an acre.

Sinuatum can also be grown as a spring greenhouse crop in the North; sow in January, and plant into a deep ground bed for a fine crop of flowers in May. Sown outdoors late in May in the Midwest, it will flower nicely later in the summer. Under good culture, it should reach a height of $2\frac{1}{2}'$.

The Russian, or rat-tail statice, known as *Suworowii*, produces lavender spike-type flowers that can be sown in October, spaced 8" by 8" in a light soil mix, grown at 45°, and will flower from late February through May.

Of the perennial sorts, *Latifolia* is probably the most popular. It is handled as almost any other perennial, requires 2 years to flower, and is very hardy. It dries well, and may be dyed after being thoroughly cured. The color is a clear blue, and its usual height is 30". *Perezi* produces exceptionally large, fine, rich blue heads, but is not dependably hardy here. *Tataricum* has silvery white flowers that are useful for cutting and drying. Much of the statice seed is now available in a decorticated or cleaned form, which lends itself to mechanical sowing.

STOCK

ANNUAL *(Mathiola incana)* 16,000–20,000 seeds per oz. Germinates in 2 wks. at 65–75°.

Columnar, or nonbranching stock, at one time a major greenhouse cut flower crop in the midwestern, eastern, and southern parts of the country, is largely produced today outdoors in California and Arizona. To compete with this market, the greenhouse grower must produce stocks of the finest quality. Toward that end, the following cultural information is presented.

Sowing Dates

Based on our own records kept over many years, the following table will give a close idea of when to sow to flower at a given time. Note that, for the Midwest and East, sowing stocks prior to July 10 or later than February 15 may mean blind, worthless growth—a result of high temperatures.

To flower	Ground beds, seedling, trans- planted, 45° nights through dark months of winter	Raised benches, direct-sown, 50° minimum temperature	Remarks
January	6½ months sow to flower	5½ months sow to flower	Buds won't set if tem- perature is above 65° for 6 hours per day
March	6¾ months sow to flower	5½ months sow to flower	For top quality, allow 7 months at 35–40° nights
April (Easter)	6½ months sow to flower	5¼ months sow to flower	Buds should show 9 weeks before cutting date
May (Mother's Day)	4½ months sow to flower	3¾ months sow to flower	
Early June	4 months sow to flower	3¾ months sow to flower	

Note: Above sowings are based on eastern and midwestern greenhouse conditions. Growers in near South (Tulsa, Nashville) find growth more rapid—Easter stocks 4 months from sowing, for example.

Minimum spacing should be 3″ by 6″. Seed may be sown direct in the flowering bench, placing three seeds at each spacing, and later thinned to the strongest-growing seedlings.

Stock must have a porous, loose soil. A heavy, slow-drying soil will not do the job. A pH range of 5.5 to 7.0 is satisfactory. Regular liquid feeding is necessary. Frequency should be determined by soil tests. Stocks do have a high potash requirement. Potash deficiency is common and shows up as a brown burning on the margin of older leaves.

Stem rot (rhizoctonia) is the big disease problem. Steam sterilization, the use of Terrachlor as a drench 10–14 days after benching at the rate of 1½ teaspoons per gallon of water, plus proper watering and ventilating practices, will go a long way toward eliminating this problem.

The best, most widely used varieties are:

- *White Christmas*—Medium-tall, large-flowered, pure white

- *No. 1 Lilac-Lavender*—Clear lavender

- *No. 22 Ball Supreme*—A long-stemmed silvery rose

Outdoor Bedding Stock

The *7-week Trysomic Dwarf Double* strain is rather widely used for bed- ding plants in some sections of the country. Growing to a height of 12″, it is the only strain that will flower under high temperatures. Plants will usually throw a central spike in May and then produce numerous side shoots which will flower later. This variety can be flowered in the pack. Seed should be sown in February. As soon as seedlings become established, they should be moved to a cold house. Chiefly grown as a color mixture, the strain is also available in separate colors.

SWEET PEA

ANNUAL *(Lathyrus odoratus) 350 seeds per oz. Germinates in 15 days at 55°.*

A major cut flower crop at one time, today "peas" are largely grown on a small scale by retail growers who still find them profitable. Their decline has largely been due to the development of longer-lasting cut flowers and the labor necessary to harvest the crop. With their sweet scent and beautiful pastel shades of color, they certainly add that "something different" to a retailer's offerings. Some growers with limited space will plant a few peas around purlin posts in benches which are producing other crops.

THUNBERGIA (Black-eyed Susan Vine)

ANNUAL *(T. species) 1,100 seeds per oz. Germinates in 12 days at 70°–75°.*

Thunbergia—colorful hanging baskets.

699

Where a splash of real color is wanted in annual climbers, porch boxes, or hanging baskets, you'll find *Alata* hard to beat. It's easy and cheap to propagate, fast-growing, and has lots of black-eyed orange, buff, and yellow flowers. It is also very useful as a screening material when planted to open ground and allowed to cover a trellis or fence. Sow 8 to 10 weeks prior to selling in 2¼"– 3" pots. Grow at 60°F. The *Susie Series,* a more recent introduction, consists of three distinct colors: orange, white, and yellow with eyes, as well as a mixture that contains both eyed and solid colors. These are especially suited for hanging baskets.

TOMATOES—FOR BEDDING

By all recent tabulations, tomatoes are number one of all U.S. bedding plants— in flats or plants sold. They are the champion of home gardeners coast-to-coast, U.S. and Canada—because they produce the most fruit for the least amount of work. And really they are the easiest to grow.

As a bedding plant, culture is quite simple. They will grow fastest at 60°F and with ample moisture and fertilizer. But generally in a bedding plant situation, growers don't want this rapid thin growth. It can easily be controlled by withholding moisture and fertilizer—and cooler temperatures. Wide extremes of temperature won't hurt the plants—they just grow faster if they are warm and wet and well fed.

For some reason, a great many, especially retail growers, produce tomatoes in 3" Jiffy-Pots—and they are widely sold in this form. Many also go in cell packs. Also, many growers produce them in 4", 6", and even larger pots or small tubs. Often, the larger plants are staked—and sold in flower or even with green fruit.

Many wholesale growers organize this crop so as to produce as many as three or even four crops of cell-pack plants on a bench during one season.

They can be retarded somewhat by use of B-Nine—but mostly by withholding water.

Tomatoes are a strictly full sunlight crop. Grown as bedding plants, they should always have full light. Probably the biggest limitation of successful tomatoes in the home garden is that maybe half of all U.S. gardeners put them in more or less of shade—and here they will make a lot of leaves and not many tomatoes.

Also, they are less successful in cool summer areas like Seattle. Or England! Such areas use earlier varieties such as *Early Girl.*

Tomatoes love heat!

Many home gardeners do them successfully in urns or tubs—up to 15" and 17" in diameter. Good, heavy plants, bearing a lot of fruit, can be grown this way.

As with many other bedding plants, breeders have made great advances in recent years—especially through use of F_1 hybrids. One result of this is the inevitable problem of winning the home gardener away from his lifetime favorite old standbys like *Marglobe* and *Rutgers*. But if such varieties are put alongside new hybrids in impartial trials (Ball Seed Company every summer) the difference is almost shocking. The old inbred or open-pollinated varieties are uneven, often diseased, and produce a small fraction of the amount of fruit of the new F_1 hybrids. The hybrids, by the way, now are almost normally bred to resist such diseases as verticillium, fusarium, and other diseases spread by nematodes. The acronym is "VFN resistant." It is important—it means a lot more success for a lot of gardeners.

Back to F_1 hybrids, here is the list of some of the old, open-pollinated varieties—and F_1 hybrids that are recommended to replace them.

Old standard	Suggested hybrid replacement
Beefsteak	Beefmaster FVN
Bonny Best (John Baer)	Super Fantastic VFN or Champion VFNT
Earliana	Early Girl V
Glamour	Champion VFNT or Better Boy VFN
Heinz 1350	Sunripe VF1&2N
Homestead 24	Sunripe VF1&2N
Jubilee	Golden Boy
Marglobe	Floramerica VF1&2
Roma	La Roma (Roma Hybrid)
Rutgers Imp. VF	Floramerica VF1&2
Super Sioux	Champion VFNT or Better Boy VFN

Lastly, with this section is a chart showing the different types of varieties available.

Probably the #1 all-around tomato as of the mid-1980s is *Better Boy*. It is VFN resistant, is an F_1.

HYBRID TOMATOES—MOST POPULAR GARDEN VEGETABLE BRED ESPECIALLY FOR DISEASE RESISTANCE, HIGHER YIELDS AND BIGGER SIZE

VARIETY	Sweet 100	Earl Girl	The Juice	Sunripe	Floramerica	Golden Boy	Pink Panther	LaRoma (Roma Hybrid)	Champion	Super Fantastic	Better Boy	Beefmaster
SIZE	1"	4-6 oz.	6-8 oz.	8-10 oz.	8-12 oz.	8-10 oz.	8-10 oz.	3 oz.	10 oz.	9-12 oz.	10-14 oz.	Over 12 oz.
GROWTH	Indeterminate (Pole)	Indeterminate (Pole)	Determinate (Bush)	Determinate (Bush)	Determinate (Bush)	Indeterminate (Pole)	Indeterminate (Pole)	Determinate (Bush)	Indeterminate (Pole)	Indeterminate (Pole)	Indeterminate (Pole)	Indeterminate (Pole)
MATURITY (DAYS)	65	52	65	75	75	80	70	62	62	70	70	80
DISEASE TOLERANCE	—	V	VF	VF1&2N	VF1&2	—	F	VF	VFNT	VFN	VFN	VFN
NOTES	Extremely sweet.	Earliest set. Good flavor. A Ball Exclusive.	Bred especially for juice. Good taste. A Ball Exclusive.	Widely adapted. Good taste. Tolerant to blossom-end rot.	Widely adapted. Grow in cages or on short stakes.	Golden yellow fruit. Very mild flavor. Only hybrid yellow.	Pink fruited. Crack tolerant. Smooth. A Ball Exclusive.	Heavy yielding Italian-type tomato. A Ball Exclusive.	Large fruited. Medium-early tomato with good disease resistance. A Ball Exclusive.	High yields. Good flavor. Continuous cropping. A Ball Exclusive.	Most popular. Excellent flavor. Smooth. Grow on stakes or sprawled.	Beefsteak type. Rough, good flavor. Tolerant of cracking or splitting.

TORENIA *(Wishbone Flower)*

ANNUAL *(T. fournieri) 375,000 seeds per oz. Germinates in 8–12 days at 70°.*

Once used as a summer pot plant, torenias are chiefly used today as a summer bedding annual, where they make a surprisingly bright showing, flowering from June until frost. They can also be used as a midwinter pot plant, at which time their bright blue blooms are most welcome. Pinching will help develop a bushy plant.

Torenias are almost always cultivated as rapid-growing annuals propagated from seed. Sown in early February and kept in a fairly warm house, at least 50°, they will make nicely sized pot material for sale as bedding stock—or for combination pots. They have no particular soil preference; grown outdoors, they do best in cool, moist, partly shaded places, but make a surprising showing in full hot sun.

The most important commercial variety is *Fournieri Compacta Blue,* a dwarf form generally preferred for pots or bedding. In addition, a white form of *Compacta* is also available.

VERBENA

ANNUAL *(V. hortensis) 10,000 seeds per oz. Germinates in 20 days at 65°. Dark.*

Verbena—a low-growing annual for summer borders.

702

One of our old standby bedding plants, the verbena owes its popularity to bright and varied colors, a delightful fragrance, low-cost propagation, and a free, all-season-flowering habit, even under full sun.

Propagation is usually from seed sown in mid-February, if 3" blooming pot plants are wanted by Memorial Day. They may be sown as late as the end of March, transplanted into packs or flats, and will still make a good showing outdoors, but not as early as when started in pots. Germination is not rapid; give them around 65° soil temperature for several weeks, and keep them on the dry side. There is some indication that overwatering at time of sowing will reduce germination. Some growers have had better success by preparing the seed flat in the late afternoon, watering it, and then sowing the seed the following morning without any further watering. Once established, they should be carried along at about 50° nights, and should be pinched back early. A February sowing kept moving and pinched should make nice bushy plants with several flower heads—not hard to sell!

There are two basic types of verbenas: the spreading type is procumbent or carpet-like, covering a fairly wide area. The upright type is free branching but distinctively bushy in habit.

Best varieties in the 8"–12" spreading *Sparkle*-type class, according to our experience, are: *Amethyst,* a mid-blue; *Blaze,* a bright scarlet; *Delight,* coral pink; *Sparkle,* red with white eye; *Crystal,* pure white; *Sangria,* wine-red with small white eye; and *Showtime Mix.*

In the upright class *Rainbow Mixture,* in a wide assortment of colors, is most popular. Because of its earliness and habit, it is valuable for pots and combination work. Similar to *Rainbow* is *Regalia Mix,* which contains some bright pastels not found in other mixes.

VINCA (Periwinkle)

ANNUAL *(V. rosea) 21,000 seeds per oz. Germinates in 15 days at 70°–75°. Dark.*

An excellent bedding plant gaining rapidly in its popularity with home gardeners, *Vinca rosea* will make a continuous show of color throughout the summer under hot, dry conditions. Even in areas of high pollution, it will thrive with a minimum of care. For 2¼" and 3" pots in bloom for sale in May, we suggest a late January/early February sowing. For pack and flat sales, sow from February 10–20. The plant is easily seed-propagated. If grown in a 60° house, vincas should fill out into good-sized flowering plants by Memorial Day. They can be hardened-off for 2 or 3 weeks at 55°, but should not be grown at temperatures below this. Vinca seedlings are slow starters and will quickly yellow and die off if grown under cold or wet conditions. Outdoors, the plants will bloom continuously until frost, if given fair exposure to the sun.

The most desirable class for general bedding-plant purposes is the dwarf (10"). Tops in this class is the *Little* series. It consists of the following four varieties and a mixture of the four:

Vinca—a champion summer annual in very hot, very dry climates—like the Southwest.

- *Little Bright Eye*—White flower with red eye
- *Little Pinkie*—A rosy pink (*Bright Eye* and *Pinkie* account for about 75% of all those sold.)
- *Little Delicata*—Pink with rose eye
- *Little Blanche*—Pure white

In recent times a new class or type of *Vinca rosea* has come into usage. Called creeping vinca, it is excellent for hanging baskets or flowering ground covers. It will spread out over 24".

Polka Dot, a white with bright red eyes, was the first in this class. Now there is a *Carpet Series* available consisting of *Dawn,* pink with rose eye; *Pink,* bright pink; *Rose,* bright rose; *Snow,* pure white; and a *Magic Carpet Mixture.*

Very popular, too, among the vinca clan, are the forms of *V. major,* a foliage vine usually seen in its variegated form. It is the traditional edging for window box and urn plantings, and, like its close relative *V. rosea,* it stands heat and drought exceptionally well. Propagation here is by cuttings, either tip or 3" sections of old stems. Finished 4" stock takes 2 years to grow which adds to its cost, but its exceptional and lasting popularity stands it well. The cuttings are stuck in October or November; as soon as rooted, they can be potted to small pots in which they will hold through the spring. From here, they usually go outdoors, over the summer until fall. Clumps are then dug, divided, tops cut back to 4" or 5", and heeled in closely in a cool house. About January 1, they are potted into 3"s or 4"s, set up along the southern edge of a bench, vines hanging downward, where they make their final growth. Frequent feedings of nitrogen-bearing fertilizer help fill them out. It is very important to break the taproot that forms through the drain hole frequently during this stage, or the plant will suffer greatly when moved out.

The most popular type grown is *V. major Variegata*, a green and white variegated sort; next in popularity is *Reticulata*, green and yellow variegated. The pure green species is sometimes seen but not highly prized.

A third, and again highly useful, vinca is *V. minor*. Unlike both *major* and *rosea*, it is completely hardy, and makes a fine ground cover, especially in deeply shaded places. It flowers profusely, having a heavy crop of 1½" single purple blooms during spring and early summer. Propagation is usually by stem cuttings rooted in June. Old clumps may be divided as a further means of propagation. The plant is also a favorite for rock gardens; often, it is commonly referred to as "myrtle" or "common periwinkle."

VIOLA

PERENNIAL *(V. cornuta) 24,000–43,000 seeds per oz. Germinates in 10 days at 65°.*

Invaluable as edging plants, violas are also very effective when used in mass plantings to front a shrub border. Although not as large as pansies, they are more free-flowering and may be obtained in a wide range of colors—yellow, red, purple, lavender, apricot, and white. Their culture is much the same as for pansies; late summer or fall sowings are, if anything, even more successful because of violas' unusual hardiness. Violas will do very well in light shade, although they prefer full sun. They will do well in any good garden soil, but in order to do their best, they should be planted in a fertile soil with a good supply of organic matter.

Among the most popular varieties are *Jersey Gem*, an attractive violet blue; *Arkwright Ruby*, a bright maroon with dark center; and *Lutea Splendens*, a clear, golden yellow. For apricot, we prefer *Chantreyland*. *White Perfection* is a clear white; *Blue Perfection*, a large-flowered medium blue.

The so-called "jump-ups" are distinctive for smaller but very freely produced blooms. They are in constant color from early spring till frost. *Helen Mount* is a violet, lavender, and canary-yellow combination.

ANNUAL *(Z. elegans) 3,000–6,000 seeds per oz. Germinates in 7 days at 75°.*

Zinnias' big claim to fame—they're really showy and they do stand summer heat! And heat is one thing you'll find plenty of during most summers in the majority of our states. If given reasonably good soil and water, they will yield quantities of the brightest-colored of all summer cut flowers. They are easy to grow.

Florists' main interest in them: sale of pack-grown or 2¼" plants in May for outdoor planting—and second, their use as a summer cut flower. Properly grown, they can be moneymakers on both scores.

For Spring Plant Sales

Sow 4 to 5 weeks before desired selling time in order to have good, husky plants for green sales in packs or 2¼" pots. Exceptions to this are *Thumbelina, Short Stuff Series, Peter Pan,* and the *Pulcino Series,* which should be sown about a month earlier to have plants in flower for pack sales. The big trick—seed flats *must* be kept at 70°, at least, till seed is through the ground. Most complaints on zinnia germination are the result of trying to germinate the seed at 50° or lower; they just won't come through—and, in fact, will soon rot in the ground. After seedlings are through, the flat may be carried along at 60°, and the trayed or potted plants will be "huskier" if grown at this temperature.

Plant breeders have done some excellent work with zinnias in recent years and have developed new and improved varieties to such an extent that today there is nearly a type, size, or color available for any conceivable garden use (see chart).

As Cut Flowers

Most popular handling for the retail florist is a late March sowing of pot or pack-grown plants carried in a 55° house and planted out in late May. These plants, if given water outdoors, will give a good crop from early July on through the summer. They should be spaced 12" × 12" outdoors. The "dahlia" and "cactus-flowered" classes are preferred, although the tiny *Lilliputs* are often included to provide variety.

A direct sowing made outdoors June 1 will be in flower by late July— they grow very rapidly if given good soil and water as needed. Sow in rows 2' apart, thin to about 6" in the row, making it easier to cultivate than if a 12" × 12" spacing were used. Later sowings may be made on through June. Disbudding will greatly improve the quality of the flowers.

GARDEN HEIGHT*	6-12"	12"	12-14"	14-18"	24-36"
VARIETY	1. Short Stuff Series 2. Thumbelina	1. Button Box Mixture 2. Dasher Series 3. Fairyland Series 4. Peter Pan Series	1. Pulcino Series 2. Small World Cherry	1. Fantastic Pink 2. Lilliput 3. Sombrero	1. Big Top Mixture 2. Ruffles Series 3. State Fair Mixture 4. Zenith Types
SPACING	6"	12"	12"	12"	18-24"
FLOWER SIZE/TYPE**	1. 4" round 2. 1½" round	1. 1½" round 2. 2½-3" round 3. 3" round 4. 3" cactus	1. 2-3" dahlia 2. 2" round	1. 2½-4" dahlia 2. 1½-2" round 3. 2-2½" single	1. 6" cactus 2. 2½" round 3. 5" broad-petaled 4. 5½-6" cactus
HABIT	Mound	Mound	Mound	Mound	Upright
BLOOM HABIT	June to frost	June to frost	June to frost	Early July to frost	Early July to frost
USE	Border	Foreground	Foreground and cut	Foreground and cut	Background and cut

Types and Varieties

The "giant cactus-flowered" class has rapidly developed into one of the most popular types. It produces huge flowers up to 6" in diameter with long, curved petals, irregularly arranged in a pleasing manner. Largely responsible for their great popularity has been the development of F_1 hybrid varieties. Prominent in this class are two series, *Big Top* and *Fruit Bowl*. Available as a mixture, they are truly outstanding and are rapidly gaining popularity over the inbred varieties. *State Fair Mix,* a giant *tetraploid* (30"–36"), produces 5"–6" flowers with broad petals in a full range of bright colors and has been very popular for many years. It has high resistance to alternaria and mildew and probably outsells all other varieties in the large-flowered class.

Ruffles Series F_1, consisting of five separate colors plus a mix, is a tall growing variety (30") that produces 2½" ruffled double flowers on long stiff stems.

In the medium height class (18"–24") are three separate color varieties worth noting: *Gold Sun F_1,* with 4" bright gold dahlia flowered blooms; *Red Sun F_1,* a 4" bright scarlet double dahlia type, and *Sombrero,* a bright colored red and gold single.

One of the most popular members of the zinnia family is the F_1 hybrid *Peter Pan,* currently available in eight colors—*Peter Pan Pink,* a coral pink; *Peter Pan Plum,* a rose; *Peter Pan Scarlet,* a brilliant scarlet; *Peter Pan Orange;*

707

The ever popular zinnia. Comes in a wide variety of heights, sizes, and colors for the summer garden. Both as a border and cut flower plant.

Peter Pan Cream; Peter Pan Flame, a brilliant red; *Peter Pan Gold,* a yellow gold; and *Peter Pan Princess,* a luminous pink. These free flowering All-America winners produce extra large, fully double, 3" flowers on very bushy plants only 10" to 12" high. The only non-All-America winner is *Princess.*

More dwarf than the *Peter Pans* but with similar flower size is the F_1 *Short Stuff Series* available in six separate, bright colors and a mix.

The *Pumilas* (2'–2½') are between the "giants" and *Lilliputs* in flower size, the latter being more widely used. It produces small pompon-type flowers (2") on bushy plants, 1½ to 2' tall. Both of these are largely grown as color mixes.

The *Pulcino Series* (12"–15") contains six very vivid colors plus a mixture. Excellent for 4" pot production.

Thumbelina (6"–8") is an extra-dwarf formulated mixture of bright colors that is particularly well adapted to edging. The compact, uniform plants flower early in packs and pots.

HOLIDAY DATES

	1985	1986	1987	1988
New Year's Day	Jan.1	Jan.1	Jan.1	Jan.1
Lincoln's Birthday	Feb.12	Feb.12	Feb.12	Feb.12
Valentine's Day	Feb.14	Feb.14	Feb.14	Feb.14
Ash Wednesday	Feb.20	Feb.12	Mar.4	Feb.17
Washington's Birthday	Feb.22	Feb.22	Feb.22	Feb.22
St. Patrick's Day	Mar.17	Mar.17	Mar.17	Mar.17
Palm Sunday	Mar.31	Mar.23	Apr.12	Mar.27
Passover	Apr.6	Apr.24	Apr.14	Apr.2
Easter Sunday	Apr.7	Mar.30	Apr.19	Apr.3
Secretaries' Day	Apr.24	Apr.23	Apr.22	Apr.27
Mother's Day	May 12	May 11	May 10	May 8
Memorial Day	May 27	May 26	May 25	May 30
Father's Day	June 16	June 15	June 21	June 19
Grandparents' Day	Sept.8	Sept.7	Sept.13	Sept.11
Rosh Hashanah	Sept.16	Oct.4	Sept.24	Sept.12
Yom Kippur	Sept.25	Oct.13	Oct.3	Sept.21
Bosses Day	Oct.16	Oct.16	Oct.16	Oct.16
Sweetest Day	Oct.19	Oct.18	Oct.17	Oct.15
Election Day	Nov.5	Nov.4	Nov.3	Nov.8
Thanksgiving Day	Nov.28	Nov.27	Nov.26	Nov.24
Christmas Day	Dec.25	Dec.25	Dec.25	Dec.25

*SPRAY DILUTION TABLE**

	1 to 50	*1 to 100*	*1 to 200*	*1 to 300*	*1 to 400*	*1 to 500*	*1 to 600*	*1 to 800*	*1 to 1000*	*1 to 1600*
1 gal.	72.5 cc. or 5 T. plus 1/4 t. or 2.56 ozs.	36.2 cc. or 2 T. plus 1 3/4 t. or 1.28 ozs.	18.1 cc. or 3 3/4 t. or .64 oz.	12.2 cc. or 2 1/2 t.	9.1 cc. or 2 t.	7.3 cc. or 1 1/2 t.	6.0 cc. or 1 1/4 t.	4.5 cc. or 1 t.	3.6 cc. or 3/4 t.	2.3 cc. or 1/2 t.
2 gals.	144.9 cc. or 10 T. plus 3/4 t. or 5.12 ozs.	72.5 cc. or 5 T. plus 1/4 t. or 2.56 ozs.	36.2 cc. or 2 T. plus 1 3/4 t. or 1.28 ozs.	24.1 cc. or 5 t.	18.1 cc. or 3 3/4 t.	14.5 cc. or 3 t.	12.2 cc. or 2.5 t.	9.1 cc. or 2 t.	7.3 cc. or 1.5 t.	4.6 cc. or 1 t.
3 gals.	217.3 cc. or 15 T. plus 1 t. or 7.68 ozs.	108.7 cc. or 7 T. plus 2 t. or 3.84 ozs.	54.3 cc. or 3 T. plus 2 1/2 t. or 1.92 ozs.	36.2 cc. or 2 T. plus 1 3/4 t. or 1.28 ozs.	27.2 cc. or 1 T. plus 2 3/4 t.	21.7 cc. or 1 T. plus 1.5 t.	18.1 cc. or 3 3/4 t.	13.4 cc. or 1 T.	10.9 cc. or 2 1/4 t.	6.9 cc. or 1.5 t.
5 gals.	362.2 cc. or 12.8 ozs.	181.1 cc. or 6.4 ozs.	90.6 cc. or 6 T. plus 1 1/4 t. or 3.2 ozs.	60.3 cc. or 4 T. plus 3/4 t. or 2.13 ozs.	45.3 cc. or 3 T. plus 1/2 t. or 1.6 ozs.	36.2 cc. or 2 T. plus 1 3/4 t. or 1.28 ozs.	30.3 cc. or 2 T. plus 1/2 t. or 1.07 ozs.	22.6 cc. or 1 T. plus 1 3/4 t.	18.1 cc. or 3 3/4 t.	11.3 cc. or 2.5 t.
10 gals.	724.5 cc. or 25.6 ozs.	362.2 cc. or 12.8 ozs.	181.1 cc. or 12 T. plus 2 1/2 t. or 6.4 ozs.	120.8 cc. or 8 T. plus 1 1/2 t. or 4.27 ozs.	90.6 cc. or 6 T. plus 1 1/4 t. or 3.2 ozs.	72.5 cc. or 5 T. plus 1/4 t. or 2.56 ozs.	60.3 cc. or 4 T. plus 3/4 t. or 2.13 ozs.	45.3 cc. or 3 T. plus 1/2 t. or 1.6 ozs.	36.2 cc. or 2 T. plus 1 3/4 t. or 1.28 ozs.	22.6 cc. or 1 T. plus 1 3/4 t. or .8 oz.

	1 to 50	1 to 100	1 to 200	1 to 300	1 to 400	1 to 500	1 to 600	1 to 800	1 to 1000	1 to 1600
25 gals.	1811.2 cc. or 64 ozs.	905.6 cc. or 32 ozs.	452.8 cc. or 16 ozs.	302.8 cc. or 10.7 ozs.	226.4 cc. or 16 T. or 8 ozs.	181.1 cc. or 12 T. plus 2½ t. or 6.4 ozs.	150.8 cc. or 10 T. plus 2½ t. or 5.33 ozs.	113.0 cc. or 8 T. or 4 ozs.	90.6 cc. or 6 T. plus 1¼ t. or 3.2 ozs.	56.5 cc. or 4 T. or 2 ozs.
30 gals.	2173.5 cc. or 76.8 ozs.	1086.6 cc. or 38.4 ozs.	543.3 cc. or 19.2 ozs.	362.4 cc. or 12.81 ozs.	271.8 cc. or 19 T. or 9.6 ozs.	217.5 cc. or 15 T. plus 1 t. or 7.68 ozs.	180.9 cc. or 12 T. plus 2 t. or 6.39 ozs.	135.9 cc. or 9 T. plus 1½ t. or 4.8 ozs.	108.6 cc. or 7 T. plus 2 t. or 3.84 ozs.	67.8 cc. or 4 T. plus 4½ t. or 2.4 ozs.
50 gals.	3622.4 cc. or 1 gal.	1811.2 cc. or 64 ozs.	905.6 cc. or 32 ozs.	602.8 cc. or 21.33 ozs.	452.8 cc. or 16 ozs.	362.2 cc. or 12.8 ozs.	302.8 cc. or 10.66 ozs.	226.4 cc. or 8 ozs.	181.1 cc. or 12 T. plus 2½ t. or 6.4 ozs.	113.2 cc. or 8 T. or 4 ozs.

*We find this table a real timesaver in figuring spray dilutions. Note that dilutions are figured both in tablespoon-teaspoons and in cubic centimeters (cc.). The cc. is simpler, more accurate. Cylinders graduated in cubic centimeters (10 cc., 50 cc. or 100 cc.) may be obtained from Central Scientific Co., 1700 Irving Park Blvd., Chicago, Ill.—or probably from your local druggist.

The table is from the Ohio Florist Association Monthly Bulletin No. 198.

t. = teaspoonful   T. = tablespoonful

The following product names are registered trademarks of Geo. J. Ball, Inc. or Divisions of Geo. J. Ball, Inc.

Containers	Other items
Jiffy-Pots	Super-Seedlings
Jiffy-Strips	Ball Crown (Lilies)
Jiffy-7	Harvest Giant (Mums)
Jiffy-9	Tag-Along (Plastic Labels)
Handi-Flats	Carefree (Geraniums)
Handi-Paks	Elfin (Impatiens)
Cell-paks	Jiffy-Mix (Soil substitute)
	Ballet Violet

INDEX

714